Teaching Reading Using Literature

Teaching Reading Using Literature

John F. Savage

Boston College

Brown & Benchmark
PUBLISHERS

Madison, Wisconsin • Dubuque, Iowa

Book Team

Managing Editor *Sue Pulvermacher-Alt*
Developmental Editor *Kassi Radomski*
Production Editor *Diane Clemens*
Photo Editor *Robin Storm*
Permissions Coordinator *Mavis M. Oeth*
Art Processor *Andrea Lopez-Meyer*
Visuals/Design Developmental Consultant *Marilyn A. Phelps*
Visuals/Design Freelance Specialist *Mary L. Christianson*
Publishing Services Specialist *Sherry Padden*
Marketing Manager *Steven Yetter*
Advertising Manager *Brett Apold*

WCB Brown & Benchmark

A Division of Wm. C. Brown Communications, Inc.

Executive Vice President/General Manager *Thomas E. Doran*
Vice President/Editor in Chief *Edgar J. Laube*
Vice President/Sales and Marketing *Eric Ziegler*
Director of Production *Vickie Putman Caughron*
Director of Custom and Electronic Publishing *Chris Rogers*

Wm. C. Brown Communications, Inc.

President and Chief Executive Officer *G. Franklin Lewis*
Corporate Senior Vice President and Chief Financial Officer *Robert Chesterman*
Corporate Senior Vice President and President of Manufacturing *Roger Meyer*

Cover illustration by Wilderness Graphics

Cover and interior designs by Silvers Design

Illustrations by Silvers Design unless otherwise noted

Copyedited by Toni L. Good

Photo Credits: Pages 32, 217: Historical Pictures/Stock Montage; Page 50: Houghton/Mifflin Company; Pages 5, 7, 100 middle, 140, 297, 340, 362, 413: © Jean Claude Lejeune; Pages 13, 62, 71, 80, 87, 100 top, 126, 164, 179, 186, 236, 258, 260, 263, 275, 283, 286, 306, 311, 331, 358, 370: © Stuart Spates; Pages 31, 48, 100 bottom, 116, 147, 200, 343, 393, 403: © James L. Shaffer; Pages 105, 237: © Michael Siluk.

Library of Congress Catalog Card Number: 92–76205

ISBN 0–697–17193–0

Printed in the United States of America by Wm. C. Brown Communications, Inc., 2460 Kerper Boulevard, Dubuque, IA 52001

10 9 8 7 6 5 4 3 2 1

Brief Contents

Preface   xi

Chapter 1   Literature and Literacy in the Elementary Classroom   1

Chapter 2   The World of Children's Literature   28

Chapter 3   Organizing and Managing a Literature-Based Program   57

Chapter 4   Early Literacy   93

Chapter 5   Word Study: Vocabulary and Learning to Read   135

Chapter 6   Reading Comprehension: Understanding Narrative Text   172

Chapter 7   Literacy Across the Curriculum: Comprehending Expository Text   212

Chapter 8   The Role of the Library in a Literature-Based Program   255

Chapter 9   Sharing Literature Through Oral Reading   270

Chapter 10   The Reading-Writing Connection   291

Chapter 11   Reading Instruction for Atypical Learners   324

Chapter 12   Multicultural Literature: Working with Diverse Learners   354

Chapter 13   Assessing Literacy Development   381

List of Children's Trade Books   419

List of Cumulative References   430

Index   443

Contents

Preface   xi

 1 LITERATURE AND LITERACY IN THE ELEMENTARY CLASSROOM   1

Introduction   3
What Is a Literature-Based Program?   4
Why Literature-Based Reading?   7
   Whole Language   8
   Advantages of Using Literature   12
How Is Literature-Based Reading Different from Conventional Reading Instruction?   15
   Skill-Development View versus Literature-Based Instruction   15
   Basal Readers   16
Achieving a Synthesis   19
Summary and Conclusions   23
Discussion Questions and Activities   24
School-Based Assignments   24
Children's Trade Books Cited in This Chapter 25
References   26

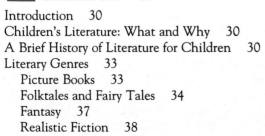 **2 THE WORLD OF CHILDREN'S LITERATURE   28**

Introduction   30
Children's Literature: What and Why   30
A Brief History of Literature for Children   30
Literary Genres   33
   Picture Books   33
   Folktales and Fairy Tales   34
   Fantasy   37
   Realistic Fiction   38

Historical Fiction   40
   Poetry   41
Literary Elements   43
   Setting   43
   Chacterization   44
   Plot   45
   Theme   45
Getting To Know Authors   49
Summary and Conclusions   52
Discussion Questions and Activities   52
School-Based Assignments   53
Children's Trade Books Cited in This Chapter   53
References   56

3 ORGANIZING AND MANAGING A LITERATURE-BASED READING PROGRAM   57

Introduction   59
Time   60
   Whole Class Work   60
   Small Group Activities   61
   Story Time   61
   Sustained Silent Reading   61
   Theme Projects   62
   Math   63
   Specialists   63
Space   64
   Reading Corner   65
   Writing Center   65
   Media Center   65
   Interest Centers   65
   Individual Reading-Study Carrels   67

Materials   67
   Trade Books   67
   Basal Readers   69
   Supplementary Literature-Based Materials   70
   Audiovisual Devices   70
   Computers   71
Pupils   73
   Large-Group Instruction   74
   Small-Group Instruction   75
   Individualized Patterns   82
   Flexibility in Grouping   85
Parents in the Classroom   86
Schoolwide Organizational Patterns   87
   Departmentalization   87
   Team Teaching   87
Summary and Conclusions   88
Discussion Questions and Activities   89
School-Based Assignments   90
Children's Trade Books Cited in This
Chapter   90
References   91

4   EARLY LITERACY   93

Introduction   95
Childhood Development and Early Literacy   95
   Physical and Mental Development   95
   Schemata   96
   Language Acquisition   98
   Early Experiences With Print   99
Reading Readiness and Emergent Literacy   99
Early Childhood Programs   103
   Nursery School   104
   Kindergarten   108
   Beginning Reading and Writing Instruction
     120
Role of the Parents in Early Literacy   121
   Parents in the Preschool Years   123
   Role of Parents When Children Come to
     School   127
Summary and Conclusions   131
Discussion Questions and Activities   131
School-Based Assignments   132
Children's Trade Books Cited in This
Chapter   132
References   134

**5   WORD STUDY: VOCABULARY AND
LEARNING TO READ   135**

Introduction   137
Word Knowledge   137
   Words and Concepts   138
   Vocabulary Development in the Classroom
     140
Word Recognition   147
   Sight Words   147
   Context Clues   152
Word Analysis   155
   Phonetic Analysis   155
   Structural Analysis   163
   The Dictionary: "Look It Up"   165
A Combination of Word-Identification Skills
167
Summary and Conclusions   167
Discussion Questions and Activities   168
School-Based Assignments   168
Children's Trade Books Cited in This
Chapter   169
References   170

**6   READING COMPREHENSION:
UNDERSTANDING NARRATIVE
TEXT   172**

Introduction   174
   Narrative and Expository Text   174
   Product and Process   175
   An Interactive Model   175
Text-Based Features   177
   Level of Text   177
   Structure of Text   178
   Content of Text   179
   Other Text-Based Features   182
Reader-Based Features   182
   Language Background   182
   Cognitive Processing   185
   Schemata   197
   Metacognition   200
   Other Reader-Based Factors   202
   Context   203
The Role of Teacher Questioning   203
Summary and Conclusions   208
Discussion Questions and Activities   208
School-Based Assignments   209

Children's Trade Books Cited in This
Chapter 209
References 210

 **7 LITERACY ACROSS THE CURRICULUM:
COMPREHENDING EXPOSITORY
TEXT 212**

Introduction 215
Trade Books and Textbooks 215
    Expository Text 215
    Textbooks 216
    Trade Books 216
    Book Clusters 218
Text-Based Features 222
    Readability 222
    Text Structure 225
    Content 228
    Other Text-Based Features 235
Reader-Based Features 239
    Language Background 239
    Cognitive Processing 243
    Schemata 244
    Metacognition 246
    Motivation 247
Summary and Conclusions 248
Discussion Questions and Activities 249
School-Based Assignments 249
Children's Trade Books Cited in This
Chapter 250
References 253

 **8 THE ROLE OF THE LIBRARY IN A
LITERATURE-BASED READING
PROGRAM 255**

Introduction 257
Teachers and Librarians 257
Reference Materials 258
    Reference Tools 259
    Learning to Use Reference Tools 260
    Organizing Information 261
Newspapers and Magazines 262
    Newspapers 262
    Magazines 264
Reading Rate/Reading Efficiency 266
    Comprehension 266
    Flexibility 266
Summary and Conclusions 267
Discussion Questions and Activities 268

School-Based Assignments 268
Children's Trade Books Cited in This
Chapter 269
References 269

 **9 SHARING LITERATURE THROUGH
ORAL READING 270**

Introduction 272
"Read with Expression" 272
    Expression 273
    Fluency 274
Reading Aloud to Pupils 276
    Advantage of Reading Aloud 276
    Conditions and Techniques for Reading
        Aloud 277
    Selecting Books for Reading Aloud 278
Reading Aloud by Pupils 280
    Round-Robin Reading 281
    Alternatives to Round-Robin Reading 282
Summary and Conclusions 287
Discussion Questions and Activities 288
School-Based Assignments 288
Children's Trade Books Cited in This
Chapter 289
References 290

 **10 THE READING-WRITING
CONNECTION 291**

Introduction 293
The Reading-Writing Relationship 293
    The Meaning Connection 294
    The Language Connection 295
    The Instructional Connection 296
Responding to Literature 297
    Responding Orally 298
    Responding Artistically 298
    Responding in Writing 298
Process Writing 303
    Prewriting 304
    Writing 305
    Editing and Revising 307
    Publishing 310
Written Products Based on Literature 312
    Stories 313
    Reports 314
    Letters 315

Poems   316
Scripts and Dialogues   316
Journals   316
Book Reports   316
Summary and Conclusions   319
Discussion Questions and Activities   320
School-Based Assignments   320
Children's Trade Books Cited in This
Chapter   321
References   322

 **READING INSTRUCTION FOR
ATYPICAL LEARNERS   324**

Introduction   326
Mainstreaming   327
Slow Learners   328
Teaching Strategies   328
Literature for the Slow Learner   331
Pupils with Learning Disabilities   334
Defining Learning Disabilities   334
Reading Programs for the Learning
Disabled   335
Holistic Reading   336
Writing   338
Pupils with Sensory and Physical Problems   339
Visual Problems   339
Auditory Problems   340
Physical Handicaps   341
Pupils with Attitude and Behavior Problems   343
Teaching Techniques   344
Bibliotherapy   345
Gifted and Talented Pupils   345
Defining Gifted and Talented   346
Challenging Reading   347
The Teacher on the Team   348
Summary and Conclusions   349
Discussion Questions and Activities   350
School-Based Assignments   350
Children's Trade Books Cited in This
Chapter   351
References   352

 **USING MULTICULTURAL
LITERATURE: WORKING WITH
DIVERSE LEARNERS   354**

Introduction   356

Cultural Dimensions of Literacy   356
Values of Multicultural Literature in the
Classroom   357
Types of Multicultural Trade Books   358
Dialect Speakers   364
Regional Dialect   364
Social Dialect   365
Standard English   366
Black English   367
Pupils Whose First Language Is Not English   369
Language Instruction   370
Reading Instruction   373
Resource Teachers   375
Summary and Conclusions   376
Discussion Questions and Activities   377
School-Based Assignments   377
Children's Trade Books Cited in This
Chapter   378
References   380

 **ASSESSING LITERACY
DEVELOPMENT   381**

Introduction   383
Reasons for Assessment   383
A General Perspective   384
Formal Assessment   387
Standardized Reading Achievement Tests   387
Skill Development Tests   390
Classroom-Based Assessment   393
Teacher Observation   394
Pros and Cons of Classroom-Based
Assessment   403
Informal Reading Inventories   406
Miscue Analysis   408
Portfolio Assessment   411
What Do Portfolios Contain   412
How Are Portfolios Used?   414
Summary and Conclusions   414
Discussion Questions and Activities   415
School-Based Assignments   416
Children's Trade Books Cited in This
Chapter   416
References   416
List of Children's Trade Books   419
List of Cumulative References   430
Index   443

Preface

MRS. CHRIS Zajak, the elementary school teacher who is the "star" of Tracy Kidder's book *Among Schoolchildren,* was interviewed in 1989 by *The Boston Globe.* When the reporter asked Mrs. Zajak, "What teaching methods have you changed since you started teaching 17 years ago?" the teacher replied, "I use a lot more literature now to teach reading."

She went on to explain how she had discovered the power of children's literature as a means of helping her pupils come to love reading and to become lifelong readers.

Teaching Reading Using Literature is designed for Chris Zajak and the thousands of teachers like her in today's elementary classrooms—teachers who are moving toward a greater use of literature as the vehicle for reading and writing instruction.

Children's literature is enjoying new popularity as an integral part of teaching children how to read and write. Literature is becoming the centerpiece of language arts instruction. Many teachers are replacing conventional reading programs altogether and using literature exclusively as the vehicle for reading and writing instruction; others are using literature as a strong supplement to their regular basal reading materials. Professional organizations are touting the idea of using real books by real people in the classroom. Teachers' journals and magazines are replete with articles about literature-based reading instruction. Conference programs are brimming with workshops demonstrating how to use literature to teach children to read, write, and think. Children's literature has become more than an enrichment feature in the language arts curriculum; it has become an essential component of literacy instruction throughout the grades.

Teaching Reading Using Literature deals with the whys and hows of this strong movement toward the greater utilization of trade books in the classroom. The book is not primarily about children's literature; it is about planning and implementing a reading and writing program for pupils that uses literature as a major component in teaching children how to read.

What Is Literature-Based Reading? Like love, literature-based reading means different things to different people. For some teachers it means abandoning conventional instructional materials for reading and writing and using only literature as the vehicle for literacy instruction. For others it means retaining features of conventional instruction but increasing the use of trade books for instructional purposes. Whether trade books are used alone or in close combination with basal readers and other instructional materials, literature is an integral part of promoting literacy in the classroom.

In the context of this book, literature-based instruction refers to the use of children's literature as the centerpiece of the reading and writing program. In a literature-based approach, teachers use literature as the *starting point* for teaching pupils how to read. Reading instruction starts with story and not with skills. Teachers begin with stories and poems, folktales and fairy tales, biographies and realistic fiction, and other genres that make up the rich montage of literature for children. From this base, teachers lead children to discover the joys and competencies of reading and writing, and to begin a lifelong love of reading.

Is literature-based instruction part of the ''whole language'' movement? Yes and no. Whole-language teachers rely a great deal on literature in teaching reading and writing. Literature-based instruction is very consistent with a whole-language philosophy, because trade books provide authentic reading material that children enjoy. However, a teacher can implement a literature-based approach without buying into the whole-language movement lock, stock, and barrel.

Does literature-based instruction ignore the traditional basic reading skills? Absolutely not! Conventional skill development can be integrated into literature-based instruction, and pupils can develop effective reading strategies as they learn to read trade books. The key to literature-based instruction is starting with story rather than starting with skills.

Is a literature-based program entirely individualized? Not necessarily. Although there is often more individualized work in a literature-based program than in a traditional ''everyone-reads-the-same-page-of-the-same-book'' program, literature-based instruction uses a variety of large-group and small-group activities and integrates a variety of teaching–learning techniques and strategies.

How successful is literature-based instruction? Very. A growing body of evidence indicates that using children's literature is a very effective way of teaching pupils how to read. Anecdotal accounts from teachers and empirical studies from researchers show that literature-based instruction produces positive results with a range of pupils— with those who learn easily as well as with those who do not.

What does a literature-based program look like in action? Read on. There is no single, simple definition of a literature-based instructional program, but the chapters that follow present the basic philosophy of literature-based instruction, along with practical suggestions on how this program can be put to work in the classroom.

A Word About Organization

Teaching Reading Using Literature is divided into thirteen chapters. The first three chapters are largely foundational. The opening chapter briefly presents an overview of literature-based reading, how it differs from conventional approaches to teaching reading, and how to achieve synthesis in a balanced program with literature at the core. Chapter 2 presents an overview of the field of children's literature, a quick review for those who have had a course in this important area and a brief introduction for those who have not yet studied the topic. Chapter 3 deals with how to organize and manage a literature-based reading and writing program in the classroom.

The next seven chapters deal with the content of developmental literacy instruction—the day-to-day topics related to teaching reading and writing in the elementary school. Chapter 4 focuses on emergent literacy, with an emphasis on how literature contributes to the developing reading and writing competencies of young children in the early years of their school lives. Chapter 5 has to do with vocabulary—instruction in word meaning and word analysis within the context of literature-based classroom instruction.

The next two chapters are about reading comprehension. Chapter 6 examines narrative text, and how teachers can help pupils develop broader and deeper understanding of the stories they read. The next chapter extends the topic of comprehension to expository text—that is, understanding and producing text written to present information rather than to tell stories. Chapter 8 focuses on the library, a central resource for children's literature and for reference materials that are used as tools for teaching reading and writing. The next chapter is about oral reading, a perennial classroom practice that has taken on new importance in light of literature-based instruction. Chapter 10 examines the reading–writing connection, since both dimensions of literacy are connected integrally in the instructional process.

The final three chapters round out the book with topics of special importance in classroom reading and writing instruction. Chapter 11 focuses on atypical learners, pupils with special learning problems, as well as on the gifted. With a focus on multicultural literature, Chapter 12 deals with children who come from diverse cultural and linguistic backgrounds. The final chapter is about assessment; it explores the tools and techniques that teachers use to measure the success of their efforts in teaching reading with literature.

An honest attempt has been made throughout the book to balance theory and practice. It is important that teachers know how to use literature to teach reading, but more important by far is their understanding of how literature contributes to the development of pupils' abilities and attitudes in learning to read and write. Chapters contain boxed sections with practical suggestions for applying theory to practice (**Putting Ideas to Work**), along with special sections that offer food for thought (**Something to Think About**) and resources such as book lists (**For Your Information**). Suggestions for in-class and field-based assignments follow each chapter.

The Audience

This book is written for teachers—those preparing to enter the teaching profession as well as current professionals who are trying to stay abreast of the field and adapt their teaching strategies in light of current research and trends in teaching reading. The book attempts to be basic enough to be appropriate for undergraduates or graduate students who may be taking their first course in teaching reading. At the same time, the content is contemporary enough to be appropriate for experienced teachers who are seeking a sound theory base and practical ideas for using literature for instructional purposes in their classrooms.

The book was written in the belief that of all the forces having an impact on education—administrative pressures, organizational patterns, materials, facilities, policies, and everything else that touches the lives of teachers and pupils—the teacher is at the heart of the instructional process. The competent professional in the classroom is the one who makes things happen.

Acknowledgments

The appreciation expressed to those who help an author is often a professional courtesy. The thanks I offer to the people who helped shape this book are a heartful expression of appreciation. Sections of this book belong to them as much as to me (although I'll take responsibility for misinterpretations of any of their ideas).

Teachers in whose classrooms I worked—professionals like Deborah Davies, Annmarie White-Hunter, Ann Carmola, and others—helped me grasp firsthand the practical realities of using literature with children. Literally hundreds of teacher–colleagues whom I encountered in classes, at in-service workshops, and at conferences provided ideas and suggestions that I begged, borrowed, or stole from them. My graduate assistants—Patricia Heimgartner and Suzanne Bresnahan—provided practical support. My friend and colleague Audrey Friedman provided creative ideas and conceptual input.

I would also like to thank those reviewers whose invaluable suggestions guided me throughout the development of this first edition: Rhoda Chalker, Florida Atlantic University; Barbara Clark, University of South Florida; Nancy Clements, Ball State University; Lane Gauthier, University of Houston; Mary Jane Gray, Loyola University of Chicago; Marjorie Hancock, Kansas State University; and John A. Smith, Utah State University.

The interest and help of Paul Tavenner and Kassi Radomski of Brown & Benchmark helped keep me going when my get-up-and-go occasionally got up and went.

More personally, thanks are due to Stacey, Jay, and Donna, my three children whose accomplishments are testimony to the power of literature in their lives, and to Mary Jane, my wife, whose love has never diminished.

Each of these people contributed time and talent to help make this book a vehicle for teachers to use in making literature part of children's instructional lives in the classroom.

Chapter 1

Literature and Literacy in the Elementary Classroom

Chapter I Outline

I. Introduction
II. What Is a Literature-Based Program?
   Characteristics of Literature-Based Instruction
III. Why Literature-Based Reading?
   A. Whole Language
      1. Immersion
      2. Modeling
      3. Holistic
      4. Authentic
      5. Purposefulness
      6. Risk-Taking
      7. Expectation of Success
   B. Advantages of Using Literature
      1. Affective Response
      2. Involvement in Reading
      3. Content
      4. Language
      5. Skills and Strategies
      6. It Works
IV. How Is Literature-Based Reading Different
   from Conventional Reading Instruction?
   A. Skill-Development View versus Literature-
      Based Instruction
   B. Basal Readers
      1. Pros and Cons of a Basal Program
         a. Advantages of Basals
         b. Disadvantages of Basals
      2. Newer Basal Programs
V. Achieving a Synthesis
   A. Basals versus Trade Books
   B. How to Synthesize
   C. Advantages of a Combined Program

VI. Summary and Conclusions
Discussion Questions and Activities
School-Based Assignments
Children's Trade Books Cited in This Chapter
References

███████████████████

Features

1.1   What Is a Trade Book?
1.2   Research-Based Qualities of Literature-Based Programs
1.3   Contrasting Whole Language Theory
1.4   Describing a Literature-Based Program
1.5   What Is a Basal Series?
1.6   Approaches to Teaching Reading
1.7   A Continuum

Key Concepts in This Chapter

Children's literature has innundated the language arts curriculum in today's schools. Literature-based instruction emphasizes the use of trade books in teaching children to read and write.

In contrast to conventional skills-based instruction, a literature-based approach places primary emphasis on story and meaning instead of on development of specific reading skills.

A literature-based approach offers compelling advantages in helping pupils learn to read and write.

Trade books can be used alone or in combination with other instructional materials to create an inspired, effective instructional program.

EARNING TO read and write has long been at the heart of education. In any literate society, the issue of how best to teach reading is a topic of concern, and instruction in this area is a major part of the educational enterprise. ''Readin' and writin' '' continue to constitute two-thirds of the 3 R's in our schools.

Methods and materials for teaching reading have evolved through the ages. Drills on letters and syllables while studying the works of the masters occupied the time of young schoolboys in ancient Greece and Rome. These practices continued through the Middle Ages for those fortunate enough to enjoy the opportunity for an education. When Johannes Gutenberg invented the printing press in the middle of the 15th century, books that were previously copied by hand and available to the select few became mechanically producible and available to many. Learning to read assumed a more important role in the lives of more people.

In early America, Pilgrim children studied the *New England Primer*

A In Adam's Fall
  we sinned all.
B Thy Life to mend,
  This Book attend.

—learning so that they could read the Bible and other religious materials. After the American Revolution children used the Noah Webster *Readers* and the *New American Spelling Book,* programs that used the same alphabetic method with content that stressed moral principles and patriotic values. In the mid-1800s, the famous *McGuffey Eclectic Readers,* the first graded reading series, appeared with prayers, psalms, and stories about children and animals that reflected the values and experiences of society at the time.

In the early years of the 20th century, an intense interest in reading instruction resulted in several new programs. These new reading series were significantly different from earlier programs—they stressed reading by learning whole words rather than letters and syllables; they emphasized reading comprehension rather than oral reading; they contained stories aimed at reflecting the experiences of middle class children, featuring story characters like the legendary Dick and Jane; they were written with the expressed purpose of helping pupils develop skills as a means of learning to read. As the instructional pendulum swung from whole word reading to phonics and linguistics, and then back again to a more eclectic approach, the content of reading books changed to reflect both social and educational trends.

As schools enter the 21st century, a new approach to literacy instruction has emerged, an approach that uses children's literature as the major vehicle for teaching children how to read and write. Increasingly, schools use real books by real authors as part of the reading program. Pupils use trade books (see 1.1 For Your Information) as a major means of developing their reading ability, and a new generation of basal readers has been infused with quality literature written for children. In short, a tidal wave of literature-based reading has hit our schools.

The move toward literature-based reading instruction has been promoted by educators and mandated by legislators. ''At the 1987 Coalition of English conference— a kind of summit meeting of language arts educators from all levels of schooling— literature was the most widely discussed topic of the entire meeting'' (Teale, 1990;

1.1
FOR YOUR INFORMATION

What Is a Trade Book?

A TRADE book is a book that is not part of a textbook series. Trade books are the picture books, storybooks, novels, and informational books found in bookstores and on library shelves. They are written to be sold to the general public and not designed primarily for school use.

Trade books may be written primarily

to entertain, as Ludwig Bemelmans' wonderful stories about *Madeline.*

to inform, as the science books by Franklyn Branley in the Let's-Read-and Find-Out series, such as *Sunshine Makes the Seasons.*

to both entertain and inform, as Jean Fritz's many humorous but historically accurate accounts of American history, such as *And Then What Happened, Paul Revere?*

Although not primarily designed for instructional purposes, trade books can be used as powerful tools to develop pupils' reading competency and positive attitudes toward reading. They are the essential elements in literature-based reading programs.

p. 808). Programs at teachers' conventions are brimming with workshops on how to use literature to teach reading. Journals are full of articles on the topic, and books about literature in the classroom flood the marketplace.

Since 1987, the California State Department of Education has mandated a literature-based language arts program for all pupils, a program that includes attention to cultural values and the integrated teaching of language processes through the reading of quality literature (California State Department of Education, 1987). Other states have followed suit. In a survey of state reading and language arts directors, Culinan (1989) found that statewide initiatives and literacy programs that hinge on literature exist in almost half the states in the U.S., and there is every indication that the trend will continue. Local initiatives are no less pervasive, as school districts move literature to center stage in their language arts curriculum.

What Is a Literature-Based Program?

Literature-based reading is a program that uses children's literature as the central core for language instruction. It is a program in which literature is an integral (rather than incidental) part of teaching pupils how to read and write. Trade books are used extensively as instructional tools. Teaching is centered on authentic texts written for meaningful purposes.

Children's literature is used in different ways for different purposes at different levels in literature-based programs. All these programs, however, use literature to help pupils develop the ability and the inclination to read. There is no designated set of trade books to be used in a prescribed fashion at particular grade levels. Programs consist of lessons and activities using a wealth of children's books and stories—picture books, fiction, informational books, folktales, poetry, fantasy, and other literary forms—to promote pupils' language development and literacy competency.

Trade books help pupils learn to read, and literature helps them learn to love reading.

Characteristics of Literature-Based Instruction

There are certain qualities or characteristics of programs in which literature is at the heart of the language curriculum.

Trade books constitute the centerpiece of the curriculum. Stories and poems serve as major vehicles of instruction in the language arts, and literature is related to other components of the school program. Activities related to literature are a regular part of each day's activities. Pupils are given time to share books, to discuss what they have read, to write and react to stories, to talk with visitors about what they are reading, and to show their enthusiasm about reading not only as a school subject but as part of their lives.

Trade books are used as primary vehicles in the instructional process. In the early stages, predictable books like Pat Hutchins's *Good Night Owl* and simple children's classics such as Wanda Gag's *Millions of Cats* are used to involve pupils in their initial reading experiences. In the upper grades, books such as Beverly Cleary's *The Mouse and The Motorcycle* or Robert Lawson's *Rabbit Hill* are used for directed reading lessons in small groups. At all levels, pupils are given time and encouragement to read and respond to literature all day long.

Reader response is an integral feature of instruction. Response is part of the meaning-making process in which pupils engage as they read. Pupils respond in a variety of ways—through discussion, drama, art, and writing in its many forms—to the literature that they experience. They laugh with Harry in Cathy Dubowski's *Cave Boy,* cry with Jemmy in *The Whipping Boy,* and share Chibi's pride and satisfaction in *Crow Boy.* Through response, they share the unique meaning and significance that they derive from their interaction with the stories and poems that they read.

"Read alouds" are part of the daily reading diet. Teachers at all levels share a steady flow of stories and poems with pupils throughout the day. At all levels, teachers open the world of literature by sharing stories in anthologies by famous writers—for example, Rudyard Kipling's *Just So Stories,* or Carl Sandburg's *Rootabaga Stories.* They also use reading aloud as a means of sharing popular chapter books—Roald Dahl's *Danny, Champion of the World* or Natalie Babbitt's *Tuck Everlasting.* From kindergarten through sixth grade and beyond, reading aloud to pupils is an essential feature of literature-based instruction.

Sustained silent reading is another daily activity, a time set aside when pupils *and teachers* read books of their own choosing. In the lower grades, children spend this special reading time engaged in old favorites like Arlene Mosel's *Tikki Tikki Tembo* and Maurice Sendak's *Where the Wild Things Are,* or getting to know newer books such as Ralph Manheim's translation of the Grimm fairytale *Dear Mili* or Angela Johnson's *Tell Me A Story, Mama.* As their independence in reading grows, pupils spend sustained silent reading time getting acquainted with Amelia Bedelia, Paddington Bear, the Boxcar Kids and the kids from the Polk Street School, Curious George, Anastasia Krupnik, Henry Huggins, Pippi Longstocking, and the rest of the wonderful cast of characters who inhabit the world of children's books. In the upper grades, they become part of the family in Mildred Taylor's *The Gold Cadillac* and part of the circle of friends in Barthe DeClements' *Fourth Grade Wizards.* Sustained silent reading is a time to truly enjoy reading. It is also a time when, by enjoying their own recreational novels, teachers become models for pupils.

Thematic units are part of content areas of the curriculum. Trade books are used extensively to support and enrich information presented in textbooks and other sources. Collections of informational trade books provide depth, breadth, and currency to the full range of topics that occupy pupils' interests and their curriculum needs. Appropriate works of fiction can also be included; for example, Jim Murphy's *The Last Dinosaur* is a fictional work, but a plausible account of why dinosaurs became extinct. These units integrate reading into all areas of the school program.

Classroom libraries are provided to put a selection of trade books at pupils' fingertips. Where budgetary restrictions limit possibilities for providing extensive classroom collections of trade books, teachers use the school or public library as a source of trade books in the classroom.

Author study engages pupils in learning about people who produce the literature that they enjoy and use in becoming literate. *Displays* document pupils' engagement with literature, with samples of pupils' artistic and written responses to the books they are reading. Book covers and posters designed by pupils about their favorite books cover display areas in the reading corner. Pupils' original poems and responses to books they have read adorn bulletin boards. Trade books on topics such as leaves or rocks are part of the science display in the corner. Posters of poems that pupils have enjoyed cover the wall. In short, there is a print-rich environment built around literature.

Teachers who are "plugged into" literature are the key to success of the program. The teacher is the most important element in any reading program. Literature-based programs need teachers who are committed to offering pupils the best in children's books, who are enthusiastic about literature, and who see themselves as readers.

Zarrillo (1989) surveyed and observed teachers who operated literature-based reading programs in their classrooms. While he found diversity in overall design and

Shared reading is an important part of the school day in any classroom.

implementation of programs, he did find five categories of activities shared by teachers who use literature successfully to teach reading: (1) the presentation of literature to pupils; (2) pupil response to that literature in a variety of ways—through writing, art, open-ended responses to interpretative questions; (3) individualized time for reading and responding to books; (4) teacher-directed lessons on word recognition and meaning strategies as needed; and (5) projects in which groups of pupils work cooperatively.

Teachers are different, of course, and so not all literature-based programs will have the characteristics identified here implemented in the same way in every classroom. Some teachers integrate these elements with a basal program; others discard the basal altogether and rely entirely on trade books. All these features, however, are part of literature-based reading and, taken together, constitute what might be called ''a literature-based program.''

In sum, a literature-based program is one in which children are immersed in literature and where literature permeates literacy instruction. Children's literature is placed at the core of the program and trade books are used as primary vehicles for teaching children how to read and write.

Why Literature-Based Reading?

The 1970s brought the first ripples of the tidal wave of literature in reading and writing instruction in schools and the wave began to peak in the 1980s. Educators began to examine critically the notion of a conventional skill-development approach to literacy instruction, an approach that emphasized mastery of a collection of discrete skills as a

1.2 Putting Ideas to Work

Research-Based Qualities of Literature-Based Programs

FROM THEIR research on literature-based reading, Tunnell and Jacobs (1989) list these basic elements of literature-based programs:

Natural reading, which involves the acquisition of reading skills in much the same way as speaking skills. ''Learning to read naturally begins when parents read to young children and let them handle books, and that process is continued with the teacher reading aloud and including books naturally in the classroom'' (p. 474).

Use of natural text, reading material written in language unencumbered by the controls imposed by basals.

Neurological impress, in which pupils follow lines of text and read along as the teacher or another pupil reads aloud.

Sustained silent reading, with pupils and teachers reading material of their own choosing without interruption.

Teacher modeling, with teachers showing themselves as enthusiastic readers.

Improving pupils' attitudes, with an emphasis on the affective dimensions of helping pupils appreciate literature and enjoy reading.

Self-selection of materials, allowing pupils a large measure of choice in what they read.

Meaning orientation, with skills taught in the meaningful context of real books and pupils' own writing.

Writing as an ''output activity'' consistently occurring with reading.

---

means of learning to read. Criticism of basal reading instruction mounted. In fact, basal bashing became a professional pastime of the 1980s. Whole language theory lent momentum to the wider use of literature in teaching children how to read. The appeal of using real books by real authors instead of contrived stories built around particular reading skills became apparent, and children's literature began to achieve greater prominence as part of literacy instruction.

Whole Language

The whole language movement had its beginnings in the work of people like Frank Smith (1988), Kenneth Goodman (1986), and others who recognized that it was psycholinguistically naive to attempt to divide language into so many discrete and isolated components in teaching children to read and write. Whole language advocates suggested that pupils be taught to read and write in a more integrated, holistic fashion. Rather than teaching reading by means of mastering separate and isolated units, an approach emerged that emphasized the close interrelationship of language components.

Despite the popular use of the expression, ''whole language'' is not an easy term to define. In search of a definition, Bergeron (1990) reviewed 64 articles pertaining to whole language. She found it variously described as an approach, a belief, a method, a philosophy, an orientation, a theory, a theoretical orientation, a program, a curriculum, a perspective on education, and an attitude of mind. Bergeron even found the same expert defining whole language differently in different sources. Taken together, the various attempts to define the concept of whole language reflect what Newman (1985) calls a ''state of mind'' and what Watson (1989) calls ''the spirit'' of whole language.

In explaining the theory of whole language, Cambourne (1989) examines the process of learning to read and write in light of the process of learning to speak. Cambourne acknowledges that learning to talk is a stunning intellectual achievement (that) ''little children with extremely immature brains have been learning successfully for thousands of years'' (p. 31). He proposes that the human brain can ''learn to process oral and written forms of language in much the same way, provided the conditions under which each is learned are also much the same'' (p. 30). What are these conditions?

Immersion   When children learn language, they are immersed in a total language environment. In the classroom, this translates into a constant focus on reading and writing activities. Pupils are surrounded and bombarded with what they are supposed to learn—printed language.

Modeling   In learning to talk, children are constantly exposed to others using language in different ways for different purposes. In school, teachers and pupils see each other as language models using print for the same variety of purposes.

Holistic   Children learn language as a whole, not in little bits and pieces. In the classroom, learning to read and write is integrated in holistic, meaningful contexts.

Authentic   Children learn to talk in authentic situations, not artificial ones. Parents do not indicate which ''20 words for the week'' their children should learn. In whole language classrooms, activities ''involve genuine communication of important meanings, not simply practice of communication skills that would be put to real use at some later time'' (Sumara and Walker, 1991; p. 283).

Purposefulness   In learning language, children learn not only what speech is but also what it can do. In learning to read and write, pupils learn the many functions that print can play in their lives and how they can use literacy in practical ways to influence their relationships with others.

Risk-Taking   In learning to talk, children are not afraid to experiment with language; they are not expected to talk like adults from the very beginning. In the classroom, there is a willingness to take risks with invented spelling and attempts to read books beyond pupils' perceived ability levels.

Expectation of Success   Although there is tolerance for error in the process of language acquisition, few parents doubt that their children will eventually learn to talk. There is a corresponding expectation of success in reading and writing in the philosophy of whole language.

Classroom instruction in reading and writing has been changed dramatically by all the attention given to whole language teaching. Even those teachers who do not consider themselves ''whole language teachers'' are being splashed, if not doused, by the wave of whole language. More writing is being taught. More trade books are being used. Language arts is becoming an integral part of instruction in content areas of the

Contrasting Whole Language Theory

THE FOLLOWING chart (Reutzel and Hollingsworth, 1988) summarizes major differences between whole language theory and conventional theories of language instruction in the classroom.

What it is . . .	What it isn't . . .

Philosophical Views about Children and Language

1. Humanism is the philosophical base.
2. Children already know how to learn.

3. Process is most important.
4. Language is indivisible.

1. Essentialism is the philosophical base.
2. Teachers must teach children how to learn.
3. Product is most important.
4. Language is divisible.

Research Support

1. Ethnographic and qualitative research predominate.
2. Instruction is based on language acquisition and development research.

1. Experimental and quantitative methods research methods predominate.
2. Instruction is based on scientific analysis of learning research.

How Children Learn Language

1. Whole to parts learning is emphasized.
2. Learning begins with the concrete and moves to the abstract.
3. Instruction is based on transactional/transformational theories in reading.
4. Instruction is associated with theories of gestalt psychology.
5. Language learning is based on personal relevance and experience.
6. Learners use language for personal purposes.
7. Inward forces motivate learning.
8. No extrinsic rewards are given for behavior.
9. Language is learned through immersion.

1. Parts to whole learning is emphasized.
2. Learning begins with the abstract and moves to the concrete.
3. Instruction is based on transmission/interactive theories in reading.
4. Instruction is associated with theories of cognitive and behavioristic psychology.
5. Language learning is based on a hierarchy of skills.
6. Learners use language to satisfy others.
7. Outward forces motivate learning.
8. Extrinsic rewards are given for learning and behavior.
9. Language is learned through imitation and shaping.

Classroom Environment

1. School learning is like home.
2. Environment is ''littered'' with children's and teacher's printed language.
3. Centers focus on a topic or theme, i.e., kites, karate, etc.
4. Groups are flexible and often formed by interest.
5. Classroom fosters cooperation and collaboration.

1. School learning is different from home.
2. Environment is often teacher made professional bulletin boards or exhibit of children's perfect papers.
3. Centers focus on skill acquisition.
4. Groups are inflexible and often by achievement.
5. Classroom fosters competitiveness and isolation.

Teacher Behavior

1. Teachers facilitate learning.
2. Teachers do not label or categorize children.
3. Instruction is informal and discovery.
4. Teachers give children choices.
5. Teachers emphasize trying and taking risks.
6. Teachers emphasize the meaning of language.
7. Instruction takes place in sentence level language units or larger.
8. Phonics principles are taught in known sight words using the analytic aproach.
9. Teachers instruct with whole stories, books or poems.
10. Brainstorming is used to build background experiences for instruction.
11. Teachers are always teaching by example.
12. Teachers participate with students in reading and writing.

1. Teachers direct learning.
2. Teachers often label children, e.g., dyslexic, buzzards, weeds, etc.
3. Instruction is formal, direct and based, systematic.
4. Teachers do not often give children choices.
5. Teachers emphasize correctness and accuracy.
6. Teachers often emphasize the isolated parts of language.
7. Instruction focuses on small steps in skill acquisition.
8. Phonics principles are often taught in isolation using the synthetic approach
9. Teachers instruct with learning letter names/sounds and basal readers.
10. Advanced organizers are used to build background for instruction.
11. Teachers often teach only by precept.
12. Teachers seldom participate in reading assigned tasks on an equal basis with children.

Child Behavior

1. Children often plan their own learning.
2. Children often choose their own topics/ purposes for writing.
3. Children often assist one another in reading and writing.
4. Children use language to learn about their language.
5. Children participate more often in discussion, etc.

1. Children follow the plan set by the teacher.
2. Children follow the assigned purposes for writing.
3. Children often compete with one another in reading and writing.
4. Children learn language conventions to use language.
5. Children often work privately and quietly at their desks.

Evaluation

1. Evaluation is informal—kid-watching, tapes, samples.

1. Evaluation is formal—standardized or criterion referenced.

From ''Whole Language and the Practitioner'' by D. Ray Reutzel and Paul M. Hollingsworth, in *Academic Therapy*, 23, 405–16, 1988. Copyright © 1988 by PRO-ED, Inc. Reprinted by permission.

curriculum. Basal reading series are moving away from rigid reliance on a skills model. As a result of these cumulative changes, literacy instruction will never be the same.

Part of the spirit of whole language is the increased use of literature in the classroom. In the very early grades, pupils learn easy-to-read stories with repeated language patterns. Children use their language skills to build stories around wordless books such as Jan Omerod's *Sunshine* and Misumasa Anno's many picture books such as *Anno's Journey* and *Anno's Flea Market.* In the primary grades, children enjoy old favorite picture books such as Esphyr Slobodkina's *Caps for Sale* and Ludwig Bemelmans' *Madeline,* along with newer titles that have quickly become favorites such as Pamela Allen's *Who Sank the Boat?* and Nancy Van Laan's *Possum Come A-Knockin'.* Throughout their school lives, pupils come to enjoy the people, places, adventures, emotions, and other experiences with books. They recognize the genius in the language and imagination of authors like Arnold Lobel, Roald Dahl, Maurice Sendak, Virginia Hamilton, Katherine Paterson, and the hundreds of other writers and illustrators who produce quality literature for children. Encounters with literature are a vital part of their daily lives in the classroom.

Consistent with whole language practice, literature is being used to cement the reading–writing connection, and informational trade books are used in thematic units at all grade levels. In short, more and more classrooms have moved closer to literature-based programs.

Advantages of Using Literature

The enormous advantages of using children's literature at the heart of a classroom language program have become apparent with widespread use. Literature has a powerful impact not only on children's reading ability, but also on their inclination to read. Literature offers many advantages, described below.

Affective Response   Literature generates enjoyment. Trade books address the affective side of reading by promoting positive attitudes. When the names of a beloved character or favorite book are mentioned, people typically respond, ''I **love** that character,'' or ''Isn't that book **wonderful.**'' Words like *love* and *wonderful* are part of the affective side of reading. Literature generates a positive attitude—a love of reading—that is the ultimate goal of teaching children how to read. The purpose of education is to create learners. The purpose of reading instruction is to create readers, not only people who can read but those who *will* read. The inclination to read is an attitude that literature promotes.

Involvement in Reading   Trade books involve pupils in the act of learning to read by reading. In skill-development programs, pupils spend lots of time doing skills-related exercises. A national survey of reading practices indicates that pupils spend as much as 70 percent of their reading instructional time doing seatwork; they spend considerably more time with their workbooks than they do with their teachers (Anderson et al., 1985). Literature involves reading, not filling out worksheets. ''Children's literature arouses children's imaginations, emotions, and sympathies. It awakens their desire to read, enlarges their lives, and provides a sense of purpose and identity'' (Trelease, 1985; p. 23). Besides, with trade books at the heart of the program, children learn to read by reading.

1.4 Putting Ideas to Work

Describing a Literature-Based Program

HEPLER (1989) poses the question, "How does a year look when you have a full-blown literature program?" and answers it in this way:

> You would have set aside time for reading aloud, Sustained Silent Reading, and group work, whether reading with you, working independently, or working in small purposeful groups. You would have decided on an author or two to study and a thematic unit or two to develop in concert with another teacher. You would have in place some form of record keeping that would include what children have read, heard read, and have made in response to books. And you would have a repertoire of experiences you would wish children to have—delight in rhyme and repetition of Mother Goose and discovery of cumulative pattern in folktales for kindergartners, or appreciation of figurative language both in poetry and in the books of Byars for fifth graders.

> Your classroom would show that children love books. There would be a reading corner, displays of books currently being worked on, perhaps a chart of books read aloud so far this year with stars by the ones most favored by the class, and bulletin boards not of canned and preprinted posters but of children's work. Of course, there would be no book report forms. Instead, writing in many modes—explanations, first-person accounts, letters, "next chapters", poetry—as well as a variety of projects would reflect the teacher's understanding of how to help children organize their literary experiences.

> Most importantly, children would be brimming with enthusiasm to tell visitors to the classroom or each other about the books they are enjoying and what they are discovering. Their ability to discuss what they read would be expanding with practice so that literary terms and patterns would be an easy part of their vocabulary. They would know and love some authors and illustrators. And they would see themselves as readers. So would you. (pp. 218–219)

Extracted with permission from S. Hepler, "A Literature Program: Getting It Together, Keeping It Going" in *Children's Literature in the Classroom: Weaving Charlotte's Web,* edited by Janet Hickman and Bernice E. Cullinan. Copyright © 1989 by Christopher-Gordon Publishers, Inc., Norwood, MA.

Classroom displays related to trade books document the fact that literature is an important part of the reading program.

Content   The content of trade books is generally appealing to children. Publishers of school books need to be careful about what they put in their reading material because they have to respond to a variety of easily offended pressure groups. School books do not have to please everybody, but they cannot offend anyone. Publishers of school texts need to shy away from topics that might offend any sensibilities. It is difficult—some say impossible—to provide an interesting diet of reading material with such constraints. Censorship and parent pressure can sometimes be an issue in selecting trade books for literature-based instruction (See 2.5, p. 44), but literature offers a far broader range of appealing material for reading.

Literature provides first-rate stories with topics that often constitute the real stuff in the real lives of real children. After a comparative analysis of elements of story structure in trade books and in conventional basal stories, one researcher concluded, ''We should expand the range of story types within basals or supplement them with trade books'' (Bruce, 1984; p. 157). Since teachers do not have it within their power to broaden the range of basal stories, they are left with the alternative of making greater use of trade books in their reading programs.

Language   Authors of quality children's books—people like Robert McCluskey and Betsy Byars, Mildred Taylor and Chris Van Allsberg—give pupils the best that language has to offer. The language of literature is rich and appealing, written for meaning without tight vocabulary control. Before publication, a trade book comes under the critical scrutiny of an editor, so there is an element of ''quality control'' instead of vocabulary control. In literature, the best children's authors produce the best of language for pupils.

Skills and Strategies   For all the benefits on the affective side of reading, children's literature can be used effectively to help pupils develop particular reading skills and strategies. ''Essential reading skills can be taught through a literature-based curriculum in a subtle, efficient manner within the context of material each child is reading'' (Fuhler, 1990; p. 314). Effective vocabulary lessons on synonyms and antonyms, for example, can be spun off from Judith Viorst's wonderful *Alexander and the Terrible, Horrible, No Good, Very Bad Day.* Folktales, fairy tales, animal stories, legends, fantasy, realistic fiction, poetry, and all the other genres that literature provides can be potent vehicles for developing the critical and creative thinking that reading comprehension requires. As pupils read trade books, they apply skills and develop strategies as they enjoy stories. As long as skill-development does not get in the way of story enjoyment, teachers can ''find'' lessons to improve reading as pupils use trade books as part of learning to read. In learning to write, literature is no less powerful in providing models for writing and material to write about.

It Works   A substantial research base is growing to support the effectiveness of literature-based reading instruction in the classroom. Anecdotal evidence and empirical studies indicate that children's literature is a viable means of teaching children how to read.

Teachers who have implemented literature-based reading programs in their classrooms repeatedly report positive results. Vida Welsh (1985), for example, describes a program in which literature was used as the core of instruction rather than as a supplement to the basal. After strong initial resistance, her opinion changed. ''I could see before my eyes a wonderful thing happening. The teachers were enthused, the kids were extremely happy and productive, and best of all, students were becoming more and more involved in their own education'' (p. 7). And from Carol J. Fuhler (1990), a junior high school teacher: ''I teach a literature-based reading program to a group of learning disabled boys who revel in the absence of worksheets and tests. Two of them showed a three-year growth in reading this year while another improved a year and a half. For students who used to dislike and distrust books, that's exciting'' (p. 315).

Beyond anecdotal accounts, research studies have also shown that using literature is an effective way to help pupils improve their reading abilities. Tunnell and Jacobs (1989) reviewed research studies on literature-based reading instruction with different ages and different types of pupils. Their conclusion: ''The success for literature-based programs is well documented'' (p. 476). Savage (1992) reviewed research on using literature with ''regular'' and with ''at-risk'' pupils. The conclusion: ''The evidence suggests that using trade books as an integral part of the reading instructional program has a strong and positive impact on increasing pupils' reading ability, even when this ability is measured by conventional skill-oriented reading achievement tests'' (p. 30).

Research indicates positive effects of literature on pupils' writing abilities as well. Based on a summary of this research, Noyce and Christie (1989) conclude, ''Children who read large amounts of children's literature are exposed to models of elaborated structures and tend to write more naturally than children whose reading diet consists mainly of basal reader stories'' (p. 5).

In sum, children's literature is having a powerful influence on the development of pupils' reading and writing abilities in the elementary grades, and the increased use of trade books promises to impact instruction in the years ahead.

How Is Literature-Based Reading Different from Conventional Reading Instruction?

Literature-based reading has enormous advantages, and direct instruction in skills and strategies can be made part of literature-based instruction. But there are differences between the contemporary literature-based approach to reading and the conventional skill-development view that has been so prevalent for so long in our schools.

Skill-Development View versus Literature-Based Instruction

For decades, the view of reading that dominated instruction was a *skill-development view;* that is, reading was seen as a series of discrete components or skills, and instruction consisted of helping children develop these skills. The two broad skills areas were vocabulary and comprehension. Each of these was broken into categories and subcategories, so that learning to read involved extensive practice on long inventories of isolated skills and subskills. Pupils spent time doing worksheets and exercises to learn vowels and consonants, synonyms and antonyms, prefixes and suffixes, main ideas and details, and other components that would, it was presumed, ''add up'' to reading. So much time, effort, and attention were devoted to learning these subskills that the bigger picture of reading tended to get lost.

This view of reading came about in large measure as a result of the spirit of the early 20th century, an age of great confidence and expectation in the power of science and technology. There was a rapid spread of scientific information. The benefits of science were being felt in all walks of life. Medical science was advancing. Scientific management principles were applied to business, producing assembly lines that were making the United States an industrial giant. Science was perceived as "the wave of the future."

In this spirit, people became interested in a "science of education." Science was invoked in attempting to discover laws of learning. Principles of scientific management and production were applied to administering schools. Experts conducted "scientific investigations" to validate classroom practices. Standardized tests were designed to measure learning "scientifically." With a scientific approach, each activity was analyzed according to its discrete parts, and each element was further analyzed. Reading was analyzed and divided into its component parts, and the skill-development view of reading was born.

This skill-development framework dominated reading instruction in the decades that followed. Reading was viewed as a combination of skills and was taught that way. Competency was measured in terms of mastering skills. Pupils who failed were given more practice in skills. This constellation of individual skills, it was believed, would come together to produce competent readers.

In contrast to this skill-development view, literature-based instruction starts with story rather than with skills. Total meaning, not mastery of a set of discrete and isolated skills, is the goal of instruction. Reading is seen as a holistic activity. Conventional skills are not ignored, since readers need to know the meaning of words and be able to figure out words they do not recognize in order to arrive at meaning. But with a literature-based approach, the primary emphasis in teaching reading is on understanding story, and the major means of helping pupils achieve this understanding is literature.

Basal Readers

The skill-development view of reading was implemented largely through the use of basal reading programs. The basal system became the technology through which science was applied to the teaching of reading. "Basal reading materials met the expectations of a public and profession enthralled with business, science and psychology" (Goodman, Shannon, Freeman, and Murphy, 1988; p. 19). The aura of scientific authority surrounding basals has persisted. Many educators continue to see basals as embodying scientific truth when it comes to teaching reading (Shannon, 1983), and many teachers still rely heavily on them as teaching tools in the classroom.

Basals are used to teach reading in over 90 percent of the classrooms in the United States, and these "reading schemes" have been used widely in English-speaking countries such as Great Britain (Arnold, 1982) and Australia (Winch, 1982) as well. They remain among the most widely used instructional tools on the educational landscape, and their popularity makes them powerful in shaping the way reading is taught in schools.

At the heart of any basal program is its *scope and sequence* of skills. For any program, a scope and sequence chart presents a comprehensive overview of the skills

1.5
FOR YOUR INFORMATION
What Is a Basal Series?

A BASAL reading program is a series of instructional materials designed specifically for teaching reading from kindergarten through sixth (and sometimes eighth) grade. The series consists of:

Readers, graded textbooks containing stories, poems, an occasional play, riddles, and other material for children to read. A series will typically contain 15 or 20 of these reading texts—several preprimers for the very early stages of reading and two books at each grade level.

Workbooks with worksheets containing exercises directly related to the stories in the readers themselves. These worksheets are designed to help pupils develop or review the reading skills and subskills presented in the program, and the exercises are often directly related to the content of particular stories in the pupils' texts.

Teacher's editions, manuals that contain detailed lesson plans, questions, teaching suggestions, activities, background information, answers to exercises, and other material designed to direct the teacher on how to use the program.

Tests to assess skill development and to monitor pupils' progress through the program.

While the readers, workbooks, teacher editions and tests constitute the four essential components of a basal series, these programs typically have additional components as well, including:

Additional tests of various kinds—placement tests, level tests, skills-mastery tests, and informal assessment devices designed to indicate where a student should begin in a program and/or how well a student has learned the skills that the program is designed to teach.

More workbooks in addition to those that are part of the basic program—reinforcement workbooks with additional worksheets for those pupils who may need additional skills practice; supplementary workbooks for enrichment exercises to address or extend skills that may not be addressed in the basic part of the program; ESL (English as a Second Language) exercises; skill sheets to be done at home; and other skill development components.

Parent materials such as newsletters, sample correspondence, and other information designed to explain the program to parents.

Record-keeping tools such as charts, forms, folders, and other devices to provide a system for recording pupils' scores and progress.

Literature-related materials such as trade books, activity cards, read-aloud libraries, and other materials that reflect the increased use of literature in the reading curriculum.

Other materials that might include Big Books, wall charts, card sets, tapes, and other materials designed to reinforce or extend the skills that the basal is designed to teach.

---

component of the series. To many, the scope and sequence chart represents the embodiment of an isolated skills philosophy. It deals with every skill at every level. It indicates where in the program a particular skill is introduced, where it is reinforced or practiced, and the point at which it should be mastered. Typically, skills are broken down according to the various strands included in the basal: comprehension, vocabulary, decoding, study skills, language skills, literature, and other skills areas. The scope and sequence chart is the blueprint upon which an entire basal program is built.

Pros and Cons of a Basal Program   Basal programs offer attractive benefits for teaching reading, particularly for the beginning teacher. Basals have not, however, escaped their share of criticism, especially in recent years.

On the positive side, basals provide comprehensive, structured tools to use in teaching reading. They contain a carefully chosen reading material, with directions on how to present this material in an orderly and sequenced manner. They address any dimensions of learning to read—oral and silent reading, narrative and expository text, strategies for developing a full range of reading competencies.

Basals help the teacher relate theory to practice. "Basal series play a critical role in reading instruction in part because of the difficulties associated with translating research findings and theory into practice" (McCallum, 1988; p. 204). Designed by reputable experts in the field of reading instruction, basals offer ready-made tools to translate current theory into instructional practice. They provide decision-making tools for teachers, with suggestions on how to present materials and extend ideas.

Basals facilitate organization, in that each part contributes to the organization and management of a classroom reading program. They provide teachers with a sense of security. Teachers feel that if they follow the basal, nothing will be omitted from the instructional diet. Basals give administrators confidence that a well-designed plan is being followed in their schools. Basals give pupils the sense of progression as they move from one level of a program to the next.

On the negative side, some heavy criticism has been leveled against basal programs. Criticism has been leveled against:

Scope and sequence, in that the tightly ordered sequence of skills does not reflect the way children acquire language in a natural and authentic manner.

Language, in that stories created specifically for skill development result in language that is artificially stiff and formal.

Content, in that too many stories present a sterile world populated by cardboard characters who hardly reflect realistic role models for pupils.

Workbooks that contain tedious skill development exercises that "distort children's view of language. Huffing and puffing at letters, marking whether vowels are glided or unglided, deciding whether *b* or *d* goes at the beginning or ending of the tattered remnant of a mutilated word rendered meaningless in its isolation—these merely leave children puzzled about what it's all about. Such Kafka-esque activities are not likely to motivate the learner, nor will they provide promise of the best repertoire of pleasure and increased social power that literacy provides" (Johnson and Louis, 1987; p. 3).

Teachers editions with scripted lessons that tend to ritualize instruction and a wealth of suggestions that turns out to be "a quagmire from which the floundering teacher must dig her own way out or sink" (Yatvin, 1980; p. 13).

Perhaps the greatest concern or criticism expressed about basal programs is the overreliance on these instructional tools. Many teachers see the basal as the only reading material that they need to provide for pupils. They are reluctant to abandon the basal even for a short time, for fear that their pupils will somehow lose out if they miss a workbook page or skip a story. So much is included in a typical basal program that teachers never run out of things to do, and many feel compelled to finish the program. With that type of thinking, pupils get very little reading material beyond the basal. "The roles of teachers and the textbook seem to be reversed . . . whereby teachers become a support system for the textbook rather than the other way around" (Shannon, 1989; p. xiv).

Newer Basal Programs   More recent basal series have responded to the concerns and criticisms. While the idea of a comprehensive graded series has remained the same, most contemporary basal programs include far fewer subskills. Model lessons and teaching suggestions reflect updated theories of learning to read. Assessment components have expanded, and workbooks contain more open-ended activities and exercises that encourage pupils to write instead of merely filling in blanks or underlining items in isolated skills-based exercises. But perhaps the most striking change that has occurred in basal programs today is the increased inclusion of literature.

Basals have been caught up in the tidal wave of literature that has swept literacy instruction. Conventional programs contained occasional selections from popular children's stories, but these stories often underwent some procrustean alterations before being made part of the series. Language was altered to conform to the intended grade level of the book, adjustments were made to bring the story in line with the skill being taught, and content was changed to eliminate possible objections to what the story contained.

Contemporary programs have far more literature than their predecessors, and though some adjustments of stories are still made, much of this literature is unexpurgated. "Freshly revised textbook series reflect a concerted effort to include recognized children's authors, a variety of literary genre, excerpts, and complete stories from award winning books" (Fuhler, 1990; p. 312). In addition to simple repetitive stories such as *The Gingerbread Man* at the kindergarten level, today's basals include folktales and fairy tales, selections from contemporary fiction, expository selections, poetry, and the full range of material that constitutes the world of literature for children.

Beyond the inclusion of more literary selections in the readers themselves, basal programs reflect other qualities of literature-based instruction. There is more attention to author awareness and more involvement in helping pupils understand qualities of good literature rather than merely developing skills. Teachers are encouraged to move pupils beyond the pages of the basal text and into books containing original versions of the stories. Some basals offer a collection of trade books as an ancillary feature of the program. Reflecting the growing emphasis on the use of literature, even the ubiquitous basal has adopted a literature-based approach to teaching reading.

Achieving a Synthesis

How best to teach children how to read has been an ongoing argument in literate societies for centuries (Mathews, 1966), sometimes with religious intensity. Eminent literacy educators have engaged in what Allington has described as "oppositional polemics and politics, us-versus-them groupings, good-guys-versus-bad-guys characterizations" (Adams, Allington et al, 1991; p. 373). Kantrowitz (1990) has termed the controversy "The Reading Wars."

What is this debate all about? The issues take different forms—decoding versus meaning, top-down model versus bottom-up model, skills-based approach versus whole language approach, text-based perspective versus reader-based perspective, use of basal versus use of trade books—and not everybody on one side of the question or the other is in complete agreement with everyone else in the same camp. Cheek (1989)

1.6
FOR YOUR INFORMATION
Approaches to Teaching Reading

Other ideas and programs for helping pupils learn to read have been used in schools in the recent past, including:

Language experience approaches that involve having children dictate stories, which are then transcribed and used for reading instruction.

Color-coded programs that utilize colors as additional visual clues to help pupils remember sound–symbol relationships.

Picture-writing aids that use simple drawings or rebus symbols in place of words and letters.

Reformed alphabet approaches that add symbols to augment or supplement the 26 letters of our alphabet.

Computer programs that use the computer as a device to present pupils with letters, words, sentences, and longer passages to help them develop basic reading competency.

Aukerman (1984) has identified 165 different approaches or programs that have been designed to teach children how to read. Each of these systems, and scores of others, has enjoyed a measure of popularity and success among devotees, and many can still be found in schools today.

summarizes the issue as a basic difference between skills-based and holistic philosophies, and he describes the impact that the debate has had on preparing teachers to teach reading and on reading programs in schools.

These arguments trace their origins to one's view of language or conceptions of the reading process. Through colonial and later periods in schools, the decoding aspects of reading instruction were emphasized. Reading was taught by having children memorize sounds and syllables, and then read by attaching the correct sounds to the symbols they encounter on the page. In the second half of the 19th century, Horace Mann questioned what he termed the "torturous practice of subjecting young children to the tedious task of first learning letters and sounds." When Mann visited Germany, he found Prussian educators teaching children to read whole words at a time, and he ardently promoted the use of this "new revolutionary" method of teaching reading when he returned home. Mann's ideas caught on, and this technique was adopted by basal reading programs published through the middle of the 20th century.

During the 1960s, the pendulum swung back to code-emphasis approaches, those that stressed sound–symbol associations as the best way to learn to read. Linguistic programs were widely used, programs in which vocabulary was controlled by consistent spelling patterns, producing sentences like *Flick the tick off the chick with a thick stick, Nick.* The pendulum subsequently swung back to a more eclectic approach, and literature-based instruction began to emerge.

Basals versus Trade Books

A major part of the current debate about reading instruction relates to questions regarding skills-based versus whole language programs. Basal reading series have been used so widely for so many years to deliver a skills model to pupils, and schools have for so long viewed reading primarily as a skill-development process, that any departure from this view is still occasionally treated with suspicion or uneasiness. At the same time, whole language theory has come to be more widely accepted by so many teachers, and the appeal of using quality trade books is so compelling, that a literature-based approach to teaching reading is sweeping schools. Those entering teaching today are faced with the important decision about determining which approach to use.

Does the decision to use a whole language or a skills-based model, or to use basal readers or trade books as primary vehicles for reading instruction, have to be an either/or proposition? Some researchers insist that the two views are so theoretically at odds with each other that they constitute "conflicting educational paradigms" that cannot be reconciled (Edelsky, 1990); others suggest that a consensus model makes practical sense. Speigel (1992) calls for building bridges between traditional, direct instruction and more holistic, literature-based programs by blending "the best of both in order to help every child reach his or her full literacy potential" (p. 43). Rather than focusing on incompatibilities and points of conflict, teachers need to see how direct teaching of reading skills/strategies can be made part of literature-based instruction.

Different theories tend to be dichotomized, and teachers are led to believe that any deviation from a theory compromises quality instruction and intellectual integrity. Instead, quality instruction comes from inspired teaching. "Inspired teaching does not originate in a particular philosophy, theory approach, or program. It originates in the creativity of teachers" (Duffy, 1992). In the practical reality of most classrooms, creative teachers skillfully synthesize skill-development and the literature-based approachs into a reading and writing program that makes sense for pupils while it helps them achieve competence as literate users of language.

How to Synthesize

The different theoretical models can be used together in various ways as part of reading and writing instruction. Strategies conventionally associated with the skill-developmental approach can be effectively integrated into instructional activities using literature. Trade books and basals can be used to complement each other in well-planned instructional segments.

Integration of reading strategies with literature occurs as teachers use trade books to illustrate and apply sound reading techniques. For example, Lapp, Flood, and Farnan (1992) illustrate how teachers can model such techniques as setting purposes, making predictions, building vocabulary, and checking for understanding—all components of a typical basal reader lesson—while using a biography that pupils may be reading.

Synthesis occurs through integrated speaking/listening/reading/writing activities that start with literature. The teacher shares a story and pupils dictate their own account of the story, which the teacher transcribes on a chart. As the group reads the story on the chart, the teacher covers certain words and asks pupils to predict what the words might be (context), to suggest other words that might be used (vocabulary), or to call attention to certain sound–symbol relationships in the words (phonics). The teacher can also help pupils see how the story progresses (story structure), the relationship between ideas in the story (cause–effect relationships, for example), or how the story might have ended differently (creative thinking). In activities such as these, literature is the starting point and strategies are modeled and applied within the context of the material, always keeping enjoyment of the story paramount.

Thematic units integrate direct skills approaches using literature. In a science unit on insects, for example, children read stories like Julie Brinckloe's *Fireflies* and the humorous verses in Nancy Winslow Parker and Joan Richards Wright's *Bugs.* Pupils write factual accounts of what they learn and imaginative stories based on information about insects. They do paintings of insects and compile lists of what bugs eat. All the while, the teacher is providing lessons on how language works, how readers and writers communicate, how to make predictions and monitor meaning while reading, how to use context and phonics when they meet words they do not know, and how to reflect on what they have learned.

Used side by side, trade books and basals provide balance in a reading program. Teachers committed to using literature are sometimes required by school policy to use a basal program. Other teachers, while recognizing the importance and appeal of quality literature, feel secure with the structure and organization of a basal series.

Basal readers and trade books can complement each other in a number of ways. The basal may be used part of the week, while trade books constitute the focus of instruction the rest of the time. Weekly units can be planned, with a two-week basal unit followed by a three-week unit based on fantasy, biography, or folklore that uses both trade books and appropriate selections from basals at different levels. One group may be reading from the basal while another is using a trade book as part of directed reading lessons.

Even when basals are closely followed, there are frequent opportunities for interactions with trade books through read-alouds, book sharing, sustained silent reading, journal writing, literature study groups, and discussions and conversations about books all day long.

Advantages of a Combined Program

Duffy (1992) identifies three advantages of combining literature-based instruction with more structured approaches. First, with trade books and authentic reading–writing opportunities, skills and strategies are learned within the context of practical experiences. The focus is on teaching and learning for understanding, not for the purpose of completing a workbook page or passing a test. Second, there is direct instruction, with the teacher playing a direct role and the pupils applying what they have learned in realistic ways. Third, pupils "do what literate people do in real life—use reading to complete genuine and useful tasks successfully" (p. 445).

A combined or synthesized program is geared to individual differences in teachers. As humans, teachers are different from one another. Some teachers, while they recognize the importance and value of literature, are more confident with the support that the structure of a basal program offers. Other teachers chafe at the bondage of a scope-and-sequenced program; they prefer to put aside basals in favor of the exclusive use of trade books. Most of us are somewhere between these two extremes, and synthesized instructional programs use literature while finding a middle ground in which we are comfortable.

As humans, we change. It is possible for teachers to move from a skills-based view to a language-based view as they gain more confidence with experience. Synthesizing instruction from different approaches suggests the possibility of a teacher changing and adapting according to the levels and needs of a particular class.

Teaching is a uniquely human enterprise. Having comprehensively reviewed 165 programs designed to teach reading, Aukerman (1984) concluded, "the answer (to

A Continuum

THE USE of trade books and basal readers for reading instruction might be viewed as two extremes on a continuum. At one extreme are teachers who see reading primarily as a skill-development activity and who rely so heavily on basal programs that they have little time to use trade books as part of their language arts program. At the other extreme are teachers who see reading as a holistic activity and who rely exclusively on trade books as instructional vehicles for teaching reading and writing.

Along this continuum, there is a considerable middle ground where teachers find an overlap between both views. It is within these areas that synthesis occurs. This model is a dynamic view adapted to the human nature of teachers.

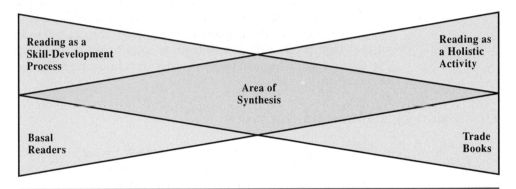

which is the best method for teaching reading) lies neither in the materials or the methods, but in the commitment that a practitioner is willing to make'' (p. 607). While recognizing human variability, today's education demands that all teachers use literature as an integral component of literacy instruction in the classroom.

What follows in this book is a further description of literature-based instruction. The ideas presented are based on the belief that, while basals may be used and direct teaching of skills and strategies may be appropriate, children's literature belongs as the centerpiece of the language arts curriculum—the heart and soul of the classroom program—and that trade books can be used as primary vehicles for helping pupils develop the ability to read and write, along with the inclination to do so.

Summary and Conclusions

Literature has become a powerful force in language arts instruction in schools. Increasingly, children's literature is being included as the centerpiece of reading and writing instruction in the elementary grades.

Teachers and researchers have sought to determine the best way to teach children how to read and write. Different approaches and philosophies have been attempted. Throughout most of the 20th century, instruction was dominated by basal programs, sets of reading books and related materials designed to provide a total instructional diet for pupils. Although the instructional emphasis of these programs differed from time to time, the nature and purpose of basals generally remained the same: namely, to help children learn to read by providing them with a structured program of skills to be learned.

As schools approach the 21st century, the widespread acceptance of whole language theory—which suggests that reading be taught as a holistic entity rather than as a set of discrete and isolated skills—has brought about the widespread use of trade books as tools for teaching reading and writing. This tidal wave of literature has swept schools, transforming instructional programs in the elementary grades. More and more schools are instituting a literature-based approach as the advantages of this approach becomes apparent. Sometimes trade books are used exclusively as basis of an instructional program; at other times, they are combined with more conventional methods and materials in a synthesized system that keeps literature at the heart of the program.

Even the best literature alone is not enough to assure success, however. Success comes from the efforts of inspired and knowledgeable teachers who can analyze the needs of their pupils and adapt instruction accordingly. That is what this text aims to help teachers learn. Inspired teachers using good literature make a strong combination for tomorrow's readers.

Discussion Questions and Activities

1. What was your favorite trade book as a child? What made it your favorite? If you were to share this book with a child today, how would you share it?
2. Do some research on the topic of whole language. (Finding references should not be difficult.) Based on your research, write a two- or three-paragraph description of what whole language involves in the classroom.
3. In your school's Curriculum Library or Educational Resource Center, review a set of basal readers. Select a sample that includes the reader, workbook, and teachers edition from the same grade level. Note how much literature is used in the material. Write a brief critique of these materials as instructional tools, telling why you would/would not use them as part of your reading instructional program.
4. How does the use of literature relate to what you know about whole language theory? With a partner or in a group, make a list of ways that trade books can be used as instructional tools in the reading program.
5. Respond to the following statement: ''My teacher uses a literature-based approach to teaching reading. Last week, she put away the basal and gave the class a book on Helen Keller with 17 worksheets to complete. This is using literature to teach reading, isn't it?''

School-Based Assignments

1. Survey the classroom in which you are working as part of your field placement. Using the descriptive characteristics listed in 1.5, how would you rate your classroom as a literature-based environment? Why?
2. Observe a reading lesson taught by an experienced teacher. Note the type of material the teacher chooses, how he or she prepares the pupils, guides their reading, and checks comprehension. What might you do differently if you were the teacher?

3. Interview teachers about the topic of whole language and the use of children's literature to teach reading. What are some of the advantages that these teachers express? What are some of their concerns?
4. Talk to the children in your class about the trade books that they are reading. Which ones are their favorites? Why? What might you do to build an instructional component around these books?
5. As a teacher, you are forming your own model or view of reading. Place yourself on the Basal/Trade Book continuum in 1.7. Tell why you place yourself at that point. Describe the implications that your position would have if you were in charge of teaching reading in your field placement.

Children's Trade Books Cited in This Chapter

Allen, Pamela. *Who Sank the Boat?* New York: Coward, 1983.

Anno, Mitsumasa. *Anno's Flea Market.* New York: Philomel, 1984.

———. *Anno's Journey.* New York: Philomel, 1978.

Babbitt, Natalie. *Tuck Everlasting.* New York: Farrar, Straus & Giroux, 1976.

Bemelmans, Ludwig. *Madeline.* New York: Viking, 1962.

Brincklow, Julie. *Fireflies.* New York: Macmillan, 1985.

Cleary, Beverly. *The Mouse and the Motorcycle.* New York: Dell, 1980.

Dahl, Roald. *Danny, Champion of the World.* New York: Knopf, 1975.

De Clements, Barthe. *The Fourth Grade Wizards.* New York: Viking, 1989.

Dumbrowski, Cathy. *Cave Boy.* New York: Random House, 1989.

Fleischman, Sid. *The Whipping Boy.* New York: Greenwillow, 1986.

Gag, Wanda. *Millions of Cats.* New York: Coward, 1928.

Grimm, Wilhelm, (Translated by Ralph Manheim). *Dear Mili.* New York: Farrar, Straus & Giroux, 1989.

Hutchins, Pat. *Good Night, Owl.* New York: Macmillan, 1972.

Johnson, Angela. *Tell Me A Story, Mama.* New York: Orchard Books, 1989.

Kipling, Rudyard. *Just So Stories.* New York: Viking, 1902.

Lawson, Robert. *Rabbit Hill.* New York: Viking, 1941.

Mosel, Arline. *Tikki, Tikki, Tembo.* New York: Holt, 1968.

Omerod, Jan. *Moonlight.* New York: Lothrop, Lee & Shepard, 1982.

Parker, Nancy Winslow, and Joan Richards Wright. *Bugs.* New York: Greenwillow, 1987.

Sandburg, Carl. *The Rootabaga Stories.* New York: Odyssey, 1968.

Sendak, Maurice. *Where The Wild Things Are.* New York: Harper and Row, 1963.

Slobodkina, Esphyr. *Caps for Sale.* New York: Harper and Row, 1947.

Taylor, Mildred. *The Gold Cadillac.* New York: Bantam, 1987.

Van Laan, Nancy. *Possum Come A-Knockin'.* New York: Knopf, 1990.

Viorst, Judith. *Alexander and the Terrible, Horrible, No Good, Very Bad Day.* New York: Macmillan, 1971.

Yashima, Taro. *Crow Boy.* New York: Viking, 1955.

References

Adams, M. J., Allington, R. L. et. al. (1991). Beginning to Read: A Critique by Literacy Professionals and a Response from Marilyn Jager Adams. *The Reading Teacher* 44:370–395.

Anderson, R. C. et al. (1985). *Becoming a Nation of Readers.* Washington, DC: National Institute of Education.

Arnold, H. (1982). *Listening to Children Read.* London: United Kingdom Reading Association.

Aukerman, R. C. (1984). *Approaches To Beginning Reading* (2nd ed.). New York: John Wiley and Sons.

Bergeron, B. S. (1990). What Does the Term Whole Language Mean? Constructing a Definition from the Literatue. *Journal of Reading Behavior* 22:301–329.

Bruce, B. (1984). A New Point of View on Children's Stories. In R. C. Anderson, J. Osborn, and R. J. Tierney (eds.), *Learning to Read in American Schools: Basal Readers and Content Texts* (pp. 153–174). Hillsdale: Lawrence Erlbaum Associates.

California State Department of Education (1987). *English Language Arts Framework for California Public Schools.* Sacramento: California State Department of Education.

Cambourne, B. (1988). *The Whole Story: Natural Learning and the Acquisition in the Classroom.* New York: Ashton-Scholastic.

Cheek, E. H. Jr. (1989). Skills-Based vs. Holistic Philosophies: The Debate Among Teacher Educators in Reading. *Teacher Education Quarterly* 16:15–20.

Culinan, B. E. (1989). Latching onto Literature: Reading Initiatives Take Hold. *School Library Journal* 35:27–31.

Duffy, G. G. (1992). Let's Free Teachers to Be Inspired. *Phi Delta Kappan* 73:442–447.

Edelsky, C. (1990). Whose Agenda Is This Anyway? A Response to McKenna, Robinson, and Miller. *Educational Researcher* 19:7–11.

Fuhler, C. J. (1990). Let's Move toward Literature-Based Reading Instruction. *The Reading Teacher* 44:312–315.

Goodman, K. (1988). *What's Whole in Whole Language?* Richmond Hill, ONT: Scholastic-TAB.

Goodman, K. S. Shannon, P., Freeman, Y. S., and Murphy, S. (1989). *Report Card on Basal Readers.* Katonah, NY: Richard C. Owens Publishers.

Hepler, S. (1989). A Literature Program: Getting It Together, Keeping It Going. In J. Hickman, and B. E. Cullinan (eds.), *Children's Literature in the Classroom: Weaving Charlotte's Web.* Norwood, MA: Christopher Gordon Publishers.

Johnson, T. D., and Louis, D. R. (1987). *Literacy through Literature.* Portsmouth, NH: Heinemann.

Kantrowitz, B. (1990). The Reading Wars. *Newsweek Special Edition: Education, A Consumer's Handbook* 64:8–14.

Lapp, D., Flood, J., and Farnan, N. (1992). Basal Readers and Literarture: A Tight Fit or a Mismatch? In K. D. Wood and A. Moss (eds.), *Exploring Literature in the Classroom: Content and Methods.* Norwood, MA: Christopher-Gordon Publishers.

Mathews, M. M. (1966). *Teaching to Read Historically Considered.* Chicago: University of Chicago Press.

McCallum, R. D. (1988). Don't Throw the Basals Out with the Bath Water. *The Reading Teacher* 42:204–208.

Newman, J., ed. (1985). *Whole Language: Theory in Use.* Portsmouth, NH: Heinemann.

Noyce, R. M., and Christie, J. F. (1989). *Integrating Reading and Writing Instruction in Grades K–8.* Boston: Allyn and Bacon.

Reutzel, D. R., and Hollingsworth, P. M. (1988). Whole Language and the Practitioner. *Academic Therapy* 23:405–415.

Savage, J. F. (1992). Literature-Based Reading Instruction: It Works! *The New England Reading Association Journal* 28: 28–31.

Shannon, P. (1989). *Broken Promises: Reading Instruction in Twentieth Century America.* Granby, MA: Bergin and Garvey Publishers.

Shannon, P. (1983). The Use of Commercial Reading Materials in American Elementary Schools. *Reading Research Quarterly* 19:68–85.

Smith, F. (1988). *Understanding Reading* (4th ed). Hilsdale, NJ: Lawrence Erlbaum Assoc.

Sumara, D., and Walker, L. (1991). The Teacher's Role in Whole Language. *Language Arts* 68:276–285.

Teale, W. (1990). Dear Readers. *Language Arts* 67:808–810.

Trelease, J. (1985). *The Read-Aloud Handbook*. New York: Penguin.

Tunnell, M. O., and Jacobs, J. S. (1989) Using ''Real'' Books: Research Findings on Literature Based Reading Instruction. *The Reading Teacher* 42:470 477.

Watson, D. J. (1989). Defining and Describing Whole Language, *The Elementary School Journal* 90:129–141.

Welsh, V. (1985). Why Change? A Teacher's Perspective. Paper presented at the 1985 Spring Conference of National Council of Teachers of English, Houston. ERIC Document ED 255 868.

Winch, G. (1982). The Use of Reading Schemes: A Comparative Study. In D. Burnes, A. Campbell, and R. Jones (eds.), *Reading, Writing, and Multiculturalism*. Sydney: Australian Reading Association.

Yatvin, J. (1980). *Trade Books or Basals? Two Programs Measured against the Standard of What a Reading Program Should Be*. Urbana, IL: ERIC Clearinghouse on Reading and Communications Skills. ED 215 336.

Zarrillo, J. (1989). Teachers' Interpretations of Literature-Based Reading. *The Reading Teacher* 43:22–28.

Chapter 2

The World of Children's Literature

Chapter 2 Outline

   I. Introduction
  II. Children's Literature: What and Why
 III. A Brief History of Literature for Children
 IV. Literary Genres
     A. Picture Books
     B. Folktales and Fairy Tales
     C. Fantasy
     D. Realistic Fiction
     E. Historical Fiction
     F. Poetry
  V. Literary Elements
     A. Setting
     B. Characterization
     C. Plot
     D. Theme
  VI. Getting to Know Authors
 VII. Summary and Conclusions
Discussion Questions and Activities
School-Based Assignments
Children's Trade Books Cited in This Chapter
References

Features

2.1   Picture Books about Teachers to Tickle the Funnybone
2.2   Sharing Folk Literature through Storytelling
2.3   Award-Winning Books
2.4   Poetry Anthologies for the Classroom Bookshelf
2.5   Censorship
2.6   Story Maps: Roadmaps to Understanding
2.7   Author/Illustrator of the Week/Month
2.8   Where Do You Find Information about Children's Authors?

Key Concepts in This Chapter

Apart from being a vehicle in the development of pupils' literacy competency, children's literature belongs as a major part of the elementary school curriculum because it is part of children's heritage.

Children's literature has a history and tradition leading up to the explosion in the publication of books for young readers in the past decade.

Pupils can experience a variety of literary forms—picture books, folktales and fairy tales, fantasy, realistic fiction, historical fiction, and poetry—as part of their school experiences.

Although literary analysis is not the purpose of using literature in the elementary grades, pupils can become aware of important literary elements such as plot, setting, characterization, theme, and the like as they come to comprehend the stories they read.

An important avenue for helping pupils come to know and appreciate literature is an awareness of the people who create this literature.

T HIS CHAPTER is about literature for children. It is no substitute for a good course in children's literature, a course that is becoming more and more essential for teachers working in today's elementary and middle schools. However, given the scope of the task at hand, this brief overview will have to suffice. Those who have already had a course in children's literature should be able to move fairly quickly through this chapter. Those who haven't had such a course will need to read more carefully.

Children's Literature: What and Why

Children's literature is the body of prose and poetry written specifically for young people. Although designed primarily for children, this body of literature appeals to readers beyond the childhood years. Children's literature also includes works that, although not originally written specifically for children, have proved to be popular with younger readers. For example, Jonathan Swift's *Gulliver's Travels* was written as a critique of humanity addressed to the mature imagination, but it became a glamorous children's adventure story.

Some of the special advantages of using literature to teach reading were presented in the previous chapter, but literature for children has values that extend well beyond those related to developing literacy competency. Literature is part of children's cultural heritage, the human attempt to record, communicate, and control experience from ancient to present times.

Literature is a rich source for feeding and enriching children's language, adding to their store of vocabulary and sharpening their sense of style. It stimulates their intellectual and emotional lives, generating both cognitive and affective responses to ideas. It nurtures children's imaginations by providing them with vicarious experiences from exploring the depths of the ocean in times long gone to reaching the remote regions of outer space in times yet to come. Books afford unlimited opportunities to foster children's personal growth, while providing a window through which children can examine their own emotions and experiences. Literature offers children a chance to weigh their own lives against a wide human spectrum and provides for the development of ethical values and insights. Charlotte Huck (1982) talks about the power of literature to make us ''more human (and) more humane.'' She also identifies literature's power to educate children's hearts as well as their heads, to develop their imaginations, and to provide a lifetime of reading pleasure.

In short, literature for children offers what Maurice Saxby (1987) calls ''The Journey To Joy,'' hours of entertainment, satisfaction, and renewal that are found through the pages of books. Literature is as essential to children's education as it is to their lives.

A Brief History of Literature for Children

The field of children's literature, as all literature, grows out of the oral tradition. Preliterate peoples gathered around the fire to hear storytellers spin tales that would teach and entertain. Many of these storytellers had priestlike powers, as they were charged

A classroom library is important to a literature based reading program.

with keeping an exact account of history alive within their minds and passing this history along to succeeding generations.

The oral tradition continued in the courts and cottages of the Middle Ages, as minstrels and balladeers roamed the countryside sharing popular tales that were later recorded by the Brothers Grimm. Even after William Caxton established a printing press in England in 1476, the oral tradition continued, with an emphasis on both entertainment and instruction. The first children's books were published solely with instructional intent, and the content was usually religious, with horribly didactic titles such as *A Token for Children of New England,* or *Some Examples of Children in Whom the Fear of God Was Remarkably Budding before They Died.*

Among the first nonreligious books published for children were chapbooks, small and crudely printed books that were sold by 17th- and 18th-century street vendors. These roughly illustrated, eight-page books had stories about the adventures of Robin Hood and other popular tales with appeal to a young audience. Mother Goose rhymes and fairy tales also found their way into print in the 1700s.

The beginning of "children's literature" per se is said to have begun in 1744 with the publication of *A Pretty Little Pocketbook* by John Newbery, the man for whom the Newbery Medal is named. Newbery's book was the first that was specifically written and published to entertain and amuse young children. Other books designed for children followed, and while a didactic focus remained, a body of literature designed for a young audience began to emerge.

The 19th century saw tremendous growth in books written for children. Jacob and Wilhelm Grimm recorded the old stories that had been popular in Europe for so long. Hans Christian Andersen wrote his famous fairy tales. American authors like Washington Irving and Nathaniel Hawthorne wrote stories that were popular with youngsters. Although the moralistic trend continued in many books, a growing number of books with no didactic or moralistic intent were written solely to entertain. Louisa

Randolph Caldecott was a 19th century illustrator for whom the annual award for the top American picture book is named.

May Alcott's *Little Women* and Mark Twain's *The Adventures of Huckleberry Finn* appeared toward the end of the century. Jules Verne introduced his popular science fiction stories; Rudyard Kipling wrote his famous animal stories; Lewis Carroll wrote the fantasy *Alice's Adventures in Wonderland*; Edward Lear produced his humorous limericks. These and other books were written and illustrated solely to entertain readers, young and old alike.

In the 1800s, color was introduced in printing, and illustrators began to gain recognition. Pictures were transformed from rough woodcuts and sketches to works of art capturing the mood and tone of the stories and the storytellers. Among the best known of these 19th-century illustrators is Randolph Caldecott, the person for whom the Caldecott medal, the award for the most distinguished American picture book, is named.

In the 20th century, the field of children's literature has truly come into its own. There has been a proliferation of books for children and the value of these books has come to be recognized and respected. In the early decades of the 20th century, picture books became exceedingly popular, while stories like L. M. Montgomery's *Anne of the Green Gables* and Kate Douglas Wiggins's *Rebecca of Sunnybrook Farm* provided reading for older children. Series books like *Tom Swift,* the *Hardy Boys,* and *Nancy Drew* were widely read. Animal fantasies like Beatrix Potter's *Peter Rabbit* and A. A. Milne's *Winnie the Pooh* arrived on the literary landscape. Special collections of poetry for children appeared. Books for children came to be part of classroom instruction.

Today's teachers are witnesses and beneficiaries of the more recent history of children's literature. The production and distribution of juvenile books is big business. Over two thousand books for young readers are published annually, and children's book sales in 1986 totaled almost $10.5 *billion* (Grannis, 1988). Authors like Dr. Seuss have become household names. Books like E. B. White's *Charlotte's Web* and Maurice Sendak's *Where the Wild Things Are* have sold well over one million copies. Children's trade books have come to be an integral part of reading instruction in schools.

Literary Genres

In a literature-based reading program, pupils encounter a range of literary genres— picture books; fairy tales, folktales and other forms of traditional literature; fantasy, including animal stories; realistic fiction; historical fiction; and poetry. Some types of books will be prevalent at one grade level rather than another (picture books in the primary grades, for example); some (like poetry) will be appropriate at all grade levels.

Picture Books

From the very early years, pupils are exposed to picture books, books in which illustrations are essential complements to the text in telling the story. In these books, the visual and the verbal work together; both illustrations and words are used to tell the story. "Picture books present the reader with a succession of images, some in the presence of written text, some alone, which taken together provide an aesthetic experience which is more than the sum of the parts" (Kiefer, 1988; p. 261).

Some experts in children's literature distinguish between a picture book and a picture storybook. The former may be an alphabet book or a counting book which merely synchronizes words and pictures without developing a story line. The latter uses words and illustrations to develop a story with setting, plot, theme, and characters. Although an awareness of this distinction may be important in using these respective books in teaching reading, the terms *picture books* and *picture storybooks* are typically used interchangeably.

As the name suggests, illustration is essential in picture books. Illustrations keep the story moving, excite children's imaginations, and enhance the text. In some picture books, the pictures themselves carry the entire meaning. In wordless books, for example, illustrations are used without text to fully develop the characters and actions. (Actually, the expression "wordless book" is a misnomer; since there may be a word or two in the book itself and since children provide words as they read these books, these books are more properly referred to as "textless books.") Even when words are used in picture books, illustrations are essential to telling the story. In a book such as Pat Hutchins's *Rosie's Walk,* for example, the entire story centers on the misadventures of an unfortunate fox who follows Rosie the hen around the barnyard, yet the fox is never once mentioned in the text. Although words are used, the pictures really tell the story. In *Black and White,* by David Macaulay, a "mystery story" is creatively integrated with the illustrations.

Artists use a variety of visual media in illustrating picture books—woodcuts, collages, paints and oils, pen and ink, water colors, crayons, and photographs. Their style and choice of color convey the mood and action of the story. Robert McCloskey's changing colors in *Time of Wonder,* for example, reflect the various moods of the changing seasons and weather conditions on the coast of Maine. By contrast, Chris Van Allsburg's dark and almost haunting drawings in *The Polar Express* reflect the mystery of the time and mood of Christmas Eve night.

Picture books cover the gamut of children's real and imagined experiences. Animals and objects come to life in William Steig's *Doctor DeSoto,* the mouse dentist who outwits the fox, and in Hardie Gramatky's gutsy tugboat *Little Toot,* who saves the ocean liner in a storm. Children face their feelings through stories like Ezra Jack Keats's *Peter's Chair,* the story of a boy who worries about the arrival of a new baby in the family, and Judith Viorst's *The Tenth Good Thing about Barney,* the story about a boy who faces grief when his pet cat dies. Children enjoy the incongruity of the concept and the hilarity of the illustrations in Judi Barrett's *Animals Definitely Should Not Wear Clothes* and cry at the end of Sally Wittman's *A Special Trade,* a very simple but sensitive story about a friendship between a young man and a little girl that develops into a friendship between an old man and a young woman. Through picture books, children encounter the reality of every day in Ezra Jack Keats's *The Snowy Day* and the fantasy of Maurice Sendak's *Where the Wild Things Are.*

The style of art found in picture books represents a range of art forms—from simple line drawings to intricate illustrations, from actual photographs to metaphorical artistic representations, from watercolors to woodcuts. These books stimulate the senses as they stimulate the imagination and the language of children.

Folktales and Fairy Tales

''Folktale is an inclusive term, referring to all kinds of narrative that has its origin in the oral tradition'' (Bosma, 1987; p. 4). The very roots of folk literature trace themselves to the stories that were part of the myths and legends, folktales and fairy tales that were shared among ancient peoples. Groups would gather in caves, castles, cottages, temples, and clearings to hear storytellers spin their yarns, some of which are as popular with children today as they were so long ago.

Folktales have their origin in the oral tradition. Part of the popularity of these traditional stories with children is that they deal with universal human themes—good and evil, cruelty and kindness, honesty and deceit, life and death. Virtue is always rewarded; wickedness is always punished. *Cinderella* lives happily ever after, as does *Tattercoats* in Joseph Jacobs's version of the rejected-and-impoverished-girl-meets-and-marries-prince story.

The fact that folktales deal with human themes accounts for the universality of these stories. Some classic European folktales such as *The Elves and the Shoemaker* and *Hansel and Gretel* have their equivalent African, Near Eastern, Far Eastern, and American Indian versions, with each version reflecting the unique flavor of the culture from which it comes. Literature provides a human link between peoples of different cultures.

The first comprehensive compendium of European folktales was recorded by the brothers Grimm, Jacob and Wilhelm. Ironically, the Grimms' primary intent was not to entertain; they were linguistic scholars who recorded the stories for the purpose of analyzing the language used to tell the tales. The Grimms' work, however, has left a literary rather than a linguistic legacy, though the brothers did make their impact in linguistics as well.

2.1

FOR YOUR INFORMATION

Picture Books about Teachers to Tickle the Funnybone

CHILDREN LOVE picture books that make them laugh, silly stories such as Babette Cole's *Princess Smarty-pants* and Robert Munsch's *Mud Puddle*. Stories that seem to especially delight children, however, are those in which teachers find themselves in outrageously impossible situations. Here are five picture books in this category:

Miss Nelson Is Missing by Harry Allard. Miss Nelson is a wonderful teacher with an obnoxious class. When she is ''replaced'' by Viola Swamp, strange things happen. (Two *Miss Nelson* sequels are available, but they cannot match the original.)

The Day the Teacher Went Bananas by James Howe. Children learn a lot of strange things when their teacher is supposed to be in the zoo.

The Hippopotamus Ate the Teacher by Mike Thaler. Instruction still goes on, even after a hippopotamus eats the teacher on a field trip to the zoo.

The Teacher from the Black Lagoon by Mike Thaler. Miss Green is *really* green, and she breathes fire and zaps kids, too.

Thomas' Snowsuit by Robert Munch. Efforts by the teacher and the principal to get Thomas into his snow-suit result in some bizarre wardrobe combinations.

Fairy tales have the qualities of folktales, but they originated in written rather than oral form. Stories like Hans Christian Andersen's *The Princess and the Pea* and Rudyard Kipling's *Just So Stories* (such as ''How the Elephant Got His Trunk'') followed the folk tradition and remain popular decades after they were written.

The appeal of traditional literature transcends the boundaries of continents and centuries. Tomorrow's generations of children will enjoy traditional stories just as much as children who heard these stories told in earlier times—for example, the French tale *Stone Soup,* the story retold by Marcia Brown of the trickster who cons the old woman into adding a series of delicious ingredients to a pot with a rock in it to create ''stone soup,'' and stories like Esphyr Slobodkina's retelling of the Slavic folktale *Caps For Sale,* the story of the hapless peddler who recovers his caps from a band of mischievous monkeys. The appeal of folktales and fairy tales is ageless.

The field of traditional literature also includes fables, myths, legends, and tall tales. Fables are stories in which animals behave like humans and in which a moral can be found. The oft-told children's stories of ''The Hare and the Tortoise'' or ''The Boy Who Cried Wolf'' are good examples of fables with lessons that children were/ are expected to absorb. Several contemporary editions of Aesop's fables are available to be enjoyed in school and at home, as are modern renditions of traditional fables, such as Marcia Brown's *Once a Mouse.*

Myths are an ancient story form, typically told to explain natural phenomena and usually containing larger-than-life characters. Different cultures had their own accounts of why the sun and moon are in the sky, where the mountains came from, and how the world got to be the way it is. Stories of gods and goddesses that have come down from the ancient Greeks and Romans are still popular today. Books such as Doris Gates's *Mightiest of Mortals: Heracles* or *Heros and Monsters of Greek Myth* by Bernard Evslin, Dorothy Evslin, and Ned Hoopes tell the story of ancient heros that today's children still enjoy.

Sharing Folk Literature through Storytelling

THE SAME qualities that made folk literature appealing fare for the ancient storyteller sitting by the fire make this genre appealing to the modern pupil sitting in the classroom—clearly defined plots, basic characters, and fast action. Folktales and fairy tales begin quickly, move rapidly, and conclude happily. Good is rewarded; evil, punished. Storytelling provides an ideal means of sharing this literature, while at the same time helping pupils develop oral language skills.

Five steps in planning and carrying out storytelling activities with folk literature are:

1. *Choosing the story.* Folktales make good subjects, but any story that pupils can enjoy is a good choice.

2. *Preparing the story.* Becoming familiar with a story to be told will require reading it two or three times beforehand.

3. *Selecting simple props.* Although props are not absolutely necessary to telling a good story, simple devices like wearing a cap, holding objects such as a stuffed animal, or using simple drawings or flannel-board figures can make the story more alive for an audience.

4. *Practicing the story.* Stories are practiced with an eye to phrases or lines to involve the audience, particular parts that need to be stressed, hand gestures, and other devices to help the story come alive. Pupils can use a tape recorder as they practice telling favorite tales.

5. *Telling the story.* As pupils relate the story, they focus on expression and other oral language qualities that make the story more enjoyable to the audience.

After the storytelling activity, copies of the story can be read independently by pupils, since the oral language activity provides a background for comprehension. Storytelling can be extended into dramatics and puppet activities as well. Older pupils can prepare stories to be told in the lower grades.

Legends are historical tales handed from generation to generation, first by word of mouth and later in written form. Related to myths, legends involve larger-than-life figures—sometimes supernatural beings—who perform heroic deeds in keeping with the traditions of the cultures from which the legends come. The Arthurian legends, for example, which chronicle the great deeds of King Arthur and his knights, still capture the imagination of children as they are retold in books such as T. H. White's *The Sword in the Stone* and Margaret Hodges's *The Kitchen Knight: A Tale of King Arthur*.

Finally, tall tales have long been a popular form of literature for children. Tall tales are accounts of exaggerated people and events that are told in a realistic manner, often with heavy doses of humor. Perhaps the best known stories of this type are accounts of the American legendary hero Paul Bunyan. Children enjoy the fantastic accounts of this giant of a man from picture books like Steven Kellogg's *Paul Bunyan* to longer accounts like Glen O. Rounds' *Ol' Paul, the Mighty Logger*. Other well-known characters from American tall tales include the cowboy Pecos Bill and the boatman Mike Fink. Stories about these characters enliven children's view of their world in books like Adrien Stoutenburg's *American Tall Tales* and Mary Pope Osborne's *American Tall Tales,* which introduces tales about female heros as well.

The heroes found in traditional literature often represent the nature of the society from which the literature comes. The epic hero Odysseus represents the ideals of intelligence and virtues valued by the ancient Greeks. Robin Hood embodies the goodness and bravery the downtrodden English peasants admired. Paul Bunyan represents the brashness and resourcefulness required for opening the American wilderness. But beyond their symbolic and cultural significance, these characters from traditional literature entertain children of all ages from one generation to the next.

Fantasy

Fantasy is another form of literature long popular with children. Fantasies are highly fanciful stories about people and places that, though sometimes believable, do not really exist. The ancients sought answers to natural and supernatural phenomena in witches and warlocks, in magic and mysteries. Modern fantasy traces its roots to these sources and many of these stories still delight children today.

Fantasy is not only an important part of children's reading experiences; it is an important part of their lives. According to psychologists, fantasy provides an important means of helping pupils deal with their emotions, their dreams, their fears, their conflicts, their worlds (Bettelheim, 1978). "Fantasy helps the child develop imagination. The ability to imagine, to conceive of alternative ways of life, to entertain new ideas, to create strange new worlds, to dream dreams are all skills vital to the survival of humankind" (Huck, Hepler, and Hickman, 1987; p. 337). Fantasy opens the world of wonder to pupils of all ages.

Children have long been fascinated by the world of kings and queens. Just as Jacob and Wilhelm Grimm recorded the actions of royalty in such popular traditional tales as *Cinderella,* so Hans Christian Andersen created such entertaining stories as *The Princess and the Pea* and *The Emperor's New Clothes.* More modern writers use royal characters for their fantasy tales as well. The young princess in Jean Yolen's *The Emperor and the Kite,* for example, rescues her father the emperor. Dr. Seuss' hilarious *The 500 Hats of Bartholomew Cubbins* involves a vain and angry king who insists that young Bartholomew remove his hat. A popular, modern fairy tales involving royalty is Antoine de Saint-Exupéry's *The Little Prince,* a lovely story full of symbolism and written at different levels of meaning. The illustrated recreation of Oscar Wilde's *The Happy Prince* is a moving story about traditional values.

Animals, too, have long played an important part in the world of fantasy literature. Writers bring animal characters to life by making them act, feel, talk, and think like humans. Beatrix Potter's Peter Rabbit, Michael Bond's Paddington Bear, and H. A. and Margaret Rey's Curious George have become as well known as they are well loved as animal fantasy characters. One of the most popular children's books ever written—E. B. White's *Charlotte's Web*—is an animal fantasy. The rabbits who inhabit the Connecticut farm in Robert Lawson's *Rabbit Hill* or the incredibly intelligent rats who create a whole culture in Robert C. O'Brien's *Mrs. Frisby and the Rats of NIMH* take on real-life qualities that make them entirely believable.

In the world of children's fantasy, authors also anthropomorphize toys and other objects by giving them human qualities. A. A. Milne's *Winnie-the-Pooh* becomes so real that we tend to forget that he is a stuffed animal. Authors like Hardie Gramatky and Virginia Lee Burton have created such delightfully believable characters as *Little Toot,* the irresponsible little tugboat who eventually saves the ocean liner in a storm, and Katy, the snow plow who single-handedly plows out the town in *Katy and the Big Snow.* In Lynne Reid Banks's more recently popular *The Indian in the Cupboard,* the plastic toy Indian comes to life to the delight and consternation of his nine-year-old owner. These objects not only delight children (and adults); they often teach valuable lessons.

Fantasy feeds on the preposterous. Children delight in reading about miniaturized characters like John Peterson's *The Littles* or Mary Norton's *The Borrowers,* characters who exist unbeknown to the people whose houses they inhabit. Astrid Lindgren's *Pippi Longstocking* is an outrageously funny character with whom children have had a love affair for a long time. Characters like James in Roald Dahl's *James and the Giant Peach* tickle children's fancy, as do events recounted by such authors as Norton Juster in *The Phantom Tollbooth* and Judi Barrett in *Cloudy with a Chance of Meatballs.* Characters with magic powers, settings that transcend the world of reality, stories that reach back in time, tales that project into the future, works of science fiction—all fill children's imaginations and extend their worlds.

A more serious type of fantasy popular with many pupils is high fantasy. These complex tales deal with ultimate values of good and evil and are often enjoyed by adults as well as upper elementary-grade pupils. Madeleine L'Engle's *A Wrinkle in Time* extends beyond the bounds of time and space as children search for their scientist-father; in C. S. Lewis's *The Lion, the Witch and the Wardrobe,* perhaps the most popular of the Narnia chronicles, children enter a world of ancient creatures and battle for the forces of good; J. R. R. Tolkien's *The Hobbit,* who battles the evil creatures of Middle-earth—all remain classic fantasies that provide compelling reading for children.

Realistic Fiction

At the other end of the literary spectrum from fantasy is reality, represented in children's literature as realistic fiction. Realistic fiction consists of stories that attempt to portray people and events as they are in real life. It mirrors children's experiences. It often deals with the problems and conflicts that children face in growing up, and it sometimes gives them insights and outlets in dealing with these issues and concerns.

Although it is a form of fiction (and therefore imaginative in nature), contemporary realistic works reflect the realities of life—death, divorce, abandonment, hostility, school failure, disabilities. But these stories also reflect the joys of life—love, happiness, friendship, satisfaction, and laughter. It is little wonder that contemporary realistic fiction tends to be the most popular story choice among children in the upper elementary and middle grades.

One of the more common themes of contemporary realistic fiction is living as part of a family. Beverly Cleary's books about Ramona Quimby and Lois Lowry's stories about the often irascible Anastasia Krupnik are stories that mirror life's problems as they entertain. More serious treatment of the complexities of family relationships are revealed in other books: Katherine Paterson's *Jacob Have I Loved,* the story of serious sibling rivalry between two sisters; Betsy Byars's *The Animal, the Vegetable and John D. Jones,* the story about two sisters who find that their vacation with their divorced father is shared by his girlfriend's son; Beverly Cleary's *Dear Mr. Henshaw,* a story told in an ingenious manner about the feelings of a boy living in a single-parent household. Not all realistic fiction about family relationships is sad and poignant. In books like the popular *Tales of a Fourth Grade Nothing* and the sequel *Superfudge,* Judy Blume tells about family relationships with humor and delight.

2.3
FOR YOUR INFORMATION
Award-Winning Books

EACH YEAR, a number of awards are given by various organizations and agencies. Among the most notable are:

The Newbery Award. The John Newbery Medal is awarded annually by the American Library Association to the author of the most distinguished contribution to American literature for children.

The Caldecott Medal. Also awarded by the American Library Association, the Caldecott Award is presented each year to the artist of the most distinguished American picture book for children.

The Laura Ingalls Wilder Award. Named after the famous "Little House" author, this award is given every three years for substantial and lasting contributions to literature for children.

The Hans Christian Andersen Prize. This is an international award given every two years to one author and one illustrator who have made contributions to children's literature the world over.

Children's Choice. While other award-winning books are selected by adults, the Children's Choice Award, given by the International Reading Association, is based on books recommended by children. These books are reviewed annually in the October issue of *The Reading Teacher.*

There are literally hundreds of other awards and prizes for quality children's books. These awards signal the type of literature that teachers can bring into the classroom for their pupils.

Getting along in school is important to children, and it is a popular theme in contemporary realistic fiction. Patricia Reilly Griff's Polk Street School series contains relatively easy books on a variety of school-related topics (including problems in learning to read). Judy Blume's *Blubber,* the story about an overweight girl; Johanna Hurwitz's *Aldo Applesauce,* the story about a boy who acquires a nickname he hates; Barthe DeClements's *Nothing's Fair in Fifth Grade,* the story of a girl who has problems entering a new school—all have incidents to which children can usually relate and stories that they can enjoy.

There are compelling works of realistic fiction about such tender topics as coping with physical and developmental disabilities and facing emotional problems associated with death and dying. Ivan Southall's *Let the Balloon Go* is about a physically handicapped 12-year-old who strives for—and achieves—independence. Betsy Byars's *Summer of the Swans* is a Newbery-Award-winning story about an adolescent girl and her mentally retarded brother. Rose Blue's *Grandma Didn't Wave Back* is a touching story of a girl who watches her beloved grandmother grow old. Katherine Paterson's deeply moving *Bridge To Terabithia,* one of the most widely read stories in the elementary grades, deals with the grief of facing the death of a friend.

Obviously, one can find more than a single theme in a work of contemporary realistic fiction. Cynthia Voigt's *Dicey's Song* is a compelling story that involves the loss of a parent, some of the difficulties of living in an extended family, the problems of poverty, the struggles of learning disabilities, an adolescent's search for independence, and friendship, all woven into a warm and beautiful story. Nor does all contemporary realistic fiction involve hardship and crises. Beverly Cleary's stories about Henry Huggins, Thomas Rockwell's account of *How to Eat Fried Worms,* and Barbara

Robinson's story about *The Best Christmas Pageant Ever* are examples of contemporary realistic fiction that constitute some of the funniest selections in the field of literature for children.

A *classic* in literature is a work that continues to appeal to readers long after the
period in which it was written. *Peter Rabbit* is a classic of children's literature. So is
Alice in Wonderland. By their nature, most books of contemporary realistic fiction
have not been around long enough to have stood the test of time. But the popularity
of books like *Bridge to Terabithia* and other works of contemporary realistic fiction
indicate that some of the recent books in this burgeoning field will likely earn the
designation of *classic* in generations to come.

Historical Fiction

Just as contemporary realistic fiction reflects life as it is (or might be) lived today,
historical fiction reflects life as it was (or may have been) lived in the past. As a field
of children's literature, historical fiction draws on both fact and imagination in allowing
children to learn about, and to enjoy, what life was like long ago.

Historical fiction leads children into the past in a way that no history textbook
can. *My Brother Sam Is Dead* by James and Christopher Collier enables children to
feel the real emotion of choosing sides in the American Revolution, and *Johnny Tremain* by Esther Forbes allows them to experience the excitement of the streets of
Revolutionary Boston. Historical fiction is based on fact, but an author's imagination
brings these facts alive.

Historical fiction reaches as far back as prehistoric times. It paints pictures of
life of a slave girl in ancient Egypt, a warrior among the early Celtic tribes, a boy in
ancient Rome, and seafaring Vikings. Tales of heros long gone and stories of life in
medieval Europe are available to capture the imagination of today's children.

Among the most popular works of historical fiction for children are those based
on American history. *The Thanksgiving Story* by Alice Dalgliesh details the life of an
early Pilgrim family and *The Courage of Sarah Noble* by the same author tells about
a young child in the wilderness. A popular story about life in early America is Elizabeth
Speare's *The Witch of Blackbird Pond,* the story about a lively girl who is forced to
make a new life for herself in a dour Puritan village.

Subsequent periods and events in American history—the Revolution, the Westward Movement, the Civil War, immigration, World War II, the 20th Century—are
chronicled by works of historical fiction for children. Jean Fritz's *And Then What
Happened Paul Revere?* and her other books about famous historical figures; Scott
O'Dell's *Sing Down the Moon,* a story of how white settlers helped destroy the life of
Native Americans; Laura Ingalls Wilder's *Little House on the Prairie* and her other
books telling about life on the American frontier; Irene Hunt's *Across Five Aprils,* the
moving story of the devastating personal affects the Civil War had on one family;
Patricia MacLachlan's *Sarah, Plain and Tall,* the beautiful story about a woman from
Maine who settled as part of a prairie family; Beth Bao Lord's *In The Year of the Boar
and Jackie Robinson,* the story of a young immigrant's early experiences in the United
States; Yoshiko Uchida's *Journey To Topaz,* a disturbing story about Japanese internment during the Second World War—these and other works of historical fiction give
children a glimpse into times and places in the past. Historical fiction is history that
touches children's lives.

Poetry

Poetry has a major place in children's literature. Poetry involves the expression of language in metrical form to convey ideas or to create images. Eleanor Farjeon defined the essence of poetry in this way:

Poetry

What is poetry? Who knows?
Not the rose, but the scent of the rose;
Not the sky, but the light from the sky;
Not the fly, but the gleam of the fly;
Not the sea, but the sound of the sea;
Not myself, but something that makes me
See, hear, and feel something that prose
Cannot. What is it? Who knows?[1]

Poetry reflects not only an object or idea or experience; it captures the essence of that object or idea or experience.

Poetry is designed to delight. It reaches into both the hearts and the heads of children, appealing to both their emotions and their thoughts. As part of children's literature in schools, the emphasis on poetry should be on the former rather than on the latter aspect; that is, poetry should be enjoyed rather than analyzed.

Why does poetry appeal to children? First, the rhythm delights the ears. The beat of lines such as "To market, to market to buy a fat pig," attracts and entertains children from the very early years. The rhythmic patterns used by poets like David McCord in his anthology *Every Time I Climb a Tree* maintain this appeal beyond the beginning years. Rhythm is the primary feature that distinguishes poetry from prose.

Rhyme is another feature that children find appealing. Not all poetry has end-line rhyme, but the strong rhyming patterns of Mother Goose—*pig-jig, hog-jog, diddle-fiddle, dock-clock*—tickle the eardrums and cause poetry to be enjoyed. Strong rhyming patterns appeal to the ears of children and adults alike.

The language of poetry is uniquely appealing as well. In addition to the qualities of rhythm and rhyme, poetry is marked by an efficiency of language, an economy of words. Poetry captures the essence of a scene, an idea, or an emotion with a phrase or a line. The language is subtle. Words are often used in special ways. Images are often (*although not always*) conveyed by means of symbolism and figurative language. "The reason a successful poem works is not easy to sum up. There is a perfection in the selection of words and word order, an effective matching of the mood to the metre; a certain balance; a reaching out with language; a wholeness. To achieve this success, the poet-craftsman works hard with language" (Winch, 1987; p. 126).

The imagery of poetry is often special to children. The poet tends to see common, everyday objects and experiences in new ways, expressing these relationships in metaphors that appeal to children's imagination and creativity. A tall apartment building becomes "a filing cabinet of human lives"; a toaster becomes a fire-breathing dragon;

---

[1]"Poetry," from *Poems for Children* by Eleanor Farjeon. "Poetry" originally appeared in *Sing For Your Supper*. Copyright © 1938 by Eleanor Farjeon; Renewed 1966 by Gervase Farjeon. Selection reprinted by permission of HarperCollins Publishers, New York.

2.4
FOR YOUR INFORMATION

Poetry Anthologies for the Classroom Bookshelf

A GOOD anthology of children's poems should never be far away from the teacher's fingertips. Among hundreds of good poetry collections available for use in the classroom, the following anthologies have proved to be particularly popular with teachers and pupils in the elementary grades:

The Random House Book of Poetry for Children selected by Jack Prelutsky is a collection of poems on a variety of topics appropriate for virtually every classroom occasion.

Where the Sidewalk Ends by Shel Silverstein is a collection of humorous poems that seem everlastingly popular with pupils in the elementary and middle grades (and their teachers too!).

A Light In The Attic, another collection by Shel Silverstein, reflects the same absurd humor and insight that pupils continually enjoy.

The Arbuthnot Anthology of Children's Literature is a collection of poems including some of the traditional classics, selected by May Hill Arbuthnot.

Sing a Song of Popcorn: Every Child's Book of Poems edited by Beatrice Schenk de Regniers is a more contemporary collection of poems arranged thematically for today's pupil, with outstanding illustrations.

Other poetry collections will depend on teacher preference and purpose. For example:

Hailstones and Halibut Bones by Mary O'Neill is an appealing anthology of poems that describe and define colors.

Nathaniel Talking by Eloise Greenfield is the poetry of a nine-year-old boy who raps and rhymes about the people in his world.

If You're Not Here, Please Raise Your Hand: Poems about School, a delightfully humorous collection of poems by Kalli Dahos, celebrates the joys and heartaches of life in an elementary school.

Animals, Animals, a collection of animal poems edited by Laura Whipple and brilliantly illustrated by Eric Carle, can be used in conjunction with this topic.

A Basketful of White Eggs is a book of riddle-poems gathered by Brian Swann from all over the world.

No early-level classroom should be without one of the many finely illustrated collections of *Mother Goose.* (See chapter 4 for specific suggestions.)

Teachers who especially enjoy the work of particular poets—Aileen Fisher or Eleanor Farjeon or John Ciardi, for example—are sure to have collections by these poets to share as treasures with pupils.

In short, any classroom bookshelf should have as wide a selection of poetry as possible so that pupils can enjoy poems throughout their school experience.

a steam shovel becomes a latter-day dinosaur. The images of poetry appeal to the sight, sound, smell, and even the touch and taste (not to mention the emotion) of readers of all ages.

Literature for children is filled with an enormous variety of poems that pupils can enjoy:

Narrative poems that tell a story, such as Clement Moore's " 'Twas the Night Before Christmas," recreated in a beautiful picture book titled *The Night Before Christmas* illustrated by Tomie de Paola.

Lyric poems, melodic poetry that creates an impression and evokes an emotion through the rhythmic use of language, typified by poems like Robert Louis Stevenson's "The Wind" and "The Swing."

Free verse, poetry that is free of the traditional elements of stress, meter, and rhyme, beautiful examples of which can be found in Richard Lewis's collection *Miracles: Poems by Children of the English-Speaking World.*

Haiku, an ancient but currently popular Japanese verse form containing three lines consisting of seventeen syllables and usually dealing with the topic of nature, a wonderful collection of which can be found in another Richard Lewis collection that was illustrated by Ezra Jack Keats, *In a Spring Garden.*

Limericks, a highly structured verse form that children enjoy, from some of the original work in Edward Lear's *The Complete Nonsense Book* to the more contemporary *The Hopeful Trout and Other Limericks* by John Ciardi.

These and other forms of poetry—including the five-line verse form cinquain; concrete poems, the shape of which follow the topic of the poem; ballads, which are part of traditional literature—open a whole new world of experiences to children. Topics of children's poetry vary from the sublime (with poems such as Robert Frost's "Stopping By Woods on A Snowy Evening") to the ridiculous (with examples like Shel Silverstein's "They've Put a Brassiere on the Camel"). The world of children's poetry is a wide world indeed. And it is a world that enriches our lives.

Helping children happily enter this world is an important job for teachers. Taste in poetry is an individual matter. A poem that appeals to one child (or adult) may have no appeal for another. Perhaps the best way to kill interest in poetry among children is to attempt to force-feed appreciation. Providing a smorgasbord of poetry which children can sample and share every day will likely lead to an appreciation that will stay with children all their lives.

Literary Elements

As they deal with literature as part of learning to read, pupils will become aware of literary elements inherent in the stories they read. The four major literary elements found in children's stories are: *setting*—the time and place in which a story takes place; *characterization*—the way in which characters in the story are presented or portrayed; *plot*—the structure of the action in a story; *theme*—the major idea or topic covering the scope of the story or poem.

There are other literary elements as well—such as mood, tone, irony, figurative language, style, and point of view—but the four that receive the most attention are plot, setting, characterization, and theme. Being aware of these four elements is important for both reading and writing. Understanding these elements in stories is an essential part of reading comprehension, and the inclusion of these elements improves pupils' writing abilities.

Setting

Setting provides the "story stage." It involves the time in which a story takes place, from the past of historical fiction to the future of science fiction. It also includes the place in which the action occurs, from as specific a locale as New York City subway tunnels to as generic a setting as a suburban middle school.

Setting is a vitally important literary element because a story derives its credibility and authenticity from the time and place in which it occurs. The entire plot of Elizabeth Speare's *The Witch of Blackbird Pond,* for example, revolves around the mood and attitudes of the people living in Puritan New England. Authors of good

Censorship

An issue that many teachers face in selecting and recommending reading material for their pupils is censorship. Censorship is the attempt to limit the opportunity of people to be exposed to certain books, films, drama, magazines, or other forms of media. It has an impact on schools when certain books are deemed inappropriate for the library or for classroom use. Throughout history, there have been repeated efforts to have books banned from schools. Efforts to exclude books whose content or language offends some segment of the population continue in the 1990s.

Censorship is a volatile, two-sided issue. Some people insist that books should be scrutinized and selected to conform to community standards, but these standards can be exceedingly variable. Although citizens in a democracy have the right to question the use of books, censorship has been seen as a violation of the rights to follow principles of diversity and professional decision-making on the part of teachers and librarians. By limiting access to print, censorship poses a threat to literacy.

Some community groups or school boards have pressed for the censorship of books on a number of different grounds. Some object to artwork. Maurice Sendak's drawing of Mickey, the little boy who "falls out of his sleeper" in the highly imaginative fantasy *In the Night Kitchen,* has generated a swarm of controversy because the boy is nude, even though the cartoonish nature of the artwork makes the illustration inoffensive to most. Some object to content. Judy Blume's very popular (with pupils) *Are You There God? It's Me, Margaret,* the story of a girl concerned with some of the bodily changes involved in approaching puberty, has generated more than twenty years of controversy. Some object to language, as children's authors occasionally use words like *damn* and *bitch* (in reference to a female canine). And objections have been raised on multiple grounds with books like Trina Schart Hyman's version of *Little Red Riding Hood* in which Red Riding Hood brings her grandmother a bottle of wine, which granny enjoys in an illustration suggesting that she's a bit tipsy. Books have been attacked on a variety of grounds indeed.

How does the classroom teacher deal with censorship? First, teachers should be prepared to justify the choice of a trade book to a parent who questions the use of the book. Teachers need to be ready to counter criticisms with sound reasons for using a particular book based on its literary or instructional merit. Although teachers need to be sensitive to parents' concerns, they also need to be sensitive to the educational and psychosocial needs of the pupils in their classrooms. Teachers deserve administrative support; school districts often have written policies and procedures to handle censorship issues.

For reference, the American Library Association and the National Council of Teachers of English are two professional organizations that have issued policies and strategies regarding censorship and the right of free access to books.

children's stories carefully craft the time and place so that the stories, even if they are fantasies, become truly believable. The same can be said for illustrators, who must carefully design their illustrations to reflect faithfully and realistically the settings that they represent.

Characterization

Into the story setting the author places characters, those who are involved in the action and those around whom the story revolves. Character development in stories is a complex process. Authors create characters in very specific ways: by the way in which the characters are described in text, by what the characters say/do/think, and by what other characters in the story say about them.

Characterization is a crucial dimension of literature for children. Folktales and fairy tales tend to have stock figures whose characters are "flat" and who simply symbolize good and evil: the cruel stepmother, for example, or the generous king.

Other forms of literature, however, need characters that are well rounded, believable, and realistic. These are the people (or animals or things) whom children come to love or hate, admire or pity, laugh at or cry with. Children often form special relationships with characters they meet in the stories that they read.

As in the case of setting, well-developed story characters behave with consistency and authenticity. Their words, thoughts, and actions are consistent with the personalities that authors breathe into them. Even animals and objects take on personalities that children remember long after they have outgrown the literature of their childhood: readers long remember the disarming charm of Winnie-the-Pooh, for example, or the loyal bond of friendship between Frog and Toad. Characters like Madeline and Henry Huggins remain our friends forever.

Plot

Plot, the action of the story, is an essential literary element. A children's book may have beautiful illustrations, attractive characters, a noble theme, a fascinating setting, and all the other qualities that characterize good literature. But to the child, one question is paramount: does the book tell an exciting, interesting, or entertaining story?

Narrative stories usually follow a fairly well-defined plot structure. There is a beginning, in which the scene is set and the characters are introduced. Characters are developed and action rises through the middle of the plot. The plot reaches its climax with conflict between the protagonist and the antagonist. Sometimes the conflict can be between the character and other people, between the character and nature, between the character and social values, or between the character and him/herself. In most children's stories the plot concludes with the successful resolution of the conflict and ends with the speedy tidying up of loose details. In most children's stories, the plot proceeds in this fairly linear fashion, although some authors use flashbacks effectively to develop action, as Robert C. O'Brien does in *Mrs. Frisby and the Rats of NIMH.*

Plot is more than a simple linear series of events, however. It is a structured plan that dynamically develops the interrelatedness of events that occur as part of the story. The events that are part of the plot also serve the other literary aspects of setting, characterization, and theme. Plot is the literary element that keeps the story moving. The setting might shift and the characters change, but plot makes the reader want to continue reading. Good plots, even in very simple stories, maintain a quality of suspense that continues to make the reader wonder what will happen next.

Theme

Theme reaches beyond the other literary elements and extends into the author's purpose in writing a story. Theme has been variously described as: the author's interpretation of the events about which he or she is writing; the "focal point" for the setting, characters, and the episodes that make up the plot; "the interconnecting thread that brings all the elements together in wholeness and harmony" (Saxby, 1987; p. 11); the ultimate outcome that emerges from the literary experience. In a word, theme involves the essential meaning of a piece of literature.

Children's books can have more than one layer of meaning. On one level, E. B. White's enormously popular *Charlotte's Web* is an animal fantasy about a spider who saves the life of a pig; on another, it is a strong statement about friendship; on a third

Story Maps: Roadmaps to Understanding

WHEN READERS understand the elements contained in a story, they have a better chance of comprehending and appreciating what they read. Davis and McPherson (1989) describe the effective use of story maps—graphic representation of story elements and the relationship to one another—as a strategy in helping pupils understand elements in stories.

Story maps can take many forms, from the simple linear design of plot to a story map that takes other elements into account to more elaborate text diagrams.

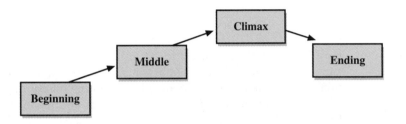

Story maps can be prepared before reading, discussed during prereading, and completed as pupils read a story. Maps can be used to guide questions during reading, or they can be used in postreading activities as pupils look back at story elements.

Although story maps have proved to be effective instructional devices, they should never be so intrusive that they get in the way of pupils' enjoyment of the literature they read.

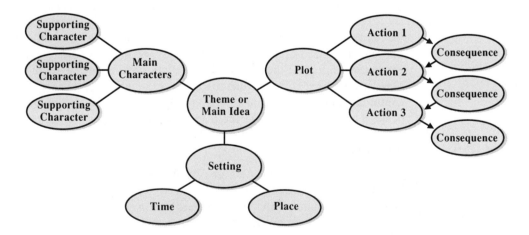

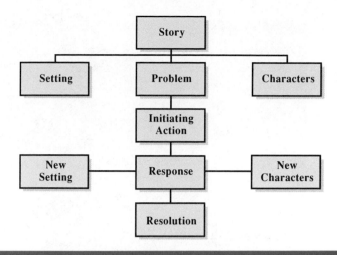

level, it can be seen as a commentary on the cycle of life and death. Some see C. S. Lewis's *The Lion, the Witch, and the Wardrobe* as an allegorical tale involving deep religious meaning, but even without ascribing any religious meaning to the story, one can enjoy it as a highly imaginative and philosophical adventure.

A single story can have more than one theme. ''The theme may be a moral one, involving acceptance of others. It may be psychological, an observation about a personality that forbids traits unlike its own. It may be sociological, an observation about peer group behavior in a suburban neighborhood. The theme may unify all these fields of inquiry, as well as some others'' (Sebesta and Iverson, 1975; p. 60).

Many children's stories have a moral. In traditional folk literature, virtues such as kindness, patience, and perseverance are always celebrated. Much contemporary children's literature also focuses on some ethical or social value as well. But in good literature, the moral is understated; the theme emerges naturally from the story. In Evaline Ness' *Sam, Bangs, and Moonshine,* for example, it is not hard to recognize the message that it is dangerous to confuse reality and fantasy and to mislead others based on this confusion, but this lesson is suggested rather than driven home with undue emphasis. Like the message in all good literature, it emerges from the context of the story and is not added on as a mini sermon.

In addition to the four elements of setting, character, plot, and theme, other literary devices are found in quality works of literature for children as well:

Irony, the technique for suggesting a message very different from, and incongruous with, the message presented in the text. For example, in Ellen Raskin's *Nothing Ever Happens on My Block,* the boy sits on the curb and complains of boredom while behind him, all kinds of exciting events are taking place in his neighborhood.

Mood, the emotional atmosphere that an author creates with language or an illustrator creates with art; that is, the mood of a story can be lighthearted or somber. In *Sounder,* William Armstrong uses setting and figurative language to create a mood of hostility and sadness.

E. B. Whites *Charlotte's Web* is a children's classic that has been enjoyed by millions of young readers.

Tone, closely related to mood (both terms are sometimes used interchangeably), reflects the author's ''attitude'' toward a topic; a story can be told as a personal experience shared with a peer (à la Judy Blume) or as an outrageous joke told by an adult to a child (à la Roald Dahl).

Style, the author's way of writing, the unique way in which an author uses language to depict setting, create characters, or describe action—the aristocratic style of speech of Father Rabbit in Robert Lawson's *Rabbit Hill,* for example, vis-à-vis the adolescent vernacular of Jill in Judy Blume's *Blubber.*

Point of view, the ''eyes'' through which the author presents the story. Although most stories are told from an omniscient or all-knowing point of view, some stories are told through the eyes of one of the characters observing or participating in the action. Jon Scieszka's *The True Story of the 3 Little Pigs!* and his *Frog Prince Continued* are clever variations of the traditional stories (the former told by the wolf and the latter by the princess who married the frog) which can be used to teach point of view from the earliest years through the upper grades. In a more serious vein, Jane Yolen's *Encounter* recounts the arrival of Columbus in the New World through the eyes of a native, Taino.

Just as elements of tone, mood, style, and point of view are all closely related in that authors create these elements through the use of language, so are the major literary elements of setting, characterization, plot, and theme closely woven together in a story. The time and place of the setting shape the characters and direct the actions. By their actions in the plot, characters achieve a depth of personality. All four elements create story unity. By synthesizing these elements, skilled authors create stories that constitute the field of literature for children.

Taking these literary elements into account gives teachers a ''set of eyes'' for examining children's stories. As teachers select books for classroom libraries or recommend books for children to read, they can use their knowledge of literary elements as yardsticks in judging the quality and characteristics of books. Librarians and reading resource specialists are usually available to help teachers make judgments and recommendations about children's books as well. Knowledge of setting, character, plot, and theme are also important for formulating questions and discussing text in instructional situations, either in reading groups or in individual conferences. These elements can suggest guidelines for questions and discussion, whether the teacher is using basal stories or trade books.

How important is a knowledge of these literary elements for children in the classroom? Clearly, an awareness of who (character) is doing what (plot) where (setting) and for what purpose (theme) is basic to the most literal level of comprehending a story. The more a reader understands the personality and motives of a character or the details of the time and place in which the story occurs, the more complete the reader's understanding and appreciation of the story will be. And recognizing the contrasting theme and mood of stories comes with understanding at the higher levels of comprehension.

Helping pupils recognize these literary elements, however, does not mean over-analysis. The point of literature in a child's life is enjoyment. Good books for children are like good wine for adults—they ought to be savored. The adult does not need to know the chemical composition or the manner of production in order to enjoy a glass of good wine, any more than the child needs to be consciously aware of the nature of the conflict or the techniques used for character development in order to enjoy a good story that he or she is reading. In-depth knowledge enhances appreciation, to be sure, but not to the point where it kills interest.

Children's literature can be an effective vehicle for helping pupils develop reading competency in the classroom, but analysis should never get in the way of enjoyment.

Getting to Know Authors

When a child (or an adult) reads a book, he or she and the author enter into a relationship with each other. The story becomes the medium that forms the bond between the two. Knowing a little about the person who has written the book helps enhance the relationship between writer and reader; it helps the child to know and to appreciate the book a little more. This awareness is part of the reading–writing connection that will be explored in Chapter 10.

A reader does not need to know an author's life story in order to read and enjoy a book. But bits and pieces of information about an author can enhance the understanding and appreciation of a piece of literature. For example, the book *And to Think That I Saw It on Mulberry Street* by Dr. Seuss is an imaginative account of what a child sees on his way to and from school, and it is a book that can be enjoyed all by itself without ever knowing who wrote it. But to know that Theodore Geisel (that's Dr. Seuss' real name) wrote the book on a boring ocean voyage as he tried to put words to the rhythm of the ship's engine gives insight into the rhythm of the language used. For aspiring authors, it is reassuring to know that this book, which was Geisel's first

Author/Illustrator of the Week/Month

ONE WAY to develop author awareness is to feature a bulletin-board display of an author or an illustrator that pupils enjoy. For example:

Author/Illustrator of the Month

BERNARD WABER

Born
September 27, 1924, in Philadelphia, PA

Went to School
University of Pennsylvania
Philadelphia College of Art

Facts about Mr. Waber
Was the youngest of four children in his family
Married with three children
Was in the Army
Works as an artist in New York City

Some of His Books
Ira Sleeps Over (1972)
Lyle, Lyle, Crocodile (1965)
The Snake: A Very Long Story (1978)
An Anteater Named Arthur (1967)
Bernard (1982)

What We Think About Bernard Waber's Books
(Here, pupils tack index cards with comments and reactions to books that they have read by Waber.)

With each display is a collection of the books that the author has written. A new author or illustrator can be featured every few weeks. (Teachers who do this typically report that pupils read the books so quickly that the display has to be changed more frequently.) Teachers of young children can enlist the help of parent volunteers in collecting information for the bulletin board. In the upper grades, gathering information can be part of a library-research assignment for pupil teams.

Where do you find information on authors for these displays? (See 2.8, p. 51.)

---

attempt at writing for children, was rejected by more than twenty-five publishers. In the early days, experts in the field of children's literature did not acknowledge the work of Seuss as worthy of mention. Ignorant of the experts' opinion, children made him a powerful force in the field.

It is interesting for children to know that there is a real person behind the books that they read—to learn, for example, that Beverly Cleary writes stories about topics that she wanted to read about when she was a child, humorous stories about problems that are small to adults but that loom large for children (like Ellen Tebbits's having to

2.8
FOR YOUR INFORMATION
Where Do You Find Information about Children's Authors?

INFORMATION ABOUT authors and illustrators of children's literature is available in a number of reference sources.

Books Are By People (1969) and *More Books By More People* (1974), two books by Lee Bennett Hopkins, contain interesting, brief biographical sketches of well-known children's authors. *Once Upon a Time: An Encyclopedia for Successfully Using Children's Literature with Young Children* by Carol Otis Hurst (1990) has biographical items related to authors and illustrators, along with teaching suggestions for the books. *An Author a Month* by Sharron McElmeel (1988) also has some interesting biographical information about authors of children's literature.

Books of Junior Authors and Illustrators are published periodically by the H. W. Wilson Company, and the Gale Publishing Company produces annual volumes of *Something about the Author,* sources that contain a wealth of information. Most children's librarians can help teachers and pupils find reference sources like these.

Some well-known children's authors have written interesting autobiographies that pupils can use to discover the thoughts and techniques of the real people whose work they enjoy, and to discover that famous authors were once young, too. A sampling of these autobiographies includes:

Bill Peet: An Autobiography, simply written and delightfully illustrated by the author in his own style;
A Girl from Yamhill, Beverly Cleary's story of her own childhood that shaped her as a writer;
How I Came to Be a Writer, Phyllis Reynolds Naylor's account of her experiences as a young person;
Boy, Roald Dahl's fascinating and personal account of growing up, told in the author's inimitable style;
Homesick, My Own Story, Jean Fritz's account of her world as a child.

Finally, some professional magazines regularly profile children's authors:

Language Arts, the journal published by the National Council of Teachers of English for teachers in the elementary grades;
The Horn Book Magazine, a bimonthly publication devoted exclusively to literature for children;
The New Advocate, another excellent magazine "for those involved with young people and their literature."

---

wear long underwear). When children learn that Beverly Cleary writes "for the little girl within her," they come to understand the source of the charm of all the wonderful characters that she created.

Krieger (1988) found that developing her pupils' author awareness—"a sense of *who* wrote the story, *how,* and *why*"—increased their interest, improved their comprehension, and enhanced their writing abilities. This author awareness develops in stages, from a knowledge that books are written by real people to more sophisticated understandings about the relationship between an author and his or her work. Awareness does not develop automatically; it requires teacher direction, careful questioning, and well-planned classroom activities.

Connecting with authors can be an aspect of the critical analysis that is part of reading comprehension. In judging the accuracy or authenticity of a piece of writing, the child may need to know about the author's qualifications or background in writing about a topic.

Children and teachers can come into contact with authors in a variety of ways. Obviously, face-to-face meetings are the best way. Popular children's authors often appear at professional conferences, bookstores, libraries, or meetings. Some even make a regular practice of visiting schools to meet with children.

Movies or videos of authors and illustrators commenting on work that they have done bring children into indirect contact and are available for classrooms. For example, the Weston Woods Company (Weston, CT) has films of authors and illustrators such as Maurice Sendak explaining where he gets his wonderfully imaginative ideas, Ezra Jack Keats discussing his work, and Robert McCloskey talking about experiences that have shaped his writing.

Teachers sometimes have pupils write letters to authors. Although many authors discourage this practice, some make an honest effort to answer their "fan mail."

Summary and Conclusions

This chapter has attempted to present a brief overview of a very extensive field, the world of children's literature. It mentions some of the significant historical developments, identifies the types of literature that elementary school pupils most often encounter in the classroom and at home, describes some of the major aspects of literature, and suggests some of the why's and where's of putting children in touch with authors.

This chapter is a microcosmic view, at best. Not addressed are many important issues related to children's literature—sexism, racism, stereotyping, censorship. Nor is there an attempt to address in any detail ways of "teaching" literature, instructional activities or devices for helping children channel their response to books in the classroom. Given the scope of the chapter, these important topics must be left for another time and place.

In the final analysis, there is no such thing as a crash course in children's literature, no real shortcut through the world of children's books. Coming to know and appreciate the field requires wide reading of a range of stories and poems. But the challenge of becoming familiar with children's literature is hardly a formidable task. Most children's books are relatively short and can be read in a reasonably brief period of time. Besides, the efforts of those who get to know children's books are rewarded by the pleasure and enjoyment derived from the search. The journey through the world of children's books is, for children and adults alike, "a journey of joy."

Discussion Questions and Activities

1. Think back to your own early experiences with children's literature. What are the books you remember most vividly from your own childhood? Why do these books stand out in your mind? Make a list of what you might do to make these stories memorable to the pupils you will teach.
2. Review four or five picture books for the primary grades. Note how text and illustrations complement each other, the styles of illustration used, how the authors tell a story with an economy of language. Make a chart summarizing your comparisons of these books.
3. Children's books such as *Peter Rabbit* have stood the test of time as classics. Other books don't make it beyond the first printing. What do you think gives a book everlasting appeal for children?
4. Review some children's poetry anthologies and make a list of six or eight poems that you might use with pupils in the elementary grades. The poems can be focused

around a particular theme (such as weather or patriotism) or they can cover a wide range of topics that would appeal to children.

5. Do some research on your favorite children's author. Select an author whose work you loved as a child. Use the references listed in 2.7 and other sources of information that the librarian can suggest. Write a brief biographical sketch of your favorite children's author and share this with a group of fellow students.

School-Based Assignments

1. What do your pupils think of children's literature? Conduct a quick, informal survey of the books they most enjoy and why they like these books. Chart the result of the survey and try to find other books that match the pupils' favorite qualities.
2. Identify a theme that your class is studying in science or social studies. Find as many trade books as you can focused on that topic and prepare a display of books related to the theme. Don't forget to include some poetry selections.
3. Review the literary elements described in this chapter. In an informal discussion with a small group of pupils, determine their knowledge or awareness of these elements in stories. Make a list of teaching suggestions that you could use to make them more aware of setting, characters, and other literary elements.
4. Interview a teacher or a librarian to see if and how they use award-winning books. How do you think the librarian can be used more effectively as a resource person in your school?
5. Who is the favorite author of the pupils in your classroom? With the help of the pupils and the librarian, locate some biographical information about that author and prepare a display similar to that suggested in 2.7.

Children's Trade Books Cited in This Chapter

Allard, Harry. *Miss Nelson is Missing.* Boston: Houghton Mifflin, 1977.

Anderson, Hans Christian. *The Emperor's New Clothes.* New York: Harper and Row, 1982. (Many other editions available.)

———. *The Princess and The Pea.* Boston: Houghton Mifflin, 1979. (Many other editions available.)

Arbuthnot, May Hill. *The Arbuthnot Anthology of Children's Literature* (4th ed.). Glenview, IL: Scott Foresman, 1976.

Armstrong, William. *Sounder.* New York: Harper and Row, 1969.

Banks, Lynne Reid. *The Indian in the Cupboard.* New York: Doubleday, 1985.

Barrett, Judi. *Animals Definitely Should Not Wear Clothes.* New York: Atheneum, 1980.

———. *Cloudy with a Chance of Meatballs.* New York: Macmillan, 1978.

Blue, Rose. *Grandma Didn't Wave Back.* New York: Franklin Watts, 1972.

Blume, Judy. *Are You There, God? It's Me, Margaret.* New York: Bradbury, 1970.

———. *Blubber.* New York: Dell, 1974.

———. *Superfudge.* New York: Dutton, 1980.

———. *Tales of a Fourth Grade Nothing.* New York: Dutton, 1972.

Brown, Marcia. *Once a Mouse.* New York: Scribner, 1961.

———. *Stone Soup.* New York: Scribner, 1947.

Burton, Virginia Lee. *Katy and the Big Snow.* Boston: Houghton Mifflin, 1943.

Byars, Betsy. *The Animal, the Vegetable and John D. Jones.* New York: Dellacourt, 1982.

———. *Summer of the Swans.* New York: Viking, 1970.

Ciardi, John. *The Hopeful Trout and Other Limericks.* Boston: Houghton Mifflin, 1989.

Cleary, Beverly. *Dear Mr. Henshaw.* New York: William Morrow, 1983.

———. *A Girl from Yamhill.* New York: Morrow, 1988.

Cole, Babette. *Princess Smartypants.* New York: Putnam, 1987.

Collier, James and Christopher. *My Brother Sam Is Dead.* New York: Four Winds Press, 1974.

Dahl, Roald. *Boy.* New York: Farrar, Straus and Giroux, 1984.

———. *James and the Giant Peach.* New York: Knopf, 1962.

Dakos, Kalli. *If You're Not Here, Raise Your Hand: Poems about School.* New York: Four Winds, 1991.

Dalgliesh, Alice. *The Courage of Sarah Noble.* New York: Scribner, 1954.

———. *The Thanksgiving Story.* New York: Scribner, 1954.

deClements, Barthe. *Nothing's Fair in Fifth Grade.* New York: Viking, 1981.

de Paola, Tomie. *The Night Before Christmas.* New York: Holiday House, 1980.

de Regniers, Beatrice Schenk. *Sing a Song of Popcorn: Every Child's Book of Poems.* New York, Scholastic, 1988.

de Saint-Exupéry, Antoine. *The Little Prince.* New York: Harcourt, 1943.

Evslin, B., Evslin, D., and Hoopes, N. *Mightiest of Mortals: Heracles.* New York: Viking, 1975.

Forbes, Esther. *Johnny Tremain.* Boston: Houghton Mifflin, 1945.

Fritz, Jean. *And Then What Happened Paul Revere?* New York: Coward, McCann and Geoghegan, 1973.

———. *Homesick: My Own Story.* New York: Dell, 1982.

Gates, Doris. *Heros and Monsters of Greek Myth.* New York: Scholastic, 1967.

Gramatky, Hardie. *Little Toot.* New York: Putnam, 1939.

Greenfield, Eloise. *Nathaniel Talking.* New York: Writers and Readers, 1989.

Hodges, Margaret. *The Kitchen Knight: A Tale of King Arthur.* New York: Holiday House, 1990.

Howe, James. *The Day the Teacher Went Bananas.* New York: Dutton, 1984.

Hunt, Irene. *Across Five Aprils.* Chicago: Follett, 1964.

Hurwitz, Johanna. *Aldo Applesauce.* New York: Wm. Morrow, 1979.

Hutchins, Pat. *Rosie's Walk.* New York: Macmillan, 1968.

Hymans, Trina Schart. *Little Red Riding Hood.* New York: Holiday House, 1983.

Jacobs, Joseph. *Tattercoats.* New York: Putnam, 1989.

Juster, Norton. *The Phantom Tollbooth.* New York: Random House, 1961.

Keats, Ezra Jack. *In A Spring Garden.* New York: Dial, 1965.

———. *Peter's Chair.* New York: Harper and Row, 1967.

———. *The Snowy Day.* New York: Viking, 1962.

Kellogg, Steven. *Paul Bunyan.* New York: Wm. Morrow, 1984.

Kipling, Rudyard. *Just So Stories.* New York: Macmillan, 1982. (Other editions available.)

Lawson, Robert. *Rabbit Hill.* New York: Viking, 1944.

Lear, Edward. *The Complete Nonsense Book.* New York: Dodd Mead, 1946.

L'Engle, Madeline. *A Wrinkle in Time.* New York: Farrar, Strauss and Giroux, 1962.

Lewis, C. S. *The Lion, the Witch and the Wardrobe.* New York: Macmillan, 1961.

Lewis, Richard, ed. *In a Spring Garden.* New York: Dial, 1989.

———. *Miracles: Poems by Children of the English-Speaking World.* New York: Simon and Schuster, 1966.

Lindgren, Astrid. *Pippi Longstocking.* New York: Viking, 1950.

Lord, Beth Bao. *In the Year of the Boar and Jackie Robinson.* New York: Harper and Row, 1984.

Macauley, David. *Black and White.* Boston: Houghton Mifflin, 1990.

MacLachlan, Patricia. *Sarah, Plain and Tall.* New York: Harper, 1985.

McCloskey, Robert. *Time of Wonder.* New York: Viking, 1957.

McCord, David. *Every Time I Climb a Tree.* Boston: Little, Brown, 1967.

Milne, A. A. *Winnie-the-Pooh.* New York: Dell, 1981. (Other editions available.)

Munsch, Robert. *Mud Puddle.* Willowdale, ONT: Firefly Books, 1982.

———. *Thomas' Snowsuit.* Willowdale, ONT: Firefly Books, 1985.

Naylor, Phyllis Reynolds. *How I Came to Be a Writer.* New York: Morrow, 1988.

Ness, Evaline. *Sam, Bangs, and Moonshine.* New York: Holt, 1966.

Norton, Mary. *The Borrowers.* New York: Harcourt Brace, 1953.

O'Brien, Robert C. *Mrs. Frisby and the Rats of NIMH.* New York: Macmillan, 1971.

O'Dell, Scott. *Sing Down the Moon.* Boston: Houghton Mifflin, 1970.

O'Neill, Mary. *Hailstones and Halibut Bones: Adventures in Color.* Garden City, NY: Doubleday, 1961.

Osborne, Mary Pope. *American Tall Tales.* New York: Knopf, 1991.

Paterson, Katherine. *Bridge to Terabithia.* New York: Crowell, 1977.

———. *Jacob Have I Loved.* New York: Crowell, 1980.

Peet, Bill. *Bill Peet: An Autobiography.* Boston: Houghton Mifflin, 1989.

Peterson, John. *The Littles.* New York: Scholastic, 1967.

Potter, Beatrix. *The Tale of Peter Rabbit.* New York: Dover, 1903. (Other editions available.)

Prelutsky, Jack. *The Random House Book of Poetry for Children.* New York: Random House, 1983.

Raskin, Ellen. *Nothing Ever Happens on My Block.* New York: Atheneum, 1966.

Robinson, Barbara. *The Best Christmas Pageant Ever.* New York: Harper, 1972.

Rockwell, Thomas. *How to Eat Fried Worms.* New York: Franklin Watts, 1973.

Rounds, Glen O. *Ol' Paul, The Mighty Logger.* New York: Holiday House, 1976.

Scieszka, Jon. *The Frog Prince Continued.* New York: Viking, 1991.

———. *The True Story of the 3 Little Pigs!* New York: Viking, 1989.

Sendak, Maurice. *In the Night Kitchen.* New York: Harper and Row, 1970.

———. *Where the Wild Things Are.* New York: Harper and Row, 1963.

Seuss, Dr. *And to Think That I Saw It on Mulberry Street.* New York: Vanguard, 1937.

———. *The 500 Hats of Bartholomew Cubbins.* New York: Vanguard, 1938.

Silverstein, Shel. *A Light in the Attic.* New York: Harper, 1981.

———. *Where the Sidewalk Ends.* New York: Harper, 1974.

Slobodkina, Esphyr. *Caps for Sale.* Reading, MA: Addison-Wesley, 1947.

Southall, Ivan. *Let the Balloon Go.* New York: St. Martin, 1968.

Speare, Elizabeth. *The Witch of Blackbird Pond.* Boston: Houghton Mifflin, 1958.

Steig, William. *Doctor DeSoto.* New York: Farrar, Strauss and Giroux, 1982.

Stoutenberg, Adrien. *American Tall Tales.* New York: Viking, 1966.

Thaler, Mike. *The Day The Teacher Went Bananas.* New York: Scholastic, 1989.

———. *The Hippopotamus Ate the Teacher.* New York: Avon, 1981.

Tolkien, J. R. R. *The Hobbit.* Boston: Houghton Mifflin, 1938.

Uchida, Yoshiko. *Journey to Topaz.* New York: Scribner, 1971.

Van Allsburg. *Polar Express.* Boston: Houghton Mifflin, 1985.

Viorst, Judith. *The Tenth Good Think About Barney.* New York: Atheneum, 1971.

Voigt, Cynthia. *Dicey's Song.* New York: Atheneum, 1983.

Whipple, Laura. *Animals, Animals.* New York: Putnam, 1989.

White, E. B. *Charlotte's Web.* New York; Harper and Row, 1952.

White, T. H. *The Sword in the Stone.* New York: Putnam, 1939.

Wilde, Oscar. *The Happy Prince.* New York: Simon and Schuster, 1989.

Wilder, Laura Ingalls. *Little House on the Prairie.* New York: Harper, 1953.

Wittman, Sally. *A Special Trade.* New York: Harper and Row, 1978.

Yolen, Jean. *The Emperor and the Kite.* Cleveland: World, 1967.

———. *Encounter.* San Diego: Harcourt, Brace, Jovanovich. 1992.

References

Bettelheim, B. (1978). *The Uses of Enchantment.* New York: Knopf.

Bosma, B. (1987). *Fairy Tales, Fables, Legends and Myths: Using Folk Literature in Your Classroom.* New York: Teachers College Press.

Davis, Z. T., and McPherson, M. D. (1989). Story Map Instruction: A Road Map for Reading. *The Reading Teacher* 43:232–240.

Grannis, C. B. (1988). ''Book Sales Statistics: Highlights from AAP Annual Survey, 1986.'' *Bowker Annual of Library and Book Trade Information* (33rd ed.) New York: R. R. Bowker.

Hopkins, L. B. (1969). *Books Are By People.* New York: Citation.

———. (1974). *More Books By More People.* New York: Citation.

Huck, C. S. (1982). I Give You the End of a Golden String. *Theory into Practice* 21:315–321.

Huck, C. S., Hepler, S., and Hickman, J. (1987). *Children's Literature in the Elementary School.* New York: Holt, Rinehart and Winston.

Hurst, C. O. (1990). *Once Upon a Time: An Encyclopedia for Successfully Using Children's Literature with Young Children.* Allen, TX: DLM.

Kiefer, B. (1988). Picture Books as Contexts for Literary, Aesthetic, and Real World Understandings. *Language Arts* 65:260–270.

Krieger, E. (1988). Developing Reading Comprehension through Author Awareness. Unpublished report, Newton, MA.

Prelutsky, J. (1983). *The Random House Book of Poetry for Children.* New York: Random House.

McElmeel, S. (1988). *An Author A Month,* Englewood, CO: Libraries Unlimited.

Saxby, M. (1987). The Gift of Wings: The Value of Literature to Children. In M. Saxby and G. Winch, (eds.), *Give Them Wings: The Experience of Children's Literature.* Melbourne: Macmillan of Australia.

Sebesta, S. L., and Iverson, W. J. (1975). *Literature for Thursday's Child.* Chicago: Science Research Associates.

Winch, G. (1987). The Supreme Fiction: On Poetry and Children. In M. Saxby and G. Winch, (eds.), *Give Them Wings: The Experience of Children's Literature.* Melbourne: Macmillan of Australia.

hapter 3

Organizing and Managing a Literature-Based Reading Program

Chapter 3 Outline

I. Introduction
II. Time
   A. Whole-Class Work
   B. Small Group Activities
   C. Story Time
   D. Sustained Silent Reading
   E. Theme Projects
   F. Math
   G. Specialists
III. Space
   A. Reading Corner
   B. Writing Center
   C. Media Center
   D. Interest Centers
   E. Individual Reading-Study Carrels
IV. Materials
   A. Trade Books
   B. Basal Readers
   C. Supplementary Literature-Based Materials
   D. Audiovisual Devices
   E. Computers
V. Pupils
   A. Large-Group Instruction
   B. Small-Group Instruction
      1. Homogeneous Grouping
      2. Heterogeneous Grouping
      3. Cooperative Learning
      4. Paired Learning
   C. Individualized Patterns
      1. Individual Activities
      2. Individualized Activities
   D. Flexibility in Grouping
VI. Parents in the Classroom
VII. Schoolwide Organizational Patterns
   A. Departmentalization
   B. Team Teaching

VIII. Summary and Conclusions
Discussion Questions and Activities
School-Based Assignments
Children's Trade Books Cited in This Chapter
References

Features

3.1   A Daily Classroom Schedule
3.2   Word Board
3.3   Sample Classroom Floor Plan
3.4   Patterns of Selecting and Using Reading Materials
3.5   Grouping
3.6   Directed Reading–Thinking Activity
3.7   Using Literature in Heterogeneous Reading Groups
3.8   Cooperative Learning Using Literature
3.9   Cooperative Integrated Reading and Composition
3.10 Grouping in the Elementary Classroom

Key Concepts in This Chapter

Organizing and managing a literature-based reading program involves the manipulation of four major variables: time, space, materials, and pupils.

Instructional time needs to be carefully planned so that pupils can enjoy maximum time for reading and writing.

The learning environment should reflect a commitment to making literature a centerpiece of literacy instruction.

Trade books constitute the mainstay of a literature-based reading program, but a range of other instructional materials can be appropriately used as well.

Pupils need to be grouped in a variety of ways for different purposes in reading and writing instruction.

G RETCHEN TREACHER, first-year teacher, sat in her third-grade classroom and stared nervously at the door. School would open in three days. Gretchen knew that in 72 hours, 23 eager eight- and nine-year-olds would come charging through the classroom door. She hadn't met any of her pupils yet, but she had reviewed their portfolios and related records from the previous year. She knew that 13 were boys and 10 were girls. Their reading levels, measured on the previous April's achievement test, ranged from seventh grade through first grade. Three of the children were from the nearby housing project, four were from the affluent Rocky Hill section of town, and the rest were from surrounding neighborhoods. One pupil would be repeating third grade. Two had been classified as learning disabled and had received resource-room services the year before. Five had received extra reading help from the Chapter I teacher.

All Ms. Treacher had to do was to set up a reading program for grade 3-T! Her emotions ran the gamut from heady excitement to raw terror.

One of the initial decisions that any teacher has to make each year is how to organize and manage a classroom reading program. There is no such thing as a "typical" reading program, just as there is no such thing as an "average" third-grade class; the average class remains a statistical abstraction. Teachers place their own special marks on their own unique programs. A classroom reading program will depend on a range of factors—the teacher and what she or he believes is the best way to foster pupils' growing competency in literacy; the expectations and resources of the school and community; the physical environment in which the teacher has to work; the teacher's own level of energy and creativity; individual style; and the like.

Gretchen's principal expected her to use the basal reading program that the school district had adopted two years before. All teachers were expected to "cover" this program. Gretchen had no objections to the basal series. As a first-year teacher she was in no position to object; she had used that program as part of her student teaching and she had liked it. Besides, the basal would give her the guidance and structure that she felt she needed as she began her professional career. The basal would be a fine place to start.

But Gretchen wanted to move well beyond the basal. She was determined to give her pupils a rich diet of literature. She remembered her own school experience and, more recently, her experience as a student teacher when she had discovered how excited her pupils became about the books she had shared with them. The basal might indeed be a fine place to start, but Gretchen fully intended to make children's literature the centerpiece of her language arts program.

Three days before the children showed up, Gretchen began to make plans for her reading program. Like veteran teachers and tyros alike, Gretchen had to take four factors into account in organizing and managing the reading program in her classroom:

Time

Space

Materials

Pupils

Although administrative and related constraints (i.e., the number of children in the class, the size of the room, materials available, school scheduling, and the like) may place the control of some of these variables beyond the direct influence of the classroom teacher, elements of time, space, materials, and pupils are the major factors that teachers must consider in organizing and managing a classroom reading program.

Time

Time—there is never enough of it. Yet it is a very important part of reading instruction for pupils. In reviewing research and descriptive reports of effective reading programs, Wolf (1977) concluded that "one of the most effective tools for teaching reading may be the simplest and most ignored: time" (p. 76). Time consistently emerges as a crucial variable of successful instructional programs in reading.

On the average, from one-third to one-half of academic time in a school day is devoted to reading, writing, and related language instruction. Reading permeates the entire curriculum. In addition to direct teacher–pupil instructional encounters over books, reading is learned and practiced through incidental vocabulary work, written language activities, recreational and content reading, discussion and related oral-language activities, and all the other activities that support literacy development.

Time alone is not enough, of course, to promote reading success. *Becoming a Nation of Readers* (Anderson et al., 1985), the report on the state of reading instruction in the U.S., contained the alarming information that silent reading time in a typical primary classroom consists of only seven or eight minutes per day, less than 10 percent of the total time devoted to reading. Concern over figures like these has led to the increasing practice of arranging for pupils to read quality children's books in place of completing workbook exercises as a means of helping them learn to read.

In addition to the amount of time, quality of time—engaged versus nonengaged time, for example—is very important. Quality is often measured by how much time is given to direct involvement in tasks related to learning to read (time on task) as opposed to time spent lining up or sitting down in moving from one activity to another, getting ready for and cleaning up after an activity, sharpening pencils, passing out paper, collecting work, or doing other noninstructional necessities that are part of the real world of classrooms. Although a certain amount of "down time" may be part of the job of working with young children, achievement increases when pupils spend their time directly and actively engaged in appropriate learning activities. It stands to reason that pupils who pay attention are more likely to learn and those who do not are less likely.

No matter how the teacher organizes blocks of classroom time, literature-based reading programs normally include: whole-class work, small-group work, story time, theme projects, math, and assistance of specialists.

Whole Class Work

Whole class work at the beginning of the day typically differs according to the age and grade level of pupils. The activity might involve talking about books or other topics, organizing daily activities, discussing current events, viewing a filmstrip or a video of a popular book, planning class projects, whole-class lessons in which the teacher demonstrates a particular reading strategy or aspect of writing, or any other activity that would provide for the exchange of language and for the stimulation of reading and writing experiences.

A Daily Classroom Schedule

P LANNING A schedule for the most effective use of time is usually an early step
in organizing a reading program. All teachers
use time differently, but a typical classroom
schedule might look something like this:

 9:00–9:20 Whole-Class Work
 9:20–10:20 Small-Group Work
10:20–10:45 Snack and Recess
10:45–11:00 Story Time (Read Aloud)
11:00–11:45 Math
11:45–12:15 Lunch
12:15–1:00 Specialist (Art, Music, Physical
Education)

1:00–1:20 Sustained Silent Reading
1:20–2:45 Science/Social Studies/Theme
Projects
2:45–3:00 Cleanup and Dismissal

No schedule is ever cast in stone, as daily
variations occur according to classroom activities. Although schoolwide schedules often
demand that certain activities be "locked in"
(for example, lunch or library time), teachers
ordinarily have opportunities to revise their
schedules according to needs and activities
that can vary on a day-to-day basis.

Small Group Activities

Small group activities "engage pupils in a range of elective and compulsory activities
that have been carefully designed according to principles that ensure plenty of social
interaction and collaborative learning. During this time, the teacher played the role of
'consultant,' interacting with and supporting as many pupils as possible as she roved
and 'hit base' with children engaged in different activities" (Cambourne and Turbill,
1990; p. 341). This is when pupils read to one another, work independently or collaboratively on writing, receive extra help as needed, practice a play they may be preparing, complete literature journals and other reader-response activities, engage in
literature circles or reading workshops, meet in groups for booktalk or directed reading
lessons, and engage in the variety of activities that constitute language-rich and literature-rich classrooms.

Story Time

The teacher reads a story, a chapter from a longer book, or some poetry to the class,
or the pupils themselves read aloud some of their own original material, during story
time. Reading aloud is vital at any level, because "the sharing of literature aloud
anchors the sounds of the language of literature in the minds of the students. Children
of all ages absorb the language they hear" (Peterson and Eeds, 1990; p. 9).

Sustained Silent Reading

Sustained silent reading (SSR) is inviolable in literature-based programs. Sustained
silent reading is a practice that involves setting a period of time aside each day in which
everybody in the classroom reads, pupils *and* teacher. SSR involves planned periods
of uninterrupted encounters with books and is another means of injecting literature
directly into the reading program. Sometimes known by other names such as Drop
Everything and Read (DEAR), the practice has proved effective for promoting interest
in reading.

Pupils can enjoy Sustained Silent Reading any place in the classroom.

SSR involves free reading; all involved choose the books and other material they want to read. There are no formal comprehension checks, questions, exercises, or other assignments attached to reading, with the possible exception of pupils' interacting with one another through conversation or discussion about books that they have read. Some schools have schoolwide SSR programs in which everyone in the school—principal, secretaries, cafeteria workers, janitors, along with teachers and pupils—puts aside assigned tasks and reads for 20 or 30 minutes, thus creating a community of readers so important to young children's literacy development.

The teacher's role in SSR is especially important. This is not a time to correct pupils' work or to put the finishing touches on report cards. By their involvement, teachers become models by demonstrating that reading is an important and enjoyable activity.

Theme Projects

Theme projects integrate literacy development with other areas of the curriculum. Through these projects, teachers can concentrate on helping pupils deal with expository writing in textbooks and informational trade books, while helping them develop research and related study skills. Thematic units integrate science and social studies with reading and writing, while allowing pupils to engage in authentic, integrated learning experiences as they explore curriculum topics in depth.

Gretchen had decided that her first theme unit would be about her favorite pets—cats. She had already gathered trade books that she knew her pupils would enjoy on the topic, books such as Mary Calhoun's *Cross Country Cat,* about the cat who learned to ski, and David McPhail's *Great Cat,* a fantasy about an oversized kitten. She had also gathered informational books such as Don Estep's *Cats and Kittens* and Simon Seymour's *Big Cats.* She would set up an attractive display of these books, overseen by a poster of the cartoon cat Garfield, to capture pupils' attention right from the first day of school. Gretchen would begin by reading Beverly Cleary's delightful *Socks* to the class and initiating a discussion about cats before having pupils work cooperatively in exploring topics related to the care and feeding of cats, species of wild cats, and other topics in which pupils could engage in authentic reading–writing activities that extended into science and social studies.

Theme teaching is based on the idea of integration—skills and strategies are developed and applied more effectively within the context of a central topic or learning experience than when done in isolation. Staab (1991) describes how a single thematic unit can include an incredible variety of oral language, reading, and writing activities. By presenting literacy opportunities in authentic learning contexts, themes give pupils the sense that reading and writing are more than ''school subjects'' to be learned from 9:00 to 10:00 in the morning and then dropped. It makes learning useful and personal.

Math

Because of its sequential nature, math is usually scheduled in its own time slot during the school day. But learning mathematics extends beyond computation and into the reasoning process involved in logical and critical thinking. Language learning occurs in math, and there are ample opportunities to integrate literature with a variety of interesting math-related trade books. (Chapter 7 briefly explores the relationship between math and reading, and presents a list of children's trade books that can be used effectively for teaching math.)

Specialists

Specialists in areas such as music, art, and physical education are often scheduled separately, although classroom teachers are becoming more and more responsible for teaching these subjects.

It is often necessary and sometimes advantageous to rotate a classroom schedule—that is, to plan the same activities at different times on different days. Reading is usually taught first thing in the morning, on the assumption that pupils are more alert and ready to learn best at that time. The learning style of some children, however, might be such that their optimum learning occurs at another time during the school day. Besides, curriculum projects or the introduction of a new topic in another curriculum area may suggest beginning a day or a week with that subject. In most classrooms, some children receive help from specialists outside the room—speech therapists, counselors, special-education resource teachers, or Chapter I teachers who provide extra reading help outside the classroom. A rotating schedule ensures that the pupil will not miss the same activity at the same time everyday.

Some teachers, when they hear about literature-based reading programs, think of literature as an ''add-on,'' something else to usurp their already limited time. Literature is not, however, an added time dimension in a crowded classroom schedule. Planning and implementing literature-based reading instruction does not require more time; it involves the use of time in a different way. Activities like sustained silent reading and storytime are already part of most sound elementary-classroom programs. Inaugurating a literature-based program involves using literature as a vehicle in already scheduled learning—using trade books instead of basals for instructional purposes, centering oral language activities on literature, including appropriate trade books to enrich learning in social studies and science, building art and drama activities around books that pupils have enjoyed—in short, integrating literature into many dimensions of the classroom program.

When basal reading programs are used, rotating units of time is an effective means of making literature a more integral part of the reading program. The teacher plans two-, three-, or four-week periods for the completion of a basal unit, depending on how many stories are in the section. During the alternating weeks, pupils spend their time reading myths and legends, poetry, biographies, plays, and other types of trade books.

In the final analysis, the amount of time available for reading instruction in the classroom is finite. The time needs to be scheduled and managed in such a way that all pupils enjoy the maximum time for reading and related language activities during the day. Economy and efficiency are the crucial elements in the time dimension of classroom management.

Space

The arrangement of space is another practical classroom-management concern for the teacher, a dimension over which the teacher maintains maximum control. A teacher's classroom is like an artist's studio; it reflects the type of activity going on therein.

The classroom environment is an important dimension to learning. ''The environments within which students learn will affect what they learn, how they learn, and how they feel about learning'' (Rhodes and Dudley-Marling, 1988; p. 95). Morrow and Rand (1991) have demonstrated how the design of a classroom environment can have an impact on literacy development in the early years of school. Learning areas that are filled with samples of print—menus and recipes in the restaurant corner, a store with labels and signs, a post office with writing materials, a gas station with posters and maps—give young children a chance to develop their emerging reading and writing abilities.

The environment of the classroom at any grade level should be lively and attractive, with displays documenting the results of pupils' interests and learning everywhere. Displays should extend beyond lists of spelling words written in columns on half sheets of paper or of math worksheets done perfectly with happy-face stickers at the top. Displays should include artwork, stories and poems that pupils have written, and a range of creative products that reflect their responses to the literature they have experienced.

Other classroom displays document the important place of literature in the pupils' classroom lives. Displays focusing on the life and work of a particular author (see 2.7, p. 50), displays with pupil-designed book covers, *book review* boards with brief responses written by pupils about the books they have read, a tree-shaped display labeled *poet-tree* with poems that pupils have written hanging from it, displays in which favorite story scenes are illustrated and described—all help create a classroom atmosphere that conveys the message that literature is well loved and well used.

A lively classroom environment usually includes plants, pictures, charts, pets, and other objects to stimulate language development, to percolate interest, and to promote learning. Pets for science become the focus of research and reporting. Mobiles

Word Board

ONE EFFECTIVE display is a *word board,* a small area in which a new "word for the day" is displayed. The word is written on a colorful, oak tag card and mounted on the board, with a sentence illustrating its meaning in context. For example:

soporific

It is said that the effect of eating too much lettuce is soporific. (This is the opening sentence from Beatrix Potter's *The Tale of the Flopsy Bunnies,* illustrated with a delightful picture of overstuffed bunnies sleeping in the lettuce patch.)

Every couple of days, the word can be replaced with the likes of *obstreperous, scintillating, supercilious,* and other fascinating words that pupils encounter in their reading and other language activities. Words like these pique pupils' interest in language, enrich their own vocabularies, and create an awareness of the power of our lexicon. After the first week or so, the pupils themselves can take responsibility for supplying the word for the day.

When taken from the word board, word cards are placed in a word file for continuing practice and use.

---

made in art are based on the characters met in books. Pupils' interests are reflected and their needs are addressed through their environment. Displays enchance pupils' ownership of their environment and promote self-empowerment in their learning.

A flexible teaching program demands the flexible arrangement and use of space. Pupils generally need an individual desk or "station," a place they can call their own. Other space should be used flexibly enough so that it suits the variety of activities and multiple learning opportunities that characterize the lively classroom. In addition to the necessary conventional arrangement of desks and chairs, special areas can be set up to facilitate the range of reading and related activities that characterize the literature-rich classroom. Special areas can include:

Reading corner, with a rug on the floor and a couple of comfortable chairs or large pillows on which pupils can relax while they enjoy reading. Here is where the classroom library is located. Posters, pupil-designed displays of book jackets, reports, and other material designed to stimulate interest in the love of reading are part of this area as well.

Writing center, with dictionaries, a thesaurus, and other aids that pupils might need in their writing. The center is supplied with an ample supply of pens, pencils, markers, and other writing implements, along with a supply of paper (including chart paper for producing Big Books in the very early grades). A typewriter or word processor can be part of the center, too. Pupils' own writing is on display, the books that they have produced are placed on tables, and individual files of their own writing are housed here as well.

Media center, containing a filmstrip projector, tape recorder, record player, and other devices that pupils can use to enjoy stories or to follow along with books presented in mediated form.

Interest centers, for displays of science materials (like rocks, plants, magnets or pupil collections of other artifacts) or other materials related to the curriculum. These centers

Sample Classroom Floor Plan

HOW A teacher arranges classroom space will depend on the number of pupils in a class, whether classroom walls are fixed or movable, the proportion of wall-to-window area, bulletin board and chalkboard space, the amount of material and equipment in the room, the type of furniture, and a number of other physical factors. This diagram is merely a suggestion of how classroom space can be used for different purposes.

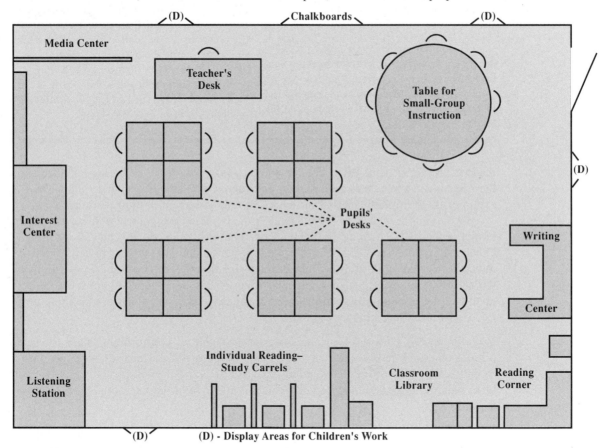

From John F. Savage and Jean F. Mooney, *Teaching Reading to Children with Special Needs.* Copyright © 1979 Allyn & Bacon, Inc., Needham Heights, MA. Reprinted by permission of the authors.

should be full of books, magazine articles, pupil-written reports, and other fiction and nonfiction material related to particular topics.

Individual reading-study carrels, where pupils who need quiet and privacy can go for independent work.

These learning centers should be more than storage areas for supplies and equipment. They should be activity centers, areas where pupils can go to engage in appropriate reading, writing, and other language-learning activities.

The fact that different areas are designated for different purposes does not imply inflexibility. Quiet reading during SSR can be done in a study carrel or in the reading center, just as well as at one's desk. And writing activities need not—in fact, *should not*—be limited to the writing center. When groups of pupils are moving around the classroom, however, organization of space is important to the efficient management of a classroom program.

Rules must be established for the use of learning centers. The number of pupils permitted in a given center at a specific time may need to be limited. Since centers are often used as independent learning areas for groups or individuals working on their own, pupils may require specific instructions in the use of each area. Centers should be located in the room so that quiet areas and noisy areas are far enough apart.

Setting up a learning environment involves the imaginative arrangement of bookcases, file cabinets, portable dividers, and maybe some ''cardboard carpentry.'' One teacher, for example, joined two large cardboard cartons (the type in which refrigerators are shipped) as a media center for her classroom so that pupils could enjoy videos and tapes of favorite stories without disturbing the rest of the class.

Since children spend hundreds of hours of their lives in classrooms, teachers owe it to them to make their learning environment as pleasant and as exciting as possible. An effective classroom atmosphere is one that promotes the notion that literacy is central to classroom life and that reading and writing are enjoyed as important, authentic activities.

Materials

Ever since the days of the New England *Primer,* materials have been a dominant force in the teaching of reading in our schools. Materials are important because they provide the vehicles by which pupils are taught to read. When a particular reading program is followed ''to the letter,'' materials can even dictate the approach used in teaching reading.

In many instances, there is a false expectation that materials will do the teaching. Shannon (1983) demonstrated that many teachers and principals believe that the basal program is the crucial element in teaching children how to read. The belief is that we can ''plug pupils in'' to a particular published program and expect the materials to do the teaching. Nothing could be further from the truth!

Despite their unquestioned importance, materials are merely tools of the trade in teaching reading. Like any tools, they are only as good as the craftsperson using them. It is the teacher and the pupils, not the materials, who make learning come alive.

A balanced and flexible reading program requires balance and flexibility in the choice and use of instructional materials. In a literature-based program, trade books will obviously play a crucial role. Basal materials may be part of this program as well. Among the other materials used for reading instruction in the classroom are supplementary, literature-related enrichment materials, supplementary skill-building materials, computers, and other devices.

Trade Books

Obviously, a literature-based reading program requires a plentiful supply of trade books in the classroom. A well-stocked classroom library will contain books at different levels. In the very early grades, wordless/textless books and picture storybooks will dominate the collection, although plenty of books for children whose independence in reading develops early should be included as well. Simple, reading textbooks that are easy to decode—with *Nat the fat cat who sits on the mat* type of material—can also be included in this collection. Decoding these simple texts can provide basic practice for beginning readers, and the success of decoding these texts can produce a positive affective response.

In the upper grades, the level of books in the classroom library must be widened to accommodate the expanding interests and increasing reading abilities of pupils. Lists recommending books for various grade levels can be found in professional references like Regie Routman's *Transitions from Literature to Literacy* (1988), Jim Trelease's well-known *The Read-Aloud Handbook* (1989), *For Reading Out Loud: A Guide to Sharing Books with Children* by Margaret Mary Kimmel and Elizabeth Segal (1983), and Beverly Korbin's *Eye Openers: Choosing Books for Kids* (1988). Reviews from magazines such as *The Reading Teacher, Language Arts,* and *The Horn Book* provide monthly reviews that suggest good leads for selecting books. Teachers use the selection guides and reviews of children's literature that appear in these magazines to stay abreast of recently published books for use in the reading program and to expand their own horizons of children's literature.

Displays of books related to various themes (for example, football, winter, or Booker T. Washington) supplement the regular classroom collection as these topics are studied. There can also be a special collection of books for reading aloud, along with some anthologies of poetry. (See 2.4, p. 42.) A classroom environment where literature is treasured will be filled with all kinds of books.

Librarians are usually enormously helpful to teachers in assembling a classroom collection of books. Most libraries have a policy of long-term loan of books for classroom use. With reasonable advance notice, librarians can put together topic-related lists and provide titles that will ensure freshness and variety in pupils' reading fare.

Permanent classroom libraries are becoming more common. As administrators in more and more school districts make a stronger commitment to literature-based reading instruction, more funds are becoming available for the purchase of trade books for classroom use. Some of the money traditionally used for buying workbooks is now being used to purchase ''real books.'' State departments of education sometimes provide grants for this purpose to teachers. Parent–teacher organizations are normally more than happy to provide funds for classroom libraries. Commercial book clubs can be another source used to supply a classroom collection. Teachers use their book club ''bonus points'' for free copies of favorite titles, and pupils can usually be convinced to contribute the books they order, once they have finished reading them. Energetic

3.4 Putting Ideas to Work

Patterns of Selecting and Using Reading Materials

HIEBERT AND Colt (1989) suggest three patterns of selecting and using trade books for instructional purposes in the classroom.

Pattern 1: "Teacher-selected literature in teacher-led groups." Here, the teacher chooses a book for instructional purposes. For example, a large-group lesson about the structure of fables might result from pupils' attempts to write fables on their own. In this pattern, pupils discuss shared content of books/stories that the teacher selects.

Pattern 2: "Teacher- and student-selected literature in teacher- and student-led small groups." The teacher recommends several books on a topic of interest and pupils choose different titles from the list. They then meet in small groups to share their interpretation of what they read, to describe their favorite books, and to talk about strategies they use.

Pattern 3: "Student-selected literature read independently." Independent reading is the ultimate test of an effective literacy program. As part of a classroom community, pupils need many opportunities to participate in authentic reading situations. These are the books that pupils read on their own for Sustained Silent Reading or for individual conferences with the teacher.

All three patterns can be used in concert with one another. Classroom programs should include combinations of teacher and student interaction and selections of literature to create thoughtful, proficient readers.

---

teachers leave no stone unturned in helping garner a collection of books that grows impressively over the years.

A practical management matter is the circulation of books in the classroom library. Classroom collections are typically housed on simple shelving or on wire racks (which are very inexpensive) in the reading corner. Usually, a simple sign-out honor system works for keeping track of books, or the task of class librarian can be assigned to a pupil helper or parent volunteer. Computers can help keep track of books. Whatever control system is used, provisions should be made so that pupils have easy access to the books available to them.

Basal Readers

For many years, basal reading materials (described more fully in Chapter 1) constituted the staple of reading instruction in most classrooms. Basals reached this position of preeminence for a number of reasons, not the least of which was that they helped facilitate classroom organization and management. Basals are well-designed packages that provide teachers with the tools they need to run a classroom program. The scope and sequence charts constitute a grand scheme for instruction. The reading books themselves provide a common core of reading material for all children. The teacher's editions contain detailed plans for carrying out lessons, and the workbooks provide materials for pupils who are not working directly with the teacher.

Although basal programs can be used to help in classroom organization and structure, no one would suggest that these teaching tools should constitute the exclusive diet of pupils' reading in school. In fact, concerns and criticism with overreliance on the basal have contributed to the more extensive use of trade books as part of formal classroom reading instruction.

Supplementary Literature-Based Materials

The increased use of literature as part of reading instruction has resulted in a plethora of supplementary programs designed for classroom use. ''The publication of lessons and worksheets to be used with children's novels has become something of a cottage industry'' (Zarrillo, 1989; pp. 23–24). These programs aim to provide both enrichment and skill-development activities related to popular children's books. Some programs provide hands-on, consumable activity sheets for pupils to use as they read the books; others are guides for teachers, with suggestions on how to use the book as a learning aid.

These supplementary literature-related programs have become very popular for a number of reasons. On the one hand, programs such as *LEAP* (Sundance Publishers), *Portals to Reading* (Perfection Form Co.), and *Novel-ties* (Learning Links) provide hands-on activities for pupils working independently. On the other hand, some packages provide a skills orientation that allows the teacher to supplement literature-based instruction of certain reading skills. But there is a real danger in this literature/skills mix: the danger that pupils will come to see literature as something to be ''worked on'' rather than to be enjoyed. Critics call it the basalization of good children's literature.

In using these materials, there is also a danger of overkill. Some of the teaching guides are longer than the books they are designed to supplement. If pupils have to complete an interminable series of uninteresting worksheets related to a book they have read, their enjoyment and enthusiasm for the book will be tempered, which is anathema to the basic purpose of literature-based reading instruction.

Supplementary literature-based programs can have a positive impact as a means of bringing literature into the reading curriculum. When used judiciously, they can help the organizational dimensions of the program by providing pupils with independent activities that will extend their understanding and deepen their appreciation of a well-liked book. As with any classroom reading materials, however, they should be used with thought and purpose.

Audiovisual Devices

Traditionally, reading has been viewed as a book-oriented activity; however, audiovisual devices have long been used in reading instruction and remain useful in literature-based reading programs. ''Audio and visual technologies and their respective media can make a significant contribution to a literature-based reading curriculum.'' Besides enhancing ''the already provocative appeal of children's literature,'' an audiovisual activity with literature ''solidifies children's concept of story, encourages the use of prediction strategies, expands receptive vocabularies, captures the imagination, and most importantly, promotes further literary involvement'' (Rickelman and Henk, 1990; p. 682).

Media provide an effective means of sharing literature with pupils. Auditory media such as tape recorders and record players allow pupils (especially young children or pupils with reading difficulties) to enjoy stories read to them. Having pupils follow a line of print as they listen to a story being read has proved to be effective in helping them learn to read. Sound effects can enhance comprehension and enjoyment, and the technology allows for repeated review of the selection. A number of cassette-and-book

Although it is a technological device, the computer can provide a focus for interaction among pupils in reading and writing.

packages are available for home and classroom use. Some of these have well-known entertainment personalities: Meryl Streep reading *Peter Rabbit,* for example, and Robin Williams reading *Pecos Bill* (Saxonville, MA: Picture Book Studio). Tape recorders can also be used effectively to develop important auditory skills associated with learning to read.

Visual media, via various types of projectors, provide opportunities for a variety of "screen reading" activities in the classroom. Filmstrips of favorite stories like *Paul Bunyan* can project illustrations as the teacher reads the story to the class, making it easier for all pupils to see the pictures without holding up the book and hearing complaints like, "Susan's head is in my way!"

Audiovisual devices—those that combine visual images with accompanying auditory input—can be used in presenting stories to pupils and in helping them develop reading competency. For a long time, 16 mm movies and sound filmstrips of popular stories have been available for classroom use. More recently, videotapes bring stories to life for pupils, although some teachers fear that the overuse of videos will deprive pupils of the inclination (and the ability) to enjoy these stories in print. Many literature-related videotapes offer the advantage of having the author or illustrator him/herself comment on and explain the story. An impressive collection of these films and videos is available from Weston Woods in Weston, Connecticut.

Computers

The ultimate "teaching machine" is, of course, the computer, and it is becoming an increasingly important instructional device in teaching reading. Rare is the classroom that does not have access to one or more microcomputers, and some schools have powerful school-based networks of these machines. Succeeding generations of hardware are becoming more and more sophisticated, and software developers are producing a flood of programs designed to be used to teach children how to read.

Although computers are widely available in schools, it is safe to say that their potential impact as instructional tools in reading has yet to be fully realized. Applied to reading, computers can be used in computer-assisted instruction (CAI) or in computer-managed instruction (CMI). In CAI, pupils interact actively with the machine as they learn. In CMI, the machine is used for diagnosis and for record keeping.

Computer-Assisted Instruction   As instructional tools, computers have a role in the skill-development aspects of reading instruction, in the literature-related aspects of the curriculum, and in word processing. As management tools, computers are used for diagnostic exercises, for record keeping, and for related aspects of classroom management.

Given the focus on reading skills when computers first came onto the scene, the early use of computers in reading instruction was to help pupils master basic elements of decoding. Programs typically included tutorials for teaching new information and drill and practice sessions to reinforce components already taught on such aspects of reading as alphabet training, short and long vowels, initial blends and digraphs, and other elements for decoding unknown words. Other more interactive programs using vocabulary exercises and problem solving, along with elements of reading comprehension, were also introduced.

With the shifting emphasis on the use of literature in classroom reading instruction, computer programs involving popular children's books quickly came onto the scene. At a basic level, these programs usually focus on the vocabulary used in the books (pupils locate synonyms or antonyms for words used in context, for example, or engage in games or crossword puzzles with words from the stories), comprehension exercises (pupils complete sentences about actions in the book or arrange events in the order in which they occurred), or exercises to test pupils' understanding of what they read. These literature-based programs can be useful when employed appropriately, but many are merely tests of whether or not pupils have read the story. Newer interactive disks enable pupils to engage more actively in stories. Developing technologies using hypertext and hypermedia hold enormous promise in making the computer a more valuable aid in literature-based reading programs (Blanchard and Rottenberg, 1990).

As an aid to literacy development, the greatest and most significant contribution of the microcomputer—both inside and outside the classroom—is word processing. Not only does word processing facilitate the job of getting thoughts down on paper, it motivates pupils to want to write more and to feel more positive about their writing. Several easy-to-use word processing programs are available for classroom use. (See 10.5, p. 00) These programs facilitate the writing process, because they allow pupils to experiment more easily with various language forms, to make revision relatively painlessly, and even to check spelling. Computers are approaching the point where they are becoming indispensable tools in classroom writing instruction.

Computer-Managed Instruction   For management purposes, the computer has long been a handy tool. Classroom management involves record keeping and maintaining ongoing accounts of pupil learning as a basis for continuous instructional planning. A computer provides teachers with fingertip access to information about pupils' reading test scores, results of formal and informal diagnostic assessment, records of previous work done, and other pertinent information. With literature-based instruction, the computer can be a useful tool in keeping a record of books read.

Beyond the record-keeping function, computers can be used to manage instruction. Computer management systems in reading typically focus on skill development. Management systems indicate skills objectives and pupils take tests (often right on the computer itself) to see which skills they have mastered. Although this type of computer management allows for precise instructional planning, the focus is on mastery of skills rather than on the more holistic dimensions of reading.

For the classroom teacher, computers have other applications in reading as well: quickly computing estimated readability levels of printed materials; gathering and analyzing data for long-term, classroom-based research on teaching reading; cataloging books and recording circulation in the classroom library; or preparing pupil reports. The immediate concern of most teachers, however, is how best to use the computer in their day-to-day work in teaching reading.

How effective is the computer as a device for teaching children how to read? Certain studies show positive results, but the computer has not proved to be a panacea. De Groff (1990) points out some of the advantages for using computers in whole language classrooms—to promote social interaction, to provide a medium for reading and writing whole and meaningful texts, to facilitate writing activities. But, computer instruction seems to be having a greater impact in science and math than in reading (Roblyer, 1988). As the explosive growth of computer use accelerates, as machines and software become more sophisticated, and as computers become a more integral part of the actual process of delivering reading instruction to pupils, their impact on literacy instruction will likely be even greater.

The choice of materials for reading instruction is almost limitless. Choosing the right material for pupils in terms of their interests, backgrounds, and learning needs—and scheduling the use of these materials in a sane and orderly fashion—make up a major part of managing reading instruction in the classroom. No matter what range of material is used, however, real books remain central to the instructional enterprise in a literature-based reading program.

Pupils

At the heart of all organization and management matters—the allocation of time, the use of furniture and space, the selection and assignment of materials, and all the rest that goes into creating and operating a learning environment—are the pupils. They are the ones for whom arrangements are made, and the success of what we do in schools must be judged in terms of how well management decisions meet their needs. Ever since teachers have been faced with twenty-five or so pupils of unequal ability, they have been confronted with the task of providing for a reasonable and orderly scheme in which pupils can best be taught.

In learning to read and write, pupils are organized or grouped in a variety of ways. Some activities are carried on with the whole class. At other times, pupils will be assigned to small groups formed on the basis of different criteria for either teacher-directed or independent learning activities. There also will be times when pupils will be expected to complete individually designed literacy-related tasks on their own.

3.5 Putting Ideas to Work

Grouping

T HERE ARE a variety of options for grouping pupils for reading and writing activities, including:

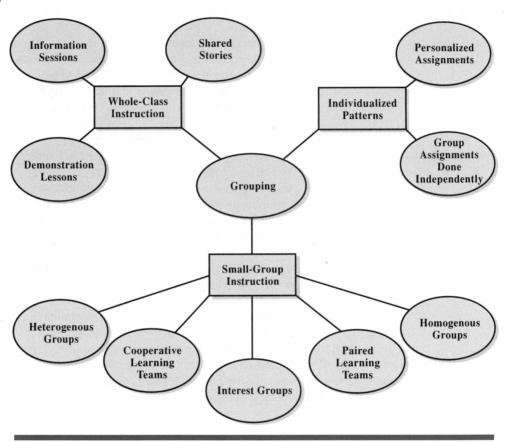

The key to any grouping pattern is flexibility. Different types of groups are needed for a balanced program that will meet curriculum requirements and at the same time meet the pupils' reading needs and interests. In any type of grouping pattern that the teacher uses, literature plays an important role as the vehicle of instruction.

Large-Group Instruction

In any classroom, the realities of school life and the nature of the curriculum are such that large-group or whole-class instruction will be appropriate at times. These occasions arise when all pupils in a class can profit from the same instruction at the same time. Large-group or whole-class sessions may be appropriate for such activities as:

literature-based language activities like storytelling, booksharing, creative dramatics or choral reading;

sharing stories by reading aloud or by viewing a filmstrip or video;

introducing a new reading strategy such as using context clues, map reading, or some aspect of dictionary use;

teaching a minilesson on an item of common need, such as recognizing and using similes and metaphors in reading and writing;

art activities like making book posters or illustrating and describing scenes from novels.

The same text can be used to demonstrate effective reading strategies to an entire class. ''With one copy of a highly interesting book with fine illustrations, the teacher can effectively demonstrate and promote reading strategies with the whole class at one time. Students have opportunities to predict text and vocabulary, integrate phonics with meaning clues, use oral and written cloze (in which pupils supply missing words in text) to predict words in context, predict and confirm events, and read orally and silently in a supportive group situation. . . . (The) emphasis is on enjoying a story together'' (Routman, 1988; p. 144). Routman describes what is often involved in a whole-class reading lesson. The teacher introduces the story aloud, asking appropriate high-level questions. The overhead projector is used frequently for displaying selected pages that pupils read aloud together, for guided silent reading, and for large-group vocabulary and context exercises. The whole class remains involved in a group reading experience.

Sometimes, whole-class instruction can be coordinated with small-group activity, as when pupil teams work on assignments that follow from large-group presentations. For example, the teacher can introduce a single story to an entire class by presenting key vocabulary, directing whole-class prereading discussion, and setting purposes for reading. Then one group listens to a version of the story on the tape recorder, another group reads with teacher direction, and a third group reads the story independently. Afterward the whole class works together in postreading discussion of the theme, in comparing the taped version to other versions, or in planning follow-up activities such as choral reading or creative dramatizations based on the story. This is an example of the flexibility that characterizes effective grouping practices.

In large-group instructional situations, the teacher still needs to be aware of individual differences that exist within the group. A group of 23 children is not one child 23 times; rather, it is 23 children ''one time each.'' Thus, different parts of large-group instruction still need to be directed at individual pupils, and differentiated follow-up is vital.

While whole-class instruction may be appropriate at times, most of the reading instruction that goes on in any classroom is done in small groups.

Small-Group Instruction

For a long time, teachers have divided their classes into smaller, more manageable organizational units for reading instruction. Research supports the idea of small-group organization for reading instruction. ''Teachers who group their students for instruction tend to have more academically engaged time and higher reading achievement. . . . Grouping students for instruction allows for more teacher-led demonstrations and practice. It also gives the students more opportunities to practice new skills under the teacher's guidance and to receive feedback concerning their performance. Grouping also makes it much easier for teachers to monitor the students' behavior, to keep them on task, and to avoid major classroom management problems'' (Rosenshine and Stevens, 1984, p. 787).

Grouping involves more than gathering pupils together; it involves interaction while moving toward a goal. ''Often, so-called 'groups' are nothing more than aggregations. . . . When a few students meet with the teacher, and each communicates only with the teacher, then they are not functioning as a group. When each student communicates with the others as well as with the teacher, a true group is functioning'' (Hittleman, 1988; p. 390). Just because pupils are *in* a group does not mean that they are functioning *as* a group.

Traditionally, reading instructional groups have been formed on the basis of pupils' perceived ability or achievement. More recently, other criteria have been used to form these groups.

Homogeneous Grouping   The most common basis for grouping pupils for reading instruction has been their reading level. Pupils are grouped according to their ability or reading achievement, creating instructional groups that are as homogeneous as possible. This ''Robins, Bluebirds, Sparrows'' arrangement was introduced and widely accepted in the 1920s, and it continued as a mainstay in grouping patterns.

The basis used for placing pupils in these ability/achievement groups typically includes their standardized reading achievement test scores, their observed reading ability from informal measures, the recommendation of their teacher from the previous year or the reading specialist, and/or the pupil's reading performance in previous grades. Teachers may divide a class into as few as two or as many as five reading groups, but the major criterion remains the same—the pupils' measured or perceived reading level.

The intent of ability grouping is to gear instruction as closely as possible to the reading levels of pupils. The teacher normally meets with each group separately every day, using materials (basal readers or trade books) at appropriate levels. Instruction focuses on the range of strategies and techniques needed for reading competency. More often than not, all children in any one group are instructed in basically the same way.

Grouping pupils by ability or achievement is commonly seen as a means of providing more manageable instruction. It facilitates the choice of materials, enables the teacher to pace instruction more appropriately, and provides for guided interaction and feedback. Homogeneous grouping aims to promote instructional efficiency. All six or eight pupils in a group can be working from the same book, thus providing a common basis of discussion and academic learning.

The practice of ability grouping is being challenged as problems with the practice are being recognized. Being in the ''low group'' year after year can have a disastrous effect on a pupil's self-concept. Placement in the slow group ''clearly sends negative messages to struggling readers—messages of limited potential and low expectations. As a result, remedial readers are often isolated from the literature-based activities of more accomplished classmates'' (Schumaker and Schumaker, 1988; p. 546).

The nature of instruction differs from group to group as well. Pupils on the fast track tend to receive more favorable treatment from teachers (Wuthrick, 1990). Pupils in the low group receive a different quality of reading instruction, with less time, less emphasis on meaning dimensions of reading, and less interesting reading materials

3.6 Putting Ideas to Work

Directed Reading–Thinking Activity

WHETHER USING trade books or basal readers as the vehicle for reading instruction in groups, a plan that has proved effective for designing lessons is Stauffer's (1969) Directed Reading-Thinking Activity (DRTA). Developed during the 1960s, the model has remained a popular way of conducting reading lessons ever since. DRTA is usable at any grade level as a plan for teacher-directed reading lessons of basal stories, trade books, or content area texts. Its twofold aim is (1) ''to teach children how to extract information of predictive value from a given context . . . [and] (2) to provide, through a group medium, ways of behaving like a thinking reader that would be useful to pupils when reading on their own'' (Stauffer, 1969; p. 60).

DRTA consists of four steps:

1. *Introducing the selection.* The first step consists of preparing pupils for reading. Discussion centering on clues in illustrations and titles aims to help pupils predict what a story might be about. Part of this stage is establishing short- and long-term purposes for reading the passage. Purpose-setting questions may focus on a particular idea, event or character; or they may relate to the hypotheses that pupils have made.

2. *Guided reading.* After reasonable preparation, pupils begin to read the passage in the group. For the teacher, this involves seeing that pupils read to meet the established purposes, helping pupils use context and graphophonic clues to figure out problem words, focusing pupils' attention on points in the selection that are essential to meaning, and perhaps rereading certain parts of a passage. Guided reading occurs with successive segments of text, maybe refining predictions as more information is acquired. Typical lessons include both silent and oral reading at this stage of DRTA.

3. *Developing comprehension.* Here the emphasis is on meaning and thought processes related to the reading lesson. Through discussion, pupils confirm their hypotheses, extend meaning, find proof, make judgments about what they have read, trace the metacognitive processes that led them to the meanings they have derived, apply their understandings, and otherwise engage in the full range of thinking skills that are part of the process of learning to read.

4. *Follow-up.* Follow-up activities typically consist of reading-skill-development activities, literature enrichment activities, language-based activities such as dramatization, follow-up research on a particular topic, writing, or other activities designed to extend and enrich reading. This follow-up starts in the group setting and is completed by pupils working independently.

Obviously, the same rigid routine need not be slavishly followed every day for every small-group reading lesson. Indeed, variations of DRTA are possible and desirable, depending on the nature of the text being read. Nevertheless, there are distinct instructional advantages to following a coherent sequence involving preparation, directed reading, and discussion in small-group reading lessons.

(Allington, 1983). Besides, research indicates that grouping pupils by their reading ability levels does not promote better reading achievement.

Paratore et al. (1991) summarize major research findings related to grouping pupils for reading instruction. They conclude that grouping pupils according to achievement or ability does not enhance reading achievement, that assignment to permanent groups based on ability affects pupils' perceptions of self and others, that alternative grouping arrangements (such as cooperative learning groups or peer tutoring) lead to significant increases in literacy learning, and that "heterogeneous groups supplemented by smaller 'needs-based' groups for providing additional help surpass homogeneous groups in reading achievement" (p. 8).

Although there may be times when grouping pupils of similar ability may be appropriate in a flexible grouping pattern, sole reliance on this practice is being questioned. The intent of grouping pupils by their ability/achievement may be positive, but the negative effects of reduced expectations, instructional practices, pupil self-concepts, and reading achievement for pupils in the low group have caused educators to reexamine the exclusive practice of homogeneous grouping. Alternative grouping patterns are being used for reading instruction in the classroom.

Heterogeneous Grouping   Any teacher who engages in whole-class instruction is necessarily dealing with a heterogeneous group. But opportunities abound for using smaller, mixed-ability groups as part of classroom organization for reading.

Activities involving multi-ability groups usually begin with teacher direction—the teacher reads part of a story demonstrating effective reading strategies, or conducts a minilesson on a component such as identifying character traits. Following this, groups reflecting different ability levels focus on targeted skills (e.g., character traits) or apply the thinking processes and reading strategies modelled by the teacher in the minilesson.

Literature can be a criterion for forming heterogeneous groups (see 3.7). Trade books provide the vehicle for the development and application of reading strategies. Interest (not achievement) is a major factor in forming groups. No matter what level the book, pupils of varying abilities can discuss their reactions, their reflections, and their reading development based on what they have read.

Pupils can be grouped heterogeneously on the basis of shared interest as well. For example, mixed-ability groups can read and discuss materials related to sports, hobbies, occupations, or curriculum-related topics. Stories, poems, magazine articles, and sometimes basal stories at different levels can be found on these topics.

Schools are moving away from a reliance on ability/achievement as the prime criterion for grouping pupils and coming to use a variety of more heterogeneous grouping patterns. Two practical ways of forming heterogeneous groups in the classroom are cooperative learning teams and mixed-ability, peer-tutoring teams.

Cooperative Learning   One of the most promising instructional practices in today's school is cooperative learning, an instructional arrangement in which pairs or small groups of pupils work together to promote one another's learning. The idea behind cooperative learning is simple: pupils often learn more while working with one another than they do while working on their own. Cooperative learning supplements teacher instruction, in that it gives pupils opportunities to work collaboratively in seeking

3.7 Putting Ideas to Work

Using Literature in Heterogeneous Reading Groups

TRADE BOOKS lend themselves especially well to pupils of different reading levels working together. For example:

Literature Study Groups. Grouping pupils according to trade books they are reading is an essential element in a literature-based reading program. At any grade level, the teacher selects several books that are sure to appeal to pupils. Levels of books range from easy to more challenging. The teacher briefly introduces each book, pupils indicate which titles appeal to them, and heterogeneous groups are formed.

Peterson and Eeds (1990) describe in some detail the rationale and procedures for literature study groups, and they detail what goes into the organization, management, and instruction of these groups, including:

parent involvement to "get literature going at home";
reading aloud as a way of making connections with authors and books;
extensive reading of appealing trade books in the classroom;
intensive reading, in which pupils are invited to extend themselves into the world of literature;
dialogue that focuses on interpretation and active involvement in the story.

Forming groups is a two-phased process. First, pupils read the book for fun with brief (five-to-seven minute) daily meetings to check progress and share meanings. Phase two involves critical interpretation, personal response, focus on literary elements, and generating involvement through a "conscious connection" to the literature. For evaluation, Peterson and Eeds suggest checklists, daily reading records, and reading response journals.

The type of activity that takes place in literature study groups is very different from that which occurs in the traditional "reading group." "Questions with predetermined correct answers are not asked. Instead, the teacher is a participant, a fellow reader who shares the joys and difficulties, insights and speculations, and asks only those questions he or she genuinely wonders about" (Eeds and Peterson, 1991; p. 119). Discussions include reflection and dialogue, as pupils reflect in their own unique ways on the stories they have read (Keegen and Shrake, 1991).

Theme Groups. The teacher selects books at different levels centered on a theme. A selection of "survival books," for example, might include:

Jean George's *My Side of the Mountain,* the story of a boy who survives by living off the land in the Catskill Mountains;
Jean George's *Julie of the Wolves,* a story about a girl who survives with the help of wolves on the Alaskan tundra;
Felice Holman's *Slake's Limbo,* a book about a boy who survives in the subway tunnels of New York City;
Cynthia Voigt's *The Homecoming,* an account of four children who survive as they walk from Connecticut to their grandmother's home in Maryland;
Armstrong Sperry's *Call It Courage,* an adventure of a boy who has to prove his manhood in the South Pacific.

Each pupil reads his or her own tale of survival at his or her reading level. Instruction focuses on vocabulary (survival or descriptive words), literary elements (the effect of the setting on the action), comprehension components (main idea or cause-effect relationships), critical thinking (how personal traits have an impact on the main character's survival), and the like.

Author Groups. Pupils of differing ability may be in the same group reading books by the same author. For example, Valerie is reading a more sophisticated Judy Blume title such as *Are You There God? It's Me, Margaret,* while Attila is reading the easier *Freckle Juice.* Based on what they read, pupils meet to share facts they have researched about the author's life and writing style, and similarities and differences in books.

Cooperative learning promotes interdependency and social skills essential in today's world.

additional information, discussing ideas, practicing skills, or extending projects begun in teacher-directed encounters.

Cooperative learning can take many forms in the literature-based classroom. For example, it might involve:

two or three pupils reading together, sharing a story, taking turns reading, figuring out words together, or just browsing through books;

a team of pupils working together on reading-related strategies, such as using context clues to determine the meaning of unfamiliar words or seeing how details support a main idea in a story;

a group of pupils cooperatively completing a reading guide based on an informational trade book or a chapter from a content area textbook;

a team of pupils writing sentences with context clues to show the meaning of new words;

a group of pupils constructing a story map or collaboratively deciding on the best way to summarize a story ''in 25 words or less'';

a team of four or five pupils finding more information about a curriculum-related topic and preparing a display to share their information with the rest of the class.

Cooperative learning occurs all the time as an integral part of process writing, as pupils confer in generating ideas, in drafting, in editing and revising, and in sharing their stories, poems and other written products.

There will be times when cooperative learning groups are formed according to similar performance levels, and times when they are formed without regard to members' reading abilities. In any cooperative learning arrangement, pupils take responsibility for checking each other's work and making sure that important knowledge and skills are acquired. Individuals are rewarded on the basis of the accomplishments of all members of the group.

3.8 Putting Ideas to Work

Cooperative Learning Using Literature

NANCY WHISLER and Judy Williams (1990) have provided a plethora of ideas and suggestions for using children's literature for cooperative learning activities. Some samples:

group prediction strategies, in which small groups brainstorm ideas related to a topic or theme before reading;

collaborative word webbing, in which cooperative learning groups construct webs related to key words in the story or related to characters;

Venn diagrams that pupils cooperatively construct for comparing story elements with their personal experiences;

literature report cards, in which groups of pupils evaluate and "grade" story characters on various qualities; for example, Barbara Cooney's wonderful *Miss Rumphius* is "graded" on her imagination, thoughtfulness, and the like.

Also included are cooperative learning activities using a variety of prediction and anticipation strategies, vocabulary activities, creative thinking experiences, classification exercises, listening activities, paired reading, story mapping, writing, discussion, and other activities that involve pupils interacting with each other as they interact with books.

In synthesizing research related to cooperative learning, Slavin (1991) reports that the most successful approaches incorporate two elements: group goals and individual accountability; that is, "groups must be working to achieve some goal or to earn rewards or recognition, and the success of the group must depend on the individual learning of every group member" (p. 76). When group goals and individual accountability are present, achievement effects are consistently positive. Slavin also reports positive effects for cooperative learning across grade levels, across subject areas, and in many of the affective dimensions of learning (such as self-esteem, social skills, attitude toward school, and the ability to work with others). Cooperative learning has also been shown to work effectively in developing and applying high-level reading-comprehension skills (Flynn, 1989), in improving comprehension of content area reading material (Uttero, 1988), and in improving reading attitudes (Madden, 1988).

Cooperative learning, when carefully planned and skillfully implemented, is a promising alternative to teacher-directed ability groups. Beyond the feelings of belonging, acceptance, and support that the practice can generate, it can improve reading and writing performance. Moreover, it can be effectively integrated with traditional practices in a flexible grouping plan.

Paired Learning   Another popular technique for cooperative work in the classroom is paired learning. Paired learning occurs when two pupils of equal ability work together in helping each other as teachers and learners simultaneously. Or it can occur as peer tutoring, in which a more capable pupil works with one who needs help.

There are plenty of opportunities for teams of pupils to work together in literature-based reading and writing activities. Equal-ability pairs can work together in previewing a story and making predictions before reading, in listening to one another read aloud to confirm hypotheses or to answer questions, and in helping one another with a discussion or writing assignment following reading. Pupils are evaluated jointly upon the completion of an assignment.

Cooperative Integrated Reading and Composition

STEVENS ET al. (1987) have demonstrated the effectiveness of cooperative learning practices in helping pupils in the elementary grades develop competency in literacy. In a program called Cooperative Integrated Reading and Composition (CIRC), third and fourth graders worked in heterogeneous learning teams for a variety of reading and writing activities. Research showed that the results of the program were impressive.

The cycle of instruction began with teacher presentation of a new skill or introduction of the story in the reading group. This was followed by teacher-guided practice with the group, in which pairs of pupils worked cooperatively to answer questions. Pupils worked in mixed-ability learning groups on activities coordinated with their group instruction. The teacher monitored pupils' work and provided feedback and reteaching as necessary. When pupils showed that they understood the work, they engaged in team practice and preassessment activities. At the end of the cycle were quizzes to test for understanding and mastery.

In comparison to pupils taught in the conventional manner (meeting in reading groups followed by independent worksheet practice), standardized test results favored the CIRC pupils on a variety of measures—reading comprehension, vocabulary, mechanics of writing, language expression, spelling, oral reading, and general writing ability.

Mixed-ability pairs can engage in cooperative learning activities such as comparing literary elements in different stories they have read or in using different print sources to locate information and note answers to questions. The effectiveness of peer tutoring has been well documented by research. ''Peer tutoring correlates with significant gains among both tutors and tutees'' (Paratore et al., 1991; p. 7).

The effects of peer tutoring are especially impressive when low-achieving older readers tutor pupils in the lower grades (Labbo and Teale, 1990). Reading aloud to younger pupils gives the poor reader a sense of purpose, along with authentic opportunities to develop vocabulary and comprehension competencies. This is true of seriously at-risk pupils (Top and Osguthrope, 1987). For younger pupils, it extends their opportunity to hear new stories and to talk about books, and it provides them with reading models with whom they can readily relate.

The various types of small-group organizational patterns described in this section are certainly not mutually exclusive. In fact, they complement one another. They provide the flexibility of allowing the best readers to work alongside the less able readers, at least some of the time, providing for true mainstreaming of the child with special needs.

More important than the grouping arrangements themselves, however, is the type of instruction and activities carried on within the groups. Directed lessons, lively discussions, and exciting supplementary work are the keys to using books for reading and writing activities in various small-grouping patterns in the classroom.

Individualized Patterns

In addition to grouping, there are ample opportunities for individual work as part of literature-based reading instruction. Individualized instruction has historical roots. ''From the very beginning, Americans have been inclined to value the individual student and to seek ways to accommodate the needs and aspirations of individuals in the

3.10 Putting Ideas to Work

Grouping in the Elementary Classroom

BERGHOFF AND Egawe (1991) describe alternatives to ability grouping in the following chart:

The authors caution, however, that these grouping patterns "work because they are connected with our understandings of literacy, learning, and community. They are not simply logistical mechanisms that can be plugged into any classroom. They are thoughtful choices of organizational patterns that support learning and the creating of meaning in the way we theorize it can best be accomplished" (p. 537).

TABLE 3.1 GROUPING IN THE ELEMENTARY CLASSROOM

	Whole Group	Small Group	Pairs	Independent
Why?	Develops the learning community; time to share culture and literacy	Common interests; strategy instructions; opportunities to plan, think, work toward a goal.	More intimate group requires less negotiation about agenda; more opportunity to construct.	Allows sustained reading and writing; allows personal choice; time for personal reflection.
How?	Possibilities include sitting in a circle, having a special chair for authors or report givers, musical signals to call the group together.	Groups of 3 or 4 self-chosen for interest; teacher planned considering social relationships, expertise, or needed language support.	Self-chosen partner; teacher assigned partner to assure success—stronger/ weaker, expert/ novice; to encourage new friendships.	Teacher specifies time for independent work; children separate themselves to work alone.
When?	Decision making—class rules, plans; problem solving—playground issues; listening to stories; choral reading; teacher or "expert" demonstrations; shared experiences—cooking, science experiments, art activities; celebrating— completion of a major project, individual accomplishments; sharing individual scholarship.	Discussion groups; literature study; content area explorations; writing support groups; instruction groups; any inquiry project.	Shared reading; study partners; cross-age tutors; letter exchanges; skill pairings— author/illustrator, reader/actor.	Sustained reading and writing; personal investigation; journal writing; alternative sign system response; gathering personally inviting resources; time for personal reflection.

TABLE 3.1 *Continued.*

	Whole Group	**Small Group**	**Pairs**	**Independent**
How does it foster literacy?	Provides a meaning-rich context where language is used to share meaning and students' individuality is explored and supported.	Opportunity to use oral language in social context to construct meaning; functional reasons to read and write; allows students to shape their own development of personal literacy.	Opportunities to practice making personal meanings public in face-to-face interaction with a peer; "two heads are better than one"—learning can go farther with two.	Allows the child to set a personal pace for thinking; allows the child to make personal connections to the class learning; time to savor language; time to use written language.
How does it support students with diverse language, cultural, ability, or experience backgrounds?	Shared experiences give the class a shared vocabulary and practice in social meaning making. Exposes differences and similarities of all students so that they are expected and accepted.	Develop awareness of multiple perspectives; peers provide support and language opportunities.	Opportunities to make connections with all class members; reasons to relate in spite of differences.	Allows time for the child to do what he enjoys without pressure to negotiate with the larger community; time to practice, to own new learning; time to work in the child's first language.
What does the teacher learn from the students?	What the children value. What energizes the group. Which children need more help in making their meanings public.	Can see the children try out different perspectives and roles; can see how the children's personal sense of power is evolving; can see what knowledge is constructed.	What the child can do with support; what kind of support the child needs; how the child accepts or rejects different perspectives.	What the child's interests are; what the child thinks about; what aspects of reading and writing make sense to the child and can be used for her/his own purposes.

From Beth Berghoff and Kathryn Egawe, "No More Rocks: Grouping to Give Students Control over Their Learning," in *The Reading Teacher* 44:536–540, (April 1991). Copyright © 1991 International Reading Association, Newark, DE. Reprinted by permission of Beth Berghoff and the International Reading Association.

practice of schooling" (Otto, Wolf, and Eldridge, 1984; p. 800). Schools today are no less concerned with the growth and development of the individual pupil. Even as they participate in a variety of small groups, pupils need activities that are *individual* and/ or *individualized.* There is a difference between these two terms.

Individual activities are those carried out by pupils working on their own; that is, when pupils are doing activities related to trade books they have read—using a map to trace the movements of the animals in Robert Lawson's *Rabbit Hill,* for example. In individual activities, pupils work independently on teacher-directed, group-related tasks.

Individualized activities are those prescribed for the child him/herself according to his or her individual interests and needs, as when pupils are working on their literature journals. These types of individualized activities are often found in literature-based reading programs.

In most classrooms, pupils are expected to work on their own for a considerable amount of time in completing seatwork, in using supplementary literature-related materials, in independent reading and research projects, and in other learning activities. All the pupils might be working on the same assignment, but each is doing it on his or her own.

Independent activities help pupils learn to function on their own and to take responsibility for some of their own learning. These activities also provide personalized learning opportunities, with assignments tailored to individual interests and needs; however, when pupils are functioning on their own, work needs to be carefully planned and closely monitored. Independent work time is full of opportunities for doodling, daydreaming, socializing, or just plain fooling around, so time-on-task is an important consideration when pupils are working on their own. That is why independent work needs teacher supervision and feedback. The more time teachers (or other adults) spend supervising pupils during independent assignments, the more pupils seem to achieve in these assignments. Also, pupils need to be held accountable for the completion of independent work assigned to them.

Practical considerations must be taken into account as pupils work on their own. Work should be within the pupil's ability to complete it. It makes little sense to have pupils doing research from an encyclopedia two or three levels beyond their reading level or struggling with a trade book that is so difficult as to be frustrating. Some pupils may need a "buddy" from whom they can seek direction, because teacher directions given at the beginning of an independent work period are often quickly forgotten. Quiet work areas may be needed for pupils who have trouble attending to a task while classmates are working around them. Computers can sometimes be effective devices in pacing independent instruction and in providing feedback.

Accommodations for each individual pupil's learning habits, along with teacher planning and supervision, make the individually oriented component of a classroom program run smoothly.

Flexibility in Grouping

Whole-class or individualized teaching? Homogeneous or heterogeneous grouping? Large-group instruction or paired learning? The answer is *yes*, all of the above.

The key to effective grouping is flexibility. One of the problems with the traditional practice of ability/achievement grouping is that pupils were locked into one group for their entire school lives. The cliche, "Once a wombat, always a wombat," too often rang true. This type of grouping contributed to an educational caste system.

A balanced literacy program in the classroom provides opportunities for pupils to work in various types of groups as part of learning to read and write. With flexible grouping, pupils are placed in different types of groups at various times. In a given day, pupils might share stories in small groups of friends who are at the same reading level, participate in whole-class lessons on topics of common needs, work on reading-related projects with classmates of dissimilar abilities, participate in writing conferences and edited sessions with one other classmate, and complete individual assignments tailored to their needs and interests.

Unsworth (1988) has suggested a set of principles to guide the use of flexible grouping in the classroom. As an alternative to permanent groups, he suggests that groups be created periodically to meet new needs as they arise. Group size can vary from two members to the whole class. The composition of groups changes according to the task of the group. The purpose of the group's task should be clear, pupils should know how their work relates to the overall program, and group assessment should be used.

In answer to the question, ''Am I allowed to group?'' Flood et al. (1992) identify the variables in using flexible grouping patterns and describe how different groups can be used in a single, literature-based lesson using Verna Aardema's *Why Mosquitoes Buzz in People's Ears*. Depending on the activity, pupils can be grouped according to several criteria. Size can vary from two pupils to a whole class. The same material can be used in all groups, or each group can use its own resources.

Flexible grouping patterns require flexibility on the part of the teacher. Rather than setting a classroom atmosphere in which some pupils ''just don't fit,'' teachers need to design literacy experiences in which pupils can work together in an environment marked by enthusiasm, support, respect, and recognition that everyone has something to contribute to one another and to the reading program.

Parents in the Classroom

Parents are a potential source of help in organizing and managing an efficient classroom reading program. By extending their considerable influence beyond the home and by providing extra sets of hands in the classroom, parent volunteers can help make literature-based reading programs run more smoothly.

Involving parents in classroom reading programs is a means of establishing home–school relationships of the first order. It allows parents to become aware of their children's reading and writing development, enables parents to better understand what literature-based instruction is all about (and where all the worksheets have gone), and encourages them to provide carryover of classroom learning experiences into their homes.

As part of helping and monitoring pupils' independent work in the classroom, parents—and grandparents, too—can do a number of jobs: listening to children read; answering the inevitable ''What do I do next?'' and other procedural questions; helping with the spelling of unfamiliar words as pupils write; helping pupils edit their writing, as long as it is done sensitively and skillfully; reading stories to small groups of pupils; assisting pupils who are having trouble with assignments; researching information for author-awareness displays; keeping track of books in and out of the classroom library; working on book projects by putting pupil-produced books together; and otherwise adding their own unique skills in their own unique ways.

Large doses of sensitivity and common sense are needed when parents work in classrooms. Often, there are schoolwide or districtwide policies to be followed. Training and orientation are essential so that parents clearly understand their roles and functions. Confidentiality of pupil records needs to remain sacrosanct.

Classroom volunteers can play many roles in helping pupils as part of literature-based reading and writing instruction.

The first parent–teacher conference or PTA meeting of the year is an effective time to recruit parent volunteers. The invitation may also be extended as part of an opening-of-school letter to pupils' homes. Since many parents do not have time for this type of activity, other community resources might be used to recruit volunteers.

Some teachers find parents to be more trouble than help in the classroom. Teachers who have used volunteers effectively, however, find that parents have become an essential part of their classroom reading programs.

Schoolwide Organizational Patterns

Other organizational patterns—such as departmentalization, team teaching, and other alternatives to self-contained classrooms—may affect the way in which reading and writing instruction are delivered.

Departmentalization is a teacher-oriented organizational pattern that is sometimes used in the upper elementary grades. Different teachers work in their academic specialty areas (science, social studies, math, language arts) in subject matter periods through the day. One teacher may be responsible for reading instruction for several classes. In the lower grades, a modified version of departmentalization is sometimes found, as when two second-grade teachers ''trade'' classes so that one teaches all the math and science and the other teaches language arts. Although this arrangement may offer the benefit of teachers with particular interest and expertise in specific areas, it hardly promotes the idea of wholeness or the integration of language arts into all areas of the curriculum.

Team teaching involves teachers with different subject specialties working together in a more coordinated effort in dealing with groups of pupils. Team teaching is characterized by close planning, which increases the chances of having language permeate experiences in other areas of the curriculum.

Each of these organizational patterns—and others that have been used over the years—reflects a different philosophy or approach to education. Each has its own advantages and disadvantages and, in practice, can represent the best or the worst of educational arrangements. None has been shown conclusively to have a significant effect on pupils' achievement in reading.

In the environments in which these patterns are used, there remains a need for balance of large-group, small-group, and independent activities as part of learning how to read and write. And though these organizational patterns decrease the flexibility typically found in a self-contained classroom, none preclude the extensive use of literature in the reading instructional program.

Summary and Conclusions

When all is said and done, a well-run classroom is conducive to pupil achievement. Efficient and effective reading instruction is the goal of organization and management. Organization and management are not ends in themselves; they are a means to an end, the end being to provide the best reading instruction possible.

When children arrive at school, they are gathered together based on a single criterion—their age. Twenty or so pupils of the same age are put together and assigned to a teacher who is charged with the responsibility of helping them become literate. Because individual differences are a fact of life, the teacher reorganizes these large groups into smaller, more manageable clusters to provide for efficient instruction.

Then the teacher faces managerial decisions and adjustments to ensure that pupils receive the best possible reading instruction. These decisions include scheduling time, arranging space, choosing and assigning materials, and keeping records of pupils' progress, not to mention establishing a "traffic pattern" for pupils who leave the room to work with specialists, keeping the milk money separate from the picture money, and assuming all the other noninstructional administrative responsibilities that go with the job of teaching. Managing classroom reading instruction is indeed a many-splendored thing!

Organizing and managing a literature-based reading program involves the same basic variables involved in any program. It requires the commitment to make literature a frequent part of pupils' classroom experiences, access to many trade books at various levels, and flexibility in grouping pupils on something other than a basal reading placement. It involves using every opportunity possible to use trade books for helping pupils become readers and writers.

In the final analysis, there is no such thing as an ideal organizational pattern. No amount of grouping will eliminate the individual differences that children carry into the classroom. No amount of high-tech equipment will generate in pupils a love of reading or real competency in writing. Although time, space, materials, and pupils influence the type of classroom program needed to teach reading, the teacher remains the mightiest force of all. Notwithstanding the advantages and disadvantages of one organizational pattern over another, reading achievement is attained by engaging in activities that go on in the classroom.

Teachers have different personalities that give rise to different teaching styles. Teachers' styles will determine in large measure their ability to work in one organizational system or another. Some teachers have a great deal of organizational ability in systematically directing the affairs of the classroom, while others are less highly organized. Some teachers are more comfortable working in a freewheeling classroom atmosphere; others are more comfortable in a structured environment. A set of materials that appeals to one teacher might have little or no appeal to another. Human diversity is, paradoxically, one of the beautiful strengths and, at the same time, one of the greatest enigmas of the educational process.

Establishing and maintaining a literature-based classroom program involves more than merely using occasional, isolated activities based on children's books. It involves a commitment to using literature as the primary basis of pupils' literacy development and a structured set of experiences that will put this commitment to work in the classroom. To this end, Johnson and Louis (1987) offer progressive, step-by-step advice to teachers who follow the traditional pattern of teaching reading with the basal, with an unrelated writing program, and with only the occasional use of literature:

1. Maintain your basal and writing programs. Develop literature-based routines for your literature program.
2. Use literature-based routines with the contents of the basal reader. Eliminate less useful workbook activities. Develop some writing activities around the literature program.
3. Increase the number of literature-based routines applied to the basal reader. Reserve workbook activities for remedial work. Increase the number of writing activities that focus on good books.
4. Eliminate the use of basal readers for your more competent children. Eliminate writing exercises and focus all writing on functional classroom activities, content areas, and literature.
5. Eliminate the use of the basal for less competent children. Fuse reading, writing, speaking, and listening activities into an information- and literature-centered literacy program.
6. Maintain your literature-based literacy program. Experience less stress, more joy, greater progress, and more satisfaction for your children. Receive approval from administration and parents. Give workshops to colleagues. Rest on your laurels! (Johnson and Louis, 1987; p. 150)[1]

The last few sentences tend to be facetious, but the steps in the process are basically sound!

Discussion Questions and Activities

1. Review Chapter 1, paying special attention to 1.4 *Describing A Literature-Based Reading Program*. List some of the ramifications of this description for organizing and managing a classroom reading program in terms of time, space, materials, and pupils.
2. Design a word board similar to that suggested in 3.2. Use children's books as the source of words that you select. What other displays related to reading, writing, and literature would you plan for your classroom?

---

[1]From T. D. Johnson and D. R. Lewis, *Literacy through Literature.* Copyright © 1987 Heinemann. Reprinted by permission of Thomas Nelson Australia.

3. How would you balance a basal program with a rich diet of literature? Make a specific plan and compare your plan to those designed by classmates.
4. From your educational resources center or curriculum library, select a piece of computer software related to children's literature or an audiovisual presentation (record, tape, video, filmstrip) of a children's story. What is the focus of the program? How is it supposed to be used in promoting pupils' interest or competency in reading? What is your opinion of the material?
5. When you were in elementary school what reading group were you in? How did you feel about being in that group? How did it affect your reading? How will these experiences influence your grouping practices as a teacher?

School-Based Assignments

1. Carefully observe the reading program in your classroom in terms of the four variables identified in this chapter: time, space, materials, and pupils. How much time is scheduled for reading each day? How is this time spent? How is the classroom arranged? What types of reading materials are available? What types are used most often? How are pupils grouped for instruction? What changes would you make if you were in charge of the classroom?
2. As you observe pupils in your classroom, note how they spend their time during reading instruction. How much time is spent in whole-group work? In small groups? Working independently? Focus your attention on one pupil and note that pupil's time on task. How do you think instructional time could be used more effectively?
3. It has been said that a teacher's classroom is like an artist's studio. Describe the "teaching studio" in which you work. Which parts of the environment indicate the emphasis on literacy instruction? What are the signs that reading is alive and well in the classroom?
4. Select a children's book, and plan a reading activity using this book with a heterogeneous group of pupils. Describe the results of your efforts.
5. What record-keeping system does the teacher/school use to keep track of pupil progress, the books they have read and heard read, and other evidence of literacy development? Briefly describe the system and the changes that you would make to improve the system.

Children's Trade Books Cited in This Chapter

Aardema, Verna. *Why Mosquitoes Buzz in People's Ears: A West African Folk Tale*. New York: Dial, 1975.

Blume, Judy. *Are You There God? It's Me, Margaret*. New York: Dell, 1972.

———. *Freckle Juice*. New York: Dell, 1978.

Calhoon, Mary. *Cross Country Cat*. New York: Morrow, 1979.

Cleary, Beverly. *Socks*. New York: Morrow, 1979.

Cooney, Barbara. *Miss Rumphius*. New York: Penguin, 1985.

Estep, Don. *Cats and Kittens*. New York: Checkerboard Press, 1990.

George, Jean Craighead. *Julie of the Wolves*. New York: Harper and Row, 1972.

———. *My Side of the Mountain*. New York: Dutton, 1959.

Holman, Felice. *Slake's Limbo*. New York: Macmillan, 1974.

Lawson, Robert. *Rabbit Hill.* New York: Viking, 1944.

McPhail, David. *Great Cat.* New York: Dutton, 1982.

Potter, Beatrix. *The Tale of the Flopsy Bunnies.* New York: Dover, 1903.

Seymour, Simon. *Big Cats.* New York: Harper Collins, 1991.

Sperry, Armstrong. *Call It Courage.* New York: Macmillan, 1940.

Voigt, Cynthia. *Homecoming.* New York: Macmillan, 1981.

References

Allington, R. L. (1983). The Reading Instruction Provided Readers of Differing Ability. *Elementary School Journal* 83:548–559.

Anderson, R. C., Hiebert, E. H., Scott, J. A., and Wilkinson, A. G. (1985). *Becoming A Nation of Readers.* Washington: National Institute of Education.

Berghoff, B., and Egawa, K. (1991). No More ''Rocks'': Grouping To Give Students Control of Their Learning. *The Reading Teacher* 44: 536–541.

Blanchard, J. S., and Rottenberg, C. J. (1991). Hypertext and Hypermedia: Discovering and Creating Meaningful Learning Environments. *The Reading Teacher* 43:656–661.

De Groff, L. (1990). Is There a Place for Computers in Whole Language Classrooms? *The Reading Teacher* 43:568–572.

Eeds, M., and Peterson, R. (1991). Teacher As Curator: Learning to Talk about Literature. *The Reading Teacher* 45:118–126.

Flood, J., Lapp, D., Flood, S., and Nagel, G. (1992). Am I Allowed to Group? Using Flexible Patterns for Effective Instruction. *The Reading Teacher* 45:608–615.

Flynn, L. L. (1989). Developing Critical Reading Skills through Cooperative Problem Solving. *The Reading Teacher* 43:664–668.

Hiebert, E. H., and Colt, J. (1989). Patterns of Literature-Based Reading Instruction. *The Reading Teacher* 43:14–20.

Hittleman, D. (1988). *Developmental Reading, K-8: Teaching from a Whole-Language Perspective.* Columbus: Merrill Publishing.

Johnson, T. D., and Louis, D. R. (1987). *Literacy through Literature.* Portsmouth, NH: Heinemann.

Keegan, S., and Sharke, K. (1991). Literature Study Groups: An Alternative to Ability Grouping. *The Reading Teacher* 44:542–547.

Kimmel, M. M., and Segal, E. (1983). *For Reading Out Loud! A Guide to Sharing Books with Children.* New York: Delacourte Press.

Korbin, B. (1988). *Eye Openers: Choosing Books for Kids.* New York: Viking.

Madden, L. (1988). Improve Reading Attitude of Poor Readers Through Cooperative Reading Teams. *The Reading Teacher* 42:194–199.

Morrow, L. M., and Rand, M. K. (1991). Promoting Literacy during Play by Designing Early Childhood Classroom Environments. *The Reading Teacher* 44:396–402.

Otto, W., Wolf, A., and Eldridge, R. G. (1984). Managing Instruction. In P. D. Pearson et al. (eds.), *Handbook of Reading Research.* New York: Longmans.

Paratore, J. R., Fountas, I. C., Jenkins, C. A., Mathers, M. E., Oulette, J. M., and Sheehan, N. M. (1991). *Grouping Students for Literacy Learning: What Works.* Boston: Massachusetts Reading Association.

Peterson, R., and Eeds, M. (1990). *Grand Conversations: Literature Groups in Action.* New York: Scholastic.

Rhodes, L. K., and Dudley-Marling, C. (1988). *Readers and Writers with a Difference: A Holistic Approach to Teaching Learning Disabled and Remedial Students.* Portsmouth, NH: Heinemann.

Rickelman, R. J., and Henk, W. A. (1990). Children's Literature and Audio/Visual Technologies. *The Reading Teacher* 43:182–184.

Roblyer, M. D. (1988). The Effectiveness of Microcomputers in Education: A Review of Research from 1980–1987. *T.H.E. Journal,* 85–89.

Rosenshine, B., and Stevens, R. (1984). Classroom Instruction in Reading. In P. D. Pearson et al. (eds.), *Handbook of Reading Research.* New York: Longmans.

Routman, R. (1988). *Transitions from Literature to Literacy.* Portsmouth, NH: Heinemann.

Schumaker, M. P., and Schumaker, R. L. (1989). 3000 Paper Cranes: Children's Literature for the Remedial Reader. *The Reading Teacher* 42: 544–559.

Shannon, P. (1983). The Use of Commercial Reading Materials in American Elementary Schools. *Reading Research Quarterly* 19:68–85.

Slavin, R. E. (1991). Synthesis of Research on Cooperative Learning. *Educational Leadership* 47:71–82.

Staab, C. (1991). Classroom Organization: Thematic Centers Revisited. *Language Arts* 68:108–114.

Stauffer, R. (1969). *Teaching Reading As A Thinking Process.* New York: Harper and Row.

Stevens, R. J., Madden, N. A., Slavin, R. E., and Farnish, A. M. (1987). Cooperative Integrated Reading and Composition: Two Field Experiments. *Reading Research Quarterly* 22:433–445.

Top, B. L., and Osguthorpe, R. T. (1987). Reverse Role Tutoring: The Effects of Handicapped Students Tutoring Regular Class Students. *The Elementary School Journal* 87:413–423.

Trelease, J. (1989). *The Read-Aloud Handbook.* New York: Penguin Books.

Unsworth, L. (1984). Meeting Individual Needs Through Flexible Whole-Class Grouping of Pupils. *The Reading Teacher* 38:298–304.

Uttero, D. A. (1988). Activating Comprehension through Cooperative Learning. *The Reading Teacher* 42:390–395.

Weaver, C. (1988). *Reading: Process and Practice.* Portsmouth, NH: Heinemann.

Whisler, N. and Williams, J. (1990). *Literature and Cooperative Learning: Pathway to Literacy.* Sacramento, CA: Literature Co-op.

Wolf, A. (1977). Reading Instruction: Time Will Tell. *Learning* 5:76–81.

Wuthrick, J. A. (1990). Blue Jays Win! Crows Go Down in Defeat! *Phi Delta Kappan* 71:553–556.

Zarrillo, J. (1989). Teachers' Interpretations of Literature-Based Reading. *The Reading Teacher* 43:22–28.

Chapter 4

Early Literacy

Chapter 4 Outline

    I. Introduction
   II. Childhood Development and Early Literacy
      A. Physical and Mental Development
      B. Schemata
      C. Language Acquisition
      D. Early Experiences with Print
  III. Reading Readiness and Emergent Literacy
  IV. Early Childhood Programs
      A. Nursery School
         1. Language Development
         2. Literature
            a. Concept Books
            b. Alphabet Books
            c. Counting Books
            d. Wordless Books
         3. Writing
      B. Kindergarten
         1. Metalinguistic Awareness
         2. Language Development
         3. Literature in Kindergarten
            a. Wordless Books
            b. Big Books
         4. Writing
         5. Perceptual and Alphabet Training
            a. Visual Perception
            b. Auditory Perception
            c. Alphabet Awareness
      C. Beginning Reading and Writing
         Instruction
   V. Role of the Parents in Early Literacy
      A. Parents in the Preschool Years
      B. Role of Parents When Children Come to
         School
  VI. Summary and Conclusions
Discussion Questions and Activities
School-Based Assignments
Children's Trade Books Cited in This Chapter
References

Features

4.1   Child's Schema of a Birthday Party
4.2   The First Three Years
4.3   Emergent Literacy and Reading Readiness
4.4   A Selected Sample of Concept Books
4.5   A Sampler of Alphabet Books
4.6   Using Literature in Kindergarten
4.7   A Cross-Grade Library Assignment
4.8   Developing a Reading Lesson with a Wordless Book
4.9   Authors Who Write Stories without Words
4.10 Steps in a Shared Reading Lesson with a Big Book
4.11 Three Reading–Writing Activities for the Emergent Literacy Classroom
4.12 First Day in First Grade
4.13 NAEYC Position Statement on Developmentally Appropriate Practice
4.14 Ten Ways Parents Can Help Children Become Better Readers
4.15 Parents Are Children's First Teachers
4.16 What Parents Can Do to Promote Literacy for Preschoolers
4.17 A Hierarchy of Home–School Relationships
4.18 A Note to Parents
4.19 Useful References for Parents about Reading in the Home

Key Concepts in This Chapter

T he ability to read and write does not happen all at once. Literacy is a process that develops and emerges over time during a child's early years. Much of what happens as part of the early literacy process will continue to influence the child as a learner.

There is a difference between the concept of emergent literacy and the conventional notion of reading readiness. The emergent literacy perspective views learning to read and write as a gradual developmental process involving all forms of language learning; readiness tends to emphasize preparedness through the teaching of specific skills.

Literature-based programs to encourage and enhance children's early literacy are provided in nursery school, kindergarten, and first grade. Although obviously different in many respects, these programs share certain qualities: a heavy emphasis on language learning and children's literature, and the integration of instruction in reading and writing.

The role of parents is crucial to the child's emerging literacy. Parents can provide a variety of literacy-related experiences in the home before, during, and following their children's entrance into an early childhood instructional program.

THE PROCESS of learning to read and write begins long before a child enters a classroom for the first time. In some ways, it begins the moment the child is born. The full range of experiences that children encounter during their early years will have a significant impact on their later development as literate individuals. Some of these experiences will influence children's literacy development more than others, but all of a child's experiences have potential for influencing that child as a learner.

Childhood Development and Early Literacy

For most children, literacy begins to emerge during the early years of life. The expressions "the early years" or "early childhood education" normally refer to the years from birth through age eight, from the early preschool years through the early years of school. Although some experts consider early childhood as ending when a child enters his or her first formal school experience, most early childhood educators are concerned with instruction through the primary grades of elementary school.

Early childhood is a time of dramatic growth and development. Children proceed through stages of physical and cognitive development that will continue to facilitate learning as they grow. Through their early experiences, children construct their first view of the world and build the background that will form the foundation of later learning. They acquire language; in fact, children learn more language in the preschool years than they will learn for the rest of their lives. Part of this language learning includes their initial encounters with print. Each area contributes to the child's later development in learning to read and write.

Physical and Mental Development

The early childhood years are important to the child's physical development. Milestones occur at different times for different children, but most learn to sit, crawl, and walk during the first year of life. By the age of two, children are running, climbing up and down stairs, and gaining more control of their large and small muscles. By age three, children have reached approximately half their adult height and have achieved the ability to run easily, ride a tricycle, and perform many physical functions independently. Their physical growth continues throughout the preschool years, into their school-aged years and beyond.

As young children's bodies develop, so do their minds (although their mental development cannot be observed as easily as their physical development). Working from an initial concrete base of experiences, children learn to confront increasingly complex intellectual tasks.

Knowledge derives from information that children glean from their immediate environments through their senses. They construct their initial knowledge of reality from sensing and manipulating objects that they encounter. With repeated and expanding contact with their immediate worlds, children begin to discriminate and perceive important features of objects and relationships from the vast flow of sensory information, and thus they form concepts. To the child, a "doggie" is everything from a favorite stuffed animal to the deer they see on a trip to a petting zoo. But children learn to differentiate between stuffed toys and real animals when they try to pull the hair on a neighbor's puppy.

Children's attention spans increase. As infants, attention is controlled by immediate aspects of a stimulus, and attention can be sustained for only short periods of time. As they grow, young children's attention spans expand, and they attend to learning-related tasks for longer periods of time and at finer levels of detail. Memory capabilities improve as well, in part because of neurological changes that occur in the early years and in part because children develop methods or strategies that help them remember things.

As they grow, children's thinking separates itself from the immediate environment. Children become capable of symbolic thought and abstract reasoning. Their perception, attention, and memory are mobilized in problem solving. They begin to develop organized plans or systematic strategies to solve problems. As they interact with others and with their environment, they begin to take an active role in selecting, organizing, and interpreting information that will help them deal with the problems they encounter. They are developing their schemata.

Schemata

Children organize the information they derive into schemata, and the schemata they develop during the preschool years will form the foundation for much of their later learning. A schema (singular form of schemata) represents an abstract concept of how humans organize and store information. A schema is a mental structure. It is an organized, generalized plan or conceptual system for arranging knowledge inside our heads. The schemata that we build are modified and expanded by subsequent experiences.

For many years, theoreticians viewed the young child's mind as a *tabula rasa,* a blank slate not yet affected by knowledge or impressions gained from experience. As children grew, knowledge that they acquired was thought to be ''written on the blank slate of their minds.'' Rather than viewing the mind as a clean slate, cognitive psychologists now see the young child's mind as a ''set of empty shelves or slots,'' which are filled, modified, or expanded by learning. These ''slots'' constitute the schemata by which the child organizes information. These are modified and expanded, and verbal labels are attached, as the child grows and learns.

How does schema theory relate to young children's learning to read and write? Here are two examples:

1. As a result of attending birthday parties, the preschooler builds a knowledge base that might be called a ''birthday party schema.'' (See 4.1) Various parts of this schema include other children, games, candy and cake, singing ''Happy Birthday,'' blowing out candles, games and prizes, presents for the birthday boy or girl, not forgetting to say ''Thank you'' when leaving, and the like. When the child subsequently reads a simple story about birthday parties, his or her comprehension of the story will be affected by the schema that he or she has. The child will be able to understand, anticipate, confirm, and relate to the story according to the information he or she already has. As the child grows and acquires more information, this birthday party schema may expand to include dancing, drinks, gag gifts, and other elements that are sometimes part of adult birthday parties, and the schema will likely be incorporated into a more generalized party schema, the parts of which will

Child's Schema of a Birthday Party

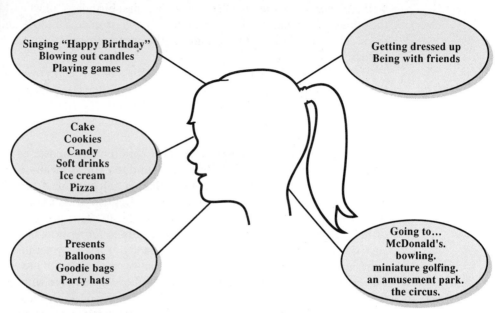

Singing "Happy Birthday"
Blowing out candles
Playing games

Getting dressed up
Being with friends

Cake
Cookies
Candy
Soft drinks
Ice cream
Pizza

Presents
Balloons
Goodie bags
Party hats

Going to...
McDonald's.
bowling.
miniature golfing.
an amusement park.
the circus.

include going-away parties, office parties, wedding parties, and the like. The more schemata the child brings to early encounters with stories, the better he or she will likely be able to understand what is read.

2. In the preschool years, children encounter stories through television and through books. These stories become part of the schemata that they will use when they learn to read. If a preschooler's experience includes classic children's fairy tales such as *Hansel and Gretel, Little Red Riding Hood,* and *The Three Pigs,* the child's comprehension and appreciation will be more complete because these stories will already be part of the child's "fairy tale schema" when the child hears these stories in an early childhood educational setting. When children achieve a measure of independence in literacy, they will likely be able to read these on their own. Previous knowledge will be activated by seeing the words in print.

The schemata built as a result of children's preschool experiences can color their view of the world. Children who have the advantage of many different experiences during the preschool years, who have opportunities for verbal interaction with others, and who experience print regularly in growing up will have a different set of schemata and a different view of reading when they start to learn to read.

Language Acquisition

Among the major areas of development in the process of early literacy is language development. As the babbling and cooing of early infancy turn into the production of vocal sound combinations that elicit a response from others, language acquisition is well under way. By the time they reach their first birthdays, most children have spoken their first words and have shown definite signs of understanding language spoken to them. They have begun to use language to meet some of their basic communication needs.

By the age of eighteen months, children's new-found power of locomotion has brought them into contact with the world around them, and they develop a repertoire of words and expressions to deal with this world. By age three, vocabulary has expanded dramatically and most of what the child has to say is intelligible, even (at times) to strangers.

More remarkable, by age three, most children have mastered syntax, the pattern or structure of word order that allows the child to express meaning in phrases, clauses, and sentences. Although they cannot define an adjective or diagram a sentence, they can intuitively apply the intricate system of English grammar to arrange words in a variety of ways to meet their communication needs. The one- or two-word utterances of holophrastic speech (the use of single words to represent whole classes of objects, such as referring to all adult males as ''daddy'') have grown through the key-word combinations of telegraphic speech (''Mommy go bye-bye.'') to a form of language that comes close to adult sentences. They still overgeneralize with expressions such as ''Three mans comed here'' or ''I cutted my finger and it bleeded,'' but they can manipulate language to meet a full range of communication purposes.

In the next two years of life, children's language is well established. The child is able to communicate within the family and other social groups and enters school with a supply of words extending into the thousands and a basic competency in language.

How this language acquisition occurs is a source of speculation and debate among the experts. There are different theories about how children acquire language. Behaviorists explain language acquisition in terms of stimulus–response. Children hear sound and respond by imitation. Meaningful sounds are reinforced; parents show delight with the sound combinations of *ma-ma* and *da-da,* so the child learns to repeat these sounds. Although this classical conditioning explains some of what takes place, it cannot account for children's inventing the many language forms they use.

The nativist theory suggests that children are born with an innate capacity to produce language. Children have an internalized set of rules that allow them to generate, refine, and expand their language performance. This inborn ability is triggered by what the child hears in his or her particular language environment.

Cognitive psychologists link language development with mental development. Although theoreticians in this field do not always agree—some say that language development enables thought to take place and others hold that language develops as a means of allowing humans to express their thoughts—all link language development to the thinking process.

No theory has been formulated to explain fully what goes on inside young children's heads as they develop the wondrous ability to communicate through language.

And language learning never stops; we learn new words all the time and we gain skill in learning the language we speak and write. But humans never learn as much language as they did when they were young children.

Early Experiences with Print

Throughout their early years, children are surrounded with environmental print. Their first encounters with print help them develop the concept of reading and writing. They see print in advertisements flashed on television and splashed on billboards. They see it on cereal boxes and milk cartons in the kitchen. They come to associate print with words that have pleasant association for them—for example, McDonald's. If they are lucky, they see print in the books that their parents buy for them and experience it translated into speech as parents and others read to them. Through these many encounters with print in their environment, children may acquire concepts of letters, words, and sentences; they come to understand what books are and what they contain; they gain the awareness that print conveys meaning.

Early encounters with print not only develop young children's knowledge about reading and writing, but these encounters also shape children's attitudes about literacy. When books have been a satisfying part of preschool experiences, children are on the way to interest and success in learning to read. If reading and writing have been absent, or if books have been the cause of criticism or unpleasantness, the child is less positively disposed about the prospects of learning to read and write.

Oral language is an essential part of the physical, mental, emotional, and social development that children experience in the preschool years. So, in many instances, is print. The nature of children's interaction with print will influence their emerging literacy.

Reading Readiness and Emergent Literacy

The expression traditionally used to refer to reading and writing experiences in the preschool years was *reading readiness*. Readiness has been defined as "a state of general maturity, based on aptitudes and learned knowledge and skills, that allows a child to learn to read under given instructional conditions" (Harris and Sipay, 1985; p. 33). Readiness was seen as a state of preparedness, a predisposition for reading, the time leading up to the "teachable moment" for reading. Readiness instruction was the type of instruction that children received before the formal teaching of reading, instruction designed to "help him/her get ready to profit from a program of instruction."

Certain factors were seen to contribute to making a child ready to learn to read:

physical factors, such as adequate vision, hearing, and general health;

social factors, such as the ability to relate to others in a group setting and to participate in learning activities;

emotional factors, such as the ability to work independently and to tolerate a reasonable amount of challenge in a learning task;

psychological factors, including attention span, general intelligence and the ability to perform certain cognitive operations;

4.2

■ **FOR YOUR INFORMATION** ▮

The First Three Years

AS CHILDREN grow physically, they also develop . . .

. . . print awareness through contact with written language in the world around them.

. . . language ability, from babbling and cooing to language that meets their daily communication needs.

. . . concepts and ideas gleaned from their immediate environments.

At no stage of the child's life will growth be as dramatic as it is in the first three years.

perceptual factors, like the ability to make visual discrimination in shapes and auditory discrimination in sounds;

language factors, such as vocabulary size and the ability to manipulate verbal concepts;

alphabet knowledge, including the ability to say the alphabet and to recognize the names and sounds of at least some letters.

Reading readiness tests were constructed to assess children's state of readiness for reading according to these factors. Checklists with items related to cognition, language, interest in reading, and knowledge of the alphabet were designed to determine a child's state of readiness. Preschool screening programs were carried out to determine children's potential placement in kindergarten and to ascertain specific readiness areas in which children would need help. Reading readiness programs in preschools and kindergartens were designed and carried out with activities to develop those factors that would "help the child get ready to learn to read when the time came."

The term (and concept) *reading readiness* implies that there is a precise point at which a child reads. Reading is seen as an occurrence, a happening. Yet reading hardly happens all at once. Literacy is a process that develops over time. It develops gradually. It emerges. The term *emergent literacy* is used to reflect the shift in orientation in viewing reading and writing development in young children (Teale and Sulzby, 1987).

Stemming from research related to the psycho-sociolinguistic theory of reading and rooted in a whole language philosophy in which the acquisition of literacy is analogous to the acquisition of speaking, emergent literacy sees the preschool stage of a child's life not as a process of "getting ready" to read and write. Rather, the young child's preschool experiences with print become part of the actual "learning-to-read-and-write" process itself. When a young child independently recognizes his own name in print, he is reading. When a young child can repeat the lines of a favorite story that she has memorized from repeatedly hearing the story read to her, she is reading. These are authentic literacy experiences for the very young child.

Young children's attempts to read and write are seen as important, viable, age-appropriate efforts at dealing with print. These attempts are not judged to the extent that they conform to the standards of adult correctness. Children reciting stories that they have heard read is not viewed merely as being "cute"; these occasions are seen as authentic and important efforts by the child to recreate meaning from written language.

The concept of readiness tends to deal with learning to read as a two-step operation involving "prereading" and "reading" as separate categories; emergent literacy tends to approach the idea of learning to read (and write) as a continuous process.

In conventional readiness programs, reading and writing are generally taught separately, the former preceding the latter. In emergent literacy, reading and writing are closely related and taught as connected operations. Young children write (it may be a scribble unintelligible to adults at the very early stages) and then they read what they have written (or they ask someone else to "tell me what this says.") They learn about reading and writing together.

4.3
FOR YOUR INFORMATION
Emergent Literacy and Reading Readiness

V ACCA, VACCA, and Gove (1991) provide the following summary comparison between emergent literacy and reading readiness.

TABLE 4.1 COMPARISON BETWEEN EMERGENT LITERACY AND READING READINESS

	Emergent Literacy	Reading Readiness
Theoretical Perspective	Children are in the process of becoming literate from birth and are capable of learning what it means to be a user of written language before entering school.	Children must master a set of basic skills before they can learn to read. Learning to read is an outcome of school-based instruction.
Acquisition of Literacy Skills and Strategies	Children learn to use written language and develop as readers and writers through active engagement with their world. Literacy develops in real-life settings in purposeful ways.	Children learn to read by mastering skills arranged and sequenced in a hierarchy according to their level of difficulty.
Relationship of Reading to Writing	Children progress as readers and writers. Reading and writing (as well as speaking and listening) are interrelated and develop concurrently.	Children learn to read first. The skills of reading must be developed before introducing written composition.
Functional-Formal Learning	Children learn informally through interactions with and modeling from literate significant others and explorations with written language.	Children learn through formal teaching and monitoring (i.e., periodic assessment) of skills.
Individual Development	Children learn to be literate in different ways and at different rates of development.	Children progress as readers by moving through a "scope and sequence" of skills.

From *Reading and Learning to Read,* 2e by Joanne L. Vacca et al. Copyright © 1991 by Joanne L. Vacca, Richard T. Vacca, and Mary K. Gove. Reprinted by permission of HarperCollins Publishers, Glenview, IL.

Freeman and Hatch (1989) summarize the differences between the traditional concept of reading readiness and the more contemporary perspective of emergent literacy in providing for children's early learning experiences.

> Reading readiness assumes the existence of a set of skills that are necessary prerequisites to formal reading instruction. Reading is viewed as a process distinct from writing. Writing should not be "taught" until children can read and spell. These reading skills, which are charted sequentially, can be learned through direct instruction. . . .
>
> An emergent literacy perspective recognizes that children begin literacy development long before school entry as they interact in their home and community. Young children develop as readers/writers; the two processes should not be taught

in isolation from each other. Instead of following a preset adult-imposed sequence of skills, children are in the process of becoming literate from a very young age and therefore are not ''getting ready to do it.'' They are actively engaged as constructors of their written language system. (p. 22)[1]

McGee and Richgels (1990) identify five current assumptions about children's literacy that underlie an emergent literacy perspective: ''(1) even young children are knowledgeable of written language; (2) young children's reading and writing are as important as adults' reading and writing; (3) reading and writing are interrelated and are also related to talking, drawing, and playing; (4) children acquire literacy knowledge by participating in meaningful activities; (5) children acquire literacy knowledge as they interact with others'' (pp. 31–32). Much of what happens in teaching reading and writing in today's early childhood settings is based on these contemporary assumptions about literacy and how young children acquire it.

Early Childhood Programs

Between the ages of two and eight, children often participate in one or more programs designed to promote their growth and development. They may attend a day-care center, a play group or other home-care program, a nursery school, a Head Start program, or a community program designed to provide a range of learning experiences and to lay a firm foundation for success in school. These early childhood education programs, which formerly were available to only a fortunate few children, have become accessible to an increasingly large number of preschoolers.

Early childhood education also includes kindergarten, although kindergarten programs are now normally included as part of children's formal compulsory education. And since reading and writing skills are still generally acquired during the first couple of years of a child's school life, early childhood education extends into the primary grades as well.

The focus of programs offered to promote and encourage emergent literacy in these various types of educational programs will differ from one level to the next. In preschool programs like day care and nursery school, the typical emphasis will be global and informal. In kindergarten, the exploration of literature and the focus on literacy development usually become more immediate and specific. By first grade, formal structured programs for teaching reading and writing begin.

Nevertheless, these programs often promote literacy development in much the same way. The same materials—wordless books or magnetized plastic letters, for example—are no less applicable for use in nursery school as they are in first grade. The nursery school teacher may engage in the same literacy-related activities as the first grade teacher—sharing stories such as Esphyr Slobodkina's *Caps for Sale,* for example. While the input for these types of activities may be similar, the output varies considerably from one level to the next. The three-year-old in nursery school can hardly be expected to respond in the same way as the six-year-old in first grade. The preschooler

---

[1]From E. B. Freeman and J. A. Hatch (1989) ''Emergent Literacy: Reconceptualizing Kindergarten Practice'' in *Childhood Education,* 66, 21–24. Reprinted with permission of Association for Childhood Education International, Wheaton, MD.

might be expected to react to *Caps for Sale* by retelling or acting out the story. The first grader, on the other hand, might be able to recognize independently some of the more familiar words, to recall the story events in sequence, to think of alternative elements in the plot (how else the peddler may have gotten his caps back, for example) to be able to explain the source of humor in the story, and/or to read the story independently.

Although preschool, kindergarten, and first grade programs are treated in different sections of this chapter, all three have a lot in common. They are developmental settings which can be designed to address the various aspects of emergent literacy of the children who attend these programs. A rich environment that stimulates language development is common to all three. All are designed to develop children's awareness of, and competency in, reading and writing. Each uses children's literature as the basis for promoting literacy development.

Nursery School

In the emergent literacy stage, nursery school provides many children with their first organized, large-group learning experience. Nursery schools focus on the development of the physical, emotional, intellectual, and aesthetic aspects of the whole child, but particular emphasis is on social development. Attention is on helping the child get along independently in the milieu of a group experience.

Language development is given a lion's share of attention in sound nursery-school programs, in part because language is an important vehicle for social interaction, and in part because development is so essential to the learning of young children. "Studies of early readers strongly support the connection between language development and literacy development" (Thomas, 1985; p. 469). The nursery school program is full of language experiences that promote fluency in speaking, accuracy in listening, and overall competency in using oral language as a learning tool.

Language experiences permeate the entire nursery school program. The constant verbal bombardment of the typically busy nursery school environment provides countless opportunities for children to develop and extend language power. Observation of nature in science is accompanied by a focus on words that can be used to describe the rocks, plants, and small animals that constitute the focus of science study. Children's language is recorded as they learn about their relationship to the community in social studies. Simple stories and poems are related to basic number learning ("One, two, buckle my shoe . . . ''). Play is obviously an important part of nursery school, but whether the play is aimed at large muscle development on the playground or at socialization in the housekeeping corner, language is central to the activity.

Nursery school programs that promote emergent literacy are saturated with literature. A library or reading corner—a ''book nook''—is part of the learning environment. Children have many opportunities to handle books, not only to enjoy the illustrations and other contents, but also to learn how to hold a book, open it, turn its pages, and take care of it. Children's book experiences usually begin with shared stories such as Margaret Wise Brown's *Goodnight, Moon* and Wanda Gag's *Millions of Cats,* which the teacher might read a number of times during the day. Stories are read in an informal, secure atmosphere, often using the Big Book versions of the stories. The atmosphere for these shared stories is an extension of the bedtime story, in which children usually want to hear favorite stories read again and again. Teachers also share books one-to-one and in small group settings.

Early in their school years, children learn to enjoy sharing literature on the way to independence in reading.

As a result of shared stories, something interesting often happens in nursery school programs. Children pick up favorite books and begin to read these books on their own. This reading does not involve verbatim repetition of the text or rote word-by-word memorization, but it does capture and recreate story meaning and often story structure. "Quite early this reading-like play becomes story-complete, page-matched, and picture-stimulated. The story tends to be reexperienced as complete semantic units transcending sentence limits" (Holdaway, 1982; p. 295). This process is particularly important to the child's emergent literacy.

In addition to a rich variety of picture storybooks, three types of books especially appropriate to nursery schools (as well as kindergarten and first grade classrooms) are concept books, alphabet books, and wordless books.

Concept books are a potential source of enjoyment and learning. "A concept book is one that describes various dimensions of an object, a class of objects, or an abstract idea" (Huck, Hepman, and Hickman, 1987; p. 172). At this age, children develop concepts primarily as a result of direct experiences. Concept books support these experiences with illustrations and simple text. There are concept books about color, size, shape, animals, opposites, travel and transportation, tools, and other topics of interest and importance to young children (see 4.4). One concept book that is especially appropriate for this level is Harlow Rockwell's *My Nursery School* in which the author describes activities in a nursery school and the good feeling that comes with being picked up at the end of the morning.

Concept books can be used to stimulate oral language, to sharpen perception, to enhance children's growing understanding of the world around them, and to provide pleasurable experiences. They allow children to see relationships between different objects and to grasp dimensions of abstract ideas.

Books that involve participation are also popular with children of nursery school age. One such book that has gained enormous popularity is Eric Carle's *The Very*

A Selected Sample of Concept Books

HERE IS a limited sample of concept books that can be enjoyed by young children and used for informational purposes in the preschool years:

Byron Barton, *Airport,* a concept book showing interesting details of a place that children find interesting.

Donald Crews, *Freight Train,* a fascinating description of a journey that illustrates color, movement, and opposites, among other concepts.

Tana Hoban, *Is It Red? Is It Yellow?,* in which colors are brightly illustrated with photographs of common objects; Ms. Hoban has written a number of other concept books popular with nursery school children.

Anne Rockwell, *First Comes Spring,* which illustrates the concept of the seasons of the year.

Harlow Rockwell, *My Kitchen,* with pictures of everyday objects that children can find in their environment.

John Reiss, *Shapes,* with colored pictures of shapes that can be found in common objects.

Peter Spier, *Fast-Slow, High-Low: A Book of Opposites,* illustrating the concept of opposites in an interesting, often sophisticated, way.

These titles represent only a small sampling of the range of topics of concept books that can be used for pleasure and for learning experiences in nursery schools.

Hungry Caterpillar, the story of a voracious caterpillar who eats holes in the book's pages as he devours the food pictured. What makes this book so much fun for children—apart from the outrageous diet that the caterpillar enjoys—is that children can poke their fingers through the die-cut holes in the pages. Beyond sheer enjoyment, the books can be the basis for focusing on many important concepts: days of the week, colors, fruits, life cycle of a caterpillar to butterfly, predication, and the like. Another long-time favorite in this category is Dorothy Hunhardt's *Pat the Bunny* which has tactile surfaces (a flannel bunny, sandpaper for Daddy's unshaven face, etc.) that extend reading beyond sight and sound.

Alphabet books have potential for a number of uses in the nursery school. They help focus children's attention on letters and awaken their awareness of the sounds the letters represent. Depending on the content of the pictures, ABC books help children learn to identify objects, animals, and concepts. With limited text on the page and plenty of picture clues to help with word identification, alphabet books often provide young children with their first independent reading experience.

The plethora of alphabet books available ranges from those that are illustrated simply with single objects on a page to those that contain incredible levels of detail and abstraction in their illustrations. Some ABC books are designed for the simple purpose of identification and naming; others incorporate themes, simple narratives, puzzles, and other informational material. Still others are accompanied by records or tapes that encourage pupils to sing along. All provide fascinating vehicles for children and parents to enjoy together.

In addition to developing enjoyment and early alphabet awareness, ABC books can be effective vehicles for developing vocabulary and stimulating language use.

In *Counting Books,* which are related to ABC books, illustrations and numerals are integrated to develop various number concepts. Books such as Tana Hoban's *Count and See* and Nancy Tafuri's *Who's Counting* illustrate number–symbol relationships and help young children develop number awareness. In addition, counting books extend

4.5
FOR YOUR INFORMATION
A Sampler of Alphabet Books

HUNDREDS OF alphabet books are available for use with young learners. Here are a handful that are highly regarded and widely used, though some may be a bit sophisticated for use with very young children:

Mitsumasa Anno, *Anno's Alphabet,* an ingeniously illustrated book full of intriguing visual illusions.

Jane Bayer, *A, My Name Is Alice,* in which the words of the old, popular jump-rope rhyme are delightfully illustrated by Stephen Kellogg

Burt Kitchen, *Animal Alphabet,* a simple alphabet book with large block letters and striking animal pictures.

Anita Lobel, *Alison's Zinnia,* an entertaining walk through a garden of flowers A to Z.

Anita and Arnold Lobel, *On Market Street,* an account of a boy who lavishly "shops" his way through the alphabet.

Bill Martin, Jr., and John Archambault, *Chicha Chicha Boom Boom,* an alphabet book with a lively, jazzy rhythm and a delightful style that children love to read.

Margaret Musgrove, *Ashanti to Zulu: African Traditions,* the only alphabet book ever to win the Caldecott Medal, focusing on objects and ideas from African culture.

Helen Oxenbury, *Helen Oxenbury's ABC of Things,* with entertaining illustrations.

Brian Wildsmith, *Brian Wildsmith's ABC,* an old favorite with brilliant illustrations by a famous illustrator.

Cathi Hepworth, *Antics! An Alphabet Anthology,* a rather sophisticated but fascinating set of alphabet entries, all of which have *ant* somewhere in the word.

Literally hundreds of other alphabet books are available for use in schools and homes, including books that extend learning in curriculum areas in the upper grades, such as Ann Whitford Paul's *Eight Hands Round: A Patchwork Alphabet,* which presents a history lesson by illustrating various types of patchwork quilts, and Anne Doublet's *Under The Sea From A to Z,* a science alphabet book featuring aquatic creatures from anemone to zebrafish.

---

knowledge beyond number awareness. Virginia Grossman's *Ten Little Rabbits,* for example, depicts activities of ten tribes of Native Americans from all regions of the U.S., and Muriel Feelings' *Moja Means One: Swahili Counting Book* has number concepts related to African cultures. Counting books can be effective devices for literacy-related learning, along with basic mathematical knowledge, in early childhood settings.

Wordless books, which will be described more fully as part of kindergarten programs, are also good books to use in the nursery school classroom. Because these books have no words, very young children have no trouble reading them. Books without words can be used to stimulate language development and to let the children handle books. Children learn to respond to the pictures depicting the story line, dictate stories based on the books, and enjoy the experience that the books provide.

Writing in nursery school usually takes the form of dictation, as teachers transcribe what the children say about pictures they have drawn or copy stories that the children tell. Children's writing can also be part of their play activity as they compile grocery lists or recreate signs in their own writing style. Large sheets of paper (newspaper rolls work well) and writing implements (large markers, crayons, paints, and pencils) are available for children's independent attempts at writing.

Nursery school programs also provide opportunities for children to develop basic visual discrimination through puzzles and other manipulatives. Music provides enjoyment and also affords opportunities for developing children's auditory perceptual skills related to pitch and patterns of sounds. Children become aware of alphabet symbols through ABC books and through environmental print, as teachers call their attention to the print on juice containers and candy wrappers that children bring in their lunch boxes. All in all, the program contributes to many dimensions of the young child's familiarity with reading and writing.

Although nursery school programs are by nature informal, they offer many opportunities for children to develop awareness and competency that will help them when they enter a more formal program in kindergarten.

Kindergarten

For some children, kindergarten is the first experience with directed learning in a large group setting during their early childhood years. For others, it is another step in a series of early-childhood educational experiences. For all children, it is a time of more intensive, literacy-related activities. Children bring a "developing form of literacy" when they enter kindergarten for the first time, and the number of activities directly related to specific factors associated with reading and writing increases.

Like nursery schools, kindergarten programs typically stress the development of the whole child, with a special emphasis on socialization. For decades, in fact, conventional wisdom suggested that no reading instruction at all should take place in kindergarten. This belief was the result of a well-publicized and widely accepted 1931 research study which concluded that children needed a mental age of 6.5 in order to learn to read (Morphett and Washburne, 1931). The conclusion that it was safer not to try to teach children to read before the mental age of 6.5 "gained almost universal acceptance and probably influenced educational programs as much as any single research investigation" (Gentile, 1983; p. 171). This conclusion was quickly disproved (Gates, 1937), as other researchers showed that instructional factors were more crucial than mental age to success in beginning reading. Nevertheless, the myth persisted that any reading instruction attempted before this magic mental age of 6.5 was at best useless and at worst harmful.

The situation today has certainly changed. Well-balanced kindergarten programs continue to attend to the full range of children's needs, but programs now provide a rich variety of experiences to promote children's growing competency in reading and writing. Most children arrive in kindergarten with a knowledge of reading and writing. As part of their attempts to make sense of their world, most have learned the place of print in that world. Kindergarten literacy training is designed to build on this knowledge.

Metalinguistic Awareness   Among the essential concepts of emergent literacy is metalinguistic awareness. Metalinguistic awareness involves the ability to reflect upon, and talk about, language concepts. At the early learning stage, this involves knowledge of such concepts as what a book is, what it contains, how it can be used, what a word is, the function and content of signs that children see all around them, what a letter is, the correspondence that exists between speech and print, the correspondence between sentence units in speech and similar units in print, the relationship between a reader's eyes and a writer's pencil as they move from left to right in a line of print, as well as other concepts about the written word. This metalinguistic knowledge about language develops as part of emergent literacy.

For many children entering school, metalinguistic awareness has been well developed in the home by parents who regularly share and talk about books, who casually but deliberately call attention to letters and sounds (''There's the *M* in *milk,* the same as in *Mommy* and *McDonalds.''*), and who demonstrate the use of reading for functional purposes (''Let's look in the cookbook to see if we can find a recipe for muffins.'').

In more formal school settings, the same kind of informal teaching can occur. In addition, there are opportunities for teachers to promote metalinguistic awareness in group and individual settings. For example, as teachers share stories in Big Books or favorite nursery rhymes written on charts, they sweep their hands over the lines of print, maintaining the rhythm of the language but pointing to key words that they read. When children are familiar with these stories and poems, the children do the pointing, indicating a general awareness of the correspondence between the markings on the line and the words that they are saying. The ability to match words or phrases written on cards to the same words or phrases in the text is another indication of the young child's awareness of the speech-to-print relationship in language.

Each time a teacher transcribes children's language, either in group or individual settings, there are opportunities for developing metalinguistic awareness in children.

Language Development   Continual attention to children's language development through speaking and listening is a vital part of literacy instruction in kindergarten, as it is in nursery school. Large- and small-group, oral language activities—show and tell, flannel-board stories, creative dramatics, choral speaking, conversation and discussion, puppetry, and other activities—are directed at helping children increase their vocabularies, build sentence structures, expand their competencies in listening and speaking, and generally improve their ability to manipulate verbal concepts.

In the language-rich classroom, print is everywhere—in displays of children's books, on word lists related to areas of interest, on charts of stories that children have dictated, on signs and posters. There are directions about keeping the housekeeping corner clean and a note pad next to the phone for ''taking messages.'' The classroom features an ''I Can Read Board,'' on which is posted everything that children can read, from bubble-gum wrappers to restaurant placemats.

Label words are a feature of many early-childhood learning environments. These are words that are written on cards and attached to common objects in the classroom: *door, window, chair, desk,* and so on. Label words serve a number of functions. They clearly establish the object–symbol relationship for children, they often become basic sight words that children can instantly recognize independently, and they can be used for teaching letter recognition and other literacy-related learning. Some teachers place single label words in the context of sentences—*I sit in my **chair.** The sun shines through the **window.***—with the target word written in a color different from that of the words in the rest of the sentence. Children help make these label words on the first day of school as they learn their way around the classroom.

Literature in Kindergarten   Much of the direct literacy-related instruction in kindergarten is literature based. The classroom library is full of books appropriate for reading in kindergarten, books like Bill Martin's *Brown Bear, Brown Bear* and Pat Hutchins's *Rosie's Walk.* Children hear about the people who wrote these stories. Children read these stories to one another in pairs and small groups. They have the

Using Literature in Kindergarten

HERE IS an example of some of the ways in which trade books can be used for literacy and related learning activities in kindergarten:

The teacher selects Maurice Sendak's *Chicken Soup with Rice,* a whimsical and imaginative poem about a boy who drinks chicken soup all year long.

The teacher reads the poem aloud in a large group setting at the beginning of the school day, sharing Sendak's delightful illustrations. Because children love this poem, the teacher will probably be asked to repeat the reading several times and the children will join in the refrain after the second or third reading.

The teacher will read the poem several times during the same day (or on subsequent days) so that the children become thoroughly familiar with the text and learn to relate the spoken form of the poem to the written form.

Since a lively version of *Chicken Soup With Rice* has been recorded in song by Carole King as part of the musical *Really Rosie,* the children can follow along the lines of the poem as they listen to the words sung on tape. Even without the music, children can read the book on their own using the illustrations.

There is a strong element of rhyming in this poem. Building on rhyming elements like *rice/ice/nice, door/floor/more,* and *peep/deep/ cheap,* children develop additional rhymes or substitute alternative rhyming words in the poem.

Since each verse begins with a month of the year, the teacher might make a list of the names of each month to be used while the poem is read. Children certainly are not required to memorize these as sight words, but they do gain an awareness of the names of the months in order. Words associated with the various months can be a direct spin-off vocabulary activity.

Sendak has filled this poem with an array of sensory images, so pupils can talk about the tastes, smells, and touches portrayed in the poem.

As an extension of the poem itself, the teacher writes on a chart and reads with the pupils a recipe for chicken soup. The teacher may even bring in the ingredients and make a pot of chicken soup in the classroom. Now children become aware of the differences between fanciful language of the poem and the practical language of expository text.

Based on their repeated exposure to the poem, children write/dictate and illustrate their own imaginative stanzas for *Chicken Soup with Rice* or other poems that strike their fancy.

These and the hundreds of other ideas that might be suggested are all appropriate means of helping children make the jump from spoken to printed language by using text that they genuinely enjoy.

opportunity to hear good stories read to them several times a day. Children in kindergarten are regular visitors to the school library, both in search of books for enjoyment and for information. They share stories they have read and act out stories they have heard. They begin to write and dictate their own versions of favorite stories. Trade books are used to find out more about dinosaurs and stars. In short, their classroom lives are permeated by encounters with whole books, and these books become the vehicles for learning to read and write.

Reading and writing done in kindergarten will focus on both narrative and expository text. Narrative text tells the stories that children traditionally enjoy, stories that have a beginning, a middle, and an ending. Expository text, reading material whose

A Cross-Grade Library Assignment

DURING THE week, the teacher had read a number of stories about the moon—Maurice Sendak's fantasy *In the Night Kitchen; Why The Sun and Moon Live in the Sky,* an African folk tale retold by Elphinstone' Dayrell; Laura Jane Coates's *Marcella and the Moon;* Jane Yolen's *Owl Moon;* and others. As a result, the kindergarten pupils had generated a number of questions about the moon: *Why does the moon change shape? What makes the moon shine? What is the moon made of?* The teacher made a list of the research questions that the children had generated, wrote them on slips of paper, and gave them to a group of five kindergartners, who were then sent off to the library to find answers to the questions.

When they arrived at the library, they were met by a group of five fifth graders who were assigned to find the answers for their younger counterparts. With the help of a library aide (who had been notified in advance of what was going on), the pupils formed pairs, researched the information together, and the kindergartners reported the answers back to the class. In this cross-grade cooperative learning activity, the fifth graders had a purposeful, authentic assignment in library research, while the younger children saw print being used for information-gathering purposes and saw the library as a place to find answers to their questions.

purpose is to convey information rather than to tell a story, also has a place in the kindergarten instructional program. Informational picture books about a variety of topics can be used effectively to expand children's developing knowledge of their world, along with their emerging literacy competencies. Pupils can do many of the same activities with informational books as they can do with storybooks. Putnam (1991) describes how dramatizing nonfiction books stimulates language development and builds important concepts for emergent readers and writers.

Wordless books are valuable teaching tools in kindergarten (and in the years beyond). As the name suggests, wordless books contain virtually no text. The entire story is presented through illustrations. Not only do illustrations carry the story idea or plot; they also develop characterization, portray setting, convey theme, and deliver other literary qualities that characterize stories told in text. Some wordless books contain detailed information in their illustrations; for example, John Goodall's *Story of an English Village* portrays changes that occurred in an English village from the 14th through 20th centuries.

Wordless books offer several unique advantages as instructional tools in the kindergarten classroom. First, they serve as a powerful stimulus for language development. Having children tell the story portrayed in the pictures is a natural language-experience activity. The illustrations provide a focus for having children suggest words to describe the people, places, and actions depicted, and the books provide a structure around which children can fashion their own stories. The children can dictate stories on a tape recorder, and the different versions of these transcribed stories can be the focus for discussion, critical thinking, and early reading experiences. Wordless books have also been used as the basis of book reports since, as one teacher joked, "The kids can't just copy words from the book for their report."

4.8 Putting Ideas to Work

Developing a Reading Lesson with A Wordless Book

WORDLESS BOOKS are effective vehicles for helping young children develop techniques for reading before they can recognize a single word of print. In *Bobo's Dream,* Martha Alexander uses only pictures to tell an amusing and captivating story about a boy and his dog. The boy buys his small dachshund a bone and they go to the park, where the bone is taken away by a larger dog. The boy retrieves the bone for his pet. The little dog sleeps and dreams about returning the favor by retrieving his master's football from a group of older bullies. Through his dream, the little dog finds the courage to intimidate his larger tormentor.

Without a word of print, the story can be used to generate a lesson that will involve a full range of important comprehension skills that can be applied to print. With careful questioning focused on the pictures, the teacher can develop a group lesson that includes:

Setting a purpose: "See if you can tell how Bobo's dream changed his attitude."
Following the literal sequence of events: "What happens after the big dog takes Bobo's bone away?"
Forming and confirming hypotheses: "What do you think the boy will do now?"

Inferring actions and feelings: "How does Bobo feel when . . . ?"
Recognizing elements of humor and irony: "Why do you think Ms. Alexander shows Bobo to be so large in this picture?"
Seeing cause-effect relationships: "Why did Bobo bark at the big dog near the end of the story?"
Recognizing theme: "What lesson can you learn from this story?"
Relating the story to the pupils' own experiences: "Can you tell about a time when you were brave?"

Wordless books provide for rich language experiences as pupils generate the text. When they recount the story based on the pictures, pupils have opportunities to use a variety of words to describe the actions and scenes depicted, to use sentences that relate the story in sequence, and to tell about their reactions to what is happening.

Beyond the speaking/thinking/reading experiences are opportunities for developing writing skills. For each simply illustrated page, children can dictate or write sentences to describe the action and produce their own versions of *Bobo's Dream.*

For young children, wordless books foster positive attitudes in that they provide a fail-safe reading experience, since there are no words "to get right or wrong." The story is told about the kindergarten pupil who, when asked by a curious classmate what the black lines on the page of a book were, replied, "Those are for people who have not learned to read pictures yet."

A group lesson with a wordless book can engage children in the full range of reading/thinking strategies that they will use when they encounter text as part of their reading (see 4.8). These books can stimulate critical and creative thinking, as children suggest other solutions to problems or think of alternative endings to stories. Illustrations in informational wordless books can be used to clarify abstract concepts and add information to the young child's developing schemata. Wordless books have even been used as cross-age tutoring devices for fifth graders working with first graders (Ellis and Preston, 1984).

Wordless books are popular at various levels of early childhood education. Obviously, the level of sophistication in response will vary according to the level of the

4.9
FOR YOUR INFORMATION
Authors Who Write Stories without Words

RATHER THAN providing a list containing scores of wordless books that can be used in kindergarten, here is a list of well-known authors/illustrators of these books. Look for these authors in selecting wordless books for the classroom.

Martha Alexander, who wrote *Bobo's Dream* and *Out, Out, Out!*

Mitsumasa Anno, whose brilliantly designed series of wordless books are among the most fascinating and popular available.

Alexandra Day, who wrote the hilarious and popular accounts of Carl, the caring rottweiler in such books as *Good Dog, Carl* and *Carl's Christmas.*

Tomie di Paola, whose *Pancakes for Breakfast* is one of the most widely enjoyed wordless books.

John S. Goodall, whose wordless books like *Jacko* delight young children and whose wordless books like *The Story of An English Village* entertain and inform older readers.

Pat Hutchins, who has designed the fascinating *Changes Changes.*

Ezra Jack Keats, who has illustrated *Clementina's Cactus.*

Fernando Krahn, whose clever illustrations contribute to lively action in a number of wordless books.

Mercer Mayer, whose *Frog* series and other wordless books are hilarious.

Jan Omerod, whose *Moonlight* and *Sunshine* represent some of the best examples of wordless books available.

Peter Spier, an author who consistently entertains and informs with his books.

David Weisner who authored the enormously engaging, Caldecott-award-winning *Tuesday.*

Some of these authors—such as Mitsumasa Anno and Jan Omerod—specialize in picture books alone; others—such as Pat Hutchins and Ezra Jack Keats—are authors of award-winning picture storybooks as well.

This list of names is designed as a starting point. Children's libraries are full of quality wordless books written by other authors for use in the kindergarten classroom and beyond.

---

child. In nursery school, wordless books might be used as a focus for describing feelings, for example. In the primary grades, they might be used for full-blown lessons on story structure. At any level, they can be used as valuable tools to enhance children's developing power of literacy.

Big Books are also popular devices being used for literature-based reading instruction in kindergarten (as well as in nursery schools and first grade classrooms). The increased use of literature in programs for helping young children acquire beginning reading competency was strengthened enormously by the introduction of these devices, which first appeared on the school scene in the early 1980s. Their use spread with incredible rapidity, so that now they are used widely in early-childhood reading programs, both for the purpose of sharing literature with children and for the purpose of fostering fluent reading.

In the simplest sense, Big Books are oversized copies of children's books. Print and illustrations are both enlarged. The size of Big Books varies slightly, but the books are large enough so that when they are mounted on an easel, they can be seen clearly by all children in a group. Seeing the print and illustrations, children in groups can participate actively in early reading experiences. Related in theory and practice to the idea of family storybook reading, ''enlarged texts allow groups of children to see and react to the printed page as it is being read aloud, a factor considered key to the effectiveness of shared reading between parent and child. . . . Fundamental concepts are acquired through actual participation in a nonthreatening, joyful manner'' (Strickland and Morrow, 1990; p. 342).

Stories that lend themselves especially well to Big-Book presentation are those that have repetitive language, stories that feature ''strong rhythm and rhyme, repeated patterns, refrains, logical sequences, supportive illustrations, and traditional story structure that provide emergent readers support in gaining meaning from text'' (Heald-Taylor, 1987; p. 6). Examples of such stories include:

Brown Bear, Brown Bear by Bill Martin, Jr. *(Brown bear, brown bear what do you see?).*

The Gingerbread Man (Run, run as fast as you can. You can't catch me, I'm the Gingerbread Man!).

The Little Red Hen (''Not I,'' said the cat. ''Not I,'' said the dog. ''Not I,'' said the pig. ''Then I'll do it myself,'' said the Little Red Hen.).

Good Night Owl, by Pat Hutchins *(And owl tried to sleep.).*

I Know an Old Lady (I know an old lady who swallowed a fly. I don't know why she swallowed a fly. Perhaps she'll die.).

This is the House That Jack Built (This is the cat that swallowed the rat that lives in the house that Jack built.)

These predicable books contain patterned language with repetitive structures that enable readers to make educated guesses as to what the author is saying and how the author is going to say it. Children use context clues to determine what the next word will be. Seeing and repeating high-frequency words and phrases in dependable contexts helps children build a sight vocabulary, a store of words that they can recognize independently in other contexts. Patterned books based on rhyme—such as Barbara Emberley's *Drummer Hoff*—can help children learn word families and phonetic elements as well. Even pupils who are having difficulty with beginning reading can participate successfully with the shared reading of a big book as they chime in on the oft-repeated refrains.

Publishing Big Books has become big business. Publishers' catalogs are full of lists of Big Books available for use in classrooms, and enlarged editions of popular stories can be found in supermarkets and discount stores. But Big Books need not always be purchased. With chart paper, pupils frequently make their own Big Books as part of classroom activities, versions of popular stories as well as their own creations.

Strickland (1988) provides a number of suggestions for reading-related learnings with Big Books, including tracking print (to develop left-to-right directionality), thinking aloud (to demonstrate thinking strategies while reading), cloze activities in which pupils fill in missing words (to promote the use of context clues), examining text features (including punctuation and other features of print), and the like.

Apart from enjoying smaller editions of the book independently, there are numerous opportunities for follow-up experiences to Big Book lessons that will promote emergent literacy. Perhaps the most common follow-up is writing, as children dictate/write and illustrate their own versions of predictable stories using the language model

Steps in a Shared Reading Lesson with a Big Book

1. *Introduce the book,* reading the title and the author's and illustrator's names, calling attention to the illustration on the cover and asking pupils to predict what the story might be about. Set a listening/reading purpose: "Let's read this book to see how. . . ."

2. *Read the book aloud* to the group, pointing to the lines of print to reinforce the writing–reading connection. Stop periodically (not so often as to disrupt the rhythm or enjoyment of the story) to ask such questions as, "What do you think will happen next? Why? How does ——— (the character) feel? How do you know? Use subsequent parts of the story to confirm hypotheses.

3. *Read the book again,* this time inviting children to join in on predictable parts to involve them actively in the reading. Children can read predictable parts in unison, or different groups can read different lines (*"Not I,"* said the fox.). After reading, talk about the story. Ask pupils what they liked about it, what problem the main character had, how he or she solved the problem, other ways that he or she might have solved the problem. But be careful about killing interest through overanalysis.

4. *Extend participation* by giving pupils cards containing words, phrases, or sentences from the story. Let individual pupils hold up their cards as their words occur in the story or match their words with the written words in the text.

5. *Follow up* by having pupils read the story on their own in free time, make puppets based on story characters, write their own versions of the story, note words that begin with the same letter or sound, use their sentences from the story written on oaktag strips to reconstruct the story, role play, or engage in other story-related activities that will promote their emergent literacy.

Not all Big Books ought to be treated in the same way. Some can simply be read in unison for the pleasure of participation and the enjoyment of the story. At other times, different lessons may be planned to develop reading strategies.

---

of the text. For example, Pat Hutchins's *Good Night Owl,* which contains strong and predictable language patterns accounting for why owl could not sleep, provides a language model for stories at Halloween ("Ghost tried to sleep"), stories about winter animals ("Bear tried to sleep"), and creative adaptations about machines ("Computer couldn't sleep"). Ideas for writing based on the patterned language of stories in Big Books are virtually limitless.

Writing   Building on young children's emerging writing ability is an integral part of today's kindergarten program. Traditionally, instruction in writing was delayed until reading ability was well established. Currently, there is a heavy emphasis on writing as part of emergent literacy in kindergarten. The reading–writing connection begins in the emergent literacy stage.

Children's early attempts at writing convey little meaning to most adults, appearing like jagged scribbles on the page. But there is usually more to these attempts than meets the adult eye, and once we ask children to read what they have written and when we view the experience as the child's early attempt to create meaning, the inherent meaning becomes apparent.

The author's chair is a special place for sharing stories in the literature-based classroom.

Taking young children's writing seriously is important, since respecting their efforts provides the foundation on which further growth is developed. "If we are not afraid of children's errors, if we give them plenty of opportunity for writing, and if their classrooms provide rich, literate environments, the children will learn quickly. By the end of kindergarten, many children are writing long stories" (Calkins, 1986; p. 43).

As literacy emerges and children gain a greater sense of the alphabetic nature of our writing system, they begin to use alphabet symbols to represent sound and meaning. They use *invented spelling,* approximations of the appropriate orthographic form of words; for example, *Once upon a time* is written as *Wns pn a tim.* This "temporary spelling" will progress from only one or two letters per word to rough approximations of the actual spellings. What is important at this stage is not that they spell the words correctly but that they get their thoughts down on paper in as meaningful a way as they can.

The *writing center* belongs in a kindergarten classroom, just as it belongs as part of the learning environment of the upper elementary grades. This learning area is filled with pencils, markers, and other writing implements, as well as with large, unlined pads of paper and other notepads on which children can record their thoughts. Interesting photographs, old greeting cards, unusual objects, toy figures, and other visual devices can be included to help stimulate writing. This learning area provides both incentive and encouragement for young children to develop their growing power of dealing with language in print.

The *author's chair* is catching on as a feature in classrooms, from kindergarten through the upper grades. Originated by Donald Graves and Jane Hansen (1983), a special chair is reserved for reading aloud to the group. Here is where the teacher sits when sharing a trade book and here is where the children sit when they want to share

Three Reading–Writing Activities for the Emergent Literacy Classroom

1. *The morning message.* Each morning, pupils dictate a simple message that the teacher writes on the chalkboard or on a chart, a simple message such as "Today Is Tuesday. It snowed last night. Eric is absent today." Within the context of the child's own language, the teacher can focus on vocabulary, sentence structure, metalinguistic features of the message, letter names and sounds, and a variety of other language-related learnings. Pupils can add their own individual sentences later in the day.

2. *Buddy journals,* in which children exchange brief written messages with others whose names they pick out of a hat at the beginning of the week. Messages can focus on books they have read, news they want to share, or anything else on their minds.

3. *All kinds of letters*—invitations to parents for open house, thank you notes to anyone who visits the class, notes to veterans on Veterans Day, letters to Santa Claus around Christmastime.

with classmates a piece of writing that they have done. Thus, from the very beginning stages, the child begins to experience the prestige of authorship.

Writing is an important part of emergent literacy at the kindergarten level. The teacher's role is to provide time, materials, and opportunities to write within the context of the language- and literature-rich learning environment. Teachers who provide many functional opportunities for writing, who encourage writing activities, and who take children's initial efforts seriously are encouraging development of this important dimension of literacy.

Perceptual and Alphabet Training   Even though kindergarten programs based on the concept of emergent literacy are different from those that emphasize specific readiness factors as discrete skills, those aspects long considered essential to success in beginning reading are not being ignored. These conventional elements include activities focusing on children's perceptual development and alphabet awareness.

Visual perceptual development is often stressed in kindergarten literacy-related instruction. Because the eyes provide a pathway to the brain for print, visual processing has received a lot of attention. Kindergarten teachers need to be aware of children with problems in visual acuity, the ability to see printed symbols clearly. Other visual processing skills that typically receive attention in kindergarten include:

visual sequencing, the ability to look at objects and letters in left-to-right sequence;

visual figure ground, the ability to focus on a particular visual image (a picture or a word) in a field of competing visual stimuli;

visual memory, the ability to recall series of visual images;

visual-motor skills, the ability to get the hands and the eyes working together in such activities as cutting and pasting, coloring, and manipulating writing implements;

visual discrimination, the ability to perceive likenesses and differences in visual forms, from gross discrimination between shapes like △ and □ to fine discrimination between letters like *b* and *d.*

Because visual processing is important and related to success in beginning reading, there has been a tendency to make visual training part of instruction in kindergarten, and a plethora of kits, games, and other materials are available for use with pupils. It is important, however, not to treat this dimension of learning as an end in itself but rather as part of the process of children's developing ability to handle print. Visual perceptual training need not be addressed in isolated workbook exercises. These visual factors can be the focus of instruction as children spend time with alphabet books, as teachers transcribe children's dictated stories, and as teachers and children share Big Books with the class. In other words, to the extent possible, visual perceptual training should be tied into real, authentic encounters with print rather than carried on as isolated exercises.

Auditory perception is no less important as part of instruction for kindergarten children. This includes auditory acuity, the ability to hear accurately and clearly. It also involves such elements as

auditory blending, the ability to recognize and blend speech sounds together into words;

auditory memory, the ability to recall sequences of auditory signals;

auditory closure, the ability to supply missing elements (sounds in words or words in sentences) in an utterance;

auditory figure ground, the ability to focus on a particular auditory stimulus in the face of competing stimuli;

auditory discrimination, the ability to recognize likenesses and differences in spoken words.

As in the case of visual processing, these auditory perceptual factors are correlated with children's beginning reading achievement, and there are plenty of tapes, kits, and other programs that focus exclusively on this aspect of learning. In most contemporary kindergarten programs, however, auditory perceptual training is carried on not as a separate entity, through separate activities, or with separate sets of instructional materials. Rather, auditory factors are developed within the context of children's emerging literacy and through real encounters with print. Auditory blending and discrimination are part of dealing with the rhymes of Mother Goose. Auditory memory comes into play as children repeat favorite stories and poems. Auditory closure is involved as they supply words in predictable stories that the teacher reads to them.

Alphabet awareness is typically a major part of literacy-related instruction in kindergarten, too. For many years, learning letter names and letter sounds has been viewed as an indispensable element for success in beginning reading, since alphabet knowledge is important to skilled reading and ranks among the best predictors of reading achievement (Bond and Dykstra, 1967; Durrell, 1980; Adams, 1990).

Alphabet awareness is part of metalinguistic knowledge that is part of the child's emerging literacy. As part of kindergarten literacy-related instruction, alphabet training is pointed more directly at competencies that children will need in basic decoding skills that are part of the process of learning to read and spell. Alphabet awareness includes more than the ability to say or sing the alphabet in order from A to Z. It includes:

knowing the names of the letters when the teacher points to them in random order;

matching uppercase (capital) letters with their lowercase equivalent forms;

being able to write letters of the alphabet;

knowing basic letter sounds; that is, being able to identify the first letter in a word based on the initial sound of the word.

Activities centered on alphabet awareness often tie into practice in visual and auditory perception. For example, matching letters that have the same shape requires visual awareness; identifying rhyming elements in *Chicken Soup with Rice* involves auditory discrimination and letter-sound recognition; tracing and writing letters requires visual-motor skills. Much alphabet knowledge can be developed through writing. As teachers transcribe dictated stories and as children begin to write independently, the question ''What sound do you hear?'' necessitates a developing awareness of sound–symbol relationships.

Alphabet books are made to order for helping children learn letter names and sounds. Beyond reading these books in the classroom, kindergarten children can create their own alphabet books by drawing or cutting out pictures for each letter. Pupil-created ABC books can focus on a number of themes—ABC and Me, The ABC of Jobs, The ABC of Transportation, The ABC of Animals, and the like (Jones, 1983). These books can be extended into a whole range of related learning beyond mastery of the symbols of written language. Joan Walsh Anglund's *In a Pumpkin Shell* is a Mother Goose alphabet book that contains letters for key words in popular nursery rhymes: C for *clock* in ''Hickory, Dickory, Dock''; D for *dog* in ''Old Mother Hubbard''; E for *early* in ''Early to Bed.'' Many children come to school without ever having met Mother Goose, and this book can be used effectively with the rich language and sound patterns of popular nursery rhymes.

Knowledge of letter names and sounds is not an end in itself. Rather, it is a specific aspect of children's emergent literacy that will help them achieve independence in decoding and encoding printed language. Children do not learn one isolated speech sound at a time when they are learning to talk; they learn language in its entirety. Alphabet instruction is only one part of a child's emergent literacy. Children's attention to meaning ought not to be diverted by their attention to letters. To the extent possible, learning letter names and sounds should be part of the larger language learning process in the kindergarten classroom.

In the traditional view of helping children learn to read and write, kindergarten was looked upon largely as ''a readiness experience,'' a time when pupils were prepared to cross the threshold into literacy. Today's kindergarten is generally looked upon as another phase in the child's literacy growth, a time when experiences are provided to help the child succeed in beginning reading and writing instruction in the first grade.

4.12 Putting Ideas to Work

First Day in First Grade

CHILDREN (not to mention their parents) enter first grade expecting to learn to read. And children can learn to read something on day one.

A good book to read on the first day of school is Miriam Cohen's *When Will I Read?,* a story about a first grader impatient to get going in reading and one that has some interesting child's-eye insights on what reading is.

As part of the first day's activities, share with pupils a short segment of familiar text— a nursery rhyme such as "Jack and Jill," the refrain from a song that all children might know, or some other sample of familiar material that is easy to read. Write the material on a chart or on the chalkboard and share it with pupils as you would share a Big Book story. When pupils are thoroughly familiar with the words, give individual copies to each pupil and have them practice reading their own copies.

Have pupils write their names on their sheets (some may need help) and send the sheets home to be read to parents. It is only the first day and already the children are reading!

Beginning Reading and Writing Instruction

After kindergarten, children enter first grade, when all children are expected to learn to read. Although people commonly accept the fact that the time for learning to walk and talk will be different for each child, parents and educators alike are anxious when a child does not learn to read at exactly the "right" time. The first grade constitutes the final stages of the child's emergent literacy phase, and this is the year when most children acquire considerable independence in reading and writing.

It has been said that no year of teaching is as challenging or as rewarding as first grade. First grade teachers meet a group of children, most of whom cannot read or write at the beginning of the year, and they leave a group that is largely literate at the end of the year. At no other level of education is such dramatic progress evident.

Although first grade programs continue to address the physical, social, and emotional development of children, the emphasis on content gradually expands according to the curriculum demands of the school and the expectations of the community. This is the year when reading and writing instruction is more formalized and the child is introduced to a basal reader.

Children will likely encounter skill-development exercises in first grade—word recognition (with sight words presented on flash cards), phonics practice (with specific attention to letter–sound relationships), and reading comprehension activities (with exercises aimed at developing and testing pupils' ability to manage meaning in printed text). The inclusion of these skills is not inappropriate nor entirely inconsistent with a literature-based program. Children need awareness of sound–symbol relationships as a backup to context when they analyze unfamiliar words they encounter in print and when they learn to write. Teachers in the second grade may well expect children to be familiar with all the protocols of using basic skills, but first graders should not be given the impression that all of these skills are important. The emphasis in first-grade reading instruction needs to remain on meaning and enjoyment, since this is where developing a positive attitude toward reading is especially important. Literature offers ample opportunities to maintain that focus.

Children's literature is as important in first grade as it is in the earlier stages of emergent literacy. All of the trade books used in nursery school and kindergarten—picture storybooks, simple informational books, wordless books, predictable stories presented in Big Books, poems and nursery rhymes, concepts books, and all the rest—can be appropriately used in the first grade classroom. In addition, most first graders are ready to enjoy "chapter books" that are read to them, books such as the ever-popular E. B. White's *Charlotte's Web* and Janwillem van de Wetering's *Hugh Pine,* the delightful story of a porcupine who tries to pass himself off as a human.

Easy-to-read books are especially appropriate as pupils gain more and more competency and independence in first grade. Designed to be read with a minimal level of reading ability, these books give children the satisfaction of an independent, whole-book reading experience, and they allow children to apply reading in an enjoyable manner. Even though all easy-to-read books do not always meet the standards of high-quality literature, these books do meet the needs of the first grader. The content of books such as Arnold Lobel's *Frog and Toad* stories and *Mousetails,* along with stories like Crosby Bonsall's *Mine's The Best,* have enormous appeal to children, while the vocabulary load and sentence structure make the books manageable for beginning readers. Dr. Seuss is a perennial favorite in the field of easy-to-read books. Many of Seuss' books are well above the level that a first grader can read independently, but books like *The Cat in the Hat, Green Eggs and Ham,* and *Hop on Pop* are appropriate for use in first grade classroom as a vehicle for helping children apply their ever-developing reading skills.

There is no precise moment at which we can say, "Emergent literacy stops here," no exact point at which we can say, "Readiness stops and reading begins." Literacy remains a developmental process, and what teachers continue to do in teaching vocabulary, comprehension, study skills, and all other dimensions of reading will continue throughout first grade and beyond.

Role of the Parents in Early Literacy

Few literacy-related issues have generated more controversy over the years than the question of parent participation in the literacy development of their children. Educators have often taken a divided and conflicting view of parents as part of the teaching-reading-and-writing process. On the one hand, it has long been recognized that parents play a vital part in the intellectual and linguistic development of their children. On the other hand, many experts have discouraged parents from helping their children learn to read before entering school, and many principals and teachers have been reluctant to involve parents once children enter school.

The "keep the parents at arm's length" attitude is quickly dissipating, however. Most parents have knowledge, insight, and commitment that are too important to ignore. Parents are being urged to take a very active role in their children's developing literacy, and educators are coming to recognize how important parents are in supporting and extending the school's mission. As the child's first and most important teachers in the preschool years, parents are seen as crucial to the awakening of children's literacy. And educators are involving parents more and more in school-based efforts to promote development of children's literacy.

4.13
■ FOR YOUR INFORMATION
NAEYC Position Statement on Developmentally Appropriate Practice

THE POSITION statement of the National Association for the Education of Young Children (NAEYC) on curric-

ulum and instructional practices that are developmentally appropriate or inappropriate for young children includes the following section on literacy instruction:

Appropriate Practice

The goals of the language and literacy program are for children to expand their ability to communicate orally and through reading and writing, and to enjoy these activities. Technical skills and subskills are taught as needed to accomplish these larger goals, not as the goal itself. Teachers provide generous amounts of time and a variety of interesting activities for children to develop language, writing, spelling, and reading ability, such as: looking through, reading, or being read high quality children's literature and nonfiction for pleasure and information; drawing, dictating, and writing about their activities or fantasies; planning and implementing projects that involve research at suitable levels of difficulty; creating teacher-made or child-written lists of steps to follow to accomplish a project; discussing what was read; preparing a weekly class newspaper; interviewing various people to obtain information for projects; making books of various kinds (riddle books, *what if* books, books about pets); listening to recordings or viewing high-quality films of children's books; being read at least one high-quality book or part of a book each day by adults or older children; using the school library and the library area of the classroom regularly. Some children read aloud daily to the teacher, another child, or a small group of children, while others do so weekly. Subskills such as learning letters, phonics, and word recognition are taught as needed to individual children and small groups through enjoyable games and activities. Teachers use the teacher's edition of the basal reader series as a guide to plan projects and hands-on activities relevant to what is read and to structure learning situations. Teachers accept children's invented spelling with minimal reliance on teacher-prescribed spelling lists. Teachers also teach literacy as the need arises when working on science, social studies, and other content areas.

Inappropriate Practice

The goal of the reading program is for each child to pass the standardized tests given throughout the year at or near grade level. Reading is taught as the acquisition of skills and subskills. Teachers teach reading only as a discrete subject. When teaching other subjects, they do not feel that they are teaching reading. A sign of excellent teaching is considered to be silence in the classroom and so conversation is allowed infrequently during select times. Language, writing, and spelling instruction are focused on workbooks. Writing is taught as grammar and penmanship. The focus of the reading program is the basal reader, used only in reading groups and accompanying workbooks and worksheets. The teacher's role is to prepare and implement the reading lesson in the teacher's guidebook for each group each day and to see that other children have enough seatwork to keep them busy throughout the reading group time. Phonics instruction stresses learning rules rather than developing understanding of systematic relationships between letters and sounds. Children are required to complete worksheets or to complete the basal reader although they are capable of reading at a higher level. Everyone knows which children are in the lowest reading group. Children's writing efforts are rejected if correct spelling and standard English are not used.

Source: National Association for the Education of Young Children (1988). NAEYC Position Statement on Developmentally Appropriate Practice in the Primary Grades, Serving 5 Through 8 Year Olds. *Young Children* 43:64–84. Reprinted by permission of the National Association for the Education of Young Children, 1834 Connecticut Avenue NW, Washington, DC 20009.

4.14 Putting Ideas to Work

Ten Ways Parents Can Help Children Become Better Readers

*B*ECOMING *A Nation of Readers,* the Report of the National Commission on Reading (Anderson et al., 1985) presents ten suggestions on how parents can help their children become better readers:

1. Help children acquire a wide range of knowledge.

2. Talk with children about their experiences.

3. Encourage children to think about events.

4. Read aloud to children.

5. Provide preschool children with writing materials.

6. Encourage children to watch TV programs that have educational value.

7. Monitor how much TV children watch.

8. Monitor children's school performance.

9. Encourage children to read independently.

10. Continue personal involvement in children's continuing growth as readers.

Parents in the Preschool Years

In the preschool years, parents were traditionally told not to get involved in teaching their children how to read for fear that they might "do something wrong," something that would do more harm than good when the "proper time" came for the child to learn in school. Besides, conventional wisdom suggested, children who already knew how to read would be bored when it came time to learn to read in school.

As society became more conscious of the importance of learning in the early years, parents were urged to take a more active role in teaching their children how to read. Some of the advantages of getting an early start on the road to literacy have been recognized—confidence, self-sufficiency, the child's development of self-concept as a reader, and the like—although some concern is often expressed that too much pressure may be put on children by exceedingly ambitious or overanxious parents who attempt to give their children an early start on reading.

That children can learn to read before they come to school has been well documented. Researchers report numerous cases of children whose parents have helped them learn to read before kindergarten (Durkin, 1966; Bissex, 1980; Lass, 1982, 1983). These studies have resulted in a greater understanding of how young children develop competency in reading and writing and what parents can do to support and encourage the process.

Relatively few parents actively set out specifically to teach their children how to read in a formal sense. Instead, they provide a stimulating environment, frequently read books to their children, and respond to their children's requests for help. They create an environment conducive to reading achievement—an environment full of verbal interaction, where reading is valued and pursued as a worthwhile activity, where children have access to reading material, where opportunities for leisure reading are provided, and where adult reading to children is practiced. These are the factors that research has shown are important to early reading development (Greaney, 1986). Parents who provide this type of environment and who respond to requests for help from their children are strongly supporting the beginnings of literacy, even though they do not set out directly to teach their children how to read.

4.15
FOR YOUR INFORMATION

Parents Are Children's First Teachers
by Joy Wilsted

PARENTS TEACH their children to walk and to talk, and they can also help youngsters learn to read. The wisdom parents use when teaching children to walk and to talk also can be used to help children become strong readers.

If we take a look at the wise things parents do in teaching the skills of walking and talking, we can apply these same things to reading. When parents teach their children to walk, they realize that the youngsters need to "get the feel" of the whole process. Parents often model walking by planting their children's feet right on top of their own feet, so the children can experience the feeling of walking.

When children first try to stand alone, parents wisely smile and praise their efforts. If the children start to fall, parents do not scold them for making mistakes. Instead, parents seem to know that their children need more confidence and they stand ready to provide support. Parents also seem to realize that all children learn to walk in different ways and at different rates.

Children rarely fail in learning the skill of walking. There is little stress in the family over how well Johnny or Jamie is doing.

When children learn to talk, parents also are children's first teachers. Parents know that children need to hear words spoken before they will speak those words themselves. Parents know how important it is to talk with children and to let children talk with them. When children say "boo" for the word "balloon," they are not scolded. Parents know that their children need to hear the word spoken many times, so they simply say "balloon" again.

These wise things that parents do in helping their children learn to walk and talk also are needed when children learn to read. Children need to "get the feel" of the reading process. When parents model reading, children can catch on more quickly if they join in and participate. When children make mistakes in reading, parents can provide another model simply by telling them the correct words. Children will be more interested in reading if the reading experience is full of meaning and if parents talk about pictures and meanings.

Parents can sense when children need reading support, just as they sense when youngsters need support in walking. There is no need to worry if one child learns to read in a different way or at a different rate than another child. Parents know that their children all didn't master walking or talking in the same month. Likewise, all children will not master reading in the same month.

Parents can find as much enjoyment and pleasure from helping their children with reading as they did with helping the youngsters learn to walk and to talk. The love and care that parents give to children in reading can make more difference to their success than any other factor because parents really are children's first teachers.

From Joy Wilsted. ''Parents Are Children's First Teachers'' in *Reading Today,* Dec. 1989/Jan. 1990. International Reading Association, Newark, DE.

Making books accessible to children in the home is also important. For very young children, publishers produce books with pages made of heavy cardboard, cloth or plastic to withstand the wear and tear that a toddler can inflict on a well-loved object. Books can be gifts for birthdays, holidays, and other occasions. The library can be a regular stop on the weekly shopping trip. Putting books in children's hands is an important part of their emergent literacy.

In addition to providing books and creating general conditions for fostering literacy development, there are specific aspects of parent–child interaction that are directly related to learning to read and write.

One of the first things that parents can do in encouraging early literacy is to help their children develop ''print awareness.'' This is part of the metalinguistic knowledge that includes learning why people read and what people do when they read. Parents can develop this awareness at home in a number of ways, both directly and incidentally: by talking about books, by casually mentioning something they may have read, by reading to children every day, by naming books by their titles while calling their children's attention to the words on the cover, and by creating innumerable experiences with print in the home.

Everyday occasions offer potential for literacy-related activities. Bathing or getting dressed offers opportunities for reciting playful poems about parts of the body. Putting away the dinner dishes provides a chance to sort the utensils according to size, shape, and function. Telling stories or playing word games such as ''I Spy'' can fill casual moments with verbal interaction. There is hardly a moment of the day that does not have the potential for some sort of literacy-related activities, however informal.

Parents can share with young children educational television programs such as ''Sesame Street,'' ''The Electric Company,'' ''Long Ago and Far Away,'' or ''Reading Rainbow.'' Shows like these are designed specifically to promote learning and to provide a foundation in school-related areas. What these shows lack is what all television lacks: the important element of feedback. Learning from these shows is best when parents or other caregivers are able to follow-up the show with shared activities such as:

''Let's see how many S-words we can find in the kitchen.''

''Can you remember what a lullaby is?''

''Let's look for things that are *empty* and things that are *full*.''

''Tell me what's *above* the TV and what's *below* the TV.''

''Can you remember three things that the girl said about monkeys?''

''Think of all the things you know that come in *pairs*.''

Follow-up questions and activities are essential to reinforce the language, cognitive, and related learnings that the show is designed to help children acquire. It also demonstrates a parent's interest in the child's learning and makes the child feel successful and important.

Parents can introduce children to the alphabet at home through thousands of planned and spontaneous activities that arise all the time. Saying the alphabet a letter at a time as children climb the stairs is a routine that helps them learn the alphabet in sequence. Calling attention to letters in the environment—''Can you see the *K* in K-Mart?'' ''Show me the *M* on the milk carton.''—reinforces awareness of letter names.

Sharing ABC books is a way of directly introducing young children to letter names and sounds, and at the same time providing early enjoyable encounters with literature. As parents and children share these books in the informal setting of the home, the experience can begin to develop alphabet awareness, concept development, successful independent reading experiences, and enjoyment.

There is perhaps no better way of helping children develop interest in and success with reading than sharing books in the home. Reading to children stimulates their interest, imagination, emotional, and linguistic development. It introduces children to literature that will be the basis of their continuing interest in reading for pleasure.

Reading together forms an important bond between parent and child, while it promotes interest and ability in literacy.

Sharing books extends beyond simply reading; it includes asking questions (but not so many that it will kill interest), talking about the pictures, discussing feelings, and enjoying the delight that good stories offer.

When preschool children choose favorite and familiar books, parents can practice paired reading, a technique in which both parents and children read together. They can read simultaneously, they can read alternate pages, they can "echo read" (with parent reading and child repeating), or they can read different parts of books ("You read what the giant says.") However it is done, paired reading actively involves young children in their emerging reading. As children achieve more reading competency and gain independence, the practice can be continued as the child enters school.

In the preschool years, parents can be effective models for reading. When impressionable children see their parents reading books and magazines for information and pleasure, they get the message early in their lives that reading is important and enjoyable.

Parents can also foster children's development as writers in the preschool years. Parents who respond enthusiastically to their children's early attempts at scribbling stories and other messages help their youngsters gain both awareness and confidence as writers. With response, children see a purpose to writing. Transcribing stories that children dictate encourages children's attempts at writing, and at the same time develops important elements of "print awareness."

What Parents Can Do to Promote Literacy for Preschoolers

HARDLY A moment goes by that does not afford opportunities for parents and other caregivers to foster the emergent literacy of young children by:

1. Talking to them, encouraging them to talk, exchanging accounts of events, patiently answering their interminable *why* questions.

2. Reading to them every day, several times a day, every chance they get.

3. Having books around, letting sturdy cardboard books be toys to be enjoyed and experienced.

4. Developing routines for learning the alphabet, naming parts of the body, playing games with sounds and words.

5. Calling attention to print in the environment—words in the supermarket, on street signs and billboards, in magazines and in books.

6. Watching ''Sesame Street'' and other instructional TV programs, while asking questions and providing information to extend concepts the programs are designed to develop.

7. Copying stories and simple messages that children dictate, and encouraging children to write their own stories.

8. Being models themselves by reading for information and enjoyment and by calling attention to their reading.

Parents are children's first teachers. Before children enter a preschool program, parents can do much to encourage and promote emergent literacy in the home.

Role of Parents When Children Come to School

Throughout the early years, the home provides a significant foundation for a child's emerging literacy. When a child enters kindergarten, the school becomes the second major influence in the child's language learning, and the home continues to support reading growth. More and more, schools are coming to recognize the importance of the continuing role of parents in their children's learning to read and write. Parents and teachers become partners in the emerging literacy of the young child.

When a child enters school, parents can reinforce and extend literacy development in the home in an unlimited variety of ways, just as they can provide support for emergent literacy in the preschool years. Through verbal interaction, parents promote their children's continuing language development. They provide access to print by continuing to make books and magazines available to their children. By reading to children, parents provide both a cognitive and emotional ''shot in the arm'' for literacy development. By listening to their children read, they convey the message that reading is important. In short, the home continues to exert a powerful influence in the development of children's emerging literacy.

More often than not, parents are more than happy to provide help at home for children learning to read, but many parents are not sure what to do. During their children's preschool years, parents seem to have an intuitive sense of fostering language learning. But their confidence seems to diminish once a child enters school and comes under the direction of a trained and expert teacher. Often, they feel that they are ''on the outside looking in.'' The confidence built while reading to their children and answering their children's questions about print dissipates a little when their child brings

4.17
FOR YOUR INFORMATION

A Hierarchy of Home-School Relationships

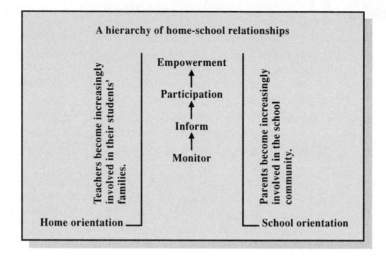

home the first phonics worksheet or word list. Feeling that they do not possess ''teaching skills,'' they often draw back and become less involved in their children's literacy development.

Not all home environments are conducive to maximum literacy development in the early years. For many children, home is a crowded place where emotional and intellectual neglect is a fact of life. Many parents struggle with the challenge of meeting the family's most basic needs. Time and material resources may be at a premium. Parents may be unaware of the importance of verbal interaction, and their own level of literacy may be limited. For children from this environment, the role of the school becomes essential in compensating for much of what the children missed during their preschool years.

Schools can take the initiative in reaching out to give parents ideas on what they can do to promote reading and writing in the home. Rasinski and Fredericks (1989) suggest a model or plan for organizing parent–teacher cooperation in promoting emergent literacy (see 4.17). At the most basic level, teacher and parents act as monitors of their pupils'/children's learning. The second level involves communication, when a two-way, home–school line of communication is established through regular and positive sharing of information. At the level of participation, parents become engaged in the school life of the child by serving as a classroom volunteer and schools participate by offering special programs for parents. The highest level of mutual involvement is empowerment, in which parents and teachers achieve an almost collegial relationship of trust and commitment.

A Note to Parents

HERE ARE ten things that parents can do at home to help children improve their reading:

1. Turn off the television for half an hour each evening. Use this time to read to your children or to listen to them read to you. Some children begin to prefer reading good stories to watching television.

2. Have children's books from the library or inexpensive books from the supermarket available, and share these books as often as possible. Let your children select some of these books.

3. Let your child help you look up numbers in the telephone book, recipes in the cookbook, or directions on the back of food containers.

4. Put a note with a ''happy message'' in your child's lunch box and exchange simple notes with him or her at home.

5. Play games involving reading and writing; for example, ''restaurant games'' in which you and your child read menus and write orders.

6. Cut pictures from magazines. Label them; describe them; classify objects (as *big* and *small,* for example); make up captions for the pictures.

7. Help your children realize that reading is important to you; let them see you using books, newspapers, and magazines as sources of information and enjoyment.

8. Share *Mother Goose* rhymes and other simple poems; emphasize the sounds and the rhythm of the language.

9. After a shared experience—a family vacation, a birthday party, a trip to the grocery store—talk about the occasion and keep a family diary; copy down what your child has to say and read the story back to him or her.

10. Encourage your child to read to you; be a good listener and don't ask too many questions; praise your child for his or her best efforts.

Each activity takes only a few minutes, yet can give your child a head start in becoming a successful reader and writer. Remember, the greatest gifts you can give your child are time and love.

Even without a formal program or plan, parents can remain a vital part of their children's emergent literacy during the primary school years. Rare indeed are parents who are not interested in their children's success as readers and writers, but they often need help and guidance. In order to encourage parents to remain involved in their children's ongoing literacy development, a list of suggestions like the one presented in 4.18 might be sent home early in the year or distributed at an open house or parents' night at school. It is important that these suggestions be practical and not require an unreasonable investment of time or money.

Informal reading instruction in the home needs no special materials. Home-based reading and writing experiences can emanate from reading the labels on soup cans and cereal boxes, checking the listings of television shows, reading the comic section of the Sunday newspaper, making out weekly grocery lists, and looking at billboards and other signs seen from the car window.

Some schools offer workshops or special programs to help parents of kindergarten pupils become more aware of what they can do to promote literacy at home. In these programs, parents learn about the type of literature appropriate for young children

4.19
FOR YOUR INFORMATION
Useful References for Parents about Reading in the Home

T HE FOLLOWING is a sampling of materials available for parents on supporting literacy in the home.

Brochures

"Choosing a Child's Book"—The Children's Book Council (67 Irving Place, New York, NY 10003).

"How to Help Your Child Become a Better Writer"—National Council of Teachers of English (1111Kenyon Road, Urbana, IL 61801).

"Good Books Make Reading Fun For Your Child," "Your Home Is Your Child's First School," "You Can Use Television to Stimulate Your Child's Reading Habits," and others—International Reading Association (P.O. Box 8139, 800 Barksdale Road, Newark, DE 19714–8139).

"Helping Children Learn About Reading"—National Association for Education of Young Children (1834 Connecticut Ave. NW, Washington, DC 20009–5780).

"Children's Classics: A Book List for Parents"—*The Horn Book Magazine* (14 Beacon Street, Boston, MA 02108).

Booklets

"Getting Involved: Your Child and Reading" and "Getting Involved: Your Child and Writing"—Government Printing Office (1511 K Street NW, Suite 740, Washington, D.C. 20005).

"How Can I Encourage My Primary-Grade Child to Read?" "Why Read Aloud To Children?" and others—International Reading Association (P.O. Box 8139, 800 Barksdale Road, Newark, DE 19714–8139).

"Parents and Children Together," a series of audio journals containing a read-along booklet with a cassette tape—ERIC Clearinghouse on Reading and Communications Skills, Indiana University (2805 East 10th Street, Bloomington, IN 47408–2698).

Books

A Parent's Guide To Children's Reading (5th ed.) by Nancy Larrick. New York: Bantam Books, 1982.

The New Read-Aloud Handbook by Jim Trelease. New York: Viking, 1989.

Home: Where Reading and Writing Begin by Mary W. Hill. Portsmouth, NH: Heinemann Educational Books, 1989.

Choosing Books for Children: A Commonsense Guide by Betsy Hearne. New York: Delacourte, 1990.

These titles and other books about reading in the home can generally be purchased in bookstores.

---

and where to find it; how to share books with children, not only by reading them but also by talking about books and sharing feelings about what they read; how to create a home reading environment; how to help children develop as writers; how to listen to children as they read. Giving parents a meaningful decision-making role in planning and implementing these programs improves the success of these efforts. In some cases, programs like these result in parents' becoming interested in working as volunteers in the classroom, as library aides, or as actively involved members of the school community.

Some basal reading series provide supplementary material—newsletters, worksheets, even videotapes—to extend their programs into the home. Although these materials can provide extension and reinforcement beyond the classroom, they are often "more of the same"; that is, they repeat skills-based activities and materials that the child deals with in school all day long. The more intimate environment of the home usually provides everyday opportunities for encounters with print that are more informal, more natural, and more authentic than those found in the typical classroom.

Teachers can also make parents aware of the many printed sources of information available to help them learn more about reading in the home and about literacy-related home activities that they can engage in with their children (see 4.19). Since many of these brochures and booklets are available free or at a minimal cost, schools can easily make them available to parents. These resources can be available for parents to examine on occasions when they visit schools for teacher conferences or open house.

As children are being introduced to writing instruction in the classroom, parents can continue to foster their youngsters' developing competency as writers at home as well. Often, the first thing that parents need to realize is that the primary focus of children's early attempts at independent writing is the meaning that the children are trying to express, not how accurately they spell or punctuate what they write. Indeed, the conventions of written language and the mechanics of writing ultimately have to be learned, but the initial focus should be on the child's willingness and confidence to attempt to express meaning in writing. Parents need to learn to respond to the message, not to be overly concerned about how neatly or correctly the message is written.

Summary and Conclusions

The early years are vitally important to children's continuing development as readers and writers, and what goes on during these years, both at home and in school, will influence the child's success in developing the power of literacy.

Under ideal circumstances, a child's early meaningful exposure to reading and writing begins in the home. The child owns books, hears stories read, and develops an awareness of the role that print plays in the environment.

Emergent literacy continues to be encouraged and developed through nursery school programs that foster language and allow children many experiences with a variety of books and early writing experiences.

In kindergarten, the emphasis on language development and exposure to print continues, but instruction takes on a more formal dimension. Specific aspects of learning directly related to reading and writing are introduced into the child's life.

In first grade, the instructional program becomes even more formalized. Here the child is expected to begin the road to independence in reading and writing.

Even after the child begins school, the role of the parent does not diminish. Parents provide support for literacy development and extend the efforts of the school in teaching the child how to read and write.

Discussion Questions and Activities

1. Think about your own preschool years. What experiences with reading and writing stand out in your mind? What were your favorite stories? In what ways did your preschool experiences influence you when you went to school?
2. Interview the parent of a young child or, if possible, observe the child in action. Note the type of language the child uses, how he or she reacts to books, the type of activities he or she enjoys most. Given the child's stage of emergent literacy, what types of activities might you suggest to foster the child's interest in reading and writing?

3. Watch an episode of "Sesame Street." Which aspects of literacy is the program designed to develop? Make a list of follow-up activities that would be appropriate to reinforce or extend the learning of a child who watched the program.

4. Get a copy of three or four wordless books. Note how the authors build the elements of plot, character, and setting into these books. Make a list of classroom learning activities that could be based on one of these books.

5. Examine the beginning textbook from a basal reading series. What reading skills does it aim to help pupils develop? What children's trade books might you use to supplement this reader? How might you integrate the use of the basal reading text with the literature you select?

School-Based Assignments

1. Visit a nursery school, kindergarten, or first grade classroom. Make a list of print found in the learning environment, print that has been produced by both adults and children. How are children using this print? What kinds of books are available and how are they being used?

2. Following the guidelines presented on p. 115, plan a reading lesson based on a predictable story in a Big Book. Teach the lesson to a group of children in an early childhood education setting. Prepare a brief report on pupils' reactions.

3. Prepare a letter about reading that might be sent home to parents the first week of school. What are the five most essential pieces of information that you might include? Get the opinion of colleagues and administrators about your letter.

4. Select a picture storybook, a wordless book, a concept book, an alphabet book, or other trade book that might be used with young children. If possible, use the book with children at different levels of emergent literacy. Be specific about the type of input you would provide at each level and the kind of output you might expect.

5. Examine the NAEYC statement regarding appropriate and inappropriate practices (p. 122) Using these standards as your guide, observe instruction in a first grade classroom over a period of time. Give the class an "appropriateness rating" according to these standards.

Children's Trade Books Cited in This Chapter

Alexander, Martha. *Bobo's Dream*. New York: Dial, 1970.

———. *Out, Out, Out*. New York: Dial, 1970.

Anglund, Joan Walsh. *In a Pumpkin Shell*. New York: Harcourt Brace, 1960.

Anno, Mitsumasa. *Anno's Alphabet*. New York: Crowell, 1975.

Barton, Byron. *Airport*. New York: Harper and Row, 1982.

Bayer, Jane. *A, My Name Is Alice*. New York: Dial, 1984.

Bonsall, Crosby. *Mine's the Best*. New York: Harper and Row, 1973.

Brown, Margaret Wise. *Goodnight, Moon*. New York: Harper and Row, 1947.

Carle, Eric. *The Very Hungry Caterpillar*. New York: Philomel, 1969.

Coates, Laura Jane. *Marcella and the Moon*. New York: Macmillan, 1986.

Cohen, Miriam. *When Will I Read?* New York: Greenwillow, 1977.

Crews, Donald. *Freight Train*. New York: Greenwillow, 1978.

Day, Alexandra. *Good Dog, Carl*. San Marcos, CA: Green Tiger Press, 1985.

———. *Carl's Christmas*. New York: Farrar, Straus and Giroux, 1990.

Dayrell, Elphinstone. *Why The Sun and Moon Live in the Sky*. Boston: Houghton Mifflin, 1968.

de Paola, Tomie. *Pancakes for Breakfast*. New York: Harcourt Brace, 1978.

de Wetering, Janwillem van. *Hugh Pine*. Boston: Houghton Mifflin, 1980.

Doublier, Anne. *Under the Sea from A to Z*. New York: Crown, 1991.

Emberley, Barbara. *Drummer Hoff*. Englewood Cliffs, NJ: Prentice Hall, 1967.

Feeling, Muriel. *Moja Means One: Swahili Counting Book*. New York: Dial, 1971.

Gag, Wanda. *Millions of Cats*. New York: Putnam, 1928.

Geisel, Theodore S. (Dr. Seuss). *Cat in the Hat*. New York: Random House, 1966.

———. *Green Eggs and Ham*. New York: Random House, 1960.

———. *Hop on Pop*. New York: Random House, 1963.

Gladone, Paul. *The House That Jack Built*. New York: McGraw Hill, 1961.

———. *The Gingerbread Boy*. New York: Clarion, 1975.

———. *The Little Red Hen*. New York: Scholastic, 1973.

Goodall, John, *Jacko*. New York: Harcourt Brace, 1972.

———. *The Story of an English Village*. New York: Macmillan, 1979.

Grossman, Virginia. *Ten Little Rabbits*. San Francisco: Chronicle Books, 1991.

Hepworth, Cathi. *Antics! An Alphabetical Anthology*. New York: Putnam, 1992.

Hoban, Tana. *Count and See*. New York: Macmillan, 1972.

———. *Is It Red? Is It Yellow? Is It Blue?* New York: Greenwillow, 1978.

Hunhardt, Dorothy. *Pat the Bunny*. New York: Western, 1942.

Hutchins, Pat. *Changes, Changes*. New York: Macmillan, 1971.

———. *Good Night Owl*. New York: Macmillan, 1972.

———. *Rosie's Walk*. New York: Macmillan, 1968.

Keats, Ezra Jack. *Clementine's Cactus*. New York: Viking, 1982.

Kitchen, Burt. *Animal Alphabet*. New York: Dial, 1984.

Lobel, Anita. *Alison's Zinnia*. New York: Greenwillow, 1990.

Lobel, Arnold. *Frog and Toad Are Friends*. New York: Harper and Row, 1970.

———. *Mouse Tails*. New York: Harper and Row, 1972.

———, and Lobel, Anita. *On Market Street*. New York: Greenwillow, 1981.

Martin, Bill, Jr. *Brown Bear, Brown Bear*. New York: Holt, 1983.

Martin, Bill, Jr., and Archambault, John. *Chicka Chicka Boom Boom*. New York: Simon and Schuster, 1989.

Musgrove, Margaret. *Ashanti to Zulu: African Traditions*. New York: Dial, 1976.

Omerod, Jan. *Moonlight*. New York: Lothrop, 1982.

———. *Sunshine*. New York: Lothrop, 1981.

Oxenbury, Helen. *Helen Oxenbury's ABC of Things*. New York: Delacorte, 1983.

Paul, Ann Whitford. *Eight Hands Round: A Patchwork Alphabet*. New York: Harper Collins, 1991.

Reiss, John. *Shapes*. New York: Bradbury, 1974.

Rockwell, Anne. *First Comes Spring*. New York: Harper and Row, 1985.

Rockwell, Harlow. *My Kitchen*. New York: Greenwillow, 1980.

———. *My Nursery School*. New York: Greenwillow, 1976.

Sendak, Maurice. *Chicken Soup with Rice*. New York: Harper and Row, 1962.

———. *In the Night Kitchen*. New York: Harper and Row, 1970.

———. *Outside Over There*. New York: Harper and Row, 1981.

———. *Where The Wild Things Are*. New York: Harper and Row, 1963.

Slobodkina, Esphyr. *Caps for Sale*. New York: Harper and Row, 1947.

Spier, Peter. *Fast-Slow, High-Low: A Book of Opposites*. New York: Doubleday, 1972.

Tafuri, Nancy. *Who's Counting?* New York: Greenwillow, 1986.

Weissman, David. *Tuesday*. New York: Clarion Books, 1991.

Wescott, Nadine Bernard. *I Know an Old Lady Who Swallowed a Fly*. Boston: Little Brown, 1980.

White, E. B. *Charlotte's Web*. New York: Harper, 1952.

Wildsmith, Brian. *Brian Wildsmith's ABC*. New York: Watts, 1962.

Yolen, Jane. *Owl Moon*. New York: Scholastic, 1987.

References

Adams, M. J. (1990). *Beginning to Read: Thinking and Learning about Print.* Cambridge, MA: MIT Press.

Anderson, R. C., Hiebert, F. H., Scott, J. A., and Wilkinson, I. A. G. (1985). *Becoming a Nation of Readers.* Washington, DC: National Institute of Education.

Bissex, G. L. (1980). *GNYS AT WRK: A Child Learns to Write and Read.* Cambridge, MA: Harvard University Press.

Bond, G. L., and Dysktra, R. (1967). The Cooperative Research Program in First-Grade Reading Instruction. *Reading Research Quarterly* 2:5–142.

Calkins, L. M. (1986). *The Art of Teaching Writing.* Portsmouth, NH: Heinemann.

Durkin, D. (1966). *Children Who Read Early.* New York: Teachers College Press.

Durrell, D. D. (1980). Letter-Name Value in Reading and Spelling. *Reading Research Quarterly* 16:159–163.

Ellis, D. W, and Preston, F. W. (1984). Enhancing Beginning Reading Using Wordless Picture Books. *The Reading Teacher* 37:692–698.

Freeman E. B. and Hatch, J. A. (1989). Emergent Literacy: Reconceptualizing Kindergarten Practice. *Childhood Education* 66:21–24.

Gates, A. (1937). The Necessary Mental Age for Beginning Reading. *Elementary School Journal* 37:497–508.

Gentile, L. M. (1983) ''A Critique of Mabel V. Morphett and Carleton Washburne's Study: When Should Children Begin To Read?'' In L. M. Gentile, M. L. Kamil, and J. S. Blanchard, eds., *Reading Research Revisited.* Columbus: Charles E. Merrill.

Graves, D., and Hansen, J. (1983). The Author's Chair. *Language Arts* 60:176–183.

Greaney, V. (1986). Parental Influences on Reading. *The Reading Teacher* 39:813–818.

Harris, A. J., and Sipay, E. R. (1985). *How to Increase Reading Ability,* 8th ed. New York: Longman.

Heald-Taylor, G. (1987). Predictable Literature Selections and Activities for Language Arts Instruction. *The Reading Teacher* 41:6–12.

Holdaway, D. (1982). Shared Book Experience: Teaching Reading Using Favorite Books. *Theory into Practice* 21:293–300.

Huck, C. S., Hepler, S., and Hickman, J. (1987). *Children's Literature in the Elementary School* (4th ed.). New York: Holt, Rinehart and Winston.

Jones, M. (1983). AB(by)C Means Alphabet Books By Children. T*he Reading Teacher* 36:646–648.

Lass, B. (1982). Portrait of My Son as an Early Reader. *The Reading Teacher* 36:20–28.

———. (1983). Portrait of My Son as an Early Reader II. *The Reading Teacher* 36:508–515.

McGee, L. M., and Richgels, D. J. (1990). *Literacy's Beginnings: Supporting Young Readers and Writers.* Boston: Allyn and Bacon.

Morphett, M. V., and Washburne, C. (1931). When Should Children Begin to Read? *Elementary School Journal* 31:496–503.

National Association for the Education of Young Children (1988). NAEYC Position Statement on Developmentally Appropriate Practice in the Primary Grades, Serving 5- Through 8-Year-Olds. *Young Children* 43:64–84.

Putnam, C. (1991). Dramatizing Nonfiction with Emergent Readers. *Language Arts* 68:463–469.

Rasinski, T. V., and Fredericks, A. D. (1989). Dimensions of Parent Involvement. *The Reading Teacher* 43:180–182.

Strickland, D. S. (1989). Some Tips for Using Big Books. *The Reading Teacher* 41:966–968.

Strickland, D. S., and Morrow, L. M. (1990). Sharing Big Books. *The Reading Teacher* 43:342–3.

Teale, W. H., and Sulzby, E. (1986). *Emergent Literacy: Writing and Reading.* Norwood, NJ: Ablex.

Thomas, K. F. (1985). Early Reading as a Social Interaction Process. *Language Arts* 62: 469–475.

Vacca, J. L., Vacca, R. T., and Gove, M. K. (1991). *Reading and Learning to Read* (2nd ed.). New York: HarperCollins.

chapter 5

Word Study: Vocabulary and Learning to Read

Chapter 5 Outline

I. Introduction
II. Word Knowledge
    A. Words and Concepts
    B. Vocabulary Development in the Classroom
        1. Integration
            a. Semantic Mapping
            b. Analogies
        2. Repetition
            a. Synonyms and Antonyms
            b. Semantic Study
            c. Word Alerts
        3. Meaningful Use
            a. Teacher Involvement
            b. Wide Reading
III. Word Recognition
    A. Sight Words
        1. Selecting Vocabulary
        2. Deciding How to Teach
    B. Context Clues
        1. Syntactic and Semantic Context
        2. Cloze Exercises
IV. Word Analysis
    A. Phonetic Analysis
        1. The Great Debate
        2. Phonics in a Literature-Based Program
            a. Connected, Meaningful Discourse
            b. Whole-to-Part Instruction
        3. Phonics and Writing
    B. Structural Analysis
    C. The Dictionary: "Look It Up"
V. A Combination of Word-Identification Skills
VI. Summary and Conclusions
Discussion Questions and Activities
School-Based Assignments
Children's Trade Books Cited in This Chapter
References

Features

5.1   Three Related Areas of Word Study
5.2   What Does It Mean to "Know" a Word?
5.3   Semantic Maps
5.4   Word for the Day
5.5   Nothing Need Ever Be Boring Again!
5.6   Books about Words
5.7   Bookwords: High Frequency Words in Storybooks for Beginning Readers
5.8   Personal Words
5.9   Teaching Sight Words
5.10 Context Clues Exercise
5.11 Using Cloze
5.12 Point-Counterpoint on Phonics
5.13 The Language of Phonics
5.14 Trade Books that Repeat Phonics Elements
5.15 Guidelines for Exemplary Phonics Instruction
5.16 Teaching Morphemic Elements through Literature

Key Concepts in this Chapter

Word knowledge is essential to reading success in literature-based reading programs. The more words pupils know, the better will be their chances for understanding what they read.

Reading requires the recognition of words in print, the ability to say a word and know what it means. Pupils can recognize words instantly by sight or through context.

Words that are not immediately recognized need to be analyzed. Pupils learn to recognize words phonetically (by letters and sounds) or structurally (by larger meaning-bearing parts).

Recognizing words in print requires a combination of strategies. The ultimate purpose of using these strategies is to arrive at meaning.

ORDS ARE the currency of communication, the main medium in the exchange of ideas through language. Words are essential to any spoken or written language experience. For this reason, vocabulary development is an essential part of language arts in the elementary grades (and beyond).

Vocabulary development begins long before formal reading instruction. Learning new words is part of the language acquisition process that takes place through the emergent literacy stage, and vocabulary growth in the early years of a child's life is dramatically rapid.

The exact size of a person's vocabulary is impossible to measure, so the number of words that children know when they come to school is a matter of debate. Measuring vocabulary size is not as easy as measuring height or weight, and the best that researchers can do is to estimate the number of words a young child knows. Although estimates of children's vocabulary size vary considerably, it is reasonable to assume that first graders will have a listening/speaking vocabulary of about 5,000 words, and that this number will grow to about 50,000 by the time the pupils enter college (Just and Carpenter, 1987).

We can be confident that, whatever the exact size of their vocabularies, children bring to school a vast repertoire as part of their mental lexicons, the total set of words that they have in their heads. This base of word knowledge provides a foundation for the meaning that pupils bring to print and forms the basis of their understanding of the trade books and other material that they read as part of literature-based programs.

As part of literacy development in the classroom, three aspects of vocabulary study/development are typically addressed. The first focuses on *word knowledge* and involves helping pupils build a store of words that they can use to meet the full range of their communication needs. In order to read, pupils not only need to ''know'' words, but they also need to be able to identify these words in print. Thus, reading instruction focuses on *word recognition,* the ability to know what a word is and what it means, and on *word analysis,* the ability to figure out the pronunciation and meaning of words that pupils do not recognize immediately in print.

All three dimensions of word study—knowledge, recognition, and analysis—are related. All are rooted in language meaning; all are aimed at helping pupils derive meaning in reading and express meaning in writing.

Word Knowledge

Knowledge of word meaning is essential to reading and writing competency. Ultimately, success at reading must be judged by how well readers understand what they read, and effectiveness in writing is determined by the appropriate use of words in written discourse. Word knowledge does not stand alone as part of the language arts curriculum; it is related to the broader context of meaning. At the same time, knowing the meaning of individual language units (words) is essential to creating total meaning in reading and writing.

Research supports what common sense suggests—that the link between vocabulary and comprehension in reading is vital. Research has shown consistently the importance of vocabulary and word knowledge as a fundamental factor in understanding what one reads.

5.1
Three Related Areas of Word Study

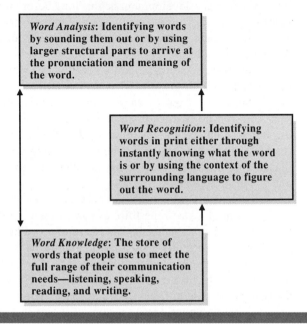

Word Analysis: Identifying words by sounding them out or by using larger structural parts to arrive at the pronunciation and meaning of the word.

Word Recognition: Identifying words in print either through instantly knowing what the word is or by using the context of the surrounding language to figure out the word.

Word Knowledge: The store of words that people use to meet the full range of their communication needs—listening, speaking, reading, and writing.

In analyzing factors related to reading comprehension, researchers such as Davis (1972), Anderson and Freebody (1985), Blachowicz (1985), and others have found repeatedly that knowledge of word meaning is an important factor in the reading comprehension process. Devine (1986) summarized research on the vocabulary–comprehension link in this way: "Of all aspects of prior knowledge, word knowledge seems to be the most important for reading comprehension" (p. 29). Based on his research, Pearson (1985) concluded that knowledge of key vocabulary predicts comprehension better than any test of reading ability or achievement. William Nagy (1988) writes, "A wealth of research has documented the strength of the relationship between vocabulary and comprehension . . . a reader's vocabulary knowledge is the single best predictor of how well that reader can understand text" (p. 1).

In sum, the more words a reader knows, the better will be his or her chances of understanding what he or she reads. That is why instruction in vocabulary is such an important part of language arts instruction.

Words and Concepts

There are different stages or steps in coming to know a word (see 5.2). Klein (1988) describes stages of word knowledge as three categories or dictionaries: "the ownership dictionary, the mid-level dictionary (accessible with contextual assistance), and the low-level dictionary (marginal; possible, but with increased risk of error. . . . Each

5.2
FOR YOUR INFORMATION
What Does It Mean to "Know" a Word?

DO PUPILS know a word when they can simply pronounce it? Do they know the word when they can give a synonym or dictionary definition? Or do they need to use the word in a number of contexts before they really know it?

Egdar Dale (1965) has produced a very useful distinction for what it means to know a word. Dale suggests five stages of word knowledge:

1. *I never saw/heard the word before.* These are totally unfamiliar words completely outside the pupil's vocabulary.

2. *I know there's such a word, but I don't know what it means.* For many adults, a word like *antidisestablishmentarianism* would fall into this category; we know that the word exists, but we don't know its meaning.

3. *I have a vague contextual placement of the word.* Words like *zither* or *beguile* or *tautology* would fit into this category for many adults. They may be familiar with the words but not familiar enough to define them in isolation.

4. *I know the word. I will be able to recognize it again if I see it and I am likely to use it.* These are words that we can be sure are part of the pupil's vocabulary.

5. *I know the word well. I can make fine and precise distinctions in its meaning.* For words at this stage, the person can distinguish between the meanings of closely related words, between *satire* and *irony,* for example, or between *misbehavior* and *misdemeanor.*

of us possesses all three dictionaries in our heads'' (Klein, 1988; p. 62). As pupils encounter new words, the words are entered into one of the ''dictionaries.'' Words normally enter into the low- or mid-level dictionaries and they work their way up to full ownership through repeated use.

Ultimately, to ''know'' a word means to understand the concept that the word represents, not just to be able to quote its dictionary definition. Vocabulary development and concept development are intimately related. Words symbolize or represent objects, events, experiences, emotions, and ideas found in the world around us. The process of attaching a word label is the final step in the process of cognition. At the same time, understanding the meaning of a word is a way of acquiring new knowledge. Within the classroom (and outside it, too), every incidence of new learning presents opportunities for learning new words.

Literature is essential to the continued vocabulary growth that pupils experience throughout their school years. The language that pupils encounter in trade books extends their knowledge of words and their ability to use this knowledge in various contexts. Peterson and Eeds (1990) use an example from Willian Steig's *Sylvester and the Magic Pebble,* the story of the donkey who turned into a rock. When pupils hear or read the words *confused, perplexed, puzzled,* and *bewildered* to describe the hungry lion who circled the donkey-turned-boulder, there is little need to teach what these words mean.

Words take on credence, worth, and accuracy in relationship to the concepts they represent. The more abstract a concept is, the harder it is to conceptualize. People can easily agree that *a doll, a shirt,* and *a chair* fall into the categories of toys, clothing, and furniture, respectively. But they cannot agree as readily on whether Tom, Dick,

As pupils deal with words in print, they develop knowledge of subject matter and competency in literacy.

and Harry are *conservative, moderate,* and *liberal,* respectively. Abstract concepts are more difficult to grasp because we cannot sense them in the same way we can touch and feel and see concrete objects. We cannot touch love or happiness, so we try to describe them in concrete terms: *Love is a warm puppy,* or *Happiness is Friday afternoon when all the children have gone home.*

Words represent concepts, and concepts are tied to experiences. A pupil who has never seen the ocean will still know the meaning of the word *ocean* by hearing about it, reading about it, or seeing it on TV. But this child's concept of *ocean* will be thin in comparison to another child who has been to the beach, seen the fury of an ocean storm, enjoyed the ocean's calm at sunset, tasted its salty brine, or felt its seaweed while swimming in its cool water. Just having an experience will not assure vocabulary growth, however. Language needs to be attached to all the direct and vicarious experiences that pupils have in and out of school. As concepts are developed, vocabulary will be broadened and deepened as well, and one of the most effective ways for promoting this concept/vocabulary growth is the use of literature in the classroom.

Vocabulary Development in the Classroom

A literature-based program needs to be saturated with planned and incidental opportunities to learn about language, to learn about words. Nagy (1988) identifies three qualities or principles of effective vocabulary instruction in the classroom: integration, repetition, and meaningful use.

Integration   Integration means teaching vocabulary in relation to what pupils already know. The meanings of new words are connected to familiar concepts and experiences. New words are taught not as separate labels or isolated items, but they are introduced and developed as their meaning relates to familiar concepts and experiences. As new words are taught, they are integrated with words that pupils already know.

Semantic mapping is one effective technique for integrating vocabulary instruction within the context of concept development. A semantic map is a web or scheme that focuses vocabulary instruction on a central object or concept. It is a visual representation of the relationships among words and concepts associated with a particular topic. New vocabulary items are connected to words and ideas with which pupils are already familiar (see 5.3). The teacher begins by writing a word on the chalkboard or on a chart. Pupils brainstorm, and the teacher writes the words that they suggest, adding new words that he or she wants to teach and perhaps indicating categories for the various classes of words. Pupils see new words in relationship to that which they already know.

Besides the format presented in 5.3, other visual designs have been used for semantic mapping, including:

Venn diagrams, intersecting circles that allow the classification of words according to concepts;

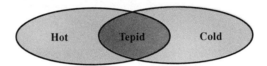

hierarchial arrays, with "branching tree" formats showing the relationships among words;

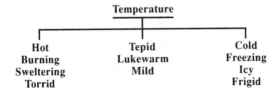

linear arrays, which allow pupils to show degrees of relationships among words and ideas.

Chilly ⟶ Cool ⟶ Frosty ⟶ Icy ⟶ Frigid

Whichever form is used, semantic maps provide for integration in vocabulary instruction in that they present new words in relationship with familiar concepts and not as isolated entities. The emphasis is on concept development as well as vocabulary development. The technique has proved very effective in promoting vocabulary growth (Johnson and Pearson, 1984).

Analogies also use the principle of integration in vocabulary study. Analogies focus not only on words but also on the mental operations that allow pupils to see conceptual relationships between words—for example, *shower:hurricane* ∷ *fire:con-flagration.* Pupils can create their own analogies for new vocabulary items. Analogies require higher-level thinking and help pupils develop and extend word meanings. They are also a means used to measure language and cognitive functioning.

5.3 Putting Ideas to Work

Semantic Maps

A SEMANTIC map can be used in developing vocabulary related to a single trade book or with several trade books centered on a theme or concept. For example:

A. As a way of introducing Miska Miles's *Annie and the Old One,* the touching story of a young Navajo girl whose efforts to forestall her grandmother's death lead to her understanding about the cycle of life, the following semantic map can be constructed:

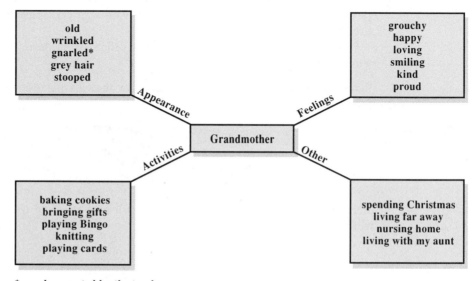

old
wrinkled
gnarled*
grey hair
stooped

grouchy
happy
loving
smiling
kind
proud

Appearance

Feelings

Grandmother

Activities

Other

baking cookies
bringing gifts
playing Bingo
knitting
playing cards

spending Christmas
living far away
nursing home
living with my aunt

* word suggested by the teacher

Semantic maps, analogies, and other activities provide integration by using pupils' prior knowledge, linking the meaning of new words to the meaning of words that pupils already know. These activities can be carried over into the second characteristic of word study in the classroom, repetition.

Repetition   A second quality of effective vocabulary instruction is repetition. Encountering a word once or twice will not guarantee that the word will become part of the pupil's mental "ownership dictionary." The pupil needs to use the word a number of times in order to "own" it.

Although vocabulary is thought of as a single entity, pupils actually have four vocabularies corresponding to the four major areas of language arts: listening, the auditory receptive function; speaking, the auditory expressive function; reading, the visual receptive function; and writing, the visual expressive function. In literature-based programs, pupils have opportunities all day long through various language activities in all these language modes. When pupils hear new words as they listen to stories or participate in dialogue as part of literature study groups, as they are encouraged to use new words in talking about books they have read, when they see these

This type of activity is integrated and multi-purposed. While introducing new words, it also activates pupils' background and motivation before reading. It is diagnostic in that the teacher can anticipate from pupil responses problems that some children might encounter in comprehending the story. It also provides experience in creative thinking (brainstorming) as well as a format for follow-up activity.

B. As pupils are reading books related to a common theme or idea—for example, Marjorie Weinman Sharmat's *Mitchell Is Moving,* Barbara Cooney's *Miss Rumphius,* and Wendy Kesselman's *Emma,* all of which deal in different ways about people being lonely—the teacher can design a semantic map such as:

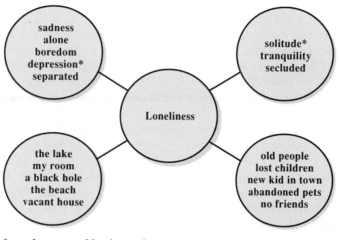

* **words suggested by the teacher**

Similar semantic maps can be constructed around other themes in children's books, themes such as courage, belonging, friendship, success, and the like.

words in print and use them in their own writing, pupils will quickly claim ownership. Here is where it becomes important for teachers to serve as models in using new words, to create "word alerts," to call attention to interesting uses of words in stories that are read aloud, and to use new words repeatedly in classroom activities. Repetition of new words in a variety of situations extends vocabulary through meaningful use and reinforcement.

There is no end to possibilities for planning classroom activities designed to increase pupils' vocabulary knowledge and use in a literature-based classroom. For example:

Synonym and antonym searches provide occasions for repeated encounters with words. Pupils can learn about synonyms very early in their school lives. After reading Margery Williams's classic *The Velveteen Rabbit* to the class, the teacher might ask how the rabbit felt when the boy abandoned him and the rabbit was condemned to be burned. The initial typical reaction "sad" can be expanded to other words that describe the rabbit's feelings: *unhappy, miserable, melancholic, woeful, heartbroken,* and the like. (In planning this activity ahead of time, the teacher might choose one of these words as the class Word for the Day or develop a semantic web based on the concept.)

5.4 Putting Ideas to Work

Word for the Day

A FOCUS and daily starting point for word study can be a class "Word for the Day." The daily word can be a new and interesting word that pupils have encountered in trade books or other reading material, such as *obstreperous (Please don't be obstreperous when the teacher leaves the classroom.)* or a key word that the teacher suggests from a content area. Pupils can quickly take responsibility for suggesting words (see 3.2, p. 65).

The Word for the Day can be written on a card and placed in its special location in the classroom. (A year's worth of multicolored word cards makes a much more interesting display than the traditional alphabet cards tacked above the chalkboard in most classrooms.) The word becomes the subject of day-long attention as pupils use it as often as they can. It also becomes a focus for word study: Where did the word come from? What other meanings does it have? What other words are related to it? Using and reusing the daily word in as many contexts as possible makes the word familiar to pupils.

Synonym searches lead naturally to antonym searches. The title of Judith Viorst's *Alexander and the Terrible, Horrible, No Good, Very Bad Day* suggests an extension of words in the title, as well as a list of "happy words" to make a title like *Alexander and the Wonderful, Terrific, Marvelous, Stupendous, Very Good Day*. (And this title might suggest ideas for a story that pupils could write about their own experiences.) Working with synonyms and antonyms obviously suggests the use of a thesaurus, a reference book containing exhaustive lists of such words. Some of the thesauri available for use in the elementary grades are: *The Clear and Simple Thesaurus Dictionary,* Harriet Wittels and Jon Greisman, eds. Putman Publishing Group, 1971 (for grades 2–7); *The Doubleday Children's Thesaurus,* Pete Stevenson. Doubleday, 1987 (for grades 3–8); and *In Other Words: A Beginning Thesaurus,* Andrew Schiller and William Jenkins. Scott Foresman, 1987 (for grades 3–4).

The use of books like these exposes pupils to a valuable language-learning and vocabulary-building tool. It starts pupils on the road to finding (in the words of Mark Twain) *just the right word* instead of *almost the right word.*

Semantic study is an important part of word work as part of literature-based instruction. Semantics is the formal study of word meaning. Semantics deals with the denotative meanings (the literal, direct, explicit dictionary definition), as well as the connotative meanings (the implied, suggested, associated meanings) of words. Some words have positive associations for children: *peppermint;* others have less positive associations: *homework.* Studying these associated meanings in language is what semantics is all about. Semantics can be part of working with synonyms. As lower-grade pupils talk about books like *Too Short Fred,* Susan Meddaugh's story of the cat who is a hero despite his diminutive stature, or upper-grade pupils discuss *Blubber,* Judy Blume's story of a girl who is overweight, words and their associated meanings can be a focus of discussion. For example, *diminutive, dwarf, runt,* and *petite* are words that can be used in lieu of *short; obese, rotund, corpulent,* and *stout* are synonyms for *fat.* Yet all have different connotations or associated meanings.

Word Alerts provide for repetition in vocabulary development. Word study and vocabulary development that are part of literature-based programs generate

5.5 Putting Ideas to Work

Nothing Need Ever Be Boring Again!

AN OVERUSED word among pupils at all levels is the word *boring.* With the help of a thesaurus, it is not hard to find alternatives to this overworked term: *vapid, tedious, uninteresting, banal, wearisome, dull,* and the like. With practice, pupils will expunge the "b-word" and use alternatives:

"Mr. Savage, this is the most vapid book I've ever read."

"This exercise is tedious. Do we have to do it?"

Vapid? Perhaps. *Tedious*? Maybe. But *Boring*? Never!

---

constant opportunities to make pupils aware of the richness of their language through literature. No opportunity need be wasted for a productive encounter with words. For example:

Etymology, the study of the origins and development of words, is a fruitful source for exploring word meanings. Pupils often get turned on to word study as they try to answer the question, "Where did this word come from?"

Curiosity about how words enter the language can also stimulate awareness and understanding. Most of our words have been borrowed, of course; there is not a language spoken on the face of the earth that has not made a contribution to our word stock. We also build our own new words, adding affixes to familiar stems (*deplane, empower*) or by combining meaning units in different ways (*astronaut, aquanaut*). We sometimes drop meaning units from the original form of words: from *creation* to *create* and from *denotation* to *denote* (which, when it was coined, was called "an American barbarism"). We shorten words in other ways: *examination* becomes *exam; dormitory* becomes *dorm.* We do the same things with acronyms: a child with learning disabilities is "an *LD* kid." We blend elements to create new words: *motel* from *motor* and *hotel; chortle* from *chuckle* and *snort.* We use proper names to represent ordinary concepts: *sandwich* and *pasteurize.* In short, our language is a vibrant, dynamic entity that adapts its lexicon to the needs of its users.

Word games bring out the fun of language: for example: "The Minister's Cat," in which pupils in turn think of adjectives in alphabetical order (The minister's cat is an *affable* cat, . . . *brave* cat, etc.); "Hinky Pinky," in which pairs of rhyming words are given to riddles (What's a smooth young hen? *a slick chick* . . . tale told in a beer factory? *brewery story*); "Swifties," in which an action word or an adverb is chosen for the context of a sentence (There goes Moby Dick!" Tom *wailed.* . . . "I'm losing my hair," the man *bawled.*); "Alliteration Game," in which pupils supply alliterative adjectives (*aggravating* alligators, *bashful* baboons); "Meaning Shifts," with questions like, "If lawyers are *disbarred,* can electricians be *delighted*? . . . cowboys *deranged*? . . . dry cleaners *depressed?*). Games like these, which are also frequently played outside of school, too, can be built from fruitful encounters with literature in the classroom.

In sum, occasions for repeated word use that will help pupils expand their awareness and knowledge of vocabulary exist in the classroom all day long. Word knowledge is built through planned and spontaneous opportunities to study and use words in meaningful situations.

5.6
FOR YOUR INFORMATION
Books about Words

A CLASSROOM with a constant attention to word study will contain books about words, such as:

Fun with Words by Maxwell Nuinberg with information about the origin and history of words.

The Weighty Word Book by Paul M. Levitt, Douglas Burger, and Elissa Gurlnick with stories of words from *abasement* to *zealot.*

Many Luscious Lollipops by Ruth Keller, one of a brilliantly illustrated series of word books with a grammatical focus as well.

A Little Pigeon Toad, A Chocolate Moose for Dinner, The King Who Rained, and other books by Fred Gwynne, with delightful plays on words.

These are only a few of the hundreds of interesting trade books that will both spark and satisfy pupils' interest in learning about words.

Meaningful use   A third characteristic of effective vocabulary instruction, one that is closely related to repetition, is meaningful use. The "Look up the dictionary meaning of words on this list and write a sentence using each word" approach to vocabulary development is not especially effective and should not be relied on as an instructional technique. Words have meanings, and their meanings are learned as they are used in meaningful contexts.

Vocabulary development is rooted in a base of meaning. Experience with words is at the heart of any language arts program, since words are essential to any language activity—expressive or receptive, oral or written. Letter writing to a favorite author; preparing a travel brochure based on France Lessac's *My Little Island*; writing an advertisement for Betsy Byars's *The Not-Just-Anybody Family,* the story of an unusual family; recreating a ghost story using Mary Downing's *The Doll in the Garden* as a model; persuading parents or teachers for special considerations, as in Judith Viorst's *Earrings,* the story about a girl who wants her ears pierced—all provide occasions for reinforcing words in meaningful contexts. Looking for opportunities to explore words and their meanings in as many ways as possible ensures that vocabulary development will be a constant focus in the literature-based classroom.

Two other elements are essential to a full and rich vocabulary development component of a reading instructional program: active involvement by the teacher and wide reading by the pupils.

Teacher involvement is a key ingredient of a rich diet of vocabulary development in the classroom. The teacher's curiosity and excitement about the world of words will be contagious. Teachers need to make words that pupils are learning part of their own language use, while they include as rich a vocabulary as possible without losing the pupils. "A significant factor for helping students develop and extend their vocabularies seems to be the excitement teachers generate about words. When teachers demonstrate enthusiasm for words and transfer this excitement to students, all instructional activities seem to be equally effective" (Hittleman, 1988; p. 166). As in other aspects of reading instruction, teacher modeling is essential to help pupils become independent word learners.

Wide reading is the idea behind literature-based instruction, one of the major reasons why trade books have become so prominent in classroom literacy programs.

Wide reading—wherever that reading is enjoyed—is a key to literacy growth.

Reading itself is a major means of acquiring word knowledge. The relationship between reading success and word meaning is a reciprocal one. Knowledge of word meaning contributes greatly to reading ability. At the same time, wide reading contributes significantly to vocabulary acquisition. The amount of free reading that pupils do has been shown as the best predictor of vocabulary growth in the elementary grades (Fielding, Wilson, and Anderson, 1986). Word knowledge may be the effect of reading success at the same time it is the cause of reading success. "Given the number of words to be learned and the number of encounters it takes to learn them thoroughly, reading is necessarily the major avenue of large-scale vocabulary growth" (Nagy, 1988; p. 31). The road that leads to reading achievement is paved with words that pupils know.

Reading competency is rooted in understanding the meaning of words in print, but in order to arrive at the meaning of words in print, pupils must be able to identify what the words are. For pupils learning to read, strategies for word recognition and word analysis are integrated into literature-based reading instruction.

Word Recognition

Word recognition is the identification of the form, pronunciation, and appropriate meaning of words in print. It involves an awareness of what the word is and what it means in the context in which it is used. As they are learning to read, pupils learn to recognize words by sight and through context.

Sight Words

Instruction in word recognition focuses on sight words, words that pupils immediately recognize as entire units on visual contact. It stands to reason that the more words pupils can recognize instantly as they read, the more smooth and efficient their reading will be. The goal of instruction in word recognition is to help pupils recognize printed words as quickly and as easily as possible. If the process of identifying words is unreasonably difficult and time consuming, the impact on enjoyment and understanding is negative.

Word recognition is a factor that separates good readers from poor readers. Some wonder if the relationship is "a chicken and egg" situation. In other words, do people read well as a result of good word recognition skills or does general reading ability make people good at recognizing words? Whatever the nature of the relationship, word recognition is related to reading competency. The initial processing of a word involves recognition of its visual form, and word recognition provides a basis for reading comprehension.

Selecting Vocabulary   Selecting vocabulary to teach as sight words is an early decision in the instructional process. Traditionally, commercial programs typically selected these words and provided suggestions on how to teach them. Stories were often written with the specific purpose of teaching a sight word through repeated use (resulting in the stereotypical *Run, Dick, run. Run, run, run*). More authentic reading material requires that teachers decide which words should be taught for instant recognition.

Meaning becomes an important criterion in the selection process. "Intensive instruction is most worthwhile when words to be covered are important, in either of two senses: important to the understanding of the selection or important because of their general utility in the language" (Nagy, 1988; p. 33). Words that are crucial to understanding text should be known before the pupil is expected to read that particular text.

Word frequency is another criterion for selecting words to be taught by sight. Lists of such frequently used words have been compiled. One of the earliest and still most well-known lists is the Dolch Basic Sight Vocabulary List (1939) which contains 220 of the words most frequently used in beginning basal readers. A number of other sight-words lists has been compiled, with the same idea in mind. For literature-based instruction, Durr (1973) and Eeds (1985) have compiled lists of high-frequency words used in trade books for children. The former list was compiled from books generally read in the upper primary and intermediate grades. The Eeds list was compiled from K–3 children's books.

Many of the words contained on sight-word lists are what structural linguists have called "function words." Syntactically, words are designated as *form* words and *function* words. Form words correspond roughly to the four "major" parts of speech: nouns, verbs, adjectives, and adverbs. Function words are all the other word classes: prepositions, conjunctions, auxiliary verbs, pronouns, and the like. Form words convey most of the meaning in language; function words have no precise lexical referents but they indicate the relationship among form words. Form and function words have been compared to a brick wall. Form words are like bricks, providing the form and substance of the wall; function words are like mortar, "cementing" the unit together as a whole entity.

What do form and function words have to do with word recognition? In the total lexicon of English, there are relatively few function words, only about 150 or so; *however*, these words constitute 30–50 percent of running words in text. In Pamela

5.7

FOR YOUR INFORMATION

Bookwords: High-Frequency Words in Storybooks for Beginning Readers

Bookwords: Final core 227 word list based on 400 storybooks for beginning readers

the	1334	good	90	think	47	next	28
and	985	this	90	new	46	only	28
a	831	don't	89	know	46	• am	27
I	757	little	89	help	46	began	27
to	746	if	87	grand	46	head	27
said	688	just	87	boy	46	keep	27
you	638	• baby	86	take	45	• teacher	27
he	488	way	85	eat	44	• sure	27
it	345	there	83	• body	43	• says	27
in	311	every	83	school	43	• ride	27
was	294	went	82	house	42	• pet	27
she	250	father	80	morning	42	• hurry	26
for	235	had	79	• yes	41	hand	26
that	232	see	79	after	41	hard	26
is	230	dog	78	never	41	• push	26
his	226	home	77	or	40	our	26
but	224	down	76	• self	40	their	26
they	218	got	73	try	40	• watch	26
my	214	would	73	has	38	• because	25
of	204	time	71	• always	38	door	25
on	192	• love	70	over	38	us	25
me	187	walk	70	again	37	• should	25
all	179	• came	69	side	37	• room	25
be	176	were	68	• thank	37	• pull	25
go	171	ask	67	why	37	• great	24
can	162	back	67	who	36	gave	24
with	158	now	66	saw	36	• does	24
one	157	friend	65	• mom	35	• car	24
her	156	cry	64	• kid	35	• ball	24
what	152	oh	64	give	35	• sat	24
we	151	Mr.	63	around	34	• stay	24
him	144	• bed	63	by	34	• each	23
no	143	an	62	Mrs.	34	• ever	23
so	141	very	62	off	33	• until	23
out	140	where	60	• sister	33	• shout	23
up	137	play	59	find	32	• mama	22
are	133	let	59	• fun	32	• use	22
will	127	long	58	more	32	turn	22
look	126	here	58	while	32	thought	22
some	123	how	57	tell	32	• papa	22
day	123	make	57	• sleep	32	• lot	21
at	122	big	56	made	131	• blue	21

have	121	from	55	first	31	• bath	21
your	121	put	55	say	31	• mean	21
mother	119	• read	55	took	31	• sit	21
come	118	them	55	• dad	30	• together	21
not	115	as	54	found	30	• best	20
like	112	• Miss	53	• lady	30	• brother	20
then	108	any	52	soon	30	• feel	20
get	103	right	52	ran	30	• floor	20
when	101	• nice	50	• dear	29	wait	20
thing	100	other	50	man	29	• tomorrow	20
do	99	well	48	• better	29	• surprise	20
too	91	old	48	• through	29	• shop	20
want	91	• night	48	stop	29	run	20
did	91	may	48	still	29	• own	20
could	90	about	47	• fast	28		

• Indicates words *not* on Durr list

List of bookwords from Maryann Eeds, ''Bookwords: Using a Beginning Word List for High Frequency Words from Children's Literature, K–3'' in *The Reading Teacher,* January 1985. Copyright © 1985 International Reading Association, Newark, DE. Reprinted with permission of Maryann Eeds and the International Reading Association.

Since this list was first published, Eeds has done extensive research in holistic classrooms where children are acquiring written language. She now believes that high-frequency words will be acquired naturally as a teacher demonstrates their use as part of the daily life of the classroom (recording plans, learning, etc.) and as the children, steeped in literature, use them in their daily writing.

Allen's genuinely funny *Who Sank the Boat?,* the opening sentence—*Beside the sea, on Mr. Peffer's place, there lived a cow, a donkey, a sheep, a pig, and a tiny little mouse.*—contains a total of 22 words, ten (or 45 percent) of which are function words. The pupil who can recognize function words instantly will be well on the way to smooth and meaningful reading.

Pupils also learn function words as they use these words in their own writing. From simple captions to cohesive stories, function words are used so frequently that pupils quickly come to realize the importance of being able to recognize and spell the words.

In the final analysis, selecting words to be taught as sight words must relate to meaning and function. The reason for learning to recognize words instantaneously by sight is to enable pupils to quickly and easily arrive at meaning in what they read. The words that most directly serve this purpose are the ones that should become part of pupils' sight vocabularies.

Deciding How to Teach   Traditionally, teachers provided for repetition of sight words with flash cards. Pupils practiced reading words that were ''flashed'' for the purpose of providing practice in rapid and accurate recognition. (Some modern programs flash the words on computer screens.) Although isolated practice with words on cards may sometimes be appropriate—as when label words are attached to objects in kindergarten classrooms both to develop an awareness of meaning–print relationships and to help pupils recognize common words in print—sight words are best taught in

Personal Words

ONE WAY of building sight vocabulary is to adopt Sylvia Ashton-Warner's idea of "organic words" (1963) and have pupils choose their own special vocabulary to be learned as sight words. On the very first day of school, the teacher asks pupils, "What word would you really like today?" The words are personal choices, taken from each pupil's own experience, words that (for whatever reason) are of immense importance to the child: *watermelon, skeleton, birthday.*

The pupil sits next to the teacher and observes the teacher writing the word on a card. The pupil then has to "do something" with the word—illustrate it, read it to a classmate, use it in a story. The words usually become sight words fairly quickly because they are the child's own words and are loaded with personal meaning and importance.

Over time, the pupil builds up a collection of personal sight-word cards, which are gathered on a ring and hung at the pupil's desk. These personal word cards find multiple uses all year long: in sentence and story writing, in word analysis practice ("See how many words in your stack have a *ch* sound" or "Do you have a compound word on your word card ring?"), in vocabulary enrichment activities ("Can you find a synonym for your word?"), and the like.

---

the context of connected text. In other words, instead of introducing sight words isolated in lists or on flash cards, new sight words should be taught as part of a semantic web or presented within the context of a larger phrase or sentence (see 5.9). Presenting words within the context of stories, poems, and informational trade books preserves the important meaning element, while helping pupils build a store of words that they can recognize instantly by sight.

Since function words are used so frequently, they may need to be taught as sight words; yet because they have no concrete meaning, they are difficult to define in isolation. These words need to be learned in the context of larger segments of text. For example, as young children share the popular finger rhyme "Eensy, Weensy Spider," and as they learn to associate printed words with the familiar spoken words of the poem, phrase cards can be used with such predictable expressions as *up the water spout, Down came the rain,* and *Out came the sun.* As children say the poem in unison, the cards can be used as the familiar phrases are spoken. The context for common function words such as *up, down,* and *out* is preserved as pupils learn to recognize these words in print.

Research supports the use of literature as a way to help pupils build a store of sight words. Bridge, Winograd, and Haley (1983) found that predictable books were especially effective for early word recognition. Moe (1989) suggests a plan for using trade books to help beginning readers increase their sight vocabularies. Noting that most of the words in early picture books are already part of the listening/speaking vocabulary of young children, Moe suggests the extensive use of trade books in early reading instruction. With a very limited sight vocabulary, pupils can independently read beginning trade books such as Nancy Tafuri's *Have You Seen My Duckling?,* Pat Hutchins' *Rosie's Walk,* or Linda Bancheck's *Snake In, Snake Out,* all of which contain a very limited number of words. By reading simple books like these, beginning readers are exposed repeatedly to words, while engaging in meaningful reading of connected text.

Teaching Sight Words

EDS (1985), who compiled the list of 227 high-frequency words from children's trade books, recommends that these words not be presented in isolation, since "it is hard to envision a less meaningful situation than subjecting children to flashcard drill or to lists of words to be memorized" (p. 421). Instead, she suggests an integrated technique for teaching the words on her list:

1. Using a Big Book or projected page, begin by focusing on words that are most irregular and most frequent, using a masking technique.

2. Cover the target word and let the children predict from the context what word is missing.

3. Uncover the masked word to show the word that goes with the one they identified.

Pupils match isolated words back into a standing context.

Word lists can be useful as an inventory of words that appear frequently in books that children read, but the payoff occurs when pupils recognize and use these words in their own reading and writing. Words have their meaning and worth as they are used in the context of authentic language. Chart poetry, language experience stories, songs and chants that are posted around the classroom are all excellent sources for helping pupils build sight vocabulary quickly and easily, with meaning always intact.

Practice in word recognition needs to be saturated with meaning. It makes little sense for a pupil to recognize a word without knowing the meaning of that word in the context in which it is used.

Context Clues

Using context clues is another strategy that mature readers rely on in interacting with print, and learning to use context clues is an important part of learning to read. Context clues consist of information presented in a passage and used to recognize the meaning (and occasionally the pronunciation) of a word.

Syntactic and Semantic Clues   In using context clues, pupils use both the syntactic and semantic components of their knowledge of language. Syntactic context clues provide information about what grammatical function a word has in a sentence. For example, in the sentence *In the old Soviet Union, Lenin's face used to be **ubiquitous,*** it is not difficult to recognize the final word as an adjective. The way it is used fits a familiar pattern and provides a syntactic clue as to the function of the word.

Syntactic clues provide only limited information about unknown words. These clues can be useful in the interpretation of potentially ambiguous sentences. For example, in the sentence *When Susan goes to the beach, she runs through the sand and **waves,*** the interpretation of *waves* as a noun or a verb will depend on syntactic context. But the full use of contextual analysis demands the use of semantic clues.

Semantic context clues provide information about the meaning of words. In the expanded sentence *In the old Soviet Union, Lenin's face used to be **ubiquitous**; it gazed from statues in public places, looked down from banners on the sides of buildings, was*

Context Clues Exercise

TO SEE how context works, try the following exercise. Jot a synonym or a brief definition for each of the following five words:

1. cynosure _____

2. polysemous _____

3. effulgent _____

4. obsequious _____

5. tyro _____

Now read the following sentences and see if you can get a better idea of the meaning of these words:

1. Jimmy was a shy and retiring person who didn't want to be noticed; his brother, on the other hand, wanted to be the *cynosure* of the group.

2. *Polysemous* words have more than one meaning.

3. Susan's *effulgent* smile and manner are a sharp contrast to her sister's dour personality.

4. The *obsequious* waiter bowed to the host and fawned on the guest as he served the meal.

5. You could tell by the way Joe sat behind the wheel for the first time and looked nervously at the dashboard that he was a *tyro* at driving.

Although these sentences do not provide full and complete definitions, the context of the language in each sentence gives clues to the meaning of the italicized words.

Answers: 1. *cynosure*—center of attention; 2. *polysemous*—diversity of meaning; 3. *effulgent*—radiant or shining; 4. *obsequious*—submissive or servile; 5. *tyro*—beginner.

---

found on stamps and medals, and appeared in pictures in every classroom, the meaning of *ubiquitous* is more clearly defined from the added information. Although syntactic clues are helpful, semantic clues are far more useful in figuring out unknown words in print.

Among the different types of context clues that can be found in text are:

definitions, in which a synonym or description for a potentially difficult word is provided right in the text itself, often as an appositive expression: *The rider gripped the* **pommel,** *the rounded hump on the front of the saddle, as the horse galloped out of control.*

comparison/contrast, in which an unknown word can be unlocked by comparing it with another key word: *My father is* **parsimonious,** *but he's not nearly as cheap as my uncle.*

summaries or examples, in which examples provide cues needed for identification: *They took all the* **paraphernalia** *they would need for a camping trip—a tent, sleeping bags, cooking utensils, and a first aid kit.*

experience, in which pupils' backgrounds and expectations suggest meanings for an unfamiliar word: *You can tell by the way she talks unkindly about her friends and tells their secrets that Kathy is a* **perfidious** *person.*

Using context involves forming a hypothesis or making an educated guess about the meaning of an unfamiliar word. The use of contextual analysis depends on semantic and syntactic information that authors provide in text. It also depends on qualities that the reader brings to print—a certain level of competency in decoding, grammatical knowledge, semantic awareness, experential background, and reasoning ability.

Although clues to the pronunciation and meaning of an unknown word may be presented in a single sentence, such neatly defined clues are not always easily found in trade books and other forms of narrative text. Pupils may need to search for meaning clues in other sentences in the surrounding passage. Pupils must get used to the idea of searching out clues they need, and cloze exercises have proved extremely useful for this practice.

Cloze Exercises   Cloze involves the systematic deletion of words from a text. Every nth (5th or 8th or 10th) word in a passage is deleted and the reader fills in the missing element. Originally designed as a measure of text readability and as a means of determining reader comprehension, cloze is an effective way to give pupils practice in contextual analysis because it forces pupils to "read beyond" the missing word and figure out what the word might be by using other information contained in the text. In initial encounters with cloze exercises in the classroom, pupils' responses should be discussed (not just checked) so that pupils get the idea of what is behind this word-identification strategy.

Pupils can be introduced to cloze in emergent literacy settings by deleting words in familiar text, as in:

To market, to _____ to buy a fat pig.

Home again, _____ again, jiggedy jig.

To market, to market to buy a _____ hog.

Home _____ , home again jiggedy jog.

As pupils become more proficient, longer cloze passages can be used to help pupils develop and practice the strategy of using context clues as a word recognition technique (see 5.10).

Cloze procedure can be modified by providing pupils with multiple choices for missing words or by deleting particular word classes—for example, adjectives. This type of "modified cloze" gives pupils clues in determining which words might fit.

In addition to cloze exercises, teacher modeling can be effective in demonstrating the use of context clues as a word recognition strategy as well. As teachers explain or "talk out" how they use context to determine the pronunciation and meaning of a new word they meet in their own reading, pupils gain insight into the process of using context clues to determine the meaning of unknown words.

Beyond being an effective word-recognition strategy for individual vocabulary items, using context plays a broader role in the process of learning to read. The figures cited earlier in this chapter on the rate of vocabulary growth—from an estimated 5,000 words to an estimated 50,000 in the school life of the pupil—can in no way be accounted for by direct teacher instruction. Research indicates that much of this vocabulary learning takes place through context (Nagy, Herman, and Anderson, 1985). Learning from context during reading is the major mode of vocabulary acquisition during the school years, and this accounts for the relationship between wide reading and vocabulary size. Learning from context while reading is a major factor in pupils' reading development.

5.11 Putting Ideas to Work

Using Cloze

THE FOLLOWING cloze exercise is based on the story *Sarah Plain and Tall,* Patricia MacLachlan's beautiful Newbery Award winner:

> Anna and Caleb lived with their father in a farmhouse on the prairie. Their mother had died (1) their father wrote a (2) to see if he (3) find a new wife. Sarah, (4) woman from Maine who (5) that she was plain (6) tall, answered his letter. (7) came to live with (8) family. Although she missed (9) brother in Maine, she (10) the children and their (11), so she decided to (12). Sarah was happy because the prairie reminded Sarah of the ocean back in Maine.

Answers: 1. and; 2. letter; 3. could; 4. a; 5. wrote; 6. and; 7. Sarah; 8. the; 9. her; 10. loved; 11. father; 12. stay.

In this passage, every fifth word was deleted. Pupils will probably need fewer deletions until they become more adept at using cloze techniques for practice in context clues.

Passages like this can be used not only to help pupils develop skill in using context clues; they can also be used in determining how appropriate a book is for a pupil's reading level.

Proficient readers rely heavily on context to determine the meaning of unfamiliar words in print. Helping pupils learn to use context clues is a way of helping them interact more effectively with print.

Word Analysis

In a literature-based program, pupils will encounter millions of running words in their experiences with books. For example, it has been estimated that an average middle grade child encounters about a million words in print each year (Nagy, Herman, and Anderson, 1985). The typical pupil will instantly recognize some of these words as sight words and will be able to determine what other words mean through context. Some words will be entirely unfamiliar, however, and the pupil will have to develop word analysis strategies in determining the pronunciation and meaning of these unfamiliar words.

Word analysis (or word attack) involves the identification of unknown words by their constituent parts, either by letter–sound relationships or by larger meaning-bearing units (roots, prefixes, and suffixes). Using letter-sound relationships is known as *phonetic analysis;* using larger morphemic elements is known as *structural analysis.* Both areas constitute major components in the reading instructional program in the elementary grades.

Phonetic Analysis

Phonics—the conscious, concentrated study of letter–sound relationships for the purpose of learning to read and spell—has long been an integral part of literacy instruction in American schools. Phonics is a means of *decoding* words, an early step in the ultimate goal of getting meaning from print.

The code or communication system of written language is the connection between printed symbols and their equivalent spoken sounds. You can pronounce a word that you have never seen—a nonsense word like *infractaneous*, for example—by "sounding it out"; that is, by using graphophonic information in attaching the appropriate sounds to the letters in the word. That is decoding; that is the process of applying phonics in reading.

The Great Debate   Phonics and its role in reading instruction is a hotly debated issue. And the controversy that surrounds phonics has been going on for centuries (Mathews, 1966). The debate centers on both theoretical and practical issues. One's view of the importance of phonics is often related to one's view of the reading process. Those who view reading as a "bottom-up" process see reading as building from parts (i.e., individual sounds and symbols in words) to the whole (i.e., larger meaning conveyed via print). Those who see reading primarily as a "top-down" process place less importance on explicit instruction in sound–symbol relationships. Skills-based advocates tend to favor a heavy emphasis on direct, systematic phonics instruction. Holistic advocates tend to place a different type of emphasis on sound–symbol relationships.

Those who favor phonics argue that English has an alphabetic writing system; that is, individual speech sounds are represented by individual written symbols. They argue that mastering this relationship is the key in learning how to read. Opponents argue that the sound–symbol relationships in English are so inconsistent and unreliable that it is impossible to rely on the alphabetic principle in learning to read. They hold that knowledge of phonics is a result, not a cause, of successful reading.

There is certainly no shortage of research and expert opinion to support arguments both pro and con. In books written for the general public, Rudolph Flesch's *Why Johnny Can't Read* (1955) blamed illiteracy on the absence of phonics in reading instruction, while Bruno Bettelhiem and Karen Zelan's *On Learning to Read* (1982) blamed poor reading performance on an overemphasis on phonics. Researchers like Jeanne Chall (1982) cite research evidence that strongly supports phonics, while researchers like Kenneth Goodman (1976) suggest that phonics may lead children away from meaning.

Materials used to help pupils master decoding skills are an issue as well. Critics point out that tightly controlled code-oriented sentences like "Can Dan fan the man?" pale in comparison to Mother Goose, Dr. Seuss, and quality literature written for young children. Phonics advocates argue that these code-based materials which focus on systematic letter–sound relationships are merely a means of opening up the world of great literature for young children.

And so it goes. Code-emphasis advocates argue on behalf of phonics and ask how anyone can read the bumper sticker I LOVE LAKE WOLOMOLOPOAG without sounding out the name of the lake. Opponents point to the idiosyncrasies of our spelling system and argue against learning to read by "huffing and puffing at letters, marking whether vowels are glided or unglided, deciding whether *b* or *d* goes at the beginning or ending of the tattered remnant of a mutilated word rendered meaningless in isolation" (Johnson and Louis, 1987; p. 3).

5.12

FOR YOUR INFORMATION

Point-Counterpoint on Phonics

Aunt Millie	*Uncle Max*
I'll tell you what's wrong with schools today. They don't teach enough about phonics.	Hogwash! Phonics is old fashioned and out of date. Besides, nobody taught me phonics and I can read.
How can you read without phonics? You *have* to sound out words you don't know.	Not really. There are often more exceptions than there are rules. Phonics can be misleading for a kid trying to learn to read.
Yes, but you have to use some phonics in reading new words, don't you?	I agree, but that doesn't mean that teachers should spend all their time teaching phonics. They should have children read more.
But phonics opens the door so that children *can* read more!	The kids will be so tired of books with sentences like ''Flick the tick off the chick with a thick stick, Nick'' that they will be turned off by the time they get to read anything interesting.
I read a book not long ago about how important phonics was in reading.	And I read one that said that phonics is not as important as everyone thought it was.
But look at cousin Alphie. He failed first grade, but once he got a teacher who taught him phonics, he quickly learned to read.	Yes, and what about cousin Rosie? The whole family thought she was stupid because she couldn't learn to read. Once they got her away from that phonics stuff, she really bloomed. No pun intended!
I think *you're* wrong.	I think *you're* wrong.

To get a better idea of some of the deep research-based issues in ''the great debate,'' and to get a sense of the intensity with which professionals carry on the debate, see the exchange of articles between Marie Carbo (1988, 1989) and Jeanne Chall (1989a, 1989b) in the highly respected professional journal *Phi Delta Kappan.*

As in many debates, the polemic that surrounds phonics often establishes false dichotomies. In practical terms, neither school of thought denies the need for phonics in learning to master an orthographic system based on the alphabetic principle. Phonics advocates see decoding as an important step along the road to getting meaning from print; those who favor literature-based instruction do not deny that knowledge of sound–symbol relationships is useful in learning to read new words. The debate is less a ''phonics or not'' question and more of a controversy that centers on the degree of emphasis that phonics deserves in a reading instructional program and how phonics should be taught.

Despite the controversy that continues to surround phonics in the process of teaching reading, the importance of graphophonic knowledge in the early stages of learning to read is supported by decades of research. Knowledge of phonics is vital not only in identifying unknown words in print, but to fluent reading and comprehension. In her comprehensive review of reading research, Adams (1990) emphasized the importance of phonics. Some statements based on a summary of this research (Stahl, Osborn, and Lehr, 1990):

> Explicit, systematic phonics is a singularly successful mode of teaching young or slow learners to read (p. 38).
>
> Knowledge of letters and phonemic awareness have been found to bear a strong and direct relationship to success and ease of reading acquisition (p. 54).
>
> Children's levels of phonemic awareness on entering school may be the single most powerful determanent of their success—or failure—in learning to read (p. 54).
>
> Activities requiring children to attend to the individual letters of words, their sequencing, and their phonological translations should be included in any beginning reading program (p. 73).
>
> Sounding out words is a way of teaching children what they need to know to comprehend text. The only reason for learning to read words is to understand text (p. 88).
>
> Good readers decode rapidly and automatically (p. 92).
>
> Phonics is of inescapable importance to both skillful reading and its acquisition (p. 117).[1]

But phonics instruction alone is not enough. The goal of phonics instruction is to help pupils acquire the ability to read connected text fluently and with understanding. Graphophonic awareness is not an end in itself but a means to a larger end.

Phonics in a Literature-Based Program   Phonics as an aid to word analysis is part of literature-based reading instruction. It is impossible to read without an awareness of the graphophonic cues of our writing system. In debunking the myths associated with whole language, Newman and Church (1990) assert that phonics *is* part of whole language programs, but not as something apart from authentic reading and writing experiences. Literature-based advocates "have no argument with the claim that children must . . . have an understanding of phonics. It is just that we disagree with much traditional practice in the manner of (its) acquisition" (Johnson and Louis, 1987; p. 13). The disagreement with traditional practice comes in two areas:

1. Literature-based instruction starts with text intended primarily to express larger language meaning rather than text designed primarily to illustrate phonetic principles; and

2. Literature-based instruction goes from whole-to-part rather than part-to-whole.

In a literature-based program, the content of graphophonic information that pupils need to develop does not change. What changes is the way in which this knowledge is presented to pupils.

---

[1]Excerpted from Marilyn Jager Adams, "Beginning to Read: A Summary" prepared by S. A. Stahl, J. Osborn and F. Lehr, 1990. Reprinted by permission of the Center for the Study of Reading, University of Illinois at Urbana-Champaign.

5.13
FOR YOUR INFORMATION
The Language of Phonics

INCLUDED HERE are some of the concepts and some of the terminology you may encounter as part of phonics instruction in the classroom.

English has an *alphabetic writing system;* that is, individual speech sounds are represented by individual letters. The sounds are called *phonemes;* the letters are called *graphemes.*

Consonants and **vowels** are the two classes of sounds. American English has approximately *24 consonant phonemes,* with 21 letters to represent these sounds. The language has *20 vowel phonemes,* with only five letters to represent these sounds. The mismatch between letters and sounds leads to the graphophonic irregularity one finds in reading and spelling Engish words.

Vowel letters are *a, e, i, o, u,* sometimes *y* and sometimes *w. Y* is a vowel when it is the only letter in a syllable representing a vowel sound (as in the word *by*) or when it follows a vowel (as in *boy*). *W* is considered a vowel letter only when it follows another vowel (as in *cow*).

Vowels can be either "short" or "long." *Short vowel sounds* are represented in the words *pat, pet, pit, pot,* and *put.* In *long vowels,* the letter name can be heard as the word is pronounced: *rate, Pete, ride, robe,* and *rude.*

Double vowels occur in combination as digraphs and diphthongs. *Digraphs* consist of two vowel letters that represent a single sound: the *oa* in *boat* or the *ea* in *seat. Diphthongs* are letter combinations that represent a "blended" vowel sound: the *ou* in *mouse* or the *oi* in *noise.*

Consonant letters are all the letters besides *a, e, i, o* and *u.* Consonants occur in blends and digraphs as well. *Blends* are two or three consonant letters that have closely related but separate sounds: **broom, droop, stream.** *Digraphs* are two letters that represent a single phoneme: **ship, thin, chop.**

Silent letters are graphemes that have no phonetic correspondence: **knee, lamb, p**sychology.

Syllables are combinations of speech sounds within words: *syl.la.ble* or *com.bin.a.tion.* The nucleus of a syllable is a vowel. Syllables are *open* when they end with a vowel (as in *ho.tel* or *be.cause*) or closed when they end with a consonant sound (as in *ho.**tel*** or *jus.tice*).

Generalizations are statements that apply to sound–symbol relationships, such as "When two vowels go walking, the first one does the talking" or "Magic *e* makes the sound of previous vowel long." The term *generalization* rather than *rule* is used to convey the idea that these principles do not apply in all cases. In fact, some of these generalizations apply in fewer than 50 percent of English words (Clymer, 1963).

Connected, meaningful discourse is the starting point for instruction when literature is used as a vehicle for developing pupils' phonetic awareness. Instead of learning isolated sounds and practicing them with stacks of worksheets containing sentences like *Can a big cat tap a tan pan?,* pupils learn phonetic elements as they encounter these elements within the context of familiar stories, poems, songs, and other segments of text that have been written to inform or entertain, and as they learn to write in response to what they read. Freppon and Dahl (1991) suggest principles that guide phonics instruction in a literature-based context. Phonics instruction:

focuses on the needs of the learner rather than on a predetermined sequence of phonics concepts;

is learned in the context of reading and writing activities;

builds upon pupils' basic knowledge of written language;

is tied to communication goals and purposes and is integrated with other language activities;

involves teacher demonstration;

uses multiple information sources—books they read, stories they write, print around the room, each other, and the teacher.

The world of children's literature offers unlimited opportunities for helping pupils acquire the graphophonic knowledge that will enable them to decode print successfully. Learning letter names and sounds is an important part of emergent literacy and a focus in the plethora of ABC books that children enjoy in the early years (see pp. 106–108). Shared stories with Big Books allow pupils to learn about the basic units of print—that is, letters and words. Pupils become aware of the relationship between spoken language (which they know) and its written representation. Directed activities during shared stories help pupils develop concepts related to phonics: the relationship between letters and sounds, the ordered sequence of sounds and letters, the relationship between the length of spoken words and the length of their written equivalents, and the like. Writing down their dictated stories necessitates attention to sound–symbol relationships. This is where instruction in phonics begins.

Sound features provide much of the appeal of nursery rhymes. As children deal with familiar Mother Goose rhymes such as "Hickory, Dickory, Dock," they can experiment with creating new words by substituting initial consonants and blends, maintaining the rhyming element: *The mouse ran up the clock (rock, sock, block, crock, lock, etc.).* Or as they read in unison the noise that the Three Billygoats Gruff made in crossing the Troll's bridge (*trip, trap, trip, trap*), they can experiment with new sounds made by substituting vowels (*trep, trop*, or *treep, troop*).

Teachers can keep an eye out for repeated phonetic elements that might be taught with a particular piece of print; for example, in the nursery rhyme "Mary Had A Little Lamb," instruction can focus on initial sound–symbol relationships in "l-words" (*little, lamb, laugh*, and *love*) or in "wh-words" (*white, where, which*, and *why*). In integrating phonics instruction into early exposure to literature, teachers need to remember that the primary purpose is meaning and enjoyment; phonics is a byproduct in the instructional process with pieces of literature like these.

The predictable graphophonic patterns found in the language of many stories for young children make these stories ideal vehicles for instruction in sound–symbol principles. The patterned, predictable lines of Barbara Emberley's *Drummer Hoff* in which people's names rhyme strongly with their activities; the more subtle rhymes of Ludwig Bemelmans' *Madeline* and subsequent stories; the unforgettable rhyming names (Foxy Loxy, Henny Penny, etc.) in Stephen Kellogg's popular "updated" version of *Chicken Little;* Deborah Guarin's rhyming story *Is Your Mama a Llama?* in which a baby llama makes inquiries of different animals; the lines of Rosemary Wells's warm and touching *Noisy Nora*—these and hundreds of other stories provide language that can be used to help pupils develop the phonetic awareness they will need to decode words in print.

Whole-to-part instruction is another feature of teaching phonics in a literature-based approach to reading. Synthetic approaches to phonics (which are sometimes called "explicit" or "direct" phonics instruction) focus on learning sound–symbol relationships and synthesizing or blending these elements in sounding out words. By contrast, analytic approaches (which are sometimes called "implicit" or "indirect" methods) start with larger units of language. A literature-based approach begins with

5.14
FOR YOUR INFORMATION
Trade Books that Repeat Phonics Elements

T RACHTENBERG (1990) suggests the following list of books that repeat common phonic elements in their text.

Short *a*

Flack, Marjorie. *Angus and the Cat.* Doubleday. 1931.

Griffith, Helen. *Alex and the Cat.* Greenwillow, 1982.

Kent, Jack. *The Fat Cat.* Scholastic, 1971

Most, Bernard. *There's an Ant in Anthony.* William Morrow, 1980.

Nodset, Joan. *Who Took the Farmer's Hat?* Harper and Row, 1963.

Robins, Joan. *Addie Meets Max.* Harper & Row, 1985.

Schmidt, Karen. *The Gingerbread Man.* Scholastic, 1985.

Seuss, Dr. *The Cat in the Hat.* Random House, 1957.

Long *a*

Aardema, Verna. *Bringing the Rain to Kapiti Plain.* Dial, 1981.

Bang, Molly. *The Paper Crane.* Greenwillow, 1985.

Blume, Judy. *The Pain and the Great One.* Bradbury, 1974

Byars, Betsy. *The Lace Snail.* Viking, 1975.

Henkes, Kevin. *Sheila Rae, the Brave.* Greenwillow, 1987.

Hines, Anna G. *Taste the Raindrops.* Greenwillow, 1983.

Short and long *a*

Aliki, *Jack and Jake.* Greenwillow, 1986.

Slobodkina, Esphyr. *Caps for Sale.* Addison-Wesley, 1940.

Short *e*

Ets, Marie Hall. *Elephant in a Well.* Viking, 1972.

Galdone, Paul. *The Little Red Hen.* Scholastic, 1973.

Ness, Evaline. *Yeck Eck.* E. P. Dutton, 1974.

Shecter, Ben. *Hester the Jester.* Harper & Row, 1977.

Thayer, Jane. *I Don't Believe in Elves.* William Morrow, 1975.

Wing, Henry Ritchet. *Ten Pennies for Candy.* Holt, Rinehart & Winston, 1963.

Long *e*

Galdone, Paul. *Little Bo-Peep.* Clarion/Ticknor & Fields, 1986.

Keller, Holly. *Ten Sleepy Sheep.* Greenwillow, 1983.

Martin, Bill. *Brown Bear, Brown Bear, What Do You See?* Henry Holt, 1967.

Oppenheim, Joanne. *Have You Seen Trees?* Young Scott Books, 1967.

Soule, Jean C. *Never Tease a Weasel.* Parents' Magazine Press, 1964.

Thomas, Patricia. *"Stand Back," said the Elephant, "I'm Going to Sneeze!"* Lothrop, Lee & Shepard, 1971.

Short *i*

Browne, Anthony. *Willy the Wimp.* Alfred A. Knopf, 1984.

Ets, Marie Hall. *Gilberto and the Wind.* Viking, 1966.

Hutchins, Pat. *Titch.* Macmillan, 1971.

Keats, Ezra Jack. *Whistle for Willie.* Viking, 1964.

Lewis, Thomas P. *Call for Mr. Sniff.* Harper & Row, 1981.

Lobel, Arnold. *Small Pig.* Harper & Row, 1969.

McPhail, David. *Fix-It.* E. P. Dutton, 1984.

Patrick, Gloria. *This Is . . .* Carolrhoda, 1970.

Robins, Joan. *My Brother, Will.* Greenwillow, 1986.

Long *i*

Berenstain, Stan and Jan. *The Bike Lesson.* Randon House, 1964.

Cameron, John. *If Mice Could Fly.* Atheneum, 1979.

Cole, Sheila. *When the Tide Is Low.* Lothrop, Lee & Shepard, 1985.

Gelman, Rita. *Why Can't I Fly?* Scholastic, 1976.

Hazen, Barbara S. *Tight Times.* Viking, 1979.

Short *o*

Benchley, Nathaniel. *Oscar Otter.* Harper & Row, 1966.

Dunrea, Olivier. *Mogwogs on the March!* Holiday House, 1985.

Emberley, Barbara. *Drummer Hoff,* Prentice-Hall, 1967.

McKissack, Patricia C. *Flossie & the Fox.* Dial, 1986.

Miller, Patricia, and Iran Seligman. *Big Frogs, Little Frogs.* Holt, Rinehart & Winston, 1963.

Rice, Eve. *"The Frog and the Ox"* from *Once in a Wood.* Greenwillow, 1979.

Seuss, Dr. *Fox in Socks.* Random House, 1965.

Long *o*

Cole, Brock. *The Giant's Toe.* Farrar, Straus, & Giroux, 1986.

Gerstein, Mordicai. *Roll Over!* Crown, 1984.

Johnston, Tony. *The Adventures of Mole and Troll.* G. P. Putnam's Sons, 1972.

Johnston, Tony. *Night Noises and Other Mole and Troll Stories.* G. P. Putnam's Sons, 1977.

Shulevitz, Uri. *One Monday Morning.* Charles Scribner's Sons, 1967.

Tresselt, Alvin. *White Snow, Bright Snow.* Lothrop, Lee & Shepard, 1947.

Short *u*

Carroll, Ruth. *Where's the Bunny?* Henry Z. Walck, 1950.

Cooney, Nancy E. *Donald Says Thumbs Down.* G. P. Putnam's Sons, 1987.

Friskey, Margaret. *Seven Little Ducks.* Children's Press, 1940.

Lorenz, Lee. *Big Gus and Little Gus.* Prentice-Hall, 1982.

Marshall, James. *The Cut-Ups.* Viking Kestrel, 1984.

Udry, Janice May. *Thump and Plunk.* Harper & Row, 1981.

Yashima, Taro. *Umbrella.* Viking Penguin, 1958.

Long *u*

Lobel, Anita. *The Troll Music.* Harper & Row, 1966.

Segal, Lore. *Tell Me a Trudy.* Farrar, Straus, & Giroux, 1977.

Slobodkin, Louis. *''Excuse Me—Certainly!''* Vanguard Press, 1959.

Although these trade books repeat phonics elements, they should not be used primarily for the sake of teaching phonics. To use *Caps for Sale,* for example, merely ''because it has a short *a* and a long *a* in the title'' is unconscionable.

List of trade books that repeat phonic elements is the appendix from Phyllis Trachtenberg, ''Using Children's Literature to Enhance Phonics Instruction,'' in *The Reading Teacher,* 43:63–654, (May 1990). Copyright © 1990 International Reading Association, Newark, DE. Reprinted with permission of Phyllis Trachtenburg and the International Reading Association.

whole words in whole stories as vehicles for helping pupils develop the graphophonic awareness that will enable them to decode unknown words.

Trachtenburg (1990) explains the whole–part–whole approach integrating phonics instruction with quality children's literature, starting with a piece of literature and zeroing in on a targed phonetic element.

1. *Whole:* Read, comprehend, and enjoy a whole, quality literature selection.

2. *Part:* Provide instruction in a high utility phonic element by drawing from or extending the preceeding literature selection.

3. *Whole:* Apply the new phonic skill when reading (and enjoying) another whole, high quality literature selection'' (p. 649).

This whole–part–whole approach makes sense, in that it connects phonics instruction with authentic reading experiences, which is the purpose of phonics instruction in the first place. The point and purpose of reading is understanding and appreciation. The point and purpose of phonics is helping readers achieve that understanding and appreciation. Teaching phonics through meaningful text makes sense in achieving both goals.

Phonics and Writing   Phonics is necessary in learning to read, and graphophonic knowledge is no less important in writing. Mastery of letter–sound relationships is essential to encoding written language. From a sound–symbol perspective, writing is the flip side of reading; that is, the reader goes from symbol to sound and the writer goes from sound to symbol. At the early stages of writing, pupils apply their knowledge of phoneme–grapheme relationships in their inventive spellings. Mastery of

5.15 Putting Ideas to Work

Guidelines for Exemplary Phonics Instruction

STAHL (1992) suggests the following nine principles of exemplary phonics instruction. Such instruction:

1. *Builds on a child's rich concepts about how print functions;* i.e. is grounded on children's knowledge of words and experiences with reading.

2. *Builds on a foundation of phonemic awareness,* pupils' awareness of sounds in spoken words.

3. *Is clear and direct,* avoiding ambiguity and focusing specifically on phonetic elements to be learned.

4. *Is integrated into a total reading program,* not taught as an isolated entity.

5. *Focuses on reading words, not learning rules,* since mature readers don't think about rules governing open and closed syllables when they are trying to figure out how to say an unfamiliar word they encounter in reading.

6. *May include onsets* (the part of the syllable before the vowel) *and rimes* (the part of the syllable after the vowel), using spelling patterns as a basis for decoding words.

7. *May include invented spelling practice,* since invented spelling necessitates an awareness of sound–symbol relationships.

8. *Develops independent word recognition strategies, focusing attention on the internal structure in words,* looking at larger spelling patterns as an aid to decoding.

9. *Develops automatic word recognition skills so that students can devote their attention to comprehension, not words,* which places phonics in its proper perspective.

From Steven A. Stahl, ''Saying the P Word: Nine Guidelines for Exemplary Phonics Instruction,'' in *The Reading Teacher* 45:618–625 (April 1992). Copyright © 1992 International Reading Association, Newark, DE. Reprinted with permission of Steven A. Stahl and the International Reading Association.

this relationship grows as pupils learn to express themselves more extensively in writing. Phonics remains part of the reading–writing connection that is addressed in Chapter 10.

Structural Analysis

When pupils can use their graphophonic knowledge to sound out an unfamiliar word they encounter in print, they can come a step closer to the meaning of the word through structural or morphemic analysis. Morphemes, which are basic and indivisible units of meaning, are the building blocks of words. The word *untidiness,* for example, is built from three morphemes:

the free morpheme *tidy,* meaning ''neat'' or ''clean'' (a free morpheme is a meaning unit that can stand alone);

the bound morpheme *un-,* meaning in this case ''not'' (a bound morpheme is a meaning unit that must be joined to another morpheme);

the bound morpheme *-ness* meaning ''a quality or state.''

Word study can be the focus of small-group or large-group instruction.

Just as phonetic analysis involves decoding unfamiliar words by their phonetic (sound) units, structural analysis involves trying to determine the meaning of words by their morphemic (meaning) units.

The major classes of morphemes in English are roots and affixes. The root (base or stem) carries the essence of word meaning. Prefixes—morphemes attached to the beginning of root words—and suffixes—morphemes attached to the end of root words—modify meaning by creating new words. Recognizing these morphemic elements enables readers to reach for the meaning of the words they read.

Children come to school with an intuitive knowledge of morphemic elements in words. Children will say, for example, "I runned and catched the ball," using the process of analogy to add the common tense-forming suffix -ed to the words they know. A good example of this type of overgeneralization is the kindergartner who complained to her teacher, "Jack *tookened* my crayons." The child began with the verb *take,* made past tense with *took,* generalized from *taken* to *tooken,* and added -ed just for good measure! This knowledge of structural elements is applied as pupils learn to read.

Learning about structural analysis typically begins with compound words, words consisting of two free morphemes, such as *afternoon* or *football.* The component parts of such words are easily identifiable. This is not to say, however, that the meaning of the word is derived from the sum of its two parts. The compound word *understand* does not mean "to stand under," nor is a *fireman* "a man made out of fire," as a *snowman* is "a man made out of snow." Once they can identify the word, pupils can probably grasp the meaning from their prior experience and language background. As compound words are encountered in the stories they read, the relationship between the two free morphemes can be the subject of some interesting discussions about word meaning.

Structural analysis also includes learning about contractions. A contraction is a verbal convention of combining separate elements into a single unit: *I am* to *I'm, cannot* to *can't, it is* to *it's.* In writing, the apostrophe is used to indicate the deletion of letters.

5.16 Putting Ideas to Work

Teaching Morphemic Elements through Literature

A S IN the case of phonics, using literature as the vehicle for helping pupils learn to use structural analysis as a word attack strategy starts with whole texts and not with lists of prefixes, suffixes and roots. Instruction becomes part of a broader base of reading.

Morphemic elements can be taught both directly and incidentally. For example, the compound words found on the first page of Jean Craighead George's *My Side of the Mountain* (snowstorm, knothole, deerskin) can be the focus of discussion for these elements. Or when pupils read about Andrew's turning "greenish" after he drinks the concoction to rid him of his freckles in Judy Blume's *Freckle Juice,* opportunities arise for talking about the meaning and function of the suffix *-ish* and pupils brainstorm for other words with this element.

Although literature provides real language for real instruction in this area, the focus remains on understanding and enjoyment. Reading to find all the compound words or all the "*-tion* words" in a story is an enormously annoying practice that detracts from the purposes of reading—understanding and enjoyment.

In learning to read, pupils certainly need to become aware of the written form of contractions. However, it is important to recognize that contractions rather than the expanded forms are more regular parts of children's language; that is, children use contractions like, "*I'm* three years old" "*That's* my cookie," and "*He's* my brother" relatively early in the language acquisition process. When contractions appear in trade books and other materials that pupils are reading, it makes sense to move from the known to the unknown, to use their spoken language as a way of helping them deal with contractions in print.

Since many words are put together or structured with morphemic units, the ability to break words down or analyze them by their structural elements is an important word-identification skill. Moreover, helping pupils learn to do this is a means of helping them expand their vocabularies and discover new word meanings on their own.

The Dictionary: "Look It Up"

Susan has just read and enjoyed E. L. Konigsburg's *From the Mixed-up Files of Mrs. Basil E. Frankweiler.* Now she wants to read another book by the same author. On the library shelf, she finds Konigsburg's *Father's Arcane Daughter.* As she reads the title, she gets stuck on the second word. It is not in her sight vocabulary. From syntactic context, she knows it is an adjective, but there are no semantic context clues to help her out. She uses phonics to sound out the word, but there are no structural units to help her figure out what *arcane* means. Susan has four choices.

1. She can ask a classmate, her teacher, or the librarian what *arcane* means.

2. She can put the book back on the shelf and forget about it.

3. She can ignore the fact that she does not completely understand the title and begin to read the book anyway.

4. She can look up *arcane* in the dictionary (to find that it means "mysterious" or "obscure").

The final choice—looking it up in the dictionary—is typically a last resort. As the ultimate word book of our language, the dictionary becomes an important and reliable aid in reading. Writers rely on the dictionary for spelling, and readers use it as a source of help in learning the pronunciation and meaning of unknown words. Like other aspects of a reading instructional program, the dictionary needs to be viewed—and used—in its proper perspective.

Traditionally, the dictionary was often used as a starting point for helping pupils expand vocabularies and develop word meanings. Pupils were given a list of new words with the assignment to look up the meaning of the words in the dictionary and write a sentence containing each word. Apart from the fact that such assignments are tedious and time-consuming, the technique has proved not to be especially effective in promoting word knowledge or vocabulary growth (Just and Carpenter, 1987; Nagy, 1988).

There are a number of problems in beginning with this definitional approach to vocabulary study. Elementary school dictionaries often do not include some of the more interesting and challenging words that pupils encounter in their reading. Dictionary definitions can be sparse, confusing, or inadequate for helping pupils discover meaning, and the definitions often contain new words that may be difficult for the pupil. Since words often have multiple meanings, the pupil requires an appropriate context to find the appropriate definition. And even when the appropriate definition is found, the dictionary tells what a word means without indicating how to use it. The story is told, for example, of the third grader who looked up the word *pregnant,* found that it meant "carrying a child," and wrote the sentence, *The fireman climbed up the ladder and came down pregnant.*

Where, then, does the dictionary fit in as part of literature-based reading instruction? The dictionary remains a valuable tool for pupils to consult after they have exhausted other strategies for attempting to determine what a word is and what it means. Because it contains a lot of interesting information about words, the dictionary becomes a fruitful reference source in exploring and extending word meanings, but it ought not to be overused as a functional vocabulary tool in the classroom.

As pupils use the dictionary to check word meanings, they acquire the competencies required for using the dictionary as a reference tool: awareness of alphabetical order, use of guide words, interpretation of symbols used to indicate pronunciation, and the ability to select the correct meaning. These elements can be developed through direct and incidental instruction as pupils use the dictionary as a functional word-finding tool in the classroom.

The dictionary requires not only knowledge and skill but also attitude. Pupils must know when it is important enough to disrupt the flow of reading to check the meaning of an unfamiliar word, and they must care enough to spend the time looking up a word. They must also know enough to recognize which words are crucial to understanding, since redundancy of text allows readers to tolerate a certain proportion of unknown words (perhaps as many as 15 percent of the words in a passage) without losing comprehension (Nagy, Herman, and Anderson, 1985; Nagy, 1988).

The dictionary might be considered the ultimate resource in vocabulary study. However, the dictionary approach needs to be enhanced and enriched, and other avenues need to be explored in helping pupils acquire new words and new meanings for old words as part of a classroom reading instructional program.

A Combination of Word-Identification Skills

These, then, are the five ways of identifying words in print:

1. immediate recognition by sight;
2. using language clues in the surrounding context to determine what the word is and what it means;
3. analyzing the word phonetically, using sound–symbol relationships;
4. analyzing the word structurally, using the morphemic building blocks of the word;
5. referring to the dictionary to find the pronunciation and meaning.

Each of these word-identification strategies is part of learning to read. None, however, is an end in itself and none can be used alone as the sole means of identifying words. All are used in flexible combination with other elements and are aimed at the broader purpose of reading for meaning. For example, young Jack sees the sentence *The circus featured an Indian chief.* He recognizes all the words up to the final one. A knowledge of phonics enables Jack to eliminate words like *squaw, village* or *teepee,* words that make sense within the context of the sentence. But if he follows the "two vowels go walking" rule of phonics, the word would be pronounced "*chiyf.*" So he must rely on a base of word knowledge and experience to come full circle in identifying the pronunciation and meaning of the word.

In conventional programs, each of these "word skills" has been taught as a separate, isolated entity. Word recognition began with lists of sight words. Phonics and structural analysis started with an inventory of elements to be learned. Context and dictionary use each involved its own set of practice materials. The practical effect was that pupils spent inordinate amounts of time alphabetizing interminable lists of words or marking the accent patterns of syllables in words that they already knew how to pronounce. Instruction began and ended with the specific component being taught. The skill became more important than the larger purpose of reading.

In literature-based programs, the act of reading itself is the starting point and ultimate aim of instruction in these aspects of word identification. The ability to sound out words, to recognize words instantly upon visual contact, to know the meaning of the prefix *un-,* to understand the correct accent pattern of a word in a dictionary—these and other word-recognition components may be included. They are important, however, only insofar as they contribute to the goal of helping children recognize words so that they can understand and enjoy what they read.

Summary and Conclusions

The world of words is important to reading, but words are merely vehicles for expressing larger meaning. Although meaning is the ultimate goal of reading, one can hardly arrive at meaning without dealing with words. To know words in print—to know what they are and what they mean—is the purpose for teaching vocabulary as part of literature-based reading and writing instruction.

Word knowledge is related to reading comprehension in a reciprocal way. On one hand, a large vocabulary contributes to reading success. At the same time, wide reading is one of the primary means of increasing word knowledge. That is why a concerted effort on vocabulary development and constant interaction with print of all kinds are two essential components of a classroom reading-instructional program. Making literature the centerpiece of the program addresses both dimensions.

Readers must not only know what words mean, but they must be able to identify words quickly and easily in print. Helping pupils learn to do this is a major focus of reading instruction. Efficient readers identify words by sight and by using clues found in the language in the surrounding text. When they encounter words that they do not know immediately, they sound out the words phonetically, analyze them structurally, and/or look up the troublesome words in the dictionary.

Pupils need to develop range and flexibility in applying these strategies as they read. It is unrealistic to memorize each of the 600,000-plus words in our lexicon, impossible to find context clues for each unfamiliar word, unthinkable to seek meaning by sounding out every new word encountered in print, impractical to rely on morphemic elements for all words, and unfeasible to look up every new word in the dictionary. No single strategy will suffice. All are needed in learning to read and all become part of literature-based reading instruction in the classroom.

Discussion Questions and Activities

1. Make a list of interesting, challenging words that you might introduce to pupils in the upper elementary grades, words such as *effulgent, lugubrious, cantankerous,* and *scintillating.* Design some activities that you might use to help pupils develop ''ownership'' of these words. Keep the qualities of integration, repetition, and meaningful use in mind as you make your plans.

2. In a magazine, you read this sentence: *The creeping kudzu spread across the hills.* Assuming you don't know what *kudzu* is, describe the strategies you could use in figuring out the word.

3. What are some important factors to keep in mind in helping primary-grade pupils develop word knowledge and word identification skills? How are these factors different for upper-elementary-grade pupils?

4. Read the exchange of opinion between Aunt Millie and Uncle Max in 5.12 (p. 157). Choose a side in the debate and defend your position.

5. Examine a trade book appropriate for use in the elementary grades. Choose words that you think you might use as vehicles for vocabulary instruction and decide how you might help pupils learn these words.

School-Based Assignments

1. Review a reading lesson from the teachers edition of a basal reading series used in your school placement. How much emphasis does the lesson place on developing vocabulary? What words are identified for instruction? What suggestions are made for teaching these words? What alternative strategies would you use in presenting these words?

2. Working with a group of three or four pupils, develop a semantic map centered on a theme from books they may be reading or words related to a curriculum topic they may be studying.

3. Observe a reading lesson being taught by one of your cooperating teachers. Note how much time is spent on developing word meaning as part of the lesson. Does the teacher emphasize the use of context clues or phonetic analysis in helping pupils figure out unknown words? What other techniques does the teacher use in teaching vocabulary?

4. Using words you have selected from pupils' experience stories or trade books that are used in the classroom, plan and teach a small-group lesson in phonetic or structural analysis. First, determine what pupils already know about the words you select. Develop your lesson in light of this.

5. Based on your experience in school, design a bulletin board display dealing with vocabulary. You might make a display on multiple-meaning words, a semantic web, or a ''word board'' related to a particular topic. If possible, involve pupils in your activity.

Children's Trade Books Cited in This Chapter

Allen, Pamela. *Who Sank the Boat?* New York: Coward-McCann, 1982.

Bancheck, Linda. *Snake In, Snake Out.* New York: Crowell, 1978.

Bemelmans, Ludwig. *Madeline.* New York: Viking, 1939.

Blume, Judy. *Blubber.* New York: Bradbury, 1974.

———. *Freckle Juice.* New York: Dell, 1971.

Byars, Betsy. *The Not-Just-Anybody Family.* New York: Dell, 1986.

Cooney, Barbara. *Miss Rumphius.* New York: Viking, 1982.

Downing, Mary. *The Doll in the Garden: A Ghost Story.* New York: Clarion, 1990.

Emberley, Barbara. *Drummer Hoff.* New York: Simon and Schuster, 1967.

George, Jean Craighead. *My Side of the Mountain.* New York: Dutton, 1959.

Guarin, Deborah. *Is Your Mama a Llama?* New York; Scholastic, 1989.

Gwynn, Fred. *A Chocolate Moose for Dinner.* New York: Simon and Schuster, 1988.

———. *The King Who Rained.* New York: Simon and Schuster, 1988.

———. *A Little Pigeon Toad.* New York: Simon and Schuster, 1988.

Hutchins, Pat. *Rosie's Walk.* New York: Macmillan, 1968.

Keller, Ruth. *Many Luscious Lollipops.* New York: Grossett and Dunlop, 1989.

Kellogg, Steven. *Chicken Little.* Boston: Houghton Mifflin, 1989.

Kesselman, Wendy. *Emma.* New York: Harper and Row, 1985.

Konigsburg, E. L. *Father's Arcane Daughter.* New York: Dell, 1986.

———. *From the Mixed-up Files of Mrs. Basil E. Frankeweiler.* New York: Antheneum, 1967.

Lessac, Frane. *My Little Island.* New York: Harper and Row, 1984.

Levitt, Paul M., Burger, Douglas, and Gurlnick, Elissa. *The Weighty Word Book.* Longmont, CO: Bookmaker's Guild, 1985.

MacLachlan, Patricia, *Sarah, Plain and Tall.* New York: Harper and Row, 1985.

Meddaugh, Susan. *Too Short Fred.* Boston: Houghton Mifflin, 1978.

Miles, Miska, *Annie and The Old One.* Boston: Little, Brown, 1971.

Nuinberg, Maxwell. *Fun With Words.* Englewood Cliffs, NJ: Prentice Hall, 1970.

Sharmat, Marjorie Weinman. *Mitchell is Moving.* New York: Macmillan, 1985.

Steig, William. *Sylvester and the Magic Pebble.* New York: Simon and Schuster, 1969.

Tafuri, Nancy. *Have You Seen My Duckling?* New York: Puffin Books, 1986.

Viorst, Judith. *Alexander and the Terrible, Horrible, No Good, Very Bad Day.* New York: Atheneum, 1972.

————. *Earrings.* New York: Atheneum, 1990.

Wells, Rosemary. *Noisy Nora.* New York: Scholastic, 1973.

Williams, Margery, *The Velveteen Rabbit.* New York: Doubleday, 1984.

Other children's trade books are listed in 5.14 (p. 161).

References

Adams, M. J. (1990). *Beginning to Read: Thinking and Learning about Print.* Cambridge, MA: MIT Press.

Anderson, R. C., Hiebert, E. H., Scott, J. A., and Wilkinson, I. A. G. (1984). *Becoming a Nation of Readers: The Report of the Commission on Reading.* Washington: National Institute of Education.

Anderson, R. C., and Freebody, P. (1985). Vocabulary Knowledge. In H. Singer and R. B. Ruddell (eds.), *Theoretical Models and Processes of Reading* (3rd ed.). Newark, DE: International Reading Assoc.

Ashton-Warner, S. (1963). *Teacher.* New York: Simon and Schuster.

Bettelheim, B., and Zelan, K. (1982). *On Learning to Read: A Child's Fascination with Meaning.* New York: Alfred Knopf.

Blachowicz, C. L. (1985). Vocabulary Development and Reading: From Research to Instruction. *The Reading Teacher* 38:876–881.

Bridge, C. A., Winograd, P. N., and Haley, D. (1983). Using Predictable Materials vs. Preprimers to Teach Beginning Sight Words. *The Reading Teacher* 36:884–891.

Carbo, M. (1988). Debunking the Great Phonics Myth. *Phi Delta Kappan* 70:226–240.

Carbo, M. (1989). An Evaluation of Jeanne Chall's Response to ''Debunking the Great Phonics Myth.'' *Phi Delta Kappan* 71:152–157.

Chall, J. S. (1989a). *Learning to Read: The Great Debate* 20 Years Later—A Response to ''Debunking the Great Phonics Myth.'' *Phi Delta Kappan* 70:521–538.

Chall, J. S. (1989b). The Uses of Educational Research: Comments on Carbo. *Phi Delta Kappan* 71:158–160.

Chall, J. S. (1983). *Learning To Read: The Great Debate.* (2nd ed.). New York: McGraw Hill.

Clymer, T. (1963). The Utility of Phonics Generalizations. *The Reading Teacher* 16:252–258.

Dale, E. (1965). Vocabulary Measurement: Techniques and Major Findings. *Elementary English* 42:895–901.

Davis, F. B. (1972). Psychometric Research on Comprehension in Reading. *Reading Research Quarterly* 7:628–678.

Devine, T. G. (1986). *Teaching Reading Comprehension: From Theory to Practice.* Boston: Allyn and Bacon.

Dolch, E. (1939). *A Manual for Remedial Readers.* Champaign, IL: Garrard.

Durr, W. R. (1973). Computer Study of High Frequency Words in Popular Trade Juvenials. *The Reading Teacher* 27:37–42.

Eeds, M. (1985). Bookwords: Using a Beginning Word List of High Frequency Words from Children's Literature K–3. *The Reading Teacher* 39:418–423.

Fielding, L. G., Wilson, P. T., and Anderson, R. C. (1986). A New Focus on Free Reading: The Role of Trade Books in Reading Instruction. In T. Raphael (ed.), *The Contexts of School-Based Literacy.* New York: Random House.

Flesch, R. (1955). *Why Johnny Can't Read.* New York: Harper and Row.

Freppon, P. A., and Dahl, K. C. (1991). Learning About Phonics in a Whole Language Classroom. *Language Arts* 68:190–197.

Goodman, K. S. (1976). The Reading Process: A Psycholinguistic View. In E. B. Smith, K. S. Goodman, and R. Meredith, *Language and Thinking in School.* New York: Holt Rinehart and Winston.

Hittleman, D. R. (1988). *Developmental Reading, K–8: Teaching From A Whole-Language Perspective* (3rd ed.). Columbus, OH: Merrill.

Johnson, D. D., and Pearson, P. D. (1984). *Teaching Reading Vocabulary* (2nd ed.). New York: Holt Rinehart and Winston.

Johnson, T. D., and Louis, D. R. (1987) *Literacy through Literature.* Portsmouth, NH: Heinemann.

Just, M. S., and Carpenter, P. A. (1987). *The Psychology of Reading and Language Comprehension.* Boston: Allyn and Bacon.

Klein, M. L. (1988). *Teaching Reading Comprehension and Vocabulary: A Guide for Teachers.* Englewood Cliffs: Prentice-Hall.

Mathews, M. M. (1966). *Teaching to Read, Historically Considered.* Chicago: University of Chicago Press.

Moe, A. J. (1989). Using Picture Books for Reading Vocabulary Development. In J. W. Stewig and S. L. Sebasta (eds.), *Using Literature In The Elementary Classroom* (2nd ed.). Urbana, IL: National Council of Teachers of English.

Nagy, W. E. (1988). *Teaching Vocabulary to Improve Reading Comprehension.* Urbana, IL: National Council of Teachers of English.

Nagy, W. E., Herman, P. A., and Anderson, R. C. (1985). Learning Words from Context. *The Reading Research Quarterly* 20:233–253.

Newman, J. M., and Church, S. M. (1990). Commentary: The Myths of Whole Language. *The Reading Teacher* 44:20–27.

Pearson, P. D. (1985). Changing the Face of Reading Comprehension. *The Reading Teacher* 38:724–728.

Peterson, R., and Eeds, M. (1990). *Grand Conversations: Literature Groups in Action.* New York: Scholastic.

Smith, F. (1985). *Reading without Nonsense* (2nd ed.). New York: Teachers College Press.

Stahl, S. A. (1992). Saying the ''p'' Word: Nine Guidelines for Exemplary Phonics Instruction. *The Reading Teacher* 45:618–625.

Stahl, S. A., Osborn, J., and Lehr, F. (1990). *Beginning To Read: Thinking and Learning about Print by Marilyn Jager Adams. A Summary Prepared by Steven A. Stahl, Jean Osborn, and Fran Lehr.* Urbana, IL: Center for the Study of Reading, University of Illinois at Urbana-Champaign.

Trachtenburg, P. (1990). Using Children's Literature to Enhance Phonics Instruction. *The Reading Teacher* 43:648–652.

Chapter 6

Reading Comprehension: Understanding Narrative Text

Chapter 6 Outline

I. Introduction
  A. Narrative and Expository Text
  B. Product and Process
  C. An Interactive Model
II. Text-Based Features
  A. Level of Text
  B. Structure of Text
  C. Content of Text
  D. Other Text-Based Features
    1. Design
    2. Illustrations
III. Reader-Based Features
  A. Language Background
    1. Metalinguistic Awareness
    2. Decoding Ability
    3. Vocabulary
    4. Sentences
    5. Paragraphs
    6. Selections
  B. Cognitive Processing
    1. Types of Comprehension
      a. Main Ideas
      b. Details
      c. Sequence
      d. Drawing Conclusions
      e. Cause–Effect Relationships
      f. Integrating Instruction
    2. Levels of Thinking
      a. Literal
      b. Inferential or Interpretative
      c. Critical–Creative
  C. Schemata
  D. Metacognition
  E. Other Reader-Based Factors
    1. Motivation
    2. State of Mind
  F. Context

VI. The Role of Teacher Questioning
V. Summary and Conclusions
Discussion Questions and Activities
School-Based Assignments
Children's Trade Books Cited in This Chapter
References

Features

6.1   Interactive Model of Reading Comprehension
6.2   Teaching Story Structure
6.3   Sentence Comprehension
6.4   Graphic Organizers for Main Ideas
6.5   Skill-Based versus Literature-Based Teaching
6.6   Question–Answer Relationships
6.7   Junior Great Books
6.8   Activating Prior Knowledge
6.9   The Metacomprehension Strategy Index
6.10 Tips on Questioning
6.11 InQuest and ReQuest
6.12 Putting It All Together

Key Concepts in This Chapter

*U*nderstanding what one reads is essential to reading. Comprehension is the result of an interaction between a reader and a piece of print in a certain context.

Text-based features such as level of text, structure of text, content, and the like can help or hinder the process of reading comprehension.

What the reader brings to print has a powerful influence on understanding text as well. Comprehension is impacted by such reader-based factors as language background, cognitive processing, schemata, and metacognition.

Teacher questioning is a key ingredient in helping pupils learn to comprehend trade books and other material that they read in a literature-based classroom.

OMPREHENSION IS the consummation of the reading process; without understanding, a person is not really reading. Everything that teachers do in reading instruction leads to the ultimate goal of comprehension.

Simply defined, reading comprehension is the process of determining meaning in text, a process by which readers reconstruct authors' intended messages in their own minds. In a broad sense, comprehension means understanding the full meaning of any communicative action, from interpreting the significance of a casual wave or a flirtatious glance, to unraveling the plot of a Victorian novel or deciphering a complicated set of written directions. In reading, it involves understanding the meaning of a printed passage by reconstructing the intended message in a text.

In literature-based instruction, a distinction might be made between comprehension and interpretation. Comprehension involves the understanding of what is contained in story text. Interpretation is the individual reaction or response to that material. Comprehension and interpretation are closely related, and both are essential to literature-based reading instruction.

Before the early 1900s, not much attention was paid to comprehension or interpretation in reading. Comprehension was taken for granted if the student could adequately read a passage aloud. The story is told about a famous educator who once visited a high school classroom and asked a student to read the front page of a newspaper. The student read the same line across columns, jumping from story to story while moving from one column to another, but nobody worried because the pupil's reading was "accurate." Since the early part of the 20th century, however, comprehension has become the primary, fundamental goal of reading instruction.

As schools move toward the early years of the 21st century, there is an intensely renewed emphasis on comprehension, "an atmosphere in which the psychic energy of the reading field has been unleashed toward the study of comprehension" (Pearson, 1985a; p. 724). This emphasis on the theory and practice of comprehension has resulted in an awarness of the varying demands of understanding different types of text, an emphasis on the process (rather than the product) of comprehension, and the development of an interactive model of reading comprehension that takes both text-based features and reader-based features into account.

Narrative and Expository Text

Even though all writing shares communicative intent and features of written language, different types of texts require varying kinds of comprehension and mental processing. Reading to find out the time of the last screening of a movie at the local theatre involves cognitive demands different from reading a critical review of that movie. Reading a recipe involves a type of comprehension different from reading a love letter. Reading a novel for pleasure during Sustained Silent Reading requires a type of comprehension different from reading an informational trade book in preparation for a thematic report in science. Comprehension differs according to the nature of the material and the reader's purpose for reading it.

In this chapter, the emphasis is on comprehending narrative text, since most of what pupils encounter for the purpose of learning to read—and much of the literature that they enjoy in the elementary grades—is narrative in nature. Narrative text is a form of writing that tells a story. Its primary purpose is to relate a series of episodes that unfold a plot. Narrative text has settings, characters, and a particular structure.

Comprehending expository text, whose primary purpose is to explain or present information, will be addressed in the next chapter.

Product and Process

Reading comprehension involves both process and product. For many years, schools dealt primarily with the products of comprehension. Although the end product of comprehension is important, schools are now coming to deal more and more with the comprehension process.

The product is the *result* of comprehension. In the classroom, for example, teachers typically make statements like ''Ramona recognized the main idea of the paragraph and stated two of the five details supporting that main idea.'' Or after a person has read a newspaper article, we hear things like ''Joe could tell us what happened at the conference, but he didn't seem to understand the more subtle implications of the article.'' These are statements that relate to the measured results or the outcomes of comprehension. These are the products.

Questions or tests measure the product of comprehension. The reader's ability to tell who the characters were, what they did, when, and why are indicators of basic understanding and recall.

The process of comprehension is more difficult to get at because it occurs inside the reader's head. The process is not as readily observable. We can tell, for example, that Ramona remembered two of five details in a paragraph (product); now we want to find out *why* she remembered those two and not the other three (process). We can say that Joe could basically understand what he read about in the newspaper (product); now we want to find out *why* he couldn't understand the implied information in the article (process).

As part of teaching pupils how to read, the focus on the comprehension process is vital. It shifts the instructional emphasis from trying to determine what a pupil has understood to helping the pupil become aware of what goes into understanding written text. It attempts to help us understand how people comprehend written discourse.

An Interactive Model

Recent research-based theories of reading comprehension have emphasized the interactive nature of the comprehension process. This view suggests that comprehension depends on three factors: reader, text, and context. Reader and text *combine* within a social context to produce meaning. Comprehension is the result of processing printed text and using experiences and expectations that the reader brings to the text. Meaning is found not in print alone; rather, it is constructed as a result of an interaction between the reader and the text.

The interactive model of reading comprehension is closely related to communication between a writer and a reader. Comprehension comes from the integration of information in the text itself—that which is ''in front of the eye''—and information in the reader's head—that which is ''behind the eye.'' Reading is an active process in which the reader uses clues found in the text to construct meaning in his or her head.

6.1

FOR YOUR INFORMATION

Interactive Model of Reading Comprehension

Interactive Model of Reading Comprehension

Reading comprehension is a process involving the interaction of:

Text-Based Features   with   Reader-Based Features

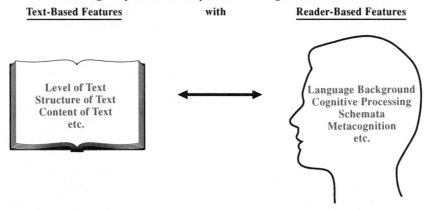

Level of Text
Structure of Text
Content of Text
etc.

Language Background
Cognitive Processing
Schemata
Metacognition
etc.

What are the factors that influence a person's reading comprehension? What enables you to understand what you are reading right now? Your understanding depends on a constellation of factors, some of which are found within the print at which you are looking and some of which you bring to the act of reading.

Text-based factors, those that are ''in front of the eye,'' include:

the level of text, the relative degree of difficulty of the language with which the ideas are presented;

the structure of text, the organizational scheme or pattern that the author uses to present the information;

content, the level of sophistication or familiarity of the material;

other factors, such as the arrangement of type and the use of graphic aids (such as the diagram presented in 6.1).

Reader-based factors, those that are ''behind the eye,'' include:

language background, the ability to recognize words, grasp sentence meaning, and deal effectively with language in larger segments of text;

cognitive processing, the ability to apply the appropriate type of comprehension and level of thinking required of understanding;

schemata, the background and knowledge that the reader already possesses;

metacognition, the awareness and control over one's mental functioning;

other factors, such as one's state of mind, level of comfort, and the like.

In a literature-based program, "teaching reading comprehension" involves taking these text-based and reader-based factors into account as pupils build reading competency by interacting with stories, poems, plays, informational trade books, and other material that they encounter in the classroom.

Text-Based Features

Meaning does not reside in text alone; it depends to a great extent on what the reader brings to the printed page. Nevertheless, features of the text can greatly influence a reader's ability to interact effectively with printed material. "Although contemporary research seems more interested in the reader than in the text, most authorities would still concur that text, its forms and structures, represents an important aspect of reading and of reading instruction" (Klein, 1988; p. 17). Aspects that are inherent in the text include the difficulty level of the writing, the structure that the author uses to organize the thoughts he or she wants to convey, and the content of the information or ideas in the text.

Level of Text

Level of text refers to the relative degree of difficulty a person can expect to experience in reading. In a nutshell, text with short, simple sentences that use familiar words is easier to read than text with long, complicated sentences using words largely unfamiliar to the reader. Level of text is commonly referred to as "readability."

Readability is the estimated ease with which a piece of print can be read and understood. Readability is normally computed by a formula that calculates the relationship between sentence length and word length/difficulty and that yields an index of how "easy" or "difficult" a text is (or is expected to be). Most formulas express this estimated readability as a grade level figure; that is, a book is reported to be at a "third grade readability level" or "at an eighth grade level of difficulty." At times, a year/month distinction is made; that is, the readability is said to be "at the 5.8 grade level."

Teachers, reading specialists, and publishers traditionally have put a great deal of faith in readability. One can still find readability figures assigned to reading text-books and quoted for popular children's books, but much of the confidence in the absolute accuracy of these numbers is beginning to dissipate. Formulas include only the measurable aspects of language. They do not take into account the reader's background, familiarity with the material, interest, or other factors "behind the eye." Different formulas often give different readability estimates for the same material. Readability figures can be arbitrary and misleading. For example, the readability level of Florence and Richard Atwater's humorous *Mr. Popper's Penguins* is listed as sixth grade; yet this book is typically read and enjoyed by third graders; most sixth graders would reject it as being "too babyish." For these reasons, schools are adhering less strictly to the guidelines that these formulas suggest, especially for narrative material.

Concerns about overreliance on readability figures notwithstanding, a text's level of difficulty will influence a reader's ability to comprehend that material. Beginning

readers find books with familiar words and repeated sentence patterns easier to understand. Traditionally, textbook authors have controlled vocabulary tightly and have ar-
tifically manipulated sentence patterns for the sole purpose of achieving a certain
readability level.

Easy-to-read trade books such as Crosby Bonsall's *Mine's The Best,* Arnold
Lobel's *Frog And Toad* stories, and some of Dr. Seuss' books such as *Green Eggs and
Ham* are appropriate instructional fare for young children. The repeated and predictable
language of books like Pat Hutchins's *Good Night Owl* and Barbara Emberley's
Drummer Hoff make these books eminently readable as well. Giving pupils ''easier''
books or easier versions of more difficult books will improve their chances of comprehending what they read and reinforce their confidence for reading more difficult
text later on.

Teachers need to be cautious, however, about assigning books to children on the
basis of a single readability figure alone. What the teacher does with a story—relating
the child's background to the story, activating prior knowledge, setting purposes,
asking directed questions, building important vocabulary, carefully guiding the
reading—will do more to enhance a child's comprehension than selecting a book based
primarily on a single readability figure.

Structure of Text

Text has structure. When authors write, they tell their stories or present their ideas in
an organized manner or pattern. This organization has been called ''the text-in-the-
head of the author.'' When the ''text-in-the-head of the reader'' corresponds to the
text-in-the-head of the author, comprehension occurs.

Different types of discourse are structured in different ways. Recognizing the
genre or type of reading material one is about to encounter can be an important initial
step to comprehension. Pupils need to recognize the nature of the text, whether it is
designed to entertain (as a narrative story), to inform (as an informational trade book
about machines), to persuade (as an editorial or advertisement), or to please (as a poem
or play). The nature of the material will often determine the structure of the writing,
so recognizing the form of what is to be read will increase chances of understanding.

Narrative text contains a structure, a ''grammar'' or set of rules for creating a
story. The elements of this structure consist of setting, plot, character, conflict, and the
like. Helping pupils recognize and understand these elements of story grammar or text
structure is important, because pupils with a knowledge of story grammar can understand and recall stories better than those who do not have this knowledge (Applebee,
1978).

The organization of narrative text follows a pattern that runs from the beginning
(*Little Red Riding Hood sets out to see her grandmother.*), through the middle part of
the story (*She meets the wolf, who races ahead to Grandma's house.*), to a conflict or
crisis (*The wolf devours Granny.*), to a solution (*The woodsman arrives and saves the
day*). Children who are exposed to stories begin to develop the sense of story structure
from a very early age. From the ''Once upon a time . . . '' to the ''. . . lived happily
ever after,'' they become aware that stories move in a predictable manner. This awareness helps them comprehend the story. For children who arrive at school without this
awareness, developing a sense of story structure is an early step in teaching reading
comprehension.

In guided reading, the teacher can build pupils' backgrounds, set purposes, and design questions to help pupils better comprehend what they read.

Pupils who are aware of the elements of story structure and are able to follow plot through its various stages are in a much better position to comprehend narrative text. Expository text is structured differently from narrative text, because the emphasis in expository writing is on the presentation of information and not on telling a story. Expository text structures will be described in the next chapter.

Content of Text

The content or subject matter will also have an impact on comprehension; however, understanding of a text depends in large measure on one's familiarity with the topic. For example, a business major reading a text on the stock market will likely have better comprehension than a music major reading the same book. Pupils who already know the story of ''The Three Little Pigs'' will have less trouble understanding it in print than someone totally unfamiliar with the story.

Most pupils have an advantage in dealing with the content of narrative text they encounter as part of learning to read. Stories often deal with content familiar to pupils. Even when some aspects of the story structure may be new to pupils, themes and experiences will often be comfortably well known. For example, Patrick Skene Catling's *John Midas In The Dreamtime* is a story set in the Australian outback about a boy who encounters a group of prehistoric aboriginal people. Although pupils may be unfamiliar with the setting and supporting characters, most will likely have experienced their own imagined trips back in time.

Part of the appeal of literature is the familiarity of the themes contained in stories. The idea of Harry Allard's goofy ghost story *Bumps in the Night* or the antics of the Herdmans in Barbara Robinson's popular *The Best Christmas Pageant Ever* will be more easily understood by children because the subject of the books have been part of children's experiences, at least their imagined if not their real experiences.

6.2 Putting Ideas To Work

Teaching Story Structure

A MONG THE techniques for helping pupils develop an awareness of story structure are:

Direct questioning that focuses specifically on story elements: *Where does this story take place?* (setting). *Who are the main characters? What does the author say about them?* (characterization). *What problem does the main character face?* (conflict). *What does the character decide to do?* (resolution). These questions are expanded depending on the nature of the story, the teacher's purposes, and the reading level of the pupils.

Literature discussions, dialogues about stories in literature study groups (see 3.7) focuses on pupils' responses to various literary elements in what they read.

Flow charts which pupils follow—as they might follow a road map—in charting the structure of a story. Pupils can create these charts. (See Fig. 6.2A.)

Plot diagrams that visually represent story action. This is similar in nature and intent to a flow chart. The one on the right is only one of many forms that can be used. (See Fig. 6.2B.)

Story frames, suggested by Fowler (1982), which are skeletal paragraphs with sequential spaces tied together by signal words and/or transitional phrases. (See Fig. 6.2C.)

These are only some of the many devices that can be used to help pupils develop an awareness of story structure that will help them better comprehend the literature they encounter as part of learning to read.

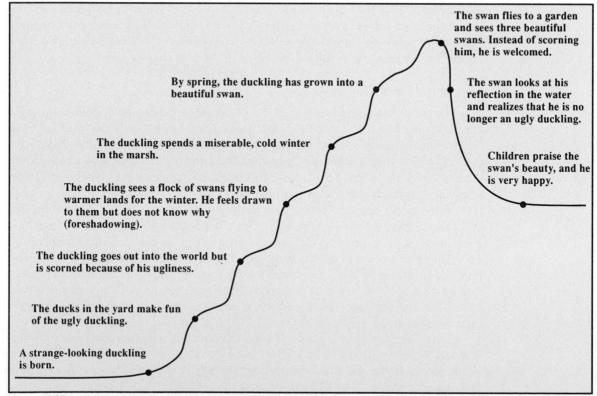

Figure 6.2B   Reprinted with the permission of Macmillan Publishing Company from *Language Arts: Contents and Teaching Strategies,* Second Edition by Gail E. Tompkins and Kenneth Hoskisson. Copyright © 1991 by Macmillan Publishing Company.

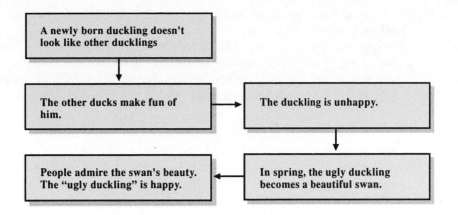

A newly born duckling doesn't look like other ducklings

The other ducks make fun of him.

The duckling is unhappy.

People admire the swan's beauty. The "ugly duckling" is happy.

In spring, the ugly duckling becomes a beautiful swan.

Figure 6.2A

Title _The Ugly Duckling_

The story starts when _one of the new ducks is very ugly._

Then, _the other ducks laugh at the new duckling and stay away from him._

The problem is solved when _the ugly duckling discovers he is a beautiful swan._

At the end, _the swan is happy because people admire his beauty._

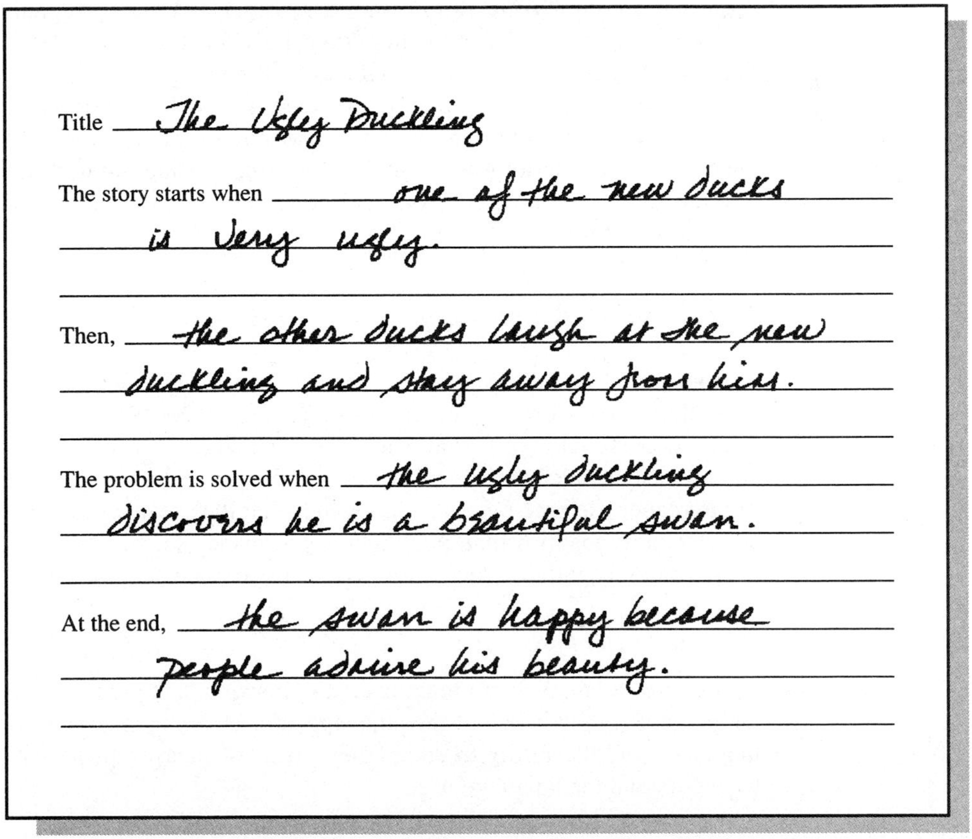

Figure 6.2C

In addressing content, teachers need to take into account both the subject matter and the knowledge and background of pupils. Teachers can help pupils better deal with content as a dimension of comprehension by activating pupils' prior knowledge of the subject, by clarifying concepts, by providing background information that may be essential to understanding the story, by making sure that pupils understand key vocabulary before they read, and by guiding reading through skillful questioning.

Other Text-Based Features

Other features of text that enhance comprehension are design and illustration. Research has "demonstrated that nonprint aspects of text such as illustrations influence comprehension and response, particularly among children" (Beach and Hynds, 1991; p. 469). These features enhance understanding by providing a visual dimension to clarify the content contained in text.

Design includes the size, amount, and arrangement of type on a page. Printed lines that are difficult to follow and large blocks of uninterrupted text might have a detrimental effect on understanding, especially for the less capable or reluctant reader. That is why design is such a crucial element in the publishing of children's books.

Illustrations can also help pupils understand what they read. Although illustrations may be more important in expository writing, pictures and drawings in narrative material help children form mental images of the settings and characters in stories. The type of illustration used helps shape the reader's perception and create the mood or tone for the story.

Reader-Based Features

Features contained in text have a powerful influence on pupils' ability to comprehend what they read. Comprehension, however, is not dependent solely on text. Readers inject meaning into the verbal symbols on the page. Text is the vehicle for conveying an author's intended meaning, but that meaning is recreated or constructed in the mind of the reader. Helping pupils comprehend what they read will involve addressing characteristics or qualities that are "behind the reader's eye," features such as language background, cognitive processing, schemata, and metacognition.

Language Background

An obvious prerequisite to reading comprehension is the reader's ability to understand language. Reading is one of the language arts. Meaning is conveyed by way of printed language, and the ability to comprehend facts or ideas in print depends on the ability to understand the language used.

Metalinguistic Awareness   The language background necessary for reading begins with the metalinguistic awareness that is developed with Big Books, language experience stories, and other reading–writing activities that are part of emergent literacy activities. Metalinguistic awareness involves understanding the nature of language as a tool of communication; learning the meaning and function of letters, words, and sentences; recognizing the connection between spoken and written language; and knowing the nature of reading itself.

Decoding Ability   Language background also includes the pupil's ability to decode with ease and fluency. Decoding ability is a "behind the eye" factor that the reader brings to the printed page, and it will influence what the reader takes away from the printed page. The relationship between decoding ability and comprehension is well documented (Adams, 1990).

More specific and extended reading comprehension requires the understanding of expanding units of language—from words and sentences to paragraphs and longer selections. Complete comprehension demands recognition of appropriate meanings at each of these language units.

Vocabulary   Words are the building blocks to meaning. Understanding the meaning of words in their proper contexts was the major focus of the previous chapter. Without knowing the meaning of words, attempts at further understanding are largely futile.

Sentences   Sentences carry the essence of meaning in language; that is, basic ideas are expressed at the sentence level. In any language, words are not strung together like beads on a string; rather, words are arranged in syntactic patterns so that their relationship to one another will convey meaning. The individual words in the sentences *Norman ate the fish.* and *The fish ate Norman.* are exactly the same; however, the meaning of the sentences is very different (especially for Norman!). The ability to understand these syntactic relationships is essential to understanding meaning in print.

When a pupil exhibits comprehension problems, it often makes sense for the teacher to look at the child's understanding of sentences as the possible root of the difficulty. Working on expressing and extracting meaning in sentences also helps cement the reading–writing relationship.

Anaphoric relationships can be important to understanding sentence meaning. Anaphora refers to the use of a word as a substitute for another word or group of words. For example, to understand the meaning of the second sentence in this pair:

Ralph took the motorcycle to the wastebasket. He decided to hide it there.

the reader must understand the anaphoric references *Ralph = he, it = motorcycle,* and *there = wastebasket.*

Anaphora is also involved in ellipitcal sentences, such as:

The mouse saw Keith riding the motorcycle. He wanted to try, too.

The reader needs to supply the invisible anaphoric element

He wanted to try (to ride the motorcycle), too.

Recognizing this type of anaphoric relationship requires inferential thinking.

Devine (1986) suggests the following strategies for helping pupils deal with anaphoric relationships: (1) direct questioning, (2) matching the terms with their antecedents, (3) encouraging pupils to make their own rules to explain anaphora, and (4) heightening their awareness by focusing their attention to anaphoric references in text.

Since anaphora is a stylistic device that authors use for organizational purposes, helping pupils understand these relationships is part of helping them understand text structure.

Sentence Comprehension

THE TEACHER can focus on comprehension of sentence units by such activities as:

locating key sentences and having pupils discuss the meaning of these sentences.

having pupils determine the deep structure of a sentence by identifying sentences with the same meaning in sets like:

> *There was a mouse in Keith's motel room.*
> *Keith knew about mice in motel rooms.*
> *A mouse was in the motel room where Keith stayed.*

having pupils change the structural patterns of sentences; for example, having them change sentences from the active voice (*Keith saw the mouse.*) to the passive voice (*The mouse was seen by Keith.*).

having pupils break long and difficult sentences apart, especially sentences with relative clauses that add multiple elements of meaning into a sentence.

having pupils rephrase sentences in their own words.

Each of these activities focuses on the pupil's ability to understand language at the sentence level. (The sentences are based on the content of Beverly Cleary's delightful fantasy, *The Mouse on the Motorcycle.*)

Paragraphs   Groups of related sentences form paragraphs. Understanding the relationship among the various sentences is the key to understanding the paragraph. Comprehending sentence relationships may also involve understanding the relationship among ideas that the author expresses, main ideas and details, sequence of ideas, cause–effect relationships, or the other relationships described in the next section.

In narrative text, paragraphs may not have a clear or specific central focus around which ideas are organized. Paragraphs may serve to provide details about the character or setting, or to add elements to the plot that keep the story moving. Understanding the meaning of narrative paragraphs often involves the ability to recognize and recall paragraph content, to understand the paragraph in relation to the rest of the narrative, and to be able to determine the paragraph's importance to the text (as, for example, when conflict is introduced or particularly important information about a character is presented).

What can be said of language understanding through the paragraph unit also applies to comprehending poetry. Word meanings may be figurative, and sentence structures may be unconventional, but comprehending the appropriate meaning of the words and seeing the relationship among the various syntactic elements that the poet uses will enable the reader to understand the meaning and import that is expressed in the poem.

Selections   Larger selections consist of chapters, stories, whole books, and other segments of text that include multiple paragraphs. Comprehension of these larger segments of language requires not only understanding of the meaning of smaller segments but also long-term recall and cognitive processing. It is in understanding these larger segments that comprehenion really occurs.

Readers bring their language backgrounds to the printed page. When problems in reading comprehension become apparent, the succeeding segments of language—

from words to sentences to paragraphs—provide the teacher with a focal point in diagnosing and addressing broader problems of reading comprehension. Instruction in using these elements of language to build understanding is part of the process of teaching reading comprehension.

Cognitive Processing

Reading is a cognitive operation, and the mental processing involved is essential to comprehending written text. This mental processing includes both the *type* of comprehension and the *level* of comprehension involved in reading.

Types of Comprehension Under the heading of *Comprehension,* basal scope and sequence charts, school curriculum guides, and skills-management systems typically contain lists of items such as recognizing main ideas and details, seeing cause–effect relationships, making comparisons and contrasts, following sequence, distinguishing fact from fancy, separating fact from opinion, determining the author's purpose, predicting outcomes, judging the validity or relevancy of material, making generalizations, and other items, numbering over one hundred in some skills inventories. Comprehension is seen as the sum total or combination of all of these elements.

These specific factors are often referred to as "comprehension skills and subskills." Calling these components "skills" implies that they can be developed and improved through isolated, repeated drill and practice. In conventional programs, skills are the starting point and primary focus in teaching reading. The result has been a plethora of instructional materials containing hundreds of exercises aimed at developing one or another of these skills, largely separated from other factors or components of the total comprehension process.

There are problems in viewing reading comprehension primarily as a series of many discrete, specific factors. The distinction between certain factors is not always clear; for example, factors like *summarizing* and *drawing conclusions* can be more alike than different. Some factors are general (*interpreting the meaning of sentences,* for example); others are more specific (*recognizing the anaphoric relationship between a pronoun and its antecedent*). Moreover, the skill-development approach often places more emphasis on mastering individual skills than on the larger act of reading.

Careful analysis of research on the distinctiveness of these skills has led to the conclusion that "there is simply no clear evidence to support the naming of discrete skills in reading comprehension" (Rosenshine, 1980; p. 552). These supposedly separate factors may involve one generalized element that can be called "reasoning while reading."

Despite the dangers inherent in viewing and trying to teach these comprehension "skills" as discrete and separate entities, it is important to recognize that different reading materials place different demands on the reader. Reading the cooking directions on the back of a frozen pizza box, for example, requires a type of comprehension that is different from reading a romantic novel or a newspaper editorial on the dangers of acid rain. The nature and purpose of each of these reading acts is quite different. Texts are organized differently, and the type of material that children (and adults) encounter impose different demands upon them as readers. And though the skill itself is not the starting point in literature-based instruction, teachers can emphasize different

Teaching reading comprehension involves more than having pupils master a set of discrete skills.

aspects of reasoning while reading as they use literature for developing pupils' competency in learning to read.

What are the different types of comprehension commonly addressed as part of teaching reading? When lists from different sources are examined, the lists are typically characterized by some commonality but great diversity. If all the different ''skills and subskills'' on published lists were itemized, the inventory of factors would extend into the hundreds. However, eight major factors seem to emerge as the ones most often included in most sources: (1) determining the meaning of words in context, (2) getting the main idea, (3) identifying details that support the main idea, (4) following sequence, (5) drawing conclusions, (6) identifying cause–effect relationships, (7) making inferences, and (8) critical reading/interpretation. Other components have been listed: predicting outcomes, identifying character's motives, summarizing, and the like. But the eight identified above are the ones that seem to be most commonly addressed as part of instructional programs.

The role of words in context was presented in the previous chapter. Making inferences and critical reading will be examined later in this chapter. The other five factors—main ideas, details, sequence, conclusions, and cause–effect relationships—become the focus of reading instruction in the literature-based classroom.

Main ideas are the central thoughts or major topics around which a paragraph or longer segment of text is organized. Since reading is a form of communication, it is obviously important that the reader be able to understand the main idea that an author is trying to convey.

A distinction is sometimes made between *main topics* and *main ideas.* The main topic is a word or a phrase that summarizes the central point; the main idea is a sentence about the major thought. This difference may be a moot distinction; no matter how it is expressed, understanding the main idea involves comprehending the major point that the author is making.

The main idea is sometimes—although not always—contained in a topic sentence. Where they occur, topic sentences are usually found as the first or last sentence of a paragraph. The opening paragraph of Judy Blume's *Freckle Juice* contains a topic sentence that sets the tone and purpose of the book: ''Andrew Markus wanted freckles.'' Clear, clean topic sentences like this one do not always exist, however, especially in narrative stories.

The main idea may not be directly stated in a paragraph or story. When not stated, the main idea must be inferred, often from the details that are provided. Getting the main idea from implied information is closely related to drawing conclusions.

Details constitute the less important information related to the main idea. In any well-written paragraph or story, the main idea will be supported by details. Details provide illustrations that help clarify concepts, complete a picture that constitutes the setting for a story, provide evidence to support a conclusion, show ways of applying an idea, fill in gaps to make a plot or character more understandable, or otherwise provide information to enhance the reader's understanding of the text. Good readers are skilled at identifying details that lead to a full and accurate understanding of the main idea.

Details should always be considered in light of their contribution to the main idea. Teachers are often criticized for spending too much time quizzing children on unimportant and trivial bits of information that have little significance in a story. Those small facts that collectively support the main idea should be the focus of a teacher's questioning and discussion.

Distinguishing between main ideas and details involves a form of reasoning and selecting as one reads. It requires the ability to see the difference between ideas of greater and lesser importance. This becomes important not only so that pupils will not become awash in an ocean of trivial facts, but also so that they can distinguish between what is relevant and irrelevant when seeking information in expository text.

Main ideas and details can be the focus of instruction for both paragraphs and longer selections of narrative text. By definition, a paragraph is one or more sentences grouped or clustered around a single topic or idea. In order to understand and later write effective paragraphs, pupils need to recognize main idea as one of the ways that authors organize their ideas.

All paragraphs may not have a main idea, but all are focused around some kind of unifying element. As pupils read paragraphs, they identify topic sentences (where these sentences exist) that contain the main idea or identify details that suggest the unifying thought or idea of the paragraph.

Paragraphs are part of longer discourse. In narrative stories, individual paragraphs carry the author's flow of ideas that constitute the main concepts or actions that the author wants to convey. In much of the literature that pupils encounter, main ideas are not directly stated, so that pupils will need to arrive at them through discussion. The main idea of a story may be the conflict/resolution that the protagonist faces/ achieves. For chapters, having pupils suggest chapter titles is a good way of focusing on main idea. For whole books, writing short summaries (25 words or less) requires pupils to capture the main idea.

The main idea in poetry nearly always requires inferential comprehension. The central thought of a poem may be a simple metaphor, like Carl Sandburg's beautiful image of fog creeping in ''on little cat's feet,'' or it may express an action, as in Shel

6.4 Putting Ideas to Work

Graphic Organizers for Main Ideas

GRAPHIC ORGANIZERS can help pupils see the relationship between main ideas and details in paragraphs.

This example focuses on the element of setting, from Sheila Burnford's *Incredible Journey:*

The Nurmi farm was neat and attractive. (Main idea)

A small cabin stood near the bank of a river.
The door was bright blue.
Scarlet geraniums grew in window boxes.
The vegetable gardens and fields were neatly fenced.

This example from Lynne Reid Banks's *The Indian in the Cupboard* focuses on the element of plot:

Little Bear and Boone had a fierce fight. (Main idea)

The two men rolled on the ground.
They grabbed and punched at one another.
Boone tried to bite the Indian.
They groaned and screamed.

Pupils can construct these visual devices based on what they read. Graphic organizers can be made for whole stories as well.

Silverstein's ludicrous image of putting a bra on a camel. Whatever the thought, image, or metaphor expressed, comprehending the main idea and details of a poem almost always requires children to go beyond the literal meaning of the lines.

In using literature to help pupils learn to recognize main ideas and details, the teacher needs to be aware of opportunities as pupils read and discuss trade books. Questions that teachers ask before, during, and after a story will help pupils focus on main ideas as a component of what they read. For example, in reading Evaline Ness' haunting *Sam, Bangs and Moonshine,* the story about a little girl who gets a friend in trouble because the girl has difficulty separating fact from imagination, questions like the following can be used:

Before—Why do you think it's important for a person to clearly see the difference between what's real and what's made-up?

During—What do you think might happen to Thomas when he goes looking for Sam's imaginary baby kangaroo?

After—What do you think Sam learned from her experiences?

Questions like these help focus pupils' attention on the main point of the story throughout.

Obviously, the nature of the story will largely determine the nature of the main idea questions that the teacher might ask. One would not ask the same type of questions with a story like *Sam, Bangs and Moonshine* as one would ask with a book like Dr. Seuss' *Green Eggs and Ham.*

Skill-Based versus Literature-Based Teaching

There is a difference between helping children learn to identify main ideas and details using trade books as compared to more conventional skill-oriented materials. Conventional programs first identify the skill they wish to develop and then provide materials in which this skill is specifically illustrated. The skill comes first; the text comes second. The designers of a basal reading program or a supplementary skill-development workbook, for example, will decide that a particular comprehension ''skill''—main ideas and details, for example—will be the focus of a particular instructional unit. Having made that decision, they then create or select material that requires children to identify main ideas—probably clearly expressed in topic sentences—and details that are specifically built around the main idea involved.

Trade books are not so tidy and contrived. A children's author starts with an idea and a story. The trade book author doesn't first identify particular components of reading comprehension that a reader will apply in understanding the story. In literature, the text comes first. Teachers need to adapt their teaching techniques and their questioning strategies to the nature of the text that the pupils are reading.

Main ideas and details can also be related to helping children understand literary elements in stories. For example, as pupils discuss the literary elements in E. L. Konigsburg's *From the Mixed-up Files of Mrs. Basil E. Frankweiler,* discussion can focus on the main ideas and details of:

character—the details that make Jamie such a good companion for his sister Claudia.

setting—the details of the museum in which they spent their time;

plot—the details of what the children did in trying to solve the mystery of the statue.

Theme, of course, relates directly to main idea, since the theme of a story is the main idea itself.

Finally, it is important to keep in mind that many pieces of children's literature do not have a ''main idea and details'' in the conventional sense. Asking children to find the main idea in one of Peggy Parish's *Amelia Bedelia* books, for example, would be counterproductive. Children's smiles and giggles while they read these books are ample evidence that they are getting the main idea!

Sequence, the order in which events or elements occur in text, is another element frequently included in lists of comprehension components, included in instructional programs, and assessed in reading tests. Sequence is sometimes referred to as the ''chaining'' of events or ideas. Anyone who has attempted to put together something with the innocuous warning ''Some Assembly Required'' recognizes the importance of understanding sequence in text.

In narrative text, sequence can be indicated in sentences, in paragraphs, or in longer segments of text. At the sentence level, the sequential order can be stated explicitly (''After Miss Nelson left, Viola Swamp arrived.'') or it can be implied (''Miss Nelson left and Viola Swamp arrived.''). Whether stated or implied, comprehending whole texts can be dependent on understanding sequential order in sentences.

In paragraphs, the order of events is usually expressed in separate sentences, and the transitions between sentences are frequently connected by signal words such as *now, before, afterward, then, finally,* and the like.

In narrative text, the sequence of events in a story constitutes the literary element of plot. Sequencing requires pupils to understand the action of a story as it leads from the beginning to the conclusion or resolution.

As in the case of main ideas, sequence in a story can be stated or implied. Inferring the sequence of events leads to predicting outcomes—that is, forecasting the events to follow based on the order of events that have already happened. A popular instructional technique for this component is having children tell or write a subsequent event for a story that they have enjoyed.

Recognizing the order of events can be the focus of using trade books such as:

Karla Kuskin's *The Philharmonic Gets Dressed,* a carefully sequenced account of how members of an orchestra prepare for a performance.

David Hall's *The Ox-Cart Man,* a book strikingly illustrated by Barbara Cooney about the sequence of the seasons; a farmer brings his goods to market in the fall, sells his goods and buys supplies for the winter, and returns home to his winter chores and preparations for a new season.

Robert Munsch's *Mortimer,* a hilarious account of a sequence of people who try to get the obstreperous Mortimer to quiet down after he goes to bed.

In selecting trade books for sequencing, it is important that sequence be essential to the plot. It makes little sense, for example, to try to teach sequencing with a book like Peggy Parish's *Amelia Bedelia,* since the sequence in which this literal-minded maid draws the drapes (with a pencil), dusts the furniture (with dusting powder), and trims the steak (with ribbons) makes little difference in the story.

Usually, events in a narrative story flow chronologically. There are occasions, however, when it becomes important for the reader to understand *flashbacks* as a means of fully comprehending a story. Flashback is a literary device that authors sometimes use to present important story information by returning to an earlier time. For example, understanding details about how the Tillerman children arrived at their grandmother's house in Maryland is important to comprehending Cynthia Voight's Newbery Award-winning *Dicey's Song.* Here is where a specific exercise that involves rearranging events according to the order in which they happened may become important to helping pupils comprehend the story.

When appropriate, prereading questions and postreading discussions can focus on the sequence of the major events in a story. The purpose of these questions is not merely to have pupils recall "what happened when," but to focus their attention on sequential elements that are important to comprehend fully significant events in the story and the relation of these events to one another.

The purpose of focusing on sequence of events in teaching reading through trade books is not to develop this "skill" as an end in itself. Rather, its purpose is to help pupils see the order of events as part of understanding and appreciating stories in literature-based programs.

Drawing conclusions is a third "type of thinking" and frequent focus of reading comprehension in the classroom. Drawing conclusions involves the ability to deduce or infer ideas from evidence presented in a piece of print. As they read, pupils piece together facts from a single source or from many sources to arrive at a conclusion—that is, to recognize a conclusion that may be stated in the text or to infer their own conclusion based on what they read. Drawing conclusions is associated closely with the ability to determine main ideas, in that both involve using information (details) to arrive at a conclusion (main idea).

Reading (or listening) with understanding involves an ongoing series of conclusions. As children read Bernard Waber's *Ira Sleeps Over,* for example, they have opportunities to draw conclusions about Ira's relationship with his mother, his father, his sister, his friend Reggie, and his teddy bear. Pupils can also draw conclusions about Ira's uneasiness, his bravado, and his return home to get Tah Tah when he realizes that Reggie sleeps with a teddy bear, too. As stories for older children get longer and more sophisticated, opportunities for drawing conclusions increase proportionately.

Drawing conclusions is not a "reading skill" alone; it is a cognitive activity that pupils need in all their school subjects and in their out-of-school lives as well. The conclusions that pupils draw from what they read will depend in large measure on their background, experience, and knowledge about a topic.

As a strategy for helping pupils draw conclusions about what they read, the teacher's questioning is key. Teachers can encourage children to think about character traits and conclude how characters may act in other situations. ("What might Homer Price say to Soup Vinson if the two characters met?") Questions during reading ("What do you think might happen next? Why?") and after reading ("Was your prediction correct? Why?") lead pupils to draw conclusions based on evidence they encounter in stories.

Humor requires the ability to draw conclusions, so books of jokes and riddles can be especially appropriate vehicles for this component of reading. Also, simple detective books like Marjorie Weinman Sharmat's *Nate the Great* series, David A. Adler's *Cam Jensen* books or his *Fourth Floor Twins* mysteries, and Donald J. Sobol's *Encyclopedia Brown* mysteries have "drawing conclusions" built in. Pupils can trace step-by-step the clues that lead these junior sleuths to draw the conclusions that enable them to solve their mysteries every time.

Cause–effect relationships are related to drawing conclusions. A cause–effect relationship is an association between an outcome and the conditions that caused the outcome to happen. Cause–effect relationships are inherent in virtually anything a child reads in the classroom.

Cause–effect elements in text are frequently indicated by signal words and phrases such as *because, so, since, thus, as a result of, therefore,* and the like. Even when these signal words are not used as part of the story, however, children can learn to understand that one event occurs as a result or consequence of the other.

Some cause–effect relationships are stated directly, and others are implied. In Maurice Sendak's modern classic *Where the Wild Things Are,* the reader is told that Max is sent to his room (effect) because he tells his mother "I'LL EAT YOU UP!" when she scolds him (cause). When he returns from his adventures in the land of the wild things, he finds his supper waiting for him (effect); the cause is implied.

In literature-based programs, cause–effect relationships can be an instructional focus from the very early stages of emerging literacy. Young children can identify the causes of the three pigs' problems or the reasons why Hansel and Gretel were sent away or how they managed to escape. From the beginning stages of learning to read, there is hardly a story where cause–effect relationships cannot be explored and developed through instruction.

Ongoing discussion and questioning engage pupils in the process of seeing cause–effect relationships as they read. In guided reading, postreading discussion, and dialogue in literature groups, *why* questions are the ones most effectively used to help pupils understand these relationships. Questions should be related to the text so that evidence of the relationship between events can be cited.

Pupils also need to be made aware of multiple cause–effect relationships or causal chains. In multiple cause–effect relationships, several effects may result from a single cause. Causal chains involve one event that causes another, which in turn causes another and so on in a chain reaction. Consider the series of causes and effects in Gene Zion's delightfully funny *Harry By the Sea:* the dog is hot so he goes into the water; when he goes into the water, he gets covered by seaweed; when people see him covered with seaweed, they think he is a sea monster; because they think he is a sea monster, they become frightened; because they become frightened, . . . and so on and so on.

An instructional device for focusing on multiple causes and effects is a chart with two columns headed **Causes** and **Effects,** with appropriate items listed under each heading. For example, using Laura Jaffe Numeroff's *If You Give a Mouse a Cookie,* a story that children (and most adults) genuinely enjoy:

Causes	Effects
You give a Mouse a cookie.	He'll want a glass of milk.
You give him a glass of milk.	He'll want a straw.
He notices his hair needs cutting.	You give him a scissors.
He needs to take a nap.	He'll want a blanket and a pillow.
etc.	etc.

Focus on cause–effect relationships is appropriate for dealing with both narrative and expository text. In narrative stories, these relationships can be the link between what the characters are like and what they do, between the setting and the action, between people and their surroundings. In understanding causes and effects, the reader understands the crucial question *Why?*

Integrating Instruction   The comprehension factors described above—main ideas and details, determining sequence, drawing conclusions, and identifying cause–effect relationships—are not separate, discrete, individual skills. They are closely integrated elements that can be thought about and taught under the umbrella of general understanding. Taken together, they enhance children's meaning-making and add a dimension to their understanding and appreciation of literature.

All these factors are closely linked. In conventional reading instructional programs, they are listed, treated, and taught as largely separate entities—a practice book on cause–effect relationships, a stack of worksheets on sequencing, some exercises on main ideas. With trade books, all these components of comprehension can be closely integrated and interwoven as elements of a single—albeit complex—entity.

There is a particular advantage in using literature to help children develop these aspects of reasoning while reading. In conventional reading programs, these elements are typically developed with paragraph-length selections. A worksheet or skills exercise book will include individual unrelated paragraphs on main ideas or sequencing or cause–effect relationships. These elements are normally tested with paragraph-length segments of print, too. Standardized tests of reading comprehension typically contain paragraphs or very short selections, followed by questions to assess particular comprehension components (''What's the best title for this story?'').

The ultimate aim of reading is not understanding at the paragraph level, however. Although comprehending the meaning of paragraphs is indeed important, the real payoff in reading comes when children can understand total selections. Using trade books enables children to develop and practice comprehension within this broader focus.

Levels of Thinking   Viewing comprehension according to the level of thinking involved is an attempt to organize a complex cognitive activity according to a taxonomy or classification scheme of the mental operations involved in understanding what one reads.

Several taxonomies have been developed in an attempt to describe a hierarchy of mental operations. Among the best known are:

Bloom (1956)	Sanders (1966)	Barrett (1974)	Guilford (1985)
Evaluation	Evaluation	Appreciation	Evaluation
Synthesis	Synthesis	Evaluation	Divergent
Analysis	Analysis	Inference	Production
Application	Application	Literal	Convergent
Comprehension	Interpretation	Recognition or	Production
Knowledge	Translation	Recall	Memory
	Memory		Cognition

These taxonomies differ in purpose. Bloom's, by far the most popular in schools, is a classification scheme for writing educational objectives. Sanders' list was produced as a criterion for formulating and judging questions. Guilford's model was an attempt to account for our intellectual structure. Barrett's taxonomy was designed to describe the reading comprehension component in a published basal-reading program and later presented in a professional text about teaching reading. The models also differ in detail, with different labels attached to different levels of thinking. When related to reading comprehension, components of these taxonomies have been adapted, renamed, and applied in different ways.

When applied to reading instruction, level of thinking is often related to understanding at the literal, inferential, and critical–creative levels. Literal comprehension involves the ability to understand information and ideas specifically expressed in text. Inferential comprehension involves the ability to infer, analyze, and question information and ideas not explicitly stated. Critical/creative comprehension demands that readers move beyond the lines in applying their higher mental processes to what they read.

Literal comprehension consists of ''reading the lines'' and involves the most basic level of understanding, the recognition and recall of information explicitly stated in text. This level of comprehension has been called ''text explicit,'' in that information is directly stated in the text.

In dealing with literal comprehension, there is an important distinction between recognition and recall of information. Recognition requires the reader to locate a piece of information; recall requires the reader to remember that information after reading it. Recognition is usually easier than recall. (That is why good readers will read the questions before they read the paragraphs in a silent reading test.) Whether the task involves recognition or recall, comprehension at this level demands understanding of information that can be found directly in the text.

Literal understanding may involve different *types* of comprehension; that is, it may involve the recognition of a main idea contained in a topic sentence or the identification of a cause–effect relationship that is directly stated. No matter what aspect of "reasoning while reading" is involved, the response to literal-level questions can be confirmed by direct reference to information contained in the text.

Some reading tasks require primary reliance on literal comprehension. Pupils need to understand what is happening in a story before they can draw inferences or react mentally or emotionally to the story. Good readers, however, quickly move on to higher levels of thinking while reading.

Inferential or interpretative comprehension, "reading between the lines," requires understanding of facts or ideas not directly stated. Inferences are reasoned assumptions about information that is implied in a text. Making inferences requires the reader to supply information that the author does not provide directly. Comprehension at this level is text implicit; that is, information is not stated directly but is implied. Since no text is totally explicit, readers make inferences virtually every time they interact with a piece of print.

In a classroom setting, children use their background knowledge and experience to help them understand that which is not stated directly. For example, in reading Bernard Waber's *Ira Sleeps Over* (the story of the little boy who wants to take his teddy bear when sleeping over at a friend's house), pupils use their backgrounds to infer how Ira felt when his sister warned him, "Reggie will laugh," and to comprehend how Ira felt when he discovered that his friend Reggie slept with a teddy bear, too. Readers play an active role in inferential comprehension as they combine the information in the text with their knowledge of the world.

Making inferences is an ongoing part of the comprehension process. As they read, children make inferences about a number of things—the details of the story setting, causes or effects of actions, time elements, motivations and emotions of characters, solutions to problems, and the like. Pupils will not always make inferences spontaneously or automatically, however. Their ability to infer meaning and supply information not directly stated in text is stimulated by teacher direction. Research has shown that pupils' inferential comprehension can be improved by strategies such as cloze exercises, teacher-pupil interviews, questions aimed at inferential understanding, background discussions that foster predictions, and encouragement of self-monitoring procedures (Johnson and Johnson, 1988). Through careful suggestions and well-chosen questions, teachers guide pupils to develop the ability to "read between the lines" in understanding what the author implies in a text.

Critical–creative comprehension, the third and highest level of thinking, involves "reading beyond the lines" to react or respond to what one has read. The ability to think critically and creatively about what one reads is the ultimate stage in the reading process.

6.6 Putting Ideas To Work

Question–Answer Relationships

RAPHAEL (1982) suggests a strategy whereby pupils are encouraged to analyze the task demands of comprehension questions before answering them, a technique she calls Question-Answer Relationships (QAR). Using the designations "right there" (literal), "think and search" (inferential), and "on your own" (critical/creative), Raphael shows pupils how to identify the response demands of questions. She suggests that teachers discuss the difference between text-based and reader-based responses to questions. Teachers provide guided group practice with short model passages, leading pupils to increased levels of independence in recognizing the demands of reading comprehension questions.

QAR has been thoroughly researched and tested, and it has proved to be a successful reading-comprehension strategy. It is an effective technique to use with both narrative and expository text.

Hard and fast distinctions between critical and creative reading are not made easily. Critical comprehension has been viewed as the logical, analytical processing of what one reads: evaluating, analyzing, synthesizing, prioritizing ideas, and the like. It involves clarifying and assessing the reasonableness of ideas. Creative thinking involves fluency, flexibility, versatility, originality, and elaboration of ideas generated in connection with reading. In the actual reading–thinking process, however, sharp lines of differences disappear quickly as one tries to identify or classify the higher mental processes involved.

The distinction between critical and creative comprehension can be expressed in another way: critical reading involves a logical, cognitive reaction; creative reading involves a more emotional reaction. In critical reading, you react with your head; in creative reading, you react with your heart. Creative comprehension is evidenced by a tear in one's eye or a lump in one's throat as Billy buries his two faithful hound dogs near the end of Wilson Rawls's heartwarming story *Where the Red Fern Grows*.

This type of emotional response to text may, in fact, be the highest form of reading comprehension. At this creative reading level, the reader not only recognizes what the characters are doing but also infers the significance of their actions. The reader is reading so well that he or she actually understands how the character feels and comes to share the same joy, sorrow, love, disappointment or other emotions that the characters are feeling. When the reader becomes one with the character, then he or she truly comprehends what is read.

Pupils engage in critical comprehension as they form judgments about what they have read. These mental operations include evaluating the adequacy or validity of the material, judging the appropriateness or acceptability of the text, comparing different sources of information, weighing the value of ideas in light of their previous experience, and otherwise thinking about the facts and ideas that they have read. Critical reading is an active mental process.

The components of critical reading that have long received specific attention in classroom reading programs are distinguishing between fact and opinion, seeing the difference between real and make-believe, and detecting propaganda in print. All

6.7
FOR YOUR INFORMATION
Junior Great Books

ONE WAY of directly using literature to develop critical reading and thinking skills in the elementary grades is the Junior Great Books program. This program aims to help pupils understand and think critically about good books. Under the direction of a trained leader, pupils discuss language and ideas of stories that range from Margery Williams's *Velveteen Rabbit* and Marcia Brown's *Stone Soup* in the early grades to Paula Fox's

Maurice's Room and works by Langston Hughes in the upper elementary grades. Discussion focuses on interpretation of meaning, support for ideas from text, questioning, and shared inquiry that requires opinion and interpretation in response—all essential elements to comprehension at the highest level.

More information about the program is available from The Great Books Foundation, 40 East Huron Street, Chicago, IL 60611.

these components are essential to the intelligent use of reading in a free society. In a literature-based program, critical reading can be effectively developed and practiced. In selecting and reading trade books, for example, pupils can determine the primary purpose of the text: to entertain, to inform, or to persuade. Although some books are more singular in their intent, others have all three purposes. Having children talk about the purpose of a book like Hardie Gramatky's classic *Little Toot* gives them a chance to practice critical thinking in connection with reading from the beginning.

From the early years, opportunities abound for critical reading. Even with picture books, there is evidence that pupils can develop critical thinking skills, not only in cognitive factors but also in aesthetic awareness (Kiefer, 1984). Primary grade pupils can relate their own experiences to the events in Russell Hoban's *A Bargain for Frances* or make judgments about the values in Bill Peet's *Big Bad Bruce,* the bear who was a bully but who was "cut down to size," literally and figuratively.

As their reading ability leads to greater independence, pupils can compare the details of frontier life as described in the many books of Laura Ingalls Wilder with those described by Patricia MacLachlan in *Sarah, Plain and Tall.* Pupils can begin to sort out reality and fantasy—which events could have happened versus which were plainly impossible—in E. L. Konigsburg's *From the Mixed-up Files of Mrs. Basil E. Frankweiler* or in John Reynolds Gardiner's *Stone Fox,* books in which young people play the central roles. They can relate their own experiences to those of characters like Beverly Cleary's lovable *Ellen Tebbits* or Joan Lowery Nixon's character Margaret Ledoux in *Maggie, Too.* Some children's books—like Evaline Ness' *Sam, Bangs, and Moonshine* and Chris Van Allsburg's *The Polar Express*—are written specifically around a critical–creative reading theme.

Critical thinking is not unique to reading, of course. It is important in all areas of the curriculum. Watching television commercials to detect propaganda techniques or to separate reality and fantasy are valuable critical listening exercises. But since reading is so essential to learning and reaches into all areas of school life, critical thinking finds its home in reading from the very early stages.

Once the teacher focuses on the importance of critical/creative reading in literature-based reading instruction, opportunities to engage children in higher-level thinking as they read will suggest themselves aplenty. ''Instructional strategies to promote the development and use of good critical and creative thinking are most effective when they involve students in forms of thinking that they will use again and again in their lives. This is best done by infusing the teaching of critical and creative thinking into regular classroom instruction'' (Massachusetts Dept. of Education, 1988; p. 7). Opportunities to stimulate critical and creative thinking need not be manufactured. Prereading activities like brainstorming ideas about the possible content of a story, sharing information related to the topic, focusing on the relationship among ideas, forming hypotheses, and setting purposes related to critical/creative thought set the stage for critical thinking while reading.

Ongoing dialogue that will lead children to evaluate what they read, to confirm hypotheses, and to refine information will guide their higher-level thought processes during the reading act itself. Follow-up questions that ask children to form judgments about what they have read, to apply, to extend, to evaluate, and to stimulate their thinking beyond the text engage children in reading as a critical thinking activity.

Schemata

Schema theory was described in Chapter 4 as a means of explaining how humans organize and store information. Schemata (the plural form of schema) are mental structures or conceptual systems for arranging information inside our heads, the mental slots in which knowledge is organized and stored.

Schema theory is a theory about knowledge, how it is organized, and how it is used. According to this theory, knowledge or information is organized into units called schemata. In addition to the knowledge itself, these ''packets of data'' contain information about how the knowledge is to be used and about the network of relationships among the various schemata inside our heads. In other words, our schemata consist of all our associated knowledge and expectations. As such, they are critical building blocks that pupils use in bringing meaning to the literature that they read.

Schemata are the ''organizational blocks'' in which information is stored. In reading, we use old information to interact with new information in text. The vicarious experiences or the information that pupils acquire through reading reshapes their prior knowledge and perceptions and enable pupils to make new connections. Reading involves building bridges between the old and the new. Readers approach text with lots of information about their world. They use this knowledge, along with the information in the text itself, to construct meaning. Pupils construct meaning by connecting new knowledge they find in text to the knowledge they already have. They combine existing knowledge with new information to achieve comprehension.

Reading comprehension and schemata are reciprocally related. People acquire their schemata through experiences. This background—the ''theory in their heads'' of a particular topic—will influence their understanding in reading about that topic. At the same time, reading a story can broaden one's background and provide vicarious experiences that will alter or enrich one's schemata. As pupils read, new material is integrated into what they already know. For example, Betsy Byars's witty and touching *The Animal, the Vegetable, and John D. Jones* is a story about two sisters who look forward to spending a seaside vacation with their divorced father, only to have their father show up with his new girlfriend and her son. On the one hand, pupils who have spent vacation at the shore, and/or children who have had the experience of unwillingly sharing the attention of a divorced parent, will be able to comprehend this story in a different way from those who have not had these experiences. On the other hand, pupils who do not have a well-defined ''seaside-vacation-schema'' or an ''unwillingly-sharing-a-single-parent-schema'' will be able to develop a background and insights (i.e., new schemata) by reading the book. ''Trade books offer opportunities for building richly elaborated schemata that go considerably beyond those offered in most school books'' (Wilson, Anderson, and Fielding, 1986; p. 6).

Schemata are absolutely essential to inferential comprehension because what a person is able to read ''between the lines'' is almost wholly determined by his or her background and expectations. To illustrate the role of schemata in inferential comprehension, the following example has been used by Anderson and Pearson (1984). If you read that the governor's wife christened a ship last Saturday, what do you think she used for the christening? And if you read at the same time last Saturday, in a church near the shipyard, the vicar was christening a child, what do you think he used for the christening? Your ability to make inferences, to infer champagne in one case and water in the other, is attributable to the fact that you have a christening schema in your head, with a ''ship christening'' subschema on one hand and a child christening subschema on the other. That is why schemata make up the ideational scaffolding for understanding what we read.

Obviously, language is an important part of schemata, too. The linguistic labels that pupils attach to their background knowledge and the language they use to make the associations between concepts will affect their comprehension as they build on these concepts through reading. *Indian in the Cupboard* is a popular story written by a British author (Lynn Reid Banks) about a uniquely American topic (cowboys and Indians). Most upper-elementary pupils have the background to understand the story, but some of the British expressions—a Matchbox *lorry* (truck), the back of the yard where the *dustbins* (garbage cans) are, or the gate to keep the *infants* (first and second graders) in the schoolyard—cause American readers to pause. The language is not, however, so unusual as to prevent comprehension.

What are some of the implications of schema theory for helping children better comprehend what they read in literature-based programs?

Schema theory emphasizes the importance of employing a prereading strategy that encourages pupils to use their own experiences to predict and evaluate the problems and actions of characters in the stories that they read. When they make these predictions before reading, they are more likely to have a more fruitful interaction with the story.

Schema theory suggests the importance of activating pupils' prior knowledge before reading a story or poem. Teachers can activate this prior knowledge in a number of ways—by informal discussions to help discover what pupils already know about a topic; by using a semantic map that focuses on both word meaning and information; by suggesting advanced organizers to focus attention on essential elements in the story pupils are about to read; by examining illustrations that contain information important to understanding.

Wide reading builds prior experience. So do media presentations. Pupils who have read Laura Ingalls Wilder's *Little House in the Big Woods* will likely be better able to comprehend *Little House on the Prairie, Farmer Boy,* and Wilder's other books

6.8 Putting Ideas To Work

Activating Prior Knowledge

GIVEN THE recognized importance of activating pupils' existing knowledge before reading, several strategies have been developed to help pupils use their schemata to improve their comprehension of text. Among these techniques are:

PreReading Plan (PReP) is designed to give pupils opportunities to access what they know about a topic before reading. Developed by Langer (1981), the strategy involves two steps. Step one engages pupils in a discussion about key concepts in a story, including brainstorming for an initial association, reflecting on that association, and extending information related to the concept. The second step involves analyzing pupil responses to determine how existing understandings can prepare them for understanding new text and to see which pupils may need extra help in comprehension. PReP is a direct way to prepare pupils to comprehend a selection by using the knowledge they already have.

Anticipation guides are designed to activate pupils' knowledge before reading, while at the same time providing a guide as they read. The teacher prepares a number of written statements about the key concepts in a story; the group discusses the statements and then pupils read to determine if the statements can be verified in the story.

Text previews both build prior knowledge and provide an organizational framework for comprehension. The text preview may contain a brief synopsis and purpose-setting questions. The preview is discussed before reading. Although they are time-consuming to construct, text previews have proved to be effective aids to comprehension (Graves, Cook and La-Berge, 1983).

These and other prereading strategies have the same intent; that is to help pupils think about what they already know in relation to a story so that they will more effectively build on this knowledge through reading.

---

because of their familiarity with background information. There is a built-in element of motivation here, too.

Seeing videos, movies or filmstrips of *Little House* or any other book will also build pupils' schemata by providing background knowledge that will enhance understanding. Using videos and books in combination can be an excellent exercise in critical reading as well. After pupils have read (or heard) a book like Marie McSwigan's exciting adventure story *Snow Treasure* and then seen the movie based on the book, they can make some critical comparisons between the print and movie versions of the story. More often than not, pupils come to the same conclusion that many adult readers do: "I saw the movie, but I liked the book a lot better."

Perhaps the ultimate schema-building device is direct, real-life experiences. For many stories, this is impossible, since topics are often removed in time and space from children's experiences. Finding a story based on an experience that children have had, however, greatly improves chances that pupils will comprehend that story. For example, children in Boston who take the "Make Way For Ducklings Tour," on which they follow the path that Mr. and Mrs. Mallard and their ducklings followed from the Charles River Basin to the Duck Pond on the Boston Common, will certainly be able to read Robert McCloskey's *Make Way for Ducklings* with greater understanding and enjoyment.

Schema theory indicates that children who have gaps in their knowledge about a topic may have trouble comprehending what they read about that topic. This suggests

Audiovisual presentations can enhance pupils' understanding and appreciation of stories they read.

the importance of the teacher's providing important information before reading and filling in pieces of information that may be important to comprehension as the pupil reads. Within the context of schema theory, reading comprehension has been likened to a jigsaw puzzle. All the information must be used, and it must fit into place without forcing it. All the important slots must contain information, and the completed picture must make sense (Anderson and Pearson, 1984). A missing "jigsaw" piece that the teacher provides may be the key to a complete understanding of the entire "puzzle."

Reading comprehension is affected by what we already know. Helping pupils to build on their schemata as they read text is an effective way of improving their chances of comprehending what they read in school.

Metacognition

An aspect of reading comprehension that has received considerable attention during the past decade or so is metacognition. The term *metacognition* means an awareness of, and control over, one's thinking; in essence, it is thinking about thinking. *Metacomprehension,* a closely related term, means an awareness of, and control over, one's understanding. Metacognition involves the ability to analyze, control, and monitor one's own cognitive activity while reading. Very simply, it is the awareness of what is going on inside your head as you read. "The key words associated with metacognition reveal its emphasis: awareness, monitoring, control, and evaluation" (Pearson, 1985b; p. 15).

Metacognition makes reading an active mental process. It begins with a basic awareness that reading is an activity that demands cognitive involvement, not just decoding. This may seem obvious, but poor readers tend to focus primarily (sometimes exclusively) on the decoding dimensions as they read. From the outset, taking metacognition into account in the classroom involves developing in pupils what has been called a "sensitivity" to the demands of reading for meaning.

6.9

FOR YOUR INFORMATION

The Metacomprehension Strategy Index

SCHMITT (1990) has developed a 25-item questionnaire to assess pupils' awareness of appropriate metacognitive activity before, during, and after they read. Called the Metacomprehension Strategy Index (MSI), the instrument is designed to measure strategies specific to narrative text comprehension. Based on the premises that metacognition is characteristic of good comprehenders and that metacomprehensive strategies can be taught, the MSI provides teachers with a means of assessing pupils' awareness of prereading, reading, and postreading metacomprehension strategies.

Even if not used as an assessment instrument, the MSI can be a useful guide to metacognitive strategies that teachers can help pupils develop in reading narrative prose. The complete questionnaire can be found in the March 1990 issue of *The Reading Teacher*.

At a very basic level, metacognition makes a person aware of whether he or she is comprehending or not. Good readers consistently monitor their own reading activity. When they realize that they are not getting meaning out of text, they take appropriate action; that is, they slow down, reread sections, or work harder to achieve meaning. Poor readers do not apply these strategies. They tend to press on, whether or not they are comprehending what they read.

How can teachers get at the metacognitive activity that goes on inside pupils' heads? Studies have tried to determine how well children monitor their own reading by determining the degree of confidence they have in their responses to reading, by monitoring their self-corrections of miscues in oral reading, by examining their performance on cloze tests which demand a total sense of a passage, and by studying their eye movements and measuring their eye–voice span while they read. In discussing reading, teachers can have pupils "think out loud" about their reading activities. This is part of the teacher–pupil dialogue that characterizes good questioning.

Metacognition is a complex activity and it is important to help pupils develop metacognitive awareness. "The research clearly indicates that good readers use these (metacognitive) strategies, and poor readers do not" (Marzano et al, 1987). Pupils learn to comprehend better when teachers help them learn how, why, and when to perform problem-solving tasks necessary for full understanding of text.

Brown (1980) incorporates as reading strategies "any deliberate planful control of activities that give birth to comprehension (including): 1. clarifying the purposes of reading . . . ; 2. identifying aspects of a message that are important; 3. allocating attention so that concentration can be focused on the major content area rather than trivia; 4. monitoring ongoing activities to determine whether comprehension is occuring; 5. engaging in review and self-interrogation to determine if goals are being achieved; 6. taking corrective action (when appropriate); 7. recovering from disruptions and distractions" (p. 456).

Metacognition can be included as a regular part of instruction in reading comprehension through a variety of formal and informal activities such as:

Questioning Questions might focus on thought processes and not just answers; that is, following up questions like "Where did the pirates hide the gold?" with such questions as "How do you know?" to help pupils become aware of their line of reasoning and thought processes.

Teacher modeling Teachers can provide pupils with their own predictions and hypotheses before and during reading, explaining their own line of reasoning and verbalizing their own thoughts as they read. This modeling should be genuine; children are quick to see through predictable behavior when the teacher always knows the right answer.

Role playing and peer teaching When pupils have the responsibility of teaching others, they must think about how they will be expected to think.

Pupil-generated questioning Given a book or a section of a book, pupils can generate questions about the text. Their questions should focus on higher levels of thinking, since children have a tendency to select trivial items in an attempt to "trick" peers.

Rating answers After pupils have answered questions about a story, they can rate how confident they are in the accuracy of their answers. This confidence rating can lead students to an awareness of what they know and do not know as a result of reading, since part of metacognition is being aware of what one needs to know.

Writing instruction Learning to write paragraphs and longer stories according to certain patterns of organization helps pupils gain metacognitive awareness of these patterns as they appear in print.

The purpose of these activities is to help pupils think, and to help them monitor their thinking as they read.

Metacognition is a complex activity, but helping pupils develop metacognitive awareness and strategies is important. Research indicates that poor readers can be taught these strategies overtly with some spectacular results (Marzano et al., 1987). Pupils learn to comprehend better when teachers help them learn how, why, and when to perform problem-solving tasks necessary for full understanding of the literature they encounter in the classroom.

Other Reader-Based Factors

Other elements "behind the reader's eye" can affect comprehension of narrative text.

Motivation is an important factor. Comprehension is an active mental process. Pupils must care enough about reading and learning to make an effort to search out and remember the essence of what they are reading. Motivation emphasizes the importance of finding reading material in which pupils are interested, which is one of the advantages of using literature extensively in the process of teaching reading.

State of mind or emotional condition will affect comprehension as well. As an adult, have you ever tried to read while you are waiting for an important phone call, or tried to study when you were preoccupied with a personal problem? Comprehension demands attention. The pupil who is worried that the class bully will be waiting to beat him up at recess or who is concerned that she has just lost her best friend will have trouble understanding the text in a reading lesson.

A host of other factors can have an impact on comprehension—physical condition, level of comfort, time of day, modality preference, personal style, environmental factors. These and other elements are identified by Carbo, Dunn, and Dunn (1986) as

Tips on Questioning

LEU AND Kinzer (1987) provide some important and useful general suggestions for using questions as part of reading instruction. These include (in an adapted form):

1. Use questions for purposes other than assessment. Questions should guide, rather than merely check children's understanding of what they read.

2. Ask higher-level (critical–creative) questions, since these questions stimulate thinking.

3. Use lower-level (literal) questions to make connections to higher-level ones.

4. Allow a wide range of acceptable answers—not just one right or wrong answer—in response to higher level questions.

5. Use different types of questions for diagnostic purposes; i.e., to determine if students can recognize cause–effect or sequential relationships.

6. Ask questions *before* reading to set a purpose for comprehension.

7. Plan questions before starting the discussion of a story.

8. Have pupils formulate their own questions as they read.

---

variables in the comprehension process for individual children. In short, much that a child brings to the printed page will affect what he or she takes away from that page. These factors are as varied as human nature itself.

Context

Besides text-based and reader-based factors, social context can affect reading comprehension. Reading occurs in a particular context. The comprehension demands of reading that is done for sheer enjoyment differ from those of reading that is done for the purpose of later discussion or sharing in a literature group, or that is done in the more directed context of an instructional group.

Many of the factors involved in organizing and managing a classroom program—providing time for reading, opportunities to talk and to write about books, displays documenting book work and author study, a variety of trade books, frequent read-aloud sessions—constitute the context in which literature-based instruction is carried on. Galda (1988) suggests the need for classroom conditions that produce ''a community of readers,'' a secure environment in which pupils have time to read and to respond to what they read in a variety of ways.

The Role of Teacher Questioning

Within a classroom instructional program, the types of questions that the teacher asks will have an enormous effect on pupils' developing comprehension. Questioning becomes a teacher–pupil dialogue about text. Questions not only foster and guide pupils' understanding; they also serve as a model for the types of questions that pupils learn to formulate on their own as they read.

As part of reading instruction, questions are used before, during, and after reading. Prereading questions focus on purpose-setting, predicting, and relating text to prior knowledge. Questions are used during reading to guide comprehension and to highlight those elements essential to the full understanding and appreciation of the story. Questions following reading are designed to stimulate discussion and critical–creative thinking about what pupils have read.

Prereading questions can have both general and specific purposes, because children who read with a purpose comprehend better than those who do not (Blanton, Wood, and Moorman, 1990). Generally, prereading questions draw on a child's background and set the stage by focusing children's thinking on the theme or main idea of a story. Specific questions give children something to look for while they read. For example, before children read Byrd Baylor Schweitzer's *Amigo,* the touching story of a boy who adopts a prairie dog because his impoverished family cannot afford the pet he so desperately wants, general questions like ''Have you ever had a pet?'' and ''What might you do if you wanted a pet but couldn't have one?'' set the general tone for reading. More specific questions/directions like ''As you read the first few pages, see if you can discover the boy's problem and what his mother suggests'' offer pupils an immediate purpose as they begin to read the book.

Questions during the reading focus pupils' attention on the major elements of the story rather than on the mere recall of bits and pieces of trivial information. Again with *Amigo,* questions like ''What did Francisco's mother suggest? What do you think he will do? What problems do you think he might have?'' give a continuing purpose for reading and help pupils engage actively in understanding what they read. Questions that help pupils integrate the major elements of a story are best because it has been shown that such questions improve comprehension and help create more useful schemata.

Postreading questions can stimulate discussion on critical elements (''How likely is it that a boy could train a prairie dog to become a pet as Francisco did?'') and creative thinking that involves fluency and elaboration of ideas (''What else do you think Francisco might have done?''). These questions are most effective when they are related directly to prereading activities.

Questions are either instructional or evaluative. Questioning is, in fact, a generic instructional strategy for comprehension (Strother, 1989). Instructional questions help pupils improve comprehension by guiding their reading activity and by helping them develop effective reading strategies. Evaluative questions, the ones that have traditionally dominated reading lessons, assess or monitor the amount and type of comprehension that has taken place.

A variety of questions at literal, inferential, and critical/creative levels is important to promoting a breadth and depth of reading comprehension. Literal questions are fairly easy to formulate and identify; these are questions whose answers can be found directly in the text. The distinction between inferential and critical/creative questions is less sharp. In general, inferential questions involve connections between pieces of evidence in the text: in Harry Allard's *Miss Nelson Is Missing,* for example, ''How do you know Miss Nelson and Miss Swamp are the same person?'' Critical/creative questions require that pupils extend beyond the lines of the text—forming value judgments, applying information, generating emotional responses, making decisions, and otherwise using their heads and hearts in responding to what they read.

InQuest and ReQuest

GIVEN THE importance of questioning in promoting reading comprehension, several strategies have been proposed to help pupils improve their own questioning techniques. Two of these strategies are:

Investigative Questioning Procedures (InQuest) is a creative idea that promotes pupils' interaction with text. Developed by Shoop (1986), the technique can be used in reading instructional groups. The group stops reading at a crucial point in a story, at which time one pupil assumes the role of a major character and others become ''on-the-scene'' investigative reporters who query the character about story events. The emphasis in InQuest is to develop pupils' high-level questioning.

Reciprocal Questioning (ReQuest) is a well-researched strategy suggested by Manzo (1969). In ReQuest, teachers and pupils read silently and then take turns asking each other questions about the material. The teacher's role is to model good questioning techniques and to provide feedback on pupils' questions. Although the strategy is easily adaptable to group reading instruction, Manzo suggests working initially with individuals and focusing questions on specific types.

The kinds of questions teachers ask will help shape pupils' responses to what they read. Questions can generate both aesthetic and efferent responses (Rosenblatt, 1982). An aesthetic response is emotional; an efferent response is more informational. Questions that stimulate an efferent response focus on the information that a pupil can carry away from reading. Questions related to ''How did you feel and why did you feel that way?'' focus on aesthetic responses. Questions used to set the purpose for reading or to stimulate postreading discussion influence the way pupils view and respond to the literature they read. When efferent questions such as ''What were the children's names?'' ''Why did Sarah travel west?'' and ''What did you learn about life on the prairie?'' are asked about *Sarah, Plain and Tall,* pupils come away with the impression that this book is used as a vehicle for comprehension check. When questions focus on aesthetic responses, pupils come to see the book as a piece of literature to be enjoyed, as well as a story to be understood.

The pattern of questioning that teachers use is very important. Klein (1988) makes the distinction between questioning *strategies, techniques,* and *activities,* three terms that are often used interchangeably in reading instruction. *Strategy* refers to the overall plan of the lesson, so questions are designed to meet the objective or goal that the teacher sets. For example, the teacher might select a ''Predict-Test-Conclude'' strategy, representing a focus for questioning at each stage of a reading lesson—predicting in prereading, testing during reading, and concluding as part of postreading. *Techniques,* which are more specific than strategies, represents a particular ''line of questioning'' that the teacher opts to use. Having decided on the Predict-Test-Conclude strategy, the teacher might decide on the technique of comparison–contrast questions. *Activities* constitute the particular format that is used as part of the overall strategy—debate, dialogue, or discussion, for example. While Predict-Test-Conclude is not the only strategy described by Klein, this idea is well adaptable to literature-based instruction in the elementary grades.

A vital objective of questioning as part of teaching reading is to have pupils learn to generate their own questions as they read. Capable readers direct their own reading.

6.12 Putting Ideas to Work

Putting It All Together

I N TEACHING pupils how to read, teachers use their professional skill, knowledge, and ingenuity to design strategies that will help children get the most out of the books that they are reading. They need to sort through the myriad of factors that affect pupils' understanding.

The following ideas are intended to suggest the application of the interactive view of comprehension in helping pupils understand Miska Miles' beautiful and touching story *Annie and the Old One,* the story of a young Navajo girl's realization, denial, and final acceptance of the impending death of the grandmother she loves so much.

Text-Based Factors

Readability Based on text analysis, the teacher would recognize this book as a story written at approximately the upper-primary-grade level.

Text Structure The story has a narrative structure and focuses on the central plot element of a young girl's conflict with herself.

Content Although the setting is a Navajo environment, the characters are family members with whom most pupils will be familiar.

Reader-Based Features

Language Background The teacher might start by constructing a semantic map for *grandmother,* including expressions like *gnarled* and a *web of wrinkles,* which are used to describe the old woman in the book. (This semantic map would also activate pupils' schemata.) The teacher would also introduce the technical vocabulary words *hogan* and *mesa.*

Schemata To activate prior knowledge, the group might examine the illustration on the cover of the book. Prereading discussion might focus on what pupils already know about Native Americans in today's world. To provide information important to comprehending this story, the patriarchal/matriarchal role of grandparents in some societies (like the Navajo society portrayed in this story) might be highlighted.

Cognitive Processing and Metacognition Using a Predict-Test-Conclude questioning strategy, the teacher might identify the central problem ("This is a story about a young girl who finds out that her grandmother will soon die."), frame questions related to this problem ("How do you think the girl in the story might react? How would you react?"), and help pupils formulate hypotheses related to the problem ("What do you think she might do?"). This type of prereading provides an advanced organizer that sets a purpose for reading.

Questions/discussion during reading can help pupils reformulate or modify hypotheses. The questioning technique can focus on cause–effect relationships, identifying the multiple causes and effects of Annie's actions. Other questioning foci are possible as well—main ideas (inferring the nature of Annie's relationship with the Old One based on the details of their actions), sequencing (ordering Annie's activities that were designed to forestall her grandmother's death), or comparison/contrast (riding the school bus versus details of old tribal lifestyle). Guide questions should also direct pupils' attention to key segments of text ("When the new rug is taken from the loom, I will go to Mother Earth."). Obviously, the number and type of questions that are asked during reading need to be limited so as not to disrupt reading or kill pupils' enjoyment of the story.

Follow-up discussion can focus on critical and creative thinking—summarizing key ideas, testing conclusions based on the hypotheses made before reading, judging the appropriateness of Annie's actions, tracing the metacognitive connections that children employed to identify the relationships between causes and effects in the story, relating the story to pupils' own experiences, generating additional questions that the story suggests, relating this story to other stories they may have read or heard, and the like.

Potential follow-up ideas for oral language and writing are legion—summarizing the story, rewriting (or retelling) it from another point of view such as Annie or the Old One, orally reading key passages, extending into writing letters to older people in nursing homes, using semantics by examining the connotations of the various terms we use to describe old people (from "Golden Agers" to "Old Fogies"), dramatizing parts of the story, and the like.

These suggestions are by no means designed to be exhaustive. What the teacher does will depend on what he or she hopes to achieve (whether the book is being used to stimulate critical thinking or just for enjoyment), the nature of class (pupils in the rural Southwest will likely understand the setting better than those in a coastal New England town), and the spontaneous opportunities that arise as pupils read. These ideas are included merely to suggest a few of the possibilities for instructional activities that exist for affording pupils more opportunities to understand what they read and for providing practice in extending understanding beyond the lines of print on a page.

They formulate hypotheses, anticipate what might be ahead, test the significance of parts of the plot, refine and restructure their understanding, and play an active role in processing information as they read. Strategies that help children pose their own questions are those that will have long-term effects on competency in comprehension and in sucessful decision-making. Pupil-directed dialogue in literature study groups, instructional techniques such as Question–Answer–Relationship (see 6.6), paired practice in formulating questions—all are techniques that teachers can use to help pupils become adept at raising questions as they read.

One essential element of caution must be exercised when asking children questions as part of literature-based reading instruction. Teachers sometimes tend to ask so many questions that children's interest in reading is diminished or killed altogether. Having to answer a dozen "motivating" questions when one is anxious to get started, being stopped at every page with interminable questions that interrupt the flow of understanding and enjoyment of the story, and having to account for every scrap of information in the book after one has finished reading it defeats many of the purposes and values that literature-based reading instruction is designed to foster.

Possibilities for comprehension-related teaching activities are virtually limitless, and judicious choice of these possibilities is important. Children's literature offers untold opportunities for affective rewards; that is one of the primary advantages of literature-based instruction. Prereading activities that help pupils interact with text more effectively, reading activities that guide them toward greater understanding of what they read, and postreading activities that help them become critical reactors to what they read are vital to effective instruction. When the list of instructional activities dulls the enjoyment of reading, however, it is time to examine what one is doing.

The teacher may be the starting point of reading comprehension, but the pupils are the finishing points. Research suggests that an instructional model "that begins with a fairly heavy reliance on the teacher and builds toward student independence and ownership *and* that includes demonstrations of how to perform the skill is superior to a model that emphasizes practice, assessment, and more practice" (Pearson, 1985b; p. 24). The same research reports, "Explicit instruction associated with guided practice, lots of opportunity to practice and apply strategies independently, as well as attention to monitoring the application of such strategies seems to help students perform better on a variety of comprehension measures" (Pearson, 1985b; p. 26).

Summary and Conclusions

Some teachers make no distinction between the terms *reading* and *reading comprehension* because without comprehension, reading does not really occur in the fullest sense of the word. Understanding is at the heart of the reading process.

Comprehension is a complex phenomenon that takes place in the mind of the reader. It is where decoding, psycholinguistics, and information processing interact. It is influenced by a constellation of factors that extend far beyond any specific reading act and involves the use of many different kinds of knowledge.

Comprehension requires active, mental involvement on the part of the reader. Understanding occurs in the mind of the reader based on information contained in text. It is dependent on factors contained in the text (the level, structure, and content of the narrative), as well as factors that the reader brings to the text (language background, cognitive processing, schemata, and metacognitive awareness). Helping pupils comprehend the literature they read demands that teachers take these factors into account as part of the instructional process.

Comprehension is not "taught" in the same way that other aspects of reading are typically taught; that is, one cannot teach comprehension as one might teach vocabulary ("*Censorship* means the supression of objectionable features on moral, political, or military grounds."), decoding principles ("When two vowels go walking, the first one does the talking."), or study skills ("When trying to quickly find a word in the dictionary, consult the guide words at the top of the page."). Comprehension can be fostered, promoted, stimulated, and aided. It involves offering pupils direct help in using their reading strategies, prior knowledge, and thinking abilities in building meaning from text. It requires modeling that leads pupils to greater degrees of independence. This is the ongoing job that teachers face when pupils interact with print as part of learning to read.

Discussion Questions and Activities

1. Review the diagram of the interactive model of comprehension presented in 6.1. Research one of the text-based or reader-based features included in this model. What additional information can you find to extend the content of this chapter?
2. Reflect on your own reading of this chapter. What text-based features helped or hindered your understanding? How did your own schemata and metacognitive awareness affect your comprehension of what you read?
3. Select a picture book or easy-to-read trade book. Describe how you might use this book to develop pupils' competency in recognizing main ideas or determining cause–effect relationships.
4. Construct a story map or other graphic device for the plot of a children's trade book with which you are familiar. Make a list of ways you might use this story map in a classroom.
5. Examine the comprehension section of the scope and sequence chart of a basal reading program. Having noted one or two of the comprehension components listed, check the lesson plan in the teachers edition to see how these components are developed.

School-Based Assignments

1. Select a trade book that you might use for instructional purposes in your classroom. Describe how the backgrounds of the pupils might influence the way you would approach comprehension with the group.

2. Observe a reading lesson designed to improve pupils' comprehension. What does the teacher do beforehand to activiate prior knowledge? What type of questions does the teacher use during reading? What kind of follow-up questions are used? Take special note of the pupils' activities and reactions during the lesson. Make a list of things you might do differently if you were teaching this lesson.

3. Review the strategies suggested in the Putting Ideas to Work sections of this chapter. Design a lesson centered on one or two of these ideas and test out the idea with a small group of pupils.

4. Talk to a group of pupils about a story they read as part of a reading lesson or about a book they read independently. Try to determine how aware they are of their meaning-getting strategies as they read. What might you do to help them improve their understanding of text?

5. Plan and teach a reading lesson to a group of pupils, with an emphasis on comprehension. Have a peer or colleague observe your lesson and provide feedback.

Children's Trade Books Cited In This Chapter

Adler, David A. *Cam Jansen Mysteries.* New York: Penguin, 1980–88 (13 titles).

———. *Fourth Floor Twins.* New York: Penguin, 1985–88 (9 titles).

Allard, Harry. *Bumps In The Night.* New York: Bantam Books, 1979.

———. *Miss Nelson Is Missing.* Boston: Houghton Mifflin, 1977.

Atwater, Florence and Richard. *Mr. Popper's Penguins.* Boston: Little Brown, 1938.

Banks, Lynne Reid. *The Indian in the Cupboard.* New York: Avon, 1980.

Blume, Judy. *Freckle Juice.* New York: Dell, 1971.

Bonsall, Crosby. *Mine's the Best.* New York: Harper and Row, 1973.

Burnford, Sheila. *Incredible Journey.* Boston: Little Brown, 1960.

Byars, Betsy. *The Animal, the Vegetable, and John D. Jones.* New York: Dell, 1982.

Catling, Patrick Skene. *John Midas in the Dreamtime.* New York: Morrow, 1986.

Cleary, Beverly. *Ellen Tebbets.* New York: Dell, 1951.

———. *The Mouse and the Motorcycle.* New York: Morrow, 1965.

Fox, Paula. *Maurice's Room.* New York: Macmillan, 1988.

Gardner, John Reynolds. *Stone Fox.* New York: Harper and Row, 1980.

Gramatky, Hardie. *Little Toot.* New York, Putnam, 1939.

Hall, Donald. *The Ox-Cart Man.* New York: Penguin, 1979.

Hoban, Russell. *A Bargain for Frances.* New York: Harper and Row, 1970.

Hutchins, Pat. *Good Night, Owl!* New York: Macmillan, 1972.

Konigsburg, E. L. *From the Mixed-Up Files of Mrs. Basil E. Frankweiler.* New York: Dell, 1967.

Kuskin, Karla. *The Philharmonic Gets Dressed.* New York: Harper and Row, 1982.

Lobel, Arnold. *Frog and Toad Are Friends.* New York: Harper and Row, 1962.

MacLauchlan, Patricia. *Sarah, Plain and Tall.* New York: Harper and Row, 1975.

McCluskey, Robert. *Make Way for Ducklings.* New York: Penguin, 1941.

McSwigan, Marie. *Snow Treasure.* New York: Scholastic, 1986.

Miles, Miska. *Annie and the Old One.* Boston, Little Brown, 1971.

Munsch, Robert. *Mortimer.* Toronto: Annick Press, 1983.

Ness, Evaline. *Sam, Bangs, and Moonshine*. New York: Henry Holt, 1966.

Nixon, Jean Lowrey. *Maggie, Too*. New York: Dell, 1985.

Numeroff, Laura Jaffe. *If You Give A Mouse A Cookie*. New York: Harper and Row, 1985.

Parish, Peggy. *Amelia Bedelia*. New York: Harper and Row, 1963.

Peet, Bill. *Big Bad Bruce*. Boston: Houghton Mifflin, 1982.

Rawls, Wilson. *Where the Red Fern Grows*. New York: Doubleday, 1961.

Robinson, Barbara. *The Best Christmas Pagent Ever*. New York: Avon Books, 1972.

Schweitzer, Byrd Baylor. *Amigo*. New York. Collier. 1963.

Sendak, Maurice. *Where the Wild Things Are*. New York: Harper and Row, 1963.

Seuss, Dr. *Green Eggs and Ham*. New York: Random House, 1960.

Sharmat, Marjorie Weinman. *Nate the Great*. New York: Putnam, 1977–89 (11 titles).

Sobol, Donald. *Encyclopedia Brown Mysteries*. New York: Bantam, 1967–84 (18 titles).

Taylor, Theodore. *The Cay*. New York: Avon Books, 1969.

Van Allsburg, Chris. *Polar Express*. Boston: Houghton Mifflin, 1985.

Voigt, Cynthia. *Dicey's Song*. New York: Fawcett, 1982.

Waber, Bernard. *Ira Sleeps Over*. Boston: Houghton Mifflin, 1972.

Wilder, Laura Ingalls. *Farmer Boy*. New York: Harper and Row, 1953.

———. *Little House in the Big Woods*. New York: Harper and Row, 1953.

———. *Little House on the Prairie*. New York: Harper and Row, 1953.

Zion, Gene. *Harry by the Sea*. New York: Harper and Row, 1965.

References

Adams, M. J. (1990). *Beginning to Read: Thinking and Learning about Print*. Cambridge, MA: M.I.T. Press.

Anderson, R., and Pearson, D. (1984). A Schema Theoretic View of Basic Processes in Reading Comprehension. In D. Pearson (ed.), *Handbook of Reading Research*. New York: Longmans.

Applebee, A. (1978). *The Child's Concept of Story*. Chicago: University of Chicago Press.

Barrett, T. T. (1974). Taxonomy of Reading Comprehension. In R. C. Smith and T. C. Barrett (eds.), *Teaching Reading in the Middle Grades*. Reading, MA: Addison-Wesley.

Beach, W., and Hynds, S. (1991). Research on Response to Literature. In R. Barr, M. Kamil, P. Mosenthal, and P. D. Pearson (eds.), *Handbook of Reading Research,* Vol. 2. New York: Longmans.

Blanton, W. E., Wood, K. D., and Moorman, G. B. (1990). The Role of Purpose in Reading Instruction. *The Reading Teacher* 43:486–493.

Bloom, B. S. (1956). *Taxonomy of Educational Objectives*. New York: Longmans Green.

Brown, A. (1980). Metacognitive Development in Reading. In R. J. Spiro, B. C. Bruce, and W. F. Brewer (eds.), *Theoretical Issues in Reading Comprehension*. Hillsdale, NJ: Lawrence Erlbaum Associates.

Carbo, M., Dunn, R., and Dunn, K. (1986). *Teaching Students to Read through Their Individual Learning Styles*. Englewood Cliffs, NJ: Prentice-Hall.

Devine, T. G. (1986). *Teaching Reading Comprehension: From Theory to Practice*. Boston: Allyn and Bacon.

Fowler, G. L. (1982). Developing Comprehension Skills In Primary Students through the Use of Story Frames. *The Reading Teacher* 36:176–179.

Galda, L. (1988). Readers, Texts, and Contexts: A Response-Based View of Literature in the Classroom. *The New Advocate* 1:92–102.

Graves, M. F., Cooke, C. L., and LaBerge, M. J. (1983). Effects of Previewing Difficult Short Stories on Low Ability Junior High School Students' Comprehension, Recall, and Attitudes. *Reading Research Quarterly* 18:262–276.

Guilford, J. P. (1985). The Structure-of-Intellect Model. In B. B. Wolman (ed.), *Handbook of Intelligence*. New York: Wiley.

Johnson, D. D., and Johnson, B. V. (1988). Making Inferences. *Massachusetts Primer* 17:4–17.

Keifer, B. (1984). *Thinking, Language and Reading: Children's Responses to Picture Books*. Champaign: ERIC Clearinghouse on Language Arts. EJ253–869.

Klein, M. L. (1988). *Teaching Reading Comprehension and Vocabulary: A Guide for Teachers.* Englewood Cliffs, NJ: Prentice-Hall.

Langer, J. A. (1981). From Theory to Practice: A Prereading Plan. *Journal of Reading* 25:2.

Leu, D. J. and Kinzer, C. K. (1987). *Effective Reading Instruction in the Elementary Grades.* Columbus, OH: Merrill.

Manzo, A. V. (1969). The ReQuest Procedure. *Journal of Reading* 2:123–126.

Massachusetts Department of Education (1988). *Reading and Thinking: A New Framework for Comprehension.* Boston: Mass. Dept. of Education.

Marzano, R. J., Hagerty, P. J., Valencia, S. W., and DiStefano, P. P. (1987). *Reading Diagnosis and Instruction: Theory into Practice.* Englewood Cliffs, NJ: Prentice-Hall.

McNeil, J. (1984). *Reading Comprehension: New Directions for Classroom Practice.* Glenview: Scott Foresman.

Pearson, P. D. (1985a). Changing the Face of Comprehension Instruction. *The Reading Teacher* 38:724–738.

Pearson, P. D. (1985b). The Comprehension Revolution: A Twenty Year History of Process and Practice Related to Reading Comprehension. *Reading Education Report No. 57.* Urbana-Champaign: Center for the Study of Reading, University of Illinois.

Raphael, T. E. (1982). Question-Answering Strategies for Children. *The Reading Teacher* 36:186–190.

Readance, J. E., Bean, T. W., and Baldwin, R. S. (1989). *Content Area Reading: An Integrated Approach.* 3rd ed. Dubuque, IA: Kendall-Hunt.

Rosenblatt, L. M. (1982). The Literary Transaction: Evocation and Response. *Theory into Practice* 21:268–277.

Rosenshine, B. V. (1980). Skill Hierarchies in Reading Comprehension. R. J. Spiro, B. C. Bruce, and W. F. Brewer (eds.), *Theoretical Issues in Reading Comprehension.* Hillsdale, NJ: Lawrence Erlbaum Associates.

Sanders, N. M. (1966). *Classroom Questions.* New York: Harper and Row.

Schmidtt, M. C. (1990). A Questionnaire to Measure Children's Awareness of Strategic Reading Processes. *The Reading Teacher* 43:454–461.

Shoop, M. (1986). InQuest: A Listening and Reading Comprehension Strategy. *The Reading Teacher* 39:670–674.

Strother, D. B. (1989). Developing Thinking Skills through Questioning. *Phi Delta Kappan* 71:324–327.

Wilson, P. T., Anderson, R. C., and Fielding, L. G. (1986). *Children's Book Reading Habits: A New Criterion for Literacy.* Champaign-Urbana: University of Illinois, Center for the Study of Reading, Rading Education Report No. 63.

Chapter 7

Literacy across the Curriculum: Comprehending Expository Text

Chapter 7 Outline

I. Introduction
II. Trade Books and Textbooks
  A. Expository Text
  B. Textbooks
  C. Trade Books
  D. Book Clusters
III. Text-Based Features
  A. Readability
  B. Text Structure
    1. Patterns of Expository Text
      a. Enumeration
      b. Time Order
      c. Comparison–Contrast
      d. Cause–Effect
    2. Teaching Text Structure
  C. Content
    1. Social Studies
    2. Science
    3. Poetry
    4. Mathematics
    5. Art
    6. Music
    7. Drama and Dance
    8. Physical Education
  D. Other Text-Based Features
    1. Design
    2. Graphic Materials
      a. Pictures and Illustrations
      b. Maps
      c. Graphs
      d. Charts, Tables, and Diagrams
IV. Reader-Based Features
  A. Language Background
    1. Decoding
    2. Word Knowledge
      a. Technical Vocabulary
      b. Specialized Words

        3. Sentences
        4. Paragraphs
        5. Selections
     B. Cognitive Processing
        1. Type of Thinking
        2. Level of Thinking
     C. Schemata
     D. Metacognition
     E. Motivation
  V. Summary and Conclusions
Discussion Questions and Activities
School-Based Assignments
Children's Trade Books Cited in This Chapter
References

Features

7.1   Book Clusters
7.2   Another Look at the Interactive Model of Reading Comprehension
7.3   Using Cloze for Readability
7.4   Teaching Text Structure
7.5   Trade Books for Social Studies
7.6   I-Charts for Critical Thinking
7.7   Trade Books for Science
7.8   Integrating Literature and Science
7.9   Trade Books for Mathematics
7.10 Eight Questions for Math-Related Trade Books
7.11 Graphic Information Lesson
7.12 Teaching Content Words
7.13 Herringbone Technique
7.14 Study Guides
7.15 K–W–L
7.16 Purpose, Classification, and Response

Nonfiction trade books are essential in literature-based reading programs. These informational books can be used hand-in-hand with textbooks as vehicles for helping pupils deal with expository text.

Comprehending expository text places demands on readers that narrative text does not. Since most reading instructional materials are narrative, pupils need special attention in learning to deal with expository writing.

Text-based features of expository writing—readability level of material, structural patterns, and the nature of the material presented—influence pupils' understanding of informational trade books and content area textbooks.

Since the purpose of expository text is to present information, reader-based features—language background, cognitive processing, schemata and metacognition—apply to informational trade books and textbooks in particular ways.

EADING AND writing are more than separate school subjects. They are integral parts of school life in all areas of the curriculum. Learning is a major purpose of schooling and reading is a major means of learning.

As adults, we learn much of what we know through reading. Scientists acquire scientific knowledge through print; in fact, communication has long been identified as a basic scientific process by the American Association for the Advancement of Science (1965). Learning in social studies relies no less heavily on communication skills. Comprehension in reading is essential to achievement in math. There is no part of the curriculum in which reading and writing do not play an integral role.

Trade Books and Textbooks

Literature-based reading involves much more than stories and poems; it includes literary nonfiction as well. Literature-based programs make extensive use of informational trade books for the dual purpose of helping pupils acquire information and develop reading abilities. "The integration of both fiction and nonfiction helps children experience two ways of knowing literature" (Crook and Lehman, 1991; p. 35).

For a long time, textbooks have been the primary vehicles for presenting information in print to pupils, and "reading to learn" was an important part of instruction in content areas of the curriculum. Although textbooks are still often used in literature-based programs, they are being supplemented—and in some cases replaced—by nonfiction trade books and fictional works that promote learning in content areas. Both trade books and textbooks can be used effectively to help pupils develop the unique strategies required of dealing with expository text.

Expository Text

Most reading material that pupils encounter early in their school lives is narrative in nature. Its purpose is to tell a story. Young children use language to fill another function, however; they use language as a vehicle to acquire information and to make meaning of their worlds. The presentation of information is the primary function of expository text that pupils encounter as part of their classroom and out-of-school reading experiences.

Expository text is written to explain, describe, and inform. This type of writing is used to convey facts, to clarify concepts, or to present arguments. Pupils encounter expository text in science, in social studies, and in other content-area textbooks. They also encounter expository text in informational trade books, including biographies, concept books, and other forms of nonfiction.

Much expository text has narrative features. Elements of "story" can be found in scientific accounts of how the earth's crust was formed or in historical accounts of how a nation was born. Pupils can respond to these narrative features with all the interest and excitement that they experience in the fiction that they read; however, not all expository text contains these narrative features, and the major purpose of expository writing remains that of presenting information.

Pupils generally find expository text more difficult to comprehend than narrative text (Mason and Au, 1990). Expository text does not typically follow the narrative story structure with which children are familiar. Expository writing tends to be more dense and is often loaded with terms and concepts unfamiliar to children. Helping pupils develop techniques for comprehending expository text through frequent encounters with this type of writing is an integral part of the process of literature-based reading instruction. Reading is best taught in a purposeful, authentic context, and reading about school subjects is a very functional purpose for reading. Reading competency develops through, not apart from, reading informational material.

Textbooks

In most classrooms, textbooks have conventionally constituted the major sources of printed material in content areas of the curriculum. Textbooks ''cover'' the subject matter that children are expected to learn. As such, these resources are integral to the instructional process.

Textbooks have distinct advantages as learning tools. They concentrate material and organize it in a way to assist learning by pupils. They provide resources for immediate use in acquiring skill in mathematics, information in science, understanding in social studies, and insight into art and other subjects. Textbooks are used as references to expand information first acquired by a pupil in a picture book or a novel. When well chosen and well used, textbooks can be valuable devices for teaching pupils how to read.

At the same time, however, there are some problems with overreliance on textbooks. Because a single textbook is likely to be beyond the reading ability of some pupils, the book may result in frustrating reading experiences. A survey of the best-selling science textbooks demonstrated a range of reading levels from first through tenth grade within the same textbook (Wood and Wood, 1968). The amount of information presented and the format of the material often make textbooks difficult for many pupils. That is why trade books are being more widely used as learning tools in content areas of the curriculum.

Trade Books

Trade books offer some compelling advantages as supplements to textbooks in content subjects. Even for pupils at the very beginning stages of learning to read, picture books provide opportunities ''for deepening literary and aesthetic responses as well as for broadening their understandings of social and cultural worlds'' (Kiefer, 1988; p. 260). Trade books can capture pupils' interest more quickly and present information in a different (and often more interesting) manner. Trade books on various topics come in a range of reading levels. They offer unique opportunities to develop pupils' critical thinking skills and they add a breadth and depth of up-to-date information about curriculum topics. Furthermore, while most textbooks focus on lower level thinking skills, trade books often provide material for higher level critical and creative thinking.

Trade books enrich the curriculum. While textbooks contain essential information, trade books can be used to expand understanding and provide a deeper dimension of learning about a subject. Many textbooks provide a collection of facts only vaguely related to one another. The balance of informational trade books and novels enhances total understanding and puts information into perspective for pupils. In studying the Civil War, for example, pupils can learn much through books like Russell Freedman's

Trade books can help pupils reach a deeper and richer understanding of curriculum topics.

Lincoln: A Photobiography and Delia Ray's *Behind the Blue and Gray: The Soldier's Life in the Civil War.* Fictional works can broaden and deepen this understanding. In *Across Five Aprils,* for example, Irene Hunt tells the story of the Civil War through the eyes of a young boy and how that terrible war affected his family. Her account not only contains historically accurate information, it also provides insights on to how the war affected the lives of so many people.

Johnson and Ebert (1992) describe how history units can be organized around children's trade books to give pupils a better sense of the past and an opportunity to share the joy and despair of historical figures. They provide suggestions for a variety of cooperative learning group projects, whole-class response activities, small group and individual projects, writing, critical thinking, problem solving, and a full range of activities that help pupils use trade books to get a better sense of what they call "time travel." They report that with the use of literature, motivation was higher, knowledge was wider, and history came alive in the minds of the pupils.

Trade books can be easily adapted to the range of reading levels typically found in an elementary classroom. While a single textbook may be well above or far below the reading level of many pupils, trade books on curriculum topics can usually be found to match the reading level of individual pupils. Easy-to-read, informational trade books can be useful in building the conceptual background that will enable less capable readers to understand more easily what they are expected to read about a topic in their content area text.

Using trade books in the content areas is an effective way to promote, as well as to teach, reading. "The greatest benefit of using literature across the curriculum is that meaningful reading is taking place all day long in a variety of settings and with a variety of texts. . . . Literature used across the curriculum extends and enriches the life of the classroom and the attitudes, knowledge, and understandings of the students who work there" (Chatton, 1989; p. 69).

Chatton (1989) identifies other values and functions of literature across the curriculum. Literature can be used to raise questions about content area topics and, at the same time, provide sources for answers to these questions. It provides a vehicle for making connections among subjects, avoiding the fragmentation that is often part of learning isolated facts. Literature can also be used to enhance pupils' problem-solving abilities and foster their critical thinking and decision-making skills.

Besides, literature entertains. It is fun. Books like those that constitute Laura Ingalls Wilder's "Little House" series not only give pupils a sense of what it was like to live at a particular time and place in American history, but these books also tell authentic stories that are appropriate to any time and place where human beings live. Even books written specifically to inform—such as Aliki's *Mummies Made in Egypt*—can often be enormously entertaining in their own right.

Book Clusters

Book clusters are collections of fiction and nonfiction trade books related to a topic being studied in the classroom. These collections can be put together for a full range of curriculum topics. A primary-grade science unit on weather might include a reading center with factual books like Franklyn M. Branley's *Sunshine Makes the Seasons,* fictional books like Marie Hall Ets's *Gilberto and the Wind,* and a book of poems such as Jack Prelutsky's *Rainy Rainy Saturday.* But "literature across the curriculum does not mean forcing connections. (It means) recognizing that some pieces of literature have a strong background of fact and provide a unique human perspective on historical, scientific, and technological subjects" (Huck, Hepler, and Hickman; 1987, p. 617).

In using book clusters, fact and fantasy need to be seen in a balanced perspective. In studying about bears, for example, pupils can use such nonfiction trade books as *The Baby Bears* by Sonja Bullatz and Angelo Lomeo or *Bears* by Mark Rosenthal, along with books like Bill Peet's delightfully humorous fantasy *Big Bad Bruce,* Paul Gladone's version of the popular fairy tale *The Three Bears,* or Robert McCloskey's popular story *Blueberries for Sal.*

In mixing fact and fiction, however, it is important to help pupils separate reality and fantasy, an important critical-reading component. Separating fact from fiction is not difficult in comparing books like Lois Slobodkin's *The Three-Seated Space Ship,* a madcap story about children who blast off with their grandmother into outer space, with Suzanne Lord and Jolie Epstein's *A Day In Space,* a photographic account of a day on a NASA space shuttle. Separating what may have happened (fiction) with what really happened (fact) may require more critical consideration in reading and discussing a book like Esther Forbes's *Johnny Tremain.*

Informational trade books can be important vehicles from the very beginning stages of learning to read. In nursery school and kindergarten, there is a rich variety of high-quality, nonfiction picture books that can be used to stimulate language, generate interest in books, and meet the other needs of an emergent literacy program. Informational books can be shared at story time, can be enjoyed by pupils independently, can be the basis of early writing and art projects, and can be used for expanding children's horizons by increasing their store of knowledge about the world in which they live.

Throughout the grades, trade books related directly to curriculum topics abound. In science, there are books on the life cycle of humans and animals, books explaining

7.1 Putting Ideas To Work

Book Clusters

BEFORE BEGINNING units on curriculum-related topics, teachers often assemble collections of fiction and nonfiction books clustered around a unit topic. For example, here is the beginning of a primary grade cluster on the topic of *flight*. It contains a combination of easy-to-read books and more challenging titles for more capable readers.

This cluster of trade books becomes a focus for study and recreational reading during the unit. Additional references can be suggested by the librarian.

Crook and Lehman (1991) have described and demonstrated the extent to which book clusters (see next page) can be built around a curriculum concept.

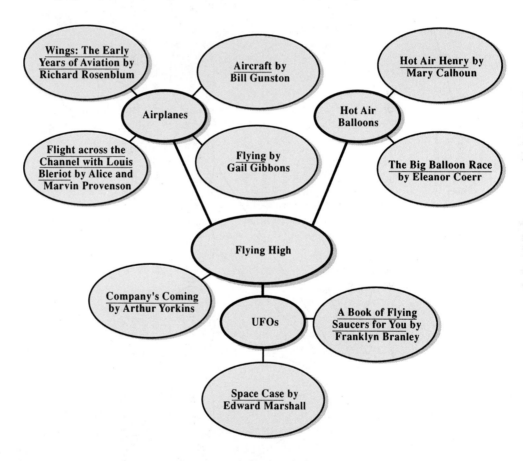

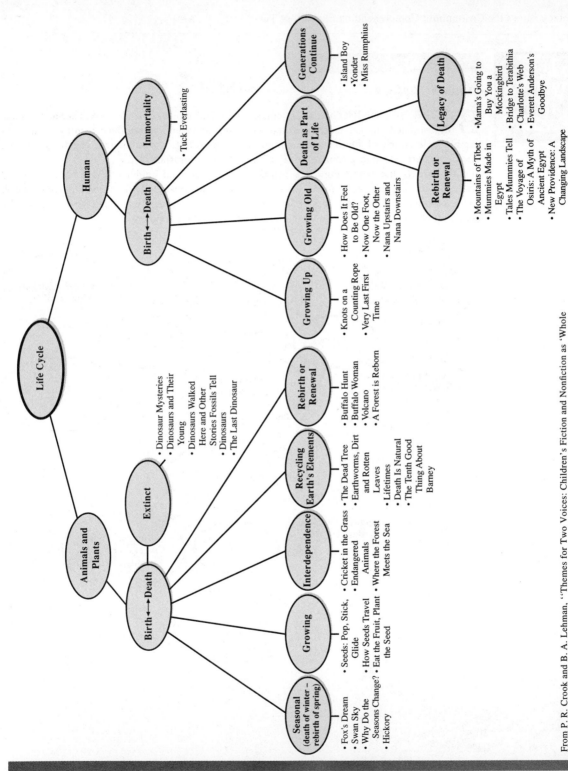

From P. R. Crook and B. A. Lehman, "Themes for Two Voices: Children's Fiction and Nonfiction as 'Whole Literature'," in *Language Arts*, 1991, 68:37. Copyright © 1991 by the National Council of Teachers of English. Reprinted by permission.

7.2 Putting Ideas to Work

Another Look at the Interactive Model of Reading Comprehension

Another Look at the Interactive Model of Reading Comprehension

Reading comprehension is a process involving the interaction of:

Text-Based Features   with   **Reader-Based Features**

Level of Text
Structure of Text
Content of Text
etc.

Language Background
Cognitive Processing
Schemata
Metacognition
etc.

how the world functions, and experiment and activity books that emphasize the scientific process. In social studies, biographies of famous people, documents and journals, photographic essays, and historical fiction bring learning to life. In math there are counting books that vary in complexity from simple enumeration of objects to those with number concepts and problem solving, along with books presenting and explaining a variety of sophisticated number concepts. In areas of general interest, there are plenty of craft and how-to books, sports stories, books of interesting and not-so-interesting trivia, and a plethora of informational trade books on topics that range from photography to aeronautics, from choosing careers to understanding human emotions. Each can be a vehicle for helping pupils acquire information while developing reading competency in the elementary grades.

How does the teacher use expository text to help pupils build reading competency and confidence? Following the interactive model of reading comprehension (described in the preceding chapter and represented in 7.2), the same factors apply to expository text as to narrative text, but in some different ways. Readers use features of the text itself to build meaning in their own minds. Reading comprehension is influenced by the level of the text, the structure of the text, the content of the material, and other textual features. Meaning is also dependent on the reader's language background, cognitive processing, schemata, and metacognitive awareness. The interaction of text-based features and reader-based features enables the reader to comprehend expository text.

Text-Based Features

Both expository and narrative text have certain features—level of difficulty, structural patterns, content, and design elements. There are differences between these features in the respective classes of text, however. The readability level of expository text used for instructional purposes in the classroom tends to be on the high side of pupils' grade placement. Organizational patterns of expository text vary greatly from those of narrative text. Content is different, too: narrative text is fictional, and expository text is loaded with facts and concepts. The design and illustrations in expository text play a more essential role. These text features need to be taken into account in using expository text to teach reading.

Readability

An important early step in teaching reading with expository text is determining the relationship between the level of the material and the pupil's reading ability. The easiest and most obvious way of doing this is to have the pupil read a portion of the text before using it as a teaching vehicle. Since this is not always possible, readability measures are commonly used.

As was briefly described in the previous chapter, readability is an estimate of the ease with which a written selection can be read and understood. Readability measures are used to predict or to determine how relatively easy or difficult a text is expected to be.

The method commonly used for estimating reading level is a readability formula, a statistically based, predictive device designed to determine level of difficulty. Typically, these formulas are based on measurable aspects of the language used in a piece of print. Most formulas rely primarily on word length (judged by the number of syllables or letters per word) and sentence length. Although some formulas also employ word lists, the number of affixes in a segment of text, or other factors in computing a readability score, most formulas still rely on word length and sentence length. Using several short samples of text, the formula is applied to produce a grade score or index indicating the expected difficulty (readability) level of the material.

Readability figures are usually expressed as grade-level equivalents, since grade level is the "coin of the realm" in our educational numbering system. Thus, based on a particular formula, a trade book or a chapter in a textbook would be said to be at a "low third grade readability level" or at a "9.8 readability level."

Although formulas have been commonly used for some time as a convenient means of computing readability, they provide very imperfect measures of text difficulty or how easily something can be read with understanding. "For a large number of readers with varying abilities, and for large numbers of texts with varying sentence and word lengths, formulas can be used to make fairly successful predictions. But for more specific cases, they become less and less sensitive to special features of texts and readers" (Davison, 1985). Formulas are not sensitive to those factors most important to influencing how well readers will comprehend what they read.

Readability formulas take language factors into account, but they deal only with measurable aspects of language. Thus, words are "weighted" by the number of letters or syllables. Formulas generally do not consider how familiar or common a word might be, so that a five-syllable familiar word like *electricity* would be computed as being much more difficult than the phonetically regular but less familiar, monosyllabic word *erg*. Similarly, because the number of words in a sentence can be easily counted, sentence length or number of sentences per sample passage is used to determine readability, without regard for sentence complexity, concept density, or literary style in a sentence. Sentence form is typically more important than sentence length in making a sentence more or less easy to understand.

Readability formulas fail to account for what is not explicitly expressed, implied material that is so crucial to understanding. Nor do these formulas account for the constellation of factors that readers bring to a piece of print—their familiarity with the material, their interest or motivation, their experiences and expectations. And since the reader's contribution is so important to the comprehension of text, any measure that does not take the reader into account is bound to be flawed.

Perhaps more dangerous than the problems inherent in the formulas themselves, however, is the way in which the concept of readability has come to be viewed by educators—with absolute, uncritical faith in the accuracy of scores. Despite repeated cautions, many teachers and administrators accept scores at face value, not as an estimate of relative difficulty. Overconfidence in readability measures has had an impact on the nature of texts used in content areas of the curriculum. Writing quality in textbooks has often been sacrificed on the altar of readability, resulting in oversimplified, choppy and unnatural language patterns written to conform to a formula. Research has shown that altering a text to "reduce its difficulty" according to a readability formula can actually make a text more difficult to understand (Davidson and Kantor, 1982). Trying too hard to conform to a readability measure can sometimes do more harm than good in producing readable and accurate text.

Despite the problems with readability formulas, these devices can be used to arrive at a general indication of the *relative difficulty* of a piece of print. Formulas are by no means absolute, but they can be useful in yielding a relative high/low readability estimate for a piece of information-related text.

Another means for judging readability that has been suggested by Vacca and Vacca (1989) is a readability checklist. Checklists take into account such elements as *understandability* (including vocabulary, conceptual background and presentation of material), *usability* (including organizational aids found in the text), and *interestability* (including attractive illustrations and motivating activities). Although useful as a means of examining curriculum-related reading materials, these checklists provide only general and subjective measures of how appropriate a book might be for a particular pupil.

Teachers need to be aware of the general level of a selection of expository text before using that material in helping pupils learn to read. Curriculum area textbooks, especially at the middle school level, are sometimes selected for their content, with not enough regard for readability. In other words, a seventh-grade science textbook might be chosen because it does a particularly good job at presenting the concepts and information contained in the science curriculum and not because it is geared to the reading ability level of seventh graders. Those responsible for selecting textbooks are becoming more sensitive to issues related to readability levels, but many classrooms still have textbooks that are very difficult for pupils to read.

At the beginning of the year, it makes sense for teachers to administer a cloze test for the purpose of establishing the readability level before using a basal class textbook in science or social studies. This measure takes only a short time to administer and a short time to correct, yet it can give the teacher an immediate overall indication

Using Cloze for Readability

A MEASURE of readability that does take the reader into account is cloze. Cloze procedures were described earlier in this book (pp. 154–155) as a means of helping pupils use context to determine the pronunciation and meaning of unknown words. Cloze exercises can also be used to determine the readability of a book in relationship to a pupil's reading level.

Cloze was proposed as a means of measuring readability by W. Taylor (1953) and further developed and applied to education by John Bormuth (1966, 1968). Cloze exercises allow readers to interact with print and to use their syntactical and semantic awareness, along with their knowledge of content, in indicating an understanding of what they read.

The directions for constructing, administering, and scoring a cloze test are:

1. Select a passage of about 250–275 words. Obviously, a shorter selection would be used for primary grade, easy-to-read informational books.
2. Leaving the first sentence intact, delete every fifth word until 50 blanks have been created. The final sentence in the passage should be left intact as well. In the primary grades, the deletion of every tenth (rather than every fifth word) is often recommended.
3. After explaining the purpose and nature of the exercise, have pupils complete the exercise independently using one word per blank. There is no time limit to the exercise.
4. In scoring, accept only the exact word that was deleted from the text. *Synonyms should not be counted* since performance criteria were established on the basis of exact word replacements. Incorrectly spelled words are acceptable (as long as they orthographically approximate the deleted word). Each correct response is multiplied by two to obtain a cloze score.

5. In interpreting the score, a score of 45–60 percent indicates that the material is at the pupils' instructional level; that is, the material may be challenging to the reader but it is at a level that can be understood with help and guidance. A score higher than 60 indicates that the material is suitable for independent reading; a score of less than 44 indicates that the material may be too difficult.

Two points are important to keep in mind regarding cloze as a measure of readability. The first relates to pupils' familiarity with the whole idea of cloze techniques. The more familiar pupils are with cloze and the more practiced they are with the procedure, the more reliable will be the readability measure. This suggests the need for practice in using cloze exercises before the technique is used as a means of measuring readability of printed material.

The second point relates to accepting only exact replacements (not synonyms) as correct responses. This seems rather harsh; however, accepting synonyms as correct responses can "muddy the water" in arriving at a readability measure. Moreover, the pupil is not unfairly punished, since a score of less than 50 percent indicates an acceptable readability level for instructional materials. In using cloze as a technique for teaching the use of context clues, the use of synonyms should not be prohibited; in fact, the use of words with similar meanings should be *encouraged!*

Cloze is an appropriate measure in judging the relationship between a reader and a piece of print. The procedure is useful because it takes the reader's background and content schemata into account. Besides, instead of relying on a predictive formula, cloze gives the teacher a measure of pupils' performance in interacting with the text that they are actually expected to read.

of the appropriateness of the textbook for the pupils. This type of cloze exercise does not necessarily validate the publisher's readability figure, but it does indicate the match between the level of the writing and the level of the reading in a classroom.

Even if the textbook is found to be beyond the readability level of most pupils, it is unlikely that the teacher will be able to abandon the use of the text altogether. After administering a cloze test, however, teachers will be in a position to know how heavily they can rely on the textbook as a source of independent assignments for pupils. Cloze also provides teachers with a thumbnail indication of which pupils will likely have the most problems with the textbook, so that the teacher can adjust instruction for these pupils and/or use alternative sources of print for content being taught.

An awareness of readability is also important as teachers set up displays of trade books on spiders, on the Westward Movement, or on some other curriculum-related topic. Trade books at different levels in these curriculum-related displays provide reading material to match the varying reading levels in a typical classroom.

Text Structure

All text has structure. Structure is the organization of the ideas, events, facts, and other content presented in a passage. Text structure specifies the logical interconnection of material in a passage. Recognizing the organization of text is a key to reading comprehension, and therefore making pupils aware of text structure is an important part of teaching reading with expository text.

The linear structure of narrative text, along with suggestions about how to make pupils aware of narrative text structure, were presented in the previous chapter. Expository text is structured or organized differently. Informational trade books and content textbooks are written primarily to inform. Exposition rather than narration is their primary mode of presentation. Ideas are related to each other in a manner different from that in the ''linear'' organization of narrative text, and good readers have learned to look for these relationships.

Patterns of Expository Text   Four patterns of organization are commonly identified in expository text: enumeration, time order, comparison–contrast, and cause–effect relationships. Other labels are sometime used for these patterns of text organization, and additional patterns (such as problem–solution or persuasive writing) have been identified as well. Teaching pupils these four patterns will give them a solid start in using text structure as an aid to comprehension.

Enumeration, the most common pattern of textbook organization, involves listing information about a topic. This pattern is closely related to the reading comprehension component of main ideas/details. Main topics are defined, explained, or expanded by pieces of related information.

Example from Textbook

Rocks look different. They are different colors. Some are shiny. Some are dull. Rocks feel different. Some are rough. Some are smooth.

From *Holt Science.* New York: Holt, Rinehart, and Winston, 1984.

Example from Trade Book

The biggest shark is the whale shark. It is longer than a bus. The whale shark has three thousand teeth. But it will never bite you. It eats only tiny shrimp and fish. The whale shark is very gentle. A diver can even hitch a ride on its back.

From *Hungry, Hungry Sharks* by Joanna Cole. New York: Random House, 1986.

Time order relates to sequence. Facts or events are arranged according to the order in which they occur, or steps are described in the order in which they are to be followed.

Example from Textbook

Do you know how to make bread? Making one loaf of bread is similar to the way a baking factory makes many loaves. At a large factory, the flour is mixed with water and yeast. The three items are mixed together to make dough. Milk, salt, and more flour and water may be added. The dough is put in a warm room. The heat sets off an action in the yeast that makes the dough rise to a larger size. Finally the dough is formed into loaves and put into pans. At last, it is baked.

From *Our Regions.* New York: Holt, Rinehart and Winston, 1983; p. 166.

Example from Trade Book

In the morning, the wind still blew. Waves rolled across Matinicus Rock. Abbie blew out each light. She trimmed each wick. She cleaned each lamp. She put in more oil. Then she went to breakfast. Then, at last, she went to bed.

From *Keep the Lights Burning, Abbie* by Peter and Connie Roop. Minneapolis: Carlrhoda Books, 1985.

Comparison–contrast, as the name suggests, involves organizing text by comparing likenesses and differences among facts and ideas.

Example from Textbook

The environment of a valley is different from the environment of a mountain top. In a valley, summer days are warm. Squirrels chatter in the tall trees. Birds sing. On the top of a mountain, the air is cold. Even in summer, there is often snow on the ground. Strong winds blow. A mountain top has a cold climate.

From *Communities Large and Small.* Lexington, MA: D.C. Heath 1987.

Example from Trade Book

A great variety of animals inhabit the earth. Like plants, their bodies are composed of cells. Unlike plants, however, these cells are not held together by rigid cell walls, but are soft and flexible. Again, unlike plants, animals cannot manufacture their own food. Instead, they are dependent on plants and other animals for nourishment.

From *Small Worlds Close Up* by Lisa Grillone and Joseph Gennaro. New York: Crown, 1978.

Cause–effect organization builds on the idea that ideas or events come about as a result of certain causes, and it explores the relationship between the causes and the events. Sometimes, this organizational pattern takes the form of a *problem–solution,* showing the development of a problem and a solution in a cause–effect relationship.

Example from Textbook

Alcohol slows down the nervous system. The nervous system controls the whole body. Too much alcohol makes people lose control over their bodies. It makes them clumsy and unable to walk in a straight line. The alcohol can make them see things as a blur. They cannot tell how far away things are. They may crash into things when they try to walk.

From *HBJ Health.* New York: Harcourt Brace Jovanovich, 1987; p. 177.

Example from Trade Book

The earth spins around, or rotates, once in twenty-four hours. That's why we have day and night. When we are on the sun side of the earth, there is daylight. As the earth rotates, we turn away from the sun. There is sunset and the night.

From *Sunshine Makes the Seasons* by Franklyn M. Branley. New York: Harper and Row, 1985.

Finding the text pattern in expository writing is not always easy. Facts are not as neatly presented nor is text as tightly organized as in the preceding samples. Chapters are often complex as authors use different organizational patterns to express the relationship among their ideas. Nevertheless, an overall pattern usually emerges in good expository writing. McGee (1982) has shown how pupils' awareness of text structure improves their comprehension of expository text.

In addition to the teaching-by-writing strategy described in 7.4, pupils can be made aware of expository text structure by:

Language experience activities, as dictated group stories are constructed according to specific expository text patterns (Kinney, 1985) and as pupils write their own class Big Books on content-related topics (Snowball, 1989).

Teacher questioning. As teachers use expository text in reading lessons, they can formulate questions according to the pattern of the text. For example, with a paragraph following a comparison–contrast pattern, teachers might have pupils identify the ideas or concepts being compared, the basis on which comparisons are being made, and how the items are alike and different. Questions that follow the pattern or ''map'' of a piece of expository writing help pupils better comprehend by focusing their attention on important relationships in the text. Often, well-designed content area textbooks will include questions in the margins to guide pupils' reading and thinking.

Signal words. Words and phrases are a natural part of certain organizational patterns. For example: *enumeration*—most important, for example, in sum, furthermore; *time order*—first, second, next, then, finally, before, after, later; *comparison–contrast*—however, but, on the other hand, nevertheless, rather, although, likewise; *cause–effect*—because, therefore, as a result, consequently, so that, hence.

Once again, the reading process is not as simple as merely looking for these words as an absolute indication of a particular text pattern. These signal words are function words that fit many different organizational patterns and, at the same time, a passage may have no explicit signal words at all. Here is where pupils need to use inferential comprehension to determine the relationship among ideas in a paragraph or selection.

Diagrams or maps of selections of expository text. Different graphic organizers are used for different text patterns. Constructing diagrams based on text structure has a dual function as part of teaching reading across the curriculum. First, graphic organizers help pupils recognize text structure as an aid in understanding what they read, in that diagrams provide a representation of the way ideas are arranged in relationship to one another. At the same time, these maps require close pupil attention to content that may be important for pupils to learn.

Writing, since awareness of text pattern is no less important as pupils develop skill in writing expository text. In their written answers to questions, their essays, and their reports on curriculum-related topics, pupils can apply their knowledge of expository text patterns in organizing their own writing.

All of these instructional techniques have one purpose—to help pupils become aware of text structure so that they can apply this knowledge in comprehending expository text.

Teaching Text Structure

M CGEE AND Richles (1985) have suggested a very practical five-step strategy for teaching about text structure in the elementary grades.

Step 1. Select a passage with a clear text structure from expository text used in the classroom.

Step 2. Prepare a graphic organizer, a visual display showing the relationship among ideas in the text similar to the one shown on the facing page.

Step 3. Introduce the graphic organizer to pupils by discussing the key ideas and the way the ideas are related to one another.

Step 4. Pupils write a passage using the graphic organizer. The teacher calls attention to the pattern being used.

Step 5. Pupils compare the passages they have written to the original passage in the text.

"After teaching about text structures using the five step teaching-by-writing strategy, you will need to provide many opportunities for students to extend and apply their newly acquired knowledge" (p. 747).

Content

Content is a text-based feature that is of paramount importance in comprehending expository text. Informational trade books and textbooks are used as vehicles to teach reading in content areas of the curriculum: social studies, science, mathematics, the arts. Helping pupils learn to understand this material is at the heart of the reading instructional process.

The competencies needed to read content from various areas of the curriculum are essentially the same as those needed to read any other material, which is why expository text can be used for reading instructional purposes. However, comprehension in different subject areas often demands adaptation in the reader's approach to the content being presented.

Social studies text is generally closer in nature and structure to the narrative style with which pupils are familiar. However, textbooks in social studies are designed primarily as sources of information, and therefore important facts and ideas are often condensed and difficult for many pupils. Words and concepts may be obscure and pupils do not always see the relevance of the information they are reading. That is why the teaching of social studies content builds pupils' schemata that will support comprehension; at the same time, reading is a powerful means of helping pupils acquire information and develop understandings in social studies.

Trade books show pupils relationships among facts and ideas, and they provide human insights that no textbook can. Trade books focus on the human side of social studies. On the topic of Japan, for example, textbooks typically present essential facts about physical and cultural features related to population, land forms, cities, imports, exports, and the like. But the study of Japan is enhanced enormously with books such as Eleanor Coerr's *Sadako and the Thousand Paper Cranes,* the moving story of a terminally ill child who engages in the Japanese art of origami; Ina Freeman's *How*

SAMPLE CAUSATION PASSAGE AND GRAPHIC ORGANIZER #1

Camels in the Desert

Camels are still ridden by the people of the desert today. They are well suited for carrying people and heavy burdens for long distances in hot, dry places because they can go for a long time without water. As a result of their thick hooves, camels can easily walk on the hot sand. Finally, camels can live off the desert because they are able to find even the smallest plant to eat hidden in the desert soil.

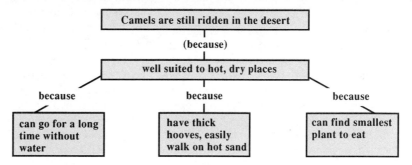

SAMPLE PROBLEM/SOLUTION PASSAGE AND GRAPHIC ORGANIZER

Forest Fires

An important problem for forest rangers is how to protect forests from being ruined by fire. Each year thousands of trees are destroyed by fire. Careless campers do not put their fires completely out. Cigarettes are left to burn on the dry ground. These small fires in dry forests can burn thousands of trees. One solution to the forest fire problem is to man lookout stations and use helicopters to spot fires. Fires that are spotted right away can be put out before they get too big to handle. Then fires will cause less damage to the forest. A second solution to the problem is to have experts and bulldozers ready to move in quickly to fight the fire. Bulldozers can throw huge amounts of dirt on a fire in a short time. The dirt helps put the fire out quicker. A third solution is to build fire lanes in the forests. Fire lanes are long breaks in the forest where there are no trees. These breaks prevent the fire from spreading and getting too large (McGee, 1982b, p. 66).

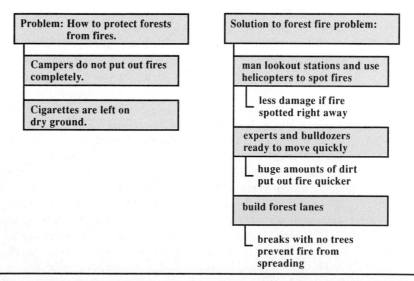

Figure 7.4   From Lea McGee and Donald Richgels, ''Teaching Expository Text Structure in Elementary Students'' in *The Reading Teacher,* 38:735–748 (April 1985). Copyright © 1985 International Reading Association. Reprinted with permission of Lea McGee and the International Reading Association.

7.5
■ FOR YOUR INFORMATION ▉▉▉▉▉▉▉▉
Trade Books for Social Studies

SOCIAL STUDIES is a broad field, and there are trade books on virtually any aspect of the subject. A full range of trade books can be found on:

American history: from picture books like Tomie de Paola's *An Early American Christmas* and Donald Hall's *The Ox-Cart Man,* through the range of Jean Fritz's popular children's books (such as *Where Do You Think You're Going, Christopher Columbus?* and *Bully For You, Teddy Roosevelt!*), to books for the upper grades such as Elizabeth Speare's *The Witch of Black-bird Pond* and Esther Forbes's classic *Johnny Tremain.*
World history: from picture books such as Aliki's brilliantly illustrated *Medieval Feast* to Marguerite de-Angeli's *Door in the Wall.*
Geography: books that inject a human dimension into learning about landforms, from picture books like William Kurelek's *A Prairie Boy's Winter* to Jean

Craighead George's detailed account of the Arctic tundra in *Julie of the Wolves.*
World culture: books such as Jean Rogers's account of an Eskimo child in *The Runaway Mittens* to John Steptoe's retelling of the African tale *Mufaro's Beautiful Daughter.*

These titles represent only a tiny fraction of trade books on topics related to various areas of social studies. The list of available books is almost endless, with quality books being published every year. Trade book titles to use in teaching social studies can be found in Laughlin and Kardaleff's *Literature-Based Social Studies: Children's Books and Activities to Enrich the K-5 Curriculum* (1991). The April/May edition of the journal *Social Education* contains an annual annotated bibliography of notable children's trade books in social studies published in the previous year.

My Parents Learned to Eat, a personal account of the courtship of the author's American father and Japanese mother; Taro Yashima's sensitive picture storybook *Crow Boy,* a hauntingly illustrated story about a lonely boy in a Japanese country school; Pearl Buck's *The Big Wave,* a traditional tale about peasant life in Japanese villages. Each of these books allows pupils to gain a glimpse of aspects of Japanese art, values, and way of life. Trade books enrich pupils' understandings by presenting the soul of a culture, not just facts about a country.

The nature of social studies content demands critical reading, especially the separation of fact and opinion, recognition of an author's bias, and the identification of propaganda techniques. Pupils can expand their horizons by comparing what is in their textbooks with what they read in trade books. Comparisons of trade books such as Jean Fritz's factual *What's the Big Idea, Ben Franklin?* with Robert Lawson's more fanciful *Ben and Me* can be both interesting and enjoyable. Determining Mildred Taylor's point of view in *Roll of Thunder, Hear My Cry;* discussing Irene Hunt's impression of the Civil War in *Across Five Aprils;* comparing Jane Yolen's story of Christopher Columbus told through the eyes of a native child in *Encounter* with Jean Fritz's more conventional version in *Where Do You Think You're Going, Christopher Columbus?*—all can be used to help pupils generate insights and critical thinking that will serve them well for a lifetime in dealing with what they read as part of social studies.

Science text is loaded with information. The intensity with which this information is presented and the interrelationships among the concepts that build upon one another can be problematic for many pupils. Concept density and technical vocabulary can be formidable obstacles to understanding as well. Newport (1990) noted that pupils meet

7.6 Putting Ideas to Work

I-Charts for Critical Thinking

HOFFMANN (1992) suggests the use of Inquiry Charts (I-Charts) as a means of nurturing critical thinking strategies through literacy in the classroom. The I-Chart procedure involves the following three phases:

1. *Planning,* which includes identifying a topic (the voyage of Columbus, for example, or the Civil War), formulating questions related to this topic, constructing the chart with questions along the top and sources of information down the left-hand side, and gathering informational materials (trade books, magazine articles, textbooks, encyclopedias, and the like).

2. *Interacting,* which includes recording pupils' prior knowledge on the topic, adding interesting facts and new questions to the questions that the pupils have already formulated, and recording on the chart information gleaned from various sources. The I-Chart needs to be large enough for pupils to fit their responses in the cells.

3. *Integrating and Evaluating,* which involves writing summary statements for each question, comparing these summary statements to pupils' prior knowledge statements, researching questions on the topic that remain unanswered, and reporting the results of this research to the class.

The I-Chart provides a practical framework for promoting pupils' critical thinking about what they read in the classroom.

---

more technical and specialized vocabulary in science textbooks than they meet in a beginning foreign language text. Adjusting instruction in light of these issues can promote comprehension.

The very nature of science content requires adjustments in how to approach text. Some material demands slow and careful reading, as when pupils read steps to be followed in an experiment in their science textbooks or in science-related trade books such as Seymour Simon's interesting *The Paper Airplane Book.* Other science material can involve more rapid reading, as when pupils read background information in a trade book about a curriculum topic, such as *Ducks Don't Get Wet* by Augusta Goldin. Pupils need to recognize differences in science reading materials, too, as when they read Eric Carle's colorfully illustrated account of *The Tiny Seed* versus the more detailed and factual account presented by Claire Merrill in *A Seed Is a Promise.*

Fictional trade books have sometimes been used to extend awareness in science. For example, William Steig's *Doctor DeSoto,* the mouse–dentist has been used to promote pupils' interest in dental hygiene. In making these leaps from fiction to fact, teachers need to be aware of anthropomorphism, the process of ascribing human characteristics to nonhuman creatures. Even in the very early grades, pupils can learn to separate fact and fiction by comparing books such as Steven Kroll's *The Biggest Pumpkin Ever,* the story of two bands of mice who take care of a pumpkin (one by day and one by night) with Douglas Florian's simple, predictable book *Vegetable Garden* or with Dorothy Hinshaw Patent's *Where Food Comes From,* which gives pupils a clear, matter-of-fact account of the sources of the food they eat. Pupils might learn that even though anthropomorphism is an effective literary technique, it is hardly scientific.

7.7
FOR YOUR INFORMATION
Trade Books for Science

AS IN the case of social studies, there is no shortage of trade books on topics that are part of the science curriculum in the elementary grades. Trade books in science include those that contain straight informational material and those that are fictional but have a strong basis in fact and contain scientifically accurate material.

Informational books that have proved popular and useful in the elementary classroom include such titles as David Macaulay's fascinating (to adults as well as to children) *The Way Things Work*; Joanna Cole's *Cars and How They Go;* Franklyn M. Branley's "Let's-Read-and-Find-Out" Series such as *The Sky Is Full of Stars* and *Sunshine Makes the Seasons;* and Simon Seymour's books that take pupils on scientific expeditions above the earth (*Galaxies*), across the earth (*Deserts*), under the earth (*Earthquakes*), and many points in between.

Information-based books of fiction include titles such as *Fireflies!*, Julie Brinckloe's first-person account of a boy's chasing these fascinating insects; *If You Are a Hunter of Fossils,* Byrd Baylor's almost lyrical account of searching for fossils; *Old Yeller,* Fred Gipson's

story of a boy and his dog that also helps pupils learn about wildlife in the southwest and the transmission of contagious diseases in the ecosystem.

There are a number of resource books related to literature and science. *Keepers of the Earth* by Michael J. Caduto and Joseph Bruchac provides a marvelous integration of literature and interesting science experiments. A valuable reference guide to the full range of science topics in children's literature is *Science and Technology in Fact and Fiction: A Guide to Children's Books* by DayAnn M. Kennedy, Stella S. Spangler, and Mary Ann Vanderwerf. Also, resource books such as *Science through Children's Literature: An Integrated Approach* by Carol and John W. Butzow are available with suggestions on how to use children's literature as part of science.

As in the case of social studies, the list of available informational trade books in science is extensive. The March issue of the journal *Science and Children* lists outstanding children's trade books in science published during the previous year.

Poetry provides another means of using literature to help pupils develop insights into science. Poetry and science have more in common than first meets the eye. Science aims to explain the world around us. A poem is the result of an attempt to interpret the world, with metaphorical images about natural phenomena. Although science is more factual and objective and poetry more lyrical and imaginative, poetry can produce insights into science, and vice versa. Reading poems can help pupils understand scientific concepts and writing poetry can help them demonstrate this understanding.

Mathematics presents unique problems for many pupils. The writing in math textbooks is generally more difficult to read than text in other content areas (Harris and Sipay, 1985). By its nature, mathematics requires slow and careful reading of short segments of text, since this text is concise and intense. Reading in math involves dealing with two symbol systems—word symbols and number symbols—and comprehension involves the ability to move from one set of symbols to the other.

Beyond textbooks, trade books provide a means of introducing and exploring mathematical concepts. "In children's literature, mathematics is viewed as a process, not merely an event; it is part of a larger experience and can only be understood in its total context" (Whitin, Mills and O'Keefe, 1990; p. 69).

In math, reading word problems can be especially difficult. Pupils typically have more problems in reading and understanding what to do than in performing the mathematical operations or calculations involved in solving word problems. Various

7.8 Putting Ideas to Work

Integrating Literature and Science

ROBB (1989) describes how literature and science can be effectively integrated in the elementary grades.

While reading Jean Craighead George's *Julie of the Wolves,* Ms. Robb's sixth grade class discovered that Julie's experiences did not match their own stereotyped version of "the big bad wolf." The pupils read everything they could get their hands on about wolves, and their discussion of the topic dominated even their lunchtime conversations.

As a result, Ms. Robb planned a unit that would combine literature with a naturalist's view of the world. Using more of George's novels and other sources, the pupils read, wrote response journals, recorded information, discussed what they had learned, and extended their reading beyond that which was originally assigned. Groups studied and shared poems about nature, researched and wrote reports on a range of related topics, and bound their writing into a class journal. They wrote letters to the Environmental Protection Agency and discussed ways that they could effect change.

Robb discovered that the issues raised during her literature/science unit "can touch the inner spirits of children and draw them to reading, discussion, research, writing, and positive action" (p. 810).

"methods of attack" or solution strategies for word problems have been suggested by Polya (1945), Earp (1970), and Forgan and Mangrum (1989). These techniques differ from one another in detail, but they usually involve five steps:

1. Read first to visualize the problem and get a general idea of what is to be done.
2. Reread more slowly, noting specific information that is provided and separating extraneous material.
3. Reread a third time to determine operations that need to be done.
4. Do the mathematical computation needed to solve the problem.
5. Reread a final time to check the reasonableness of the solution.

The relationship between mathematics and literacy extends beyond reading. Kliman and Kleiman (1992) have demonstrated how pupils can write creative word problems in mathematics based on literature that they have enjoyed. There is overlap between children's literature and other curriculum content areas in the elementary grades.

Art deals primarily with nonprint media, yet this curriculum area certainly involves visual processing. Even very young children use terms such as *color, line,* and *shape* in directed discussion about the illustrations in picture books. Expository text related to art often requires following directions and critical reading. Trade books in art—such as John J. Reiss' simple *Shapes,* James F. Seidman and Grace Mintoyne's *Shopping Cart Art,* or M. B. Goffstein's *An Artist*—can provide enrichment and background for expanding interest in this area. Art can also be used as an entry into such books as Wendy Kesselman's warm and touching *Emma,* the story of an elderly woman living in a city apartment who overcomes her loneliness when she begins painting.

7.9

FOR YOUR INFORMATION

Trade Books for Mathematics

DIFFERENT TYPES of trade books can be used effectively to develop important mathematical concepts.

Counting books, such as Anno Mitsumasa's well-known *Anno's Counting Book* and Tana Hoban's alphabet-and-number book *26 Letters and 99 Cents* are among the hundreds of counting books available. Some, such as Peter Sis's brilliantly colorful *Going Up,* present ordinal numbers.

Concept books, such as David M. Schwartz's two works *If You Made a Million* and *How Much Is a Million?,* help pupils grasp mathematical concepts with text and illustration.

Storybooks sometimes illustrate mathematical concepts and operations in a narrative context, such as Pat Hutchins's humorous *The Doorbell Rang,* which is based on the idea of sharing cookies (division); Judy Viorst's delightful *Alexander, Who Used to Be Rich Last Sunday* in which a boy sees his money disappear (subtraction); David Birch's *The King's Chessboard* in which a wise man who wants a grain of rice to be doubled each day for as many days as there are squares on a chessboard (multiplication).

Music involves a special type of reading in its own right, as pupils learn to interpret the special symbol system of musical notation. Text-processing in this curriculum area involves mastery of technical and specialized vocabulary, along with understanding of appropriate critical concepts. Music also offers opportunities for background and interest reading of such trade books as Karen Ackerman's Caldecott-Award-winning *Song and Dance Man,* a brilliantly illustrated account of an old vaudeville performer, or *The Philharmonic Gets Dressed,* Karla Kurstein's amusing account of musicians getting dressed for a performance. Trade books with musical themes can help pupils explore the world of music while providing another avenue of reading. Children's books that are set to music—Maurice Sendak's *Chicken Soup with Rice,* for example, or John Langstaff's *Frog Went a-Courtin'*—can be used to provide a delightfully integrated, musical classroom experience.

Drama and dance can be integrated with literature as pupils pantomime or dramatize the actions while the teacher reads a story like *Shadow,* the African folk-tale translated and brilliantly illustrated by Marcia Brown. Sebesta (1987) provides a wealth of practical suggestions for enriching the humanities and reading curricula at the same time through interviews, dance, art, writing, drama, and a range of other activities based on children's trade books.

Physical education typically does not involve very much expository text processing, but there are a variety of how-to books on virtually any sport in which pupils are interested. Pupils are also often drawn to the biographies of famous athletes, from books like the relatively easy *Wonder Women of Sports* by Betty Millsaps Jones to biographies written at a higher readability level such as *Babe Didrickson: Athlete of the Century* by R. R. Knudson. Moreover, physical education teachers can also have a powerful influence in recommending trade books, particularly for reluctant readers.

There is no part of the school curriculum in which reading does not play a part. Although comprehension in every area will depend on pupils' overall reading competency and their ability to reconstruct meaning, pupils have to make adjustments from

Eight Questions For Math-Related Trade Books

SCHIRO (in press) has developed a comprehensive set of criteria for evaluating children's trade books that contain mathematical ideas. The following eight questions have been adapted from Schiro's criteria:

1. Is the book's mathematics correct and accurate?
2. Are mathematical ideas presented effectively and attractively?
3. Does the book use language and symbols appropriate for the age and grade level of pupils?
4. Is the mathematical content appropriate for the intended audience?
5. How involved does the pupil get with the mathematics in the book?
6. How well do the story and the math content complement each other?
7. Are the book's ideas presented so that pupils can apply and generalize them?
8. How much time and effort must a teacher expend to help the pupil benefit from the mathematics in the book?

---

carefully reading the terse text of a mathematical word problem to a descriptive account in a book of historical fiction that they are reading for enrichment and enjoyment. Text in each of these areas, however, can be used to teach reading across the curriculum. Learning to read and reading to learn are part of the same process.

Other Text-Based Features

In narrative text, design and illustration are text-based features that can enhance understanding. In expository text, these features are even more important for helping pupils comprehend. Narrative stories are broken into chapter-length segments, and illustrations usually consist of pictures designed to help pupils visualize what characters or scenes look like.

In expository material, design enhances comprehension to a far greater extent. Headings and subheadings highlight important information and provide road signs for pupils as they read. Illustrative material such as maps, charts, graphs, and diagrams are essential means of presenting information to reinforce or extend the content presented in text. These devices need to be understood as pupils deal with textbooks and trade books to expand their knowledge and to extend their reading ability.

Design   All textbooks and some informational trade books contain:

a table of contents, which is a chronological organizational summary of content and is presented at the beginning of the book;

an index, a systematic and detailed guide to content, presented at the end of the book;

a glossary, a ''mini-dictionary'' of the pronunciation and definition of technical and potentially difficult words used in the text.

Recognizing the purpose of each feature can be an aid to understanding expository text that pupils encounter in the classroom. Teachers can help pupils develop competency in the effective use of these features through both planned and spontaneous

Trade books can be used as effectively in art and music as they can in other areas of curriculum.

occasions in the overall reading instructional program. For example, when textbooks are distributed, the nature and function of these features can be explained to the group as a whole. Instead of the usual direction, ''Open your books to page 48,'' a teacher can say, ''Open your books to the chapter on transportation,'' thus directing pupils to the table of contents. In a small group reading lesson with a social studies book, a question such as, ''Who can most quickly find the pages with information of forestry products?'' will help pupils discover that the index is an efficient tool to use in quickly locating information on specific topics. As individual pupils encounter difficult technical words in science material, they can be made aware of the glossary as a means of helping them deal with this vocabulary. In short, teachers need to be aware of the many opportunities that present themselves for weaving these elements into instruction in content area reading.

Individual chapters in textbooks and some informational trade books frequently have elements such as:

introductory statements that provide an overview of the chapter content;

introductory questions that attempt to provide a purpose for reading;

headings and subheadings which divide the chapter into logical units and provide an indication of text organization;

guide questions highlighting important concepts in specific segments of text;

summary statements to recap the major points presented in the chapter.

Because each element can be used to enhance pupils' comprehension by providing clues to text organization, pupils need to become adept in using these features. As in the case of teaching parts of a book, the first instructional step is creating an awareness. Teachers should point out these chapter elements and discuss their purposes and uses.

Knowledge acquired from maps and globes are important to comprehending expository text in social studies and other subjects.

Graphic Materials Expository writing often includes a variety of illustrations, maps, tables, charts, graphs, diagrams, and cartoons. Even though these devices are information-laden, pupils often ignore them as aids to understanding because pupils do not know how to interpret them.

  Pictures and illustrations, the most widely used of all graphic aids, are part of all children's books. In early narrative picture books, illustrations are integrated with print as a direct means of telling the story and are at least as important—if not more important—than text. As the amount of print in children's books increases, illustrations become more incidental. Yet pictures remain important in helping young readers capture in their minds' eyes the images conveyed through words. In expository writing, illustrations can be used directly to build pupils' backgrounds and to help develop and clarify concepts. They need to be examined and discussed as they help pupils learn ideas presented in text.

  Maps occur frequently, especially in social studies textbooks. Teachers sometimes take these maps for granted, assuming that pupils will use them as learning resources. But, map reading needs to be taught with the same perspective as text reading: that is, to decode map symbols, to interpret the literal meaning of maps, and to use maps to make inferences, draw conclusions, and think critically about information presented.

  Maps represent the earth's physical features, and pupils need to be aware of the distortions that occur as the spherical shape of the globe is "flattened" in a two-dimensional map. Some teachers have used half an orange or half a hollow rubber ball to illustrate this concept. In learning about maps and how to use them in content areas, pupils need to understand the nature and purpose of:

map projections (Mercator versus polar versus Peter's projections) and the effect that these projections have on the size and shape of geographic features represented;

types of maps (such as physical maps, political maps, population maps, product maps, climate maps, and the like) and the kind of information each type contains;

legends, with keys to the symbols that cartographers use to represent various features;

scales and location, with the use of grids and keys to indicate various distances and directions.

Just as decoding sound–letter relationships and interpreting print is essential for constructing meaning from text, so decoding symbols and interpreting information is essential for comprehending maps. Just as the skilled text readers move beyond text, skilled map readers develop critical thinking skills with the use of these graphic aids.

For pupils who are interested, there are informational trade books about maps and globes. For example, Jack Knowlton's *Maps and Globes* gives pupils a historical account of map making, as well as information about the types of maps typically found in books, and Harvey Weiss' *Maps: Getting from Here to There* is an instructional account of maps and their various purposes.

Graphs constitute another important source of information in curriculum-related reading materials. Direct instruction in making and interpreting graphs occurs in math, but graph reading also needs attention as pupils encounter these devices in expository text.

Pupils need to be aware of the nature and purpose of various types of graphs:

line graphs, which are common and familiar to most pupils, and which show relationships among various types of data with a simple line;

bar graphs, which compare items using solid vertical and horizontal bars;

pictographs, which present information by the use of simple representative pictures or drawings;

circle or pie graphs, in which proportionate parts of a whole are represented as a "slice" or percentage of a 360° circle.

Spontaneous teaching of graph reading typically occurs as pupils encounter graphs in their content area reading. Skillful, purposeful questions can lead pupils from literally "reading" the information to inferences about the data to the critical thinking skills of application and prediction based on the data.

Charts, tables, and *diagrams* are other graphic devices typically found in curriculum-related reading material. Like graphs, charts systematically arrange information, often using pictures to show relationships among sets of facts or ideas. Tables constitute organized presentation of raw data in rows and columns. Diagrams are drawings used to illustrate pictorially relationship among concepts or steps in a process to be followed. All of these graphic devices support text and often provide visual summaries of information presented in print.

Tables, charts, and diagrams condense information and require careful reading. As pupils encounter these graphic devices in expository text, teachers need to discuss the information presented and to formulate questions that will lead pupils to interpret the information accurately and meaningfully.

Since graphic devices contain large amounts of information, it is imperative that teachers and pupils pay attention to these devices in reading expository text in the

Graphic Information Lesson

REINKING (1986) suggests a strategy called a Graphic Information Lesson (GIL). This strategy was designed for occasional postreading use to help pupils interpret and use graphic information in relation to text information. The three stages of a Graphic Information Lesson are:

1. *Determining graphic information.* After reading the text, the teacher leads a discussion of information found in graphic aids, focusing on higher-level thinking skills. With the help of teacher modeling, pupils learn to determine if graphic information is supplemental, redundant, or complementary to text.

2. *Integrating and synthesizing.* The teacher introduces *pseudographs,* graphic displays of information related to, but not contained in, the text. Pupils decide the accuracy of the pseudographs, based on information in text.

3. *Reinforcing and applying.* Pupils engage in a variety of activities, from constructing their own pseudographs to selecting graphs that are most important to text.

elementary classroom. Graphic devices are too important to be ignored. Because maps, charts, graphs, tables, and diagrams will become more important as learning aids in the middle and high school grades, and because these devices will remain potential sources of information in the reading material that pupils will encounter as adults, it makes sense to develop pupils' awareness and skill in using graphic aids in expository text early in their school lives.

Reader-Based Features

As in the case of narrative text, what is "behind the eye" of the reader will have an enormous impact on the reader's comprehension of expository text. Major reader-based features include language background, cognitive processing, schemata, and metacognitive awareness.

Language Background

Pupils' understanding of language will have a huge impact on their ability to comprehend expository text. The same elements in language that affect understanding of narrative text—the ability to decode, knowledge of word meaning, comprehension of paragraphs, and understanding total selections—impact comprehension of expository text.

Decoding   The ability to recognize or figure out the meaning of unknown words in print is an essential competency in all reading. Informational trade books and content area textbooks can be used in helping pupils develop and apply effective decoding strategies.

Structural analysis—the ability to identify unknown words by their prefixes, suffixes, and roots—can be especially important in content area materials. The structure of a word might often indicate its definition: the meaning of *dioxide,* for example, can be found in the meaning of the prefix *di-* and the root *-oxide*. A word that illustrates this nicely, and one that pupils enjoy, is the longest word in the English language:

pneumonoultramicroscopicsilicovolcanocontiosis which is "a lung disease caused by breathing extremely fine siliceous dust particles," can be illustrated by examining the meaning of the various word elements:

pneumono—having to do with the lungs

ultra—very

micro/scopic—tiny

silico—containing silicon

volcano—floating in air as dust from a volcano

conti/osis—diseased condition

This type of exercise not only builds on pupils' fascination with unusual words, it also effectively demonstrates how syllabication and structural analysis can be used in attacking some of the seemingly formidable terminology they may encounter in text.

Word Knowledge   The strong link between vocabulary knowledge and comprehension was addressed earlier in this book. Vocabulary development in content areas is doubly important. Not only does word knowledge contribute to understanding in reading, but words represent concepts and ideas that are at the heart of content areas of the curriculum.

Apart from the general store of words that pupils need for all their communications activities, two types of vocabulary are uniquely important to learning in content areas: technical words and specialized words.

Technical vocabulary consists of those words that are unique to a particular subject field. When, for example, was the last time you heard the word *iambic* used outside an English classroom or *longtitude* used other than in reference to maps? Each area of the curriculum has its own core of technical words, and mastering these words is important in comprehending expository text in that area.

Specialized words are those words that have a generally common meaning but which take on specialized meaning in a particular content area. Most people pay *bills*; legislatures pass *bills*; ducks have *bills*. With specialized words, pupils need to adjust their understanding of the word according to its use in a curriculum context.

Since specialized vocabulary takes on a special meaning as part of content being studied, multiple-meaning word exercises are a natural part of teaching reading with expository text, activities such as the following on "map words:"

Can you think of a word that means:

to slide or ride down a hill on a sled	*(coast)*	a strip of land next to the sea
land drained by a river	*(basin)*	a bowl for containing liquid
a strip of leather worn around the waist	*(belt)*	a region with a similar type of vegetation or climate
a large break or fracture in a rock formation	*(fault)*	a defect in a person or thing

7.12 Putting Ideas to Work

Teaching Content Words

BUILDING WORD meaning with expository text involves many of the same techniques and principles suggested in Chapter 5. In a language-rich classroom, vocabulary from content areas will be part of ongoing word work—part of word alerts, semantic study, and other activities related to building word meaning. As expository text is used for instructional purposes, word work will be related to technical and specific terms that are part of subject areas, such as:

Word sorts, in which pupils "sort out" words related to particular topics (Separate the following into *Weather Words* and *Plant Words:* humid, erosion, algae, barometer, cell, chlorophyll, horizon, seed, stem, moisture . . .).

Analogies, with terms related to curriculum areas (biology:humans :: zoology: [animals] astronaut:space :: aquanaut:[water]).

Synonyms and antonyms, although many technical terms do not have specific synonyms. Knowledge of terms (and concepts) such as *barter* can be enhanced with a synonym search (*trade, exchange, convey, swap,* etc.) or an antonym activity (*keep, retain, hold,* etc.).

Categorizing, in which pupils determine relationships among technical terms—
Circle the word that best describes the other words:

dictator   king   president   ruler   czar (Social Studies)
dog   whale   mammal   bat   horse (Science)
color   red   fuchsia   purple   mauve (Art)

Direct teaching is often appropriate, given the relationship between words and concepts. Opportunities to use words in different contexts following direct teaching and dictionary work is important, however.

Graphic organizers similar in nature and purpose to semantic maps (pp. 142–143), which show words connected to ideas and related concepts.

Exercises like these stimulate pupils' thinking while focusing their attention on the specific meaning of words in relation to a content area of the curriculum. These activities can also extend pupils' awareness of words from specialized meanings to more generalized meanings: a *gulf* (between two people), a *harbor* (for a fugitive), a *tidal wave* (of opinion).

In teaching vocabulary in content areas, teachers can help pupils build conceptual background while reinforcing word meaning. Herein is the reciprocal relationship between developing reading competency and acquiring information at the same time. Vocabulary activities can be done to build schemata before using a chapter in a science book for a guided reading activity, or as a postreading exercise to review and reinforce important concepts.

Sentences   Just as understanding the sentence is essential to comprehending narrative text, it is equally important in comprehending expository text. Sentences remain the key language units for conveying meaning in connected discourse.

Most sentences in expository text are packed full of information. As part of reading instruction using expository material, teachers need to focus on sentence understanding by having pupils:

identify topic, summary, and other key sentences in paragraphs;
restate the meaning of important sentences in their own words;

explain relationships in sentence parts that express meaning;
break longer sentences apart and combine the parts in new ways;
identify technical and specialized vocabulary items and write them in new sentences.

These are reading and writing activities that reinforce both information acquisition and sentence mastery as part of comprehending expository text.

Paragraphs   As in narrative text, paragraphs are groups of sentences focused on a central idea. In well-written expository text, the idea or main point of a paragraph is clear and focused.

Helping pupils learn text structure (pp. 225–229) is an integral part of instruction in paragraph comprehension. Simple graphic organizers such as the following can be used in helping pupils understand the structure of paragraphs in expository text:

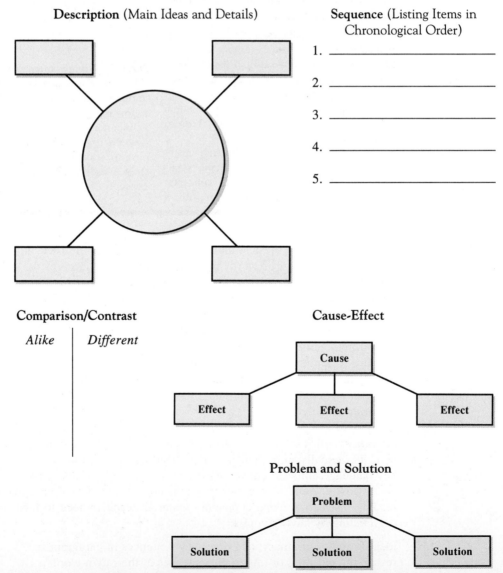

Description (Main Ideas and Details)

Sequence (Listing Items in Chronological Order)

1. _____

2. _____

3. _____

4. _____

5. _____

Comparison/Contrast

Alike | *Different*

Cause-Effect

Cause

Effect   Effect   Effect

Problem and Solution

Problem

Solution   Solution   Solution

Focusing on organizational patterns in this way increases pupils' comprehension and recall of what they read in paragraphs.

Selections   Understanding words, sentences, and paragraphs leads to comprehending larger selections of expository text—chapters in content area textbooks and entire informational trade books. Sound teaching practices—setting purposes for reading, guiding reading through a variety of multilevel questions, and directing postreading discussions on information acquired in reading—will help build pupils' understanding of larger segments of expository text.

A pupil's language background at all levels—from word knowledge and basic decoding skills to understanding the meaning of large segments of expository text—is essential to reading comprehension. While building language background at these various levels, the teacher is teaching reading and content concurrently, helping pupils learn to read and read to learn at the same time.

Cognitive Processing

As with narrative text, cognitive processing is another ''behind the eye'' factor inherent in the comprehension process. In reading informational material, pupils are applying thinking with expository text, including both the type and aspect of thinking involved in interacting with ideas in print.

Type of Thinking   This dimension of cognitive processing involves reading for main ideas and details, cause–effect relationships, sequence, and the like. Type of thinking becomes a specific focus in helping pupils come to recognize text structure in informational material that they encounter as part of learning to read.

Different types of expository text require different types of thinking. Reading a word problem in mathematics or a set of directions for a science experiment or an art project requires careful, deliberate reading to follow a sequence of directions. Sequence of events is also involved in historical fiction such as Alice Dagliesh's *The Courage of Sarah Noble,* but in a more general and less deliberate way. A textbook chapter on urban and rural life suggests a specific focus on comparison and contrasts. Most textbooks and informational trade books suggest a focus on more than one type of thinking. For example, a full range of types of thinking can be applied in reading Oz Charles's fascinating, factual account of *How Does Soda Get into the Bottle?*

Deciding which type of cognitive processing is most appropriate for a piece of expository text is part of the process of using informational material in teaching reading. Types of thinking are part of various stages of reading lessons that use expository text—part of the prereading purpose-setting and schema building, part of the questions to guide the reading, part of the postreading discussions and exercises designed to reinforce and extend content presented in text.

Level of Thinking   Literal, inferential, and critical–creative levels of thinking are as vital (if not more important) in comprehending expository text as in dealing with narrative text.

Teachers direct pupils' level of thinking in interacting with expository text largely through the questions they ask. Questions that are part of guided reading

7.13 Putting Ideas to Work

Herringbone Technique

THE HERRINGBONE Technique is a strategy that has been used to help pupils organize and recall information and ideas presented in larger segments of expository text. The technique focuses on six essential comprehension questions: Who? What? When? Where? Why? and How? Information is arranged in this format:

The Herringbone format can be introduced on a chart or an overhead projector. Teachers can direct groups of pupils through the process as part of guided reading instruction using content textbook chapters or informational trade books. Follow-up discussion can focus on pupil responses and extend into sentence and paragraph writing activities.

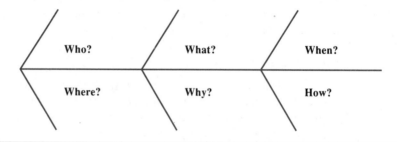

lessons—before, during, and after reading—help pupils reach toward higher levels of thinking. Strategies such as Question–Answer Relationships (see 6.6, p. 195), teacher modeling, study guides (see 7.14), and other techniques help pupils develop the habit of independent questioning as they read on their own.

Schemata

Pupils' schemata—the conceptual organizational structure of their knowledge background—provides an important foundation for understanding material read in expository text. Reading activates existing knowledge as newly acquired information is integrated with what we already know, so lack of existing knowledge can be a formidable obstacle to reading comprehension.

Vacca and Vacca (1989) identify three schema-related problems that can interfere with understanding in reading:

schema availability, in which pupils lack the relevant background knowledge and information needed to comprehend a text;

schema selection, failure to bring background knowledge to bear as they read; and

schema maintenance, in which pupils are not aware or skilled enough at recognizing when shifts in schema occur during reading.

Schema theory suggests the importance of assessing background knowledge before reading. Readers bring a reservoir of experience to the printed page. If what is in the text is aligned with these experiences, comprehension is enhanced. If not, comprehension is not as easy. Determining what pupils already know about a topic and

Study Guides

STUDY GUIDES can be used to address both the type and level of thinking while reading. Study guides provide pupils with a "road map" that will guide them through important segments of expository text by focusing their attention on major ideas presented.

Preparation. Teachers first decide which parts of an informational trade book or a chapter in a textbook they want pupils to concentrate on. They then decide which type and aspect of thinking they want to emphasize.

Construction. Teachers formulate questions that are centered on particular information or ideas to be emphasized and that are directed at the type and level of thinking they want pupils to use.

Use. Study guides should be used in the context of well-planned reading lessons. Prereading should include vocabulary activity and schema building. Teachers explain the purpose of the guides, which pupils can use independently or cooperatively as they read. Postreading discussion should focus on pupil responses to questions and directions in the guide.

---

setting purposes that will determine what they can acquire from text (that is, to see how their schemata may be altered) is an important prereading activity in content-related reading lessons.

Addressing pupils' schemata as part of reading instruction involves teaching reading and content at the same time. As teachers help pupils acquire and organize background information that will lead to better reading comprehension, they are simultaneously helping pupils learn material that is normally part of the school curriculum.

Building a knowledge background is essential to further comprehension. Besides reading, knowledge is acquired in a variety of ways: through direct experience, through dramatized or vicarious experiences, through audiovisual presentations, or through discussions and related verbal interactions. Background knowledge acquired through these various means will support comprehension when reading about a topic.

Humans learn best through direct experience; schemata are built by dealing with the world around us. In studying a unit on the Florida Everglades, for example, a pupil who has lived or visited there will have a richer schema about that subject. Pupils who have watched a movie or visited a model of the Everglades in a science museum will have a more concrete basis of understanding as well. While it is obviously not possible for teachers to provide direct or vicarious experiences for everything that pupils are expected to study in content areas of the curriculum, it is possible for teachers to use classroom discussion and other means to provide some prior knowledge about a topic before pupils read about that topic. Prior knowledge will support their reading comprehension.

Building knowledge is one of the functions of trade books in the content areas. A collection of attractive books about a topic will provide pupils with a potential supply of information that will build their schemata to support their comprehension as they read.

K–W–L

DESIGNED BY Ogle (1986), K–W–L is a structured teaching technique for helping pupils access prior knowledge as part of reading lessons with expository text. K–W–L involves three steps:

1. *K—Assessing What I Know.* This step involves brainstorming and categorizing ideas related to the topic of an expository reading selection. The teacher notes pupils' ideas on the chalkboard or on a chart.

2. *W—What Do I Want to Learn?* Based on what pupils already know, the teacher provokes questions on what they might want to learn. Pupils then read the selection.

3. *L—What I Learned.* As pupils finish reading, they note what they learned about a topic and list questions that still need to be addressed.

Metacognition

Metacognition—the awareness of and control over one's mental functioning—is another "behind the eye" factor that is crucial to reading comprehension. Metacognition involves thinking while reading. It includes not only pupils' abilities to think about the content contained in text, but also about the processes used to understand the ideas that the author is expressing and the ability to use this knowledge to monitor their own reading.

Pupils' ability to monitor their own reading is an important part of metacognition. Experienced readers know when they are running into trouble with understanding text, and they know what to do about it. In this respect, reading has been compared to driving. When everything is going smoothly, the process of reading (and driving) is fairly automatic for the experienced and skilled practitioner. But when problems develop, the reader (or driver) must attend more closely to the process itself. The reader attends to those problems that are blocking attempts to build meaning from text and develops strategies to overcome those problems.

How can teachers begin to promote this metacognitive awareness as part of reading instruction? With informational reading materials, teachers can use:

metacognitive discussions before reading assignments to develop an awareness of the reading task and how best to handle it effectively;

schema-building activities that will lead to pupils' awareness of what they might expect to learn;

teacher modeling, demonstrating their own reading behaviors as pupils follow a segment of expository text projected on a screen;

careful questioning, with questions focused not only on content but also on process (*What does the author say were three reasons for the American Civil War? How do you know? Where did you find the answer to that question? What language does the author use to express this view? Do you think the author might give other reasons later on?*).

7.16 Putting Ideas to Work

Purpose, Classification, and Response

MARY LOU Hess (1991), a teacher in an inner-city elementary school, has described a three-step strategy that she developed to help her pupils comprehend nonfiction material. The strategy involves:

Developing a purpose. Pupils brainstorm to raise questions about what type of information may be in their reading material. Questions are written on paper, and reading to find answers provides a purpose for reading.

Classifying. Pupils sort their questions into categories and generate their own text headings for classifying questions. With animals, for example, categories can include *habitat, food, appearance,* and the like. After pupils read and take notes, they work in pairs cutting out and sorting facts. These classification activities increase pupils' comprehension of nonfiction by making them aware of text structure.

Responding through talk. Pupils are given opportunities to talk about the information they are collecting, since exchanging information helps them incorporate new learning into their existing mental framework. By talking about the information they gained, pupils explain facts to peers, raise questions that involve rereading to verify or adjust understandings, and gain ownership of the new information.

"It became clear to me that having a purpose, classifying, and talking worked simultaneously to increase my students' ability to comprehend nonfiction. . . . Pupils used these strategies to become more proficient, independent readers" (p. 231.).

With a constant classroom focus on metacognitive activity while reading, pupils are apt to begin to apply these learning strategies themselves as they read. "The key to metacognition is moving from teacher-directed to student-directed reading activities, a shift from teacher-developed questions to student-developed questions, questions that students ask *themselves* during the act of reading" (Dupuis et al., 1989; p. 55).

This type of prereading and postreading discussion related to metacognitive processing is not entirely new or revolutionary. It is part of directed or guided reading lessons that skilled teachers have carried out as long as reading has been taught. Metacognition adds the dimension of helping pupils look at the act of reading, as well as the content being read, as part of these discussion/questioning procedures.

Motivation

The level of interest or motivation that pupils bring to reading can have a powerful effect on their comprehension of expository reading material. Pupils who are especially interested in a particular topic will usually extend themselves or "read beyond their level" in reading about that topic. Conversely, pupils with no special interest will approach reading with less enthusiasm and less concentration than may be required for understanding what they read.

Interest and motivation belong to the affective domain of reading, the area that is often the most difficult to develop and to measure. In dealing with informational materials, attitudes will be influenced by pupils' interest in reading itself, by their interest in the subject matter being studied, and by the way in which content is presented.

Although writers of textbooks often assume that pupils want to learn about the subject of their writing, teachers recognize that this assumption is not necessarily valid. Even pupils who are capable and enthusiastic readers of narrative material are not always interested in reading assignments related to school subjects. Then it becomes important for teachers to inject some of the motivational spark needed to fire pupils' interest by making material personal and meaningful through trade books.

Both intrinsic and extrinsic motivation are at work in a classroom. Extrinsic motivation includes rewards and punishments—the fear of poor grades, for example, or the chance to use free classroom time in a desirable activity. By contrast, intrinsic motivation involves interest and success in dealing with a particular topic. Material that pupils choose to read for fun—such as a book by their favorite author or material they select for Sustained Silent Reading—has an intrinsic motivational element of interest built in.

Motivation is part of some of the instructional techniques for content area reading lessons suggested earlier. For example, selecting trade books at their reading level gives pupils a better shot at success that is likely to improve motivation. Showing pupils how to succeed in a textbook reading assignment is motivational. Schema-building activities that help forge a link between content being studied and pupils' real-world needs can produce an element of interest. Allowing pupils to make choices from lists of topics or to generate personal choices for curriculum reports provides a dimension of motivation. Finally, although it is a cliché, enthusiasm is catching; teachers who are enthusiastic about topics being studied in content areas will likely generate interest and motivation among pupils.

Summary and Conclusions

In school as in life, reading fulfills two major functions: to entertain and to inform. Just as pupils are exposed to the former purpose in narrative materials, they are introduced to the latter through the expository text they encounter throughout their early school years. "Let's read to find out" with nonfiction trade books needs to be part of instruction from the emergent literacy stage.

Each part of the school curriculum requires reading competency. Reading is a vehicle for learning in all school subjects; at the same time, curriculum-related printed materials are vehicles for the development of reading and writing competency. Dealing with expository text fuses the learning-to-read and reading-to-learn functions of literacy.

Children's trade books are effective and appealing sources of information for reading and learning in today's classrooms. Informational trade books are available on virtually all topics included in content areas. They can be used apart from or in conjunction with textbooks that are often prescribed for curriculum content.

Comprehension occurs as a result of the interaction of what is "in front of the reader's eye" (text-based factors) and what is "behind the reader's eye" (reader-based factors). Level (or readability) of textbooks tends to be high in relation to pupils' grade placements. The content of each curriculum area involves its own unique demands in understanding text. Because maps, charts, diagrams, and other graphic aids are especially important to expository writing, these devices require a specific instructional focus.

Reader-based features include language background, cognitive processing, schemata, metacognitive awareness, and motivation. Understanding successively large units of language is necessary for comprehension. Technical and specific vocabulary require particular attention. Teaching pupils to comprehend expository material involves questioning that focuses on both the type and level of thinking. Because pupils often lack the schemata essential to understanding curriculum topics, building background information is vital as well. Developing metacognitive awareness is part of the particular demands of reading expository text. Both extrinsic and intrinsic factors can be used to stimulate pupils' interest in reading in the content areas.

Discussion Questions and Activities

1. From a third or fourth grade social studies or science textbook, select a topic and locate two or three trade books on the subject. Or locate some of the informational trade books listed in *Science and Children* or *Social Education* (see 7.5 and 7.6). What are some of the differences you notice between the two sources? List the advantages and disadvantages of using trade books versus a textbook as instructional tools for reading.
2. Research the topic of readability. Using a microcomputer software package, compute the readability of a piece of expository text designed for use in the elementary grades. What conclusions can you draw?
3. Examine a sample of expository writing with an eye to text structure. Design a graphic organizer that you might use to make pupils aware of this structural pattern in text.
4. Using the ideas presented in 7.13 and 7.14, make a herringbone or a study guide that would help pupils comprehend a selection of expository text related to a curriculum topic.
5. Prepare a reading lesson using an informational trade book. What might you do to build pupils' schemata before reading? List the questions you would use to guide reading. What postreading strategies or activities would you use?

School-Based Assignments

1. Interview a small group of pupils concerning their favorite curriculum topics. Then find a trade book related to that topic. Share the book with the group and note the instructional adjustments you would need to make in order to use the book to teach reading.
2. Examine the teachers edition of a mathematics, science, or social studies text used in your classroom. What suggestions are made for helping pupils develop word knowledge with the material in the text? What provisions are made for using the book as a vehicle for teaching reading?
3. Select an expository selection from a basal reader. Locate informational trade books or magazine articles on the topic of the basal selection. Describe how you might use the material to extend the basal reading experience. Try out your ideas with a small group.

4. Using the components of the interactive model of reading comprehension as a framework for your observation, observe a supervising teacher or colleague teach a reading lesson using an expository text selection. Note how the teacher prepares the pupils, the type of guided instruction he or she provides during reading and postreading activities. Pay particular attention to the pupils. In your log or journal, make a record of your observations, including what you might have done differently.

5. Identify a particular component of the reading curriculum—a dimension of vocabulary development or an aspect of comprehension. Select a piece of expository writing and use it to plan a lesson directly related to that component. Try your lesson with a small group.

Children's Trade Books Cited In This Chapter

Ackerman, Karen. *Song and Dance Man.* New York: Knopf, 1988.

Anno, Mitsumasa. *Anno's Counting Book.* New York: Putnam, 1977.

Aliki, *The Medieval Feast.* New York: Harper and Row, 1986.

———. *Mummies Made In Egypt.* New York: Crowell, 1979.

Baylor, Byrd. *If You Are a Hunter of Fossils.* New York: Antheneum, 1980.

Birch, David. *The King's Chessboard.* New York: Dial, 1988.

Branley, Franklin. *The Sky Is Full of Stars.* New York: Harper and Row, 1981.

———. *Sunshine Makes the Seasons.* New York: Harper and Row, 1985.

Brinckloe, Julie. *Fireflies!* New York: Macmillan, 1986.

Brown, Marcia. *Shadow.* New York: Macmillan, 1982.

Buck, Pearl. *The Big Wave.* New York: Harper and Row, 1986.

Bullatz, Sonja, and Lomeo, Angelo. *The Baby Bears.* New York: Golden Books, 1983.

Carle, Eric. *The Tiny Seed.* New York: Scholastic, 1986.

Charles, Oz. *How Does Soda Get into the Bottle?* New York: Simon and Schuster, 1988.

Coerr, Eleanor. *Sadako and the Thousand Paper Cranes.* New York: Putnam, 1977.

Cole, Joanna. *Cars and How They Go.* New York: Harper and Row, 1983.

———. *Hungry, Hungry Sharks.* New York: Random House 1986.

Dalgliesh, Alice. *The Courage of Sarah Noble.* New York: Macmillan, 1986.

de Angeli, Marguerite. *Door in the Wall.* New York: Doubleday, 1949.

de Paola, Tomie. *An Early American Christmas.* New York: Holiday House, 1987.

Ets, Marie Hall. *Gilberto and the Wind.* New York: Viking, 1963.

Florian, Douglas. *Vegetable Garden.* Orlando: Harcourt Brace Jovanovich, 1991.

Forbes, Esther. *Johnny Tremain.* Boston: Houghton Mifflin, 1946.

Freeman, Ina. *How My Parents Learned To Eat.* Boston: Houghton Mifflin, 1984.

Freeman, Russell. *Lincoln: A Photobiography.* New York: Clarion, 1987.

Fritz, Jean. *And Then What Happened, Paul Revere?* New York: Putnam, 1973.

———. *Bully for You, Teddy Roosevelt!* New York: Putnam, 1991.

———. *What's the Big Idea, Ben Franklin?* New York: Coward-McCann, 1976.

———. *Where Do You Think You're Going, Christopher Columbus?* New York: Putnam, 1980.

George, Jean Craighead. *Julie of the Wolves.* New York: Harper and Row, 1972.

Gipson, Fred. *Old Yeller.* New York: Harper and Row, 1956.

Gladone, Paul. *The Three Bears.* New York: Scholastic, 1977.

Goffstein, M. B. *An Artist.* New York: Harper and Row, 1980.

Goldin, Augusta. *Ducks Don't Get Wet.* New York: Crowell, 1965.

Grillone, Lisa, and Gennaro, Joseph. *Small Worlds Close Up.* New York: Crown, 1978.

Hall, Donald. *The Ox-Cart Man.* New York: Viking, 1979.

Hoban, Tana. *26 Letters and 99 Cents.* New York: Greenwillow, 1987.

Hunt, Irene. *Across Five Aprils.* Chicago: Follett, 1964.

Hutchins, Pat. *The Doorbell Rang.* New York: Greenwillow, 1986.

Jones, Betty M. *Wonder Women of Sports.* New York: Random House, 1981.

Kesselman, Wendy. *Emma.* New York: Doubleday, 1980.

Knolton, Jack. *Maps and Globes.* New York: Harper and Row, 1985.

Knudson, R. R. *Babe Didrickson: Athlete of the Century.* New York: Viking, 1985.

Kroll, Steven. *The Biggest Pumpkin Ever.* New York: Scholastic, 1986.

Kurelek, William. *A Prairie Boy's Winter.* Boston: Houghton Mifflin, 1973.

Kuskin, Karla. *The Philharmonic Gets Dressed.* New York: Harper and Row, 1982.

Langstaff, John. *Frog Went a-Courtin'.* New York: Harcourt Brace, 1955.

Lawson, Robert. *Ben and Me.* Boston: Little Brown, 1951.

Lord, Suzanne and Epstein, Jolie. *A Day in Space.* New York: Scholastic, 1986.

Macaulay, David. *The Way Things Work.* Boston: Houghton Mifflin, 1988.

McClosky, Robert. *Blueberries for Sal.* New York: Viking, 1963.

Merrill, Claire. *A Seed Is a Promise.* New York: Scholastic, 1973.

Patent, Dorothy Hinshaw. *Where Food Comes From.* New York: Holiday House, 1991.

Peet, Bill. *Big Bad Bruce.* Boston: Houghton Mifflin, 1978.

Prelutsky, Jack. *Rainy, Rainy Saturday.* New York: Greenwillow, 1980.

Ray, Delia. *Behind the Blue and Gray: The Soldier's Life in the Civil War.* New York: Lodestar, 1991.

Reiss, John J. *Shapes.* New York: Macmillan, 1974.

Rogers, Jean. *The Runaway Mittens.* New York: Greenwillow, 1988.

Roop, Peter and Connie. *Keep the Lights Burning, Abbie.* Minneapolis: Carlrhoda Books, 1985.

Rosenthal, Mark. *Bears.* Chicago: Children's Press, 1983.

Schwartz, David M. *How Much Is a Million?* New York: Lothrup, 1987.

———. *If You Made a Million.* New York: Lothrup, 1989.

Seidman, James F., and Mintoyne, Grace. *Shopping Cart Art.* New York: Macmillan, 1970.

Sendak, Maurice. *Chicken Soup with Rice.* New York: Harper and Row, 1962.

Seymour, Simon. *Deserts.* New York: Morrow, 1990.

———. *Earthquakes.* New York: Morrow, 1991.

———. *Galaxies.* New York: Morrow, 1988.

———. *The Paper Airplane Book.* New York: Penguin, 1971.

Sis, Peter. *Going Up.* New York: Greenwillow, 1989.

Slobodkin, Louis. *The Three-Seated Space Ship.* New York: Macmillan, 1962.

Sperry, Armstrong. *Call It Courage.* New York: Macmillan, 1940.

Steig, William. *Doctor DeSoto.* New York: Farrar, Straus and Giroux, 1982.

Steptoe, John. *Mufaro's Beautiful Daughters: An African Tale.* New York: Lothrup, 1987.

Taylor, Mildred. *Roll of Thunder, Hear My Cry.* New York: Dial, 1976.

Viorst, Judith. *Alexander, Who Used to Be Rich Last Sunday.* New York: Macmillan, 1978.

Weiss, Harvey. *Maps: Getting from Here to There.* Boston: Houghton Mifflin, 1991.

Yashima, Taro. *Crow Boy.* New York: Viking, 1955.

Children's Books Cited in the Webs in 7.1

Aliki. *Mummies Made in Egypt*. New York: Harper and Row,1985.

Andrews, Jan.*Very Last First Time*. New York: Macmillan. 1986.

Babbitt, Natalie. *Tuck Everlasting*. New York: Farrar, Straus & Giroux, 1975.

Baker, Jeannie. *Where the Forest Meets the Sea*. New York: Greenwillow, 1988.

Bender, Lionel. *Volcano!* New York: Franklin Watts,1988.

Branley, Franklin. *A Book of Flying Saucers For You*. New York: Crowell, 1973.

Brown, Palmer. *Hickory*. New York: Harper and Row,1978.

Calhoun, Mary. *Hot Air Henry*. New York: Morrow, 1981.

Codrington, Kenneth deBurgh. *Cricket in the Grass*. London: Faber and Faber, 1959.

Coerr, Eleanor. *The Great Balloon Race*. New York: Harper and Row,1981.

Cooney, Barbara. *Island Boy*. New York: Viking Kestrel, 1988.

———. *Miss Rumphius*. New York: Viking, 1982.

dePaola, Tomie. *Nana Upstairs and Nana Downstairs*. New York: Puffin, 1978.

———. *Now One Foot, Now the Other*. New York: Putnam, 1981.

Elting, Mary, and Goodman, Ann. *Dinosaur Mysteries*. New York: Putnam, 1980.

Farber, Norma. *How Does It Feel to be Old ?* Illustrated by Trina S. Hyman. New York: Dutton. 1985.

Freedman, Russell. *Buffalo Hunt*. New York: Holiday, 1988.

———. *Dinosaurs and Their Young*. New York: Holiday, 1983.

Gerstein, Mordicai. *Mountains of Tibet*. New York: Harper and Row,1987.

Gibbons, Gail. *Dinosaurs*. New York: Holiday, 1987.

———. *Flying*. New York: Holiday House, 1966.

Goble, Paul. *Buffalo Woman*. New York: Bradbury,1984.

Gunston, Bill. *Aircraft*. New York: Watts, 1986.

Johnston, Tony. *Yonder*. New York: Dial, 1988.

Lauber, Patricia. *Dinosaurs Walked Here and Other Stories Fossils Tell*. New York: Bradbury, 1987.

———. *Tales Mummies Tell*. New York: Crowell, 1985.

Lauber, Patricia, and Wexler, Jerome. *Seeds, Pop, Stick, Glide*. New York: Crown, 1987.

Little, Jean. *Mama's Going to Buy You a Mocking Bird*. New York: Penguin, 1986.

Marshall, Edward. *Space Case*. New York: Dial, 1982.

Martin, Bill Jr., and Archambault, John. *Knots on a Counting Rope*. New York: Henry Holt, 1987.

McLaughlin, Molly. *Earthworms, Dirt and Rotten Leaves: An Exploration in Ecology*. New York: Macmillan. 1986.

Murphy, Jim. *The Last Dinosaur*. New York: Scholastic,1988.

Newton, James. *A Forest Is Reborn*. New York: Harper and Row,1982.

Overbeck, Cynthia. *How Seeds Travel*. Minneapolis: Lerner,1982.

Paterson, Katherine. *Bridge to Terabithia*. New York: Avon, 1977.

Penny, Malcom. *Endangered Animals*. New York: Watts,1988.

Pringle, Laurence. *Death Is Natural*. New York: Macmillan. 1977.

Provensen, Alice, and Provensen, Marvin. *The Glorious Flight across the Channel*. New York: Viking, 1983.

Rosenblum, Richard. *Wings: The Early Years of Aviation*. New York: Four Winds Press, 1980.

Tejima, Keizaburo. *Fox's Dream*. New York: Putnam, 1987.

———. *Swan Sky*. New York: Putnam, 1988.

Tresselt, Alvin. *The Dead Tree*. New York: Parents Magazine Press,1972.

Tscharner, Renata Von, and Fleming, Ronald L. *New Providence: A Changing Landscape*. San Diego: Harcourt Brace, 1987.

Viorst, Judith. *The Tenth Good Thing about Barney*. New York: Macmillan. 1971.

White, E. B. *Charlotte's Web*. New York: Harper and Row,1952.

Whitfield, Philip, and Pope, Joyce. *Why Do the Seasons Change?* New York: Penguin,1987.

Yorkins, Arthur. *Company's Coming*. New York: Crown, 1988.

References

AASA (1965). *The Basic Science Processes.* Washington: American Association for the Advancement of Science.

Bormuth, J. R. (1966). Readability: A New Approach. *Reading Research Quarterly* 1:79–132.

Bormuth, J. R. (1968). The Cloze Readability Procedure. *Elementary English* 45:429–436.

Butzow, C. M., and Butzow, J. W. (1989). *Science through Children's Literature.* Englewood, CO: Teacher Ideas Press.

Caduto, M. J., and Bruchac, J. (1989). *Keepers of the Earth.* Golden, CO: Fulcrum, Inc.

Chatton, B. (1989). Using Literature across the Curriculum. In J. Hickman and B. Cullinan, (eds.), *Children's Literature in the Classroom: Weaving Charlotte's Web.* Needham, MA: Christopher Gordon Publishers.

Crook, P. R., and Lehman, B. A. (1991). Themes for Two Voices: Children's Fiction and Nonfiction as ''Whole Literature.'' *Language Arts* 68:34–41.

Davison, A. (1985). *Readability— The Situation Today.* Technical Report No. 359. Champaign: University of Illinois, Center for the Study of Reading.

Davidson, A., and Kantor, Robert N. (1982). On the Failure of Readability Formulas to Define Readable Texts: A Case Study from Adaptations. *Reading Research Quarterly* 17:187–209.

Dupuis, M. M., Lee, J. W., Badiali, B. J., and Askov, E. N. (1989). *Teaching Reading and Writing in the Content Areas.* Glenview, IL: Scott, Foresman.

Earp, N. W. (1970). Procedures for Teaching Reading in Mathematics. *Arithmetic Teacher* 17: 575–579.

Forgan, H. W., and Mangrum, C. T. (1989) *Teaching Content Area Reading Skills* (4th ed.). Columbus, OH: Merrill Publishing.

Gere, A. A. (ed.) (1985). *Roots in the Sawdust: Writing to Learn across the Disciplines.* Urbana, IL: National Council of Teachers of English.

Harris, A. J., and Sipay, E. R. (1985). *How to Increase Reading Ability* (8th ed.). New York: Longmans.

Hess, M. L. (1991). Understanding Nonfiction: Purposes, Classification, Responses. *Language Arts* 68:228–232.

Hoffman, J. V. (1992). Critical Reading/Thinking across the Curriculum: Using I-Charts to Support Learning. *Language Arts* 69:121–127.

Holmes, B. C., and Ammon, R. I. (1985). Teaching Content with Trade Books: A Strategy. *Childhood Education* 61:366–370.

Huck, C., Hepler, S., and Hickman, J. (1987). *Children's Literature in the Elementary School* (4th ed.). New York: Holt, Rinehart and Winston.

Johnson, N. M., and Ebert, M. J. (1992). Time Travel Is Possible: Historical Fiction and Biography— Passport to the Past. *The Reading Teacher* 45:488–495.

Kennedy, D., Spangler, S., and Vanderwerf, M. (1990). *Science and Technology in Fact and Fiction: A Guide to Children's Books.* New York: Bowker.

Kiefer, B. (1988). Picture Books as Contexts for Literacy, Aesthetic, and Real World Understandings. *Language Arts* 65:260–271.

Kinney, M. A. (1985). A Language Experience Approach to Teaching Expository Text Structure. *The Reading Teacher* 39:854–856.

Kliman, M., and Kleiman, G. W. (1992). Life among the Giants: Writing, Mathematics, and Exploring Gulliver's World. *Language Arts* 69:128–136.

Lamme, L. L. (1990). Exploring the World of Music through Picture Books. *The Reading Teacher* 44:294–300.

Laughlin, M., and Kardaelff, P. (1991). *Literature-Based Social Studies: Children's Books and Activities to Enrich the K-5 Curriculum.* Phoenix: Oryx Press.

Mason, J. M., and Au, K. H. (1990). *Reading Instruction for Today* (2nd ed.). Glenview, IL: Scott Foresman.

McGee, L. A. (1982). Awareness of Text Structure : Effects on Children's Recall of Expository Text. *Reading Research Quarterly* 17:581–90.

McGee, L. A., and Richgels, D. J. (1985). Teaching Expository Text Structure to Elementary Students. *The Reading Teacher* 39:739–748.

Newport, J. F. (1990). What Is Wrong with Science Textbooks? *National Elementary Principal* 69:22–24.

Ogle, D. (1986). K–W–L: A Teaching Model That Develops Active Reading of Expository Text. *The Reading Teacher* 39:564–570.

Polya, G. (1945). *How to Solve It.* Princeton, NJ: Princeton University Press.

Raphael, T. E., Englert, C. S., and Kirschner, B. W. (1989). Acquisition of Expository Writing Skills. In Jana M. Mason (ed.), *Reading and Writing Connections.* Boston: Allyn and Bacon.

Reinking, D. (1986). Integrating Graphic Aids into Content Area Instruction: The Graphic Information Lesson. *Journal of Reading* 30:146–151.

Robb, L. (1989). Books in the Classroom. *The Horn Book Magazine* 65:808–810.

Robinson, F. P. (1946) *Effective Study.* New York: Harper.

Row, B. D., Stoodt, B. D., and Burns, P. C. (1978). *Reading Instruction in the Secondary School.* Chicago: Rand McNally.

Schiro, M. (in press) *In Search of Excellence: Criteria for Evaluating Children's Mathematics Books.* Chestnut Hill, MA: Boston College.

Sebestia, S. L. (1987). Enriching the Arts and Humanities through Children's Books. In B. E. Cullinan (ed.), *Children's Literature in the Reading Program.* Newark, DE: International Reading Association.

Snowball, D. (1989). Classroom Big Books: Links between Reading and Writing Nonfiction. *The Reading Teacher* 43:267.

Taylor, W. (1953). Cloze Procedure: A New Tool for Measuring Readability. *Journalism Quarterly* 30:415–433.

Vacca, R. T., and Vacca, J. L. (1989). *Content Area Reading* (3rd ed.). Glenview, IL: Scott Foresman.

Whitin, D. J., Mills, H., and O'Keefe T. (1990). *Living and Learning Mathematics.* Portsmouth, NH: Heinemann.

Wood, T. L., and Wood, W. (1988). Assessing Potential Difficulties in Comprehending Fourth Grade Science Textbooks. *Science Education* 72:561–574.

hapter 8

The Role of the Library in a Literature-Based Reading Program

Chapter 8 Outline

I. Introduction
II. Teachers and Librarians
III. Reference Materials
   A. Reference Tools
   B. Learning to Use Reference Tools
   C. Organizing Information
IV. Newspapers and Magazines
   A. Newspapers
   B. Magazines
V. Reading Rate/Reading Efficiency
   A. Comprehension
   B. Flexibility
VI. Summary and Conclusions
Discussion Questions and Activities
School-Based Assignments
Children's Trade Books Cited in This Chapter
References

Features

8.1   Children's Trade Books about the Library
8.2   Ten Ways to Use the Newspaper
8.3   Magazines that Publish Children's Writing
8.4   Selective Reading Guide

Key Concepts in This Chapter

T he library or media center is the epicenter of a school in which literature is at the heart of the reading program. In addition to being the source of books for information and pleasure, the library provides additional reading resources for pupils' use.

Reference materials are sources of information that supplement informational trade books in a balanced reading program.

Newspapers and magazines are also valuable instructional resources that provide up-to-the-minute material for learning to read.

As competency and independence increases, rate of reading may be a concern. Rate, however, is governed by comprehension and flexibility in light of purpose for reading.

A LTHOUGH CHILDREN'S literature is at the heart of a classroom reading program and trade books are used as essential vehicles in literacy instruction, pupils also need to learn to deal with material that extends beyond the normal diet of reading materials in the classroom. These materials include reference tools, newspapers and magazines, and other sources of print typically found in the school library or media center.

Teachers and Librarians

In a literature-based reading program, pupils will be familiar with the library or media center. The library is the epicenter of a school in which literature is valued and used as an integral part of literacy instruction. During story hours children travel to the library to enjoy stories shared by the librarian, by a parent volunteer, or by an upper-grade pupil. For those who come to love literature, libraries become very special places.

The school librarian or media center coordinator remains an important member of the instructional team in literature-based programs. As the resident expert on books, the librarian is in a unique position to have an important impact on reading. The key to maximizing this impact is cooperation between the classroom teacher and the librarian. Although they have different jobs, teachers and librarians have similar goals—to develop in pupils the ability and the inclination to read. An active, trusting relationship is essential to both professionals' meeting these goals (Dales, 1990).

Librarians, whose job it is to keep up-to-the-minute with books, can recommend newly published trade books that can be used for different purposes in the classroom—an especially good book for read-aloud, just the right reference on snakes, a newly published book that would be perfect for third graders on a rainy day. Some librarians compile lists of new acquisitions to be circulated to teachers and parents. Librarians (including public librarians in some communities) can also prepare collections of books that can be checked out for weeks at a time to supplement the classroom library or to support a thematic unit.

Opportunities also exist for the teacher and the librarian to co-teach aspects of the reading program. Classes typically make weekly visits to the library for storytime or for instruction in how to utilize various library resources. Instead of dropping the class at the library door and heading for the teachers' lounge (however tempting or well deserved that respite might be), the teacher can coordinate efforts with the librarian to provide a double dose of instruction with activities such as:

The librarian reads a book during shared storytime; the teacher follows up with classroom enrichment activities related to the book.

The classroom teacher begins a thematic unit with preplanning help from the librarian; the librarian gears instruction in library use directly to the unit theme.

The librarian introduces one book in a series during storytime—Michael Bond's *A Bear Called Paddington* in the primary grades, for example, or Robert Newton Peck's *Soup* in the upper elementary grades; the classroom teacher continues with other books in the series.

The librarian can play an important part in introducing young children to literature.

The librarian introduces a reading-related component as part of library time—for example, the metaphorical riddles in Brian Swann's strikingly illustrated *A Basketful of White Eggs;* the teacher continues the direct instructional focus by having pupils write and illustrate their own riddles.

The librarian plans a display of pupils' reviews and commentaries about books; the teacher plans a reading–writing activity to produce the "stuff" for the display.

The librarian shares a book based on a song, such as John Langstaff's *Frog Went a-Courtin';* the music teacher uses this song in class.

The key to this successful collaboration is planning. The primary responsibility for the reading program rests with the teacher in the classroom. But most librarians are more than happy to become involved and provide all the help and support they can. Teachers who involve librarians in this way add an incredibly enriched dimension to their classroom reading programs.

Reference Materials

As an extension of literature-based reading programs, there will be times when pupils will have occasion to use the rich source of reference materials that school and community libraries or media centers contain. Instruction will be needed to help pupils

8.1
FOR YOUR INFORMATION
Children's Trade Books about the Library

SOME SIMPLY written and informative children's trade books about libraries are available, including:

Carol Green's *I Can Be A Librarian*
Patricia Fujimoto's *Libraries*
Claire McInerney's *Find It! The Inside Story at Your Library*

Cherry Gilcrest's *A Visit to the Library*
Anne Rockwell's *I Like the Library*

The school or public librarian may suggest some additional titles as well. Although these books introduce library services, explain how to use the library, and/or tell about the role of the librarian, they are no substitute for firsthand encounters.

---

locate and use this material efficiently and effectively. In addition to information in informational trade books, pupils will have occasion to use encyclopedias, almanacs, and other sources of printed information to satisfy their curiosity or curriculum needs.

Reference Tools

A useful reference source that most pupils encounter in school is an encyclopedia, a multivolume series of books containing articles on a wide variety of topics. Pupils need to learn what to look for in this reference tool, how to find what they need to know (including using the separate volume that contains the index), how to use the headings and subheads to determine text organization (which is a carryover from classroom instruction on the structure of expository text). Pupils often find it interesting that different answers to the same question can be found in different encyclopedias, which is itself a lesson in critical reading.

In addition to the conventional comprehensive sets of encyclopedias such as *World Book* or *Compton's,* there are multiple-volume, single-purpose encyclopedias such as *The Raintree Illustrated Science Encyclopedia* (Milwaukee: Raintree, 1984), along with single-volume encyclopedias like Enzo Angelucci's *World Encyclopedia of Civil Aircraft* (New York: Crown, 1982) with illustrations and information about flying from Leonardo da Vinci to space exploration. Though limited in scope, these single-purpose encyclopedias are useful sources of information on specific topics that pupils need or want to research.

Pupils need to be aware that while encyclopedias are valuable reference tools, these books are not the only sources of information available. As part of becoming literate citizens, pupils learn the nature and purpose of reference tools that include:

atlases, books of maps and other geographic information;

almanacs, annual references containing up-to-date information on an incredible range of topics;

other reference sources, such as books about children's authors (see p. 51) or reference books about specific topics such as Reginald Bragomer, Jr., and David Fisher's *What's What: A Visual Glossary of the Physical World* (Maplewood, NJ: Hammond, 1981), which has illustrations and descriptions of physical objects from an aba to a zipper.

Learning to use reference tools has long-term benefits for reading and learning.

It is reasonable to expect that dictionaries, an atlas, an almanac, and perhaps a set of encyclopedias will be available in the classroom for immediate use, but a larger collection of reference tools is housed in the library or media center.

Learning to Use Reference Tools

Libraries contain mountains of printed information on vast arrays of topics. Finding their way through the labyrinth of informational material can be a daunting task for some pupils.

For pupils, finding information involves knowing where to look for what they need to know and having strategies to dig out the information. Pupils need at least a rudimentary knowledge of how fiction and nonfiction are classified and arranged, and how to gain access to available resources. Finding information often requires familiarity with the card catalog or one of the electronic access systems that more and more learning resource centers are now using. It includes learning the range of services available for seeking out information.

How can pupils learn to use the library effectively? Too often, instruction in using the library as part of literature-based reading programs consists of early-in-the-year visits when pupils are bombarded with information that ranges from library protocol to the difference between the Dewey Decimal and the Library of Congress cataloging systems. Even if pupils pay attention during these visits, there is almost always too much information presented at one time to make any practical sense.

Pupils can learn to use library resources through authentic opportunities that bring them into contact with what the library has to offer. For example:

as they engage in purposeful searches for information based on thematic units that they are developing in the classroom;

as older pupils provide instructional sessions for younger pupils on the use of reference tools (see 4.7, p. 111);

as they search out answers to questions of interest that arise on the playground, over lunch, or in the classroom.

Ultimately, pupils acquire knowledge in how to use the library purposefully as they seek information on topics of interest related to their school work or their lives.

Just as literature-based reading instruction is aimed at developing a lifelong interest in reading, the attitudes and strategies developed in using research tools for informational purposes are used throughout a pupil's life. Every time we use the phone book to find the number of the closest pizza parlor or use ERIC to prepare a term paper for a college course, we use the competencies developed as part of learning to read for information.

Organizing Information

When pupils have located information in nonfiction trade books or in reference books, they may need to extract what they read and to organize it in an efficient and usable way. This requires strategies in taking notes and in arranging the information in some systematic format.

Notetaking involves making brief written records of ideas and facts gathered from printed (and other) sources of information. Research indicates that ''notetaking has great potential as a studying aid, for it allows the student to record a reworked (and perhaps more deeply processed) version of text'' (Anderson and Armburster, 1984; p. 666).

Effective notetaking is based on a range of prerequisite comprehension components including recognizing main ideas and details, separating relevant from irrelevant information, summarizing, and the like. In taking notes, pupils need to recognize essential information in informational trade books and other sources of expository text, and to make a brief written record of this information for later use.

Some pupils equate notetaking with copying word-for-word from an encyclopedia or other reference source. More often than not, copying verbatim results when reference sources that pupils are expected to use are too difficult and pupils often do not have the prerequisite strategies to separate out what is essential in text. When they do find it necessary to copy, pupils should be made aware of the principles and practices of giving credit.

Notetaking is most effective when it is done with a specific purpose. It is best done when pupils are seeking information that meets their authentic interests or needs. When all the information is gathered, it needs to be organized in order to be remembered and/or presented to others.

Organizing information into a systematic format enables pupils to better use the information they have gathered. Organization of material begins with recognizing expository text structure and comprehending the relationships among ideas.

The conventional outline format of numbers and letters to indicate coordinate and subordinate ideas has been the means most often used for organizing information. But devices such as story maps (pp. 179–180) for narrative text, graphic organizers (p. 242) for expository text, or the Herringbone Technique (p. 244) are alternative means of expressing the relationship among ideas. Pupils can use graphic devices such as chapter subheads in nonfiction trade books and textbooks as an example of how to organize material systematically.

Pupils can become aware of the strategies involved in organizing information through direct and incidental attention in literature-based reading programs. For example:

as they are introduced to the table of contents in nonfiction trade books they are using in the classroom;

as they learn about text structure as part of classroom reading and writing activities;

as they organize their class schedules at the beginning of the school day;

as they prepare curriculum-related written reports as part of thematic units.

Obviously, not all expository text that pupils encounter will require taking notes and organizing information in a systematic form. There will be times when pupils will read trade books for specific information without needing to copy it down, or when they browse through reference materials in search of information on sports, careers, music, or other topics of interest. When needed, however, strategies for taking notes and organizing information can serve valuable purposes in pupils' literacy development in literature-based reading programs.

Newspapers and Magazines

In addition to informational trade books and school texts, up-to-the-minute sources of printed information that are available to pupils all their lives are newspapers and magazines. As reading instructional tools, newspapers and magazines provide a full range of narrative and expository text that can be used effectively in the classroom for helping pupils develop reading competency.

Newspapers

Over the years, the daily newspaper has proved to be a practical tool in teaching reading. Teachers from kindergarten through high school have developed thousands of ideas for using the newspaper for a full range of reading and writing activities, while at the same time helping pupils acquire information related to all areas of the curriculum. The newspaper has been called ''the thinking child's textbook,'' and it can be no less valuable in literature-based programs.

Newspapers offer the unique advantage of being a single source of many different kinds of texts: news to inform, editorials to persuade, reviews to promote critical thinking, features to enrich, comics to entertain, puzzles to stimulate language development, advertisements to convince. Calling them ''indispensable in the teaching of language arts,'' du Boulay (1988) identifies other values of newspapers in the classroom:

They provide purposeful, relevant information.

They are associated with life beyond the classroom.

They are inexpensive and easy to obtain.

They provide interesting examples of narrative and nonnarrative text.

The newspaper — which has been called "the thinking child's textbook" — has a place in the reading instructional program.

In sum, newspapers provide a resource for integrating language instruction across the broad spectrum of the curriculum.

Conrad (1989) addresses the use of the newspaper as an authentic and functional medium for reading and language instruction in the whole language classroom. The newspaper provides interesting examples of narrative and nonnarrative text and is a resource for an integrated approach to teaching reading and writing. Newspapers contain information related to thematic units. They also provide current, relevant information on a variety of curriculum-related topics, along with background information that teachers can use to activate prior knowledge that will help pupils build meaning as they read. The newspaper is related to literature, in that it contains themes, plots, and character traits that pupils encounter in the stories they read. In sum, the newspaper addresses real issues that affect pupils' lives and that reflect the pupils' culture and environment.

Beyond its general value as an essential source of information in a democratic society, the newspaper can be used for a variety of specific purposes in the reading/ writing program, including:

letter recognition, word recognition, and oral language development with younger pupils;

critical thinking, propaganda, and verbal problem solving in the upper elementary grades;

research skills for pupils seeking information on specific subjects on all levels;

writing, as the news is used as a writing model to forge the reading-writing connection (Kossack, Kane, and Fine, 1987).

There is no part of the reading/writing curriculum in which the newspaper cannot be a productive tool.

8.2 Putting Ideas to Work

Ten Ways to Use the Newspaper

SPECIFIC READING and writing activities using the newspaper are virtually limitless. The ten activities suggested here can easily be expanded a hundredfold.

1. Using "the 5 Ws and an H" format of news stories (who, what, when, where, why, and how), pupils can rewrite accounts of their favorite episodes in trade books or write their own narrative accounts of events in their lives.

2. Pupils match headlines to stories (main idea), write headlines based on stories, or write stories based on headlines.

3. Pupils can read editorials or letters to the editor to determine reasons for the writer's thinking and write their own letters to the editor based on a classroom discussion of current issues, or they can write an editorial-style review of a book that they read.

4. Pupils can examine display and classified ads with an eye to vocabulary and propaganda techniques used, and create advertisements for trade books that they have enjoyed.

5. Pupils can rearrange the frames of comic strips or design their own comic strips based on their favorite story characters.

6. Pupils can use back issues of newspapers to research items of interest from local or state history.

7. Pupils can interview community members who are experts on specific topics and write the account of the interview in the form of a news story, or they can write stories based on real or imagined interviews with authentic authors.

8. Pupils can examine book reviews from their local papers and use these as models for submitting their own reviews of new books.

9. Pupils can develop word banks related to specific topics (politics, finance, travel, or sports, for example) based on newspaper sections.

10. Pupils can produce their own classroom newspaper, with school or neighborhood news, editorials on local policies, advertisements for school events, reviews of books, and samples of their original writing.

These ten suggestions relate to language arts. The newspaper can also be used for math, social studies, science, and other areas of the curriculum.

A wealth of materials about using the newspaper as a tool for literacy development can be obtained from the American Newspaper Publishers Association Foundation, Box 17407, Dulles International Airport, Washington, DC 20041. Most local newspapers also provide information and material for classroom use.

In the final analysis, the newspaper is more than a daily teaching tool for reading and writing. It is a vehicle for the dissemination of information and the expression of opinion in a democratic society. Even where reading instruction is centered largely on literature, it makes good sense to give pupils a headstart in developing a skilled and critical approach to reading the newspaper.

Magazines

Another potentially valuable source of reading materials found in the library or school media center are magazines, such as:

Info Power (Sundance Publications, Newtown Road, Littleton, MA 01460)

8.3

FOR YOUR INFORMATION

Magazines that Publish Children's Writing

PUBLICATION IS the consummation of the writing act, and having one's writing appear in a national magazine is the ultimate in publication. A number of national magazines accept stories, poems, letters, essays, plays, and other products written by elementary school pupils. A short list of these magazines includes:

Boys' Life (1325 Walnut Hill Lane, Irving, TX 75602)

Children's Digest (P.O. Box 567, Indianapolis, IN 46206)

Highlights for Children (803 Church Street, Honesdale, PA 18431)

Jack and Jill (P.O. Box 567, Indianapolis, IN 46206)

Kids Magazine (P.O. Box 3041, Grand Central Station, New York, NY 10017)

Scholastic Magazines (50 W. 44th Street, New York, NY 10036)

Young World (P.O. Box 567, Indianapolis, IN 46206)

Junior Scholastic (50 W. 44th Street, New York, NY 10036)

World (National Geographic Society, Washington, DC 20036)

Ranger Rick (National Wildlife Federation, 8925 Leesburg Pike, Vienna, VA 22184)

These and other similar publications provide a wealth of interesting and valuable material that pupils can enjoy and, at the same time, can be used for instructional purposes.

Magazines offer unique advantages as supplements to trade books in literature-based reading programs. Selections are manageably short. Content typically deals with topics of current interest to pupils. Articles can provide a springboard for further reading about high-interest topics. The writing provides a model for teachers to use in writing lessons. Magazines often appeal more readily to reluctant readers.

Magazines provide material that supplements literature-based instruction. With multiple copies of the same magazine in a classroom reading lesson, articles can be used in reading groups in much the same way as trade books and textbooks. For example, after hearing a Chinese legend about how pandas got their black and white fur, the class can share informational magazine articles about pandas. With a balance of literature and magazine articles, pupils have opportunities to enjoy relevant samples of narrative and expository text.

Adults fall into three reading categories: book readers, nonbook readers, and nonreaders. Many adults, even those who do not frequently read books, devour daily newspapers and regularly read magazines like *Time, Good Housekeeping, Popular Mechanics, Business Week,* and other publications that seem to overpopulate newsstands. Using magazines as reading instructional tools in a literature-based program gives pupils a headstart in learning to use this material critically and well.

Reading Rate/Reading Efficiency

As pupils learn to read widely and as the volume of their reading increases, rate of reading becomes a concern. In enjoying a good piece of literature, the speed at which one reads is less important than comprehension and enjoyment (unless the rate is inordinately slow). As the volume of text to be read increases, however, rate becomes a concern.

By itself, speed of reading—the number of words read per minute—is not of primary importance. More important by far is comprehension and the ability to adjust rate to the nature of the text and one's purpose for reading it.

Comprehension

Reading quickly may be important at times, but comprehension is more vital all the time. Rapid reading is of little use if pupils do not understand what they are reading. Reading for speed alone suggests the old line, ''I took a speed reading course and read *War and Peace* in 20 minutes. It's about Russia.'' Comprehension involves more than rate; understanding is influenced by all the text-based and reader-based factors described in the previous two chapters.

Flexibility

In literature-based reading, pupils need to learn to adjust their reading rate according to purpose. Pupils become aware of using a different speed in reading a favorite novel, for example, from that in reading a difficult word problem in math. The ability to adjust rate to the nature of the material being read is a metacognitive competency, an awareness of which can be developed early in a pupil's reading life. In group reading lessons in the classroom, prereading discussion can center on how best to approach a text selection, deciding whether quick perusal, careful reading, or a combination of both may be best.

Two types of rapid reading that are sometimes the focus of instruction with informational trade books and other types of expository text in the elementary grades are skimming and scanning. Both are special types of rapid reading.

Skimming refers to the process of reading to pick up the main idea or to get a very general overview of text. It involves a superficial survey for the purpose of forming an overall impression of a trade book or other reading material.

Scanning means reading rapidly to find a specific piece of information, as when we look for a name in a telephone book or when pupils quickly locate an item in an index.

In a reading instructional setting, skimming can be taught by asking pupils:

to survey a few pages in a trade book to see if the story is appealing or appropriate for independent reading;

to find quickly the main idea of a passage in a nonfiction trade book or textbook;

to look quickly over a newspaper article and match it with an appropriate headline;

to skim a selection to see if it might be a useful source of information for a theme unit.

Selective Reading Guide

FOR UPPER elementary pupils, Cunningham and Shablak (1975) suggest the use of Selective Reading Guides as a means of achieving flexibility and comprehension in expository reading material. Based on the assumption that not all content is of equal significance in content area textbooks, the teacher previews chapters to determine which ideas are particularly important and which are not.

In a reading group, the teacher then guides pupils through the chapter with directions such as, "Look at the heading on page 100. Read this paragraph about pioneer life slowly and carefully"; or "On pages 101 and 102, there is a story about a pioneer family. It is interesting but not especially important. Read it quickly and move on to page 103."

This type of guided reading is characteristic of purpose setting and questioning that is part of well developed reading lessons using content area material. These guided directions can be tape recorded and used by pupils working independently.

Scanning can be developed as pupils read as quickly as possible to find a topic in an index or to find a specific piece of information such as a name or a date in a chapter. As part of reading instruction, teachers can prepare a list of factual questions and pupils can be assigned to find answers as quickly as possible as a prereading or postreading activity.

Beyond the elementary grades, reading rate extends into the realm of "speed reading," accompanied by audacious (some say outrageous) claims of programs that can "triple your reading speed or double your money back." Although there are indeed techniques and devices that people can use to speed up their reading pace, the same principle applies to adults in speed reading programs as to children learning to read more quickly: how fast a person reads depends on the nature of the material and the person's purpose for reading it.

Summary and Conclusions

In a literature-based reading program, pupils will encounter fact and fiction in the trade books they read. They will also extend their reading for information into reference books, newspapers and magazines, and other types of reading material that they will continue to encounter throughout their lives. Given the flood of information that pupils will face as they enter adulthood during the 21st century, early encounters with this type of print will be important.

With story hours and other literature-related activities, pupils come to see the library as a treasured place from their early school years. With graduated instruction, pupils' awareness is expanded to include the library as a rich source of reference materials that they can use to find information on virtually any topic. Learning to use these references effectively and efficiently is part of literacy instruction in the elementary grades.

Beyond library reference tools, newspapers and magazines are learning tools that can be used for literacy development. These current sources of information can be used in an incredible variety of ways to develop reading, writing, thinking, and knowledge to supplement literature used in teaching reading.

As reading competency and independence develops, the volume of printed material that pupils are expected to read usually increases, thus suggesting the need to learn to increase reading rate. Although techniques of skimming and scanning are rapid reading strategies that can be taught in the elementary grades, rate of reading always must be judged in light of the nature of the material, the reader's purpose for reading it, and comprehension.

Discussion Questions and Activities

1. In preparing for a research assignment that you might have for one of your college courses, make a list of strategies that you need to complete the assignment. (Don't take anything for granted; you need to understand the concept of alphabetical order.) With the help of a librarian, fully explore the range of resources available to you in researching your topic.
2. Examine your local or national newspaper or children's magazine. Make a list of the activities you might plan for using this material as a vehicle for teaching reading and writing in the classroom or resource room.
3. How important is reading rate to you? With a classmate, compare how you adjust your reading speed with the different types of reading you do throughout the day—for example, reading the newspaper, the lunch menu in the cafeteria, course material in preparation for a test. How does your reading rate differ from that of someone just learning to read?

School-Based Assignments

1. Observe a science or social studies lesson or talk to pupils about a topic in which they are particularly interested. Then visit the school library or media center and/or the local public library to locate trade books and other reference materials on the topic. Prepare a list of resources that might be used in your classroom.
2. In the school library or media center, locate a magazine written for elementary pupils, and select (perhaps with the help of some pupils) an article that would appeal to the grade level in which you are interested. Design a directed reading lesson using the article. If possible, try the lesson with a small group of pupils.
3. How quickly do the pupils in your classroom read? Give a small group of pupils a brief timed test and check their comprehension. Make a list of suggestions to help them improve their reading rate.

Children's Trade Books Cited in This Chapter

Bond, Michael. *A Bear Called Paddington*. Boston: Houghton Mifflin, 1960.

Fujimoto, Patricia. *Libraries*. Chicago: Children's, 1984.

Gilcrest, Cherry. *A Visit to the Library*. New York: Cambridge University Press, 1985.

Green, Carol. *I Can Be A Librarian*. Chicago: Children's, 1988.

Langstaff, John. *Frog Went a-Courtin'*. New York: Harcourt Brace, 1955.

McInerney, Claire. *Find It! The Inside Story at Your Library*. Minneapolis: Lerner, 1989.

Peck, Robert Newton. *Soup*. New York: Knopf, 1974.

Rockwell, Anne. *I Like the Library*. New York: Dutton, 1977.

Swann, Brian. *A Basketful of White Eggs*. New York: Orchard Books, 1988.

References

Anderson, T. H., and Armbruster, B. B. (1984). Studying. In P. D. Pearson (ed.), *Handbook of Reading Research*. New York: Longmans.

Conrad, S. (1989). Newspaper in the Whole Language Classroom. In *A Whole Language Primer*. Quincy, MA: The Patriot Ledger.

Cunningham, D., and Shablak, S. L. (1975). Selective Reading Guide-o-Rama: The Content Teacher's Best Friend. *Journal of Reading* 18:380–382.

Dales, B. (1990). Trusting Relationships between Teachers and Librarians. *Language Arts* 67:732–734.

du Boulay, G. (1988). Newspapers: Text for Non-Narrative and Narrative Reading and Writing. *Australian Journal of Reading* 11:206–210.

Kossack, S., Kane, S., and Fine, J. (1987). Use the News: The Reading–Writing Connection. *Journal of Reading* 30:730–732.

Chapter 9

Sharing Literature through Oral Reading

Chapter 9 Outline

I. Introduction
II. "Read with Expression"
   A. Expression
      1. Expression and Meaning
      2. Punctuation
   B. Fluency
      1. Modeling
      2. Repeated Reading
      3. Marking Phrases
III. Reading Aloud to Pupils
   A. Advantages of Reading Aloud
   B. Conditions and Techniques for Reading Aloud
   C. Selecting Books for Reading Aloud
IV. Reading Aloud by Pupils
   A. Differences between Oral and Silent Reading
   B. Round-Robin Reading
   C. Alternatives to Round-Robin Reading
      1. Group Oral Reading
      2. Individual Conferences
      3. Paired Practice
      4. Echo Reading
      5. Audience Reading
      6. Choral Reading
      7. Reading Plays and Scripts
V. Summary and Conclusions
Discussion Questions and Activities
School-Based Assignments
Children's Trade Books Cited in This Chapter
References

Features

9.1   The Suprasegmental Phoneme System
9.2   Suggestions for Reading Aloud
9.3   Good Books to Read Aloud
9.4   One-Liners
9.5   Radio Reading
9.6   Play Week

Key Concepts in This Chapter

For centuries, oral reading has been part of education, and it is still practiced widely in elementary schools today. Sharing stories by reading aloud is one of the cornerstones of a literature-based program.

Expression and fluency are essential qualities of oral reading; these qualities enable the reader to convey meaning to listeners.

Reading aloud to pupils opens the world of literature to them. It stimulates their imagination and enhances their language background.

Helping pupils become skilled oral readers involves techniques other than the conventional practice of "round-robin" reading traditionally carried on in so many classrooms.

A|S PART of formal education, oral reading has enjoyed a position of prominence for a very long time. The ancient Greeks and Romans thought of reading exclusively as an oral process. To many ancient learners, the lines of writing represented ''rivers of speech'' and the nature of reading was ''to recapture the actual speech, the sounds, the author's actual words. . . . To get the full benefit of what the reader read, he had to read aloud'' (Mathews 1966; p. 12).

In the centuries that followed, this view of reading as an oral activity persisted. Throughout the Middle Ages and the Renaissance, and during the Industrial Revolution in England and the Colonial period in America, silent reading was considered a peculiar habit and the instructional emphasis remained on reading aloud. In fact, in the New World, reading was equated with ''elocutionary delivery'' from the very early years of education. Reading was taught mainly for the purpose of ''exercising the organs of speech'' and for providing practice in ''just and distinct articulation.'' The goal of developing eloquent oral reading overshadowed the more important goals of comprehension or enjoyment. Oral reading was taught as a social skill because the few who knew how to read were expected to read the Bible and other books aloud to others (Smith, 1965).

During the first quarter of the 20th century, a shift occurred in educational emphasis from oral reading to silent reading. The pendulum swung from reading for *articulation* to reading for *meaning*. As group standardized reading achievement tests were being developed, comprehension became a primary concern. Silent reading replaced oral reading as the aim of instruction in the classroom.

Although the emphasis in teaching reading continues to be on silent reading, oral reading still is part of reading instruction in the elementary school. When people recall their early school experiences in learning to read, reading aloud in front of a group of classmates—and mostly being embarrassed by it—is one of their most frequent and vivid memories (Savage, 1978). Pupils and teachers spend so much classroom time reading aloud and listening to others read that oral reading as part of an instructional program deserves careful examination.

Reading aloud is one of the basic characteristics of literature-based instruction. ''Reading aloud gives teachers the opportunity to open up the world of literature to students who may not discover it on their own'' (Peterson and Eeds, 1990; p. 9). In literature-based classrooms, oral reading involves both: (1) reading aloud *to* pupils for the purpose of sharing literature, while modeling mature, effective reading behaviors; and (2) reading aloud *by* pupils to teach them to use effective reading strategies and to use reading as a means of communicating to others.

The third major purpose of oral reading—assessment—will be addressed in Chapter 13.

"Read with Expression"

Oral reading involves more than the tedious task of standing in front of others trying to get all the words correct. The goal of all reading—silent and oral—is comprehension. Oral reading involves not only the comprehension of an author's message but also the communication of that message to others. Meaning is derived and communicated to others through expressive, fluent oral reading.

9.1
FOR YOUR INFORMATION
The Suprasegmental Phoneme System

THE SUPRASEGMENTAL phoneme system consists of three elements: pitch, stress, and juncture.

Pitch is the level of the voice as one speaks/reads aloud. There are four levels of pitch in American English: /1/ the level to which the voice falls at the end of a statement, /2/ the normal pitch level, /3/ the level to which the voice rises at the end of most questions, and /4/ the level saved to express extreme surprise or shock.

Stress is the relative force of articulation, or loudness, with which sounds are made. American English uses four degrees of stress: /'/ primary, /^/ secondary, /ˋ/ tertiary, and /˘/ weak.

Juncture is the transition between one speech sound and the next in a stream of speech. Included here are internal junctures /+/, which represent pauses within sentences, and terminal junctures— /↓/ (falling) and /↑/ (rising)—which represent end-sentence pauses.

These sound features operate closely together to produce an "overlay" that gives total meaning to the language one speaks/reads aloud.

Expression

Teachers and parents have long urged children to "read with expression." But what makes for expression in oral reading? How does expression come into play as pupils render lines of print into the spoken equivalent?

Expression in oral reading comes from the same elements that make up intonation in speech, the three elements of what is technically known as the *suprasegmental phoneme system* of any language: pitch, stress, and juncture (see 9.1).

Expression and Meaning Speakers use intonation to convey total meaning in speech: readers use expression to convey total meaning in oral reading. There is a reciprocal relationship between expression and meaning. On the one hand, pupils have to fully grasp the total meaning of a passage in order to be able to read the passage with appropriate expression. Struggling with individual words distracts from the larger meaning in text and results in word-by-word performance characteristic of young or immature readers. On the other hand, expression allows the reader to transmit full meaning to others.

Holdaway (1972) explores the relationship between expression and meaning and illustrates the role that expression plays in conveying full meaning with the sentence *He was a little boy.* Taken out of context, this sentence likely would be read with a normal intonation pattern. But in the larger context of:

Poor Herman! He wasn't a bear. He was a little boy.

the expression would change to convey the full meaning. "These sentences have not been *read* until the appropriate intonation patterns have been perceived" (Holdaway 1972; p. 98).

In the extreme, expression in oral reading—the way in which a passage is read—alters meaning drastically. Consider the conflicting interpretations possible with the following segment of print:

a woman without her man is lost

If one interprets the meaning of this line of print as, "A woman is lost without a man," the sentence would be written

A woman without her man is lost.

and would be read with a normal intonation pattern:

/2/ _____ /3/ ↘/↓/ /1/

If, on the other hand, one interprets the meaning as, "A man is lost without a woman," the sentence would be written

A woman—without her, man is lost.

and would be read with an intonation pattern like this:

/2/ ___ /3/ ↘/+//2/ ___ /3/ ___ /↓//2/

The two interpretations of this line of print are diametrically different. In the first, the woman is lost without the man. In the second, the man is lost without the woman. The different meanings do not reside in the language, but rather in the way the language is expressed. The difference well illustrates the old cliché, "It's not what he said but how he said it!"

Punctuation   From the preceding example, the role that punctuation and other graphic devices (such as capital letters, italics, boldface print, and other typographical devices) play in writing and in oral reading becomes apparent. End-sentence punctuation marks (periods, question marks, and exclamation points) indicate not only sentence function but also the intended direction of the voice in reading. Internal punctuation (commas, colons, semicolons, dashes, ellipsis points) indicate the expressional shifts that occur within sentences. Punctuation, of course, represents only the most obvious intonational elements. There is a relationship between punctuation and the suprasegmental phonemes, but as is the case of the relationship between letters and sounds, the relationship is far from perfect.

The suprasegmental phoneme system of English, as in any language, is quite complex. Children learn to use it in speech very early as part of the language acquisition process. When they come to school, they learn how the system applies to the process of reading aloud.

Fluency

Fluency involves the ability to read aloud smoothly and easily. Expression is certainly an essential ingredient of fluent reading, and fluency is also related to word recognition. Pupils who do not recognize the words they encounter and who cannot easily decode

Sharing literature by reading aloud is an essential mark of literature-based reading programs.

these words will often "bump along," reading in a word-by-word manner. Fluent readers, on the other hand, are able to identify words easily and quickly. This is the reason for the strong relationship between fluent oral reading and good overall reading ability.

There is, however, an irony in helping pupils achieve fluency via the word identification route. Teachers often try to improve fluency by focusing on letters, sounds, and words in isolation "in the mistaken belief that more attention to this area will result in improved (oral) reading" (Allington 1983; p. 557). Merely learning to recognize words quickly does not automatically produce fluent oral reading.

In order to help pupils achieve fluency, teachers need to use strategies that focus specifically on fluency. They can use such techniques as modeling, repeated reading, and phrase marking to help pupils become more fluent oral readers.

Modeling   Sharing stories by reading aloud every day is one of the essential characteristics of a literature-based reading program. The teacher's reading aloud to pupils provides pupils with a model of fluent oral reading. When the teacher reads the first hundred or so words as a selection is introduced to a reading group, the pupils' fluency improves and their oral reading errors decrease in number (Smith, 1979).

Repeated Reading   This is a simple rehearsal strategy that allows pupils to practice reading the same passage several times. Evidence shows that when pupils have a chance to preview text silently before reading it aloud, and when they have opportunities to read the material more than once, fluency, accuracy, and speed in oral reading improve (Dowhower, 1989). Repeated reading also has a positive impact on comprehension. Passages should be relatively brief (50–100 words) and within the pupil's reading ability. Pupils can engage in repeated reading sometimes with a partner as a cooperative learning activity and sometimes independently (Samuels, 1978).

Marking Phrases   Fluent readers put words together in meaningful phrases. When the teacher lightly marks phrases in oral reading material, pupils learn to read this grouping of words in ''meaningful chunks.'' The use of phrase marking helps pupils develop an eye–voice span—the distance that the eye is ahead of the voice—that contributes to both expression and fluency in oral reading.

Reading Aloud to Pupils

Reading aloud to pupils is recognized as an important part of teaching children how to read, and it is one of the distinguishing characteristics of a literature-based reading program. ''These are the goals of reading aloud with the total group:

> To make the language of word artists a part of students' lives.
> To make students aware of the delight which can be found in literature.
> To help students discover and entertain all genres and styles of writing (such as poetry, non-fiction, fantasy and science fiction, folk and fairytale, realistic stories, satire, classics, picture books) they might never discover on their own;
> To develop community through building a common literary history.
> To provide a forum for the making and sharing of connections which have been inspired by reading.
> To provide an opportunity for you to help build children's awareness of literary elements.'' (Peterson and Eeds, 1990; p. 49)[1]

Children first experience the world of literature as they listen to stories, and sharing this literature through oral reading continues as an essential part of literacy instruction throughout the grades.

Advantages of Reading Aloud

Reading aloud to pupils has a number of distinct advantages. It is one way of sharing literature with pupils, literature that some children may otherwise have no other way of enjoying. Reading aloud stimulates pupils' imaginations and allows them to engage in experiences vicariously. Hearing good stories read well has an enormously positive effect on pupils' language and reading development. Reading to pupils is a powerful device for stimulating vocabulary growth, since new words are introduced and used in meaningful contexts (Elley, 1989). Careful questioning can focus on the many dimensions of comprehension as well. A shared reading experience can be the basis of group discussion, as when a class examines prejudice after hearing Theodore Taylor's *The Cay,* a book in which a warm relationship develops between a young white boy and an old black man. But for all of its instructional benefits, the primary purpose of reading aloud to pupils is enjoyment. Reading to pupils provides positive experiences that ignite pupils' interest to read on their own.

---

[1]Excerpted from R. Peterson and M. Eeds, ''Grand Conversations: Literature Groups in Action'' in *Scholastic,* 1990. Reprinted by permission of Scholastic, Inc.

By the time they begin nursery school or kindergarten, some children will have discovered the pleasure of being read to at home or in other child-care settings. These pupils will arrive in the classroom already having escaped Mr. McGregor's garden with Peter Rabbit, having been to the ball with Cinderella, and having sailed away for a year and a day with the Owl and the Pussycat in their beautiful pea green boat. Other children will not have been so lucky. But since teachers have little or no direct control over the experiences that pupils have had with books at home, it becomes the teacher's job to make sure that storytime is a regular and important part of life in the classroom.

Conditions and Techniques for Reading Aloud

A teacher does not need to be an Academy Award nominee to read aloud to pupils, but sharing books does take some good oral reading skills. Preparation is important. If possible, the teacher should preview stories to note the points of high suspense (a good place to terminate a daily oral reading period) or to mark long passages that are not essential to the story and are likely to tax the pupils' collective attention span. Preparation also enables teachers to spot words or incidents in the story that may prove embarrassing or otherwise unfortunate to one of the pupils—a cruel nickname that might be pinned on a pupil, for example, or an incident that might reflect a child's unhappy home experience.

A comfortable environment enhances oral reading. The primary purpose of storytime is enjoyment, so pupils should sit where they can listen comfortably. Pupils should have a chance to see illustrations that are essential to the story. In continuing stories, the teacher can set the tone by asking pupils to briefly recall what had happened in the previous episode or to predict what might happen next. These introductions need to be brief, however, so that they do not take away from the primary purpose of enjoyment.

Not every pupil will enjoy every story a teacher reads, but pupils owe it to each other not to ruin storytime for the rest of the group. Art supplies can keep uninterested pupils quietly engaged, but more often than not, these pupils will get involved in the story as it progresses. A large number of disinterested pupils suggests that the book was an inappropriate choice in the first place. If this is the case, teachers should not hesitate to abandon a book and select another. Lack of success in arousing interest is not necessarily a sign that a book is not good or should be abandoned forever. For a number of reasons, a well-written book that meets one teacher's purposes in one classroom may not be a good choice for reading aloud in another classroom.

Reading should be done slowly enough for pupils to savor the language and to visualize the settings and actions. Slow reading is especially important during suspenseful parts, with changes in tone during dialogue (as long as the teacher is comfortable doing so). Tone, volume, and expression ought to convey humor, mystery, sadness, and other moods created by the story. And the reader should keep the story moving without long interruptions such as pupils' anecdotes or questions. If the story lends itself to discussion, the class can talk after reading, as long as the discussion is not turned into a quiz.

9.2 Putting Ideas to Work

Suggestions for Reading Aloud

SLOAN AND Latham (1981) offer some direct and practical advice on the techniques of reading aloud to pupils:

1. Define new words in introducing a story or after reading it, but let context carry the meaning during the reading.

2. Let the pupils know a little about the author—this information makes the story more interesting and may lead pupils to read other works by the author.

3. Group pupils so that they can see you easily.

4. Read with feeling that comes from a genuine enthusiasm for the story.

5. Hold the book so that the pupils can see your facial expressions.

6. If you use gestures, make them slight.

7. Summarize long descriptive passages to give the story "more vitality and movement as a read-aloud tale."

8. Maintain eye contact to personalize reading and to keep the audience involved.

9. Stop at interesting places to heighten excitement for the next episode.

10. Use ongoing evaluation, keeping the dialogue related to pupils' interests.

Selecting Books for Reading Aloud

Selecting books for reading aloud is a practical concern. Selections will vary according to classroom demographics—the age, grade level, interests, and backgrounds of the pupils. A good rule of thumb to follow in selecting books is this: Any book that teachers and pupils can enjoy together is a good book to read aloud.

In the very early grades, picture books are most appropriate, favorites like Bernard Waber's *Ira Sleeps Over* or Robert McCloskey's *Make Way for Ducklings*. Picture books need not be limited to the beginning reading stages, however; upper grade pupils—even "upper grade" college students and experienced teachers—enjoy hearing books read aloud as part of classes or in-service sessions. These picture books are often shared as part of instructional sessions with Big Books. Here, reading aloud to (or with) pupils can have a more direct instructional focus.

From short picture books, teachers can move to chapter books, such as some old favorites like *The Littles* by John Peterson, Michael Bond's *Paddington Bear,* A. A. Milne's *Winnie-the-Pooh,* and Betty McDonald's *Mrs. Piggle Wiggle.* Reading books like these to primary grade pupils enables children to enjoy the language and the stories before they are able to read the books independently. Moreover, it whets their appetite for more of the delightful material that literature provides.

The range of read-aloud selections for pupils in the middle grades is as great as the field of children's literature itself. Read-aloud selections can range from old favorites like Norton Juster's *The Phantom Tollbooth* and John Steinbeck's *The Red Pony* to newer titles like Stephen Manes's *Be a Perfect Person in Just Three Days* and Phyllis Reynolds Naylor's *Shiloh.*

Obviously, teachers' choices will depend on the grade level of pupils, but it is difficult (and often dangerous) to pinpoint a specific grade level to a particular book. Although the background and schemata of a primary grade child may not allow him

9.3 Putting Ideas to Work

Good Books to Read Aloud

PUPILS NEED to hear many types of books read aloud:

humorous books, like Thomas Rockwell's *How to Eat Fried Worms* or Dick King-Smith's *Ace, the Very Important Pig;*

improbable stories, like Oliver Butterworth's *The Enormous Egg* and Deborah and James Howe's *Bunnicula;*

mysteries, like E. L. Konigsburg *From the Mixed-Up Files of Mrs. Basil E. Frankweiler* or Bill Brittain's *The Wish Giver;*

fantasies, like Roald Dahl's *Charlie and the Chocolate Factory* or Robert O'Brien's *Mrs. Frisby and the Rats of NIMH;*

sad books, like Doris Smith's *A Taste of Blackberries* or Wilson Rawls' *Where the Red Fern Grows;*

adventure books, like John Gardiner's *Stone Fox* or Armstrong Sperry's *Call It Courage;*

curriculum-related books, such as Alice Dalgliesh's *The Courage of Sarah Noble* or James and Christopher Collier's *My Brother Sam Is Dead;*

biographies, such as Donald Sobol's *The Wright Brothers at Kitty Hawk* and Carl Sandburg's *Abe Lincoln Grows Up;*

animal stories, like Sheila Burnford's *The Incredible Journey* and Jim Kjelgaard's *Big Red;*

historical tales, such as Marguerite de Angeli's *The Door in the Wall* and Elizabeth George Speare's *The Sign of the Beaver;*

fantasies, like Tolkien's *The Hobbit* or C. S. Lewis's *The Lion, the Witch and the Wardrobe;*

science fiction, such as Madeleine L'Engle's *A Wrinkle in Time* and Caroline MacDonald's *The Lake at the End of the World;*

classics, such as Robert Louis Stevenson's *Treasure Island* or Mark Twain's *Tom Sawyer.* (Teachers often find that they have to do a bit of ''editing'' or explaining some of the content and language of these classics to modern-day pupils.)

recent books that have become popular, such as Sid Fleischman's *The Whipping Boy* or Jerry Spinelli's *Maniac McGee.*

There is no end to possibilities for read-aloud titles in the classroom! Selections for reading aloud to pupils are suggested in books like Jim Trelease's popular *The New Read-Aloud Handbook* (1989), Charlotte S. Huck's popular children's literature text *Children's Literature in the Elementary School* (1987), and Eden Ross Lipson's *Parent's Guide to the Best Books for Children* (1991). Also, a list of read-aloud books passed from one year's teacher to the next will give a running record of what a class has heard read aloud, although favorite books can certainly be repeated.

---

or her to fully comprehend such realistic fiction as Katherine Paterson's *The Great Gilly Hopkins* or Betsy Byars's *The Pinballs,* books like E. B. White's *Charlotte's Web* or Patricia MacLachlan's *Sarah, Plain and Tall* have proved popular with pupils at different grade levels. And the myths contained in books like Virginia Hamilton's *In the Beginning: Creation Stories from around the World* make marvelous read-aloud material across the grades.

When a teacher introduces an author to a class by reading the author's book aloud, pupils often want to read (or hear) more selections by the same author. For example, after hearing Robert Newton Peck's very funny story *Soup,* pupils will likely search out Peck's follow-up books with the same puckish character, *Soup and Me* and *Soup for President.*

The read-aloud fare need not be limited to storybooks, of course. Poetry—from the humor of Edward Lear and Shel Silverstein, to the rhythm of David McCord and

Robert Louis Stevenson, to the beauty of Aileen Fisher and Eleanor Farjeon—ought to be a staple in the read-aloud diet. Poetry anthologies, with poems for different occasions, can be kept at the teacher's fingertips as ready resources to be used at a moment's notice. (A list of poetry anthologies is presented on page 42.) Reading poetry aloud to pupils is especially important because pupils need to hear poetry read *well* in order to learn to enjoy its beauty and understand its significance. Other selections of print—interesting items in newspapers, magazine articles, jokes and riddles, and the like—often are appropriate material for reading aloud to pupils as well.

In a literature-based reading program, reading aloud to pupils is much more than a "time filler" or a "fun activity" to break up the day. It is not an extra. Reading to pupils helps them make a favorable connection between the stories they hear and the stories they read themselves. It is also a way to inject literature directly into the life-blood of reading instruction, a means of creating an awareness and love of books. As such, reading aloud to pupils is an integral component of literature-based classroom reading instruction.

Reading Aloud by Pupils

Adults engage primarily in silent reading. Children in classrooms spend a significant amount of time reading aloud. Oral reading is an important part of classroom instructional programs. Beyond being an effective means of sharing literature, oral reading plays a role in pupils' developing reading competency.

Differences between Oral and Silent Reading

Reading aloud and reading silently both involve the interpretation of printed messages, but there are important differences between the two. Silent reading involves one-to-one communication between a writer and a reader; oral reading involves one-to-many communication as the reader conveys the author's message to an audience. Silent reading is rapid; oral reading is slower because it takes longer to articulate the speech sounds. In oral reading, the reader must accurately pronounce each word; thus he or she relies heavily on graphophonic cues. In silent reading the reader can use context to guess at certain words. Silent reading is aimed primarily at comprehension, and though comprehension is also important in reading aloud, the related demands of oral reading sometimes get in the way of understanding and recalling what is read.

These differences notwithstanding, teachers often judge a pupil's reading competency by oral reading performance. Pupils have been considered "good readers" if they could smoothly read a passage from their basal readers; conversely, pupils who did not do well in reading aloud were said to be "poor readers," irrespective of their ability to comprehend what they had read. Oral reading thus became a simple and straightforward way of checking on pupil progress.

The assumption that good oral reading strategies are automatically transferred to silent reading is not necessarily valid. Although oral and silent reading are indeed related, and though competent readers usually read well both orally and silently, oral reading is not simply an outward manifestation of silent reading. Oral reading relies heavily on facility in word recognition; overall reading competency is defined primarily in terms of comprehension.

When one considers the relatively small amount of time that people spend reading aloud as adults, the time pupils spend reading aloud in the classroom seems disproportionate. Competency in oral reading is important during adulthood when, for example, reading the minutes of a meeting, reading an announcement or a report to colleagues, or sharing a snippet of print with family or friends, but the values of oral reading in the classroom extend beyond these functional situations.

Teachers use oral reading both as a diagnostic and as an instructional tool. In the learning-to-read stage, for example, reading aloud is important in making the transition from word-by-word reading to the natural flow that indicates comprehension of text. Reading the predictable text in Big Books is itself an important way of helping young children learn to read. If the full value of oral reading is to be achieved, however, the way in which the practice is conducted needs to be consistent with appropriate purposes. In other words, *what* teachers do needs to be consistent with *why* they do it.

Round-Robin Reading

The technique that has traditionally been used for classroom oral reading instruction and practice is the ''round-robin'' method, described by Austin and Morrison (1963) as:

Around the circle	'Round the circle
Or up the row	Out of the text
You read orally	You read aloud
'Til I say, ''Whoa!''	'Til I say, ''Next.''[2]

Just about anyone who has gone to school is familiar with round-robin reading. One pupil begins reading at a designated point in the text while all the others (supposedly) follow along and monitor their classmate's reading. After a paragraph or two, the teacher calls on the next pupil, and so on until all have had a chance, until the end of the passage is reached, or until the bell rings (whichever comes first).

Memories of this type of performative oral reading are unpleasant for most people. They remember the dread of waiting to be called on, making mistakes in front of classmates, or being laughed at as they read. Adults recall furtively looking ahead in anticipation of being called on to read, only to be chided by the teacher for failing to ''keep the place.''

Despite the wide popularity of the practice, research suggests ''that the practice of round-robin reading is suspect. (Researchers) conclude that its use in the classroom is not defensible if comprehension is the goal'' (Tierney, Readence, and Dishner 1990; p. 423).

When one considers the different instructional purposes of oral reading—diagnosing reading needs, developing expression, listening, providing auditory feedback, interacting with others—it is obvious that round-robin reading falls short in many areas. Diagnosis is an individual process and many pupils feel embarrassed about having to expose their oral reading ability (or lack thereof) in a reading group. Expression is best developed in other settings. Listening can actually be hampered in round-robin reading, because following the lines of print can be a distraction instead of an aid to listening.

---

[2]Reprinted with permission of Macmillan Publishing Company from *The First R: The Harvard Report on Reading in the Elementary Schools* by Mary C. Austin and Coleman Morrison. Copyright © 1963 by Macmillan Publishing Company.

One-Liners

AN ESPECIALLY effective group activity for helping pupils develop the skills of oral reading is "one-liners." The teacher selects lines spoken by the characters from a popular children's trade book. For example, the following is a very brief sample selected from *The BGF* by Roald Dahl:

Don't be sad.

Do you like vegetables?

You mustn't feel bad about it.

Giants is everywhere around.

Aren't you really a little mixed up?

Let's go back inside.

I cannot help thinking about your poor mother and father.

For oral reading practice, pairs of pupils read the lines with differing interpretations. For example:

Don't be sad.   Read pleadingly.   Read as a command.

Let's go back inside.   Read eagerly.   Read reluctantly.

I can't help thinking about your poor mother and father.   Read casually.   Read sadly.

Using lines like this for practice in interpreting print allows pupils to focus directly on the elements of expression—pitch, stress and juncture—that make for effective oral reading. Teachers can choose books according to the reading level and interests of pupils, or the pupils themselves can create these exercises based on books that they have read and enjoyed.

In short, "In terms of listening and meaning-making, this strategy (round robin) is a disaster. The children are being reinforced for tuning out," not listening in (Sloan and Latham 1981; p. 135). The practice of round-robin oral reading fails to meet the legitimate purposes for reading aloud and alternatives to round-robin reading need to be explored and practiced in the literature-based classroom.

Alternatives to Round-Robin Reading

There are a number of practical alternatives to round-robin oral reading using trade books. Some of these alternatives include purposeful oral reading in groups, reading aloud in individual conferences, paired practice, echo reading, audience reading, choral reading, and reading plays and scripts. Each of these activities offers opportunities for pupils to share literature with those around them.

Group Oral Reading   Pupils can practice oral reading in instructional groups with trade books as the vehicles of instruction; however, instead of circling the group round-robin fashion, pupils can read aloud selections of text for specific purposes; for example, "Read the sentence that proves that Keith was happy in his new home." Pupils can share parts of stories that show how characters felt, descriptive passages related to settings, segments that summarize points of conflict, or other parts that are essential to the story. Pupils can also read with a focus on affective response, as when they share selections that strike them as especially beautiful, fascinating, humorous, or otherwise noteworthy. Pippi Longstocking's very creative account of "schools in Argentina" in Astrid Lindgren's *Pippi Longstocking* is one such selection.

Through paired practice, pupils share literature by reading aloud to each other.

Individual Conferences   In addition to group work, one-to-one pupil–teacher conferences provide appropriate settings in which to work on oral reading. Individual conferences are certainly the most appropriate times for determining the strategies on which pupils rely as they read. Conferences also provide opportunities for valuable one-to-one instructional sessions—opportunities for teachers to combine direct instruction on strategies when using trade books. In this less threatening situation, the teacher can help the pupil use context as a meaning-based strategy and to explore different means of attacking new words (Taylor and Nosbush 1983). One-to-one sessions are also opportunities for individual discussion and feedback on a pupil's response to literature.

The tape recorder is a handy device to use in these oral reading conferences. Tape recordings give pupils direct feedback on their oral reading performance. Individual tapes for each pupil supply a cumulative record of pupil growth throughout a school year, and teachers can discuss these recorded records of pupil progress with parents during conferences as part of portfolio assessment (see pp. 411–414). Tapes also allow the teacher to review a pupil's performance several times.

Conferences offer opportunities for personal conversations about books. The conference can be the time for the teacher to introduce a book that he or she suspects would be ideal for a particular pupil, to discuss the stories that pupils have been reading, to ask critical-level questions, and to otherwise interact with pupils using literature as the basis of the interaction.

Individual conferences are part of the personalized activity that makes teaching a very special profession. Conferences fill a range of functions, not the least of which is the development of oral reading skills.

Paired Practice   As its name suggests, paired reading takes place when two pupils take turns reading aloud together. Both pupils are given material consistent with their reading levels and seated side by side so that each can follow what the other is reading. One pupil reads while the other listens, following along in the text. After ten minutes or so, the roles change. As pupils finish reading, they retell each other what they have just read. Retelling is a means of monitoring comprehension without using specific questions based on text.

Paired reading is another dimension of cooperative learning. More fluent readers become models, and less fluent readers practice oral reading in an atmosphere more relaxed than the typical reading group. Teachers can monitor oral reading as pupils read in pairs.

Echo Reading   The practice of echo reading is related to paired reading. In echo reading, however, the teacher, aide, or other competent reader, rather than a peer, models oral reading. The teacher sits slightly behind the pupil and both read in unison, with the student attempting to read along as quickly and as accurately as possible. At the outset, the teacher reads slightly louder and faster than the pupil, although the pupil eventually takes the lead. The purpose of this gradual takeover is to help the pupil achieve a fluent reading pattern.

Audience Reading   Communicating messages via reading to a large group of people for a specific purpose is the essence of oral reading. Reading to an audience for the purpose of information or entertainment can give pupils practice in oral reading for authentic purposes in the classroom.

A very practical application of audience reading occurs when older pupils read stories to groups of younger children. Teachers can arrange, for example, for third graders to read to groups of kindergarten children. The teacher helps the older pupils select appropriate books and prepare the story. Even the slowest reader in a class can participate by reading a relatively ''easy'' book to a lower grade class. Upper grade pupils can also make tape recordings of favorite books for use in primary classrooms. This type of pupil–pupil reading provides models for younger children, and it gives older pupils opportunities to practice effective oral reading skills for a very real purpose.

There are plenty of planned and spontaneous opportunities to practice audience reading in the classroom. Teachers can appoint a pupil each week to read the announcements that frequently arrive at the classroom door. An upper grade class can be responsible for reading the morning announcements over the school's public address system. (In some schools, where literature is especially valued, a very brief book report can be made part of these morning announcements.) Teachers can appoint a pupil each day to read something at the opening of class—a poem, a quote of the day, or the daily weather forecast, for example. Pupils practice audience reading when they read their own written work to the class or when they read short excerpts from books on which they are reporting. In short, teachers can be on the lookout for the multiple opportunities that arise to give pupils a chance to practice their oral reading in front of classmates.

Content areas of the curriculum involve occasions for audience reading of non-fiction material as well. With prior practice, pupils read aloud selections from informational trade books as classmates listen for the ideas and information contained in

Radio Reading

SEARFOSS (1975) recommends radio reading as an alternative to conventional round-robin reading in the classroom. The primary instructional goal of this strategy is comprehension rather than word-perfect reading. The four steps in the process are

1. *Getting started.* This involves selecting material to be read aloud (short informational pieces from newspapers or magazines or brief narrative passages are appropriate) and explaining ground rules to pupils.

2. *Communicating the message.* The reader reads; the audience listens. Since the reader's job is to convey information, the reader can change particular words, insert new words, and omit or substitute words when warranted.

3. *Checking for understanding.* The audience briefly discusses content as a check on comprehension. If the meaning is clear, the reader is free to continue, or the role of the radio reader rotates to another member of the group.

4. *Clarifying unclear messages.* If audience discussion indicates that meaning has not been conveyed accurately, the reader returns to the text and reads those parts needed for audience understanding.

Prompting or correcting have no place in radio reading. When readers make errors in reading aloud, listeners need to listen skillfully enough to adjust to the meaning.

---

the passages. This type of oral reading practice is another means of extending literacy into all areas of the curriculum.

Choral Reading   Related to the oral language activity of choral speaking, choral reading involves the group rendition of a text—a poem or story passage, for example. In choral reading, everybody reads the same material aloud together. This type of group oral reading is good for shy or retiring pupils because the experience and the support of reading aloud as part of a group bolsters their reading confidence. The practice is an effective means of helping pupils develop interpretation and meaning, while sharing books such as Bill Martin, Jr., and John Archambault's popular *Chicka, Chicka, Boom, Boom* or Glen Rounds's version of the old favorite *I Know an Old Lady Who Swallowed a Fly.*

Choral reading can be either rehearsed or spontaneous. When rehearsed, pupils receive the material ahead of time, discuss its meaning, and decide how it can be read to reflect its interpretation. Different arrangements can be planned: *antiphonal,* with two groups of readers balanced against each other reading alternative segments; *refrain,* involving a solo voice for some lines and groups responding in refrain; *cumulative,* adding or reducing the number of readers for successive parts of the text; *unison,* reading an entire selection together. These rather formal, choral reading presentations require the careful selection of material and some preparation time.

Spontaneous choral reading requires less preparation. Occasionally the teacher might say, "Let's read together the poem we've all been talking about," or "I want you all to read that final paragraph aloud together, because it sums up nicely the main points that the author is trying to make." Books such as Nadine Bernard Wescott's

Dramatizing parts of a favorite story is an effective way of bringing literature alive in the classroom.

adaptation of the delightful old song *The Lady with the Alligator Purse* or Paul Fleischman's *A Joyful Noise: Poems for Two Voices* make for enjoyable choral reading experiences.

Reading Plays and Scripts   No material is better suited for oral reading in the classroom than plays. In contrast to narrative and expository text, plays are specifically written to be performed or read aloud, and therefore the genre provides an ideal vehicle for the development and practice of oral reading skills. In a literature-based program, this activity introduces another literary genre—drama—into the reading program. Besides, reading plays directly addresses the affective dimensions of reading instruction—pupils *love* it.

   Reader's theatre is a technique that can be used effectively in reading plays and scripts. Productions can be relatively simple (as when pupils read their parts seated on chairs or stools in a ''stage'' area) or they can be fairly elaborate (as when upper grade groups stage a program in which they read Mother Goose rhymes or fairy tales for kindergartners, complete with lollipops and balloons). Presenting literature as a simple reader's theatre production is a motivational device for pupils and an opportunity to practice oral reading in an authentic setting.

   Pupils can often adapt popular children's trade books to be read aloud in a dramatic form. For example, the writing style of *The Pinballs,* Betsy Byars's moving account of three foster children, lends itself to a three-part, oral reading performance. The style in which certain books are written—for example, Bill Martin, Jr., and John Archambault's *Knots on a Counting Rope,* a story told in an exchange of dialogue between a Navaho grandfather and his blind grandson; Crosby Bonsall's *Mine's the Best* a simply written back-and-forth exchange between two boys; and Angela Johnson's *Tell Me a Story, Mama,* a mother and child exchange that can be read in two

9.6 Putting Ideas to Work

Play Week

A "play week" is a five-day period devoted to drama and oral reading. In preparation, the teacher selects plays that are appropriate for classroom use. On Monday, different groups receive copies of the plays; plays are matched to different groups according to reading level and the number of characters. Pupils select (or are assigned) roles and begin reviewing their respective parts. Vocabulary is taught as needed and meaning is discussed. On Tuesday, pupils continue to practice reading their play together. The last three days of the week are performance days, as pupils stage their plays *readers' theatre* style—pupils read, not memorize and recite, their lines to an audience. Simple props can be used: "May we borrow your briefcase?"

(Yes). "Can I bring in my brother's hunting knife?" (No!).

Play weeks take a little extra planning on the teacher's part. Plays need to be located and reviewed. The number of characters in the play need to be matched with the number of pupils in the group, although adjustments are not hard to make. The reading level of the play needs to be matched to that of the pupils, and the whole process needs to be monitored closely. But when the teacher sees the enjoyment and the enthusiasm that play weeks generate, and when the pupils begin asking for another play week on the Monday morning after the last one, the rewards are well worth the effort.

---

parts—adapts well to paired oral reading. As they enjoy other books, pupils can be alert to possibilities for sharing books with classmates through paired dramatic reading.

There is no shortage of opportunities for pupils to share literature through oral reading. The range of activities that teachers can use should reflect the variety of purposes that they have in bringing literature into the reading program and in helping pupils improve oral reading competency.

Summary and Conclusions

Much emphasis is placed on oral reading in the elementary classroom. Teachers spend a significant amount of their time listening to pupils read aloud. Although oral reading has a number of functions, "the main emphasis is on cognitive learning; hearing reading is not mainly for social interaction or for maintaining the individual contact with a child as a means of 'individualized teaching.' Its purpose should be to show children how to use all the cueing systems available to them through positive reinforcement" (Arnold 1982; p. 81).

Oral reading remains an essential part of literature-based reading instruction throughout the grades. In addition to its diagnostic and instructional value, it is a primary vehicle for sharing literature in the community of readers.

Much teaching takes place as part of the teacher–pupil interaction that typically characterizes shared oral reading experiences. In the context of oral reading, teachers can demonstrate and discuss how pupils can use appropriate strategies in processing text. Reading aloud provides a basis for analyzing and discussing various dimensions of meaning. The purposes that teachers establish and the questions that they ask help pupils develop a reflective approach characteristic of thoughtful, critical readers.

Beyond direct instruction, stories shared through oral reading provide a vehicle for enjoyment and a springboard to additional reading.

Reading aloud is a valuable instructional activity. It extends beyond the ritual of public performative practice and into a variety of opportunities for functional educational experiences. Viewed in this way, teachers and pupils have a purpose for reading out loud.

Discussion Questions and Activities

1. Reading to children in the home during the emergent literacy stage is extremely important. Research some of the material on the topic of reading aloud to young children, and prepare a document that could be shared with parents on the importance of reading aloud with their children.
2. Recall your own school experiences. What role did oral reading play? How did you react to reading aloud in the classroom? What do you see as the advantages and disadvantages of oral reading?
3. Examine a lesson in the teachers edition of a basal reading series. What suggestions are provided for oral reading of the story? How might you adapt or expand the lesson to include oral reading as part of the instructional focus?
4. Select a trade book and develop a lesson plan or series of ideas on how you could use this book to help pupils develop oral reading fluency, using some of the techniques suggested in the chapter (echo reading, paired practice, one liners, etc.).
5. Make a videotape of your reading of a ten-minute segment of a children's book. Have a classmate view the tape and offer suggestions on how you might improve your delivery to an audience.

School-Based Assignments

1. Based on interviews with teachers from different grade levels, make a list of ten books that are popular read-aloud titles. Familiarize yourself with these books.
2. Based on classroom observation, how much time do pupils spend reading aloud during a school day? What procedures or strategies does the teacher typically use? Write one or two alternative strategies that you could use if you were in charge of the classroom.
3. Informally interview a group of pupils about their perceptions of oral reading. Make a list of their reactions, along with some of the instructional implications that their perceptions suggest.
4. Using the techniques suggested in 9.2 (p. 278), read a story aloud to a group of pupils. Videotape your performance or have a colleague observe you and provide feedback on your reading.
5. Observe a pupil reading aloud in a one-to-one setting and, if possible, make an audio or videotape recording of his or her performance or tape record your own reading to a group of pupils. What strategies would you suggest to help this pupil improve the oral reading you hear on the tape?

Children's Trade Books Cited in This Chapter

Bond, Michael. *Paddington Bear*. New York: Random House, 1973.

Bonsall, Crosby. *Mine's the Best*. New York: Harper and Row, 1973.

Brittain, Bill. *The Wish Giver*. New York: Harper and Row, 1983.

Burnford, Sheila. *The Incredible Journey*. Boston: Little and Brown, 1961.

Butterworth, Oliver. *The Enormous Egg*. Boston: Little and Brown, 1956.

Byars, Betsy. *The Pinballs*. New York: Harper and Row, 1977.

Collier, James, and Collier, Christopher. *My Brother Sam Is Dead*. New York: Macmillan, 1974.

Dahl, Roald. *Charlie and the Chocolate Factory*. New York: Penguin, 1983.

————. *The BFG*. New York: Penguin, 1989.

Dalgliesh, Alice. *The Courage of Sarah Noble*. New York: Macmillan, 1954.

de Angeli, Marguerite. *The Door in the Wall*. New York: Doubleday, 1949.

Fleischman, Paul. *A Joyful Noise: Poems for Two Voices*. New York: Harper and Row, 1988.

Fleischman, Sid. *The Whipping Boy*. New York: Greenwillow, 1986.

Gardiner, John. *Stone Fox*. New York: Harper and Row, 1980.

Hamilton, Virginia. *In the Beginning: Creation Stories from Around the World*. New York: Harcourt Brace, 1988.

Howe, Deborah, and Howe, James. *Bunnicula*. New York: Atheneum, 1979.

Johnson, Angela. *Tell Me a Story, Mama*. New York: Franklin Watts, 1989.

King-Smith, Dick. *Ace, the Very Important Pig*. New York: Crown, 1990.

Kjelgaard, Jim. *Big Red*. New York: Holiday House, 1956.

Konigsburg, E. L. *From the Mixed-up Files of Mrs. Basil E. Frankweiler*. New York: Atheneum, 1967.

L'Engle, Madeleine. *A Wrinkle in Time*. New York: Farrar, Straus & Giroux, 1962.

Lewis, C. S. *The Lion, The Witch, and the Wardrobe*. New York: Macmillan, 1950.

Lindgren, Astrid. *Pippi Longstocking*. New York: Viking Press, 1950.

McCloskey, Robert. *Make Way for Ducklings*. New York: Viking, 1941.

MacDonald, Betty. *Mrs. Piggle Wiggle*. New York: Harper and Row, 1957.

MacDonald, Caroline. *The Lake at the End of the World*. New York: Dial, 1989.

MacLachlan, Patricia. *Sarah, Plain and Tall*. New York: Harper and Row, 1985.

Manes, Stephen. *Be A Perfect Person in Just Three Days*. New York: Bantam, 1982.

Martin, Bill, Jr., and Archambault, John. *Chicka, Chicka, Boom, Boom*. New York: Simon and Schuster, 1989.

————. *Knots on a Counting Rope*. New York: Henry Holt, 1987.

Milne, A. A. *Winnie the Pooh*. New York: Dutton, 1926.

Naylor, Phyllis R. *Shiloh*. New York: Macmillan, 1991.

O'Brien, Robert. *Mrs. Frisby and the Rats of NIMH*. New York: Macmillan, 1971.

Paterson, Katherine. *The Great Gilly Hopkins*. New York: Harper and Row, 1978.

Peck, Robert Newton. *Soup*. New York: Knopf, 1974.

————. *Soup and Me*. New York: Knopf, 1975.

————. *Soup for President*. New York: Knopf, 1978.

Peterson, John. *The Littles*. New York: Scholastic, 1986.

Rawls, Wilson. *Where the Red Fern Grows*. New York: Doubleday, 1978.

Rockwell, Thomas. *How to Eat Fried Worms*. New York: Franklin Watts, 1973.

Rounds, Glen. *I Know an Old Woman Who Swallowed a Fly*. New York: Holiday House, 1991.

Sandburg, Carl. *Abe Lincoln Grows Up*. New York: Harcourt Brace, 1954.

Smith, Doris. *A Taste of Blackberries*. New York: Crowell, 1973.

Sobol, Donald J. *The Wright Brothers at Kitty Hawk*. New York: Scholastic, 1961.

Speare, Elizabeth George. *The Sign of the Beaver*. Boston: Houghton Mifflin, 1983.

Sperry, Armstrong. *Call It Courage*. New York: Macmillan, 1968.

Spinelli, Jerry. *Maniac Magee*. Boston: Little Brown, 1990.

Stevenson, Robert Louis. *Treasure Island*. New York: Scholastic, 1972. (One of several editions available)

Taylor, Theodore. *The Cay*. New York: Doubleday, 1969.

Tolkien, J. R. R. *The Hobbit.* Boston: Houghton Mifflin, 1938.

Twain, Mark. *Tom Sawyer.* New York: Simon and Schuster, 1982. (One of several editions available)

Waber, Bernard. *Ira Sleeps Over.* Boston: Houghton Mifflin, 1973.

Wescott, Nadine Bernard. *The Lady with the Alligator Purse.* Boston: Little Brown, 1988.

White, E. B. *Charlotte's Web.* New York: Harper and Row, 1952.

References

Allington, R. L. (1983). Fluency: The Neglected Reading Goal. *The Reading Teacher* 36:556–61.

Arnold, H. (1982). *Listening to Children Read.* London: United Kingdom Reading Association.

Austin, M., and C. Morrison (1963). *The First R.* New York: Macmillan.

Dowhower, S. L. (1989). Repeated Reading: Research into Practice. *The Reading Teacher* 42:502–7.

Elley, W. (1989). Vocabulary Acquisition from Listening to Stories. *Reading Research Quarterly* 24:174–87.

Holdaway, D. (1972). *Independence in Reading.* Auckland, New Zealand: Ashton-Scholastic.

Huck, C. S., S. Hepler, and J. Hickman. (1987). *Children's Literature in the Elementary School* (4th ed.). New York: Holt, Rinehart and Winston.

Mathews, M. M. (1966). *Teaching to Read: Historically Considered.* Chicago: University of Chicago Press.

Lipson, E. R. (1991). *Parent's Guide to the Best Books for Children.* New York: Random House.

Peterson, R., and Eeds, M. (1990). *Grand Conversations: Literature Groups in Action.* New York: Scholastic.

Samuels, S. J. (1979). The Method of Repeated Reading. *The Reading Teacher* 32:403–8.

Savage, J. F. (1978). What Do You Remember about Learning to Read? *New England Reading Association Journal* 13:6–10.

Searfoss, L. W. (1975). Radio Reading. *The Reading Teacher* 29:295–96.

Sloan, P., and Latham, R. (1981). *Teaching Reading Is . . .* Melbourne: Thomas Nelson.

Smith, D. D. (1979). The Improvement of Children's Oral Reading through the Use of Teacher Modeling. *Journal of Learning Disabilities* 12:39–42.

Smith, N. B. (1965). *American Reading Instruction.* Newark, DE: International Reading Association.

Taylor, B. M., and Nosbush, L. (1983). Oral Reading for Meaning: A Technique for Improving Word Identification Skills. *The Reading Teacher* 37:234–237.

Tierney, R. J., J. E. Readence, and Dishner, E. K. (1990). *Reading Strategies and Practices: A Compendium.* Boston: Allyn and Bacon.

Trelease, J. (1989). *The New Read-Aloud Handbook* (2nd ed.). New York: Penguin.

Chapter 10

The Reading–Writing Connection

Chapter 10 Outline

I. Introduction

II. The Reading–Writing Relationship
   A. The Meaning Connection
   B. The Language Connection
   C. The Instructional Connection

III. Responding to Literature
   A. Responding Orally
   B. Responding Artistically
   C. Responding in Writing
      1. Personal Perspectives
      2. Buddy Journals
      3. Writing in the Literature-Rich
         Classroom

IV. Process Writing
   A. Prewriting
   B. Writing
   C. Editing and Revising
   D. Publishing

V. Written Products Based on Literature
   A. Stories
   B. Reports
   C. Letters
   D. Poems
   E. Scripts and Dialogues
   F. Journals
   G. Book Reports

VI. Summary and Conclusions

Discussion Questions and Activities
School-Based Assignments
Children's Trade Books Cited in This Chapter
References

Features

10.1   Oral Language Responses to Literature
10.2   Pupils Respond to Books
10.3   A Practical Payoff
10.4   "I Don't Have Nothin' to Write About"
10.5   Using Word Processing
10.6   Revising, Editing, and Proofreading Checklist
10.7   The Author's Chair
10.8   Decisions in the Writing Process
10.9   Using Big Books as Writing Models
10.10 Literature-Based Writing
10.11 A Writing Web
10.12 Children's Trade Books about Writing

Key Concepts in This Chapter

Reading and writing are closely related. Both are active, meaning-making processes that require common areas of knowledge. Literature is a glue that holds the reading–writing connection.

Literature generates a response in readers. When this response takes the form of writing, opportunities arise for helping pupils develop competence in the many aspects of written language.

Most teachers follow a process writing model of instruction. Process writing involves a series of stages or steps that writers follow: making a series of prewriting decisions, writing a first draft, and engaging in a series of postwriting activities that lead to publication.

Literature can be used as the focus for classroom writing instruction—the "glue" that forges the reading–writing connection.

NE OF the direct effects of the whole-language movement in schools all over the English-speaking world has been the emphasis on the close connection between reading and writing. The closer integration of reading and writing has been called "the single most important change in language instruction" today (Pearson, 1985).

In conventional language arts programs, writing instruction followed reading instruction. Not only were reading and writing taught separately in traditional programs, but even the various components of writing were separated. Spelling, handwriting, grammar, punctuation, capitalization—each "owned" a separate part of the school program. There were separate curriculum guides, separate textbook series, and occasionally different teachers for each of these areas. The net effect of this practice was providing skill-and-drill exercises on grammar, punctuation, spelling, and other mechanical aspects of writing, with little time devoted to producing continuous, connected, and meaningful text.

Reading and writing were largely compartmentalized as two separate entities, with little instructional relationship between the two. The words that were learned in spelling were different from the vocabulary in the basal reader. The phonics that was taught as part of reading was rarely viewed as an aid in spelling. Paragraph-writing techniques were taught with little attention to how this awareness could lead to better comprehension in reading. In short, programs were operated in considerable isolation.

In classrooms today, reading and writing are more closely linked. "A growing body of research has demonstrated that reading and writing are closely related and that both processes can be learned better in connection with each other rather than in isolation" (Noyce and Christie, 1989; p. 3). This close relationship has a lot to do with how both reading and writing are taught in the classroom.

What does the reading–writing connection have to do with literature-based reading instruction? Indeed, the link between reading and writing can be forged whether one uses basal readers, trade books, or the print on cereal boxes as vehicles for teaching pupils how to read. Literature, however, more powerfully forges the reading–writing connection by providing a generous source of ideas and a focus for writing. Moreover, fostering the processes of reading real books by real people, and having pupils produce purposeful written products that others take seriously, add authenticity to teaching reading and writing simultaneously.

The Reading–Writing Relationship

Reading and writing are related in a number of ways. Building on these relationships is the key to literacy development in the classroom.

Reading and writing deal with written language. Reading involves the intake of ideas through print; writing, the output of ideas through print. Literacy is defined as the ability to read *and* write. In addition to being related aspects of language, reading and writing are connected through meaning and through instructional activities in the classroom.

The Meaning Connection

Meaning is central to both reading and writing. Meaning-making is at the core of the reading–writing connection. Writers construct meaning as they select words and craft language structures that will convey on paper (or on the side of a wall or in some other medium) this meaning to others. Readers construct meaning as they use their knowledge of language and their schemata in shaping their own versions of the author's intended message in their own minds. "At the heart of understanding reading and writing connections one must begin to view reading and writing as essentially similar processes of meaning construction" (Tierney and Pearson, 1983; p. 568). The reader's goal is similar to the writer's goal; that is, to represent meaning in a comprehensible, coherent framework.

Awareness of the meaning element in reading and in writing develops simultaneously in young children. Instead of the "first-reading-then-writing" view that prevailed in early childhood education for such a long time, emergent literacy involves the development of both aspects of literacy together (see chapter 4).

Both reading and writing are cognitive activities, and the thinking processes involved in both are closely connected. Hittleman (1988; p. 28) focuses on the thinking processes connecting the two: "The act of composing text allows students to learn how texts work. They learn how to organize information, how to present ideas clearly and without ambiguity, how to establish purposes for communicating, and how to address their writing to particular audiences. The current thinking and research on the integration of reading and writing programs support this conclusion." Reading and writing both involve critical thinking. Writing in combination with reading has proven to be a very effective means of developing pupils' critical thinking abilities, better than either activity alone (Tierney et al., 1989).

Reading and writing are both active, thinking operations. Competent readers and writers approach texts in similar ways. Both set goals and mobilize their prior knowledge. Both make certain assumptions about their respective audiences. Both tentatively construct meaning, monitor their efforts, and revise according to how well they are meeting their goals.

In answer to the question "How are reading and writing related?" Rubin and Hansen (1984) identify five areas of knowledge that both have in common:

1. *information knowledge,* including knowledge and grammatical background. This is what both readers and writers use to construct text. Besides, "information that is gained in reading is one possible source of content for writing" (Rubin and Hanson, 1984; p. 6).

2. *structural knowledge,* which includes the organizational patterns that writers use when they write and that readers recognize when they read. "Writers produce text with structures; readers use these structures when they construct meaning" (Rubin and Hanson, 1984; p. 7).

3. *transactional knowledge,* which is an awareness of writing as a medium of communication between an author and a reader.

4. *aesthetic knowledge,* which is knowledge of the aesthetic devices such as style or topics that generate appeal.

5. *process knowledge,* which is an awareness of what elements are common to both reading and writing.

Meaning, then, is the crucial element in the reading–writing connection. Readers construct meaning from text while they interact with print. Writers construct meaning as they build language structures that will convey their thoughts and ideas in written form.

The Language Connection

In addition to the link through meaning, reading and writing are connected through language. Within the context of writing about literature, pupils develop competencies in both areas together. Evidence suggests that pupils who write about what they read comprehend better (Kelly, 1990). At the same time, when pupils write about books, they learn to process successive units of language. They develop skill in the following areas:

encoding/decoding words. Writing requires that pupils attend to the details of words. The same sound–symbol relationships that are required in decoding unfamiliar words in reading are the ones that pupils need to know to spell the words they write. Pupils need to know that the letter *b* represents the phoneme /b/ in sounding out the unfamiliar word *baboon,* just as in writing a story about *balloons.*

writing sentences. Sentence construction is essential to both reading and writing. It is axiomatic that effective writing is characterized by well-constructed sentences. At the same time, sentence comprehension is essential to reading comprehension. In fact, the ability to match sentences with similar meanings has been used as a measure of pupils' reading comprehension ability (Simons, 1971; Brown, Hammill, and Wiederholt, 1986).

developing paragraphs. In paragraphs, reading and writing are related through discourse structure and text organization. Writers produce text with structure; readers who understand those structures better comprehend what they read. Pupils apply the knowledge of these structural patterns as they read *and* as they write.

writing longer selections. Beyond paragraphs, pupils develop awareness of story structure as they deal with literature. They become aware of the ''concept of story''; that is, they learn that a well-constructed story has a beginning, a middle, and an end, and that stories revolve around a conflict or a problem. With developing sophistication, they become aware of the role of character and setting. They see the place of description and the role of dialogue in telling stories. Being aware of these elements in the stories that they read makes pupils sensitive to these elements in the stories that they write.

Reading and writing are not only two sides of the same coin of written language, they are aspects of learning that can develop simultaneously with the use of literature in classroom instruction.

The Instructional Connection

Reading and writing are related instructionally as well, in that teaching one necessarily involves teaching the other. Shanahan (1988) suggests seven instructional principles based on research about the connection between reading and writing:

1. *Reading and writing both need to be taught.* Although closely related, they are independent enough to merit direct, daily separate attention in the classroom.

2. *Both should be introduced from the earliest years.* Since reading ability is not a prerequisite of writing development, writing can be a focus of instruction from the early stages of a child's school (or preschool) life.

3. *Relationships between reading and writing need to be emphasized in different ways at different stages of a pupil's development.* At the very early stages, the decoding–encoding connections may need to be stressed; later on, cognitive connections—linking the meaning-making processes in both—may need to be emphasized.

4. *Reading–writing connections need to be made explicit.* Transfer between reading and writing ability is not automatic; teachers need to focus specifically on the relationship to heighten pupils' awareness.

5. *Content and process relationships should be emphasized.* Knowing *what* to do and *how* to do it are both important in approaching reading and writing. For example, in both reading and writing, pupils need to be aware of whether meaning is clear, and if not, how to take action.

6. *Communicative aspects of reading and writing should be stressed.* Reading and writing involve a communicative connection between a reader and an author. This connection should be stressed through such activities as author awareness.

7. *Reading and writing should be taught in meaningful contexts.* Both should be practiced for a variety of purposes in the classroom.

These, then, are the major connections between reading and writing: both are meaning-making processes that involve language; both involve common understandings essential to processing print; and both can be taught congruently in the classroom. "Reading and writing need to be viewed as supportive and interactive processes whereby what is learned from reading can be used when writing, and what is learned by writing can foster an appreciation for authorship and reading" (Kolczynski, 1989; p. 76).

Writing cements this reader–writer relationship. "Research advancing this perspective has suggested that reading, like writing, is composition, that both writing and reading involve 'transactions' between a reader and a text, that an awareness of the author-reader relationship is central to both reading and writing, and that the writing process includes reading. This view recognizes the central fact of reading and writing—they are instances of communication between people" (Rubin and Hansen, 1984; p. 4).

Young children often show their delight by joining in stories or by physically reacting to the stories they hear.

Responding to Literature

Literature typically generates a response. Often, that response is emotional. Young children show delight by clapping their hands to the rhythm of language and with the repeated request of "Read it Again!" Children's literature can also evoke an emotional response in adults. Many mature adults get misty-eyed when they read Robert Munsch's simple *Love You Forever* or Tomie de Paola's *Now One Foot, Now The Other,* two children's stories about the relationship between young people and old people. Few are immune to shedding a tear at the death of Leslie in Katherine Paterson's *Bridge to Terabithia* or at the fate of the animals at the end of Wilson Rawls's *Where the Red Fern Grows.* That authors can make us care so much about what we read is evidence of the power and value of literature as part of classroom reading programs.

Reader response is an essential component of literature-based reading. Reader response theory is based on the notion of a transaction between a reader and a text, a relationship described earlier in chapters 6 and 7. Rosenblatt (1982) distinguishes between *efferent* responses and *aesthetic* responses. The former focuses on knowledge or information taken away from a text; the latter focuses more on an emotional reaction. "Any reading event falls somewhere on the continuum between the aesthetic and the efferent poles" (Rosenblatt, 1982; p. 269). There can be elements of both aesthetic and efferent response to any encounter with print. Although a reader's response may be primarily aesthetic at the death of Wilbur in E. B. White's *Charlotte's Web,* readers also come away with knowledge about spiders and pigs and the type of man Farmer Zukerman was. Similarly, readers carry away information about how fossils were created in Byrd Baylor and Peter Parnall's *If You Are a Hunter of Fossils,* but the poetic nature of the language creates an aesthetic response as well.

Literary response is not a simple, singular process. It depends on a constellation of factors including readers' "cognitive abilities, their stance toward reading, personality orientations, social–cognitive competencies, knowledge of literature, and language conventions" (Beach and Hynds, 1991; p. 480). All these factors that influence how readers infuse meaning into text as part of the comprehension/interpretation process. Classroom responses to literature are an integral part of literacy development. These include oral language responses, artistic responses, and written language responses.

Responding Orally

Pupils' response to literature can take the form of a variety of oral language activities in the classroom. Competency in oral language is the foundation for literacy. Classroom oral language activities provide vehicles for the development of thinking, vocabulary, audience awareness, listening, and fluent expression that are essential to effective communication.

Talking about books is a natural response among children. Focusing that talk on books in the classroom can stimulate pupils' interest in literature, while providing opportunities for the development of oral language and related skills.

Responding Artistically

Another common response mode to literature in the elementary grades is art. Pupils produce a variety of artistic products from simple illustrations to detailed dioramas in response to books that they have read and enjoyed. Teachers engage pupils in using a variety of media—from paints and crayons to fabric and metal—to produce artistic products in response to literature. As they dictate or write summary captions for their artwork, pupils move toward the common response mode of writing.

Some teachers have also helped pupils respond musically. The class selects a musical selection to accompany a scene or chapter.

Responding in Writing

Written response to literature is the foundation of the reading–writing connection in a literature-based program. Pupils can respond to literature through various forms of writing, from personal-response journals that reflect spontaneous feelings and attitudes (Karolides, 1992), to more detached forms of responses such as reports or letters. Each written response offers opportunities to develop skills in reading and writing at the same time.

Personal Perspectives   Response journals are generated when pupils write about books from a personal perspective. Kelly (1990) describes a program in which personal

10.1 Putting Ideas to Work

Oral Language Responses to Literature

ORAL RESPONSES to literature can take many forms in the classroom. For example:

Storytelling. Pupils can take turns retelling different parts of a serial folktale such as *Why Mosquitoes Buzz in People's Ears,* an African tale retold by Verna Aardema, or they might retell a familiar fairy tale from another point of view, as John Scieszka did in *The True Story of the Three Little Pigs,* the hilarious account told through the eyes of the wolf, who is now in jail.

Creative dramatics. Pupils can act out old favorites like *The Three Billygoats Gruff,* or they can improvise stories like Nonnie Hogrogian's *One Fine Day,* an ideal story for dramatization about a fox who goes on a prolonged search to have his amputated tail sewn back on.

Discussion. Groups can engage in critical thinking and problem solving by discussing the fairness of Thelma's actions in Russell Hoban's *A Bargain for Frances* or the racial prejudice that the Logan family encountered in Mildred Taylor's *Roll of Thunder, Hear My Cry.*

Dialogue. Referring to teachers as "curators of literature," Eeds and Peterson (1991) suggest ways of focusing pupils' attention on literary elements (structure, character, time and place, point of view, mood, and symbolism) through dialogue, as pupils share their reactions in literature study groups. They describe the literary insights that pupils develop in talking about such books as John Gardiner's *Stone Fox,* Frances Hodgson Burnett's *The Secret Garden,* and Allan Eckert's *Incident at Hawk's Hill.*

Oral reports. Pupils can report orally on informational trade books that they have found especially interesting, such as Robert Quackenbush's *What an Awful Mess!,* the biographical account of Charles Goodyear's inventing rubber, or R. R. Knudson's biography *Babe Didrickson, Athlete of the Century.*

Choral speaking. Pupils can select poems that lend themselves especially well to large group recitation—poems with dialogue and contrasts in mood, question-and-answer poetry ("Who has seen the wind?"), ballads, poems with humor and repeated language ("I know an old woman who swallowed a fly"), and the like.

Opportunities for classroom oral language experiences with books are virtually limitless with songs, puppets, finger plays, sharing, news time, readers' theatre adaptations of favorite stories, and other activities.

---

response was used very effectively with third graders to add "a substantive element to the literature program." Building on the work of Bleich (1987) and Petrosky (1982), the teacher provided three prompts, "(a) What did you notice in the story? (b) How did the story make you feel? and (c) What does the story remind you of in your own life?" (p. 466) to provide a framework for focusing discussion and writing. After they practiced group responses orally, the third graders moved to responding through writing. As they became practiced, their written responses increased in length and fluency, and responses showed greater depth of understanding and higher levels of comprehension.

Tomkins (1990) suggests a similar plan for generating pupil response to literature. Each day the teacher reads a chapter of a popular book to the class. Pupils spend ten minutes writing an entry in a log or journal about the chapter. Their entries are personal responses; that is, instead of summarizing the chapter, pupils write about their favorite characters, ways in which the story relates to their own lives, how the story

10.2 Putting Ideas to Work

Pupils Respond to Books

HERE ARE some samples of pupils' responses to books. These samples should be considered examples of how some pupils reacted to what they read; they are not intended to be used as standards against which other pupils' responses should be judged.

Sample #1

After reading stories about teddy bears—*Corduroy, Ira Sleeps Over, Hi Bears, Bye Bears*, and others—Janie wrote the following in her journal:

> The bear stories made me think of Fuzz. Fuzz is my stuffed bear. He's precshous to me because my dad gave him tome before he moved to Huston. He is two feet tall and has fluffy gray hair. When I am full of sad, Fuzz understands. When no one is home, I think of my dad and hug Fuzz.

makes them feel, or how they might change the events in the story. In other words, their writing involves them in the story.

Buddy Journals   Related to this type of personal written response are buddy journals (Bromley, 1989). After citing three important reasons for making connections between reading and writing—"First, we know that reading and writing develop simultaneously. Second, reading and writing reinforce each other. Third, through reading and writing, language is used for communication" (p. 122)—Bromley describes buddy journals as a way to make the reading–writing connection. As the name suggests, a buddy journal is a written diary or log that pairs of pupils share with each other. By exchanging journals, pupils carry on a "written conversation" with real and meaningful communication. The writing is functional, the activity is interactive, and the feedback is immediate. When books are used as the basis of the exchange of ideas, literature cements the reading–writing connection.

Writing in the Literature-Rich Classroom   To what extent does writing flourish in a literature-rich classroom? Phillips (1989) compared the writing of two groups of pupils, one that had been exposed to a rich diet of literature and one that had progressed through a normal basal reading program. She analyzed 1,200 samples of the children's writing and found that the literature group "was much more sophisticated in this

Sample #2
The following journal entry was written in response to *The Secret Garden:*

Dear Miss Carmola,
In The Secret Garden colin meets Dickon
and his animals, two squirrels, (Nut and Shell)
a hawk, (Soot), a-little fox cub, (Captain) and a
baby lamb. At 2:00 o'clock Colin will go outside
and Dickon will push his carriage.
Before they go out Colin thinks about the
outside . of the world. He thinks about big
jamborees of music and people dancing and
laughing children playing and telling jokes.
Mary says that's what it feels like. I think
she feels like that because she has been
in the garden so much!
She has grown to like it, like she likes Colin.
I have a woods in my back yard and I've
been in it many times! I'm growing to
like my woods like Mary is growing to like
her garden.
                              Lexi

Used with permission of Alexis Green and Esme Green.

writing as evidenced in the increasing complexity in vocabulary and sentence structure. The length, fluency and literary quality of the literature class's writing flourished'' (p. 1).

Such dramatic results are hardly surprising. Children tend to mimic language they see and hear. If basals are the only language models to which they are exposed, pupils' writing will likely be characterized by controlled use of words, simple sentence structure, and repeated ideas. With frequent exposure to high-quality writing, and the

Sample #3
Responding in the form of a letter to the teacher gives the teacher a chance to respond.

Dear Miss Carmola,

Where The Sidewalk End is

wonderful. I love poetry, do you?

My favorite poems are "Warning" and

"Afraid of the dark" what are

yours?

Kiara

Feb. 24

Dear Kiara,
        Yes, I do like poetry.
I like Shel Silverstein's poems
because most of them are
silly. I think that silly poems
are fun to read when you
need a good laugh.
                    Miss Carmola

A Practical Payoff

There was a practical payoff for Jay Stacey in writing about children's books. In the process of applying to a highly competitive college, Jay responded to the standard application essay question, "What book has most deeply influenced your life and how has this book affected your thinking?" Passing on the classics of the ages, Jay wrote that the most influential book he had ever read was Dr. Seuss' *Green Eggs and Ham.* He explained that this was the first book that he had ever read completely on his own. He told how this book had helped open the world of literacy to him, that the experience had helped him develop a view of himself as a reader, that reading *Green Eggs and Ham* all by himself had helped him discover the joy and satisfaction of independent learning.

Jay was accepted at the college of his choice.

opportunity to take themselves seriously as authors, pupils develop more meaningful learning through written expression. Words that pupils encounter in their reading appear in their writing over and over again.

One way of promoting the reading–writing connection is to let pupils learn about what famous authors were like as children. Some delightful autobiographical accounts of well-known children's authors (see 2.8 for a sample of these books) describe the early experiences that shaped their lives as authors. Through activities that promote author awareness (pp. 49–52), pupils come to see the connection between everyday experiences and stories produced by people like Roald Dahl, Beverly Cleary, and other authors that they know and love.

In using literature (or any other topic) to develop pupils' writing abilities, schools today almost universally utilize a model or approach called process writing. Process writing involves a series of steps or stages, and literature has its place at every point along the way.

Process Writing

Process writing is a theory, along with a set of instructional practices based on that theory, about teaching pupils how to write. Instead of focusing primarily on written *products*—stories, poems, reports, letters, and other "pieces" of writing that pupils produce—the instructional focus is on the writing *process,* the steps that writers follow as they produce a written product. "The idea of writing as a process arrived on the educational scene in the mid-1960s. Its swift and almost universal acceptance marked it as a 'paradigm shift,' a new way of understanding, which at once rendered traditional 'product-centered composition teaching' as obsolete" (Walshe, 1988; p. 212).

The writing process starts long before the teacher says, "Take out your pencils and papers," and it does not conclude when the pupils add the inevitable "The End" with a flair of finality at the conclusion of what they have written. Process writing involves all the thoughts and activities that occur from the time a decision is made to write until the time when the final written product has been completed. Generally, the process can be divided into four stages: (1) prewriting, (2) drafting, (3) editing/revising, and (4) publishing.

"I Don't Have Nothin' To Write About"

T HE COMMON complaint "I don't have nothin' to write about" can often be overcome by invoking stories based on imaginative accounts so frequently found in children's stories; for example, the outrageous improbability of the actions of such animals as:

the cat who wreaks havoc in Dr. Seuss' widely known and greatly loved *The Cat in The Hat;* the bear who wakes up the little boy in the middle of the night and asks the boy to remove his sore tooth in David McPhail's delightful fantasy *The Bear's Toothache;*

the exotic animals who invade the girl's home in Mercer Mayer's wonderfully written and illustrated *What Do You Do with A Kangaroo?;* the jungle animals who appear in the living room of Judy and Peter's home as the children play the intriguing board game in Chris Van Allsburg's *Jumanji.*

These stories can provide a springboard of ideas for stories by children who have imagined animals in improbable situations.

Prewriting

Prewriting is the first stage of the writing process. This planning and organizational stage consists of a series of decisions. It involves decisions about why to write, what to write about, which aspect of the topic to focus on, who the audience will be, and which approach to take.

In many instances, the decision to write is reached because the teacher says, "Take out your pencils" (or the professor says, "Term projects are due next Tuesday"). Classroom writing experiences should take place to meet the range of authentic purposes for literacy—social, imaginative, informative, persuasive. Literature can be the springboard for many writing experiences. Ideas from literature often provide the motivation to write. Having enjoyed stories from the best of their literary heritage, pupils often feel motivated to engage in story-making themselves. The key here is the spark of motivation that turns "have to" into "want to."

Literature provides models as well as motivation. In the beginning stages of writing, models of form can be important, even essential. In using literature as models, a prewriting discussion might involve the quality of reproduction versus innovation— that is, the extent to which pupils should maintain what they find in the models versus the extent to which they should move out on their own. Pupils who are exposed to fairy tales and fantasy in the very early grades begin to include sophisticated writing features in their own writing (Phillips, 1989). Having been exposed to stories about Paul Bunyan and Mike Fink, pupils in the upper elementary grades are more ready to write their own tall tales based on the exaggeration and humor they find in these models. Models are essential in writing poetry, especially in poems like limericks and haiku, which adhere more strictly to form than other types of poetry.

Finding something to write about is an early step in the prewriting process. Pupils' lives are full of experiences and their heads are full of dreams, but they often need to be convinced that the content of their lives constitutes an appropriate topic for their writing. Prewriting includes opportunities to brainstorm about ideas in stories, with a specific focus on the vocabulary that is a necessary part of this brainstorming. Pupils' familiarity with literature can often help them realize that wonderful stories can be generated from everyday ideas, events, and feelings. Reading a book like Beverly Cleary's *Dear Mr. Henshaw* or Patricia Reilly Giff's *The Beast In Ms. Rooney's Room* can give pupils a sense that their ordinary home or school experiences are indeed worthy subjects for written work.

Trade books also show pupils how to approach a topic, which aspects to include, and how to focus on detail in relating incidents from their lives. The writer's focus on detail is like the photographer's angle when using a camera. The photographer must decide whether to take a picture of the entire castle or a close-up of a gargoyle under the eaves. The author must decide whether to write about a larger experience ("What I Did on Summer Vacation") or on only one aspect of that experience ("The Day I Pitched for the Mets"). As part of the writing process, trade books can be used to help pupils learn this sense of focus. Only a few of us haven't dreamed of taking to the air and flying above our neighborhoods. Pupils can see how Peter Spier treated this fantasy in his *Bored—Nothing To Do.*

Deciding on form is another prewriting decision; often the same topic can be treated as a narrative story, an expository text, a poem, a personal letter, an advertisement, or another form of written response. *Dear Mr. Henshaw,* for example, is a story told in the form of personal letters, and many of Shel Silverstein's poems tell a story as well.

Identifying an audience is an important prewriting decision. "The purpose of writing is not to arrange ink on paper, to provide a mirror for the author's thoughts, but to carry ideas and information from the mind of one person into the mind of another" (Murray, 1968; p. 3). Audience helps in deciding tone, form, and style. In responding to a book, for example, pupils can write a journal entry about how the book made them feel, a recommendation for the book in a letter to a pen pal, a concise and factual "index card" report to be used by classmates in deciding whether or not to read the book, or a story about a character or episode that would be displayed in the school corridor for all to read. Possibilities for choices are enormously varied.

Prewriting also includes an incubation time, a time for pupils' ideas to jell and take shape. In some ways, the entire prewriting stage is a time for mental and verbal gestation. During this stage of the writing process, pupils have the opportunity to share and discuss with the teacher and with peers possible focus, format, and voice that are open to them and to organize their ideas into a meaningful structure.

The components of the prewriting stage of the writing process cannot be reduced to any predetermined order, anything that will suggest a cup of motivation, a pound of critical analysis, a pinch of brainstorming, and ten minutes of conferencing with the teacher. What goes on as part of prewriting will depend on the nature of the writing activity, the grade and ability level of pupils, the goals of the teacher, and many other factors. What is important is that prewriting be part of classroom writing activities.

Writing

Writing is the second stage of the process, the time when pupils commit their ideas to paper. Having made some prewriting decisions on what they want to say and how they want to say it, pupils now practice using the tools of the writer's trade. In their writing,

Literature is used to cement the reading-writing connection as pupils respond in writing to stories and poems that they read.

their ideas take on form. Details are reduced to words, key points to phrases. Thoughts are forged into sentences and sentences are gathered into paragraphs. The act of composing is going on. Atwell (1987) suggests ways of promoting the reading–writing connection in the writing workshop, since pupils look at what they have written from a reader's point of view, and she suggests some practical ways to promote this concept.

The writing time is a busy time. The classroom takes on a workshop atmosphere. Not all pupils are sitting and quietly writing. While some are still "fiddling" with ideas and deciding on form, others are busily engaged in the writing act itself. The teacher is an active participant in the workshop environment. This is not the time to straighten out the lunch and picture money, to correct math homework, or to tidy up the desk. Rather, the teacher is a mobile and visibly available observer and consultant, an adult audience to provide reaction, a resource to advise one pupil about the choice of a word and another about the organization of a paragraph, a coach to provide a few words of encouragement here and a little prodding there, a referee to adjudicate conflicting peer responses, a diagnostician to give instruction on specific areas of writing where individual pupils need a little extra help. What the teacher encounters during this time often suggests areas of widespread instructional need—problems with punctuation, run-on sentences, subject–predicate agreement, or other troublesome aspects that might be addressed in large- or small-group instruction.

In addition to offering an opportunity for conferencing with pupils, the writing time provides teachers with an opportunity to do a little writing themselves. "There is nothing better for increasing awareness of the true artistry in words than attempting the process yourself" (Eeds and Peterson, 1991; p. 175). Teacher modeling is a powerful way of influencing pupil behavior. When teachers write, they have a vehicle for discussing their own writing in group conferences.

It should be clear from the outset that in their written responses to literature, as in all their classroom writing experiences, pupils start writing in first-draft form.

Writing rarely results in a finished product the first time around. Rare and talented indeed is the writer—whether a Pulitzer Prize winner, a young child, or an undergraduate student—who can take pen in hand and produce a polished product on the first attempt. The first version of writing should be a draft in which pupils have opportunities to experiment with putting meaning on paper.

If pupils and teachers understand that every writing experience starts with a first draft, there is no need to worry about things like spelling, usage, punctuation, handwriting, and other mechanical matters of form at the beginning. The first draft is a starting point. The best advice that teachers can give pupils during the writing phase is to get their ideas down on paper. ''For now, write your story so that *you* can read it to an audience. If you can't spell a word, write it down the way it sounds and we can get it right later on.''

Correctness in writing is important because it contributes to the ultimate effectiveness of written communication. Mechanical matters of form can be taken care of during the editing/revising stage, because review and revision are integral components of the writing process.

Editing and Revising

Editing and revising are important parts of writing. Editing involves proofreading and working on aspects of writing that focus on surface levels of correctness to ensure that all words are spelled correctly, to see that all sentences are complete and begin with capital letters and end with proper punctuation marks, and to make sure that the writing is mechanically sound. Proofreading is more than a search for errors; it is a chance to help pupils develop an *attitude* of independent self-appraisal. A major aim of proofreading is to help pupils develop responsibility for putting their own writing into an effective form.

Revising focuses on meaning and clarity, with an eye to interesting word choice, sentence variety and linguistic complexity, paragraph organization, clarity of ideas, and sensitivity to form and content that contribute to overall effectiveness in writing.

Revising is part of the act of reading, too, though we do not often think of it as such. As good readers engage in reading, they ''examine their developing interpretations and view the model they build as draft-like in quality'' (Tierney and Pearson, 1983; p. 576). The more serious the reader or writer is, the more thoughtful the reading is likely to be. In jotting a note to your roommates to tell them that you have gone shopping or in reading a note from them telling them where they have gone, there is not much need for careful drafting or revision. But in reading a letter from a loved one or in preparing a piece of important work on which you will be judged, there is cause to reflect and develop interpretation that may require several revisions as you go along.

Fitzgerald (1989) describes how the revision stage of the writing process is closely related to critical reading, in that both draw on similar thinking processes. Throughout the writing process, writers cast a critical eye on what they are writing. At the revision stage, authors examine what they have written in reference to the anticipated expectations of their readers; that is, to judge the ''degree of fit'' between what they have written and what they expect their readers to understand. This type of careful examination of text is the essence of critical reading.

Part of the editing/revising stage of the writing process is conferencing. As time allows, the teacher meets with individual pupils to discuss their writing. The teacher's

Using Word Processing

IF THE computer has influenced one area of classroom literacy instruction more than others, that area is writing. Word processing is especially useful in the postwriting stage of the writing process.

Most pupils are motivated when using computers. Once basic keyboard skills have been mastered, they often find typing easier than using pencils and pens. There is no part of the writing process in which the computer is not an aid: brainstorming and listing ideas at the prereading stage, composing first drafts at the writing stage, and editing and revising at the postwriting stage. Programs guide proofreading; vagrancies in spelling can be quickly corrected, especially with the aid of a spellchecker; more colorful words can be quickly substituted for more interesting ones; sentences can be easily revised by adding words or combining sentences; whole blocks of print can be moved effortlessly. Conferencing, peer editing, and revising become relatively painless as pupils view their writing on a screen.

Beyond revision, computers allow pupils to print their writing so that their stories, poems, letters, and reports take on a more professional appearance. Computers can be used to promote the communicative aspects of writing as well, in that telecommunications allow students to send their word-processed writing to readers across town or around the country.

Scores of word processing programs are available for young writers. Some that have proved user friendly to teachers and pupils are:

Bank Street Writer (Scholastic Publications), one of the original word processing programs available for use in classrooms and one that has kept pace with developments in the field.

Magic Window II (Artsci), an intermediate-level program that primary pupils can learn to use rather quickly.

PFS Write (Software Publishing), a program with some sophisticated features that is appropriate for first-time users.

Milliken Word Processor (Milliken Publishing), a basic program for young users.

Other word processing programs are available for use in the elementary classroom, and with the astounding speed with which this field is developing, more are sure to follow.

---

role is not primarily to find where errors occur but to show how improvements can be made, to identify problems in such a way that pupils see that they have some chance of overcoming them. Graves (1983) and Calkins (1986) have effectively detailed the role of the teacher in the conference.

Effective writing conferences focus on the writing process as well on the product. That is, the teacher talks about where pupils got their ideas, how they decided on their approach to the topic, why they selected the language they used, and how they might go about editing. In addition to these process-oriented matters, the conference also focuses on such issues as completeness of sentences, spelling, and grammatical structure.

Peer conferencing is also appropriate, as pupils share and discuss each other's writing with partners or in small groups. With demonstration, modeling, discussion, and guided practice, pupils become adept at helping each other in postwriting activities. In the safe and supportive atmosphere of the classroom writing workshop, pupils can let each other know whether the writing has been successful in entertaining, informing, or convincing (depending on its purpose), and they can suggest ways in which the writing can be improved. When pupils read and react to each other's writing, they

10.6 Putting Ideas to Work

Revising, Editing, and Proofreading Checklist

		YES	NO
	Sentences		
R	Is my sentence a complete thought that makes sense?		
	Have I made the words lively, colorful, and interesting?		
E	Does my sentence begin with a capital letter?		
	Does it end with the correct punctuation mark?		
	Are all the words spelled correctly?		
	Paragraphs		
R	Does the topic sentence state the main idea of my paragraph?		
	Do the supporting sentences tell about the topic sentence?		
	Does my paragraph have a clincher sentence?		
	Do all the sentences flow in a logical or sensible order?		
	Did I use different kinds of sentences in my paragraph?		
	Is there only one main idea in my paragraph?		
E	Did I indent at the beginning of my paragraph?		
	Is my paragraph neatly written and easy to read?		
	Writing Selections		
R	Does my writing selection have an interesting title?		
	Does it contain words that paint a clear picture for my readers?		
	Does my writing selection have enough action?		
	Have I included all the details that I want to include?		
E	Can I answer **YES** to all the EDITING questions for the sentences and paragraphs in my writing selection?		
P	**Proofreading Sentences, Paragraphs, and Writing Selections**		
	Have I marked all corrections carefully?		

R = Revising   **E** = Editing   **P** = Proofreading

From *CONNECT/Writing, Revising, Editing, and Proofreading Checklist*. Copyright © 1992 Sundance Publishers and Distributors, Littletown MA. Reprinted by permission.

become more aware of what makes their own writing more effective. Here is a place where the link between reading and writing is forged, as pupils read each other's writing with an eye to constructing meaning in text.

Fitzgerald (1989) suggests group thinking conferences on pupils' own writing as a way to help them become better critical readers and writers. In a supportive and trusting environment, small groups of pupils take turns reading aloud what they have written. To stimulate discussion, the teacher asks questions such as the following: "What was the piece about? What do you like about the piece? Do you have any comments, questions or suggestions for the author?" Pupils revise their writing based on the feedback they receive in these group thinking conferences.

Feedback and comments need to be made in a constructive, positive fashion. Pupils can learn to focus with questions such as "What other words might you use?" rather than such comments as "That's a dumb word to use!" Teachers need to model this constructive approach, always sans red pen.

Based on feedback and revision, pupils produce a final draft. Rewriting has been looked upon conventionally as punishment, the price one must pay for carelessness or stupidity (or both) in one's attempts at writing. Revising demands a price, all right, but it is the price one pays for effectiveness in written expression. Rewriting what one has written is not evidence of failure but a way to achieve a greater measure of success in writing.

Publishing

Publishing is the culmination of the writing process. In conventional writing instruction, school writing assignments were typically done for an audience of one (the teacher), and then primarily as a vehicle for correction. Writing, however, is a communication activity, and the circle of communication is not complete until the writing is read by the intended audience. Publication involves finding readers, "not 'pretend readers' but the real kind who will show interest in writing and let the writer know what they think" (Walshe, 1988; p. 213).

There are a number of options for publishing pupils' writing. A simple and rather intimate form of publication occurs when pupils read each other's writing as part of a classroom community of writers, and when their work is posted on the classroom bulletin board for classmates and visitors to read. Publication is extended beyond the classroom with stories posted in the school lobby or cafeteria, when writing is reproduced as part of a classroom newspaper, or when it is sent home for parents and others to read. Arrangements can also be made to have pupils record their stories on cassette tapes for use in listening centers, or to make videotapes of pupils as they read their stories. Sharing stories in these ways is part of writing for communication.

More formal publication takes place as pupils' writing is gathered into class books. "For many children, book publishing is the most exciting part of the literature program. Frequently, the first reading that some children do is their own published story, so being an author makes as much of an impact on the child as being a reader" (Routman, 1988; p. 110). In the very early grades, before pupils' independent writing competency has developed, teachers, parent volunteers, student teachers, or pupils from upper grades transcribe children's stories, which are then, typically, illustrated by the original authors. As independent writing skills develop, the final drafts of pupils' own

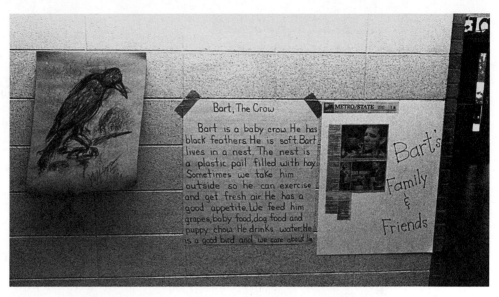

Publication of children's writing is the culmination of the writing process.

writing can be used. Stories are taped inside laminated covers, mounted inside heavy cardboard covered by wallpaper, stitched by hand or with a sewing machine, or otherwise bound in a sturdy enough form to withstand repeated handling by pupils in the elementary grades.

Affording status as literature to pupil-written books and other writing is important. This level of respect solidifies the reading–writing connection in pupils' minds and encourages them to take themselves more seriously as authors, as producers of stories as well as consumers of stories. This perception can be a powerful motivation and ego-enhancing dimension of a classroom literacy program.

This, then, is the writing process, a process that includes the steps of prewriting, writing, editing/revising, and publishing. The stages and steps will vary from activity to activity, from grade to grade, from classroom to classroom, and from pupil to pupil within any classroom. There are pupils who will be able to skip over various steps along the way—pupils who arrive in the classroom with a keen sense of story, pupils with facile expressional skills, pupils with easy mastery of the mechanics of writing. For most pupils, however, writing competency grows as they follow these steps used by professional writers.

DeGroff (1989) describes how literature can be used ''to support the process that take writers from topic selection to a final model form.'' Using Ezra Jack Keats's popular story *The Snowy Day,* she shows how pupils can be led to see how focus can be given to the events of a perfectly ordinary day in shaping a story topic. Discussion of the book can focus on why the author chose to include some incidents and not others, the tone of the writing, and the author's choice of words, all of which are prewriting decisions that writers make.

DeGroff describes how discussion of the story can lead to an awareness of how pupils draft meaning as they read in much the same way that authors draft meaning as they write. She also describes how literature discussions can provide a model for

The Author's Chair

T HE AUTHOR'S chair is a concept/ device suggested by Donald Graves and Jane Hansen (1982). In the classroom, a special chair is designated as ''The Author's Chair.'' The teacher sits in this chair while reading to children, and pupils are afforded the honor of sitting in it as they read their writing to classmates. Pupils read their own stories aloud, just as the teacher shares the works of famous authors. Thus, children gain a sense of themselves as authors and a feeling of genuine worth about their writing.

---

writers' conferences in which teachers and pupils engage as part of process writing. ''During literature discussion we want students to notice how respondents comment and question but respect writer's ownership of their work. . . . We do not tell Ezra Jack Keats that he must change his book. We simply comment and raise questions that reflect our understanding and response'' (p. 118).

Using Keats's story, DeGroff explains how readers and writers practice revision as they encounter new information in text, consider alternative word choice in the book, and examine how the author might have written the story differently. Pupils also examine the editorial decisions that Keats must have made about *A Snowy Day:* size, shape, title, illustration, and design of the book. Examining works of children's literature in this way opens pupils' eyes to the options that they can exercise in their own classroom writing activities. The idea can be extended by having pupils discuss ways in which the story could have changed:

if the story had taken place on a sunny day in the summer;

if the main character had been a girl instead of a boy;

if the setting had been the country instead of the city.

Having pupils talk about stories in this way opens their eyes to wider possibilities in their writing, while it focuses on critical reading and an awareness of elements of story structure in literature.

Each stage of the writing process involves the reading–writing connection. Wide reading gives pupils impressive models and helps them generate ideas that they can use as topics in the prewriting stage of the process. The act of writing itself involves pupils in the construction of meaning in text that is essential to both composing and comprehending. Editing and revising alerts them to the language standards and qualities that will make them keener processors of print. Publishing what they have written gives pupils a sense of authorship that influences them as readers.

Written Products Based on Literature

The writing process results in written products, which can include imaginative stories, informational reports, journals and logs, friendly letters, various types of poetry, scripts and dialogues, and other forms of writing. Each of these products can be directly related to literature in the classroom.

10.8 Putting Ideas to Work

Decisions in the Writing Process

WHETHER WRITING an imaginative story in the third grade or writing a term paper for a course in teaching reading, the writing process consists of four steps or stages, each of which involves a series of decisions.

Stages	Decisions
Prewriting	Stimulus for writing—*Why am I writing this?*
	Finding a topic—*What will I write about?*
	Focus on detail—*What aspect of the topic will I emphasize?*
	Deciding on form—*Will I write a story or a poem?*
	Deciding on audience—*Who will read what I write?*
Writing	Drafting—*What ideas and details will I include?*
	Vocabulary—*What words will I use to express actions and feelings?*
	Sentences—*How can I write so others will be interested and entertained?*
Editing/Revising	Sentences—*Do my sentences make sense? Are they clear? Do they begin with capitals and end with periods?*
	Paragraphs—*Do they have topic sentences? Are they too long? Do I have enough details?*
	Selection—*Does it have an interesting title? Did I include exciting action and interesting details?*
Publishing	Personal—*Will it be a diary or journal for me only?*
	Intimate—*Will it be shared with only select people; parents or classmates?*
	Public—*Will it be posted on a bulletin board or published in a class book?*

Stories

Storywriting is stimulated by the full range of narratives that pupils encounter in the world of children's literature. They can create their own witches and goblins, heroes and villains, friends and foes based on the characters that they find in books. They can write their own versions of favorite stories, write new endings, write sequences, or produce a variety of imaginative tales and realistic accounts of their own lives. An awareness of narrative story structure—how problems develop in stories and how these problems are solved—provides a structural dimension that children's writing often lacks.

Using Big Books as Writing Models

BIG BOOKS can be used in virtually thousands of ways to stimulate written language activities in the classroom. Some teachers have used the predictable and repeated language patterns found in many Big Books as the basis for writing activities. For example:

1. The language patterns in Pat Hutchins's *Good Night, Owl* can be repeated in writing Halloween stories (*The skeleton shook, rattle, rattle, and Ghost tried to sleep.*), science stories about winter animals (*The rabbit hopped, hop, hop, and Bear tried to sleep.*), or in stories focused on another primary grade theme or topic.

2. The patterned language in Bill Martin's *Brown Bear, Brown Bear, What Do You See?* can be the model for end-of-the-month summaries of activities: *Grade 1, grade 1, what did we do? In January, we celebrated Julie's and Juan's birthdays, we took a field trip to the bakery, we had an assembly on safety,* and so on.

Reports

Written reports provide pupils with opportunities to develop expository writing, and informational trade books are essential in gathering content for these reports. As part of a thematic unit on dinosaurs, for example, written reports will include information found in such nonfiction trade books as:

Aliki, *My Visit to the Dinosaurs*

Franklyn Branley, *What Happened to the Dinosaur?*

Kathy Lasky, *Dinosaur Digs*

Patrice Laubner, *News about Dinosaurs*

Bernard Most, *If the Dinosaurs Came Back*

Peter Zallinger, *Dinosaurs*

Using trade books for research on thematic topics is a direct link in the reading–writing connection. Building expository text structure into the report by organizing the writing according to the text structure in the informational books cements the connection.

Sometimes a fictional story that pupils read can stimulate their interest in a topic enough to lead them to research and reporting. Robb (1989) tells about a fifth grade class that developed "an all consuming curiosity about wolves and their environment" after reading Jean Craighead George's *Julie of the Wolves*. The pupils spent a year researching the topics of animal behavior and the environment based on the interest that the literature had sparked (see 7.8, p. 233).

10.10 Putting Ideas to Work

Literature-Based Writing

THE IDEA of writing a friendly letter to an author illustrates the difference between a literature-based focus and a more conventional approach to language teaching in the classroom. Teaching the form and protocol of writing friendly letters and business letters is typically part of the elementary school curriculum in most districts, and lessons on letter writing are normally included in most language arts textbook series. In conventional programs, these lessons become the starting point and focus in teaching this important writing skill.

With literature-based instruction, children's books become the starting point for this aspect of the language arts curriculum. The pupils' response to the literature or the questions that they raise as a result of their reading stimulate the lessons on how to write a letter.

With both approaches, the content of the lesson does not differ dramatically. The focus does.

Letters

Writing letters is an authentic language and social skill, and writing letters to favorite authors has long been a classroom practice. Some authors encourage letters from their young readers and make an honest attempt to respond to this correspondence. Others do not. When an author does respond to a letter written by a class, the excitement among pupils is usually high and another element in the reader–writer connection is established. Even when the class receives an apologetic ''We're-sorry-but-Mr.-Author-is-so-busy-writing-a-new-book-that-he-does-not-have-time-to-respond-to-all-the-wonderful-mail-he-receives'' reaction from a publisher, at least their letters generate an authentic response.

Prewriting activities for letters to authors need to include discussions about the number and type of questions that are appropriate (with cautions about questions like ''How much money do you make?'') and about outlandish requests (''Please use my name in your next book''). This type of discussion is part of the social aspect of using language well.

Literature suggests opportunities for imaginative letter-writing activities as well, as when pupils write notes of condolence to Beatrix Potter's beloved *Peter Rabbit* or letters to Alexander (from Judy Viorst's *Alexander and the Terrible, Horrible, No Good, Very Bad Day*) telling him about their very bad days. Nor are opportunities for ''epistolary communication'' limited to those suggested by literature. Teachers and pupils have plenty of opportunities to write thank-you notes to class guests, get-well messages to classmates who may be absent for prolonged periods, letters of appreciation to the school secretary, letters to pen pals across the miles or to senior citizens across town, and the like.

Another form of letter writing occurs when pupils exchange letters through a classroom mailbox about the books that they have read. This type of activity is an extension of buddy journals, with the added dimension that pupils are expected to follow the conventional letter form—heading, salutation, body and closing, all punctuated appropriately.

As a deeper dimension of learning about letter writing, Beverly Cleary's warm and sensitive award-winning *Dear Mr. Henshaw* can be used to show how a whole story is told through a series of personal letters, as can Rosa Guy's *The Ups and Downs of Carl Davis III.*

Poems

Writing poetry is another popular and important writing activity in the literature-based classroom. Pupils who are exposed to the full range of lyric poems, descriptive poems, narrative poems, humorous poems, fanciful poems, and free verse will likely want to respond to literature in poetic form. Although conventional elements of rhythm and rhyme have enormous appeal to pupils, teachers need to maintain a focus on meaning as their pupils write poems.

Some forms of poetry necessarily start with direct modeling. In order to learn the form of limericks or haiku, for example, pupils must be exposed to models of these poems found in books such as John Ciardi's collection of absurd limericks *The Hopeful Trout and Other Limericks* and one of Ann Atwood's beautiful collections of haiku such as *Fly with the Wind, Flow with the Water.* Having been exposed to the form of these structured poems, pupils will be able to produce some versions of their own.

When writing less structured forms of poetry, pupils need considerable freedom in putting their thoughts, ideas, emotions, and images into poetic form.

Scripts and Dialogues

Scripts and dialogues provide opportunities to integrate reading, writing, and speaking, as pupils produce their own versions of stories to be staged. Many stories like Arnold Lobel's *Frog and Toad Are Friends* and *Knots on a Counting Rope* by Bill Martin, Jr. and John Archambault provide models of dialogue for pupils to follow as they write. Wordless books provide ideal vehicles for having pupils at any level produce dialogue. Supplying words for the old woman in Tomie de Paola's popular *Pancakes for Breakfast* or lines for the various characters in Martha Alexander's *Bobo's Dream* offer natural opportunities for pupils to create written products to cement the reading–writing connection through meaning.

Journals

Response journals, logs, and other personal written responses to literature are an integral and regular part of literature-based instruction. These personal forms of writing provide an ongoing record of stories, poems, and other materials that pupils have experienced, along with their responses to this literature. Pupils may recall their own struggles with handwriting in response to Beverly Cleary's *Muggie Maggie* or tell why they find Susan Pearson's *Well, I Never!* so funny. Unlike other forms of writing produced in response to literature, journals take a personal perspective. More detached responses take the form of book reports.

Book Reports

A common form of writing in response to literature is, of course, "the good old book report." Traditionally, book reports were occasional assignments, given for the apparent purpose of making sure that pupils had read the books they were supposed to

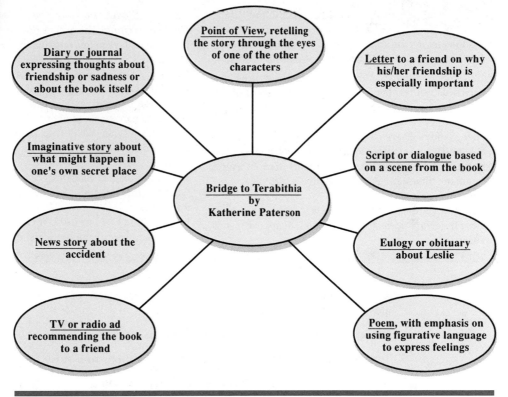

10.11 Putting Ideas to Work

A Writing Web

read. When book-reading is an everyday classroom occasion and when responding to literature is a regular part of language instruction, book reports become less of a big deal for pupils. Reports can be done in personal and creative ways that include:

index card reports, two-sentence summary/response statements written to recommend (or not recommend) the book to others;

character reports, written through the eyes of one of the book's characters, sometimes delivered ''in costume'' as an oral report to the class;

author reports, written as an interview with the author, perhaps delivered as a press conference with classmates asking questions about the book;

advertisements, written as print, radio, or television ads for the book, with an emphasis on using propaganda techniques as a critical thinking activity as well;

letters, written to be actually sent to the author or to be exchanged with classmates through a ''classroom mailbox.''

10.12
▌FOR YOUR INFORMATION▐▬▬▬▬▬
Children's Trade Books about Writing

A NUMBER of children's trade books dealing directly with the subjects of writing and publishing are available for use with pupils. A small sampling of these books is:

Aliki, *How a Book Is Made.* With simple writing and lively illustrations, the author explains the steps of the book-publishing process and the roles of the people involved.

Asher, Sandy. *Where Do You Get Your Ideas?* This is a book about developing ideas for stories and poems, some supplied by well-known authors like Marjorie Weinman Sharmat, Patricia Reilly Giff, and Lois Lowry.

Benjamin, Carol Lea. *Writing for Kids.* This book provides advice and ideas for pupils about many aspects of writing.

Cassedy, Sylvia. *In Your Own Words: A Beginner's Guide to Writing.* The author provides ideas for writing poetry and plays in this book which is suggested for ages 10 and up.

Colligan, Louise. *Scholastic's A+ Junior Guide to Good Writing.* More appropriate for upper grade pupils, this guide emphasizes process writing, with how-to's related to narrative and expository text.

Dubrovin, Vivian. *Write Your Own Story.* This is a practical guide on writing for pupils in the upper elementary grades.

Juster, Norman. *A Surfeit of Similes.* This book is just what the title suggests, by the author of *The Phantom Tollbooth.*

Mahon, Julia C. *First Book of Creative Writing.* This is a direct and specific guide, with lots of ideas for writing.

posters, in the form of a baseball card for a sports hero or a "Wanted, Dead or Alive" poster for the character in a mystery book.

news reports, recalling part of a book in the form of a TV, radio, or newspaper report.

taped reading, in which pupils tape record sections of a story for others to enjoy.

illustrations from the story, with appropriate captions.

book cover or jacket, with illustration and information about both the book and the author.

report card, giving a grade and comment about some aspect of the character in the story (honesty, resourcefulness, humor, etc.)

conversations between characters from different books.

puppets, made from socks, sticks, or coffee cans, reflecting characters from the book.

Book reports can take other forms as well. In a classroom full of literature, there will be no shortage of creative ideas that teachers can suggest and that pupils can use in responding to, and reporting on, what they read.

Even in a literature-based reading program, not all the writing that pupils do will be about the books they have read. They will write about their personal experiences, both real and imagined; they will write about the most interesting characters they have ever met and what they hope to do when they become adults; they will write letters to the residents of nursing homes nearby and pen pals far away; they will write about the ideas that fill their heads and the emotions that fill their hearts.

Literature, however, does provide a fruitful vehicle for topics and a rich language model for writing. Using a process writing model, pupils can produce an infinite variety of poems, stories, reports, letters, advertisements, essays, biographies, scripts, and other written products in response to the literature they read. Literature provides a force that forges the reading–writing connection.

The professional literature is full of practical ideas on ways to make the reading–writing connection through literature in the classroom (Tway, 1985; Criscuolo, 1988; Noyce and Christie, 1989; Mason, 1989). Creative teachers will find numerous other ways to make this important connection, including giving pupils a chance to participate in the planning of literature-based writing activities. Pupils have original ideas, and with responsibility for planning writing activities, they feel a heightened sense of ownership of the final product.

Summary and Conclusions

Three basic premises of the reading–writing connection are: (1) that there is an integral connection between the process of learning to read and the process of learning to write; (2) that competency in both areas can be developed simultaneously; and (3) that development of one can have a powerful influence on the development of the other. Literature provides an ideal vehicle for forging the reading–writing connection, since pupils' writing is strongly influenced by what they read.

Process writing is a movement that has dramatically changed the way writing is taught in schools. The writing process includes a prewriting stage that involves a series of decisions, a writing stage in which a draft is produced, and a postwriting stage that involves editing and revision, and finally publication of a finished product. Literature can be used to support each step in the process, from helping pupils generate ideas and explore forms through publishing the written product.

The written products that pupils produce can take a variety of forms, from imaginative stories and informational reports to personal expressions of emotions through poetry. All provide possibilities for written responses to the literature that pupils read in and out of school.

The most obvious link between reading and writing exists at the level of decoding and encoding words.

> But just as there is more to reading than word recognition, there is more to writing than spelling, and there is far more to the reading–writing connection than just reciprocal exercise with individual words. . . .
>
> As children become authors, as they struggle to express, refine, and reach audiences through their own writing, they actively come to grips with the most important reading insights of all.
>
> Through writing, children learn that text is not preordained or immutable truth. It is human voice. . . . Children learn that the purpose of text is not to be read but to be understood. They learn that text does not contain meaning but is meaningful only to the extent that it is understood by its reader. They learn that different readers respond differently to the same text. They also learn that sometimes understanding comes only through hard work even for the best readers. They learn that cogent writing may depend on consulting other sources, inviting the insight that cogent reading may do this too.
>
> They learn that text is written about an underlying organization, inviting the insight that it may be productively read in that way too.

They learn, in short, that reading is about thinking, and that lesson is critical. (Adams, 1990; pp. 404–405)[1]

And that is the basis of the reading–writing connection!

Discussion Questions and Activities

1. After doing additional reading and research, make a list of ways in which reading and writing are related and how literature cements this relationship.
2. Think of the last writing assignment that you encountered—a research report or term paper for a class that you are taking, for example. Trace the process you followed in writing the paper, from your prewriting decision of choosing (or being assigned) a topic to the final product.
3. Using a children's trade book that you know well, plan a process writing lesson that you would use in the classroom. Be sure to include prewriting activities, ideas for the writing workshop, and provision for editing and publication.
4. Select a children's trade book that you have especially enjoyed. Using the model suggested in 10.11, design a ''writing web'' for this book.
5. Recall your own writing experiences from elementary school. Compare these early experiences to the ideas presented in this chapter.

School-Based Assignments

1. Examine a sample of pupils' writing in your school placement. What can you tell about the pupils' writing abilities and instructional needs based on what you observe? How might you address these needs in a class lesson?
2. Work with a small group of pupils in developing part of a writing lesson or in designing a writing web (see 10.11) based on a trade book that they have read or that you have read to them.
3. After reading a chapter of a book to a class, plan a lesson in which pupils respond in writing to the story. Remind pupils that they should react to the story rather than merely tell what happened. Select one or two of the pupils' responses and plan a writing conference.
4. In a classroom you visit, what written evidence indicates that literature is alive and well in that classroom? Are pupils' written responses to literature displayed around the room? If you were the teacher in that classroom, what activities would you plan to involve pupils in literature-based writing encounters?
5. Select a children's trade book and discuss it with pupils in the manner suggested by DeGroff's discussion of A Snowy Day (see pp. 312–313).

---

[1]Excerpted from M. J. Adams, *Beginning to Read: Thinking and Learning about Print*. Copyright © 1990 MIT Press, Cambridge MA.

Children's Trade Books Cited in This Chapter

Aardema, Verna. *Why Mosquitoes Buzz in People's Ears.* New York: Dial, 1978.

Alexander, Martha. *Bobo's Dream.* New York: Dial, 1970.

Aliki. *How a Book Is Made.* New York: Harper and Row, 1988.

———. *My Visit to the Dinosaurs.* New York: Harper and Row, 1985.

Asher, Sandy. *Where Do You Get Your Ideas?* New York: Walker, 1987.

Atwood, Ann. *Fly with the Wind, Flow with the Water.* New York: Scribner, 1979.

Baylor, Byrd, and Parnall, Peter. *If You Are a Hunter of Fossils.* New York: Scribner's, 1980.

Benjamin, Carol Lea. *Writing for Kids.* New York: Harper and Row, 1985.

Branley, Franklyn. *Whatever Happened to the Dinosaurs?* New York: Crowell, 1989.

Burnett, Frances Hodgson. *The Secret Garden.* New York: Harper and Row, 1912.

Cassedy, Sylvia. *In Your Own Words: A Beginner's Guide to Writing.* Garden City: Doubleday, 1979.

Ciardi, John. *The Hopeful Trout and Other Limericks.* Boston: Houghton Mifflin, 1989.

Cleary, Beverly. *Dear Mr. Henshaw.* New York: Morrow, 1983.

———. *Muggie Maggie.* New York: Morrow, 1991.

Colligan, Louise. *Scholastic's A+ Junior Guide to Good Writing.* New York: Scholastic, 1988.

de Paola, Tomie. *Now One Foot, Now the Other.* New York: Putnam, 1981.

———. *Pancakes for Breakfast.* New York: Harcourt, Brace Jovanovich, 1978.

Dubrovin, Vivian. *Write Your Own Story.* New York: Franklin Watts, 1984.

Eckert, Allan. *Incident at Hawk's Hill.* Boston: Little, Brown, 1971.

Gardiner, John. *Stone Fox.* New York: Harper and Row, 1980.

George, Jean Craighead. *Julie of the Wolves.* New York: Harper and Row, 1972.

Giff, Patricia Reilly. *The Beast in Mrs. Rooney's Room.* New York: Dell, 1984.

Guy, Rosa. *The Ups and Downs of Carl Davis III.* New York: Dellacourt, 1989.

Hoban, Russell. *A Bargain for Frances.* New York: Harper and Row, 1970.

Hogrogian, Nonny. *One Fine Day.* New York: Macmillan, 1971.

Hutchins, Pat. *Good Night, Owl.* New York: Macmillan, 1972.

Juster, Norman. *A Surfeit of Similes.* New York: William Morrow, 1989.

Keats, Ezra Jack. *The Snowy Day.* New York: Penguin, 1962.

Knudson, R. R. *Babe Didrickson, Athlete of the Century.* New York: Viking, 1985.

Lasky, Kathy. *Dinosaur Dig.* New York: Morrow, 1990.

Laubner, Patrice. *News about Dinosaurs.* New York: Bradbury Press, 1989.

Lobel, Arnold. *Frog and Toad Are Friends.* New York: Harper and Row, 1979.

Mahon, Julia C. *First Book of Creative Writing.* New York: Franklin Watts, 1968.

Martin, Bill, Jr. *Brown Bear, Brown Bear, What Do You See?* New York: Henry Holt, 1983.

Martin, Bill, Jr., and Archambault, John. *Knots on a Counting Rope.* New York: Henry Holt Co., 1987.

Mayer, Mercer. *What Do You Do with a Kangaroo?* New York: Scholastic, 1987.

McPhail, David. *The Bear's Toothache.* Boston: Little, Brown, 1972.

Most, Bernard. *If the Dinosaurs Came Back.* New York: Harcourt Brace Jovanovich, 1978.

Munsch, Robert. *Love You Forever.* Scarborough, ONT: Firefly Books, 1986.

Paterson, Katherine. *Bridge to Terabithia.* New York: Harper and Row, 1977.

Pearson, Susan. *Well, I Never!* New York: Simon and Schuster, 1991.

Quackenbush, Robert. *Oh, What an Awful Mess!* Englewood Cliffs: Prentice Hall, 1980.

Rawls, Wilson. *Where the Red Fern Grows.* New York: Doubleday, 1973.

Seuss, Dr. *Cat In The Hat.* New York: Random House, 1957.

———. *Green Eggs and Ham.* New York: Random House, 1960.

Spier, Peter. *Bored—Nothing To Do.* New York: Doubleday, 1978.

Taylor, Mildred. *Roll of Thunder, Hear My Cry.* New York: Dial, 1976.

Van Allsburg, Chris. *Jumanji*. Boston: Houghton
    Mifflin, 1981.
White, E. B. *Charlotte's Web*. New York: Harper and
    Row, 1952.
Wolf, Alexander (Jon Scieska, pseud.). *The True Story
    of the Three Little Pigs*. New York: Penguin,
    1989.

Yektai, Niki. *Hi Bears, Bye Bears*. New York:
    Orchard, 1991.
Zallinger, Peter. *Dinosaurs*. New York: Random
    House, 1988.

References

Adams, M. J. (1990). *Beginning to Read: Thinking
    and Learning about Print*. Cambridge, MA:
    MIT Press.
Atwell, N. (1987). *In the Middle: Writing, Reading,
    and Learning with Adolescents*. Portsmouth,
    NH: Heinemann.
Beach, R., and Hynds, S. (1991). Research on
    Response to Literature. In R. Barr, M. L.
    Kamill, P. Mosenthal, and P. D. Pearson (eds.),
    Handbook on Reading Research. Vol. 2. New
    York: Longman.
Bleich, D. (1978). *Subjective Criticism*. Baltimore:
    John Hopkins University Press.
Bromley, K. D. (1989). Buddy Journals Make the
    Reading–Writing Connection. *The Reading
    Teacher* 43:122–129.
Brown, V. L., Hammill, D. D., Wiederholt, J. L.
    (1986). *Test of Reading Comprehension*. Austin,
    TX: Pro-Ed.
Calkins, L. M. (1986). *The Art of Teaching Writing*.
    Portsmouth: Heinemann Educational Books.
Criscuolo, N. P. (1988). Twelve Practical Ways to
    Make the Reading/Writing Connection. *The New
    England Reading Association Journal* 24:30–32.
DeGroff, L-J. (1989). Developing Writing Processes
    with Children's Literature. *The New Advocate*
    2:115–123.
Eeds, M., and Peterson, R. (1991). Teacher as Curator:
    Learning to Teach about Literature. *The
    Reading Teacher* 45:118–126.
Fitzgerald, J. (1989). Enhancing Two Related Thought
    Processes: Revision in Writing and Critical
    Reading. *The Reading Teacher* 43:42–48.
Graves, D. H. (1983). *Writing: Teachers and Children
    at Work*. Portsmouth, NH: Heinemann.
Graves, D. H., and Hansen, J. (1982). The Author's
    Chair. *Language Arts* 60:176–183.
Hittleman, D. R. (1988). *Developmental Reading,
    K–8: Teaching from a Whole-Language
    Perspective*. 3rd ed. Columbus, OH: Merrill
    Publishing.

Karolides, N. J. (ed.) (1992). *Reader Response in the
    Classroom: Evoking and Interpreting Meaning
    in Literature*. New York: Longman.
Kelly, P. R. (1990). Guiding Young Students'
    Response to Literature. *The Reading Teacher*
    43:464–470.
Kolczynski, R. G. (1989). Reading Leads to Writing.
    In J. W. Stewig and S. L. Sebesta (eds.), *Using
    Literature in the Elementary Classroom*.
    Urbana: National Council of Teachers of
    English.
Mason, J. M. (ed.) (1989). *Reading and Writing
    Connections*. Boston: Allyn and Bacon.
Murray, D. M. (1968). *A Writer Teaches Writing*.
    Boston: Houghton Mifflin.
Noyce, R. M., and Christie, J. F. (1989). *Integrating
    Reading and Writing Instruction in Grades K–8*.
    Boston: Allyn and Bacon.
Pearson, P. D. (1985). Changing the Face of Reading
    Comprehension Instruction. *The Reading
    Teacher* 38:724–728.
Petrosky, A. R. (1982). From Story to Essay: Reading
    and Writing. *College Composition and
    Communication* 33:19–36.
Phillips, L. M. (1989). *Using Children's Literature to
    Foster Written Language Development*.
    Technical Report No. 446. Champaign:
    University of Illinois at Urbana–Champaign,
    Center for the Study of Reading.
Robb, L. (1989). Books in the Classroom. *The Horn
    Book* 65:808–810.
Rosenblatt, L. M. (1982). The Literary Transaction:
    Evocation and Response. *Theory Into Practice*
    21:268–277.
Routman, R. (1988). *Transitions from Literature to
    Literacy*. Portsmouth, NH: Heinemann.
Rubin, A., and Hansen, J. (1984). *Reading and
    Writing: How Are the First Two 'R's' Related?*
    Reading Education Report No. 51. Champaign:
    University of Illinois at Urbana–Champaign,
    Center for the Study of Reading.

Shanahan, T. (1988). The Reading–Writing Relationship: Seven Instructional Principles. *The Reading Teacher* 41:636–647.

Simons, H. D. (1971). Reading Comprehension: The Need for a New Perspective. *Reading Research Quarterly* 7:340–361.

Tierney, R. J., and Pearson, P. D. (1983). Toward a Composing Model of Reading. *Language Arts* 60:568–580.

Tierney, R. J., Soter, A., O'Flahoran, J. F., and McGinley, T. (1989). The Effects of Reading and Writing upon Thinking Critically. *Reading Research Quarterly* 24:134–173.

Tomkins, G. E. (1990). *Teaching Writing: Balancing Process and Product.* Columbus: Merrill Publishing.

Tway, E. (1985). *Writing Is Reading: 26 Ways to Connect.* Urbana, IL: National Council for Teachers of English.

Walshe, R. D. (1988). Questions Teachers Ask about Teaching Writing K–12. In R. D. Walshe and P. March (eds.), *Teaching Writing K–12.* Melbourne, Australia: Dellastar.

Chapter 11

Reading Instruction for Atypical Learners

Chapter 11 Outline

I. Introduction
II. Mainstreaming
III. Slow Learners
  A. Teaching Strategies
    1. Direct Instruction on Comprehension Components
    2. Semantic Mapping
    3. Focus on Metacognition
    4. Think Alouds
    5. Strategy Training
    6. Reading to Younger Pupils
    7. Taped Books
  B. Literature for the Slow Learner
IV. Pupils with Learning Disabilities
  A. Defining Learning Disabilities
  B. Reading Programs for the Learning Disabled
  C. Holistic Reading
  D. Writing
V. Pupils with Sensory and Physical Problems
  A. Visual Problems
  B. Auditory Problems
  C. Physical Handicaps
VI. Pupils with Attitude and Behavior Problems
  A. Teaching Techniques
  B. Bibliotherapy
VII. Gifted and Talented Pupils
  A. Defining Gifted and Talented
  B. Challenging Reading
VIII. The Teacher on the Team
IX. Summary and Conclusions
Discussion Questions and Activities
School-Based Assignments
Children's Trade Books Cited in This Chapter
References

Features

11.1 Reading Recovery
11.2 The "Curious George" Strategy
11.3 Instructional Story Plans
11.4 Using Literature With Learning Disabled Pupils
11.5 Literature As Part of Language Therapy
11.6 Books about Children with Sensory and Physical Handicaps
11.7 Shared Stories for Handicapped Learners
11.8 Literature-Based Reading for Emotionally Handicapped Pupils
11.9 Children's Books on "Tender Topics"

Key Concepts in This Chapter

A *full range of abilities can be found among pupils in any classroom; literature helps meet this range of literacy needs in special ways.*

Because of cognitive functioning or a learning disability, some pupils experience greater-than-normal difficulty in learning to read. Reading instruction can be adjusted with literature to meet the needs and levels of these pupils.

Pupils with sensory or physical challenges need instructional adjustments as part of a regular classroom program.

Some children display attitude and behavior problems that get in the way of learning to read. For these pupils, trade books become vehicles both for reading instruction and for reflecting some of their emotional experiences to themselves and to others.

Pupils who are gifted learners can use literature in a variety of ways to extend their learning as part of classroom literacy instruction.

LL CHILDREN are different. Individual differences among pupils are a fact of life in any classroom. Although the age range of pupils tends to be relatively narrow, the differences in other human characteristics will be great. The differences in height, weight, hair color, and other physical characteristics are outward reflections of the enormous range of internal differences that are not so readily observable.

The range of human characteristics includes learning abilities. Most children arrive at school with physical, emotional, and cognitive competencies that will allow them to learn to read with regular instruction. Others arrive with fewer, or more, of the characteristics needed for success in achieving literacy.

Because each child is unique in his or her own special way, there is no such thing as a "standard" or "typical" pupil. Nevertheless, some pupils differ substantially from their age-mates in those characteristics considered important in learning how to read. These atypical learners include:

slow learners, pupils whose basic abilities may delay their expected progress in acquiring literacy;

learning disabled children, pupils who have a "glitch" in their central nervous system that makes learning to read and write unusually difficult;

physically challenged children, pupils whose orthopedic or sensory handicaps impede the learning process or limit full participation in classroom programs;

emotionally bothered children, pupils who have attitude or behavior problems that impact their learning to read.

As a group, these pupils are considered *at risk.* Because of physical, cognitive, or emotional problems, they are likely to experience difficulty in learning to read and write.

Pupils exhibit different degrees of problems that affect learning to read, from mild to severe. "At the mild end of the continuum, the behavioral and educational differences (among groups) are blurred at best. . . . In fact the overlap of underachievement and social/emotional problem behavior commonly found in mild and moderate learning disabled and emotionally disturbed students makes differentiating between the two groups sometimes little more than the flip of a diagnostic coin. With respect to reading behaviors, similar difficulties occur" (McCoy and Prehm, 1987; pp. 256–257).

In addition to at-risk pupils in the classroom, atypical learners include:

gifted pupils, children whose high level of ability facilitates the process of learning to read.

Pupils who are atypical in one dimension may be very typical in other aspects of learning and of life. For example, a pupil may be talented in reading but not so gifted in math. Or a child who has a learning disability that makes reading inordinately difficult may be an especially gifted artist. In such cases, the key is to help the pupil use areas of strength to develop interest and competency in reading. This chapter deals with those characteristics that most directly influence learning to read.

Atypical learners need high-quality instruction that does not differ substantially in nature from that provided as part of a normal classroom reading program. Certain aspects of the reading instructional program may need to be adjusted to meet the special learning needs of the atypical learner in the classroom, but no matter what their learning characteristics, pupils need instruction that stresses meaning from the very beginning, that provides direct instruction for reading strategies, that integrates reading and writing, that extends reading into content areas of the curriculum, that is permeated with fine literature—in short, a program that involves good teaching and the use of strategies that have proved effective in teaching reading and writing.

Mainstreaming

Exceptional children have always been part of society. At first, they were excluded from schools and kept hidden away at home. Through the late 1800s and into the 20th century, special educational institutions were established for children with more obvious needs—schools for the blind, for example, or schools for the severely mentally retarded. Later, separate classes in public schools were set up for pupils characterized as "special." As the fields of medicine, psychology, and education have learned more about the unique characteristics of exceptional children, and as society has become more sensitive to the importance of addressing the needs of *all* learners, the practice of integrating pupils with special learning needs into the regular school settings developed.

In 1975, Congress passed Public Law 94–142, legislation designed to ensure that all children, whatever their special needs, receive appropriate education from the ages of three to 21. This law was updated in 1990 with the Individuals with Disabilities Education Act (IDEA). These laws require that the education of pupils with disabilities be based on a full assessment of each individual's learning needs and that it be outlined in an Individualized Educational Plan (IEP) indicating what special services the pupil should receive as part of his or her education. This legislation also stipulates that education of special-needs learners be conducted "in the least restrictive environment"; that is, to the extent possible, special needs children are to be integrated into the normal school life that all children experience.

Federal and state laws related to pupils with special needs led to the widespread practice of mainstreaming these pupils into regular classrooms. Although pupils with severe special needs are still educated in substantially separate settings, and though support services are provided to meet special needs of pupils in neighborhood schools, the time of completely segregating children with special needs has passed and many atypical learners spend substantial amounts of their instructional time in regular classrooms.

The practice of mainstreaming has had an impact on reading instruction. Professionally, the lives of teachers are both enriched and challenged by the need to provide reading instruction for pupils with a variety of learning needs—those who are well equipped to learn and those who are less well equipped, those who are tuned into reading and those who are not, those who learn easily and those who do not.

Mainstreaming is important to the educational life of special-needs pupils because these pupils benefit both socially and academically by interacting with peers.

Placement in regular classrooms results in shared responsibility between so-called "regular" and "special" pupils. At the same time, it is important that intensive, supportive reading instruction be provided. O'Sullivan, Ysseldyke, Christensen, and Thurlow (1990) observed the reading instruction of three groups of mildly handicapped learners (learning disabled, emotionally/behaviorally disturbed, and slow learners) in both regular and special education settings. They found that these special-needs pupils were more actively involved in learning for higher proportions of time in special reading classes than in regular reading classes. Given the fact that the proportion of time devoted to reading instruction is greater in special education than in mainstreamed settings, direct and intensive literacy instruction needs to be provided for the at-risk pupil, instruction that should include frequent use of high-quality literature.

Slow Learners

Slow learners are, by definition, pupils who learn more slowly. These are pupils whose intellectual ability or learning capacity is below others of the same chronological age. Although factors other than cognitive processing can cause a pupil to learn less easily, intellectual functioning is the chief criterion conventionally used in identifying slow learners in school. Slow learners need the same skills and strategies that good readers do. They need to decode unfamiliar words and figure out meaning from context. They need to draw on their schemata to build meaning. They need to monitor their own comprehension as they proceed through text. They need to apply comprehension strategies in reading informational materials. And they need lots and lots of literature. Development of competencies in these areas moves less quickly for the slow learner than for the more typical pupil.

McCoy and Prehm (1987) emphasize the importance of direct instruction, time on task, and classroom management techniques in teaching reading to slow learners. In direct instruction, specific objectives are set, direct teaching is aimed at helping pupils generalize, lessons are carefully sequenced, familiar examples are used to build comprehension, and plenty of practice allows pupils to apply what they have learned. Particular attention needs to be given to time-on-task for slow learners in the classroom, with concentrated attention to reading-related activities that are at an appropriate level of difficulty. Classroom management considerations include providing enough instructional time for reading, giving slow learners the extra attention they need, and involving them in a variety of instructional groups. (These topics are addressed in Chapter 3.)

Teaching Strategies

Although attention to vocabulary and decoding strategies is important, improving comprehension is the goal in teaching reading to the slow learner. A variety of techniques have proved effective in helping less-able readers improve their reading comprehension with the use of trade books.

Direct Instruction on Comprehension Components   Explicit instruction on essential elements is appropriate with a literature-based approach. By focusing directly and specifically on causal relationships in stories, Varnhagen and Goldman (1986) helped a group of extremely slow learners improve their ability to identify and understand the

Reading Recovery

READING RECOVERY is an early inter-vention program that is being used with young children who are experiencing reading problems. Designed by the New Zealand ed-ucator Marie M. Clay, the program aims to reach first graders who are having difficulty learning to read, in the hope that early inter-vention will help them succeed before they fall into a pattern of failure.

The program involves one-to-one lessons for 30 minutes each day. Pupils are selected based on teacher recommendation and a di-agnostic survey that measures the child's knowledge of letters and words, concepts about print, writing, and text reading. Al-though tutoring sessions differ according to the teacher and the needs of the child, each Reading Recovery lesson normally consists of:

1. *Reading familiar books.* The child reads trade books that he or she has enjoyed before. The teacher observes and assesses the child while reading these familiar stories.

2. *Assessing reading strategies.* The child reads a book that was new to him or her the previous day. The teacher keeps a running record of the child's reading behavior to determine the strategies that the child uses while reading.

3. *Writing messages and stories.* The child composes and writes a message, assisted as needed by the teacher. The teacher copies this message and uses it in various ways for instructional purposes. Time is also spent working with letters and teaching decoding strategies.

4. *Reading new books.* The teacher introduces the child to a new book that he or she will be expected to read the next day. Child and teacher discuss the book and set the stage for meaning before reading.

Reading Recovery is a literature-based reading program for problem readers in that trade books containing stories rather than a controlled vocabulary are used extensively in the instructional process. Reported results of the program have been extremely positive (Pinnell, Ford, and Lyons, 1988; Pinnell, Fried, and Estice, 1990).

A full description of the diagnostic and in-structional procedures involved in Reading Recovery are contained in *The Early Detec-tion of Reading Difficulties* by Marie M. Clay (1988).

---

relationship among ideas and events in text. This understanding was reinforced as pupils wrote stories with an emphasis on the relationship among episodes in stories. This focus could be extended to other components of comprehension as well.

Semantic Mapping Working with reading disabled pupils, some of whom were from special classes, Sinatra, Stahl-Gemake, and Berg (1984) found semantic mapping to be an effective means of improving reading comprehension. A semantic map is a graphic representation of the relationships among ideas or events in text (see pp. 141–142), and is a cognitive strategy that helps pupils comprehend what they read. Teachers can present maps before reading a text, or they can help pupils construct a map as they read a selection of narrative or expository text.

Focus on Metacognition Pogrow (1990) used a program called HOTS (Higher Order Thinking Skills) to help high-risk pupils improve reading comprehension. HOTS is based on the premise that a fundamental problem with at-risk pupils is that they do not understand ''understanding''; that is, they lack metacognitive strategies involved in linking new information with the knowledge they already have. Pogrow developed a program that focuses on higher-level thinking processes of consciously applying meta-cognitive strategies in problem solving, making inferences, generalizing ideas, and synthesizing information, instead of the traditional drill and practice that characterizes remedial instruction. The program uses questioning strategies extensively, engaging pupils in conversations that sound like Socratic dialogue. By modeling the problem-solving process through questioning and dialogue, teachers show pupils how to tackle concepts by building on what they already know. The HOTS program has produced very positive effects on the reading of high-risk pupils, leading to the conclusion that ''a thinking skills program can improve achievement as much as a good remedial approach—and probably a great deal more'' (Pogrow, 1990; p. 391).

Think Alouds   Davey (1983) has identified aspects of cognitive processing that good readers have and poor readers lack: making predictions, visualizing, building on prior knowledge, monitoring, and self-correction. She proposes that poor readers can acquire these competencies through modeling and practice, and she suggests ''Think-Alouds'' that help slow learners approach reading more strategically, systematically, and thoughtfully. The steps in the Think-Aloud Process are:

1. As pupils follow silently in a text, the teacher makes predictions, discusses visual impressions, comments on prior knowledge, and verbalizes the mental processes that the teacher uses while reading.
2. After modeling experiences, pupils read aloud in pairs, following the same procedures.
3. Pupils then move to independent practice and they integrate the Think-Aloud procedures into other classroom reading experiences.

Strategy Training   Hahn (1985) found that remedial readers benefited from instruction in strategic behavior in how to comprehend text better. Pupils were taught to use the following text strategies: ''(a) asking themselves questions while reading expository text, (b) practicing recall of these same texts, and (c) learning how to write text-based and reader-based questions'' (Hahn, 1985; p. 73). Metacognitive activities such as self-questioning and recall/review of what they read helped slow learners understand and remember more of what they read.

Reading to Younger Pupils   For pupils who are reading well below their peers in the regular classroom, reading a trade book that other pupils consider ''too easy'' or ''a baby book'' can be embarrassing. Making arrangements for pupils to read these books to pupils in the lower grades in a cross-grade cooperative activity provides a motivational dimension to learning.

Taped Books   Many trade books popular with pupils at a particular grade level will be above the reading level of slow learners in the class. These pupils can use the listening center to listen to tapes as they follow the text of books that other pupils in the class are reading. Following the lines of a story while listening to a tape produces

Cross grade tutoring—with older pupils reading to younger ones— has proved to be an effective technique for promoting literacy.

double benefits: it helps establish the speech–print connection of the text in the pupil's mind, and exposure to the book allows the pupil to engage in literature discussions and other reading-related activities.

The ideas suggested here—direct instruction, semantic mapping, metacognitive processing, Think-Alouds, strategic approaches to text, and others—are not intended for the slow learner alone. A literature-based reading program will address the needs of both good and poor readers. These techniques are sometimes overlooked, however, and they have proved effective in helping to improve the reading comprehension of the less able reader.

In reading instruction for slow learners, isolated skill development is often heavily emphasized, with dittoed worksheets and other materials that can discourage extensive reading. Poor readers need explicit instruction in reading strategies, but this instruction needs to be tied to authentic reading experiences rather than to practice exercises removed from the connected discourse of a good story. For slow learners, as for any reader, the purposeful application and integration of skills and strategies in reading for meaning are more important than the mastery of the skills themselves.

Literature for the Slow Learner

The integration and application of reading strategies come through reading trade books. Slow learners deserve to be exposed to literature just as all children do. With literature, less able pupils learn that reading can be a pleasure, not always a chore.

Gentile and McMillen (1990) identify some of the values of using literature to help at-risk pupils make sense out of print. Literature ''provides them with the means to apply skills contextually, using rich material that educates and entertains. Moreover, good literature is knowledge based and furnishes these students with a broad range of historical, geographical, political, scientific, mathematic, religious, biographical, and

The "Curious George" Strategy

RICHEK AND McTague (1988) suggest a literature-based remedial approach that they call "The Curious George Strategy for Students With Reading Problems." The strategy involves carefully planned, small-group reading lessons using trade books in series such as H. A. and Margaret Rey's mischievous monkey *Curious George,* Norman Bridwell's imaginative *Clifford* the big red dog, and Gene's Zion's engaging pooch *Harry.* (Since vocabulary and language patterns remain consistent, pupils find successive books in a series progressively easier to read.)

As a first step, the teacher introduces the book and reads it aloud. Pupils are invited to assist in the reading by providing predictable words. Word cards are made from the vocabulary in the story. This procedure is repeated with successive sections of each book that pupils enjoy until the book has been read. At that point, pupils dictate their own versions of

the story. This same strategy is carried out with successive books in the series.

Richek and McTage report that the technique generates enthusiasm and a willingness to read more independently. Other activities emerge from the strategy—sentence building with word cards, shared reading with pupil-initiated discussion, and a plethora of writing activities.

Beyond the observed excitement that the strategy generates among otherwise reluctant readers, statistical data supports the success of the program. In comparison with a control group, pupils in the *Curious George* group performed significantly better in tests of oral reading and comprehension. Informal observations of teachers and parents reaffirmed the success of the strategy.

With highly motivating books such as *Curious George,* remedial readers can read well above the level of their expected achievement.

---

literary information. It stirs wonderment and imagination, facilitates these students' understanding of themselves and others and the world in which they live, and offers them a sense of identity or control that can empower the spirit and motivate them to express their thoughts and feelings'' (Gentile and McMillen, 1990; p. 389). In short, literature has the same power for at-risk pupils as it does for other learners inside and outside of school.

Shumaker and Shumaker (1988) , in an article that describes how a project based on Eleanor Coerr's *Sadako and the Thousand Paper Cranes* brought a group of upper-grade remedial readers out of the academic shadows and into the spotlight, identify the advantages of using trade books as vehicles for reading instruction for slow learners. By reading *real* books, these pupils realize that reading and writing are not only school subjects but means of empowerment in the real world. Literature revitalizes and enhances the reading experience of slow learners, communicates acceptance and recognition of them as readers, and exposes great authors to pupils who might not otherwise encounter them. Children who are remedial readers in the upper elementary grades need literature most of all. "Literature offers neutral ground, free of classroom competition, grouping and grades. It emphasizes the worth of remedial activity. It . . . enhances the child's self concept and reduces the isolation of the struggling student. Finally, it has the look, sound, and rhythm of language as used by masters, unlike the artificial language constructs of workbooks and the anonymous voices of textbooks'' (Shumaker and Shumaker, 1988; pp. 547–548).

Instructional Story Plans

THE CHAPTER I teachers in New Bedford, Massachusetts, have developed Instructional Story Plans, guides that help teachers adapt quality literature to the instructional needs and levels of slow learners. For example, the Instructional Story Plan for Mary Ann Hobertman's delightful and popular *A House Is a House for Me* suggests ways of using the story to help pupils:

develop visual discrimination;

learn vocabulary related to shelters;

focus on a range of comprehension components;

share in the story through prediction and oral reading;

extend knowledge in the area of social studies; engage in a range of art activities related to the story.

And all of this is done within the context of preserving the element of enjoyment for pupils who do not read as well as their peers.

The purpose of these Instructional Story Plans, which have been developed for books from the very beginning stages of reading through the upper grades, is to provide a means of enabling below-average readers in Chapter I programs to enjoy literature while building essential reading and related competencies.

Instructional materials for poor readers need to be adjusted to the pupil's reading level; however, this adjustment often results in at-risk pupils' reading books obviously easier than books being read by classmates. The unfortunate consequence can be merciless comments such as ''Jack is reading baby books,'' or ''I read that book two years ago!'' To provide authentic reading experiences of lower-level materials in the regular classroom, the teacher can:

arrange to have upper grade pupils read easier books aloud to children in the lower grades;

use author groups, in which pupils read books by authors who have written books at different difficulty levels;

provide supplementary instructional support that will allow the less-able pupils to handle books a little above their expected levels;

plan whole-group and cooperative learning projects in which less-able readers are given meaningful assignments in line with their abilities.

In remedial settings such as Chapter I or resource rooms, easier trade books can be used with less risk of insensitive comments from peers, since all pupils are reading books at approximately the same level.

In the final analysis, slow learners profit from quality and innovative instruction just as all pupils do. And like all pupils, they deserve literature as part of that instruction. ''A literature-based approach . . . becomes a program of prevention rather than remediation. Even our low-ability readers benefit from an understanding of good literature'' (Routman, 1988; p. 18).

Pupils with Learning Disabilities

Another group of at-risk pupils includes those with learning disabilities.

Defining Learning Disabilities

The term *learning disability* is not easy to define. The expression was coined in the 1960s to describe pupils who had problems learning to read despite average or above-average intelligence, normal emotional development, and no sensory impairments. Different terms have been used to describe the condition (including *dyslexia, specific language disability, minimal brain damage, neurological impairment,* and literally scores of other expressions). Experts still use different definitions, depending on their psychological, educational, linguistic or medical orientations. The following definition is the ''legal'' one accepted and used in federal laws related to special education:

> ''Specific learning disability'' means a disorder in one or more of the basic psychological processes involved in understanding or in using language, spoken or written, which may manifest itself in an imperfect ability to listen, think, speak, read, write, spell, or to do mathematical calculations. The term includes such conditions as perceptual handicaps, brain injury, minimal brain dysfunction, dyslexia, and developmental aphasia. The term does not include children who have learning problems which are primarily the result of visual, hearing, or motor handicaps, of mental retardation, of emotional disturbance, or of environmental, cultural, or economic disadvantage. (U.S. Office of Education, Section 5[b]4)[1]

Concerned with the exclusionary nature of some definitions, a Joint Committee for Learning Disabilities, consisting of experts in various fields related to studying and educating children, formulated the following definition:

> Learning disability is a generic term that refers to a heterogenous group of disorders manifested by significant difficulties in the acquisition and use of listening, speaking, reading, writing, reasoning, or mathematical abilities. These disorders are intrinsic to the individual and presumed to be due to central nervous system dysfunction.
>
> Even though a learning disability may occur concomitantly with other handicapping conditions (e.g., sensory impairment, mental retardation, social and emotional disturbance), or with socioenvironmental influences (e.g., cultural differences, insufficient/inappropriate instruction, psychogenic factors), and especially attention deficit disorders, all of which may be causing learning problems, a learning disability is not the direct result of those conditions or influences. (Hammill et al., 1981)[2]

Although technical definitions vary, learning disabilities are generally thought to be neurologically based; that is, learning problems are related to problems in the child's central nervous system, causing otherwise capable pupils inordinate problems in learning to read and write. There is considerable debate about the incidence, the nature, and the best instructional techniques to use with learning disabled pupils (Coles, 1987),

---

[1]From U.S. Department of Education (1991). *13th Annual Report to Congress on the Implementation of the Education of the Handicapped Act.* Washington, D.C.

[2]D. D. Hamill, et at., ''A New Definition of Learning Disabilities'' in *Learning Disabilities Quarterly* 4:331–342, 1981. Reprinted with permission.

yet classroom reading teachers are left with the challenge of finding ways of providing reading instruction to pupils who experience difficulties for reasons that are not readily observable.

For many pupils, learning disabilities become manifest for the first time in the process of learning to read. Throughout the preschool years, the child's development may have been normal—sometimes even advanced—in every way. It is not until reading instruction begins that learning problems begin to emerge. In most dictionaries, in fact, the word *reading* is included in the definition of *dyslexia* (Savage, 1985).

Reading Programs for the Learning Disabled

Special reading programs have been developed for use with learning disabled pupils. Perhaps the most widely known of these programs is the Orton-Gillingham method, "a phonics approach to beginning reading (as well as being a remedial method), using a multisensory routine of visual, auditory, kinesthetic, and tactile exercises as children learn grapheme-phoneme relationships and blend letters and sounds into more complex wholes (words)" (Auckerman, 1984; p. 236). The technique involves learning symbol–sound combinations through a series of sounding, blending, tracing, and writing exercises. "The use of context to aid a child in word identification is *discouraged* . . . ; the purpose being to have the pupils rely upon their phonics instead of 'guessing' from contextual clues" (Auckerman, 1984; p. 239).

Like Orton-Gillingham, most programs that have been used extensively with learning disabled pupils emphasize the decoding aspects of learning to read. All tend to be highly structured, stress a sequential approach to phonics, and are typically carried out in clinical or tutorial settings outside the regular classroom.

In addressing the reading needs of the learning disabled pupil, teachers and specialists have examined various components of the cognitive and perceptual processes and directed instruction at these components. For example, diagnosticians examined learning modalities (whether the pupil learned better visually or auditorally) and mental functioning (whether there was a problem with remembering or sequencing information, for example). Instruction aimed at weak areas was provided in an attempt to strengthen reading competency. This diagnostic–prescriptive approach had merit, in that it allowed specialists to address very specific areas of learning.

There has been a move away from this approach to reading instruction for learning disabled pupils. Adams (1990) reviewed the research on "whether reading acquisition can be accelerated by training various nonlinguistic perceptual and motor skills such as spatial relations, visual memory, visual discrimination, visual–motor integration, gross and fine motor coordination, tactile–kinesthetic activities, auditory discrimination, and auditory-visual integration." Her conclusion: "Despite the energy invested in such endeavors, and despite the fact that many of the activities may be good for children in any number of ways, they seem not to produce any measurable pay-off in learning to read" (Adams, 1990; p. 61).

Besides, this diagnostic–prescriptive approach focusing on perceptual processing had the same effect as the conventional skills-based techniques of teaching reading; that is, discrete aspects of learning were addressed in an isolated manner that critics have called "an almost manic desire to fragment learning tasks, . . . a strong predilection for explaining reading and writing failure in terms of strange conditions with strange names: *Nigel suffers from dysphonetica because of psycho-neural malintegration and auditory short term memory deficits''* (Cambourne, 1985; p. 86).

Holistic Reading

More recently, there has been a tendency to approach reading instruction for learning disabled pupils in a more holistic manner. ''Contemporary approaches to teaching learning disabled students and remedial learners tend to focus directly on the academic area in which the student is having difficulty. Thus, if a student has reading difficulties, instruction focuses on working with sound/letter relationships, word recognition, and/or reading texts as opposed to teaching an underlying ability like perceptual skills'' (Rhodes and Dudley-Marling, 1988; p. 7). In approaching instruction for the learning disabled (and other pupils with reading problems), a four-step sequence is suggested:

1. *developing summary statements* based on specific observations of what the pupil does as a reader and a writer; for example, ''When Vladamir encounters an unfamiliar word, he relies exclusively on graphophonic cues to identify the word'' or ''Aphrodite's independent writing rarely exceeds one or two sentences.''

2. *developing learner objectives* based directly on pupils' observed needs, statements that reflect what the teacher hopes the pupil will accomplish; for example, ''Vladamir will begin to examine context clues in identifying words he does not recognize in print'' or ''Aphrodite will begin to produce longer independent writing passages.''

3. *developing teaching goals* that suggest specifically what the teacher will do to help pupils achieve these objectives; for example, ''The teacher will use cloze passages to introduce Vladamir to the use of context clues'' or ''In writing conferences, the teacher will encourage Aphrodite to elaborate on one idea in her writing.''

4. *conducting ongoing evaluation,* close monitoring and careful record-keeping that enables the teacher to reexamine and revise goals in light of pupils' daily reading and writing performance.

With this more holistic approach, the focus is directly on reading and writing rather than on an underlying perceptual disorder that influences literacy development. Explicit instruction on reading strategies is delivered, but it is done within the context of authentic stories rather than skills-based exercises.

As a group, learning disabled pupils need extra assistance in mastering basic decoding skills, and they will likely receive considerable help in this aspect of reading in resource rooms. In the classroom, the teacher needs to reinforce these skills and help the pupil to apply decoding strategies as one means of identifying unfamiliar words as part of reading authentic text. Word identification techniques that are presented for all pupils need to be aimed especially at, and constantly reinforced with, the learning disabled pupil, since fluent and automatic processing of words is necessary before comprehension is achieved.

To help pupils achieve comprehension, the same techniques that are effective for all learners can be used effectively with the learning disabled pupil. Although word

11.4 Putting Ideas to Work

Using Literature with Learning Disabled Pupils

HERE ARE some of the reflections/reactions from Carol J. Fuhler (1990), a junior high school teacher of learning disabled students:

> I teach a literature-based reading program to a group of learning-disabled boys who revel in the absence of worksheets and tests. Two of them showed a three-year growth in reading this year while another improved a year and a half. For students who used to dislike and distrust books, that's exciting.
>
> My students have taught me that daily reading, even for a mere 10 minutes, is a special time spent sharing a good book together.
>
> I believe that based on hearing a variety of stories read well, students are better able to build their own sense of story, to improve linguistic development, and eventually, to foster enthusiasm and a growing love of reading on their own.
>
> I have found that essential reading skills can be taught through a literature-based curriculum in a subtle, efficient manner within the context of the material each child is actively reading.

Excerpted from Carol J. Fuhler, "Let's Move Toward Literature-Based Reading Instruction" in *The Reading Teacher,* January 1990. Copyright © 1990 International Reading Association, Newark DE.

skills may need a more intense emphasis, the greater emphasis remains on the meaning-building process with direct teaching and application of comprehension strategies. Before reading a story, purposes are set, schemata are activated, and metacognitive awareness is set in motion with guided practice in such techniques as Think-Alouds and study procedures such as Herringbone outlines are used with learning disabled pupils just as they are with all pupils.

To help learning disabled (and other remedial) readers achieve fluency and learn to connect spoken language with its written equivalent, modeling techniques are often suggested. These include:

neurological impress, in which the teacher sits near the pupil and reads aloud while pointing to the part of the text being read. The pupil attempts to read along with the teacher as quickly and as accurately as possible. Over time, the teacher decreases speed and volume so that the student can gradually take the lead.

taped reading, in which a pupil reads along silently with a recorded text.

repeated reading, in which a pupil reads a passage aloud to the teacher, and is then given a tape recording of the passage to practice for fluency. This technique is recommended for pupils whose word recognition is appropriate to the level of the text being read.

In each of these procedures, literature is made a direct part of reading instruction of the learning disabled pupil. As in the case of reading instruction for slow learners, children's literature and trade books are essential. Resource room instruction has so often focused almost exclusively on skill-development materials that the joy of reading good stories is sometimes overlooked. But pupils who have trouble with learning to read deserve literature, too, and it has been shown that literature works to their advantage. A case could be made for using *more* literature with less-capable readers.

11.5 Putting Ideas to Work

Literature As Part of Language Therapy

SINCE READING is a language activity, speech and language problems can seriously impede the process of learning to read, and language therapy is frequently part of the instructional program for pupils with learning disabilities. Literature can be made an integral part of this instructional component. Here is an account from one speech-language pathologist.

> I utilize literature during language therapy sessions in lieu of traditional picture cards that depict action verbs, spatial relations, and story sequences. Individualized Educational Plans written for pupils with language delays or disorders typically contain goals and objectives aimed at improving their verb tense usage, their understanding of spatial relations, story sequence skills, pronoun usage and vocabulary development. Literature can be used to integrate and reinforce all of these skills and make instruction more motivating and memorable. The rhythm, rhyme, humor and repetition in a good children's story can capture a pupil's attention far better than a stack of picture cards monotonously flipped to produce a desired response. Besides, quality literature is rich with language and linguistic forms.

> Stories can be used in a variety of ways. Using a Big Book, for example, past tense verbs can be hidden using self-sticking memo sheets. As pupils hear the story retold, they supply the missing verbs. Correct responses are rewarded. This cloze procedure can be adapted to be used with auxiliary verbs, prepositional phrases, pronouns, and selected vocabulary items. Having pupils predict what happens next or asking them to explain what happened before an event in a story are effective scaffolding techniques aimed at strengthening storytelling or narrative discourse capabilities.

> Any book containing good language is a good book to use. I love books by Chris Van Allsberg—*The Stranger, Jumanji, The Garden of Abdul Gasazi, The Wreck of the Zephyr*. I also like poetry, books like John Prelutsky's *New Kid on the Block* and Shel Silverstein's *Where the Sidewalk Ends* and *Light in the Attic*. I've also used *Lon Po Po* by Ed Young and *What Do You Do with a Kangaroo?* by Mercer Mayer. In any quality children's book one can find language to work with.

> Reading is enjoyable! Apart from addressing specific language needs, literature in language therapy sessions can provide a motivating and pleasurable experience for both the pupils and the speech pathologist.
>
> Jacalyn R. Costello, CCC-SP
> Speech/Language Pathologist

While the nature and cause of the slow learner's problems may differ from those of the learning disabled pupil, the difficulties that they encounter in learning to read are often similar, and many of the instructional techniques suggested for classroom reading instruction are the same. Quality instruction will include an emphasis on building vocabulary, direct instruction in applying word-recognition strategies (along with intensive instruction in decoding skills), an explicit focus on comprehension, and the use of thinking skills as pupils learn to read through literature-based instruction.

Writing

Since a learning disability can influence writing as much as reading, learning disabled pupils need special attention. The handwriting of many dyslexic pupils can be virtually illegible. Spelling is a particular problem, where the order of letters is often reversed and familiar words are frequently misspelled. These spelling problems interfere with getting words and ideas on paper in an interesting, organized manner commensurate with the pupil's intellectual ability.

Adjustments can be made for written language activities in the classroom. Pupils can dictate into a tape recorder or directly to a scribe for fluency of stories. Typewriters and word processors can be used to alleviate problems of handwriting that is difficult to produce and even more difficult to interpret. Peer conferencing and team proof-reading can be cooperative learning experiences in preparing final drafts. The spell-checker that is part of so many word processing programs is an incredible convenience for the learning disabled pupil (and adult). In short, the learning disabled pupil needs every help possible in classroom writing activities.

Although slow learners and pupils with learning disabilities may not have the same disorder, the manifestation of their problems is often similar. In reviewing research related to reading, Kirk, Kliebhan, and Lerner intermingled research findings related to slow learners and learning disabled pupils because "the characteristics, learning patterns, and diagnostic and teaching procedures for these two groups of children overlap to a great extent. The research findings for one group have obvious implications for the other" (Kirk, Kliebhan, and Lerner, 1978; p. 198). Reading instructional strategies that work for slow learners will not be dramatically different for the learning disabled pupil in the regular classroom; literature serves both groups well.

Pupils with Sensory and Physical Problems

The senses are the pathways to the brain. Sight and sound are the two primary senses involved in reading, and pupils who have serious impediments in either of these sensory channels will experience difficulty in learning to read. Physical problems resulting from injury or from a congenital condition can also cause language-related or other problems that can interfere with the acquisition of literacy. Pupils with major problems in these areas will likely receive considerable support and instructional help outside the classroom, but many pupils with sensory and physical difficulties may be mainstreamed in the regular classroom, at least for part of the day.

Visual Problems

The sense of sight is essential in reading, since pupils need to see print before they can read it. Blind pupils learn to use an alternative sensory pathway to the brain—the sense of touch with Braille symbols—as a means of reading. Visually impaired pupils in the regular classroom use glasses to compensate for their lack of visual acuity.

Although the reading instructional program may not differ substantially for the visually impaired pupil, teachers need to be aware of accommodations that may need to be made for the pupil with problems in this area, accommodations such as:

advantageous seating so that the pupil can see Language Experience charts and other areas where print is displayed. A front row, center seat is usually suggested, although certain visual conditions might suggest another location. (Consultation with the resource teacher will be beneficial.)

encouraging the use of optical aids such as magnifiers or telescopic devices. The pupils themselves can explain how these devices work to curious classmates. Large-print books and other adjusted materials may be needed. (Again, the resource teacher can recommend and secure these materials.)

Technology enables visually impaired pupils to participate more fully in literature-based instruction in mainstream classrooms.

assigning a classmate to provide visual assistance; reading the subtitles on a filmstrip of a story, for example.

adjusting time for reading assignments.

using large-print books. Many popular children's trade books are available in large-print editions as well as in Braille.

Vision screening programs in the school identify some pupils with eye problems; many others "fall through the cracks." The classroom teacher, as the professional who sees the pupil day in and day out, needs to be on the lookout for symptoms that may indicate visual difficulties—squinting, constantly rubbing the eyes, holding the book at odd angles or at unusual distances, excessive blinking, or showing a preference for one eye. If a vision problem is even remotely suspected, appropriate referral is essential.

Auditory Problems

Hearing is another sensory pathway that is essential in learning to read. Most hearing-impaired pupils mainstreamed into regular classrooms will be equipped with hearing aids or other mechanical devices designed to enhance sound intake. But pupils sometimes arrive in the classroom with undiagnosed problems, and these problems become manifest in the process of learning to read. It is important for classroom teachers to refer pupils quickly for appropriate testing once problems are suspected.

As in the case of visually impaired pupils, classroom accommodations need to be made for the hard-of-hearing pupil in the regular classroom, accommodations such as:

making sure that directions are given clearly and loudly enough to be heard and arranging a "buddy" to provide help as necessary.

11.6
FOR YOUR INFORMATION
Books about Children with Sensory and Physical Handicaps

A NUMBER of trade books in which handicapped children are major characters in the story are available for use in the classroom. A small sampling of these books includes:

Ada B. Litchfield, *A Cane in Her Hand,* the story about how a visually impaired child adjusts to her problem of being different.
Bill Martin, Jr., and John Archambault, *Knots on a Counting Rope,* the story of a blind American Indian child, told in an interesting narrative style.
Edith Fisher Hunter, *Child of the Silent Night,* a simply written, moving biography of Laura Bridgeman, a child whose illness left her both blind and deaf.
Ivan Southall, *Let the Balloon Go,* an Australian book about a boy with cerebral palsy and the reluctance of his mother to let him experiment with his own capabilities.
Eleanor Spense, *October Child,* a courageous story that reveals the effects of an autistic child on his family.

Patricia MacLachlan, *Through Grandpa's Eyes,* which tells how a young boy sees the world around him much differently through his grandfather's blindness.
Theodore Taylor, *The Cay,* a survival tale of a boy who learns to use his other senses when he loses the ability to see.

These are not just books about exceptional children; they are compelling stories that happen to center on children with handicaps. Betsy Byars did not win the coveted Newbery Award for her *Summer of the Swans* because the book was about a girl's relationship with her severely retarded brother; she won the award because of the quality of the book as a piece of children's literature.

Portraying the Disabled: A Guide to Juvenile Fiction by Debra Robertson and *Portraying the Disabled: A Guide to Juvenile Non-Fiction* by Joan Brest Friedberg et al. are two annotated bibliographies that list books about individuals with special needs.

looking directly at the pupil when giving directions.

making sure that amplification devices such as hearing aids (when prescribed) are used and encouraging the use of headphones and cassettes as needed.

providing visual reinforcement for vocabulary words, directions, and other instructional components.

Hearing-impaired pupils especially profit from the natural language found in good literature as part of reading instruction. McCoy and Prehm (1987) question the use of contrived language often found in basal readers as the most effective tools for teaching pupils who are hard of hearing. These authors suggest that appropriate language levels and reasonable phonetic emphasis are the cornerstones of a suitable reading program. Vocabulary development with semantic mapping, the use of contextual analysis, effective word attack, and monitoring of comprehension are all suggested as effective techniques as well.

As in the case of the visually impaired pupil, the classroom teacher should be alert to hearing loss that some pupils may develop. A runny nose, draining ears, mouth breathing, and the general look of an unwell child may be symptoms that hearing may be (or may become) a problem.

Physical Handicaps

Pupils with physical handicaps and other health-related problems are also mainstreamed into the regular classroom. These problems interfere to various degrees with the learning-to-read process. Some health problems may cause chronic absenteeism

Shared Stories for Handicapped Learners

BLYDEN (1988) cites the advantages of sharing stories with multihandicapped learners and suggests procedures for using literature with pupils in multihandicapped classrooms. Through shared stories, literature becomes the base to improve receptive language competency, and reading is a pleasurable experience.

Blyden recommends the use of Big Books, with one teacher reading while the other signs for hearing-impaired pupils. Wheelchairs are arranged in a semicircle and ambulatory pupils are seated on chairs or mats. Pupils are encouraged to participate through gestures, language, questions, and discussion. Follow-up activities can be planned, just as with more typical pupils, in light of pupils' abilities and needs.

Story hours for multihandicapped pupils exemplify principles and practices of the total communication strategy necessary with these pupils, and shared literature promotes socialization along with the joys of language.

---

and fatigue that make learning to read difficult; other physical factors may have nothing directly to do with reading; for example, limitation in lower limb involvement does not normally cause a direct impediment in learning to read.

Even when physical disabilities keep the pupil from full participation in the school setting, classroom teachers can play a role by providing suggestions to parents and nursing staffs, both to promote reading development during convalescence and to establish a vehicle for emotional expression during recovery (Schuman and Fitzsimons, 1990). Careful record keeping is also important for pupils whose health-related absenteeism is a chronic problem.

Working in conjunction with the resource specialist, the classroom teacher can make accommodations for physically challenged pupils. Adjustments need to be made in light of pupils' needs. For example:

pupils with severe motor problems may need wheelchairs, special typewriters, separate desks or workspaces, or other adaptive equipment.

pupils whose neuromuscular problems make speech production difficult need a system of nonverbal communication.

pupils with motor coordination problems may need some sort of physical support for holding books.

Obviously, related factors such as emotional problems, cognitive deficits, or learning disabilities also need to be taken into account while working with pupils with sensory or orthopedic handicaps. The teacher needs to look beyond the more obvious handicap to discover other impediments that the pupil might have in learning to read.

The classroom teacher and the specialist need to work together in selecting literature and in identifying strategies and arrangements for what works best in light of the pupil's reading needs. Technical advancement in computers and other communications devices holds enormous promise for equipment that will facilitate the learning of the physically disabled pupil. But as these advances are being made, teachers need patience, sensitivity to the frustration that the pupil so often feels, willingness to give

Through cooperative learning activities, mainstreamed pupils can be an integral part of literature-based reading and writing instruction.

pupils time to produce a response, and a knack for using what works to promote the pupil's learning.

Beyond instructional adjustments and classroom accommodations for reading, it is important that handicapped pupils be accepted and treated as part of the regular class. This means including pupils in all activities, applying the same rules for appropriate behavior, integrating them into the social life of the classroom, and encouraging independence. Teachers need to be sensitive to the fact that some children with handicaps prefer to be inconspicuous so as not to appear different at an age when conformity is important, and many nonhandicapped pupils shy away from those who are disabled. Teachers need to apply a measure of support and TLC in making the handicapped pupil as much a part of the life of the classroom as possible. Full participation is the goal.

Pupils with Attitude and Behavior Problems

No learning is ever devoid of emotion. Attitude and behavior, the emotional or affective dimensions of learning, can directly influence the process of learning to read. Pupils' self-concepts, the relationships they maintain with others, the attitudes they bring to school, and the process of learning to read will have a strong impact on their learning experiences.

Trying to determine how emotional problems and reading problems are related is analogous to asking the question ''Which came first, the chicken or the egg?'' On the one hand, fear or a low self-image will lead to problems in learning to read. At the same time, failure causes frustration, embarrassment, hostility, and a range of emotions that are marks of personality problems. Success breeds confidence, which leads to continuing success in reading. No matter which is cause and which is effect, attitude and learning to read are inseparable.

11.8 Putting Ideas to Work

Literature-Based Reading for Emotionally Handicapped Pupils

D'ALISSANDRO (1990) describes how she initiated a literature-based reading program in a self-contained classroom of emotionally handicapped pupils, many of whom had other disabilities that compounded their learning to read. As an alternative to the conventional basal reading and language experience approaches, the teacher focused her reading program on novels that accommodated pupils' varying reading levels, books such as Aesop's *Country Mouse–City Mouse,* Judy Blume's popular *Tales of a Fourth Grade Nothing,* E. B. White's classic *Charlotte's Web.*

Pupils sat in groups for 40 minutes. All—including the teacher—read aloud. The story became the focus of discussion, additional reading, and other related activities for concept building.

Results were extremely positive. Pupils' word identification improved significantly, even though very little time was spent in direct instruction on word attack. Standardized test scores rose. Interests and attitudes improved demonstrably. Pupils gained in their ability to sustain interest and maintain comprehension while reading. But for these pupils with emotional problems, "the full integration of the program takes place when the experiences gained from the readings are attached to personal experiences and become meaningful insights" (D'Alissandro, 1990; p. 292).

The program was a success, and the success was long-lasting.

Teaching Techniques

Instructional techniques suggested for pupils with problems in attitude and behavior often relate more to behavior management strategies than to strategies for processing print. These include:

using Language Experience activities (often based on stories that teachers read aloud) as vehicles for reading acquisition;

using the lyrics of popular songs or the scripts of television shows as motivational devices;

employing a behavior modification program that involves structured techniques that identify acceptable behaviors, define conditions for learning, and reward success;

contracting, with a pupil–teacher agreement for the completion of reading-related tasks;

making charts that document progress or record short-term growth in learning or behavior patterns;

role playing to help pupils discover how their behavior affects others;

adjusting assignments to accommodate for the shorter-than-normal attention spans of some pupils.

In short, quality reading instruction must be delivered in a way that will provide plenty of successful learning experiences and encouragement to reinforce both learning and behavior. A reading technique that has proved successful with pupils with attitude and behavior problems is bibliotherapy.

Bibliotherapy

Books often contribute to more than the academic development of emotionally troubled pupils; books can contribute to their personal and emotional development as well. Skilled teachers often use trade books to help pupils deal with some of their own personal problems. This process is known as bibliotherapy.

Bibliotherapy is the dynamic interaction between a person and a piece of literature, an interaction through which the person satisfies emotional needs or finds solutions to personal problems in stories. Bibliotherapy is a means of helping pupils work through some of their personal, social, and affective problems through literature.

The three steps in the process of using books to help identify and deal with personal problems include:

1. universalization and identification, as pupils discover that they are not the only ones with a particular problem;

2. catharsis, as pupils identify with the characters and share their feelings; and

3. insight, when pupils become aware of the motivation and behavior of story characters, and develop a realistic view of themselves and their problems.

Through bibliotherapy, pupils can see book characters with problems similar to their own. By identifying with the problems of these characters, pupils may develop insights into their own problems. They may see how book characters cope with problems and relate the solutions to their own lives. The insights pupils develop into how characters solve problems in stories are often transferred to the reality of their own worlds. Pupils thus develop heightened knowledge of themselves and insights into their own behaviors. A child from a special class, for example, frightened other pupils away with his overly aggressive behavior on the playground. When his teacher read Margaret Howell's *The Lonely Dragon,* the story of a friendly dragon who frightened children away because he breathed smoke and fire when he became excited, the child began to realize the effect that his own excited behavior was having on others.

Over the years, it has been shown that books shape pupils' attitudes and influence their behavior (Kimmel, 1970; Sullivan, 1987; Shumaker and Shumaker, 1988). Bibliotherapy can be a successful dimension of reading instruction for pupils with emotional problems.

Although bibliotherapy is an attempt to promote emotional health through literature, books do not stand alone in helping pupils find solutions to problems through reading. Bibliotherapy requires the careful guidance of teachers in story selection and in interpretation through follow-up questions and discussions, retelling and role playing, writing and art projects that will highlight and reinforce the positive therapeutic effects of a book.

Gifted and Talented Pupils

Atypical pupils who add another dimension to classroom reading programs are the gifted and talented. Who are the gifted and talented?

11.9
FOR YOUR INFORMATION
Children's Books on "Tender Topics"

AUTHORS OF books for children and young adults often deal with sensitive issues in their writing. Such tender topics as death, divorce, or family problems are addressed in skillful and insightful ways. Here is a small sampling of books that deal with some of these issues:

Death
Judith Viorst, *The Tenth Good Thing about Barney,* a picture book that deals sensitively with a child's grief about the death of a pet.

Jane Rush Thomas, *Saying Good-bye to Grandma,* a story about a seven-year-old who attends her grandmother's funeral and comes to grips with many of the associations of death.

Doris Buchanan Smith, *A Taste of Blackberries,* a story about the shock and grief of a boy who witnesses the accidental death of his best friend.

Katherine Patterson, *Bridge to Terrabithia,* the moving story of a young boy who has to deal with the death of his best friend.

Mary Kate Jordan, *Losing Uncle Tim,* a story about the death of an uncle from AIDS.

Realignment of Family Structures
Beverly Cleary, *Dear Mr. Henshaw,* a boy's insightful reflection of some of the emotions of going through a divorce.

Betsy Byars, *The Animal, the Vegetable, and John D. Jones,* the story of two sisters who have to share their annual vacation with their father with his new girlfriend and her son.

Barbara Williams, *Mitzi's Honeymoon with Nana Potts,* an amusing account of a girl who is sent to stay with her new stepfather's mother while her own mother goes on a honeymoon.

Patricia MacLachan, *Journey,* a poignant story in which a mother leaves her son and daughter at their grandparents' house and the family has to deal with the issue of abandonment.

Abuse
Jeanette Caines, *Chilly Stomach,* a simply written story about a child's reaction to an overly friendly uncle.

Linda Barr, *I Won't Let Them Hurt You,* the story of a babysitter who learns that the child in her care is being physically abused.

Betsy Byars, *The Pinballs,* in which three foster children learn that they can take control of their own lives.

Homelessness
Eve Bunting, *Fly Away Home,* a touching story of a boy and his father who live in an airport because "the airport is better than the streets."

Karen Ackerman, *The Leaves in October,* a portrayal of how children learn to grow up quickly in a homeless shelter.

Vicki Grove, *Fastest Friend in the West,* an upper-grade book in which friendship leads to insights into the problems of homelessness.

Jerry Spinelli, *Maniac MacGee,* an upper-level book about an adolescent who uses his unique talents to overcome the problems of living on his own.

These books are sometimes troubling for adults, since they can contain strong stuff about the often painful life experiences involved in growing up. With careful guidance, many of these books can, nevertheless, allow pupils to encounter characters with problems similar to their own and the way in which these problems might be faced.

The above titles are only a fraction of books that might be used for the purpose of bibliotherapy. For additional titles, annotated by problem areas, check the American Guidance Council's *The Bookfinder.*

Defining Gifted and Talented

The traditional standard for designating a pupil as gifted was the score on an IQ test; however, giftedness and academic talent extend beyond the single criterion of cognitive ability and into the area of creativity.

Not all gifted learners are the same, but they share certain characteristics that influence their literacy development. They learn quickly. They consistently read above grade level. Many enter school already able to read and they continue to make rapid progress in reading. They are usually very interested in reading and writing. They have larger-than-average vocabularies, owing largely to their wider-than-average reading. They have good recall of what they read. They are quick to understand relationships, facile with abstract concepts, and creative in making jumps in abstract thinking and problem solving. They have the gifts of higher intellectual ability and academic aptitude.

Like all children, gifted pupils come in all shapes and sizes. Not all excel in reading. Some may be talented in athletic ability, gifted as artists, or brilliant in mathematics. But those who have above-average talent in factors related to reading and writing are the ones of concern in this chapter.

Often, gifted pupils in the regular classroom are given larger amounts of work rather than more challenging and enriching assignments. ("Now that you've learned the names of all the U.S presidents, memorize the names of their vice presidents.") More is not necessarily better, however. A curriculum for the gifted and talented is expected to offer something other than the normal fare. These pupils need some different kinds of reading experiences consistent with their abilities.

Challenging Reading

Because gifted and talented pupils do not demand the same type of attention as learning disabled or behaviorally disordered pupils, they often get lost in the larger educational landscape. Classroom programs that stress enrichment and acceleration can be designed to meet the needs of these atypical pupils in the regular classroom. *Books for the Gifted Child* by Paula Hauser and Gail A. Nelson is a two-volume bibliographic reference of fiction and nonfiction titles that have been identified as particularly appropriate for talented pupils. Using quality literature, the teacher can plan such activities as:

deep reading in areas of interest from different sources; for example, reading not only biographies of famous people but books about their times in history;

focusing on the author's craft, looking at how authors achieve their intended purposes;

problem solving, exploring two or three different versions of the same story, or reading to find answers to questions consistent with their own needs, purposes, and interests;

inquiry reading, long-term reading projects in which pupils select their own topics, do extensive reading and research, and communicate their findings to others (Cassidy, 1981);

Junior Great Books (described on page 196), a program that enriches the reading diet and promotes discussion and critical thinking on which many gifted pupils thrive;

writing, with stories, poems, and responses to literature that show elaboration of ideas and depth of critical and creative reaction;

In short, gifted and talented pupils in the regular classroom should be given freedom to expand beyond the bounds of narrow curriculum requirements and engage in reading and writing activities that encourage exploration and invention.

Literature is an especially important part of reading for gifted and talented pupils. A literature-based program provides breadth and depth of stories needed to challenge the ability of exceptionally bright and creative pupils. Trade books offer an attractive alternative to more routine instructional materials and allow these pupils to explore worlds of fantasy and reality consistent with their abilities

Certain notable prodigies notwithstanding, pupils who are remarkably gifted in factors related to reading are often no different from their agemates in their physical, social, and emotional development. Thus, young pupils who may be capable of reading a story several years above grade placement may not possess the schemata or enjoy the social maturity that would allow them to comprehend or appreciate the story at a level that the teacher might expect.

As in any learning situation, the teacher is the key in planning reading programs for gifted and talented pupils in the regular classroom. What Nelson and Cleland wrote more than 20 years ago is no less true today: "It is the teacher who sets the environment which inspires or destroys self-confidence, encourages or suppresses interests, develops or neglects abilities, fosters or banishes creativity, stimulates or discourages critical thinking, and facilitates or frustrates achievement" (Nelson and Cleland, 1971; p. 47). And these words will remain true as long as there are teachers and pupils in schools.

The Teacher on the Team

Atypical learners usually receive help and support services outside the regular classroom. Special services available in many schools include:

remedial reading instruction, intensive programs for pupils who are reading below grade level or expected achievement level;

Chapter I programs, federally funded programs for extra services, including reading and language instruction and greater parent involvement;

resource room programs where special teachers and tutors provide programs for pupils who have been diagnosed as learning disabled;

speech and language therapy for pupils with articulation problems and other language difficulties;

guidance and counseling for pupils who need special service in the affective dimensions of learning and life;

special programs for gifted or talented learners that offer resources and challenge that these pupils might not experience in the classroom.

Sometimes the specialist involved in providing supplementary instruction is "mainstreamed" to work with the atypical learner within the classroom. But most often, these services are provided through "pull-out" programs offered outside the regular classroom. With all the coming and going in the regular classroom, however, it is important that pupils who need extra help not miss regularly scheduled reading instruction. And it is vital that these pupils not miss recess, art, or other activities that they especially enjoy.

Beyond issues of scheduling, special services provided for atypical learners make the classroom teacher part of a professional team providing reading instruction. The teacher shares responsibility with other professionals so that individual learning needs can be met more fully. In reality, however, "a common pattern in the public schools is that one or two 'specialists,' usually including a school psychologist, see the child briefly, hold a meeting at which the child's teacher says little, and produce a report" (Bateman, 1992; p. 33).

As a member of a multidisciplinary team, the regular classroom teacher must become a full participant in the decision-making process. This means not being intimidated by the extra credentials or areas of expertise that many learning specialists have. It means having a loud voice in planning the reading instruction of the pupil. It means involvement in preparing the Individual Educational Plan mandated by PL 94–142, since implementation of much of the plan will be accomplished in the classroom. It means being a champion who will speak and act on behalf of the pupil.

In making maximum use of available services, communication and coordination are crucial. Classroom teachers need to be aware of what services the pupil is receiving in special programs and how these services can be extended and reinforced through their own classroom instruction. Based on their observation of atypical learners in classroom settings, they need to suggest leads for specialists to follow in out-of-class instruction. This two-way communication is absolutely vital to the reading instruction of the atypical learner.

In many ways, classroom teachers are the stars of interdisciplinary teams, since they are the central force in the education of the child. While successful performance in the one-to-one setting of a special program can be important, the ultimate payoff comes when the pupil succeeds in the classroom. This is why teachers need to assume a central role in planning reading instruction for the atypical learner.

Summary and Conclusions

Helping all pupils achieve their full potential is a major aim of education in any society. Achieving this goal in the face of the diverse needs and characteristics of pupils in the classroom is a challenge that all teachers face.

Most pupils acquire the ability to read and write with a routine of normal instruction. For others, achieving literacy is more difficult. Educators have many names for this latter group—remedial readers, learning disabled pupils, slow learners, underachievers, dyslexics, handicapped learners, and the more generic term *at risk*. What schools do not have is an easy solution to the problems that these atypical pupils encounter in acquiring literacy competency.

An essential beginning to meeting the needs of the atypical learner is to see the pupil first as a learner and not primarily as atypical. The next step is to provide quality instruction—instruction that involves selecting appropriate trade books and other instructional materials, building language, developing schemata, setting purposes, making pupils aware of their own active involvement in the reading process, extending reading into the many facets of their school and out-of-school lives, saturating instruction with literature; in short, doing well what we already know how to do. "America will become a nation of readers when verified practices of the best teachers in the best schools can be introduced throughout the country" (Anderson et al., 1985; p. 120).

The final step in meeting the reading instructional needs of all pupils is making adjustments in light of pupils' unique learning needs—adjusting the level and pace of instruction for pupils who learn more slowly, adapting presentations for pupils who have difficulty processing information, building a backlog of successful experiences with appropriate materials in an attempt to turn around negative attitudes and behaviors, making adjustments in light of the physical disabilities of handicapped pupils, allowing gifted pupils the freedom and flexibility to develop to their full potential. In these efforts, the classroom teacher can expect the direct assistance and support of other professionals who work with atypical learners.

A Massachusetts law providing for special education for all children is based on the premise that:

(a) all children are normal,
(b) all children are different,
(c) the differences in children are normal. (Audette, 1974)

Taking these normal differences into account is what makes teaching reading a fine art and a precise science.

Discussion Questions and Activities

1. From the special education section of the library, read a reference on one of the areas of exceptionality contained in this chapter—slow learners, learning disabled, emotionally disturbed, physically handicapped, or gifted and talented pupils. How are the areas described in the reference? What implications are suggested for teaching reading?
2. What do you think are the advantages and disadvantages of having specialists work with atypical pupils in the classroom versus removing these pupils for special services?
3. Based on research, identify specific characteristics of pupils with learning and behavior problems. Describe how these characteristics affect learning to read and write.
4. Someone has suggested that classroom teachers should "get out of the light" of gifted and talented pupils and let them develop to their maximum potential on their own. What do you think of this idea? What are ways that teachers can promote this maximum development in the classroom?
5. Based on the content of this chapter, your own school experiences, and other sources you may have consulted, make a list of DOs and DON'Ts of teaching reading to slow learners, special-needs children, or gifted pupils. Compare your list to lists that other students might have made and make a class "master list" of suggestions.

School-Based Assignments

1. In your field-based setting, identify a pupil who might be termed atypical in the classroom. Observe the pupil during reading instruction. What types of adjustments or accommodations are made in light of his or her needs? What other adaptations would you recommend on the basis of what you observe?

2. Interview (and if possible, observe) a special-needs or resource-room teacher in your school. How much reading instruction does this teacher provide to pupils referred for special services? How much is literature used as part of this instruction? What type of communication or coordination takes place between the specialist and the classroom teachers?

3. Find a book on one of the "Tender Topics" identified in 11.9. Share the book with a group of pupils. Note their reactions and responses to the story.

4. Interview two or three pupils with reading problems in your school. What are their perceptions of reading? How do they feel about going to remedial reading or other instructional settings? Based on what you find out, what recommendations would you make to the teacher or principal?

5. Based on what you have read and what you see in schools, what are the three most challenging problems you anticipate in teaching reading to atypical learners in the classroom? How can you prepare yourself to meet these challenges?

Children's Trade Books Cited in This Chapter

Ackerman, Karen. *The Leaves in October*. New York: Atheneum. 1991.

Aesop. *City Mouse–Country Mouse and Two More Mouse Tales*. New York: Scholastic, 1970.

Barr, Linda. *I Won't Let Them Hurt You*. Worthington, OH: Willowisp Press, 1988.

Blume, Judy. *Tales of a Fourth Grade Nothing*. New York: Dell, 1972.

Bunting, Eve. *Fly Away Home*. New York: Clarion, 1991.

Byars, Betsy. *The Animal, the Vegetable, and John D. Jones*. New York: Dell, 1983.

———. *The Pinballs*. New York: Harper and Row, 1977.

———. *Summer of the Swans*. New York: Viking, 1970.

Caines, Jeanette. *Chilly Stomach*. New York: Harper and Row, 1986.

Cleary, Beverly. *Dear Mr. Henshaw*. New York: Morrow, 1983.

Grove, Vicki. *The Fastest Friend in the West*. New York: Putnam, 1991.

Hoberman, Mary Ann. *A House Is a House for Me*. New York: Penguin, 1982.

Howell, Margaret. *The Lonely Dragon*. London: Longman, 1972.

Hunter, Edith Fisher. *Child of the Silent Night*. New York: Dell, 1963.

Jordan, Mary Kate. *Losing Uncle Tim*. Morton Grove, IL: Albert Whitman, 1989.

Litchfield, Ada B. *A Cane in Her Hand*. Morton Grove, IL: Albert Whitman, 1977.

MacLachlan, Patricia. *Journey*. New York: Delacorte, 1991.

Martin, Bill, Jr., and Archambault, John. *Knots on a Counting Rope*. New York: Henry Holt, 1987.

Mayer, Mercer. *What Do You Do with a Kangaroo?* New York: Scholastic, 1987.

Patterson, Katherine. *Bridge to Terabithia*. New York: Avon, 1977.

Silverstein, Shel. *Light in the Attic*. New York: Harper and Row 1981.

———. *Where the Sidewalk Ends*. New York: Harper and Row, 1974.

Smith, Doris Buchanan. *A Taste of Blackberries*. New York: Crowell, 1973.

Southall, Ivan. *Let the Balloon Go*. New York: Bradbury Press, 1968.

Spence, Eleanor. *October Child*. London: Oxford University Press, 1976.

Spinelli, Jerry. *Maniac Magee*. Boston: Little Brown, 1990.

Taylor, Theodore. *The Cay*. New York: Doubleday, 1989.

Thomas, Jane Resh. *Saying Good-Bye to Grandma*. New York: Houghton Mifflin, 1988.

Van Allsburg, Chris. *The Garden of Abdul Gasazi.*
Boston: Houghton Mifflin, 1979.
———. *Jumanji.* Boston: Houghton Mifflin, 1981.
———. *The Stranger.* Boston: Houghton Mifflin,
1986.
———. *The Wreck of the Zephyr.* Boston: Houghton
Mifflin, 1983.

Viorst, Judith. *The Tenth Good Thing about Barney.*
New York: Macmillan, 1971.
White, E. B. *Charlotte's Web.* New York: Harper and
Row, 1952.
Williams, Barbara. *Mitzi's Honeymoon with Nana
Potts.* New York: Dell, 1983.

References

Adams, M. J. (1990). *Beginning to Read: Thinking
and Learning about Print.* Cambridge, MA:
MIT Press.

Anderson, R. C., Hiebert, E. H., Scott, J. A., and
Wilkinson, I. A. G. (1985). *Becoming a Nation
of Readers: Report of the Commission on
Reading.* Washington, DC: National Institute of
Education.

Auckerman, R. C. (1984). *Approaches to Beginning
Reading.* 2nd ed. New York: John Wiley &
Sons.

Audette, R. (1974). Concept Paper. In *Core
Evaluation Manual.* Bedford, MA: Institute for
Educational Services.

Bateman, B. (1992). Learning Disabilities: The
Changing Landscape. *Journal of Learning
Disabilities* 25:29–36.

Blyden, A. E. (1988). Shared Story Reading for
Severely Handicapped Learners. *Reading
Improvement* 25:67–70.

Cambourne, B. (1985). Change and Conflict in
Literacy Education: What It's All About.
Australian Journal of Reading 8:77–88.

Cassidy, J. (1981). Inquiry Reading for the Gifted. *The
Reading Teacher* 35:17–21.

Clay, M. M. (1988). *The Early Detection of Reading
Difficulties.* Portsmouth, NH: Hienemann.

Coles, G. (1987). *The Learning Mystique: A Critical
Look at "Learning Disabilities."* New York:
Pantheon Books.

Davey, B. (1983). Think-Aloud—Modelling the
Cognitive Processes of Reading Comprehension.
Journal of Reading 27:44–47.

Friedberg, J. B. (1992). *Portraying the Disabled: A
Guide to Non-fiction.* New Providence, NJ:
Bowker.

Fuhler, C. J. (1990). Let's Move toward Literature-
Based Reading Instruction. *The Reading
Teacher* 43:312–316.

Gentile, L. M., and McMillan, M. M. (1990). Literacy
through Literature: Motivating At-Risk Students
to Read and Write. *Journal of Reading, Writing,
and Learning Disabilities* 6:383–393.

Hahn, A. L. (1985). Teaching Remedial Students to Be
Strategic Readers and Better Comprehenders.
The Reading Teacher 39:72–77.

Hammill, D. D., Leigh, J. L., McNeill, G., and Larson,
S. C. (1981). A New Definition of Learning
Disabilities. *Learning Disability Quarterly*
4:336–42.

Hauser, P., and Nelson, G. (1988). *Books for the
Gifted Child.* New Providence, NJ: Bowker.

Kimmel, E. (1970). Can Children's Books Change
Children's Values? *Educational Leadership*
28:209–211.

Kirk, S. A., Kliebhan, J. M., and Lerner, J. W. (1978).
*Teaching Reading to Slow and Disabled
Learners.* Boston: Houghton Mifflin.

McCoy, K. M., and Prehm, H. J. (1987). *Teaching
Mainstreamed Students: Methods and
Techniques.* Denver: Love Publishing.

Nelson, J. B., and Cleland, D. L. (1971). The Role of
the Teacher of Gifted and Creative Children. In
P. A. Witty (ed.), *Reading for the Gifted and the
Creative Student.* Newark, DE: International
Reading Association.

O'Sullivan, P. J., Ysseldyke, J. E., Christenson, S. L.,
and Thurlow, M. L. (1990). Mildly Handicapped
Elementary Students' Opportunities to Learn
During Reading Instruction in Mainstreamed
and Special Education Settings. *Reading
Research Quarterly* 25:131–146.

Pinnell, G. S., DeFord, D. E., and Lyons, C. A. (1988).
*Reading Recovery: Early Intervention for At-
Risk First Graders.* Arlington, VA: Educational
Research Service.

Pinnell, G. S., Fried, M. D., and Estice, R. M. (1990).
Reading Recovery: Learning How to Make a
Difference. *The Reading Teacher* 43:282–295.

Pogrow, S. (1990). The Effects of Intellectually Challenging At-Risk Elementary Students: Findings from the HOTS Program. *Phi Delta Kappan* 71:389–397.

Rhodes, L. K., and Dudley-Marling, C. (1988). *Readers and Writers with a Difference: A Holistic Approach to Teaching Learning Disabled and Remedial Students.* Portsmouth, NH: Heinemann.

Richek, M. A., and McTague, B. K. (1988). The ''Curious George'' Strategy for Students with Reading Problems. *The Reading Teacher* 42:220–226.

Robertson, D. (1991). *Portraying the Disabled: A Guide to Juvenile Fiction.* New Providence, NJ: Bowker.

Routman, R. (1988). *Transitions: From Literature to Literacy.* Portsmouth, NH: Heinemann.

Savage, J. F. (1985). *Dyslexia: Understanding Reading Problems.* New York: Julian Messner.

Savage, J. F., and Mooney, J. F. (1979). *Teaching Reading to Children with Special Needs.* Boston: Allyn and Bacon.

Schuman, D. R., and Fitzsimons, V. M. (1990). Reading As an Intervention for the Orthopedic Convalescent Child. *New England Reading Association Journal* 26:2–8.

Schumaker, M. P., and Schumaker, R. C. (1988). 3,000 Paper Cranes: Children's Literature for Remedial Readers. *The Reading Teacher* 46:544–548.

Sinatra, R. C., Stahl-Gemake, J., and Berg, D. N. (1984). Improving Reading Comprehension of Disabled Readers Through Semantic Mapping. *The Reading Teacher* 38:22–29.

Sullivan, J. (1987). Read-Aloud Sessions: Tackling Sensitive Issues through Literature. *The Reading Teacher* 41:874–878.

U.S. Department of Education (1991). Report to the 13th Congress on the Implementation of the Education of the Handicapped Act. Washington, DC: U.S. Department of Education.

Varnhagen, C. K., and Goldman, S. R. (1986). Improving Comprehension: Causal Relations Instruction for Learning Handicapped Learners. *The Reading Teacher* 39:896–904.

Chapter 12

Using Multicultural Literature: Working with Diverse Learners

Chapter 12 Outline

I. Introduction
II. Cultural Dimensions of Literacy
   A. Values of Multicultural Literature in the Classroom
   B. Types of Multicultural Trade Books
      1. Picture Books
      2. Folktales and Traditional Literature
      3. Realistic Fiction
      4. Biographies and Informational Books
      5. Poetry
III. Dialect Speakers
   A. Regional Dialect
   B. Social Dialect
   C. Standard English
   D. Black English
IV. Pupils Whose First Language Is Not English
   A. Language Instruction
   B. Reading Instruction
   C. Resource Teachers
V. Summary and Conclusions
Discussion Questions and Activities
School-Based Assignments
Children's Trade Books Cited in This Chapter
References

354

Features

12.1   AHANA
12.2   An Indian Father's Plea
12.3   Integrating Multicultural Literature into the Curriculum
12.4   Red Riding Hood or Lon Po Po?
12.5   A Multicultural Sampler
12.6   Teaching Multicultural Literature
12.7   Dialects
12.8   Dialect in Print
12.9   Children's Books with a Black Perspective
12.10 Principles of Second Language Learning
12.11 Literature from a Hispanic Perspective
12.12 Children's Literature and Second Language Learning

Key Concepts in This Chapter

Culture, language, and literacy are closely related. Multicultural literature brings all three elements together.

All languages are a collection of dialects. Pupils who speak a nonstandard dialect may need instructional adjustments as they learn to deal with the standard language of print.

For pupils whose first language is not English, special provisions need to be made in helping them learn to read and write. Once again, literature becomes an important part of their reading instruction.

Multicultural literature is not intended solely for linguistically and culturally diverse pupils; it is an important part of reading and writing instruction for all children.

T ODAY'S EDUCATIONAL scene is becoming more and more a multicultural mosaic. The percentage of children in schools who are culturally and linguistically different is rising. Not long after the year 2000, pupils who are black, Hispanic, Asian, and Native American will constitute one-third or more of the school population. In many areas today, these children constitute a substantial majority of pupils in schools.

As education moves toward and into the 21st century, schools need to be increasingly aware of the needs of AHANA (See 12.1) pupils. These pupils bring diverse backgrounds, experiences, perspectives, and skills to their education. They also bring a culture and language that influences their learning to read and write. Although it is expected that education will respect and value each pupil's cultural and linguistic heritage, schools are required to teach all pupils to read and write in English.

Traditionally, schools often have trouble meeting the needs of AHANA pupils. Scores on achievement tests for these pupils are generally lower and dropout rates are higher. Some school districts have gone so far as to set up separate schools and classes to reflect the culture and environment of the pupils' homes. Although such programs are established in an attempt to promote achievement of AHANA pupils, they raise the specter of racial and ethnic discrimination. And so in more and more classrooms, the teacher has the responsibility of educating pupils to live in a multicultural world, no matter what the cultural background or language patterns of the pupils are.

Multicultural literature has become an important part of pupils' classroom experiences. Books that reflect diverse cultural groups, along with stories and poems written by AHANA children's authors, are vital to literature-based reading instruction. Quality multicultural literature contributes to the literacy development of all pupils, those who are members of AHANA groups and those who are not.

Cultural Dimensions of Literacy

Edward Tylor's famous definition of culture is ''that complex whole which includes knowledge, belief, art, morals, law, customs, and any other capabilities and habits acquired by man (humans) as a member of society'' (Tylor, 1929; p. 1). It has been described as ''the prism through which members of a group see the world and create 'shared meanings' '' (Bowman, 1989; p. 118). In the technological world in which today's pupils live, literacy is certainly part of that complex whole that they are expected to acquire. Cultural issues need to be part of the language arts curriculum.

Culture plays a part in learning to read. Although some reading-related issues are more culturally determined than others—for example, the common research finding that girls read better than boys in the primary grades is true in only a handful of countries, including the U.S. and England—culture determines much about a people's lifestyles and values, and literacy is part of the values that people have.

Literature has a special place in the cultural life of any people. Stories passed down from one generation to another reflect the values that a group of people treasured—bravery, honesty, integrity, cunning, respect for elders, wisdom, and the like. In American literature, for example, the stories of Paul Bunyan represent the strength, confidence, and ingenuity required to open the rugged American wilderness. That is

12.1
FOR YOUR INFORMATION
AHANA

THE TERM *AHANA* is used in this chapter in lieu of the more conventional term *minority*. Coined in 1979 by two undergraduate students at Boston College, AHANA is an acronym for African American, Hispanic, Asian, and Native American. The term is coming to be used increasingly on U.S. campuses.

AHANA is used here because it gets away from the pejorative connotations that often surround the word *minority*. Reflecting on what the world might be like for black Americans in the year 2035, Bill Cosby says, "The word *minority* has connotations of weakness, lesser value, self-doubt, tentativeness, and powerlessness" (Cosby, 1990; p. 61). Thus, the use of the alternative term *AHANA*.

Besides, when one walks into a school in which 40 percent of the pupils are black, 30 percent are Hispanic, 20 percent are Asian, and 5 percent are Native American, these pupils hardly constitute a "minority" of the population in that school.

why literature has long been part of education and why it is assuming a more important role in today's elementary school.

AHANA pupils bring to schools a set of experiences not always reflected in the curriculum of the school (see 12.2). Pupils' schemata are built from these experiences, and it is important to have books available that reflect familiar experiences that are important to their school lives. AHANA pupils need to see their world reflected in trade books as part of learning to read. In the words of a white middle-class mother who had adopted a very young Korean orphan, "I want picture books in which my son can at least see faces that look like his own."

Values of Multicultural Literature in the Classroom

Through the 1950s, AHANA cultures were sometimes stereotyped, but more often ignored, in children's trade books. With the increased social consciousness that the Civil Rights Movement helped generate, a body of multicultural literature—books that authentically reflect non-Western cultures, with characters and experiences other than those of mainstream America—began to appear. An extensive and ever-growing body of multicultural literature exists for classroom use.

Emphasizing the importance of using children's books with a multicultural perspective in the classroom, Bishop (1987) identifies three values of literature in a multicultural society: (1) literature can show how people are connected with common human experiences; (2) books can help pupils understand the unique differences that make cultural groups distinctive; and (3) literature can help pupils understand "the effects of social issues and forces on the lives of ordinary individuals" (Bishop, 1987; p. 60).

Multicultural literature has special values for AHANA and mainstream pupils alike. These books help all pupils better understand themselves and others, learn the literary heritage that comes from different cultures, and discover values that connect the present to the past. Multicultural literature can also help pupils expand their understanding of geography and history, and it can broaden their awareness of social

Multicultural literature is becoming more and more important in reflecting the multicultural landscape of today's schools.

issues and literary techniques (Norton, 1990). Further, literature from other lands is a powerful medium for developing the concept of global interdependence in understanding our developing world (Diakiw, 1990).

Multicultural literature is appropriate for all pupils, not just pupils who are culturally and linguistically distinct. "For minority and immigrant children, these books can be a mirror, reflecting and validating familiar cultures and experiences. For mainstream children, these books can be a window, revealing a multicultural vista that juxtaposes the familiar and the less familiar" (Cox and Galda, 1990; p. 582).

Beyond the level of awareness, literature can lead pupils to deep understanding and even action over issues of social concern. "Textbooks touch the mind with sanitary descriptions of events: stories, told from the points of view of persons who lived through the events, have the power to touch the hearts of readers and move them to the type of action that characterizes the highest level of multicultural study. . . . Multicultural learning achieves its pinnacle when students are inspired to challenge and act upon their beliefs and values about people who are different from them or from the mainstream" (Rasinski and Padak, 1990; pp. 579–580).

Types of Multicultural Trade Books

Multicultural literature includes the full range of literary genres—picture storybooks, folktales and traditional stories, realistic fiction, biographies and informational books, and poetry.

Picture Books   The use of books that reflect diverse cultures can begin with ABC and counting books such as Muriel Feelings' *Jambo Means Hello: Swahili Alphabet Book,* which not only introduces Swahili words but also cultural aspects of life in African villages where Swahili is spoken. John Agard's *The Calypso Alphabet* does the same thing with a Caribbean flavor, as does Rosario's *Idalia's Project ABC* with

12.2 Something to Think About

An Indian Father's Plea

In the September 1990 issue of *Teacher Magazine,* Robert Lake, a member of the Seneca and Cherokee Indian tribes, wrote an open letter regarding his son's education. The letter begins,

Dear Teacher,

I would like to introduce you to my son, Wind-Wolf. He is probably what you would consider a typical Indian kid. He was born and raised on the reservation. He has black hair, dark brown eyes, and an olive complexion. And like so many Indian children his age, he is shy and quiet in the classroom. He is 5 years old, in kindergarten, and I can't understand why you have already labeled him a "slow learner."

Very poignantly, the letter goes on to describe how difficult it is for Wind-Wolf to adjust to a new cultural environment that demands learning new things. Mr. Lake talks about all the science, social studies, music, math, and language that his son has learned as part of his upbringing in a Native American culture, and the father pleads for an educational experience that will help his son maintain pride in his cultural heritage and share his cultural diversity, while at the same time develop the skills necessary to succeed in the wider society. The letter concludes,

My son, Wind-Wolf, is not an empty glass coming into your class to be filled. He is a full basket coming into a different environment and society with something special to share. Please let him share his knowledge, heritage, and culture with you and his peers.

From Robert Lake, "An Indian Father's Plea," in *Teacher,* Vol. II, No. 1, September 1990. Copyright © 1990 Teacher Magazine. Reprinted with permission.

a Hispanic flavor. Feelings' *Moja Means One: A Swahili Counting Book* extends the multicultural concept to numbers.

Primary grade teachers have available an extensive selection of multicultural picture storybooks, beginning reading books, and trade books for pupils beginning to achieve independence in reading. Books reflecting a multicultural focus should be a regular and normal part of literature-based instruction—books such as Ann Gilfranconi's *Osa's Pride* and Tololwa M. Mullel's *The Orphan Boy,* stories that reflect African traditions; Sally Scott's *The Magic Horse,* a tale told from Persia; Jinko Marimoto's *Mouse's Marriage,* a simply written story with illustrations that reflect Japanese customs; Paul Goble's *Her Seven Brothers* and Peggy Parish's *Good Hunting, Blue Sky,* books that reflect the cultures of different Native American groups; Edna O'Brien's *Tales for the Telling,* a book of Irish stories; Lina Mao Wall's *Judge Rabbit and the Tree Spirit,* a folktale from Cambodia; Ann Tompert's *Grandfather Tang's Story,* a story rooted in the ancient Chinese tradition; Jeanne M. Lee's *Ba-Nam,* a story about the culture of Vietnam.

These books and others suggested in this chapter reflect only a small fraction of the multicultural literature available for use in the primary grades. These early level trade books reflect the broader multicultural mosaic that can be found in so many elementary classrooms and can be enjoyed by all pupils in learning to read and write.

Folktales and Traditional Literature   Folk literature addresses universal themes that transcend cultural boundaries and appeal to people of different backgrounds; folktales are grounded in particular cultures. These stories reflect the values and traditions of the people from whom they come. Folk literature reveals the heart and soul of a people. Since it springs from the oral tradition, this type of literature also lends itself especially well to reading aloud, storytelling, dramatization, and other language activities.

Integrating Multicultural Literature into the Curriculum

BANKS (1989) has identified four approaches to the integration of ethnic content into the curriculum:

1. *The Contributions Approach,* which focuses on heros, holidays, and discrete cultural elements; for example, pupils read about the life of Dr. Martin Luther King, Jr., or observe a period such as Black History Month.

2. *The Ethnic Additive Approach,* in which ethnic content and issues are added to the curriculum without changing its basic structure—studying the internment of Japanese-Americans as part of the study of World War II, for example.

3. *The Transformation Approach,* which changes the basic structure of the curriculum by having pupils view concepts or themes from diverse ethnic perspectives; pupils examine the Westward Movement, for example, through the eyes of Native Americans.

4. *The Social Action Approach,* which includes all the aspects of the Transformation approach and adds the element of decision making on social issues; pupils are given opportunities to reflect on their values as these values relate to diversity in their culture.

Rasinski and Padek (1990) relate the use of children's literature to Banks's four approaches:

1. In the *Contributions Approach* pupils encounter the lives of famous people through biographies or the customs of different cultures through trade books.

2. In the *Ethnic Additive Approach* books such as Mildred Taylor's *Roll of Thunder, Hear My Cry,* the story of prejudice experienced by a black family in the rural South is read and discussed, or a book like Beth Baylor's *Francisco,* the story about an empoverished Hispanic child who adopts a prairie dog, would be included in a unit on pets.

3. In the *Transformation Approach* pupils might compare accounts of the American Revolution by reading Esther Forbes' *Johnny Tremain,* the story of a heroic young boy closely involved in the Revolution, and the perspective presented in James and Christopher Collier's *War Comes to Willy Freeman,* the story of a newly emancipated black female who witnesses the death of her father in battle with the British and then finds her mother kidnapped by the Redcoats.

4. In the *Social Action Approach,* having read about the treatment of Japanese-Americans in Yoshiko Uchida's *Journey to Topaz* and *Journey Home,* pupils further explore the issue of sanctioned bigotry and decide what they might do in the face of similar experiences.

Fairy tales and legends add to the multicultural fabric of the classroom. African folk literature is reflected in such books as *Abiyoyo,* Pete Seeger's adaptation of the South African lullaby and folk story of the trickster-turned-hero when he made a monster disappear; Verna Aardema's retelling of the West African story *Why Mosquitoes Buzz in People's Ears;* or Veronique Tadjo's *Lord of the Dance: An African Retelling.* Folk literature represented in stories like these gives African-American pupils a keen awareness of the antiquity and richness of their culture.

Similarly, books such as Gerald McDermott's *Arrow to the Sun* is a strikingly illustrated folk story from the Pueblo Indians. Paul Goble's *The Gift of the Sacred Dog*

Red Riding Hood or Lon Po Po?

AS YOUNG children delight in familiar fairy tales, their experiences can be enriched by comparing fairy tales that they know with equivalent fairy tales from other lands. For example:

Ed Young's *Lon Po Po: A Red-Riding Hood Story from China* is a Caldecott winner that tells the age-old story of the cunning of the wolf, with an interesting cultural twist.

Another Chinese fairy tale is Louie Ai-Ling's *Yeh-Shen: A Cinderella Story from China*. The Cinderella theme is carried through John Steptoe's *Mufaro's Beautiful Daughters,* a story set in the high civilization of ancient Africa; Shirley Climo's *Egyptian Cinderella* casts that story in the setting of that ancient civilization; Charlotte Huck's *Princess Furball* is a version of Cinderella in which a clever princess escapes marriage to an ogre. These variations of a popular story show the cross-cultural nature of traditional themes and the universality of folk literature.

Mats Rehnman's *The Clay Flute* is a Persian variation of the fairy tale about the Frog Prince. *Vasilissa the Beautiful* by Elizabeth Winthrop is a Russian folktale (illustrated by the Soviet artist Alexander Koshkin) with a Cinderella and Hansel and Gretel theme. Each of these versions of favorite stories reflects the unique cultural perspective from which the story is told.

Chinese Mother Goose Rhymes, edited by Robert Wyndham, is a collection of nursery rhymes and ballads for children that illustrates the universal nature of the language, content, and themes of children's poetry across cultures.

Using well-known stories and poems like these broadens pupils' view of their world, enhances their understanding, and heightens their appreciation.

and other stories give a sense of tradition about the Indians of the Plains. Diane Hoyt-Goldsmith's *Pueblo Storyteller* offers information about Indians of the Southwest. Each story is part of the tradition of the Native American culture.

Books such as Tom Birdseye's *A Song of the Stars,* Diane Snyder's version of the Japanese trickster tale *The Boy of the Three Year Nap,* and Lawrence Yep's *The Rainbow People,* a collection of traditional tales carried by Chinese workers who came to America in the 1800s—all represent Asian folk legends as part of literature for children.

Folk literature might also include religious themes such as John Bierhorst's translation of *The Spirit Child,* an intriguing Aztec story of the Nativity, or Adele Gera's anthology *My Grandmother's Story: A Collection of Jewish Folk Tales.* Pupils can develop critical reading skills as they enjoy comparing Tomie de Paola's version of the Italian folktale *The Legend of Old Barara* with Ruth Robbins's award-winning adaptation of the Russian folktale *Baboushka and the Three Kings,* both of which are stories about the gift-giving tradition of January 6. These stories deal with religious themes, but they make up part of the ethnic diversity that characterizes the cultural pluralism of our society.

Although the United States cannot boast the antiquity of other cultures, it has its own folk tradition. Beyond the Paul Bunyan, Pecos Bill, and Johnny Appleseed stories, pupils can enjoy books such as *The Diane Goode Book of American Folk Tales and*

All children need to experience literature that reflects a variety of multicultural experiences.

Songs, Ann Durell's collection of traditional literature from various ethnic groups (blacks, Pueblo Indians, Hispanics) and regions (Appalachia, New England) of the U.S.

Realistic Fiction   Pupils in the middle grades devour realistic fiction, and this genre is especially important in their developing independence as readers. In reflecting AHANA cultures, realistic fiction should be just that—*realistic.* Teachers should be especially wary of books that present cultural groups in a single, stereotyped manner. Historically, some trade books for children perpetuated negative images; contemporary literature tends to avoid such stereotyping.

Among the plethora of realistic fiction books written for middle grade pupils, a number focus on experiences of AHANA cultures. Black characters appear in different settings, from the farm in Virginia Hamilton's *Zeeley* to the ghetto in Paula Fox's *How Many Miles to Babylon.* So do Hispanic characters in books like Nicholasa Mohr's *Felita,* a story about hatred experienced in a city neighborhood, and Joseph Krumgold's *And Now Miguel,* a story that takes place on a New Mexico sheep farm. In realistic fiction dealing with Native Americans, the theme often focuses on traditional and contemporary values that young characters face, as in Virginia Driving Hawk Sneve's *Jimmy Yellow Hawk.*

Multiethnic realistic fiction—for example, stories that reflect specific cultural experiences or focus on nonwhite characters—have the same universal conflicts and themes contained in all contemporary realistic fiction. No matter what their ethnic background, pupils face conflicts with themselves, with adults and peers, with nature, and with society in the process of becoming an adult in today's world.

Biographies and Informational Books   Multicultural literature for children is full of biographical and autobiographical accounts of famous and not-so-famous people, from

12.5
FOR YOUR INFORMATION
A Multicultural Sampler

A S THE cultural diversity of society widens, so does the need for books that reflect that cultural diversity. The following is a tiny sample of the range of children's trade books available about various AHANA groups. (Separate samplings of trade books dealing with black and Hispanic cultures will be presented later in this chapter.) The total inventory of trade books with a multicultural focus is far too extensive to list here; the following list represents only a handful of titles that are appropriate for use in a literature-based reading program.

Native American
Primary Grades
The Legend of Bluebonnet, retold by Tomie DiPaola, a beautifully illustrated version of a Comanche tale.
Hawk, I'm Your Brother by Byrd Baylor, describing the kinship between a young boy and a hawk.
Brother Eagle, Sister Sky, with beautiful paintings by Susan Jeffers illustrating the powerful words of Chief Seattle reflecting respect for the beauty of the environment.
Intermediate Grades
Annie and the Old One by Miska Miles, a story about the love between a girl and her grandmother, told against a backdrop of contemporary Navajo life.
Knots on a Counting Rope by Bill Martin, Jr., and John Archambault, a beautifully told tale in which a boy learns about his name and his heritage.
Upper Grades
Sign of the Beaver by Elizabeth George Speare, a popular story about a Native American boy who teaches a friend both survival skills and values.
Owl's Song by Janet Hale, in which a young boy experiences loneliness and prejudice as he searches for his identity as a Native American and as an American.
Japanese
Primary Grades
Anna In Charge by Yoiko Tsutsui, a simple, contemporary picture story about an older and a younger sister.
Crow Boy by Taro Yashima, a haunting story about a boy rejected by his peers in school, with striking illustrations.
Intermediate Grades
The Big Wave by Pearl Buck, a compelling story of human tragedy and friendship, in which a famous writer tells much about a culture she understands well.
Upper Grades
Sadako and the Thousand Paper Cranes by Eleanor Coerr, the popular story about a girl who develops leukemia as a result of the Hiroshima bombing.

Journey to Topaz by Yoshiko Uchida, the moving and tragic story of the internment of Japanese-Americans in the early days of World War II.
Chinese
Primary Grades
The Magic Leaf by Winifred Morris, a picture book that reflects many aspects of the culture.
Tikki, Tikki, Tembo retold by Arlene Mosel, a humorous folktale that children (and adults) delight in repeating.
The Empty Pot by Demi, a delicately illustrated story about an ancient Chinese emperor in search of a successor.
Intermediate Grades
In the Year of the Boar and Jackie Robinson by Beth Bao Lord, a story of a girl who finds friends in Brooklyn after the hardship of immigration.
The Chinese Word for Horse and Other Stories by John Lewis, a book that combines information about the Chinese writing system and Chinese culture.
Upper Grades
Dragonwings by Lawrence Yep, a compelling story with strong characters that reflect Chinese cultural values and way of life.
Angel Island Prisoner 1922 by Helen Cherin, the story about the struggles of brave and wise Chinese immigrant women.

Native Americans, Chinese, and Japanese are not the only cultural groups represented in today's classroom. Children's trade books with other cultural perspectives need to be included in pupils' reading diet, books such as:

Aekyung's Dream by Min Paek, the story of the first experiences of a young Korean girl in the United States.
The Land I Lost: Adventures of a Boy in Vietnam by Quang Nhong Huynh, the sometimes funny and sometimes poignant portrait of village life in prewar Vietnam.
Angel Child, Dragon Child by Michele M. Suart, in which a Vietnamese child relies on her mother's gift of a silver matchbox to help her through the prejudice she encounters as a new pupil in school.

There are literally thousands of books with a multicultural perspective available for use in the elementary reading program, and more are being published every year. Updated lists of multicultural trade books are available regularly from the Children's Book Council, 568 Broadway, Suite 404, New York, NY 10012, and from the Council on Interracial Books for Children, 1841 Broadway, Room 608, New York, NY 10023.

easy reading books such as *Ragtime Trumpie,* Allan Schroeder's account of the child-hood of the black entertainer Josephine Baker, to longer books like Beth Bao Lord's autobiographical account of a Chinese child's adjustment to living in a new land in *In the Year of the Boar and Jackie Robinson.* These books add a personal dimension to what it is like to grow up in another culture.

Informational books provide descriptions and accounts of the customs and traditions of AHANA cultures. *Lion Dancer: Ernie Wan's Chinese New Year* by Kate Waters and Madeline Slovenz-Low is an informative and entertaining account of ancient customs of the Chinese, and Joan Hewett's very realistic *Hector Lives in the United States Now: The Story of a Mexican-American Child* gives a realistic description of the life of one Hispanic family living in the United States. Books like these, which are often illustrated with photographs, promote cultural awareness while providing material for learning to read.

For pupils who have recently arrived from foreign lands (and for those whose ancestors arrived a long time ago), William Jay Jacobs's factual account of *Ellis Island: New Hope in a New Land* gives a sense of both history and personalness to the emotions of arriving in a new land. A fictional but nonetheless realistic account of more recent immigration is Eve Bunting's *How Many Days to America? A Thanksgiving Story,* an account of the journey of a group of political refugees who come to the United States as "boat people."

Poetry   Poems also provide literature for children from a multicultural perspective—Virginia Driving Hawk Sneve's *Dancing Teepees,* a collection of poetry of American Indian youth, for example, and Frane Lessac's *Caribbean Canvas,* a collection of colorful paintings and charming poetry from that part of the world.

A full range of ethnic literature can enrich the reading program in any classroom. For pupils whose culture is reflected in trade books, stories contribute to their strengthened self-concepts, deepening their sense of pride and appreciation for their cultural identity. At the same time, quality literature that has characters and settings related to diverse cultural populations can lead *all* pupils to a better understanding of cultures different from their own, while giving them reading material with genuine appeal.

Dialect Speakers

Dialect is a fact of language. All languages have dialects and all native speakers of any language speak one dialect or another of that language. In fact, a language may be defined as a collection of dialects that are mutually understandable among a group of native speakers.

There are two types of dialects: regional and social. Within these categories, dialects differ from each other in three respects: phonology, vocabulary, and syntax.

Regional Dialect

Regional dialect, as the name indicates, is a variety of language used by speakers living in the same geographic area. The area may be relatively large (like the state of Maine) or relatively small (like the lower east side of Manhattan Island); yet natives of these areas share the same general speech features.

Teaching Multicultural Literature

NORTON (1990) details a sequence for the study of multicultural literature as part of the language arts curriculum in the upper elementary grades. The model includes five steps or phases.

Phase 1 begins with literature that comes from the oral tradition. The folktales, fables, myths, and legends of a group of people (such as Native Americans or African Americans) are shared and discussed. Pupils develop their own storytelling activities that replicate the literature they have been reading.

Phase 2 narrows the focus on folklore to the literature of a specific group—one or two Native American people, for example, or black folk literature from the American slave era. Pupils develop their critical awareness as they search for deeper cultural values reflected in the stories they read.

Phase 3 takes pupils into other areas of literature—informational books such as history and biography related to the culture being studied. Pupils extend their critical analysis with such activities as comparing the values and beliefs expressed in folk literature with those reflected in the biographies they read, or judging the authenticity of information presented.

Phase 4 involves historical fiction, as pupils "read, analyze, and evaluate historical fiction according to their authenticity of setting, credibility of conflict, believability of characterization, authenticity of traditional beliefs expressed by characters, and appropriateness of themes and authors' style" (Norton, 1990; p. 34).

Phase 5 moves into contemporary poetry, fiction, and biography, as pupils search for continuity from one type of writing to another and as they compare literature written by members of cultural groups with that written by nonmembers. In this final phase, pupils also trace the threads across genres.

Norton provides extensive examples of books and activities for the study of Native American cultures, with suggestions for using her model in the study of black and Hispanic literature as well.

Social Dialect

Social dialects exist within every geographic region. A social dialect is a variety of language that distinguishes people from different social strata or levels of society.

Dialects differ from each other in three ways:

phonologically, with clearly marked sound differences distinguishing one dialect from another; Bostonians pronounce words like *car* and *yard* as "*cah*" and "*yahd.*"

lexically, with different words used to name the same object or action from one dialect to the next; a sandwich on an Italian roll is variously known as a *submarine* (or *sub*), *hoagie, hero, grinder, torpedo,* or *po'boy* in various parts of the United States.

syntactically, with certain grammatical forms characterizing one dialect or another; "*How be you?*" is a greeting in some regional dialects, while "*He be here*" is a syntactical feature of some social dialects.

This type of linguistic diversity is part of the fascination of language.

12.7
FOR YOUR INFORMATION
Dialects

> D IALECT IS not an "inferior brand" of language. All languages have dialects; all native speakers speak them.

Dialects differ in areas of
PHONOLOGY
VOCABULARY
SYNTAX

Dialects can be either
REGIONAL
or
SOCIAL

Standard English

Out of this linguistic pluralism that characterizes any language there emerges a form of language described as "standard." *Standard English* is the speech that is free of the variations that characterize regional and social dialects. It has been called the language of public life because it generally includes the language conventions that govern communication beamed at the general public across geographic, social, ethnic, and other lines. Standard language forms are used by broadcasters as they deliver the national network news each evening.

Standard English has long been the language of schools, just as it is the language of business, commerce, government, and all other aspects of public life. Schools are rightly expected to teach Standard English. But in so doing, they sometimes perpetuate a negative view of dialect, a notion that dialects are inferior language forms. Dialects are *different* language forms, but they are not *deficient* language forms. They are not ineffective approximations of Standard English, but rather systematic language forms that speakers use to meet the full range of their daily communication needs. Rather than being inferior versions of the standard form, dialects are fully developed language systems that differ in systematic ways from Standard English.

Schools have sometimes attempted to replace pupils' dialects with Standard English; however, schools often fail to realize how closely pupils' dialect is tied to their cultural identity. Language is part of culture. To denigrate pupils' language is to denigrate part of their very being. Although Standard English needs to be used and taught in the classroom, pupils' dialect must be recognized and respected for what it means, what it does, and what it is.

What does all this discussion about dialect have to do with teaching reading and writing with literature? As a group, dialect speakers—whether they are black youngsters from the inner city, Native American children from reservations, or white pupils from impoverished rural areas—tend not to score as well on reading measures as their mainstream, middle-class counterparts. Complicating factors such as nutrition, home background, educational level of parents, economic factors and other elements compound the educational problems of these pupils. But their dialect impacts learning as well, since language is a factor in their learning to read. This is especially true of black pupils in schools today.

12.8 Something to Think About

Dialect in Print

Dialect is unique to spoken language. No matter how many ways the word *car* is pronounced—*cah, caw, cour, cayr*—it is still written *c-a-r*. In using multicultural literature in the classroom, teachers need to be aware of *eye dialect*. Eye dialect is writing that reflects unique phonological, lexical, and syntactic features of dialect in print. For example, Mark Twain reflected the dialect of the slave Jim in *The Adventures of Huckleberry Finn* ("We's safe, Huck. I jis knows it!") and Theodore Taylor did the same thing with the language of the old Virgin Islander Timothy in *The Cay* ("Many schooner go by dis way, 'an dis also be d'ship track to Jamaica an' on.").

Authors of contemporary children's stories sometimes use eye dialect to reflect the spoken language of characters as well. For example, John Steptoe's *Daddy Is a Monster . . . Sometimes* contains lines such as "Daddy, you ain't gonna knock me out 'cause I'm gonna give you a knuckle sandwich" and "He be real nice and read you a story, but then—when the story be over and he kiss you good-night and cut off the lights, he start to do it again." The grandmother in Valerie Flournoy's warm and touching book *The Patchwork Quilt* says, "Stuff? This ain't stuff. These little pieces gonna make me a quilt," and "A year ain't that long, honey. Makin' the quilt gonna be a joy."

The use of eye dialect in stories written for children is controversial. Reflecting a reasonable representation of colloquial speech patterns can add an element of authenticity and enjoyment to a story, but it can also stereotype dialect speakers and offend readers—black and white alike. In children's books where eye dialect is used, language ought not to be the only matter of concern; the quality and appeal of the story are more important considerations.

Black English

Not all blacks speak "Black English." Yet there is a dialect variation of American English that is shared by large numbers of African-American speakers. Known as Black English or Vernacular Black English (VBE), this dialect variation has been defined and described (Dillard, 1972; Burling, 1973; Smitherman, 1981).

As with any dialect, Black English has its own unique phonological features (for example, the dropping of a *t* or *d* in a consonant cluster at the end of a word, so that *desk* may be pronounced *des'*), vocabulary items (*hood* as a word meaning "neighborhood"), or grammatical features (use of the verb *be* to distinguish between a state or condition that is permanent—"My brother be sick [every day]."—or only temporary—"My brother sick [today but he should be better tomorrow]." It is important to remember that these variations are systematic, that not all features are characteristic of the language of all black Americans, and that many of these features are common among white speakers as well.

In teaching reading to pupils who speak a dialect of Black English, teachers need to maintain a high level of respect for the pupils and their language background and to continue to realize that their dialect is a bona fide communication system that meets their needs outside the classroom. However, teachers also need to be aware that there may be dialect "conflict points" between the standard language of print and the natural language that the pupil brings into the classroom. For example, the vowel phonemes in words such as *pen* and *pin* sound the same in some dialects, so insisting that the young child "hear the differences in the sounds" in developing decoding strategies may be futile. Similarly, when a dialect speaker pronounces the word *ten'* for *tent,* insisting that the pupil repeat the word "until he says it right" is inappropriate.

Barnitz (1980) suggests these five implications of dialectology for the teaching of reading:

1. The use of the home dialect in oral reading is natural.
2. Because dialects differ in their homonym pairs, the use of context must be encouraged.
3. Because dialects and languages vary in the contrasts made by native speakers, auditory discrimination test items must be interpreted cautiously.
4. Phonological differences exist across dialects. The nature of phonics generalizations may vary.
5. Communication of meaning is part of all dialects. Reading instruction should emphasize meaning by incorporating all the language arts and the cultural background of the child.

As pupils read, they should not be penalized for reading in their own dialect, even when apparent discrepancies between the language of the text and the language of the pupil occur (as when the pupil reads *asked* as "*axed*," for example, or when the pupil reads "*they was*" instead of *they were*). Allowing dialect speakers to render print in their natural language is not only instructionally sound; it is good common sense. Few of us read *Charlie and the Chocolate Factory* or *James and the Giant Peach* with a British accent, even though Roald Dahl, the Englishman who wrote these delightful stories, spoke with a British accent. Similarly, it makes sense to allow pupils who speak dialects of Black English to read stories in their natural language patterns. As pupils read, teachers should be aware of which miscues are dialect-related and which result from inaccurate processing of text. Enjoyment and meaning of the stories remain paramount.

Literature-based reading demands the use of books that reflect black cultural experiences. These books should be part of the reading diet of all pupils, no matter what the color of their skin or ethnic background. Children's trade books by and about African Americans provide opportunities for cross-cultural awareness as part of the classroom reading program.

Sims (1982) studied children's literature from a black perspective and classified books by orientation as:

1. *socially conscious literature*—books to raise the social awareness of non-black readers about such issues as prejudice. A book like Beverly Naidoo's *Journey to Jo'burg,* for example, tells a story about a young black South African girl and her brother, against a background of apartheid.
2. *melting pot literature*—books that stress the universality of human experiences such as friendship, family relations, and everyday life. The characters that Ezra Jack Keats creates in *Peter's Chair,* for example, are black, but their race is incidental to the concern that Peter expresses about the imminent arrival of a new baby and his father's sensitive reassurances.
3. *cultural conscious literature*—books that celebrate the unique quality of the black experience, the traditions that are part of growing up black in the United States. For example, *Let the Circle Be Unbroken* by Mildred Taylor is a heartwarming story about growing up black in the segregated South of the 1930s.

12.9
FOR YOUR INFORMATION
Children's Books with a Black Perspective

CLASSROOM LIBRARIES need to be amply supplied with trade books that provide a black perspective. These include such books as:

Primary Grades

Grandpa's Face by Eloise Greenfield, a beautiful story of intergenerational love and respect in an extended family.

Wagon Wheels by Barbara Brenner, the realistic account of a black family's migration west.

The Black Snowman by Phil Mendez, an intriguing tale that connects the present with the past, as a black snowman helps a boy discover the beauty of his heritage.

Intermediate Grades

Sister by Eloise Greenfield, a strong personal account of growing up black.

Nellie Cameron by Michele Murray, a story about a girl's triumph in learning to read.

The Hundred Penny Box by Sharon Bell Mathis, a tender story about a young boy's compassion and sensitivity toward his 100-year-old great-great-aunt.

Upper Grades

Roll of Thunder, Hear My Cry by Mildred Taylor, a powerful story of a black family growing up in the rural segregated South, winner of the Newbery Award as the most notable contribution to children's literature in 1977.

Finding Buck McHenry by Alfred Slote, a baseball story with accounts of the old Negro League and a commentary about discrimination.

Sounder by William Armstrong, the popular story of a young boy's experience with prejudice and security.

Reading Aloud

The People Could Fly: American Black Folktales by Virginia Hamilton, a critically acclaimed collection of African-American folk literature reflects the richness of the black culture.

Listen Children by Dorothy Strickland, a collection of poems, short stories and plays that can be read aloud or acted out.

Again, lists of other titles reflecting the black perspective are available from the Interracial Council of Children's Books.

Each of these categories provides a perspective on black culture to enhance the reading program in the classroom. Walker-Dalhouse (1992) has demonstrated the effectiveness of reading aloud books in which the major character is black (Virginia Hamilton's *Zeeley,* for example, and Bette Greene's *Phillip Hall Likes Me, I Recon Maybe*) and using these books as a focus of discussion on ethnicity.

Dialect variation is a natural sociolinguistic phenomenon between regional areas and social classes. Although dialects need to be taken into account in teaching children how to read, they also need to be recognized as legitimate language systems that are part of pupils' cultures. As such, they need to be accepted and understood in literature-based reading programs.

Pupils Whose First Language Is Not English

For many pupils, the process of becoming literate is influenced by the fact that English is not their first or native language. These may be the children of immigrants from Mexico or other Latin American countries, from the Philippines or Southeast Asia, from newly democratized nations in Eastern Europe, or from other nations whose citizens seek the hope of a better life in the United States. With their varied backgrounds, these pupils contribute to the rich multicultural mosaic of today's educational

Pupils whose first language is not English can enjoy popular children's trade books written in their own language.

scene, and demographic projections indicate that their numbers will continue to grow into the next century.

Apart from the fact that their first language is not English, these pupils constitute a very diverse group. Some will be bilingual, more comfortable in their native language but able to communicate adequately in English. For others, English will be a second or "foreign" language. Some will be able to speak and understand the language of their homes but will not be able to read it. Others have had the benefit of an excellent education before immigrating and will be fully literate in their first language. Levels of language competency will vary among bilingual or ESL (English as a Second Language) pupils, but all will likely have a degree of limited English proficiency that will influence their learning to read and write.

How to help ESL and bilingual pupils become literate in English is a matter of debate. Some experts claim that it is better to teach pupils to read first in their native language, with the belief that it is better to have pupils become literate in a language with which they are familiar before attempting to become literate in a second language. It has been argued that pupils can learn to apply effective strategies in learning to read the language they know best before applying these strategies to reading English.

An equally strong (or even stronger) case, however, has been made for beginning literacy instruction in English for non-native speakers even before they can read or write their native language. In the final analysis, "current research suggests that it is *not* necessary to delay teaching children to read in the second language before they have learned to read in the first" (Mason and Au, 1990; p. 329). This is especially true when the emphasis is on comprehending text.

Language Instruction

Literature fits many of the needs of the non-English-speaking pupil in learning to read. Bilingual and ESL pupils need a strong background in oral language to build word meanings and sentence patterns that will support comprehension in reading. This

Principles of Second Language Learning

SUMMARIZING A wealth of research on ESL teaching, Early (1990) suggests the following principles of second-language learning:

1. ESL pupils' learning should build on the experiences and language they bring to school. Pupils should be encouraged to use their first language as a means of developing proficiency in English.

2. Learning a language means learning to use that language for a range of purposes and functions. This takes many years, so ''expecting quick and full-fledged competence'' is unrealistic.

3. Integrating language teaching with subject areas of the curriculum is a promising procedure in developing language, thought, and academic knowledge.

4. Integrated activities hold more promise than isolated exercises as a means of teaching English as a second language.

5. Although verbal language is the major means of communicating, pupils also communicate through drawing and other forms of meaning-making.

6. Parent participation is especially important to both school achievement and social growth of ESL pupils.

Early describes thematic units that integrate content and language as particularly effective ways of developing language competencies and promoting academic learning at the same time. Trade books remain an integral part of the process.

---

instruction needs to be provided in meaningful context rather than with lists of isolated words or pronunciation drills.

For many LEP (Limited English Proficiency) pupils, the first step in literacy instruction is building an oral language background solid enough to support success in learning to read and write. This occurs, in part, through a range of book-related activities typically carried on as part of literature-based instruction. Language development takes place in a classroom environment in which pupils can feel free to express their thoughts without fear of ridicule and/or constant correction. Instruction in oral language involves developing a familiarity with the sound system of American English, building vocabulary that will provide a store of word meanings, and helping pupils acquire language structures that will enable them to capture and communicate the meaning of what they read.

The pronunciation system that LEP pupils bring to school is apt to be different from the sound system used by native speakers. Different languages have different sound systems (which is why a non-native speaker of any language has ''an accent''). Spanish, for example, does not have the /š/ phoneme (the initial sound in *sheep*), so that Latino pupils may pronounce the word *sheep* as ''*cheep*.'' Pupils need to become basically aware of sound elements before sound–symbol instruction takes place.

Phonetic elements of English should not be taught as isolated exercises, however. Sounds are contained in words, and the best practice in English pronunciation takes place in the context of meaningful discourse. For the LEP pupil, good reading does not equal perfect pronunciation. The same principle applies to non-native speakers as to dialect speakers; that is, pupils should render text into their natural language pattern.

Meaning is more important than the exact form used to express it. For LEP pupils, accents are a normal part of speaking and reading.

Word knowledge is essential to all reading and writing. Since English may not be the language spoken in the LEP pupils' homes and neighborhoods, word knowledge will likely not be as wide or as deep as that of pupils who come from English-speaking environments. The semantic webs, word alerts, and other vocabulary-building activities that are important for all pupils in the classroom are particularly important to the LEP pupil. Especially in the early years, concept books (see pp. 105–106) become important to helping pupils attach word labels to objects and experiences, and to build a store of vocabulary as schemata to be used in learning to read.

Syntax is also important to the pupil's knowledge of language. LEP pupils need to acquire the language patterns that convey meaning. Instruction here extends beyond the narrow grammatical focus of proper usage (such as avoiding expressions like *ain't* and double negatives) to understanding the underlying grammatical relationships by which meaning is conveyed in connected discourse. This involves exposure to a variety of language patterns in trade books and in oral language exercises, and an examination of how the same idea can be expressed in a number of ways.

Literature is a vehicle for fostering the language competency of the LEP pupil. Traditionally, language and reading instruction for the bilingual and ESL pupil has consisted of context-free, skill development activities, with workbooks and similar materials. Good trade books involve these pupils in encounters with meaningful units of text, while providing interesting material for pupils to share and discuss. "ESL programs that emphasize skills and workbook activities can deprive these young learners of the richly supportive context offered by good children's books" (Allen, 1989; p. 58).

The concentrated instruction involved in language development for bilingual and ESL pupils often can be done more effectively with trade books than with a stack of cards or isolated drills. (See 11.5, which addresses language help for special needs children.) Besides, not only do trade books provide interesting material for the development of pupils' English competency, these books also provide a multicultural dimension to the classroom reading program.

Allen (1989) points out some of the ways in which literature supports the many dimensions of language development for bilingual and ESL pupils. A trade book provides pupils with "a large, cohesive, uninterrupted chunk of language." Predictable and patterned stories with repeated refrains are especially appropriate for younger LEP pupils, since these books allow pupils to function quickly as readers of English text. Stories are made comprehensible by illustrations, by repeated language patterns, and by predictable story structure. Good children's literature also provides pupils with models for developing their writing proficiency in English.

Informational trade books support second language learners in content areas of the curriculum. These books often provide a more readable alternative to content area textbooks, and they convey an enormous amount of information with the combination of illustration and text.

Pupils with limited English proficiency can share trade books in a number of ways. For example:

Shared stories. Pupils' language power grows as they participate in conversation and informal discussion of familiar stories shared in group settings. Small-group settings are more advantageous for sharing sessions for LEP pupils, since they will have more

12.11
FOR YOUR INFORMATION

Literature from a Hispanic Perspective

CHILDREN'S TRADE books written from a Hispanic perspective are important to classroom reading programs. Although the language spoken by Hispanic pupils is Spanish, the cultural traditions of these pupils can be very diverse. Respective groups of Hispanic pupils trace their cultural traditions from Cuba, Puerto Rico, Mexico, and other Latin American nations, and teachers need to be sensitive to the range of literature that reflects these cultural traditions.

A sample of books that reflect Hispanic experiences and can be used in the classroom include:

Primary Grades

Maria Teresa by Mary Atkinson, a picture book that describes the struggles of a Spanish child.

Hello, Amigos! by Tricia Brown, a photographic exploration of the day in the life of a young Hispanic boy.

Gilberto and the Wind by Marie Hall Ets, a picture book that fits nicely into science as well.

Intermediate Grades

Jo, Flo, and Yolanda by Carol de Poix, the story of three sisters who look alike but behave differently

Cesar Chavez by Ruth Faucher, a biography that relates the story of this leader's childhood.

Upper Grades

The House on Mango Street by Sandra Cisneros, the story of a young girl's experiences with family, friends, and the neighborhood.

Felita by Nicholasa Mohr, describing the prejudice and isolation felt by a girl when her family moves to a "better" neighborhood.

As in the case of black and other multiethnic literature, additional titles can be suggested by the Council on Interracial Books for Children.

---

occasions to speak and feel more comfortable. "Books can do more than provide an input of vocabulary and structure. They give pupils something to talk about by providing a very special kind of shared experience" (Allen, 1989; p. 59).

Read Alouds. Frequently listening to good stories read well by the teacher will help LEP pupils develop vocabulary and grammatical patterns, not to mention a sense of story structure and enjoyment.

Filmstrips and story boards. For bilingual and ESL pupils, visual referents are sometimes important for vocabulary and concepts that may be unfamiliar. Illustrations in picture books can be the focus for discussion, language, and concept building as well.

None of these techniques is unique for LEP learners. Each, however, can be geared specifically to help the language development in the literature-based classroom.

Reading Instruction

As pupils whose dominant language is other than English begin to achieve more independence in dealing with print, trade books remain essential vehicles for the continuing development of their reading competency. Trade books directly related to the pupil's ethnic or cultural background have a built-in element of interest. Pupils often have the schemata to build comprehension of these books to which they can relate.

A variety of trade books can be used in numerous ways to promote enjoyment and comprehension for ESL and bilingual pupils. For example:

Songs and chants. Pupils can share some of their own cultural backgrounds with teachers and peers as they share songs and chants that are part of their own experiences.

These items can be written on a chart and learned by the group. A good trade book in this area for Hispanic pupils is Lulu Delacre's *Arroz con Leche: Popular Songs from Latin America,* a bilingual collection of traditional folk songs and rhymes from Mexico, Puerto Rico, and Argentina.

Repetition and patterns. Repetitious poetry and predictable pattern books such as Pat Hutchins's *Good Night, Owl* provide pupils with printed text that they can easily learn to read independently through repetition, thus building confidence in their ability to handle the text on their own.

Language experience activities. Pupils' personal accounts of their own experiences, or their own versions of favorite stories, are valuable vehicles for reading instruction. The teacher transcribes what the pupils dictate and uses this material for vocabulary practice, using context, decoding strategies, and other instruction.

Taped books. Pupils with limited ability in English can follow the lines as they listen to a recorded or taped version of the story.

Choral reading. Using the work of such favorite children's poets as Shel Silverstein and Jack Prelutsky, McCauley and McCauley (1992) have demonstrated that choral reading is a highly effective technique for promoting language learning and reading success for children whose first language is not English.

Bilingual texts. Books with parallel versions of two languages—such as Rebecca Emberley's English/Spanish books *Taking a Walk/Cammandro* and *My Home/Mi Casa*—allow Hispanic pupils to build vocabulary and concepts by matching text in their native language to text in English. These bilingual texts not only promote second language learning; they provide an indication that the pupil's native language and culture are valued in the classroom. Stories such as Alberto Blanco's *The Desert Mermaid/La sirena del desierto* or Harriet Rohmer and Mary Anchondo's Aztec legend *How We Came to the Fifth World/Como vinimos al quinto mundo* contain good stories that reflect cultural traditions as well. Trade books in Spanish, such as *Flecha al Sol,* the Spanish edition of Gerald McDermott's *Arrow to the Sun,* allow Spanish-speaking pupils to enjoy classic literature in their native tongue.

Figurative language. LEP pupils usually need special help with idiomatic expressions and figures of speech, since they often interpret the meaning of expressions such as "It's raining cats and dogs" in a literal sense. Peggy Parish's *Amelia Bedelia* books provide a wealth of material in this area. Pupils can illustrate their own figures of speech and write original sentences illustrating the meaning of idiomatic expressions.

There are no mystical, magical techniques for helping bilingual and ESL pupils learn to read with literature. Making sure that there is a sound basis of language and understanding; providing a variety of multicultural trade books; using pupils' own backgrounds to build understanding; being aware of points where pupils' language and experience will create problems in understanding; providing well-planned direct instruction in applying effective reading strategies—these are the best procedures for teaching reading to pupils whose first language is not English.

As language competence and reading ability develop, ESL and bilingual pupils need to be involved in writing, since the reading–writing connection is no less important to these pupils than to those whose native language is English. LEP pupils develop

12.12 Putting Ideas to Work

Children's Literature and Second Language Learning

THE EFFECTIVENESS of using an infusion of literature in reading programs for pupils whose first language is not English has been clearly demonstrated.

To test the hypothesis that repeated exposure to high-interest, illustrated storybooks will produce rapid second-language learning, Elley and Mangubhai (1983) placed hundreds of high-interest trade books written in English into classrooms in rural schools in the South Pacific island nation of Fiji. The researchers then determined the effect of this "book flood" on the general language competence of the pupils for whom English was a second language.

In various classes, the trade books were used in teacher-directed, shared reading sessions followed by book-related activities, and in daily periods of sustained silent reading. Results showed that pupils who were exposed to literature progressed in reading and in listening comprehension at a dramatic rate, demonstrating the role that literature can play in helping pupils learn English as a second language.

In the United States, Roser, Hoffman, and Farest (1990) conducted a project in which children's literature was infused into a tradi-tional language arts program serving primarily limited-English-speaking pupils from economically disadvantaged environments. The project involved introducing literature units (including trade books on focused topics and teaching suggestions) into kindergarten, first, and second grade classrooms in which over 80 percent of the pupils were Hispanic. Books were shared, enjoyed, and discussed; pupils talked, drew, and wrote in response to stories; trade books became the focus of formal reading lessons. In short, literature became an integral part of the reading program.

The results? Very positive! Pupils' scores increased on both the standardized reading achievement test administered in the district and on the state test of basic skills. Teachers developed insights and teaching techniques that they had not had before. "Our results indicate that a literature-based program can be implemented successfully in schools that serve at-risk students. Further, there is every indication that these students respond to such a program in the same positive ways as any student would—with enthusiasm for books, with willingness to share ideas, and with growth in language and literacy" (Hoffman and Farest, 1990; p. 559).

writing ability through process writing activities, through dialogue journals, and through other techniques that have proved effective for all pupils (Hudelson, 1987).

Multicultural literature can be a powerful force in enhancing literacy experiences and in leading to personal empowerment for all children.

Resource Teachers

As is the case with special needs pupils, most school systems offer special instruction and support services for ESL and bilingual pupils. Sometimes, pupils leave the classroom and receive extra help in small groups or tutorial settings. In other situations, pupils receive support as part of the regular classroom program. Some bilingual programs provide special periods of instruction in pupils' native language as well as in English.

In all cases, the teacher becomes a member of a team providing literacy instruction for pupils with limited English proficiency. And as is the case with resource specialists who work with special needs learners, coordination and communication are vital. Since resource specialists for LEP pupils are often speakers of the pupil's first language, these specialists can prove to be valuable sources of information about pupils' family backgrounds, cultural background, and native language—information that the teacher can use in planning a successful reading program in the classroom.

Resource teachers can also be effective contacts with the home, since parent involvement is essential in the literacy development of the LEP pupil. For a variety of culturally and linguistically related reasons, parents of ESL and bilingual pupils are sometimes reluctant to approach the school as full partners in their children's education. Yet because family values reinforce school expectations, "interpreting the school's agenda for parents is one of the most important tasks teachers face" (Bowman, 1989).

Parent involvement is important for reasons more directly related to literacy. When English is not the native language spoken at home, pupils can lose opportunities for language development and schema building that support success in learning to read. That is why partnership programs have been developed to include parents and children working cooperatively in reading and related language-instructional activities (Quintero and Huerta-Macias, 1990).

Summary and Conclusions

North America has always been considered an ethnic and cultural melting pot, a place where people from many nations, languages, and cultures have come together. In recent years, the metaphor of a "melting pot" has given way to that of a "salad bowl," a society in which different ethnic and cultural groups retain their own values and identities while still being part of "one nation under God." It is in this context that schools are educating pupils to form the society of the 21st century, and multicultural children's literature needs to be part of that education.

Multicultural literature opens windows of understanding and sharpens pupils' appreciation for the "taste" of the salad of which we are all a part. Literature that reflects different multicultural perspectives allows racially and ethnically diverse pupils to realize that they have a rich cultural heritage of which they can be proud, while it allows all pupils to realize the literary diversity of the society in which we live.

The language that pupils bring to school affects their learning to read and write. Pupils arrive in the classroom with different regional and social varieties of speech, and these dialects need to be taken into account in teaching them how to read. Some aspects of instruction may need to be adjusted in light of the phonological, lexical, and syntactical features of pupils' language; the strategies used to create meaning in printed text remain the same for all pupils. No matter what dialect pupils speak, they should be allowed to render print into their natural language pattern.

When the language that pupils bring to the classroom is not English, further adjustments are required. Instruction in reading and writing English needs to be rooted firmly in oral language competency. The emphasis in literacy instruction needs to remain on understanding and appreciating print.

No matter what the pupil's language—be it a dialect of English or a language other than English—that language is rooted in the pupil's cultural roots and traditions. These traditions are tied to, and illustrated by, the literature that is part of that culture. Multicultural literature reflects something of value for all pupils and constitutes meaningful material that is essential to reading instruction in today's elementary school.

Discussion Questions and Activities

1. Select several books of a well-respected AHANA author of children's literature—Virginia Hamilton, John Steptoe, Virginia Driving Hawk Sneve, or Lawrence Yep, for example. You can also find some background information on the author him/herself. What special qualities do the works have that reflect the author's understanding of the culture?

2. Do a little sociolinguistic research. Using a linguistic atlas or other reference book from the library, investigate the speech pattern of the language of your area. How are these language patterns manifested in the language of your friends and fellow students?

3. Prepare a reading lesson plan based on a trade book with a multicultural focus. What type of adjustments might you have to make if you were teaching this lesson to a group of inner city or rural dialect speakers, or to a group of pupils with limited English proficiency?

4. Compile a list of trade books that you might use in planning a program like *Teaching Multicultural Literature* (see 12.6). Suggest one or two ideas on how you might use different books at each phase. Compare your list of books and your ideas with those compiled by classmates.

5. In a group, respond to the following discussion question: If you were teaching in a mostly white, middle-class community, why would it be important to have a strong focus on multicultural literature in your reading program? Have a recorder take notes on your group's discussion and the conclusions you reach.

School-Based Assignments

1. Interview a teacher on the topic of how the teacher views language differences in his or her classroom. What adjustments does he or she think necessary for pupils who speak a nonstandard dialect or who speak English as a second language?

2. Take a look at the classroom library with an eye to its selection of multicultural books. How many books are available with a multicultural perspective? How do these books reflect their respective cultures?

3. Select a children's trade book appropriate to your grade level, one that has a distinct multicultural focus or flavor. Share the book with a group of pupils, either by reading it to them or by using it in a directed reading activity. Determine if pupils notice the elements contained in the story and note their reaction. What type of activity, beyond reading and writing, would be appropriate with this book to focus on the diversity it reflects?

4. Multicultural literature has an important place in thematic units in social studies. Select a social studies topic that is part of the curriculum in your school setting. Make a list of children's trade books that could be used in this unit, along with one or two activities that can be planned for each book.

5. Since they come from the oral tradition, ethnic folktales typically have qualities that make them appealing for storytelling. With the help of the librarian (if necessary), select a piece of folk literature and work with a small group of pupils in preparing to share it orally with a younger class.

Children's Trade Books Cited in This Chapter

Agard, John. *The Calypso Alphabet.* New York: Henry Holt, 1989.

Armstrong, William. *Sounder.* New York: Harper and Row, 1969.

Ai-Ling, Louie. *Yeh-Shen: A Cinderella Story from China.* New York: Philomel, 1982.

Baylor, Byrd. *Amigo.* New York: Macmillan, 1989.

———. *Hawk, I'm Your Brother.* New York: Macmillan, 1976.

Bierhorst, John. *The Spirit Child.* New York: Morrow, 1984.

Blanco, Alberto. *The Desert Mermaid/La sirena del desierto.* San Francisco: The Children's Press, 1992.

Brenner, Barbara. *Wagon Wheels.* New York: Harper and Row, 1978.

Brown, Tricia. *Hello, Amigos!* New York: Henry Holt, 1986.

Buck, Pearl. *The Big Wave.* New York: Harper and Row, 1986.

Bunting, Eve. *How Many Days to America? A Thanksgiving Story.* New York: Clarion, 1988.

Cadato, Michael, and Joseph Bruchae. *Keepers of the Earth.* Golden, CO: Fulcrum, 1989.

Cheltin, Helen. *Angel Island Prisoner.* Berkeley, CA: New Seed Press, 1982.

Chief Seattle. *Brother Eagle, Sister Sky.* New York: Dial, 1991.

Cisneros, Sandra. *The House on Mango Street.* Houston: Arte Publico, 1989.

Climo, Shirley. *Egyptian Cinderella.* New York: Harper and Row, 1989.

Coerr, Eleanor. *Sadako and the Thousand Paper Cranes.* New York: Dell, 1977.

Collier, James, and Christopher Collier. *War Comes to Willy Freeman.* New York: Dell, 1983.

Dahl, Roald. *Charlie and the Chocolate Factory.* New York: Bantam, 1977.

———. *James and the Giant Peach.* New York: Knopf, 1962.

Delacre, Lulu. *Arroz con Leche: Popular Songs and Rhymes from Latin America.* New York: Scholastic, 1989.

Demi. *The Empty Pot.* New York: Holt, 1991.

dePaola, Tomie. *The Legend of the Bluebonnet.* New York: Putnam, 1983.

de Poix, Carol. *Jo, Flo and Yolanda.* Carrboro, NC: Lollipop Power, 1979.

Durrel, Ann. *The Dianne Goode Book of American Folk Tales and Songs.* New York: Dutton, 1989.

Emberley, Rebecca. *Taking a Walk/Cammandro.* Boston: Little, Brown, 1990.

———. *My Home/Mi Casa.* Boston: Little, Brown, 1990.

Faucher, Ruth. *Cesar Chavez.* New York: Harper and Row, 1988.

Feelings, Muriel. *Jambo Means Hello: Swahili Alphabet Book.* New York: Dial, 1974.

———. *Moja Means One: A Swahili Counting Book.* New York: Dial, 1971.

Flournoy, Valerie. *The Patchwork Quilt.* New York: Dial, 1985.

Fox, Paula. *How Many Miles to Babylon.* New York: White, 1967.

Gera, Adele. *My Grandmother's Stories: A Collection of Jewish Folk Tales.* New York: Knopf, 1990.

Goble, Paul. *The Gift of the Sacred Dog.* New York: Bradbury Press, 1980.

———. *Her Seven Brothers.* New York: Bradbury, 1989.

Green, Bette. *Philip Hall Likes Me. I Recon Maybe.* New York: Dial, 1974.

Greenfield, Eloise. *Grandpa's Face.* New York: Philomel, 1988.

———. *Sister.* New York: Crowell, 1974.

Grifalconi, Ann. *Osa's Pride.* Boston: Little, Brown, 1990.

Hale, Janet. *Owl's Song.* New York: Avon, 1976.

Hamilton, Virginia. *The People Could Fly: American Black Folktales.* New York: Knopf, 1985.

———. *Zeeley.* New York: Macmillan, 1967.

Hewett, Joan. *Hector Lives in the United States Now: The Story of a Mexican-American Child.* New York: Lippincott, 1990.

Hoyt-Goldsmith, Diane. *Pueblo Storyteller.* New York: Holiday House, 1991.

Huck, Charlotte. *Princess Furball.* New York: Greenwillow, 1989.

Huynh, Queng Nhuong. *The Land I Lost: Adventures of a Boy in Viet Nam.* New York: Harper and Row, 1982.

Jacobs, William Jay. *Ellis Island: New Hope in a New Land.* New York: Charles Scribner's Sons, 1990.

Keats, Ezra Jack. *Peter's Chair.* New York: Harper and Row, 1967.

Krumgold, Joseph. *And Now Miguel.* New York: Crowell, 1953.

Lee, Jeannie, M. *Ba-Nam.* New York: Henry Holt, 1987.

Lessae, Frane. *Caribbean Canvas.* New York: Lippincott, 1987.

Lewis, John. *The Chinese Word for Horse, and Other Stories.* New York: Schocken Books, 1980.

Lord, Beth Bao. *In The Year of the Boar and Jackie Robinson.* New York: Harper and Row, 1984.

Martin, Bill, Jr., and John Archambault. *Knots on a Counting Rope.* New York: Henry Holt, 1987.

Mathers, Petra. *Maria Teresa.* New York: Harper and Row, 1985.

Mathis, Sharon Bell. *The Hundred Penny Box.* New York: Viking, 1975.

McDermott, Gerald. *Arrow to the Sun.* New York: Viking, 1974.

———. *Flecha al Sol.* New York: Viking, 1991.

Mendez, Phil. *The Black Snowman.* New York: Scholastic, 1989.

Miles, Mishka. *Annie and the Old One.* Boston: Little, Brown, 1971.

Mohr, Nicholasa. *Felita.* New York: Dial, 1979.

Morimoto, Junko. *Mouse's Marriage.* New York: Viking Kestrel, 1986.

Morris, Winnifred. *The Magic Leaf.* New York: Atheneum, 1987.

Mosel, Arline. *Tikki, Tikki, Tembo.* New York: Henry Holt, 1968.

Mullel, Tololwe M. *The Orphan Boy.* New York: Clarion, 1990.

Murray, Michele. *Nellie Cameron.* Minneapolis: Seabury, 1971.

Naidoo, Beverley. *Journey to Jo'burg.* New York: Lippincott. 1985.

O'Brien, Edna. *Tales for the Telling.* New York: Penguin, 1988.

Paek, Min. *Aekyung's Dream.* San Francisco: Children's Book Press, 1988.

Parrish, Peggy. *Good Hunting, Blue Sky.* New York: Random House, 1989.

Rehnman, Mats. *The Clay Flute.* New York: Farrar, Straus & Giroux. 1989.

Rohmer, Harriet, and Mary Anchondo. *How We Came to the Fifth World/ Como vinimos al quinto mundo.* San Francisco: Children's Book Press, 1988.

Rosario, Idalia. *Idalia's Project ABC.* New York: Henry Holt, 1987.

Schroeder, Alan. *Ragtime Trumpie.* Boston: Little, Brown, 1989.

Scott, Sally. *The Magic Horse.* New York: Morrow, 1988.

Seeger, Pete. *Abiyoyo.* New York: Macmillan, 1986.

Slote, Alfred. *Finding Buck McHenry.* New York: Harper Collins, 1991.

Sneve, Virginia Driving Hawk. *Dancing Teepees: Poems of American Indian Youth.* New York: Holiday House, 1989.

———. *Jimmy Yellow Hawk.* New York: Holiday House, 1972.

Snyder, Dianne. *The Boy of the Three-Year Nap.* Boston: Houghton Mifflin, 1988.

Speare, Elizabeth George. *Sign of the Beaver.* Boston: Houghton Mifflin, 1983.

Steptoe, John. *Daddy Is a Monster . . . Sometimes.* New York: Lippincott, 1980.

———. *Mufaro's Beautiful Daughter: An African Tale.* New York: Lothrup, 1987.

Strickland, Dorothy. *Listen, Children.* New York: Bantam, 1986.

Suart, Michele. *Angel Child, Dragon Child.* Milwaukee: Raintree, 1983.

Taylor, Mildred. *Let The Circle Be Unbroken.* New York: Dial, 1981.

———. *Roll of Thunder, Hear My Cry.* New York: Dial, 1976.

Tompert, Ann. *Grandfather Tang's Story.* New York: Crown, 1990.

Tsutsui, Yoiko. *Anna In Charge.* New York: Viking Kistrel, 1989.

Uchida, Yoshiko. *Journey to Topaz.* New York: Scribner, 1971.

———. *Journey Home.* New York: Macmillan, 1982.

Wall, Lina Mao. *Judge Rabbit and the Tree Spirit.* San Francisco: Children's Press, 1991.

Waters, Kate, and Madeline Slovenz-Low. *Lion Dancer: Ernie Wan's Chinese New Year.* New York: Scholastic, 1990.

Winthrop, Elizabeth. *Vasilissa the Beautiful.* New York: Harper Collins, 1991.

Wyndham, Robert, ed. *Chinese Mother Goose Rhymes.* New York: Philomel, 1968.

Yashima, Taro. *Crow Boy.* New York: Viking, 1969.

Yep, Lawrence. *Dragonwings.* New York: Harper and Row, 1985.

———. *The Rainbow People.* New York: Harper and Row, 1989.

Young, Ed. *Lon Po Po: A Red-Riding Hood Story from China.* New York: Philomel, 1989.

References

Allen, V. G. (1989). Literature as Support to Language Acquisition. In P. Rigg and V. G. Allen (eds.), *When They Don't All Speak English: Integrating the ESL Student into the Regular Classroom.* Urbana, IL: National Council of Teachers of English.

Banks, J. A. (1989). Integrating the Curriculum with Ethnic Content: Approaches and Guidelines. In J. A. Banks and C. A. McGee Banks (eds.), *Multicultural Education: Issues and Perspectives.* Boston: Allyn and Bacon.

Barnitz, J. G. (1980). Black English and Other Dialects: Sociolinguistic Implications for Reading Instruction. *The Reading Teacher* 33:779–786.

Bishop, R. S. (1987). Extending Multicultural Understanding through Children's Books. In B. Cullinan (ed.), *Children's Literature in the Reading Program.* Newark, DE: International Reading Association.

Boman, B. T. (1989). Educating Language-Minority Children: Challenges and Opportunities. *Phi Delta Kappan* 71:118–120.

Burling, R. (1973). *English in Black and White.* New York: Holt, Rinehart and Winston.

Cosby, B. (1990). 45 Years From Today. *Ebony* 46:61.

Cox, S., and Galda, L. (1990). Multicultural Literature: Mirrors and Windows on a Global Community. *The Reading Teacher* 43:582–589.

Diaakiw, J. Y. (1990). Children's Literature and Global Education: Understanding the Developing World. *The Reading Teacher* 44:296–300.

Dillard, J. L. (1972). *Black English.* New York: Random House.

Early, M. (1990). Enabling First and Second Language Learners in the Classroom. *Language Arts* 67:567–575.

Elley, W. R., and Mangubhai, F. (1983). The Impact of Reading on Second Language Learning. *Reading Research Quarterly* 19:53–67.

Hudelson, S. (1987). The Role of Native Language Literacy in the Education of Language Minority Children. *Language Arts* 64:827–841.

Lake, R. (1990). An Indian Father's Plea. *Teacher Magazine* 2:48–53.

Mason, J., and Au, K. (1990). *Reading Instruction for Today.* New York: Harper Collins.

McCauley, J. K., and McCauley, D. S. (1992). Using Choral Reading to Promote Language Learning for ESL Students. *The Reading Teacher* 45:526–537.

Norton, D. E. (1990). Teaching Multicultural Literature in the Reading Curriculum. *The Reading Teacher* 44:28–40.

Quintero, R., and Huerta-Macias, A. (1990). All in the Family: Bilingualism and Biliteracy. *The Reading Teacher* 44:306–312.

Rasinski, T. V., and Padak, N. D. (1990). Multicultural Learning through Children's Literature. *Language Arts* 67:576–580.

Roser, N. L., Hoffman, J. V., and Farest, C. (1990). Language, Literature, and At-Risk Children. *The Reading Teacher* 43:554–559.

Sims, R. (1982). *Shadow and Substance: Afro-American Experiences in Contemporary Children's Fiction.* Urbana, IL: National Council of Teachers of English.

Smitherman, G., ed. (1981). *Black English and the Education of Black Children and Youth.* Detroit: Center for Black Studies, Wayne State University.

Tylor, E. B. (1992). *Primitive Cultures.* 5th ed. London: J. Murray Co.

Walker-Dalhouse, D. (1992). Using African-American Literature to Increase Ethnic Understanding. *The Reading Teacher* 45:416–422.

Chapter 13

Assessing Literacy Development

Chapter 13 Outline

I. Introduction
  A. Reasons for Assessment
  B. A General Perspective
    1. Assessment Is Part of Learning
    2. The More Abstract an Element Is, the More Difficult It Is to Measure
    3. The Face of Reading Assessment Is Beginning to Change
II. Formal Assessment
  A. Standardized Reading Achievement Tests
    The Pros and Cons of Standardized Reading Achievement Tests
  B. Skill-Development Tests
    1. Criterion-Referenced Tests
      The Pros and Cons of Criterion-Referenced Tests
    2. Standardized Skills Tests
III. Classroom-Based Assessment
  A. Teacher Observation
    1. Reciprocal Teaching
    2. Interactive Assessment
    3. Think Alouds
    4. Book Discussions
    5. Conferences
    6. Checklists
    7. Written Records
    8. Literature Journals and Logs
  B. Pros and Cons of Classroom-Based Assessment
  C. Informal Reading Inventories
    Pros and Cons of Informal Reading Inventories
  D. Miscue Analysis
    Pros and Cons of Miscue Analysis

IV. Portfolio Assessment
    A. What Do Portfolios Contain?
    B. How Are Portfolios Used?
 V. Summary and Conclusions
Discussion Questions and Activities
School-Based Assignments
Children's Trade Books Cited in This Chapter
References

███████████████████

Features

13.1   Dimensions of Assessment
13.2   New Views of Reading Assessment
13.3   National Assessment of Educational Progress
13.4   Competency Testing
13.5   Assessing Attitudes toward Reading
13.6   Assessment of Emergent Literacy
13.7   Comprehension Matrix and Profile
13.8   Sample Checklists
13.9   Literature Reading Behavior Inventory
13.10 Informal Reading Inventories
13.11 Using Trade Books as "Benchmark" Measures
13.12 Using the Tape Recorder

Key Concepts in This Chapter

*L*iteracy assessment has many purposes; a variety of tools and techniques are needed to reflect the different purposes that assessment has in a literature-based program.

Formal reading tests are used widely in schools. These norm-referenced instruments are used both to measure individual pupil progress and to assess the status of reading programs.

Classroom performance measures provide an ongoing indication of pupils' reading and writing competencies, along with their instructional needs.

Portfolio assessment involves the compilation of multiple measures to monitor and record pupil progress in reading and writing.

███████████████████

ASSESSMENT OF learning is a major concern of anyone associated with education—teachers, administrators, parents, pupils, school boards, state legislators, and the general public. Everyone is anxious to know, ''How are we doing?'' This is no less true of literature-based instruction than in more conventional reading programs.

Because of this widespread concern, testing is a pervasive part of schooling. For a long time, standardized testing has dominated the educational landscape. It has been estimated that 105 million standardized tests are administered every year—an average of 2½ tests per pupil per year, and this is a conservative estimate (Neill and Medina, 1989). Also, the amount of testing that we do seems to be increasing (Haney and Madaus, 1989). Schools have a heavy philosophical and financial investment in formal testing.

Of all curriculum areas, testing seems to impact reading most of all. Because reading is so close to the heart of the educational process and because success in school is so closely related to literacy development, everyone is interested in the results of reading tests. Reports on local performance on achievement tests make the front page of the newspaper, and important educational decisions are based on reported test results. ''The influence of (reading) testing is greater now than at any time in our history'' (Valencia and Pearson, 1987; p. 727).

Assessment, however, extends well beyond the narrow concept of testing. Although the terms *testing, assessment, measurement,* and *evaluation* are often used interchangeably, there are differences among them. *Evaluation* refers to the process of gathering information to see how well pupils have achieved objectives. *Testing* is the technology we use to gather this data. *Measurement* is the process of quantifying the data we gather. *Assessment* is a broad term that includes the gathering *and* the use of this information for the purpose of instructional improvement. Part of assessment is *diagnosis,* the process of determining strengths and weaknesses for the purpose of planning instruction. These terms are related, to be sure, and definitional arguments exist. The point is, however, that assessment has many dimensions and many purposes in literacy programs.

In using literature to teach pupils how to read and write, maintaining a broad perspective on assessment is important. Formal tests are only one (some say distorted) part of the assessment scene. One-time measures may be appropriate for some purposes, but ongoing classroom-based assessment that teachers conduct and the instructional decisions that they make as a result of their assessment activities are far more important.

Reasons for Assessment

Why does so much testing go on in schools? The reasons for assessment include:

accountability to the public for the money it spends on schooling, to let the taxpayers know that they are getting a return on their educational investment;

gathering information to let parents know that learning has taken place, to indicate how well their children are progressing, and to compare the performance of various groups;

getting information to help teachers assess instructional outcomes and to indicate direction for teaching aimed at pupils' needs and interests.

13.1
FOR YOUR INFORMATION
Dimensions of Assessment

Dimensions of Assessment

Formal Tests

including
norm-referenced
achievement tests

skills-related
criterion-referenced
tests

competency
tests

Classroom Assessment

including teacher
observation,
conferences and
written records

informal reading
inventories

miscue
analysis

Portfolios

with samples of
pupils' work
showing growth over
time in
different dimensions
of literacy
development

To achieve these purposes, different types of assessment tools and procedures are needed.

For decades, education has relied heavily on a variety of formal instruments to provide data on pupils—norm-referenced reading tests to measure levels of achievement, criterion-referenced tests aimed at determining mastery of specific skills, diagnostic instruments to indicate pupils' strengths and weaknesses, basal reading tests to monitor learning from the reading series, and other formal measures designed to determine the amount and/or kind of learning that has taken place. Beyond these formal measures, teachers have long used their own informal techniques of observation and record-keeping to keep track of pupils' progress and problems. More recently, portfolios have been used as part of assessment to indicate pupils' reading and writing development. Each of these elements constitutes a part of the total picture in assessing pupils' progress and problems in learning to read.

A General Perspective

Before examining the specifics of formal, informal, and portfolio dimensions of assessment, the whole process of assessment needs to be examined in a general perspective. Any view of assessment needs to consider three points:

1. Assessment extends beyond testing; it is a continuous part of learning.
2. The more abstract an element is, the more difficult it is to measure with confidence.
3. The face of reading assessment is beginning to change dramatically.

Assessment Is Part of Learning   Assessment extends beyond the narrow concept of "testing" and becomes an integral element in the total instructional process. It is the beginning and end of the learning cycle that constitutes good teaching; that is, teachers assess in order to set goals and objectives for lessons, provide instruction to meet these goals and objectives, and assess to determine if the goals have been met. Assessment is also a means of helping teachers reflect on their own teaching and what is happening in their classrooms.

Formal tests are administered only periodically; assessment takes place each day. It happens before the teacher recommends a trade book to a pupil for independent reading, and as the teacher solicits the pupil's reaction to the story. It goes on in reading groups as the teacher tries to find out what pupils already know about a topic before they read, and as part of postreading questions and discussion. It is an inherent part of such instructional strategies as InQuest, ReQuest and K-W-L (described on p. 204 and 246). In short, assessment is an integral part of the teaching-learning process.

By themselves, tests will not improve teaching. Tests measure learning outcomes. They will improve learning outcomes only to the extent that they lead to improved instruction. "Collecting data about students is an empty exercise unless the information is used to plan instruction" (McKenna and Kear, 1990; p. 627).

The More Abstract an Element Is, the More Difficult It Is to Measure   Assessment involves measurement. Tests and other assessment tools are educational yardsticks that are used to quantify reading development. But reading ability cannot be measured with the same precision and confidence that physical qualities can be measured. It is easier to measure a pupil's height or weight with absolute accuracy than to measure intelligence or reading ability, and it is more difficult still to measure the affective dimensions of learning.

Yardsticks exist to measure every human characteristic—tape measures to determine height, standardized reading tests to measure reading level, scales to assess such qualities as empathy and appreciation. But it is not easy to quantify what is inside a pupil's head (or heart). To assess the more abstract human qualities, the best we can do is estimate. It is presumptuous to consider a reading level of 3.4 as an absolute measure of a pupil's reading ability or to say that a pupil has "mastered" a comprehension skill such as main ideas based on a single measure alone. Intangible human qualities are far more complex than that.

The Face of Reading Assessment Is Beginning to Change   Research on the nature of the reading process has affected reading instruction, and the theory and practice of assessment is starting to catch up with these changes. Although some newly developed reading assessment instruments are beginning to reflect the findings of recent reading research (Peters and Wixon, 1989; Tierney, Carter, and Desai, 1991), many conventional standardized measures of reading achievement still look the same as they did in the 1920s.

As the view of reading has shifted from mastery of a discrete set of separate skills to more dynamic interaction between a reader and text, assessment dimensions are changing to reflect that view. As literacy development is seen as a multifaceted process, assessment is taking on a multidimensional focus. As whole language theory has influenced classroom instruction, new tools of assessment are advancing to the forefront. "The assessment of reading seems best described as being in a state of *transition*" (Pikulski, 1989; p. 80).

New Views of Reading Assessment

VALENCIA AND Pearson (1987) identify a "litany of conflicts" that contrast
new views of reading and conventional practices in assessing reading.

A SET OF CONTRASTS BETWEEN NEW VIEWS OF READING AND CURRENT PRACTICES IN ASSESSING READING

New views of the reading process tell us that	Yet when we assess reading comprehension, we . . . .
Prior knowledge is an important determinant of reading comprehension.	Mask any relationship between prior knowledge and reading comprehension by using lots of short passages on lots of topics.
A complete story or text has structural and topical integrity.	Use short texts that seldom approximate the structural and topical integrity of an authentic text.
Inference is an essential part of the process of comprehending units as small as sentences.	Rely on literal comprehension test items.
The diversity in prior knowledge across individuals as well as the varied causal relations in human experiences invite many possible inferences to fit a text or question.	Use multiple choice items with only one correct answer, even when many of the responses might, under certain conditions, be plausible.
The ability to vary reading strategies to fit the text and the situation is one hallmark of an expert reader.	Seldom assess how and when students vary the strategies they use during normal reading, studying, or when the going gets tough.
The ability to synthesize information from various parts of the text and different texts is hallmark of an expert reader.	Rarely go beyond finding the main ideas of a paragraph or passage.
The ability to ask good questions of text, as well as to answer them is hallmark of an expert reader.	Seldom ask students to create or select questions about a selection they may have just read.
All aspects of a reader's experience, including habits that arise from school and home, influence reading comprehension.	Rarely view information on reading habits and attitudes as being as important information about performance.
Reading involves the orchestration of many skills that complement one another in a variety of ways.	Use tests that fragment reading into isolated skills and report performance on each.
Skilled readers are fluent; their word identification is sufficiently automatic to allow most cognitive resources to be used for comprehension.	Rarely consider fluency as an index of skilled reading.
Learning from text involves the restructuring, application, and flexible use of knowledge in new situations.	Often ask readers to respond to the text's declarative knowledge rather than to apply it to near and far transfer tasks.

What will these changes mean as schools move into the 21st century? A different approach to reading will demand a different approach to assessment. Reliance on a single standardized measure of reading ability will disappear. Different kinds of reading assessment techniques will be used. Tests will expand conventional multiple-choice formats and include alternative response modes for pupils. Assessment will become less test-centered and more teacher-centered and pupil-centered.

Literature-based reading instruction lends itself especially well to this changing view of assessment. Teachers who use literature as the centerpiece of their reading instructional program do not abandon the components of conventional programs. However, with trade books as instructional tools, reading becomes an authentic encounter with text. As enjoyment and meaning are the primary goals of instruction, these elements are the primary concerns in assessment.

As these trends develop, classroom teachers will continue to interpret the results of formal measures, engage in informal assessment processes, and compile portfolios to assess the reading and literacy development of pupils.

Formal Assessment

Formal measures of reading commonly used in schools include norm-referenced, standardized reading-achievement tests, criterion-referenced tests, and tests of specific components related to literacy.

Standardized Reading Achievement Tests

Most college students are well familiar with standardized reading-achievement tests, because they have had years and years of experience with "What's-the-best-title-for-this-story?" These are the test batteries that all pupils take once a year, with levels that cover kindergarten through twelfth grade. They are timed tests with a multiple choice format. They are the tools that American education has traditionally relied on to monitor pupil progress in reading; to compare, rank, and sort pupils; and to pass judgment on the quality of education that our schools provide.

Each of the words used to describe these measurement tools tells about the instruments themselves. They are:

Standardized. Reading achievement tests are designed to be used on a national basis. Test items are specified, procedures for administering the tests are set, and rules about the test are enforced so that comparable measures can be obtained by people using the tests in different areas and under different circumstances. Just as measuring devices for weight and height are standardized with commonly consistent units of measurement, so are measuring devices for reading.

Reading. Achievement tests aim to assess reading. All contain separate sections for vocabulary (or word meaning) and comprehension. Some have additional sections as well—for example, sections on decoding skills or on reading speed. Pupils' performance on these separate sections are combined in an attempt to provide a measure of their overall reading level.

Achievement. Achievement involves the amount of information gained or level of proficiency attained. The pupil's level of achievement is based on norms. Standardized reading achievement tests are *norm-referenced* measures; that is, test results are determined by how well the pupil compares to others in a norming sample selected to represent a national cross section of pupils. Pupils' performances are judged in relation to how their scores compare to a large representative group of pupils at the same age and grade level in the national norming sample. Norm-referenced reading-achievement test scores indicate a pupil's relative standing in the general school population.

Tests. A test is defined as "a set of systematic tasks or questions to which responses may be quantified and performance interpreted" (Harris and Hodges, 1981; p. 327). The items to which pupils respond reflect their purported levels of achievement in these norm-referenced tests.

Standardized tests are written by experts in the fields of reading and measurement and are published by commercial publishing companies, independent of particular instructional programs. They report figures to indicate statistical validity and reliability and they are used in virtually every school in this country.

The Pros and Cons of Standardized Reading Achievement Tests

Those who favor the use of standardized reading achievement tests view them as objective instruments that can be used as "national yardsticks," tools that provide a measure that can be used to determine the reading level of pupils from diverse geographical, ethnic, social, economic, and demographic backgrounds. The tests provide uniform standards that supposedly avoid the vagrancies inherent in subjective judgments. They allow schools to gauge how their pupils perform in comparison to pupils nationwide.

At the same time, a whirlwind of criticism surrounds the theory and practice of standardized reading-achievement testing. The common concerns or complaints about these tests are:

They are product-oriented and ignore important elements of the reading process.

They are anachronistic, given what we know about literacy and about learning to read and write.

They often provide downright erroneous information about pupils' reading abilities and misleading information about schools.

They unfairly discriminate against certain groups of pupils, with disproportionate negative impacts being felt by minority, low-income, and linguistically different learners.

They are too narrow in scope; that is, they test reading skills and not reading.

They focus too heavily on low-level skills, drawing a focus away from higher-level thinking and creative activities.

The machine-scorable, multiple-choice format is limiting in the kind of information it can generate about pupils.

They treat pupils as objects—"as if their education and thought processes were similar and as if their reasons for their answers were irrelevant" (Wiggins, 1989; p. 708).

Besides, "there is normally considerable waste of time in standardized group tests because able children spend most time on items that are too easy, and less able readers spend most time on items that are too difficult" (Johnson, 1984; p. 156).

13.3
FOR YOUR INFORMATION
National Assessment of Educational Progress

THE NATIONAL Assessment of Educational Progress (NAEP) is a national testing program designed to monitor reading (and other) achievement of American students. A federally mandated project conducted at present by the Educational Testing Service, the program assesses samples of nine-, 13-, and 17-year-old pupils and charts their performance over time. (Reading has been assessed in 1971, 1975, 1980, 1984, and 1988.) The results produce a kind of national "satellite photo" of the nation's level of reading proficiency, a broad picture of the educational achievement of the nation as a whole. NAEP also gathers information about pupils' reading attitudes and behaviors.

What are the results of the most recent NAEP testing? *The Reading Report Card, 1971–88* (Mullis and Jenkins, 1990) indicates that even though gains in reading proficiency for the nation were not dramatic,

trends were generally positive. The overall picture shows a nation of pupils reading better now than in the past, albeit only slightly better. Advances by minority pupils in the latest testing are particularly impressive.

With regard to attitudes and experiences in reading, pupils of all ages were more aware of reading in content areas of the curriculum. And although reading is not a frequent or highly valued activity for many pupils, older pupils reported reading more today than did those in the early 1970s. It is not surprising that the data indicate that pupils who read most display the highest reading proficiency.

In writing performance, NAEP testing indicates little overall change, with pupils performing at only minimal levels of proficiency on informative, persuasive, and imaginary writing tasks (Applebee, Langer, Mullis, and Jenkins, 1990).

Perhaps the most serious problems associated with norm-referenced, standardized reading achievement testing rest not in the tests themselves but rather in the uncritical faith with which results are viewed and in the effects that test results can have on instruction. People often see the single quantification of a standardized test score as an infallible indicator of a pupil's reading ability. With this unquestioning stance, vital decisions such as promoting pupils from grade to grade, providing financial support for schools, rewarding teachers, and ranking school districts or schools within districts are inappropriately made based on test results.

These kinds of decisions can lead to pressures to adjust reading programs in light of standardized test results. Standardized tests are built on a skill-based model of reading. When instruction is defined narrowly in terms of test content, the educational process is corrupted. Reading instruction degenerates into having pupils work on skills exercises and answer low-level questions based on short passages, because these are the types of items contained on the tests. At worst, pressures lead to using the test itself as the basis for reading instruction.

Reading extends well beyond the realm of what is measured on conventional, standardized reading achievement tests. Standardized tests take a pupil's "reading pulse," but pulse is only one manifestation of a healthy or unhealthy condition. As new tests are designed in light of what we know about reading, and as the concept of assessment extends beyond mere testing, the bondage of standardized achievement tests will likely be broken, and horizons on reading assessment will be broadened.

Whatever their form and however they report their results—as grade level, standard score, percentile, or level of proficiency—the purpose of achievement tests is the same: to indicate "how well" a pupil reads. The test samples behavior and reports a score that indicates overall reading ability. While analyzing the results of various parts of a reading achievement battery can produce information about sub-areas of reading development, more specific information about component parts of the reading process is produced by skill-development tests.

Skill-Development Tests

As the name indicates, reading skill-development tests are designed to measure pupil progress in particular reading skills areas. These assessment tools include criterion-referenced measures and standardized instruments that focus on particular components of the reading process.

Criterion-Referenced Tests   Criterion-referenced tests are formal measures designed to assess pupils' progress in specific skills—for example, phonics, vocabulary, or different dimensions of reading comprehension. Rather than compare a pupil's performance to that of others, criterion-referenced tests focus on a pupil's ability to reach a certain level of performance in areas that these tests are designed to measure. Norm-referenced measures are designed to indicate how a pupil compares with others in a sample group; criterion-referenced tests yield results in terms of specific performance standards.

Sometimes called *mastery tests,* criterion-referenced tests get their name from the fact that the pupil needs to attain a certain score as a criterion for mastery. For example, if pupils are asked to identify which of ten words have short vowel sounds and if 90 percent is set as the criterion, pupils who can identify nine of the ten words are said to have "mastered" this dimension of word attack. Or if 80 percent is the criterion for mastery for identifying the main idea of a paragraph, pupils who can answer four of five main idea questions correctly are said to have "mastered" this component of comprehension. The acceptable score is the criterion measure.

Because criterion-referenced tests are less concerned with whether the pupil is better or worse than other pupils in reading, they provide less-global measures and are very closely related to the view of reading as a skill-development process.

Basal reading tests are usually criterion-referenced instruments. Included as part of basal reading programs, these tests are designed to be administered as pupils complete units in the basal text. Typically these tests focus on skills emphasized in the instructional component of the program, and include such goals as determining pupils' knowledge of the meanings of new vocabulary items included in the stories and mastery of skills included in workbook exercises. As basals change to a more literature-based orientation, the focus of these tests is beginning to change as well.

Basal reading tests are part of the overall structure of these series. They give the teacher a means of monitoring pupils at various stages of the program. Like all assessment tools, they have their own advantages and disadvantages.

The pros and cons of criterion-referenced tests. Although criterion-referenced tests have been used as objective-based evaluation measures, these tests have received their share of criticism. Like any one-time measure, they sample only a small slice of behavior that may or may not accurately reflect a pupil's true capacity. One lucky guess on a criterion-referenced test can mean the difference between "mastery" and "nonmastery."

13.4
Competency Testing

A DIMENSION of reading assessment that arrived on the educational scene in the 1970s is competency testing. Usually mandated by state-level political governing bodies, competency tests are designed to ensure that pupils have developed an adequate degree of reading (and other academic) proficiency by the time they graduate from high school. Some states use scores from norm-referenced standardized reading tests as indicators of reading competency; other states have designed their own criterion-referenced measures. No matter what type of yardstick is used, these tests are intended to indicate if pupils can read at least well enough to meet the daily demands of living in a democratic society before they leave school.

The stakes of competency testing are high. In some states, pupils are denied a high school diploma based on their test score. In other instances, their progress from one educational level to another is affected by their performance on intermediate competency measures that are used to monitor grade-to-grade progress.

A spin-off from pupil competency testing is teacher competency testing. A majority of states now require admission or certification tests (or both) for teachers, and the number of states requiring such tests is growing (Eissenberg and Rudner, 1988). Admissions tests are used to screen people before they enter a teacher education program; certification tests are used before states grant someone a license to teach. Although there is a tendency for states to rely on existing standardized instruments for both admissions and certification testing, some states use custom-designed measures in both areas. Although certification tests focus on subject knowledge and professional skills, over half the states continue to require teachers to demonstrate basic competency in reading, writing, and mathematics.

To its proponents and critics, teacher competency testing reflects what is best and worst about education, respectively. Proponents point out that these tests screen out incompetent individuals who really ought to be excluded from the teaching profession. Critics argue that a paper-and-pencil test is an arbitrary and invalid means of determining whether or not an individual can deal effectively with children.

In contrast to norm-referenced measures, criterion-referenced measures provide a breakdown that achievement tests do not. These more precise data generate specific skills information rather than the "big picture" that other assessment tools and techniques provide.

On the other hand, criterion-referenced tests are based on the view that learning to read involves learning a series of isolated skills, arbitrarily sequenced and largely unrelated to one another. The concept of "mastery" is also open to question; that is, although a person may master some aspects of language learning (using the correct punctuation mark at the end of a written sentence, for example), some aspects of reading defy mastery (for example, the ability to interpret a poem). Besides, the skills inventories that make up most formal criterion-referenced instruments take an incredibly large amount of time to administer.

For teachers who emphasize the skills dimension of reading, criterion-referenced tests are useful measures. In literature-based reading instruction, they are rarely, if ever, used.

Beyond the fairly shallow focus of criterion-referenced tests that take small samples of many different skills, there are skills tests that are diagnostic measures that attempt to provide in-depth and detailed information in areas related to reading.

Assessing Attitudes toward Reading

BECAUSE DEVELOPING a positive attitude toward reading is a major goal of any classroom program—especially one in which literature is valued and widely used—measuring attitude toward reading should be an important part of the assessment agenda. Attitude toward reading will have a lot to do with a pupil's reading performance, yet attitude typically is ignored in most performance measures.

McKenna and Kear (1990) have devised a scale, the *Elementary Reading Attitude Survey,* to determine how pupils feel about reading and learning to read. The instrument has 20 items designed to gather information about pupils' recreational and academic reading, with brief and simply worded questions like "How do you feel about spending free time reading?" and "How do you feel when you read out loud in class?" The four-point response mode is very interesting. Pupils indicate their response to each question by circling one of four drawings of the popular cartoon cat Garfield, each with a pose and facial expression that convey emotions from delight to disgust.

The instrument can be administered quickly in a large-group setting, and separate norms for recreational and academic reading are provided. The results can be used to get a quick indication of attitude that can be used in combination with teacher observations and judgments as the basis for assessment and instructional planning. The scale can be used on a pre-/post-test basis at the beginning and end of the year to determine changes in attitude toward reading that may be related to an emphasis on literature in the reading program.

The *Elementary Reading Attitude Survey* is a public domain instrument; that is, it can be used free of charge by teachers in the classroom. The five-page instrument itself, along with directions for administering it and details regarding technical aspects of its development, can be found in *The Reading Teacher,* May 1990, pages 626–639.

Standardized Skills Tests   Standardized skills tests concentrate in detail on particular components of reading competency. These are tests such as:

Test of Reading Comprehension (Brown, Hammill, and Wiederholt, 1986), a comprehensive measure of understanding in reading, with subtests on word meaning, paragraph meaning, sentence matching, sequencing, and comprehension of content-related materials.

Peabody Picture Vocabulary Test (Dunn and Dunn, 1981), a test that requires pupils to name objects in pictures as a means of measuring vocabulary size.

Test of Written Language (Hammill and Larsen, 1988), a comprehensive measure of written language that assesses both stylistic features (syntactic maturity, logical sentences, thematic maturity, etc.) and mechanical aspects (spelling, vocabulary, etc.) of writing.

Woodcock-Johnson Psycho-Educational Battery (Woodcock and Johnson, 1989), a comprehensive battery designed to measure cognitive functioning and academic achievement, with a reading subtest that includes tests of letter and word identification, along with passage comprehension.

These tests, and others like them, focus in depth on particular aspects of literacy. They are normally administered to one pupil at a time by specialists qualified to administer the test and interpret the results. They are usually reserved for pupils who

Assessment is more than testing; it is an integral part of on-going reading activities.

experience greater-than-average difficulty in learning to read. These tests and others like them are reviewed regularly in *Buros Mental Measurements Yearbook* (Kramer and Conoley, 1992).

The ammunition in the arsenal of reading assessment is extensive and impressive. Formal measuring devices exist for virtually every aspect of pupils' developing competencies. But in a literature-based reading program, the on-the-spot informal assessment that the teacher does in the classroom is more valuable by far for guiding the instruction of pupils learning to read. ''The best possible assessment of reading would seem to occur when teachers observe and interact with students as they read authentic texts for genuine purposes'' (Valencia and Pearson, 1987; p. 728).

Classroom-Based Assessment

Teachers typically do not need batteries of formal standardized reading tests to evaluate their pupils' progress and problems in learning to read. A test is a one-shot event that may or may not reflect what a pupil knows or can do. Ongoing assessment involves the use of a variety of classroom-based tools and techniques that include observation, conferences, checklists, reading records, journals and logs, anecdotal records, and performance-based devices that indicate pupil performance in reading and writing on a day-to-day basis.

This type of classroom assessment has come to be widely known as ''kid watching'' (Goodman, 1978). Information gathered as a result of kid watching provides the basis for the instructional decisions that teachers make as part of literature-based reading.

The teacher's role in classroom-based assessment is vital. Speaking of the teacher as evaluator, Johnson (1987) says, ''The most fundamental goal of all educational evaluation is optimal instruction for all children and evaluation practices are legitimate

13.6 Putting Ideas to Work

Assessment of Emergent Literacy

F OR MANY years, kindergartners and beginning readers were assessed by standardized norm-referenced reading readiness
tests. These tests consisted of items designed
to measure the child's competency in such
areas as visual discrimination, auditory discrimination, knowledge of letter names and
sounds, visual-motor ability, and beginning
word recognition as indicators of the child's
readiness for formal reading instruction.

Consistent with the concept of emergent
literacy, current early assessment focuses
more on the young child's awareness of, and
ability to deal with, print in a more functional
context. Clay (1985) has developed a widely
used measure that includes assessment of
pupils' letter identification, concepts about
print, simple word recognition, and beginning
reading skills. Designed as part of Reading
Recovery (see 11.1), Clay's instrument can be
used as a diagnostic measure in any emergent
literacy program.

Rather than depending on a single instrument to provide a single measure of a pupil's
knowledge of reading and writing, assessment
in the early years becomes an ongoing process
that focuses on a broad range of skills and
knowledge reflecting the various dimensions
of early literacy development. Fisher (1989)
has developed a three-phase, systematic assessment framework for kindergarten:

Beginning of Year Assessment involves interviewing each child, observing reading and
writing behaviors, and assessing letter
recognition.

Ongoing Assessment requires continual observations of literacy-related activities in a
wide range of contexts; observations are recorded and summarized monthly.

End of Year Assessment involves an interview
focusing on what the children can tell about
themselves as readers and writers, a review
of assessment records compiled throughout
the year, and a measure of letter–sound
knowledge.

---

only to the extent that they serve this goal'' (p. 744). Since most classroom decision-
making takes place on a moment-to-moment basis, and since the teacher is the one
making these decisions, the ongoing informal assessment that the teacher conducts is
a key element in the assessment process.

Rather than ''The Great Administrator of Tests,'' the teacher's role in the assessment process is an active and dynamic one in literature-based programs. Teachers
select the assessment tools or techniques according to the pupil behaviors they want
to sample. Standardized evaluation measures put the responsibility for assessment on
the instrument itself; classroom-based evaluation empowers teachers and students and
places assessment at the heart of the instructional process.

Teacher Observation

Observing pupils as they read is a powerful method of gathering data, and one that is
essential to developing a complete picture of pupils' literacy development. Through
observation, teachers determine pupils' reading behaviors within the context in which
these behaviors normally occur, not in a strained and artificial testing situation. Opportunities for observation occur constantly in the classroom.

Observation involves more than passively watching pupils as they read. It involves active involvement in gathering data and making judgments based on this information. Some structured strategies for observation that have proved effective include:

Reciprocal Teaching (Palinscar, 1984), in which teachers observe pupils as they engage in an interactive dialogue about what they have read, focusing their ability to predict, question, and critically evaluate.

Interactive Assessment (Paratore and Indrisano, 1987), a strategy that integrates teaching practices into an assessment model by having the teacher explain the purpose of assessment and guide the pupil through a series of assessment/instructional steps.

Think Alouds (Alvermann, 1984), in which pupils tell what they are thinking while they read as an indication of their ongoing processing of text.

Book Discussions (Paradis et al., 1991), a technique in which teachers use a combination of comprehension matrices, anecdotal records, journals and logs, tape recordings, and other devices to record the results of discussion to determine pupils' understanding of what they read.

All these techniques—Reciprocal Teaching, Interactive Assessment, Think Alouds, and Book Discussions—are effective classroom strategies in literature-based programs. All can be used as pupils read trade books. The activities are authentic, in that they involve pupils reading real books for real purposes. Material for assessment is derived from the classroom program, not from an outside test. The strategies are based ''on the assumption that the 'human-as-instrument' is as effective and valued as the 'test-as-instrument' when assessing human behaviors'' (Cambourne and Turbill, 1990; p. 340). Each strategy is focused on the reading process and not on the production of a single answer. Each integrates instruction with assessment.

In literature-based programs, observing pupils as they read literature validates assessment of their ability far better than a single standardized measure does.

As a method of classroom assessment, observation extends beyond the reading act itself. It can involve the use of cloze exercises, story maps, and other devices that teachers use for instructional purposes. It includes listening to what pupils say about reading and writing as part of ''grand conversations'' in literature groups, learning how they see reading and writing as part of their lives, having them talk about the kind of metacognitive strategies they use—thus extending self-evaluation into the assessment process.

Although pupils' literacy development can be observed and assessed any time a pupil reads or writes, *conferences* are especially important to classroom assessment. Conferences occur when teachers meet pupils for assessment purposes. They can be conducted individually when teachers meet pupils one-to-one to talk about a trade book the pupil may be reading; or they can be done with several pupils at once, as when the teacher participates in a literature study group. They can be scheduled sessions with structured questions and activities for the purpose of evaluation and diagnosis; or they can be casual encounters as teachers discuss books that pupils are enjoying.

Comprehension Matrix and Profile

WOOD (1988) provides useful models of recording devices for observation in either reading groups or in individual conferences.

The Group Comprehension Matrix allows the teacher to focus on the performance of a whole group or on the performance of individuals within the group.

Group Comprehension Matrix

Story *The Mandarin and the Magician* Date *October 14th*

Genre: Narrative (realistic, (fantasy)) Grade *4th*
       Poetry
       Plays
       Exposition

* New student - Oct. 1st

	Kelly	Ryan*	Marti	Tonya	Jason	David	Teresa
Makes predictions about story	S	+	—	S	—	+	—
Participates in the discussion	S	+	S	S	—	+	S
Answers questions on all levels	—	+	S	S	S	+	S
Determines word meanings through context	—	+	—	—	—	S	—
Reads smoothly and fluently	+	+	+	S	—	+	S
Can retell selection using own words	S	+	+	S	S	S	—
Comprehends after silent reading	N	N	N	N	N	N	N
Can read "between the lines"	—	S	S	—	—	S	—
Possesses broad background knowledge	S	S	—	—	—	S	—

Comments: *The students had much difficulty comprehending the story until I provided much more background information. Their predictions were not as accurate and abundant as usual—largely due to their lack of knowledge of Chinese dynasties. Jason remains very quiet unless asked specific questions. He is much more responsive one-to-one. While his recall is good, his oral reading is very choppy. Teresa is always willing to volunteer any answers although her recall is on the literal level. Ryan may need to move up another level—will test individually.*

Often	+	Words to review:
Sometimes	S	*dynasty*
Seldom	—	*Mandarin*
Not observed	N	*queue*

Individual Comprehension Profile

Name __Eric Matthews__   Date __September 3__   Grade __3__

Overall compr.: 1 = none, 2 = some, 3 = most, 4 = all

	Reading type: Oral	Reading type: Silent	Genre: Poetry	Genre: Plays	Genre: Realistic fiction	Genre: Fantasy	Genre: Nonfiction	Recall mode: Free recall	Recall mode: Probed recall	Recall mode: Infer, predict	Degree of guidance: Background knowl.	Degree of guidance: Preteaching vocab.	Degree of guidance: Assist during rdg.	Overall compr.	Comments
Level 2_2 p. 41	✓				✓			✓	✓		–	–	–	3	A little choppy at first, then very fluent with accurate recall
Level 2_2 p. 76	✓	✓		✓				✓	✓	✓	–	–	–	4	Very fluent reading and retelling
Level 2_2 p. 168		✓					✓	✓	✓	✓	–	–	–	4	Needs no assistance – has control over word recognition and comprehension
Level 3_1 p. 101	✓				✓			✓	✓	✓	–	–	–	2	Some fluency problems & sketchy recall (e.g., misread "trail" for "trial," "beautiful" for "body")
Level 3_1 p. 96	✓					✓		✓	✓	✓	✓	✓	–	3	With help, recall is improved; can predict and infer (e.g., Why do you think...)
Level 3_1 p. 66		✓					✓	✓	✓	✓	✓	✓	✓	4	Had difficulty recognizing "ambulance" – "emergency." Defined "Red Cross" & "swerved." This helped!
Level 3_1 p. 119		✓					✓	✓	✓	✓	✓	✓	✓	4	Tried with and without guidance. Comprehension is improved with help.

Overall assessment: Eric's comprehension while reading silently seems better than while reading orally. Can retell in own words at level 3, but gives more detail when probed or prompted. With assistance, seems to benefit from instruction in this material.

Appropriate placement level __3_1__

From Karen D. Wood, "Techniques for Assessing Students' Potential for Learning," *The Reading Teacher*, 41:440–447 (January, 1988). Copyright © 1988 International Reading Association, Newark DE. Reprinted with permission of Karen D. Wood and the International Reading Association.

The Individual Comprehension Profile is designed to assess how pupils handle different types of reading. The group matrix and individual profile can be used with a variety of reading materials—trade books, basal stories, content area textbooks, or other reading material. Both are designed "to assess the student in the act of comprehending while the teacher is in the act of teaching," and are intended to fit a view of assessment "as a dynamic ongoing process," not as a one-shot deal.

Different types of pupil conferences have different purposes. Intense, individual attention occurs when conferences are planned to observe strategies pupils use when they encounter challenging material or when the teacher wants to determine reading levels or the amount of progress a pupil has made. More casual conferences can reveal pupils' responses to what they are reading and how their attitudes are being shaped. Although different in nature and intent, all conferences can be sources of valuable information that teachers use for assessing pupils' progress and problems.

Observation can be supported, focused, and organized through the use of *checklists*. "Checklists are used . . . to keep the observer focused, to provide a method of recording observations that requires a minimum of writing, and to provide consistency from one observation to the next" (Cockrum and Castillo, 1991; p. 76).

The purpose of a checklist is not to indicate whether or not pupils have "measured up." Rather, checklists provide a profile of qualities and characteristics that suggest leads for future instruction. Moreover, they serve as record-keeping devices that show growth from month to month or term to term in a school year, and from year to year in a pupil's school life.

As tools of classroom-based assessment in literature-based programs, checklists can focus on many dimensions of reading, from pupils' abilities to apply decoding strategies to their understanding of literary elements in stories. They can be customized according to pupils' level of literacy development, according to the dimensions of literacy in which they engage, and according to aims that the teacher has in an instructional program. The sample checklist in 13.8 is merely an example of the thousands of checklists that can be used for classroom-based assessment.

Written records provide evidence of the growth of pupils as readers and writers. Anecdotal records, journals, logs, and other written accounts of pupil performance are part of the complete assessment picture in the literature-based classroom.

Keeping daily records of observations provides an ongoing account of classroom-based assessment. These anecdotal records include observations about material that pupils are reading, how well pupils are progressing, how they are using reading and writing, how they are responding to literacy activities, and unique notations about literacy events that occur in the classroom. These notes can be kept in a loose-leaf notebook, with pages devoted to individual pupils and a section for general reflections. Anecdotal notes document the kid-watching and related activities that are an integral part of classroom assessment.

Anecdotal records provide more than a record of pupils' growth as learners; they also give reflective teachers information to consider in focusing attention on their own classroom performance. Often these records become part of the journals that more and more teachers are beginning to maintain.

The records that pupils keep in response to their reading—*literature journals and logs*—can be valuable sources of data to assess pupils' development as readers and writers. In literature-based programs, pupils keep logs listing books they have read and notations of their reactions to these books. These notations can reveal information such as a pupil's depth of understanding or awareness of literary elements. Building on the reading–writing connection, pupils' reactions to what they read are often more detailed in such responses as buddy journals (see p. 300), exchanges with teachers (Atwell, 1987) and other forms of writing. These responses are potential gold mines of information that can be used for classroom-based assessment.

13.8 Putting Ideas to Work

Sample Checklists

Early to Beginning Stages

	1st	2nd	3rd	4th
Name _____ Dates				

Indicators of Developing Control and Comprehension

Code: M = Most of the time   S = Sometimes   N = Not yet

Talking and Listening

	Code				Comments
– Communicates with others about own activities					
– Explains ideas clearly					
– Uses expanded vocabulary related to classroom activities					
– Communicates in a group setting					
– Repeats nursery rhymes, chants, poems, etc.					
– Responds to and talks about stories					
– Sings songs					
– Dictates stories, personal messages					
– Listens attentively to class activity					
– Listens and responds in community talk					
– Talks about reading and writing					

Reading

– Displays interest in books					
– Chooses to spend time with books					
– Asks for rereading of favorite stories					
– Anticipates and joins in on repetitive phrases					
– Displays sense of story					
– Understands environmental print					
– Possesses knowledge about letters					
– Pretend or memory reads					
– Recognizes some words					
– Focuses on deriving meaning from text					

Writing

– Displays interest in print					
– Pretend writes and attaches meaning					
– Spends time writing					
– Attaches print to art work and other work					

Writing (con't)	Code				Comments
– Understands a variety of purposes and kinds of writing					
– Uses inventive spelling					
• random letters					
• some representative letters					
• phonetic spelling					
• correct spelling of high frequency words					
– Writes on own for personal communication					
– Patterns writing after literary structures					

Indicators of attitudes and social behaviors

– Is willing to be challenged					
– Is productive and involved during work periods					
– Expresses enjoyment as a result of hard work and achievement					
– Cooperates with others					
– Contributes to group work					
– Displays sensitivity and respect for others					
– Learns from watching others					

Indicators of thinking skills

– Articulates ideas clearly					
– Generates solutions and ideas to solve problems					
– Considers suitable resources					
– Differentiates between relevant and non-relevant information					
– Considers other points of view					
– Spends time reading, writing, constructing, researching, reflecting, etc.					
– Talks about information discovered					
– Explains, shows or helps others to understand learning					
– Asks worthwhile questions					
– Plans, organizes and carries through on tasks					
– Understands not all problems have simple solutions					

Source: Church, J. C. (1991). Record Keeping in Whole Language Classrooms. Reprinted with permission of Christopher-Gordon Publishers, Inc. from *Assessment and Evaluation in Whole Language Programs,* edited by Bill Harp. © 1991 by Christopher-Gordon Publishers, Inc., Norwood MA.

Developing to Independent Stages

	1st	2nd	3rd	4th
Name _____ _____ Dates				

Indicators of Developing Control and Comprehension

Code: M = Most of the time   S = Sometimes   N = Not yet

Talking and Listening

	Code				Comments
– Expects what is heard to make sense					
– Monitors understanding of spoken language by asking questions, seeking clarification, etc.					
– Uses a variety of speaking patterns to adjust to audience					
– Speaks confidently before a group and within the community					
– Communicates clearly and effectively					

Reading

– Selects reading material with confidence					
– Reads for literary experience					
– Reads to be informed					
– Reads to perform a task					
– Constructs meaning, develops interpretation and makes judgements					
– Compares and contrasts, makes application					
– Understands story features - irony, humor, organization, point of view					
– Uses a variety of strategies - prediction, rate, background, information, etc.					
– Rereads for different purposes					
– Displays an expanding vocabulary					

Writing

– Initiates writing for specific and personal purposes					
– Incorporates models from literature					
– Participates in writing conferences by asking questions and giving comments					
– Is aware of voice, sense of audience, sense of purpose					

Writing (con't)   Code   Comments

– Displays control over mechanics					
• punctuation					
• grammatical constructions					
• spells high frequency words correctly					
– Pieces are well developed and organized					
• style					
• characters					
• setting					
• detail					
• logical progression of events					
– Informative pieces are well developed					
– Displays research skills					
– Edits and proofreads					
– Talks confidently about writing					

Indicators of attitudes and social behaviors

– Is willing to be challenged					
– Is productive and involved during work periods					
– Expresses enjoyment as a result of hard work and achievement					
– Cooperates with others					
– Contributes to group work					
– Displays sensitivity and respect for others					
– Learns from watching others					

Indicators of thinking skills

– Articulates ideas clearly					
– Generates solutions and ideas to solve problems					
– Considers suitable resources					
– Differentiates between relevant and non-relevant information					
– Considers other points of view					
– Spends time reading, writing, constructing, researching, reflecting, etc.					
– Talks about information discovered					
– Explains, shows or helps others to understand learning					
– Asks worthwhile questions					
– Plans, organizes and carries through on tasks					
– Understands not all problems have simple solutions					

Source: Church, J. C. (1991). Record Keeping in Whole Language Classrooms. Reprinted with permission of Christopher-Gordon Publishers, Inc. from *Assessment and Evaluation in Whole Language Programs,* edited by Bill Harp. © 1991 by Christopher-Gordon Publishers, Inc., Norwood MA.

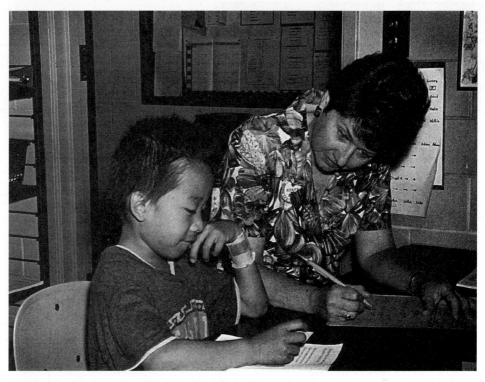

Informal performance-based assessment allows the teacher to measure progress and guide instruction as part of literature-based reading.

Pros and Cons of Classroom-Based Assessment

Like every other dimension of assessment, classroom observation has its advantages and disadvantages. The advantages are strong. Informal assessment is tailored to the individual pupil, the text, and the teacher's instructional purposes. Attention focuses on the processes that pupils use as they read; thus, the focus extends beyond the right answer itself to finding out how pupils arrive at answers based on what they read. The results of classroom assessment provide immediate feedback that teachers can use in planning the next steps in instruction.

The down side of classroom-based assessment is lack of objectivity. Two teachers can make different interpretations about a pupil's response to a question or performance in reading a passage. Observation is labor-intensive and time-consuming as well.

Factors of validity and reliability are other concerns. People tend to have more faith in numbers than in qualitative judgments. Cambourne and Turbill (1990) argue that traditional criteria of ''scientific rigor'' cannot be applied to informal assessment techniques; they do suggest qualities of credibility, transferability, dependability, and confirmability as characteristics to safeguard the trustworthiness of conclusions derived from classroom assessment. Besides, most parents will accept a teacher's observation of progress even without the reinforcement of test results (Aiex, 1988), especially when results are documented by the results of the child's work (Linek, 1991).

Criticism and concern over classroom-based assessment notwithstanding, this dimension of assessment remains a key element in the overall assessment of pupils'

Literature Reading Behavior Inventory

IN A literature-based reading program, trade books are the vehicles for many of the teacher's informal assessment activities. Gail Heald-Taylor (1987) has designed an inventory to guide teachers in evaluating reading for young children who learn to read with literature.

The behaviors are not listed sequentially, so teachers ought not expect that pupils will acquire these behaviors in a neat, linear fashion.

LITERATURE READING BEHAVIOR INVENTORY

Book Awareness	Beginning	Secure	Date
The Child: • listens to stories • shares reading with others (unison reading) • begins looking at books as a self-initiated activity • holds the book right side up • turns pages in sequence from right to left, front to back • examines pictures in book • enjoys having stories read to him or her			
Comprehension	**Beginning**	**Secure**	**Date**
The Child: • recalls the main idea of the story • recalls details from the story • can name events in the story • understands cause and effect in the story • predicts			
Readinglike Behavior	**Beginning**	**Secure**	**Date**
The Child: • attempts to read the selection (oral response may or may not reflect the exact text or pictures) • attempts to read using pictures as the cue to story line • attempts to read by retelling a remembered text (attends to memory and pictures) • attempts to read matching the retelling to particular pages (page matching using pictures and memory as clues)			
Directionality	**Beginning**	**Secure**	**Date**
The Child: • consistently turns pages from right to left • recognizes where print begins on a page • recognizes where print ends on a page • begins to move his/her eyes and finger left to right across the print while attempting to read (finger does not stop at individual words) • develops awareness of line directionality (child's finger moves left to right across line of print and then moves to the far left of the page and down to track the next line of print)			

Print and Word Awareness	Beginning	Secure	Date

• begins to point to clumps of letters and assigns an oral response (each oral response may not accurately match the text)
• begins to accurately word match:
  √ beginning of sentences
  √ names of people and things
  √ end of sentences
• holistic remembering—uses memory, picture and text to recall the story line
• accurately word matches a repetitive pattern in the story
• tracks (word points) to find a specific word
• word points according to oral language syllables
• recognizes common words in stories
• integrates many strategies to get meaning (picture clues, memory, tracking, word recognition, context and syntax)
• begins to accurately word match familiar literature pattern books (uses picture clues, memory, word recognition, context and syntax)
• begins to self-correct for meaning			

Use of Cueing Systems	**Beginning**	**Secure**	**Date**
The Child: • uses memory, picture clues, tracking, syntax and semantic systems well • becomes aware of letter and sound symbol relationships • recognizes letter names in familiar words • talks about his or her own reading behaviors ("That's 'dog.' I know because it begins like my name—David.") • begins to use the phonetic cueing system with familiar materials • integrates picture, memory, tracking, syntax, semantics and phonetics to read familiar material • uses a variety of cueing systems to read new material			
Texts	**Beginning**	**Secure**	**Date**
The child: • reads familiar predictable texts • reads unfamiliar pattern texts • reads unfamiliar texts (without pattern) • reads factual texts (functional, fantasy) • chooses to read for enjoyment			

literacy development. Observation empowers the teacher as the ultimate decision maker in the process of teaching children how to read and write, bringing us one notch higher in true professionalism in teaching.

Classroom assessment is performance based; that is, it is rooted in pupil performance. Data gathered through observation in conferences and recorded on checklists and anecdotal notes extend beyond raw test scores. This information is based on what pupils do and say when they read and write. Two procedures that have been used to focus more sharply on classroom reading performance to assess progress and problems are Informal Reading Inventories and the process of Miscue Analysis.

Informal Reading Inventories

An Informal Reading Inventory (IRI) consists of series of sequentially graded paragraphs that increase in difficulty from primer to sixth-grade level or beyond, along with a set of questions based on the material. The inventory is a curriculum-based measure that determines a pupil's reading level through actual reading performance rather than by filling in a set of bubbles on the answer sheet of a standardized test.

The reading levels determined by informal reading inventories are designated as *independent, instructional,* and *frustration.* Criteria for determining these levels are:

Independent—99%–96% accuracy in Word Recognition; 90% accuracy in Comprehension; Good reading behaviors. This means that pupils make no more than one to four oral reading errors in every 100 words in a passage, can understand most of what they read, and show no signs of physical inefficiencies (like finger pointing or head movement) or evidence of unusual anxiety.

Instructional—95%–93% accuracy in Word Recognition; 75% accuracy in Comprehension; Adequate reading behaviors. In other words, pupils make no more than five or six mistakes per 100 words, understand at least three-quarters of what they read, and show no evidence of inefficiency or nervousness as they read.

Frustration—90% or less in Word Recognition; 50% or less in Comprehension; Poor reading behaviors. Material at this level is considered too difficult for pupils to handle, even with support and help from the teacher.

Administering the inventory is an individual enterprise. Pupils read words on a graded word list to determine their beginning point for reading. The teacher asks the pupil to begin reading at an appropriate entry point, usually a grade level or two below the pupil's reading level. The pupil then reads paragraphs at higher and lower levels until it is determined which level of reading material constitutes the pupil's independent, instructional, and frustration levels.

As the pupil reads, the teacher marks areas that indicate word recognition difficulties—insertions or the addition of extra words, omissions of words or word parts, substitutions, mispronunciations, or words pronounced by the examiner. After the reading, the pupil is asked specific questions based on the content of the passages. Scores are computed, and the independent, instructional, and frustration levels are determined based on these scores.

More detailed information about constructing and administering informal reading inventories is provided by Johnson, Kress, and Pikulski (1987).

13.10
FOR YOUR INFORMATION

Informal Reading Inventories

ALTHOUGH IT is frequently recommended that teachers construct their own informal inventories for use in their classrooms, a number of commercially produced IRIs are available in the marketplace, among the most popular of which are:

Classroom Reading Inventory (5th ed.) by Nicholas J. Silvaroli. Dubuque: Wm. C. Brown Publishers, 1986.
Informal Reading Inventory: Preprimer to Twelfth Grade (4th ed.) by Paul C. Burns and Betty D. Roe. Boston: Houghton Mifflin, 1993.

Group Assessment in Reading: Classroom Teacher's Handbook by Edna W. Warncke and Dorothy A. Shipman. Englewood Cliffs, NJ: Prentice-Hall, 1984.
Flynt-Cooter Reading Inventory for the Classroom by E. Sutton Flynt and Robert Cooter, Jr., Scottsdale, AZ: Gorsuch Scarisbrick Publishers, 1993.
Analytical Reading Inventory (2nd ed.) by Mary Lynn Woods and Alden J. Moe. Columbus, OH: Merrill Publishing, 1985.
Basic Reading Inventory by J. Johns. Dubuque: Kendall-Hunt, 1985.

Teachers do not need to formally administer an informal reading inventory, however, to achieve the purposes that the IRI was designed to accomplish. The teacher can use IRI guidelines as an ''ear'' in listening to pupils read aloud, noting the type of oral reading practices with which pupils seem to need assistance. Even if the inventory itself is not used as a diagnostic device, the guidelines provide a benchmark for listening to pupils' oral reading.

Pros and Cons of Informal Reading Inventories   The IRI is a functional diagnostic tool, a means of assessing pupil performance by observing actual reading. IRIs represent authentic performance-based reading assessment, in that these tools require the actual performance of the task being measured. Results can be used as a basis for matching pupils to appropriate reading material. In helping pupils select trade books, for example, the teacher can use the suggested criteria for Independent/Instructional levels to determine if the book can best be read independently at home or if it might better be read with the support of a reading group.

There are legitimate criticisms and practical problems regarding the theory and use of the IRI, however. Some consider the criteria for determining reading levels too arbitrary, rigid, and high. The procedure relies extensively on oral reading performance, although most inventories provide a parallel set of passages for silent reading as well. One paragraph per grade provides only a very narrow sample of reading behavior. Pupils' performances on informal inventories may not reflect their ability to deal with other printed material (expository text in content areas, for example). Pupils' performances can be inconsistent; a pupil can do well in reading a passage at one level, completely bog down at the next higher level, and read well at the level above that. Pupils' interest in what they read influences their performance. Inconsistent performance can be caused by many factors, and such inconsistency makes it difficult for the teacher to determine which grades constitute the pupil's independent, instructional, or frustration level.

Using Trade Books as "Benchmark" Measures

WHEN LITERATURE is an important part of instruction, trade books need to be an important part of assessment. The Whole Language Council of the Milwaukee Public Schools (1990) has developed an assessment guide that puts literature at the heart of the assessment process.

Certain popular trade books are designed as benchmark books at different grade levels, two or three books per grade; for example:

Grade 2—Frog and Toad Together by Arnold Lobel;
Grade 4—Sarah, Plain and Tall by Patricia MacLachlan;

Grade 5—James and the Giant Peach by Roald Dahl.

Pupils are expected to read most of the book independently. A section of the book is designated to be used for assessment purposes—the story "The Dream" in *Frog and Toad Together,* for example, or the two final chapters of *Sarah, Plain and Tall.* The teacher asks six or more verification questions on the designated section, all focusing on comprehension. Responses determine if the book is at the pupil's independent, instructional, or frustration level. This guide contains directions and forms for other assessment techniques as well.

A serious concern raised frequently about informal reading inventories relates to their emphasis on word skills as a means of assessing reading. In interpreting an IRI, word skills are heavily emphasized. Performance in word recognition is balanced equally with comprehension, yet getting meaning is far more important in reading than merely saying the words.

Instead of relying solely on IRI criteria in listening to pupils read aloud for diagnostic purposes, teachers can gain much information about reading performance through the use of miscue analysis.

Miscue Analysis

Miscue analysis is a procedure that takes the assessment process a step further than the IRI. A "miscue" is a response in oral reading that does not match the words on the page. It is an inaccuracy in oral reading that traditionally would be called an error or a mistake.

Kenneth Goodman (1965, 1969) introduced the term *miscue* into the professional literature in the 1960s to replace the terms *error* or *mistake* in describing a reader's departure from printed text. The intent in using the term *miscue* was to remove the onus associated with *error* and to get away from the idea that all departures from print indicate weaknesses or problems in reading. Listening to oral reading with an ear to miscues involves noting which cueing system may have led the reader away from the exact reading of the words on the page.

Miscue analysis involves noting not only that the pupil does not read exactly what is printed in the text; it also involves examining the type of departure a pupil makes while reading orally. The three major categories of miscues are:

Semantic, a miscue based on word meaning in which the pupil might substitute a word that means the same as the word in the text.

Example: That apple pie ~~certainly~~ *sure* tasted good.

Syntactic, a miscue in which the departure from print corresponds to an equivalent grammatical form.

Example: "I am going home right now," Linda said.

Graphophonic, a miscue based on sound–symbol similarities in the text.

Example: The children saw a h̶o̶u̶s̶e̶ *horse* in the field.

Miscue analysis helps the teacher get more insight into the reading process by looking at the nature of a departure from text rather than just noting the fact that the pupil misread a word or a phrase. For example, the sentence in a passage is: The *children* went to the beach to go swimming. Adam reads, "The *chicken* went to the beach to go swimming." Beth reads, "The *kids* went to the beach to go swimming."

With an IRI, both would simply be counted as "substitutions," yet the nature of the miscues is very different. Alan is depending on graphophonic cues and largely ignoring context. On the other hand, Beth is virtually ignoring graphophonic clues and is relying primarily on meaning-based context in reading the word. Sometimes a substitution might be a calculated response rather than a random guess at a word. Miscue analysis involves a qualitative rather than a quantitative look at pupils' oral reading.

Conducting miscue analysis, like administering an IRI, is an individual enterprise. Unlike IRIs, however, a longer passage that is complete in itself is used: one or two chapters from a trade book, an entire basal reading story, a chapter from a content text, or an article from a magazine. Reading is thus based in the holistic context of a selection that contains larger meaning than that which is typically contained in a paragraph or two. The level of the material is about a year above the pupil's reading grade level, challenging enough to promote miscues but not so difficult as to be frustrating. The intent of miscue analysis is not to locate a particular reading level; rather, it is to determine the types of language cueing systems that the pupil is using while reading. The content can be familiar to the reader, but the pupil should not have already read the particular passage.

As the pupil reads, the teacher marks the miscues, codes each according to its type (semantic, syntactic, and graphophonic), notes if the pupil self-corrects or not, notes whether or not the miscue fits the context of the passage, and notes if the miscue preserves the meaning of the text. Miscues resulting directly from a pupil's dialect—reading *creek* as "crick," for example, or reading "they was" when the text is *they were*—are not counted. Following the reading, pupils recount what they have read as a check on comprehension.

A formal instrument for miscue analysis is the *Reading Miscue Inventory* (Goodman and Burke, 1972). Although recognized as a valuable diagnostic tool, in practice this test has proved very complicated and time-consuming for the busy classroom teacher to administer, and the authors have suggested a more streamlined procedure for using the inventory (Goodman, Watson, and Burke, 1987). More complete directions for formally analyzing pupils' miscues during oral reading are also provided by Hittleman (1988), by Weaver (1988), and by Watson and Henson (1991).

Even without the formal procedures, miscue analysis provides a focus for listening to pupils read aloud. Analyzing miscues enables the teacher to listen to oral reading with a fine-tuned ear in order to gain information about the type of strategies pupils use while reading—whether pupils are using context and language cues or whether they are relying on other strategies as they read. Less proficient readers, for example, tend to rely heavily on graphophonic cues (sounding out) and less on semantic and syntactic cues in reading words that they do not recognize. This kind of information suggests the kind of instruction that might be appropriate for the pupil.

The miscues that pupils make can also indicate their ongoing processing of meaning as they read aloud. Some miscues get in the way of meaning; others preserve the essential meaning of text. Sometimes a pupil who miscues in one part of the text will make a second miscue to preserve meaning. For example, look at the two miscues in the following sentence:

and   it
Jack took an apple⌃wrapped⌃in paper.

Technically these insertions would be counted as "two errors," but the second insertion indicates that the pupil is comprehending. After the reader inserted the word *and,* the second insertion (*it*) became necessary to preserve the meaning and syntactic structure of the sentence. That is why *miscue* is an appropriate term to get away from all the negative connotations of *mistake*. Miscues indicating departure from meaning in text are the ones that should be attended to closely and quickly.

Of course, miscue analysis is only one indication of pupils' ability to derive meaning, and other techniques such as retelling and postquestioning need to be used. For example, this miscue changed the meaning of a text:

When the boat docked, the sailors were waiting to go on shore.

Yet, when recounting what he had read, the pupil who omitted the expression *to go* was able to tell exactly where the sailors were waiting (and why). Some pupils can fracture oral reading and still manage to comprehend much of what they read. These are the pupils who suffer when teachers judge reading competency and progress on the basis of oral reading alone.

Pros and Cons of Miscue Analysis   Miscue analysis involves more than the simple tabulation of mistakes. It is a complex process that involves examining pupils' reading performance as a means of getting at the psycholinguistic processing that goes on while they read. Although it can be complex and time-consuming, miscue analysis reveals the type of strategies that pupils use while reading, thus revealing information that can be useful in planning instruction. It carries reading diagnosis beyond the ad hoc recording of "faults" to be noted for remediation and on to strategies that can be used to help pupils improve reading competency.

Miscue analysis requires skill, expertise, and confidence on the part of the teacher. It also demands knowledge of the reading process in order to make judgments about responses that pupils make to print. There are those who would argue that readers should produce verbatim what is on a page of print and that no deviation from print

Using the Tape Recorder

FOR BOTH informal reading inventories and miscue analysis procedures, the use of a tape recorder is recommended. Tape recording pupils' oral reading relieves much of the pressure and anxiety (and curiosity, too) that pupils experience while watching the teacher make mysterious marks as they read. It also frees the teacher to direct full attention to the pupil and alleviates the problem of trying to record in written form the reading of a pupil who reads rapidly. The tape recording of the pupil gives the teacher a chance to listen and reflect on the reading several times outside the distracting atmosphere of the typically busy classroom.

While listening to the tapes, however, teachers should give an ear to their own performance as well. "Until a teacher listens to herself in action, she may not realize that she has become predominantly a 'prompter' or a 'sound-it-outer' or an over-zealous 'corrector' " (Arnold, 1982; p. 37). Assessment is most useful when it leads to improvement of instruction. Teachers can listen to their own responses during oral reading with an ear to determining how they are helping pupils with the full range of cues available, cues both in the text and "behind the reader's eye."

---

should be excused or "rationalized." These concerns notwithstanding, miscue analysis provides a powerful means of analyzing pupils' oral reading performance as a means of assessing their progress and problems in learning to read.

Classroom assessment—including teacher observation, informal inventories, miscue analysis, and other formal and informal procedures that teachers follow—is an essential dimension of reading assessment. Even though policymakers and the general public frequently put their faith in standardized tests, and even though these measures can provide information for teachers, the day-to-day assessment that goes on in the classroom is what should direct the reading instructional process.

Portfolio Assessment

In the past several years, there has been a strong movement toward the portfolio approach to literacy assessment. Portfolios are cumulative collections of material that detail pupils' literacy achievement and development. Just as artists use portfolios to demonstrate their artistic ability, pupils use portfolios to demonstrate their growth and competency in reading and writing. More than a single grade score or a checklist, portfolios contain a combination of evidence that can be used for short- and long-term assessment. They are dynamic showcases of the pupil's literacy achievements.

Valencia (1990) has identified four theoretical cornerstones on which the concept of portfolio assessment is built: (1) good assessment should come from a variety of literacy experiences in which pupils engage in the classroom; (2) assessment should be continuous to chronicle ongoing development; (3) assessment should be multidimensional, reflecting the multifaceted nature of literacy development; and (4) assessment should include "active, collaborative reflection by both teacher and students" (p. 330). A portfolio is a means of getting away from a single measure—a standardized reading-achievement test score or simple letter grade—as an indication of how well pupils are doing in reading. It measures growth over time; it is not a single sample of performance on a given day.

What Do Portfolios Contain?

Portfolios are not merely work folders. The contents are chosen selectively for the purpose of showing pupil growth over time. Each work sample is dated so that teachers, parents, and pupils know when the work was performed.

There is no prescribed list of contents for pupils' assessment portfolios. The collections should contain a variety of materials designed to reflect pupils' developing competency in reading and related language areas. The contents might contain:

samples of the pupils' work—originally written stories at various stages of completion, story maps or exercises on which pupils have worked, reading logs or other written responses to literature, additional writing samples, and other examples of work that reflects achievement;

observational notes made by the teacher—the results of interviews about books that pupils have read, for example, or other anecdotal notations;

test scores, checklists, or the results of standardized norm-referenced or criterion-referenced tests that pupils might have taken;

audio (and perhaps video) tapes of pupils' reading performance;

lists of trade books that pupils have read on their own, with pupils' responses to these books;

self-assessment indicators, personalized statements from pupils to enhance both the teacher's and the parent's understanding. ''The instrument can be a written report by the child describing strengths and weaknesses . . . or a series of answers to questions (such as): 1. How well do you think you do in reading? 2. What do you do when you try to read a hard word? 3. How do you select your own reading material?'' (Flood and Lapp, 1989; p. 513). Self-evaluation comments can be placed on 3×5 index cards. These can also include a teacher–pupil generated list of objectives for the next assessment period.

Some of the work samples in a portfolio might include ''captions,'' brief teacher comments as to why the sample was included and what the sample demonstrates about particular pupils and their achievements. There might also be provision for written comments by parents and others who review the material.

Including a portfolio summary sheet is often useful to suggest an organization of the material in the folder. This summary sheet provides a guide for administrators and others who have neither the time nor the need to review the contents in great detail. The summary sheet is also useful to pass along to next year's teacher.

A portfolio ought not be a potpourri of every piece of work that a pupil has completed in a school term. Just as an artist does not include every piece of art that he or she ever created, so pupils should choose samples of work that reflect their development as readers and writers. The content might, for example, contain a spontaneous writing sample done in September with a similar sample done in December or a tape

In preparing portfolios, pupils and teachers need to collaborate to select work that reflects the child's development as a reader and a writer.

recording of a passage read in January and the same passage read in March. The key to selection is choosing material that will clearly reflect pupil growth—a collection of work not so extensive as to be unmanageable but large enough to provide valid evidence of pupil progress. The two-part question that might guide the selection process is "Why am I including this material and for whom is it intended?"

Portfolios are packaged in expandable file folders and kept in an accessible place in the classroom. Sometimes, different portfolios might be kept for different subjects—a social studies or science portfolio, for example. Different portfolios might sometimes be appropriate for different purposes; for example, the principal will view a portfolio differently than will the parent. Confidentiality of portfolio contents needs to be maintained, although pupils often share their portfolios with friends.

Pupils themselves should have a say in what to include in their portfolios. Pupils should be given opportunities to select their best work or work that is especially important to them. A teacher–pupil collaborative effort in selecting portfolio samples focuses cooperative attention on pupil effort and achievement. It allows pupils to understand more fully teacher expectations in the area of literacy. At the same time, collaboration allows the teacher to gain insight into pupils—how they perceive themselves as learners and how they understand the metacognitive dimensions of learning to read and write.

Collaboration also gives pupils a voice in the whole assessment process. It gives pupils a chance to reflect on their own work. Collaboration takes the sole responsibility for assessment off the teacher's shoulders and enables pupils to develop confidence in their ability to evaluate their own learning and set their own goals (Levi, 1990). It helps make pupils realize that assessment should not always come from the outside, that they have a measure of personal responsibility, a stake in achieving and assessing the quality of their own work.

How Are Portfolios Used?

Portfolios are both assessment tools and learning devices. They need to be reviewed fairly frequently for the purpose of adding new material and removing older samples, thus encouraging integration between assessment and instruction.

Portfolios are especially valuable during parent conferences. Instead of handing parents a simple grade or a single standardized test score as an indication of all the work that their children have done, portfolios provide parents with a more complete picture of their children's efforts and accomplishments. They provide validation for the instructional decisions that the teacher has made and tangible evidence of what the pupil has done.

Portfolios are no less valuable in meetings with administrators. Samples of work reflect pupil achievement and evidence of learning far better than a printout of test scores. They let the principal know what is going on in the classroom. They provide the principal with details of how the curriculum is being implemented, information that any administrator can use with constituencies outside the school.

Pupil portfolios are a dimension of teacher assessment as well; teachers use these devices to look at their own development as professionals. A set of pupil portfolios reflects the variety of an enriched classroom instructional program. "The result is not a score on a teachers' exam. Instead, it is a reflection of a sample of work (that) offers a humane, useful and generative portrait of development—one that a teacher, like a student, can learn from long after the isolated moment of assessment" (Wolf, 1989; p. 39).

Portfolio assessment involves work. Portfolios can be messy and putting them together is a lot more effort than relying on a single measure to reflect the effort of a teacher and pupils for all the work during a year or term. Although the process is time-consuming, efforts are rewarded in that portfolios reflect the many variables involved in learning to read and write. Besides, portfolios reflect an attitude toward assessment. "Portfolios reflect a philosophy that demands that we view assessment as an integral part of our instruction, providing a process for teachers and students to use to guide learning" (Valencia, 1990; p. 340).

Summary and Conclusions

Accountability is a catchword in education. Schools are expected to answer to elected officials, parents, taxpayers, and policymakers to justify their efforts in terms of cost-effectiveness and pupil progress. The pupil progress for which we are held accountable is most often judged by tests. Norm-referenced measures have become the premier means of pupil, school, district, state, and national assessment. Schools are compared, teachers are unfairly judged, and educational decisions are made based on how well pupils perform on standardized tests. Thus, these tests take on a larger-than-life specter for many teachers.

The general public puts great faith in these tests, not realizing that these instruments are imperfect measures that do not always reflect accurately what is inside a pupil's head or heart. When classroom instruction is tailored to the test—when the teacher "teaches to the test" by focusing narrowly on test items and test content—then the tail is wagging the dog. "There is a place for the more intrusive norm-referenced, product-oriented approach (to assessment) but it is a small one, certainly much smaller than the pretentious position it currently occupies'' (Johnson, 1987; p. 748).

Formal tests are only one part of assessment. Standardized achievement tests can generate data to indicate trends, but they are generally inappropriate for judging the performance of individual pupils. Teacher judgment, interviews with pupils, listening to them read, analyzing their miscues and their responses to print—these are the assessment tools that should guide instruction in the elementary grades. In answer to the question ''How can teachers monitor a student's progress in literature-based programs without skills workbooks or tests to grade?'' Aiex (1988) suggests writing samples, checklists, observation, and other informal devices as alternatives to conventional instruments. These informal measures will not make formalized tests go away; they constitute different yardsticks for measuring pupil progress. But informal assessment is gaining impetus with the changing views of literacy and the methods of assessment related to these views.

As part of teacher observations, portfolios containing samples of pupils' work are important, both as a means of assessment and as a means of reporting progress in reading and writing skills. The writing samples, tape recordings, and other work contained in a portfolio are tangible evidence of pupil progress on the road to reading and writing competency.

Pupils are complex human beings. Reading and writing are complex human behaviors. A full range of tools and techniques is necessary to account for an accurate and effective picture of how literacy learning takes place.

Discussion Questions and Activities

1. What do you remember about standardized reading-achievement testing? Make a list of your most vivid recollections about these tests. As a teacher today, what special provisions would you make for administering these tests to your class? Why would you make these provisions?

2. Take a position—pro or con—on criterion-referenced testing. Be prepared to defend your opinion. How does your position relate to your view of the reading process?

3. Prepare a brief explanation of miscue analysis that you might give parents of some of the children in your class. Explain to the parents why you might use miscue analysis as part of your assessment of their children. Explain how the information you would gather with miscue analysis supports other assessment information you gather from formal tests and other types of informal assessment.

4. What do you think about skills-competency testing for elementary teachers? Do you think that it is a valid and effective way to ensure quality instruction for today's pupils, or do you think it might exclude some excellent candidates from the teaching profession? What assessment alternatives can you suggest for those who want to become teachers?

5. Prepare your own teaching portfolio. Include lesson plans you have developed, teaching materials you have made, notes and journals you may have kept about your educational experiences, a videotaped excerpt of a lesson you have taught, and other material that shows your developing professionalism as a teacher. Get ready to use this portfolio in job interviews.

School-Based Assignments

1. Examine a formal test used in your classroom—a standardized norm-referenced achievement test, the test that is part of your basal program, a criterion-referenced skills test. What components of reading are being assessed? Interview your co-operating teacher about how he or she uses the results of the test. How might you use results differently?

2. Using a selection from a basal reading textbook or a trade book, conduct an informal reading inventory or a miscue analysis with a pupil in your classroom. Find out if the material is at the child's independent, instructional, or frustration level. What language systems does the pupil appear to be using when dealing with text? Write a brief account of your experience.

3. Assess your pupils' attitudes toward reading. Include pupil attitudes toward both academic and recreational reading. Based on pupil responses, what instructional activities might you plan?

4. How are the results of assessment used in your classroom? List all the assessment devices and activities that are used and indicate how the results of these assessment activities are used to plan instruction for pupils.

5. Working with one or two pupils, begin to build a portfolio, or review the contents of the pupils' portfolios if these are already used in the classroom. What type of material is included? How does this material show growth in reading and writing development?

Children's Trade Books Cited In This Chapter

Dahl, Roald. *James and the Giant Peach*. New York: Knopf, 1961.

Lobel, Arnold. *Frog and Toad Are Friends*. New York: Harper and Row, 1970.

MacLachlan, Patricia. *Sarah, Plain and Tall*. New York: Harper and Row, 1965.

References

Aiex, N. K. (1988). Literature Based Reading Instruction. *The Reading Teacher* 41:458–461.

Alvermann, D. (1984). Second Graders' Strategic Preferences while Reading Basal Stories. *Journal of Educational Research* 77:184–189.

Applebee, A. N., Langer, J. A., Mullis, I. V. A., and Jenkins, L. V. (1990). *The Writing Report Card, 1984–88*. Washington, DC: U.S. Dept. of Education.

Arnold, H. (1982). *Listening to Children Read*. London: United Kingdom Reading Association.

Bertrand, J. E. (1991). Student Assessment and Evaluation. In Bill Harp (ed.), *Assessment and Evaluation in Whole Language Programs*. Norwood, MA: Christopher Gordon Publishers.

Brown, V. L., Hammill, D. D., and Wiederholt, J. L. (1986). *Test of Reading Comprehension*. Austin, TX: Pro-Ed.

Cambourne, B., and Turbill, J. (1990). Assessment on Whole-Language Classrooms: Theory into Practice. *The Elementary School Journal* 90:338–349.

Clay, M. M. (1985). *The Early Detection of Reading Difficulties*. 3rd ed. Portsmouth, NH: Heinemann.

Cockrum, W. A., and Castillo, M. (1991). Whole Language Assessment and Evaluation Strategies. In Bill Harp (ed.), *Assessment and Evaluation in Whole Language Programs*. Norwood, MA: Christopher Gordon Publishers.

Dunn, L. M., and Dunn, L. M. (1981). *Peabody Picture Vocabulary Test.* Pines, MN: American Guidance Service.

Eissenberg, T. E., and Rudner, L. M. (1988). State Testing of Teachers: A Summary. *Journal of Teacher Education* 39:21–22.

Fisher, B. (1989). Assessing Emergent and Initial Readers. *Teaching K–8* 20:56–58.

Flood, J., and Lapp, D. (1989). Reporting Reading Progress: A Comparison Portfolio for Parents. *The Reading Teacher* 42:508–514.

Goodman, K. (1965). A Linguistic Study of Cues and Miscues in Reading. *Elementary English* 42:639–643.

———. (1969). Analysis of Reading Miscues: Applied Psycholinguistics. *Reading Research Quarterly* 5:126–135.

Goodman, Y. M. (1978). Kid-Watching: An Alternative to Testing. *National Elementary School Principal* 57:41–45.

Goodman, Y., Watson, D., and Burke, C. (1987). *Reading Miscue Inventory: Alternative Procedures.* New York: Richard C. Owen.

Hammell, D. D., and Larsen, S. C. (1988). *Test of Written Language.* Austin, TX: Pro-Ed.

Haney, W., and Madaus G. (1989). Searching for Alternatives to Standardized Tests: Whys, Whats, and Whithers. *Phi Delta Kappan* 70:683–687.

Harris, T. L., and Hodges R. E., eds. (1981). *A Dictionary of Reading and Related Terms.* Newark, DE: International Reading Association.

Heald-Taylor, G. (1987). Predictable Literature Selections and Activities for Language Arts Instruction. *The Reading Teacher* 41:6–12.

Hittleman, D. (1988). *Developmental Reading, K–8: Teaching from a Whole-Language Perspective.* 3rd ed. Columbus, OH: Merrill.

Holdaway, D. (1972). *Independence in Reading.* Auckland, NZ: Ashton Scholastic.

Huck, C. S., Hepler, S., and Hickman, J. (1987). *Children's Literature in the Elementary School.* 4th ed. New York: Holt, Rinehart and Winston.

Johnson, M., Kress, R., and Pikulski, J. (1987). *Informal Reading Inventories.* 2nd ed. Newark, DE: International Reading Association.

Johnson, P. (1984). Assessment in Reading. In P. D. Pearson (ed.), *Handbook of Reading Research.* New York: Longman.

———. (1987). Teachers As Evaluation Experts. *The Reading Teacher* 41:744–748.

Kramer, J. J., and Conoley, J. C. (1992). *Buros Mental Measurements Yearbook.* Lincoln, NE: University of Nebraska, Buros Institute of Mental Measurement.

Levi, R. (1990). Assessment and Educational Vision: Engaging Learners and Parents. *Language Arts* 67:267–274.

Linek, W. M. (1991). Grading and Evaluation Techniques for Whole Language Teachers. *Language Arts* 68:125–132.

Madaus, G. F. (1990). *Testing As a Social Technology.* Chestnut Hill, MA: Boston College.

McKenna, M. C., and Kear, D. J. (1990). Measuring Attitude toward Reading: A New Tool for Teachers. *The Reading Teacher* 43:626–639.

Mullis, I. V. S., and Jenkins, L. B. (1990). *The Reading Report Card, 1971–88.* Washington, DC: U.S. Office of Education.

Neill, D. M., and Medina, N. J. (1989). Standardized Testing: Harmful to Educational Health. *Phi Delta Kappan* 70:688–697.

Palinscar, A. S. (1984). The Quest for Meaning from Expository Text: A Teacher-Guided Journey. In G. G. Duffy, L. R. Roehler, and J. Mason (eds.), *Comprehension Instruction.* New York: Longman.

Paradis, E., Chatton, B., Boswell, A., Smith, M., and Yovich, S. (1991). Accountability: Assessing Comprehension during Literature Discussions. *The Reading Teacher* 45:8–17.

Paratore, J. R., and Indrisano, R. (1987). Intervention Assessment of Reading Comprehension. *The Reading Teacher* 41:778–783.

Peters, C. W., and Wixson, K. K. (1989). Smart New Reading Tests Are Coming. *Learning89* 17:43–44,53.

Pikulski, J. J. (1989). The Assessment of Reading: A Time for Change? *The Reading Teacher* 43:80–81.

Tierney, R. J., Carter, M. A., and Desai, L. E. (1991). *Portfolios in the Reading–Writing Classroom.* Norwood, MA: Christopher-Gordon Publishers.

Valencia, S. (1990). A Portfolio Approach to Classroom Reading Assessment: The Whys, Whats, and Hows. *The Reading Teacher* 43:338–340.

Valencia, S., and Pearson, P. D. (1987). Reading Assessment: Time for a Change. *The Reading Teacher* 41:726–732.

Watson, D., and Henson, J. (1991). Reading Evaluation—Miscue Analysis. In Bill Harp (ed.), *Assessment and Evaluation in Whole Language Programs.* Norwood, MA: Christopher–Gordon Publishers.

Weaver, C. (1988). *Reading Process and Practice.* Portsmouth, NH: Heinemann.

Whole Language Council, Milwaukee Public Schools (1990). *Whole Language Assessment Guide.* Milwaukee: Milwaukee Public Schools.

Wiggins, G. (1989). A True Test: Toward More Authentic and Equitable Assessment. *Phi Delta Kappan* 70:703–713.

Wixson, K. K., Bosky, A. B., Yochum, M. N., and Alvermann, D. E. (1984). An Interview for Assessing Students' Perceptions of Classroom Reading Tasks. *The Reading Teacher* 37:354–359.

Wolf, D. P. (1989). Portfolio Assessment: Sampling Students' Work. *Educational Leadership* 36:35–40.

Wood, K. D. (1988). Techniques for Assessing Students' Potential for Learning. *The Reading Teacher* 41:440–447.

Woodcock, R. W., and Johnson, M. B. (1989). *Woodcock-Johnson Psycho-Educational Battery.* Rev. ed. Allen, TX: DLM/Teaching Resources.

Cumulative List of Children's Trade Books Cited in This Text

Aardema, Verna. *Why Mosquitoes Buzz in People's Ears.* New York: Dial, 1978.

Ackerman, Karen. *The Leaves in October.* New York: Atheneum, 1991.

Adler, David. *Cam Jansen Mysteries.* New York: Penguin, 1980–88 (13 titles).

———. *Fourth Floor Twins.* New York: Penguin, 1985–88 (9 titles).

Aesop. *City Mouse–Country Mouse and Two More Mouse Tales.* New York: Scholastic, 1970.

Agard, John. *The Calypso Alphabet.* New York: Henry Holt, 1989.

Ai-Ling, Louie. *Yeh-Shen: A Cinderella Story from China.* New York: Philomel, 1982.

Alexander, Martha. *Bobo's Dream.* New York: Dial, 1970.

———. *Out, Out, Out.* New York: Dial, 1970.

Aliki. *How a Book Is Made.* New York: Harper and Row, 1988.

———. *Mummies Made In Egypt.* New York: Crowell, 1979.

———. *My Visit to the Dinosaurs.* New York: Harper and Row, 1985.

———. *The Medieval Feast.* New York: Harper and Row, 1986.

Allard, Harry. *Bumps In The Night.* New York: Bantam Books, 1979.

———. *Miss Nelson Is Missing.* Boston: Houghton Mifflin, 1977.

Allen, Pamela. *Who Sank the Boat?* New York: Coward, 1983.

Anderson, Hans Christian. *The Emperor's New Clothes.* New York: Harper and Row, 1982. (Many other editions available.)

———. *The Princess and The Pea.* Boston: Houghton Mifflin, 1979. (Many other editions available.)

Andrews, Jan. *Very Last First Time.* New York: Macmillan, 1986.

Anglund, Joan Walsh. *In a Pumpkin Shell.* New York: Harcourt Brace, 1960.

Anno, Mitsumasa. *Anno's Alphabet.* New York: Crowell, 1975.

———. *Anno's Counting Book.* New York: Putnam, 1977.

———. *Anno's Flea Market.* New York: Philomel, 1984.

———. *Anno's Journey.* New York: Philomel, 1978.

Arbuthnot, May Hill. *The Arbuthnot Anthology of Children's Literature* (4th ed.). Glenview, IL: Scott Foresman, 1976.

Armstrong, William. *Sounder.* New York: Harper and Row, 1969.

Asher, Sandy. *Where Do You Get Your Ideas?* New York: Walker, 1987.

Atwater, Florence and Richard. *Mr. Popper's Penguins.* Boston: Little Brown, 1938.

Atwood, Ann. *Fly with the Wind, Flow with the Water.* New York: Scribner, 1979.

Auckerman, Karen. *Song and Dance Man*. New York: Knopf, 1988.

Babbitt, Natalie. *Tuck Everlasting*. New York: Farrar, Straus & Giroux, 1976.

Baker, Jeannie. *Where the Forest Meets the Sea*. New York: Greenwillow, 1988.

Bancheck, Linda. *Snake In, Snake Out*. New York: Crowell, 1978.

Banks, Lynne Reid. *The Indian in the Cupboard*. New York: Doubleday, 1985.

Barr, Linda. *I Won't Let Them Hurt You*. Worthington, OH: Willowisp Press, 1988.

Barrett, Judi. *Animals Definitely Should Not Wear Clothes*. New York: Atheneum, 1980.

———. *Cloudy with a Chance of Meatballs*. New York: Macmillan, 1978.

Barton, Byron. *Airport*. New York: Harper and Row, 1982.

Bayer, Jane. *A, My Name Is Alice*. New York: Dial, 1984.

Baylor, Byrd. *Amigo*. New York: Macmillan, 1989.

———. *Hawk, I'm Your Brother*. New York: Macmillan, 1976.

Baylor, Byrd, and Parnall, Peter. *If You Are a Hunter of Fossils*. New York: Scribner's, 1980.

Bemelmans, Ludwig. *Madeline*. New York: Viking, 1939, 1962.

Bender, Lionel. *Volcano!* New York: Franklin Watts, 1988.

Benjamin, Carol Lea. *Writing for Kids*. New York: Harper and Row, 1985.

Bierhorst, John. *The Spirit Child*. New York: Morrow, 1984.

Birch, David. *The King's Chessboard*. New York: Dial, 1988.

Blanco, Alberto. *The Desert Mermaid/La sirena del desierto*. San Francisco: The Children's Press, 1992.

Blue, Rose. *Grandma Didn't Wave Back*. New York: Franklin Watts, 1972.

Blume, Judy. *Are You There God? It's Me, Margaret*. New York: Dell, 1972.

———. *Blubber*. New York: Bradbury, 1974.

———. *Freckle Juice*. New York: Dell, 1971, 1978.

———. *Superfudge*. New York: Dutton, 1980.

———. *Tales of a Fourth Grade Nothing*. New York: Dutton, 1972.

Bond, Michael. *A Bear Called Paddington*. Boston: Houghton Mifflin, 1960.

———. *Paddington Bear*. New York: Random House, 1973.

Bonsall, Crosby. *Mine's the Best*. New York: Harper and Row, 1973.

Branley, Franklin. *A Book of Flying Saucers For You*. New York: Crowell, 1973.

———. *Sunshine Makes the Seasons*. New York: Harper and Row, 1985.

———. *The Sky Is Full of Stars*. New York: Harper and Row, 1981.

———. *Whatever Happened to the Dinosaurs?* New York: Crowell, 1989.

Brenner, Barbara. *Wagon Wheels*. New York: Harper and Row, 1978.

Brincklow, Julie. *Fireflies!* New York: Macmillan, 1985.

Brittain, Bill. *The Wish Giver*. New York: Harper and Row, 1983.

Brown, Marcia. *Once a Mouse*. New York: Scribner, 1961.

———. *Shadow*. New York: Macmillan, 1982.

———. *Stone Soup*. New York: Scribner, 1947.

Brown, Margaret Wise. *Goodnight, Moon*. New York: Harper and Row, 1947.

Brown, Palmer. *Hickory*. New York: Harper and Row, 1978.

Brown, Tricia. *Hello, Amigos!* New York: Henry Holt, 1986.

Buck, Pearl. *The Big Wave*. New York: Harper and Row, 1986.

Bullatz, Sonja, and Lomeo, Angelo. *The Baby Bears*. New York: Golden Books, 1983.

Bunting, Eve. *Fly Away Home*. New York: Clarion, 1991.

———. *How Many Days to America? A Thanksgiving Story*. New York: Clarion, 1988.

Burnett, Frances Hodgson. *The Secret Garden*. New York: Harper and Row, 1912.

Burnford, Sheila. *The Incredible Journey*. Boston: Little Brown, 1960.

Burton, Virginia Lee. *Katy and the Big Snow*. Boston: Houghton Mifflin, 1943.

Butterworth, Oliver. *The Enormous Egg*. Boston: Little and Brown, 1956.

Byars, Betsy. *The Animal, the Vegetable, and John D. Jones*. New York: Dellacourt, 1982.

———. *The Not-Just-Anybody Family*. New York: Dell, 1986.

———. *The Pinballs*. New York: Harper and Row, 1977.

———. *Summer of the Swans*. New York: Viking, 1970.

Cadato, Michael, and Joseph Bruchae. *Keepers of the Earth*. Golden, CO: Fulcrum, 1989.

Caines, Jeanette. *Chilly Stomach*. New York: Harper and Row, 1986.

Calhoon, Mary. *Cross Country Cat*. New York: Morrow, 1979.

Calhoun, Mary. *Hot Air Henry*. New York: Morrow, 1981.

Carle, Eric. *The Tiny Seed*. New York: Scholastic, 1986.

———. *The Very Hungry Caterpillar*. New York: Philomel, 1969.

Cassedy, Sylvia. *In Your Own Words: A Beginner's Guide to Writing*. Garden City: Doubleday, 1979.

Catling, Patrick Skene. *John Midas in the Dreamtime*. New York: Morrow, 1986.

Charles, Oz. *How Does Soda Get into the Bottle?* New York: Simon and Schuster, 1988.

Cheltin, Helen. *Angel Island Prisoner*. Berkeley, CA: New Seed Press, 1982.

Chief Seattle. *Brother Eagle, Sister Sky*. New York: Dial, 1991.

Child's Book of Poems. New York: Scholastic, 1988.

Ciardi, John. *The Hopeful Trout and Other Limericks*. Boston: Houghton Mifflin, 1989.

Cisneros, Sandra. *The House on Mango Street*. Houston: Arte Publico, 1989.

Cleary, Beverly. *A Girl from Yamhill*. New York: Morrow, 1988.

———. *Dear Mr. Henshaw*. New York: Morrow, 1983.

———. *Ellen Tebbets*. New York: Dell, 1951.

———. *The Mouse and the Motorcycle*. New York: Dell, 1980.

———. *Muggie Maggie*. New York: Morrow, 1991.

———. *Socks*. New York: Morrow, 1979.

Climo, Shirley. *Egyptian Cinderella*. New York: Harper and Row, 1989.

Coates, Laura Jane. *Marcella and the Moon*. New York: Macmillan, 1986.

Codrington, Kenneth deBurgh. *Cricket in the Grass*. London: Faber and Faber, 1959.

Coerr, Eleanor. *Sadako and the Thousand Paper Cranes*. New York: Putnam, 1977.

———. *The Great Balloon Race*. New York: Harper and Row, 1981.

Cohen, Miriam. *When Will I Read?* New York: Greenwillow, 1977.

Cole, Babette. *Princess Smartypants*. New York: Putnam, 1987.

Cole, Joanna. *Cars and How They Go*. New York: Harper and Row, 1983.

———. *Hungry, Hungry Sharks*. New York: Random House, 1986.

Collier, James, and Christopher Collier. *War Comes to Willy Freeman*. New York: Dell, 1983.

———. *My Brother Sam Is Dead*. New York: Four Winds Press, 1974.

Colligan, Louise. *Scholastic's A+ Junior Guide to Good Writing*. New York: Scholastic, 1988.

Cooney, Barbara. *Island Boy*. New York: Viking Kestrel, 1988.

———. *Miss Rumphius*. New York: Penguin, 1985.

Crews, Donald. *Freight Train*. New York: Greenwillow, 1978.

Dahl, Roald. *Boy*. New York: Farrar, Straus and Giroux, 1984.

———. *Charlie and the Chocolate Factory*. New York: Penguin, 1983.

———. *Danny, Champion of the World*. New York: Knopf, 1975.

———. *James and the Giant Peach*. New York: Knopf, 1962.

———. *The BFG*. New York: Penguin, 1989.

Dakos, Kalli. *If You're Not Here, Raise Your Hand: Poems about School*. New York: Four Winds, 1991.

Dalgliesh, Alice. *The Courage of Sarah Noble*. New York: Scribner, 1954.

———. *The Thanksgiving Story*. New York: Scribner, 1954.

Day, Alexandra. *Carl's Christmas*. New York: Farrar, Straus and Giroux, 1990.

———. *Good Dog, Carl*. San Marcos, CA: Green Tiger Press, 1985.

Dayrell, Elphinstone. *Why The Sun and Moon Live in the Sky*. Boston: Houghton Mifflin, 1968.

de Angeli, Marguerite. *The Door in the Wall*. New York: Doubleday, 1949.

DeClements, Barthe. *Nothing's Fair in Fifth Grade*. New York: Viking, 1981.

———. *The Fourth Grade Wizards*. New York: Viking, 1989.

de Paola, Tomie. *An Early American Christmas*. New York: Holiday House, 1987.

———. *The Legend of the Bluebonnet*. New York: Putnam, 1983.

———. *Nana Upstairs and Nana Downstairs*. New York: Puffin, 1978.

———. *Now One Foot, Now the Other*. New York: Putnam, 1981.

———. *Pancakes for Breakfast*. New York: Harcourt Brace, 1978.

———. *The Night Before Christmas.* New York: Holiday House, 1980.

de Poix, Carol. *Jo, Flo and Yolanda.* Carrboro, NC: Lollipop Power, 1979.

de Regniers, Beatrice Schenk. *Sing a Song of Popcorn: Every Child's Book of Poems.* New York: Scholastic, 1988.

de Saint-Exupéry, Antoine. *The Little Prince.* New York: Harcourt, 1943.

de Wetering, Janwillem van. *Hugh Pine.* Boston: Houghton Mifflin, 1980.

Delacre, Lulu. *Arroz con Leche: Popular Songs and Rhymes from Latin America.* New York: Scholastic, 1989.

Demi. *The Empty Pot.* New York: Holt, 1991.

Doublier, Anne. *Under the Sea from A to Z.* New York: Crown, 1991.

Downing, Mary. *The Doll in the Garden: A Ghost Story.* New York: Clarion, 1990.

Dubrovin, Vivian. *Write Your Own Story.* New York: Franklin Watts, 1984.

Dumbrowski, Cathy. *Cave Boy.* New York: Random House, 1989.

Durrel, Ann. *The Dianne Goode Book of American Folk Tales and Songs.* New York: Dutton, 1989.

Eckert, Allan. *Incident at Hawk's Hill.* Boston: Little Brown, 1971.

Elting, Mary, and Goodman, Ann. *Dinosaur Mysteries.* New York: Putnam, 1980.

Emberley, Barbara. *Drummer Hoff.* Englewood Cliffs, N.J.: Prentice Hall, 1967.

———. *My Home/Mi Casa.* Boston: Little, Brown, 1990.

———. *Taking a Walk/Cammandro.* Boston: Little, Brown, 1990.

Estep, Don. *Cats and Kittens.* New York: Checkerboard Press. 1990.

Ets, Marie Hall. *Gilberto and the Wind.* New York: Viking, 1963.

Evslin, B., Evslin, D., and Hoopes, N. *Mightiest of Mortals: Heracles.* New York: Viking, 1975.

Farber, Norma. *How Does It Feel to be Old?* Illustrated by Trina S. Hyman. New York: Dutton, 1985.

Faucher, Ruth. *Cesar Chavez.* New York: Harper and Row, 1988.

Feeling, Muriel. *Moja Means One: Swahili Counting Book.* New York: Dial, 1971.

———. *Jambo Means Hello: Swahili Alphabet Book.* New York: Dial, 1974.

Fleischman, Paul. *A Joyful Noise: Poems for Two Voices.* New York: Harper and Row, 1988.

Fleischman, Sid. *The Whipping Boy.* New York: Greenwillow, 1986.

Florian, Douglas. *Vegetable Garden.* Orlando: Harcourt Brace Jovanovich, 1991.

Flournoy, Valerie. *The Patchwork Quilt.* New York: Dial, 1985.

Forbes, Esther. *Johnny Tremain.* Boston: Houghton Mifflin, 1945.

Fox, Paula. *How Many Miles to Babylon.* New York: White, 1967.

———. *Maurice's Room.* New York: Macmillan, 1988.

Freedman, Russell. *Buffalo Hunt.* New York: Holiday, 1988.

———. *Dinosaurs and Their Young.* New York: Holiday, 1983.

Freeman, Ina. *How My Parents Learned To Eat.* Boston: Houghton Mifflin, 1984.

Freeman, Russell. *Lincoln: A Photobiography.* New York: Clarion, 1987.

Fritz, Jean. *And Then What Happened, Paul Revere?* New York: Coward, McCann and Geoghegan, 1973.

———. *Bully for You, Teddy Roosevelt!* New York: Putnam, 1991.

———. *Homesick: My Own Story.* New York: Dell, 1982.

———. *What's the Big Idea, Ben Franklin?* New York: Coward-McCann, 1976.

———. *Where Do You Think You're Going, Christopher Columbus?* New York: Putnam, 1980.

Fujimoto, Patricia. *Libraries.* Chicago: Children's, 1984.

Gag, Wanda. *Millions of Cats.* New York: Putnam, 1928.

Gardiner, John Reynolds. *Stone Fox.* New York: Harper and Row, 1980.

Gates, Doris. *Heros and Monsters of Greek Myth.* New York: Scholastic, 1967.

Geisel, Theodore S. (Dr. Seuss). *Cat in the Hat.* New York: Random House, 1966.

———. *Green Eggs and Ham.* New York: Random House, 1960.

———. *Hop on Pop.* New York: Random House, 1963.

George, Jean Craighead. *Julie of the Wolves.* New York: Harper and Row, 1972.

———. *My Side of the Mountain.* New York: Dutton, 1959.

Gera, Adele. *My Grandmother's Stories: A Collection of Jewish Folk Tales.* New York: Knopf, 1990.

Gerstein, Mordicai. *Mountains of Tibet.* New York: Harper and Row, 1987.

Gibbons, Gail. *Dinosaurs.* New York: Holiday, 1987.

———. *Flying.* New York: Holiday House, 1966.

Giff, Patricia Reilly. *The Beast in Mrs. Rooney's Room.* New York: Dell, 1984.

Gilcrest, Cherry. *A Visit to the Library.* New York: Cambridge University Press, 1985.

Gipson, Fred. *Old Yeller.* New York: Harper and Row, 1956.

Gladone, Paul. *The Gingerbread Boy.* New York: Clarion, 1975.

———. *The House That Jack Built.* New York: McGraw Hill, 1961.

———. *The Little Red Hen.* New York: Scholastic, 1973.

———. *The Three Bears.* New York: Scholastic, 1977.

Goble, Paul. *Buffalo Woman.* New York: Bradbury, 1984.

———. *Her Seven Brothers.* New York: Bradbury, 1989.

———. *The Gift of the Sacred Dog.* New York: Bradbury Press, 1980.

Goffstein, M. B. *An Artist.* New York: Harper and Row, 1980.

Goldin, Augusta. *Ducks Don't Get Wet.* New York: Crowell, 1965.

Goodall, John. *Jacko.* New York: Harcourt Brace, 1972.

———. *The Story of an English Village.* New York: Macmillan, 1979.

Gramatky, Hardie. *Little Toot.* New York: Putnam, 1939.

Green, Bette. *Philip Hall Likes Me. I Recon Maybe.* New York: Dial, 1974.

Green, Carol. *I Can Be A Librarian.* Chicago: Children's, 1988.

Greenfield, Eloise. *Grandpa's Face.* New York: Philomel, 1988.

———. *Nathaniel Talking.* New York: Writers and Readers, 1989.

———. *Sister.* New York: Crowell, 1974.

Grifalconi, Ann. *Osa's Pride.* Boston: Little, Brown, 1990.

Grillone, Lisa, and Gennaro, Joseph. *Small Worlds Close Up.* New York: Crown, 1978.

Grimm, Wilhelm, (Translated by Ralph Manheim). *Dear Mili.* New York: Farrar, Straus & Giroux, 1989.

Grossman, Virginia. *Ten Little Rabbits.* San Francisco: Chronicle Books, 1991.

Grove, Vicki. *The Fastest Friend in the West.* New York: Putnam, 1991.

Guarin, Deborah. *Is Your Mama a Llama?* New York: Scholastic, 1989.

Gunston, Bill. *Aircraft.* New York: Watts, 1986.

Guy, Rosa. *The Ups and Downs of Carl Davis III.* New York: Dellacourt, 1989.

Gwynn, Fred. *A Chocolate Moose for Dinner.* New York: Simon and Schuster, 1988.

———. *The King Who Rained.* New York: Simon and Schuster, 1988.

———. *A Little Pigeon Toad.* New York: Simon and Schuster, 1988.

Hale, Janet. *Owl's Song.* New York: Avon, 1976.

Hall, Donald. *The Ox-Cart Man.* New York: Penguin, 1979.

Hamilton, Virginia. *In the Beginning: Creation Stories from Around the World.* New York: Harcourt Brace, 1988.

———. *The People Could Fly: American Black Folktales.* New York: Knopf, 1985.

———. *Zeeley.* New York: Macmillan, 1967.

Hepworth, Cathi. *Antics! An Alphabetical Anthology.* New York: Putnam, 1992.

Hewett, Joan. *Hector Lives in the United States Now: The Story of a Mexican-American Child.* New York: Lippincott, 1990.

Hoban, Russell. *A Bargain for Frances.* New York: Harper and Row, 1970.

Hoban, Tana. *Count and See.* New York: Macmillan, 1972.

———. *Is It Red? Is It Yellow? Is It Blue?* New York: Greenwillow, 1978.

———. *26 Letters and 99 Cents.* New York: Greenwillow, 1987.

Hoberman, Mary Ann. *A House Is a House for Me.* New York: Penguin, 1982.

Hodges, Margaret. *The Kitchen Knight: A Tale of King Arthur.* New York: Holiday House, 1990.

Hogrogian, Nonny. *One Fine Day.* New York: Macmillan, 1971.

Holman, Felice. *Slake's Limbo.* New York: Macmillan, 1974.

Howe, Deborah, and Howe, James. *Bunnicula.* New York: Atheneum, 1979.

Howe, James. *The Day the Teacher Went Bananas.* New York: Dutton, 1984.

Howell, Margaret. *The Lonely Dragon.* London: Longman, 1972.

Hoyt-Goldsmith, Diane. *Pueblo Storyteller.* New York: Holiday House, 1991.

Huck, Charlotte. *Princess Furball.* New York: Greenwillow, 1989.

Hunhardt, Dorothy. *Pat the Bunny.* New York: Western, 1942.

Hunt, Irene. *Across Five Aprils.* Chicago: Follett, 1964.

Hunter, Edith Fisher. *Child of the Silent Night.* New York: Dell, 1963.

Hurwitz, Johanna. *Aldo Applesauce.* New York: Wm. Morrow, 1979.

Hutchins, Pat. *Changes, Changes.* New York: Macmillan, 1971.

———. *Good Night Owl.* New York: Macmillan, 1972.

———. *Rosie's Walk.* New York: Macmillan, 1968.

———. *The Doorbell Rang.* New York: Greenwillow, 1986.

Huynh, Queng Nhuong. *The Land I Lost: Adventures of a Boy in Viet Nam.* New York: Harper and Row, 1982.

Hymans, Trina Schart. *Little Red Riding Hood.* New York: Holiday House, 1983.

Jacobs, Joseph. *Tattercoats.* New York: Putnam, 1989.

Jacobs, William Jay. *Ellis Island: New Hope in a New Land.* New York: Charles Scribner's Sons, 1990.

Johnson, Angela. *Tell Me A Story, Mama.* New York: Orchard Books, 1989.

Johnston, Tony. *Yonder.* New York: Dial, 1988.

Jones, Betty M. *Wonder Women of Sports.* New York: Random House, 1981.

Jordan, Mary Kate. *Losing Uncle Tim.* Morton Grove, IL: Albert Whitman, 1989.

Juster, Norman. *A Surfeit of Similes.* New York: William Morrow, 1989.

Juster, Norton. *The Phantom Tollbooth.* New York: Random House, 1961.

Keats, Ezra Jack. *Clementine's Cactus.* New York: Viking, 1982.

———. *In A Spring Garden.* New York: Dial, 1965.

———. *Peter's Chair.* New York: Harper and Row, 1967.

———. *The Snowy Day.* New York: Penguin, 1962.

Keller, Ruth. *Many Luscious Lollipops.* New York: Grossett and Dunlop, 1989.

Kellogg, Steven. *Chicken Little.* Boston: Houghton Mifflin, 1989.

———. *Paul Bunyan.* New York: Wm. Morrow, 1984.

Kesselman, Wendy. *Emma.* New York: Doubleday, 1980.

King-Smith, Dick. *Ace, the Very Important Pig.* New York: Crown, 1990.

Kipling, Rudyard. *Just So Stories.* New York: Macmillan, 1982. (Other editions available.)

Kitchen, Burt. *Animal Alphabet.* New York: Dial, 1984.

Kjelgaard, Jim. *Big Red.* New York: Holiday House, 1956.

Knolton, Jack. *Maps and Globes.* New York: Harper and Row, 1985.

Knudson, R. R. *Babe Didrickson: Athlete of the Century.* New York: Viking, 1985.

Konigsburg, E. L. *Father's Arcane Daughter.* New York: Dell, 1986.

———. *From the Mixed-up Files of Mrs. Basil E. Frankweiler.* New York: Atheneum, 1967.

Kroll, Steven. *The Biggest Pumpkin Ever.* New York: Scholastic, 1986.

Krumgold, Joseph. *And Now Miguel.* New York: Crowell, 1953.

Kurelek, William. *A Prairie Boy's Winter.* Boston: Houghton Mifflin, 1973.

Kuskin, Karla. *The Philharmonic Gets Dressed.* New York: Harper and Row, 1982.

L'Engle, Madeleine. *A Wrinkle in Time.* New York: Farrar, Straus & Giroux, 1962.

Langstaff, John. *Frog Went a-Courtin'.* New York: Harcourt Brace, 1955.

Lasky, Kathy. *Dinosaur Dig.* New York: Morrow, 1990.

Lauber, Patricia. *Dinosaurs Walked Here and Other Stories Fossils Tell.* New York: Bradbury, 1987.

———. *Tales Mummies Tell.* New York: Crowell, 1985.

Lauber, Patricia, and Wexler, Jerome. *Seeds, Pop, Stick, Glide.* New York: Crown, 1987.

Laubner, Patrice. *News about Dinosaurs.* New York: Bradbury Press, 1989.

Lawson, Robert. *Ben and Me.* Boston: Little Brown, 1951.

———. *Rabbit Hill.* New York: Viking, 1944.

Lear, Edward. *The Complete Nonsense Book.* New York: Dodd Mead, 1946.

Lee, Jeannie, M. *Ba-Nam.* New York: Henry Holt, 1987.

Lessac, Frane. *Caribbean Canvas.* New York: Lippincott, 1987.

———. *My Little Island.* New York: Harper and Row, 1984.

Levitt, Paul M., Burger, Douglas, and Gurlnick, Elissa. *The Weighty Word Book.* Longmont, CO: Bookmaker's Guild, 1985.

Lewis, C. S. *The Lion, the Witch and the Wardrobe.* New York: Macmillan, 1961.

Lewis, John. *The Chinese Word for Horse, and Other Stories.* New York: Schocken Books, 1980.

Lewis, Richard, ed. *In a Spring Garden.* New York: Dial, 1989.

Lewis, Richard. *Miracles: Poems by Children of the English-Speaking World.* New York: Simon and Schuster, 1966.

Lindgren, Astrid. *Pippi Longstocking.* New York: Viking Press, 1950.

Litchfield, Ada B. *A Cane in Her Hand.* Morton Grove, IL: Albert Whitman, 1977.

Little, Jean. *Mama's Going to Buy You a Mocking Bird.* New York: Penguin, 1986.

Lobel, Anita. *Alison's Zinnia.* New York: Greenwillow, 1990.

Lobel, Arnold. *Frog and Toad Are Friends.* New York: Harper and Row, 1962, 1970, 1979.

———. *Mouse Tails.* New York: Harper and Row, 1972.

Lobel, Arnold, and Lobel, Anita. *On Market Street.* New York: Greenwillow, 1981.

Lord, Beth Bao. *In the Year of the Boar and Jackie Robinson.* New York: Harper and Row, 1984.

Lord, Suzanne and Epstein, Jolie. *A Day in Space.* New York: Scholastic, 1986.

Macaulay, David. *Black and White.* Boston: Houghton Mifflin, 1988.

———. *The Way Things Work.* Boston: Houghton Mifflin, 1990.

MacDonald, Betty. *Mrs. Piggle Wiggle.* New York: Harper and Row, 1957.

MacDonald, Caroline. *The Lake at the End of the World.* New York: Dial, 1989.

MacLachlan, Patricia. *Journey.* New York: Delacorte, 1991.

———. *Sarah, Plain and Tall.* New York: Harper and Row, 1985.

Mahon, Julia C. *First Book of Creative Writing.* New York: Franklin Watts, 1968.

Manes, Stephen. *Be A Perfect Person in Just Three Days.* New York: Bantam, 1982.

Marshall, Edward. *Space Case.* New York: Dial, 1982.

Martin, Bill, Jr. *Brown Bear, Brown Bear, What Do You See?* New York: Henry Holt, 1983.

———. *Knots on a Counting Rope.* New York: Henry Holt, 1987.

Martin, Bill, Jr., and Archambault, John. *Chicka Chicka Boom Boom.* New York: Simon and Schuster, 1989.

———. *Knots on a Counting Rope.* New York: Henry Holt Co., 1987.

Mathers, Petra. *Maria Teresa.* New York: Harper and Row, 1985.

Mathis, Sharon Bell. *The Hundred Penny Box.* New York: Viking, 1975.

Mayer, Mercer. *What Do You Do with a Kangaroo?* New York: Scholastic, 1987.

McClosky, Robert. *Blueberries for Sal.* New York: Viking, 1963.

———. *Make Way for Ducklings.* New York: Viking, 1941.

———. *Time of Wonder.* New York: Viking, 1957.

McCord, David. *Every Time I Climb a Tree.* Boston: Little, Brown, 1967.

McDermott, Gerald. *Arrow to the Sun.* New York: Viking, 1974.

———. *Flecha al Sol.* New York: Viking, 1991.

McInerney, Claire. *Find It! The Inside Story at Your Library.* Minneapolis: Lerner, 1989.

McLaughlin, Molly. *Earthworms, Dirt and Rotten Leaves: An Exploration in Ecology.* New York: Macmillan, 1986.

McPhail, David. *Great Cat.* New York: Dutton, 1982.

———. *The Bear's Toothache.* Boston: Little, Brown, 1972.

McSwigan, Marie. *Snow Treasure.* New York: Scholastic, 1986.

Meddaugh, Susan. *Too Short Fred.* Boston: Houghton Mifflin, 1978.

Mendez, Phil. *The Black Snowman.* New York: Scholastic, 1989.

Merrill, Claire. *A Seed Is a Promise.* New York: Scholastic, 1973.

Miles, Miska. *Annie and the Old One.* Boston, Little Brown, 1971.

Milne, A. A. *Winnie-the-Pooh.* New York: Dell, 1981. (Other editions available.)

Mohr, Nicholasa. *Felita.* New York: Dial, 1979.

Morimoto, Junko. *Mouse's Marriage.* New York: Viking Kestrel, 1986.

Morris, Winnifred. *The Magic Leaf.* New York: Atheneum, 1987.

Mosel, Arline. *Tikki, Tikki, Tembo.* New York: Henry Holt, 1968.

Most, Bernard. *If the Dinosaurs Came Back.* New York: Harcourt Brace Jovanovich, 1978.

Mullel, Tololwe M. *The Orphan Boy.* New York: Clarion, 1990.

Munsch, Robert. *Love You Forever.* Scarborough, ONT: Firefly Books, 1986.

———. *Mortimer.* Toronto: Annick Press, 1983.

———. *Mud Puddle.* Willowdale, ONT: Firefly Books, 1982.

———. *Thomas' Snowsuit*. Willowdale, ONT: Firefly Books, 1985.

Murphy, Jim. *The Last Dinosaur*. New York: Scholastic, 1988.

Murray, Michele. *Nellie Cameron*. Minneapolis: Seabury, 1971.

Musgrove, Margaret. *Ashanti to Zulu: African Traditions*. New York: Dial, 1976.

Naidoo, Beverley. *Journey to Jo'burg*. New York: Lippincott, 1985.

Naylor, Phyllis R. *How I Came to Be a Writer*. New York: Morrow, 1988.

———. *Shiloh*. New York: Macmillan, 1991.

Ness, Evaline. *Sam, Bangs, and Moonshine*. New York: Henry Holt, 1966.

Newton, James. *A Forest Is Reborn*. New York: Harper and Row, 1982.

Nixon, Jean Lowrey. *Maggie, Too*. New York: Dell, 1985.

Norton, Mary. *The Borrowers*. New York: Harcourt Brace, 1953.

Nuinberg, Maxwell. *Fun With Words*. Englewood Cliffs, NJ: Prentice Hall, 1970.

Numeroff, Laura Jaffe. *If You Give A Mouse A Cookie*. New York: Harper and Row, 1985.

O'Brien, Edna. *Tales for the Telling*. New York: Penguin, 1988.

O'Brien, Robert C. *Mrs. Frisby and the Rats of NIMH*. New York: Macmillan, 1971.

O'Dell, Scott. *Sing Down the Moon*. Boston: Houghton Mifflin, 1970.

O'Neill, Mary. *Hailstones and Halibut Bones: Adventures in Color*. Garden City, NY: Doubleday, 1961.

Omerod, Jan. *Moonlight*. New York: Lothrop, 1982.

———. *Sunshine*. New York: Lothrop, 1981.

Osborne, Mary Pope. *American Tall Tales*. New York: Knopf, 1991.

Overbeck, Cynthia. *How Seeds Travel*. Minneapolis: Lerner, 1982.

Oxenbury, Helen. *Helen Oxenbury's ABC of Things*. New York: Delacorte, 1983.

Paek, Min. *Aekyung's Dream*. San Francisco: Children's Book Press, 1988.

Parish, Peggy. *Amelia Bedelia*. New York: Harper and Row, 1963.

Parker, Nancy Winslow, and Joan Richards Wright. *Bugs*. New York: Greenwillow, 1987.

Parrish, Peggy. *Good Hunting, Blue Sky*. New York: Random House, 1989.

Patent, Dorothy Hinshaw. *Where Food Comes From*. New York: Holiday House, 1991.

Paterson, Katherine. *Bridge to Terabithia*. New York: Harper and Row, 1977.

———. *Jacob Have I Loved*. New York: Crowell, 1980.

———. *The Great Gilly Hopkins*. New York: Harper and Row, 1978.

Paul, Ann Whitford. *Eight Hands Round: A Patchwork Alphabet*. New York: Harper Collins, 1991.

Pearson, Susan. *Well, I Never!* New York: Simon and Schuster, 1991.

Peck, Robert Newton. *Soup*. New York: Knopf, 1974.

———. *Soup and Me*. New York: Knopf, 1975.

———. *Soup for President*. New York: Knopf, 1978.

Peet, Bill. *Big Bad Bruce*. Boston: Houghton Mifflin, 1978, 1982.

———. *Bill Peet: An Autobiography*. Boston: Houghton Mifflin, 1989.

Penny, Malcom. *Endangered Animals*. New York: Watts, 1988.

Peterson, John. *The Littles*. New York: Scholastic, 1967, 1986.

Potter, Beatrix. *The Tale of Peter Rabbit*. New York: Dover, 1903. (Other editions available.)

———. *The Tale of the Flopsy Bunnies*. New York: Dover, 1903.

Prelutsky, Jack. *Rainy, Rainy Saturday*. New York: Greenwillow, 1980.

———. *The Random House Book of Poetry for Children*. New York: Random House, 1983.

Pringle, Laurence. *Death Is Natural*. New York: Macmillan, 1977.

Provensen, Alice, and Provensen, Marvin. *The Glorious Flight across the Channel*. New York: Viking, 1983.

Quackenbush, Robert. *Oh, What an Awful Mess!* Englewood Cliffs: Prentice Hall, 1980.

Raskin, Ellen. *Nothing Ever Happens on My Block*. New York: Atheneum, 1966.

Rawls, Wilson. *Where the Red Fern Grows*. New York: Doubleday, 1961, 1973, 1978.

Ray, Delia. *Behind the Blue and Gray: The Soldier's Life in the Civil War*. New York: Lodestar, 1991.

Rehnman, Mats. *The Clay Flute*. New York: Farrar, Straus & Giroux, 1989.

Reiss, John J. *Shapes*. New York: Macmillan, 1974.

Robinson, Barbara. *The Best Christmas Pageant Ever*. New York: Harper, 1972.

Rockwell, Anne. *First Comes Spring*. New York: Harper and Row, 1985.

———. *I Like the Library*. New York: Dutton, 1977.

Rockwell, Harlow. *My Kitchen*. New York: Greenwillow, 1980.

———. *My Nursery School*. New York: Greenwillow, 1976.

Rockwell, Thomas. *How to Eat Fried Worms*. New York: Franklin Watts, 1973.

Rogers, Jean. *The Runaway Mittens*. New York: Greenwillow, 1988.

Rohmer, Harriet, and Mary Anchondo. *How We Came to the Fifth World/ Como vinimos al quinto mundo*. San Francisco: Children's Book Press, 1988.

Roop, Peter and Connie. *Keep the Lights Burning, Abbie*. Minneapolis: Carlrhoda Books, 1985.

Rosario, Idalia. *Idalia's Project ABC*. New York: Henry Holt, 1987.

Rosenblum, Richard. *Wings: The Early Years of Aviation*. New York: Four Winds Press, 1980.

Rosenthal, Mark. *Bears*. Chicago: Children's Press, 1983.

Rounds, Glen O. *Ol' Paul, The Mighty Logger*. New York: Holiday House, 1976.

———. *I Know an Old Woman Who Swallowed a Fly*. New York: Holiday House, 1991.

Sandburg, Carl. *Abe Lincoln Grows Up*. New York: Harcourt Brace, 1954.

———. *The Rootabaga Stories*. New York: Odyssey, 1968.

Schroeder, Alan. *Ragtime Trumpie*. Boston: Little, Brown, 1989.

Schwartz, David M. *How Much Is a Million?* New York: Lothrup, 1987.

———. *If You Made a Million*. New York: Lothrup, 1989.

Schweitzer, Byrd Baylor. *Amigo*. New York: Collier, 1963.

Scieszka, Jon. *The Frog Prince Continued*. New York: Viking, 1991.

———. *The True Story of the 3 Little Pigs!* New York: Viking, 1989.

Scott, Sally. *The Magic Horse*. New York: Morrow, 1988.

Seeger, Pete. *Abiyoyo*. New York: Macmillan, 1986.

Seidman, James F., and Mintoyne, Grace. *Shopping Cart Art*. New York: Macmillan, 1970.

Sendak, Maurice. *Chicken Soup with Rice*. New York: Harper and Row, 1962.

———. *In the Night Kitchen*. New York: Harper and Row, 1970.

———. *Outside Over There*. New York: Harper and Row, 1981.

———. *Where the Wild Things Are*. New York: Harper and Row, 1963.

Seuss, Dr. *And to Think That I Saw It on Mulberry Street*. New York: Vanguard, 1937.

———. *Cat In The Hat*. New York: Random House, 1957.

———. *Green Eggs and Ham*. New York: Random House, 1960.

———. *The 500 Hats of Bartholomew Cubbins*. New York: Vanguard, 1938.

Seymour, Simon. *Big Cats*. New York: Harper Collins, 1991.

———. *Deserts*. New York: Morrow, 1990.

———. *Earthquakes*. New York: Morrow, 1991.

———. *Galaxies*. New York: Morrow, 1988.

———. *The Paper Airplane Book*. New York: Penguin, 1971.

Sharmat, Marjorie Weinman. *Mitchell is Moving*. New York: Macmillan, 1985.

———. *Nate the Great*. New York: Putnam, 1977–89 (11 titles).

Silverstein, Shel. *A Light in the Attic*. New York: Harper, 1981.

———. *Where the Sidewalk Ends*. New York: Harper and Row, 1974.

Sis, Peter. *Going Up*. New York: Greenwillow, 1989.

Slobodkin, Louis. *The Three-Seated Space Ship*. New York: Macmillan, 1962.

Slobodkina, Esphyr. *Caps for Sale*. New York: Harper and Row, 1947.

Slote, Alfred. *Finding Buck McHenry*. New York: Harper Collins, 1991.

Smith, Doris Buchanan. *A Taste of Blackberries*. New York: Crowell, 1973.

Sneve, Virginia Driving Hawk. *Dancing Teepees: Poems of American Indian Youth*. New York: Holiday House, 1989.

———. *Jimmy Yellow Hawk*. New York: Holiday House, 1972.

Snyder, Dianne. *The Boy of the Three-Year Nap*. Boston: Houghton Mifflin, 1988.

Sobol, Donald. *Encyclopedia Brown Mysteries*. New York: Bantam, 1967–84 (18 titles).

———. *The Wright Brothers at Kitty Hawk*. New York: Scholastic, 1961.

Southall, Ivan. *Let the Balloon Go*. New York: Bradbury Press, 1968.

Speare, Elizabeth George. *The Witch of Blackbird Pond*. Boston: Houghton Mifflin, 1958.

———. *The Sign of the Beaver*. Boston: Houghton Mifflin, 1983.

Spence, Eleanor. *October Child.* London: Oxford University Press, 1976.

Sperry, Armstrong. *Call It Courage.* New York: Macmillan, 1940, 1968.

Spier, Peter. *Bored—Nothing To Do.* New York: Doubleday, 1978.

———. *Fast-Slow, High-Low: A Book of Opposites.* New York: Doubleday, 1972.

Spinelli, Jerry. *Maniac Magee.* Boston: Little Brown, 1990.

Steig, William. *Doctor DeSoto.* New York: Farrar, Straus and Giroux, 1982.

———. *Sylvester and the Magic Pebble.* New York: Simon and Schuster, 1969.

Steptoe, John. *Daddy Is a Monster . . . Sometimes.* New York: Lippincott, 1980.

———. *Mufaro's Beautiful Daughters: An African Tale.* New York: Lothrup, 1987.

Stevenson, Robert Louis. *Treasure Island.* New York: Scholastic, 1972. (One of several editions available)

Stoutenberg, Adrien. *American Tall Tales.* New York: Viking, 1966.

Strickland, Dorothy. *Listen, Children.* New York: Bantam, 1986.

Suart, Michele. *Angel Child, Dragon Child.* Milwaukee: Raintree, 1983.

Swann, Brian. *A Basketful of White Eggs.* New York: Orchard Books, 1988.

Tafuri, Nancy. *Have You Seen My Duckling?* New York: Puffin Books, 1986.

———. *Who's Counting?* New York: Greenwillow, 1986.

Taylor, Mildred. *Let The Circle Be Unbroken.* New York: Dial, 1981.

———. *Roll of Thunder, Hear My Cry.* New York: Dial, 1976.

———. *The Gold Cadillac.* New York: Bantam, 1987.

Taylor, Theodore. *The Cay.* New York: Avon Books, 1969.

Tejima, Keizaburo. *Fox's Dream.* New York: Putnam, 1987.

———. *Swan Sky.* New York: Putnam, 1988.

Thaler, Mike. *The Day The Teacher Went Bananas.* New York: Scholastic, 1989.

———. *The Hippopotamus Ate the Teacher.* New York: Avon, 1981.

Thomas, Jane Resh. *Saying Good-Bye to Grandma.* New York: Houghton Mifflin, 1988.

Tolkien, J. R. R. *The Hobbit.* Boston: Houghton Mifflin, 1938.

Tompert, Ann. *Grandfather Tang's Story.* New York: Crown, 1990.

Tresselt, Alvin. *The Dead Tree.* New York: Parents Magazine Press, 1972.

Tscharner, Renata Von, and Fleming, Ronald L. *New Providence: A Changing Landscape.* San Diego: Harcourt Brace, 1987.

Tsutsui, Yoiko. *Anna In Charge.* New York: Viking Kistrel, 1989.

Twain, Mark. *Tom Sawyer.* New York: Simon and Schuster, 1982. (One of several editions available)

Uchida, Yoshiko. *Journey Home.* New York: Macmillan, 1982.

———. *Journey to Topaz.* New York: Scribner, 1971.

Van Allsburg, Chris. *Jumanji.* Boston: Houghton Mifflin, 1981.

———. *The Garden of Abdul Gasazi.* Boston: Houghton Mifflin, 1979.

———. *Polar Express.* Boston: Houghton Mifflin, 1985.

———. *The Stranger.* Boston: Houghton Mifflin, 1986.

———. *The Wreck of the Zephyr.* Boston: Houghton Mifflin, 1983.

Van Laan, Nancy. *Possum Come A-Knockin'.* New York: Knopf, 1990.

Viorst, Judith. *Alexander and the Terrible, Horrible, No Good, Very Bad Day.* New York: Atheneum, 1972.

———. *Alexander, Who Used to Be Rich Last Sunday.* New York: Macmillan, 1978.

———. *Earrings.* New York: Atheneum, 1990.

———. *The Tenth Good Thing about Barney.* New York: Macmillan, 1971.

Voigt, Cynthia. *Dicey's Song.* New York: Fawcett, 1982.

———. *Homecoming.* New York: Macmillan, 1981.

Waber, Bernard. *Ira Sleeps Over.* Boston: Houghton Mifflin, 1973.

Wall, Lina Mao. *Judge Rabbit and the Tree Spirit.* San Francisco: Children's Press, 1991.

Waters, Kate, and Madeline Slovenz-Low. *Lion Dancer: Ernie Wan's Chinese New Year.* New York: Scholastic, 1990.

Weiss, Harvey. *Maps: Getting from Here to There.* Boston: Houghton Mifflin, 1991.

Weissman, David. *Tuesday.* New York: Clarion Books, 1991.

Wells, Rosemary. *Noisy Nora.* New York: Scholastic, 1973.

Wescott, Nadine Bernard. *I Know an Old Lady Who Swallowed a Fly.* Boston: Little Brown, 1980.

———. *The Lady with the Alligator Purse.* Boston: Little Brown, 1988.

Whipple, Laura. *Animals, Animals.* New York: Putnam, 1989.

White, E. B. *Charlotte's Web.* New York: Harper and Row, 1952.

White, T. H. *The Sword in the Stone.* New York: Putnam, 1939.

Whitfield, Philip, and Pope, Joyce. *Why Do the Seasons Change?* New York: Penguin, 1987.

Wilde, Oscar. *The Happy Prince.* New York: Simon and Schuster, 1989.

Wilder, Laura Ingalls. *Farmer Boy.* New York: Harper and Row, 1953.

———. *Little House in the Big Woods.* New York: Harper and Row, 1953.

———. *Little House on the Prairie.* New York: Harper and Row, 1953.

Wildsmith, Brian. *Brian Wildsmith's ABC.* New York: Watts, 1962.

Williams, Barbara. *Mitzi's Honeymoon with Nana Potts.* New York: Dell, 1983.

Williams, Margery. *The Velveteen Rabbit.* New York: Doubleday, 1984.

Winthrop, Elizabeth. *Vasilissa the Beautiful.* New York: Harper Collins, 1991.

Wittman, Sally. *A Special Trade.* New York: Harper and Row, 1978.

Wolf, Alexander (Jon Scieszka, pseud.). *The True Story of the Three Little Pigs.* New York: Penguin, 1989.

Wyndham, Robert, ed. *Chinese Mother Goose Rhymes.* New York: Philomel, 1968.

Yashima, Taro. *Crow Boy.* New York: Viking, 1955, 1969.

Yektai, Niki. *Hi Bears, Bye Bears.* New York: Orchard, 1991.

Yep, Lawrence. *Dragonwings.* New York: Harper and Row, 1985.

———. *The Rainbow People.* New York: Harper and Row, 1989.

Yolen, Jane. *Owl Moon.* New York: Scholastic, 1987.

Yolen, Jean. *Encounter.* San Diego: Harcourt, Brace, Jovanovich. 1992.

———. *The Emperor and the Kite.* Cleveland: World, 1967.

Yorkins, Arthur. *Company's Coming.* New York: Crown, 1988.

Young, Ed. *Lon Po Po: A Red-Riding Hood Story from China.* New York: Philomel, 1989.

Zallinger, Peter. *Dinosaurs.* New York: Random House, 1988.

Zion, Gene. *Harry by the Sea.* New York: Harper and Row, 1965.

References

AASA (1965). *The Basic Science Processes.* Washington: American Association for the Advancement of Science.

Adams, M. J. (1990). *Beginning to Read: Thinking and Learning about Print.* Cambridge, MA: MIT Press.

Adams, M. J., Allington, R. L. et. al. (1991). Beginning to Read: A Critique by Literacy Professionals and a Response from Marilyn Jager Adams. *The Reading Teacher* 44:370–395.

Aiex, N. K. (1988). Literature Based Reading Instruction. *The Reading Teacher* 41:458–461.

Allen, V. G. (1989). Literature as Support to Language Acquisition. In P. Rigg and V. G. Allen (eds.), *When They Don't All Speak English: Integrating the ESL Student into the Regular Classroom.* Urbana, IL: National Council of Teachers of English.

Allington, R. L. (1983). Fluency: The Neglected Reading Goal. *The Reading Teacher* 36:556–61.

Allington, R. L. (1983). The Reading Instruction Provided Readers of Differing Ability. *Elementary School Journal* 83:548–559.

Alvermann, D. (1984). Second Graders' Strategic Preferences while Reading Basal Stories. *Journal of Educational Research* 77:184–189.

Anderson, R., and Pearson, D. (1984). A Schema Theoretic View of Basic Processes in Reading Comprehension. In D. Pearson (ed.), *Handbook of Reading Research.* New York: Longmans.

Anderson, R. C., and Freebody, P. (1985). Vocabulary Knowledge. In H. Singer and R. B. Ruddell (eds.), *Theoretical Models and Processes of Reading* (3rd ed.). Newark, DE: International Reading Assoc.

Anderson, R. C., Hiebert, E. H., Scott, J. A., and Wilkinson, I. A. G. (1984). *Becoming a Nation of Readers: The Report of the Commission on Reading.* Washington: National Institute of Education.

Anderson, R. C., Hiebert, E. H., Scott, J. A., and Wilkinson, I. A. G. (1985). *Becoming a Nation of Readers: Report of the Commission on Reading.* Washington, DC: National Institute of Education.

Anderson, T. H., and Armburster, B. B. (1984). Studying. In P. D. Pearson (ed.), *Handbook of Reading Research.* New York: Longmans.

Applebee, A. (1978). *The Child's Concept of Story.* Chicago: University of Chicago Press.

Applebee, A. N., Langer, J. A., Mullis, I. V. A., and Jenkins, L. V. (1990). *The Writing Report Card, 1984–88.* Washington, DC: U.S. Dept. of Education.

Arnold, H. (1982). *Listening to Children Read.* London: United Kingdom Reading Association.

Ashton-Warner, S. (1963). *Teacher.* New York: Simon and Schuster.

Atwell, N. (1987). *In the Middle: Writing, Reading, and Learning with Adolescents.* Portsmouth, NH: Heinemann.

Auckerman, R. C. (1984). *Approaches to Beginning Reading.* 2nd ed. New York: John Wiley & Sons.

Audette, R. (1974). Concept Paper. In *Core Evaluation Manual.* Bedford, MA: Institute for Educational Services.

Austin, M., and C. Morrison. (1963). *The First R.* New York: Macmillan.

Banks, J. A. (1989). Integrating the Curriculum with Ethnic Content: Approaches and Guidelines. In J. A. Banks and C. A. McGee Banks (eds.), *Multicultural Education: Issues and Perspectives.* Boston: Allyn and Bacon.

Barnitz, J. G. (1980). Black English and Other Dialects: Sociolinguistic Implications for Reading Instruction. *The Reading Teacher* 33:779–786.

Barrett, T. T. (1974). Taxonomy of Reading Comprehension. In R. C. Smith and T. C. Barrett (eds.), *Teaching Reading in the Middle Grades.* Reading, MA: Addison-Wesley.

Bateman, B. (1992). Learning Disabilities: The Changing Landscape. *Journal of Learning Disabilities* 25:29–36.

Beach, R., and Hynds, S. (1991). Research on Response to Literature. In R. Barr, M. L. Kamill, P. Mosenthal, and P. D. Pearson (eds.), *Handbook on Reading Research.* Vol. 2. New York: Longman.

Beach, W., and Hynds, S. (1991). Research on Response to Literature. In R. Barr, M. Kamil, P. Mosenthal, and P. D. Pearson (eds.), *Handbook of Reading Research,* Vol. 2. New York: Longmans.

Bergeron, B. S. (1990). What Does the Term Whole Language Mean? Constructing a Definition from the Literature. *Journal of Reading Behavior* 22:301–329.

Berghoff, B., and Egawa, K. (1991). No More ''Rocks'': Grouping To Give Students Control of Their Learning. *The Reading Teacher* 44:536–541.

Bertrand, J. E. (1991). Student Assessment and Evaluation. In Bill Harp (ed.), *Assessment and Evaluation in Whole Language Programs.* Norwood, MA: Christopher Gordon Publishers.

Bettelheim, B., and Zelan, K. (1982). *On Learning to Read: A Child's Fascination with Meaning.* New York: Alfred Knopf.

Bettelheim, B. (1978). *The Uses of Enchantment.* New York: Knopf.

Bishop, R. S. (1987). Extending Multicultural Understanding through Children's Books. In B. Cullinan (ed.), *Children's Literature in the Reading Program.* Newark, DE: International Reading Association.

Bissex, G. L. (1980). *GNYS AT WRK: A Child Learns to Write and Read.* Cambridge, MA: Harvard University Press.

Blachowicz, C. L. (1985). Vocabulary Development and Reading: From Research to Instruction. *The Reading Teacher* 38:876–881.

Blanchard, J. S., and Rottenberg, C. J. (1991). Hypertext and Hypermedia: Discovering and Creating Meaningful Learning Environments. *The Reading Teacher* 43:656–661.

Blanton, W. E., Wood, K. D., and Moorman, G. B. (1990). The Role of Purpose in Reading Instruction. *The Reading Teacher* 43:486–493.

Bleich, D. (1978). *Subjective Criticism.* Baltimore: Johns Hopkins University Press.

Bloom, B. S. (1956). *Taxonomy of Educational Objectives.* New York: Longmans Green.

Blyden, A. E. (1988). Shared Story Reading for Severely Handicapped Learners. *Reading Improvement* 25:67–70.

Boman, B. T. (1989). Educating Language-Minority Children: Challenges and Opportunities. *Phi Delta Kappan* 71:118–120.

Bond, G. L., and Dykstra, R. (1967). The Cooperative Research Program in First-Grade Reading Instruction. *Reading Research Quarterly* 2:5–142.

Bormuth, J. R. (1966). Readability: A New Approach. *Reading Research Quarterly* 1:79–132.

Bormuth, J. R. (1968). The Cloze Readability Procedure. *Elementary English* 45:429–436.

Bosma, B. (1987). *Fairy Tales, Fables, Legends and Myths: Using Folk Literature in Your Classroom.* New York: Teachers College Press.

Bridge, C. A., Winograd, P. N., and Haley, D. (1983). Using Predictable Materials vs. Preprimers to Teach Beginning Sight Words. *The Reading Teacher* 36:884–891.

Bromley, K. D. (1989). Buddy Journals Make the Reading–Writing Connection. *The Reading Teacher* 43:122–129.

Brown, A. (1980). Metacognitive Development in Reading. In R. J. Spiro, B. C. Bruce, and W. F. Brewer (eds.), *Theoretical Issues in Reading Comprehension.* Hillsdale, NJ: Lawrence Erlbaum Associates.

Brown, V. L., Hammill, D. D., and Wiederholt, J. L. (1986). *Test of Reading Comprehension.* Austin, TX: Pro-Ed.

Bruce, B. (1984). A New Point of View on Children's Stories. In R. C. Anderson, J. Osborn, and R. J. Tierney (eds.), *Learning to Read in American Schools: Basal Readers and Content Texts* (pp. 153–174). Hillsdale: Lawrence Erlbaum Associates.

Burling, R. (1973). *English in Black and White.* New York: Holt, Rinehart and Winston.

Butzow, C. M., and Butzow, J. W. (1989). *Science through Children's Literature.* Englewood, CO: Teacher Ideas Press.

Caduto, M. J., and Bruchae, J. (1989). *Keepers of the Earth*. Golden, CO: Fulcrum, Inc.

California State Department of Education (1987). *English Language Arts Framework for California Public Schools*. Sacramento: California State Department of Education.

Calkins, L. M. (1986). *The Art of Teaching Writing*. Portsmouth, NH: Heinemann.

Cambourne, B. (1985). Change and Conflict in Literacy Education: What It's All About. *Australian Journal of Reading* 8:77–88.

Cambourne, B. (1988). *The Whole Story: Natural Learning and the Acquisition in the Classroom*. New York: Ashton-Scholastic.

Cambourne, B., and Turbill, J. (1990). Assessment on Whole-Language Classrooms: Theory into Practice. *The Elementary School Journal* 90:338–349.

Carbo, M. (1988). Debunking the Great Phonics Myth. *Phi Delta Kappan* 70:226–240.

Carbo, M. (1989). An Evaluation of Jeanne Chall's Response to "Debunking the Great Phonics Myth." *Phi Delta Kappan* 71:152–157.

Carbo, M., Dunn, R., and Dunn, K. (1986). *Teaching Students to Read through Their Individual Learning Styles*. Englewood Cliffs, NJ: Prentice-Hall.

Cassidy, J. (1981). Inquiry Reading for the Gifted. *The Reading Teacher* 35:17–21.

Chall, J. S. (1983). *Learning To Read: The Great Debate*. (2nd ed.). New York: McGraw Hill.

Chall, J. S. (1989a). *Learning to Read: The Great Debate* 20 Years Later—A Response to "Debunking the Great Phonics Myth." *Phi Delta Kappan* 70:521–538.

Chall, J. S. (1989b). The Uses of Educational Research: Comments on Carbo. *Phi Delta Kappan* 71:158–160.

Chatton, B. (1989). Using Literature across the Curriculum. In J. Hickman and B. Cullinan, (eds.), *Children's Literature in the Classroom: Weaving Charlotte's Web*. Needham, MA: Christopher Gordon Publishers.

Cheek, E. H. Jr. (1989). Skills-Based vs. Holistic Philosophies: The Debate Among Teacher Educators in Reading. *Teacher Education Quarterly* 16:15–20.

Clay, M. M. (1985). *The Early Detection of Reading Difficulties*. 3rd ed. Portsmouth, NH: Heinemann.

Clay, M. M. (1988). *The Early Detection of Reading Difficulties*. Portsmouth, NH: Heinemann.

Clymer, T. (1963). The Utility of Phonics Generalizations. *The Reading Teacher* 16:252–258.

Cockrum, W. A., and Castillo, M. (1991). Whole Language Assessment and Evaluation Strategies. In Bill Harp (ed.), *Assessment and Evaluation in Whole Language Programs*. Norwood, MA: Christopher Gordon Publishers.

Coles, G. (1987). *The Learning Mystique: A Critical Look at "Learning Disabilities."* New York: Pantheon Books.

Conrad, S. (1989). Newspaper in the Whole Language Classroom. In *A Whole Language Primer*. Quincy, MA: The Patriot Ledger.

Cosby, B. (1990). 45 Years From Today. *Ebony* 46:61.

Cox, S., and Galda, L. (1990). Multicultural Literature: Mirrors and Windows on a Global Community. *The Reading Teacher* 43:582–589.

Criscuolo, N. P. (1988). Twelve Practical Ways to Make the Reading/Writing Connection. *The New England Reading Association Journal* 24:30–32.

Crook, P. R., and Lehman, B. A. (1991). Themes for Two Voices: Children's Fiction and Nonfiction as "Whole Literature." *Language Arts* 68:34–41.

Culinan, B. E. (1989). Latching onto Literature: Reading Initiatives Take Hold. *School Library Journal* 35:27–31.

Cunningham, D., and Shablak, S. L. (1975). Selective Reading Guide-o-Rama: The Content Teacher's Best Friend. *Journal of Reading* 18:380–382.

Dale, E. (1965). Vocabulary Measurement: Techniques and Major Findings. *Elementary English* 42:895–901.

Dales, B. (1990). Trusting Relationships between Teachers and Librarians. *Language Arts* 67:732–734.

Davey, B. (1983). Think-Aloud—Modelling the Cognitive Processes of Reading Comprehension. *Journal of Reading* 27:44–47.

Davidson, A., and Kantor, Robert N. (1982). On the Failure of Readability Formulas to Define Readable Texts: A Case Study from Adaptations. *Reading Research Quarterly* 17:187–209.

Davis, F. B. (1972). Psychometric Research on Comprehension in Reading. *Reading Research Quarterly* 7:628–678.

Davis, Z. T., and McPherson, M. D. (1989). Story Map Instruction: A Road Map for Reading. *The Reading Teacher* 43:232–240.

Davison, A. (1985). *Readability— The Situation Today.* Technical Report No. 359. Champaign: University of Illinois, Center for the Study of Reading.

DeGroff, L. (1990). Is There a Place for Computers in Whole Language Classrooms? *The Reading Teacher* 43:568–572.

DeGroff, L. J. (1989). Developing Writing Processes with Children's Literature. *The New Advocate* 2:115–123.

Devine, T. G. (1986). *Teaching Reading Comprehension: From Theory to Practice.* Boston: Allyn and Bacon.

Diaakiw, J. Y. (1990). Children's Literature and Global Education: Understanding the Developing World. *The Reading Teacher* 44:296–300.

Dillard, J. L. (1972). *Black English.* New York: Random House.

Dolch, E. (1939). *A Manual for Remedial Readers.* Champaign, IL: Garrard.

Dowhower, S. L. (1989). Repeated Reading: Research into Practice. *The Reading Teacher* 42:502–7.

du Boulay, G. (1988). Newspapers: Text for Non-Narrative and Narrative Reading and Writing. *Australian Journal of Reading* 11:206–210.

Duffy, G. G. (1992). Let's Free Teachers to Be Inspired. *Phi Delta Kappan* 73:442–447.

Dunn, L. M., and Dunn, L. M. (1981). *Peabody Picture Vocabulary Test.* Pines, MN: American Guidance Service.

Dupuis, M. M., Lee, J. W., Badiali, B. J., and Askov, E. N. (1989). *Teaching Reading and Writing in the Content Areas.* Glenview, IL: Scott, Foresman.

Durkin, D. (1966). *Children Who Read Early.* New York: Teachers College Press.

Durr, W. R. (1973). Computer Study of High Frequency Words in Popular Trade Juveniles. *The Reading Teacher* 27:37–42.

Durrell, D. D. (1980). Letter-Name Value in Reading and Spelling, *Reading Research Quarterly* 16:159–163.

Early, M. (1990). Enabling First and Second Language Learners in the Classroom. *Language Arts* 67:567–575.

Earp, N. W. (1970). Procedures for Teaching Reading in Mathematics. *Arithmetic Teacher* 17: 575–579.

Edelsky, C. (1990). Whose Agenda Is This Anyway? A Response to McKenna, Robinson, and Miller. *Educational Researcher* 19:7–11.

Eeds, M. (1985). Bookwords: Using a Beginning Word List of High Frequency Words from Children's Literature K–3. *The Reading Teacher* 39:418–423.

Eeds, M., and Peterson, R. (1991). Teacher As Curator: Learning to Talk about Literature. *The Reading Teacher* 45:118–126.

Eeds, M., and Peterson, R. (1991). Teacher as Curator: Learning to Teach about Literature. *The Reading Teacher* 45:118–126.

Eissenberg, T. E., and Rudner, L. M. (1988). State Testing of Teachers: A Summary. *Journal of Teacher Education* 39:21–22.

Elley, W. (1989). Vocabulary Acquisition from Listening to Stories. *Reading Research Quarterly* 24:174–87.

Elley, W. R., and Mangubhai, F. (1983). The Impact of Reading on Second Language Learning. *Reading Research Quarterly* 19:53–67.

Ellis, D. W, and Preston, F. W. (1984). Enhancing Beginning Reading Using Wordless Picture Books. *The Reading Teacher* 37:692–698.

Fielding, L. G., Wilson, P. T., and Anderson, R. C. (1986). A New Focus on Free Reading: The Role of Trade Books in Reading Instruction. In T. Raphael (ed.), *The Contexts of School-Based Literacy.* New York: Random House.

Fisher, B. (1989). Assessing Emergent and Initial Readers. *Teaching K–8* 20:56–58.

Fitzgerald, J. (1989). Enhancing Two Related Thought Processes: Revision in Writing and Critical Reading. *The Reading Teacher* 43:42–48.

Flesch, R. (1955). *Why Johnny Can't Read.* New York: Harper and Row.

Flood, J., and Lapp, D. (1989). Reporting Reading Progress: A Comparison Portfolio for Parents. *The Reading Teacher* 42:508–514.

Flood, J., Lapp, D., Flood, S., and Nagel, G. (1992). Am I Allowed to Group? Using Flexible Patterns for Effective Instruction. *The Reading Teacher* 45:608–615.

Flynn, L. L. (1989). Developing Critical Reading Skills through Cooperative Problem Solving. *The Reading Teacher* 43:664–668.

Forgan, H. W., and Mangrum, C. T. (1989). *Teaching Content Area Reading Skills* (4th ed.). Columbus, OH: Merrill Publishing.

Fowler, G. L. (1982). Developing Comprehension Skills In Primary Students through the Use of Story Frames. *The Reading Teacher* 36:176–179.

Freeman, E. B. and Hatch, J. A. (1989). Emergent Literacy: Reconceptualizing Kindergarten Practice. *Childhood Education* 66:21–24.

Freppon, P. A., and Dahl, K. C. (1991). Learning About Phonics in a Whole Language Classroom. *Language Arts* 68:190–197.

Friedberg, J. B. (1992). *Portraying the Disabled: A Guide to Non-fiction.* New Providence, NJ: Bowker.

Fuhler, C. J. (1990). Let's Move toward Literature-Based Reading Instruction. *The Reading Teacher* 44:312–315.

Galda, L. (1988). Readers, Texts, and Contexts: A Response-Based View of Literature in the Classroom. *The New Advocate* 1:92–102.

Gates, A. (1937). The Necessary Mental Age for Beginning Reading. *Elementary School Journal* 37:497–508.

Gentile, L. M. (1983). ''A Critique of Mabel V. Morphett and Carleton Washburne's Study: When Should Children Begin To Read?'' In L. M. Gentile, M. L. Kamil, and J. S. Blanchard, eds., *Reading Research Revisited.* Columbus: Charles E. Merrill.

Gentile, L. M., and McMillan, M. M. (1990). Literacy through Literature: Motivating At-Risk Students to Read and Write. *Journal of Reading, Writing, and Learning Disabilities* 6:383–393.

Gere, A. A. (ed.) (1985). *Roots in the Sawdust: Writing to Learn across the Disciplines.* Urbana, IL: National Council of Teachers of English.

Goodman, K. (1965). A Linguistic Study of Cues and Miscues in Reading. *Elementary English* 42:639–643.

Goodman, K. (1969). Analysis of Reading Miscues: Applied Psycholinguistics. *Reading Research Quarterly* 5:126–135.

Goodman, K. (1988). *What's Whole in Whole Language?* Richmond Hill, ONT: Scholastic-TAB.

Goodman, K. S. (1976). The Reading Process: A Psycholinguistic View. In E. B. Smith, K. S. Goodman, and R. Meredith, *Language and Thinking in School.* New York: Holt Rinehart and Winston.

Goodman, K. S., Shannon, P., Freeman, Y. S., and Murphy, S. (1989). *Report Card on Basal Readers.* Katonah, NY: Richard C. Owens Publishers.

Goodman, Y., Watson, D., and Burke, C. (1987). *Reading Miscue Inventory: Alternative Procedures.* New York: Richard C. Owen.

Goodman, Y. M. (1978). Kid-Watching: An Alternative to Testing. *National Elementary School Principal* 57:41–45.

Grannis, C. B. (1988). ''Book Sales Statistics: Highlights from AAP Annual Survey, 1986.'' *Bowker Annual of Library and Book Trade Information* (33rd ed.) New York: R. R. Bowker.

Graves, D., and Hansen, J. (1983). The Author's Chair. *Language Arts* 60:176–183.

Graves, D. H. (1983). *Writing: Teachers and Children at Work.* Portsmouth, NH: Heinemann.

Graves, D. H., and Hansen, J. (1982). The Author's Chair. *Language Arts* 60:176–183.

Graves, M. F., Cooke, C. L., and LaBerge, M. J. (1983). Effects of Previewing Difficult Short Stories on Low Ability Junior High School Students' Comprehension, Recall, and Attitudes. *Reading Research Quarterly* 18:262–276.

Greaney, V. (1986). Parental Influences on Reading. *The Reading Teacher* 39:813–818.

Guilford, J. P. (1985). The Structure-of-Intellect Model. In B. B. Wolman (ed.), *Handbook of Intelligence.* New York: Wiley.

Hahn, A. L. (1985). Teaching Remedial Students to Be Strategic Readers and Better Comprehenders. *The Reading Teacher* 39:72–77.

Hammell, D. D., and Larsen, S. C. (1988). *Test of Written Language.* Austin, TX: Pro-Ed.

Hammell, D. D., Leigh, J. L., McNeill, G., and Larsen, S. C. (1981). A New Definition of Learning Disabilities. *Learning Disability Quarterly* 4:336–42.

Haney, W., and Madaus, G. (1989). Searching for Alternatives to Standardized Tests: Whys, Whats, and Whithers. *Phi Delta Kappan* 70:683–687.

Harris, A. J., and Sipay, E. R. (1985). *How to Increase Reading Ability* (8th ed.). New York: Longmans.

Harris, A. J., and Sipay, E. R. (1985). *How to Increase Reading Ability,* 8th ed. New York: Longman.

Harris, T. L., and Hodges R. E., eds. (1981). *A Dictionary of Reading and Related Terms.* Newark, DE: International Reading Association.

Hauser, P., and Nelson, G. (1988). *Books for the Gifted Child.* New Providence, NJ: Bowker.

Heald-Taylor, G. (1987). Predictable Literature Selections and Activities for Language Arts Instruction. *The Reading Teacher* 41:6–12.

Hepler, S. (1989). A Literature Program: Getting It Together, Keeping It Going. In J. Hickman, and B. E. Cullinan (eds.), *Children's Literature in the Classroom: Weaving Charlotte's Web.* Norwood, MA: Christopher Gordon Publishers.

Hess, M. L. (1991). Understanding Nonfiction: Purposes, Classification, Responses. *Language Arts* 68:228–232.

Hiebert, E. H., and Colt, J. (1989). Patterns of Literature-Based Reading Instruction. *The Reading Teacher* 43:14–20.

Hittleman, D. R. (1988). *Developmental Reading, K–8: Teaching from a Whole-Language Perspective.* 3rd ed. Columbus, OH: Merrill Publishing.

Hoffman, J. V. (1992). Critical Reading/Thinking across the Curriculum: Using I-Charts to Support Learning. *Language Arts* 69:121–127.

Holdaway, D. (1972). *Independence in Reading.* Auckland, New Zealand: Ashton-Scholastic.

Holdaway, D. (1982). Shared Book Experience: Teaching Reading Using Favorite Books. *Theory into Practice* 21:293–300.

Holmes, B. C., and Ammon, R. I. (1985). Teaching Content with Trade Books: A Strategy. *Childhood Education* 61:366–370.

Hopkins, L. B. (1969). *Books Are By People.* New York: Citation.

Hopkins, L. B. (1974). *More Books By More People.* New York: Citation.

Huck, C., Hepler, S., and Hickman, J. (1987). *Children's Literature in the Elementary School* (4th ed.). New York: Holt, Rinehart and Winston.

Huck, C. S. (1982). I Give You the End of a Golden String. *Theory into Practice* 21:315–321.

Hudelson, S. (1987). The Role of Native Language Literacy in the Education of Language Minority Children. *Language Arts* 64:827–841.

Hurst, C. O. (1990). *Once Upon a Time: An Encyclopedia for Successfully Using Children's Literature with Young Children.* Allen, TX: DLM.

Johnson, D. D., and Johnson, B. V. (1988). Making Inferences. *Massachusetts Primer* 17:4–17.

Johnson, D. D., and Pearson, P. D. (1984). *Teaching Reading Vocabulary* (2nd ed.). New York: Holt Rinehart and Winston.

Johnson, M., Kress, R., and Pikulski, J. (1987). *Informal Reading Inventories.* 2nd ed. Newark, DE: International Reading Association.

Johnson, N. M., and Ebert, M. J. (1992). Time Travel Is Possible: Historical Fiction and Biography—Passport to the Past. *The Reading Teacher* 45:488–495.

Johnson, P. (1984). Assessment in Reading. In P. D. Pearson (ed.), *Handbook of Reading Research.* New York: Longman.

Johnson, P. (1987). Teachers As Evaluation Experts. *The Reading Teacher* 41:744–748.

Johnson, T. D., and Louis, D. R. (1987). *Literacy through Literature.* Portsmouth, NH: Heinemann.

Jones, M. (1983). AB(by)C Means Alphabet Books By Children. *The Reading Teacher* 36:646–648.

Just, M. S., and Carpenter, P. A. (1987). *The Psychology of Reading and Language Comprehension.* Boston: Allyn and Bacon.

Kantrowitz, B. (1990). The Reading Wars. *Newsweek Special Edition: Education, A Consumer's Handbook* 64:8–14.

Karolides, N. J. (ed.) (1992). *Reader Response in the Classroom: Evoking and Interpreting Meaning in Literature.* New York: Longman.

Keegan, S., and Sharke, K. (1991). Literature Study Groups: An Alternative to Ability Grouping. *The Reading Teacher* 44:542–547.

Keifer, B. (1984). *Thinking, Language and Reading: Children's Responses to Picture Books.* Champaign: ERIC Clearinghouse on Language Arts. EJ253–869.

Kelly, P. R. (1990). Guiding Young Students' Response to Literature. *The Reading Teacher* 43:464–470.

Kennedy, D., Spangler, S., and Vanderwerf, M. (1990). *Science and Technology in Fact and Fiction: A Guide to Children's Books.* New York: Bowker.

Kiefer, B. (1988). Picture Books as Contexts for Literacy, Aesthetic, and Real World Understandings. *Language Arts* 65:260–271.

Kiefer, B. (1988). Picture Books as Contexts for Literary, Aesthetic, and Real World Understandings. *Language Arts* 65:260–270.

Kimmel, E. (1970). Can Children's Books Change Children's Values? *Educational Leadership* 28:209–211.

Kimmel, M. M., and Segal, E. (1983). *For Reading Out Loud! A Guide to Sharing Books with Children.* New York: Delacourte Press.

Kinney, M. A. (1985). A Language Experience Approach to Teaching Expository Text Structure. *The Reading Teacher* 39:854–856.

Kirk, S. A., Kliebhan, J. M., and Lerner, J. W. (1978). *Teaching Reading to Slow and Disabled Learners.* Boston: Houghton Mifflin.

Klein, M. L. (1988). *Teaching Reading Comprehension and Vocabulary: A Guide for Teachers.* Englewood Cliffs, NJ: Prentice-Hall.

Kliman, M., and Kleiman, G. W. (1992). Life among the Giants: Writing, Mathematics, and Exploring Gulliver's World. *Language Arts* 69:128–136.

Kolczynski, R. G. (1989). Reading Leads to Writing. In J. W. Stewig and S. L. Sebesta (eds.), *Using Literature in the Elementary Classroom.* Urbana: National Council of Teachers of English.

Korbin, B. (1988). *Eye Openers: Choosing Books for Kids.* New York: Viking.

Kossack, S., Kane, S., and Fine, J. (1987). Use the News: The Reading–Writing Connection. *Journal of Reading* 30:730–732.

Kramer, J. J., and Conoley, J. C. (1992). *Buros Mental Measurements Yearbook.* Lincoln, NE: University of Nebraska, Buros Institute of Mental Measurement.

Krieger, E. (1988). Developing Reading Comprehension through Author Awareness. Unpublished report, Newton, MA.

Lake, R. (1990). An Indian Father's Plea. *Teacher Magazine* 2:48–53.

Lamme, L. L. (1990). Exploring the World of Music through Picture Books. *The Reading Teacher* 44:294–300.

Langer, J. A. (1981). From Theory to Practice: A Prereading Plan. *Journal of Reading* 25:2.

Lapp, D., Flood, J., and Farnan, N. (1992). Basal Readers and Literature: A Tight Fit or a Mismatch? In K. D. Wood and A. Moss (eds.), *Exploring Literature in the Classroom: Content and Methods.* Norwood, MA: Christopher-Gordon Publishers.

Lass, B. (1982). Portrait of My Son as an Early Reader. *The Reading Teacher* 36:20–28.

Lass, B. (1983). Portrait of My Son as an Early Reader II. *The Reading Teacher* 36:508–515.

Laughlin, M., and Dardaelff, P. (1991). *Literature-Based Social Studies: Children's Books and Activities to Enrich the K-5 Curriculum.* Phoenix: Oryx Press.

Leu, D. J. and Kinzer, C. K. (1987). *Effective Reading Instruction in the Elementary Grades.* Columbus, OH: Merrill.

Levi, R. (1990). Assessment and Educational Vision: Engaging Learners and Parents. *Language Arts* 67:267–274.

Linek, W. M. (1991). Grading and Evaluation Techniques for Whole Language Teachers. *Language Arts* 68:125–132.

Lipson, E. R. (1991). *Parent's Guide to the Best Books for Children.* New York: Random House.

Madaus, G. F. (1990). *Testing As a Social Technology.* Chestnut Hill, MA: Boston College.

Madden, L. (1988). Improve Reading Attitude of Poor Readers Through Cooperative Reading Teams. *The Reading Teacher* 42:194–199.

Manzo, A. V. (1969). The ReQuest Procedure. *Journal of Reading* 2:123–126.

Marzano, R. J., Hagerty, P. J., Valencia, S. W., and DiStefano, P. P. (1987). *Reading Diagnosis and Instruction: Theory into Practice.* Englewood Cliffs, NJ: Prentice-Hall.

Mason, J., and Au, K. (1990). *Reading Instruction for Today.* New York: Harper Collins.

Mason, J. M. (ed.) (1989). *Reading and Writing Connections.* Boston: Allyn and Bacon.

Mason, J. M., and Au, K. H. (1990). *Reading Instruction for Today* (2nd ed.). Glenview, IL: Scott Foresman.

Massachusetts Department of Education (1988). *Reading and Thinking: A New Framework for Comprehension.* Boston: Mass. Dept. of Education.

Mathews, M. M. (1966). *Teaching to Read Historically Considered.* Chicago: University of Chicago Press.

McCallum, R. D. (1988). Don't Throw the Basals Out with the Bath Water. *The Reading Teacher* 42:204–208.

McCauley, J. K., and McCauley, D. S. (1992). Using Choral Reading to Promote Language Learning for ESL Students. *The Reading Teacher* 45:526–537.

McCoy, K. M., and Prehm, H. J. (1987). *Teaching Mainstreamed Students: Methods and Techniques.* Denver: Love Publishing.

McElmeel, S. (1988). *An Author A Month,* Englewood, CO: Libraries Unlimited.

McGee, L. A. (1982). Awareness of Text Structure : Effects on Children's Recall of Expository Text. *Reading Research Quarterly* 17:581–90.

McGee, L. A., and Richgels, D. J. (1985). Teaching Expository Text Structure to Elementary Students. *The Reading Teacher* 39:739–748.

McGee, L. M., and Richgels, D. J. (1990). *Literacy's Beginnings: Supporting Young Readers and Writers.* Boston: Allyn and Bacon.

McKenna, M. C., and Kear, D. J. (1990). Measuring Attitude toward Reading: A New Tool for Teachers. *The Reading Teacher* 43:626–639.

McNeil, J. (1984). *Reading Comprehension: New Directions for Classroom Practice.* Glenview: Scott Foresman.

Moe, A. J. (1989). Using Picture Books for Reading Vocabulary Development. In J. W. Stewig and S. L. Sebesta (eds.), *Using Literature In The Elementary Classroom* (2nd ed.). Urbana, IL: National Council of Teachers of English.

Morphett, M. V., and Washburne, C. (1931). When Should Children Begin to Read? *Elementary School Journal* 31:496–503.

Morrow, L. M., and Rand, M. K. (1991). Promoting Literacy during Play by Designing Early Childhood Classroom Environments. *The Reading Teacher* 44:396–402.

Mullis, I. V. S., and Jenkins, L. B. (1990). *The Reading Report Card, 1971–88.* Washington, DC: U.S. Office of Education.

Murray, D. M. (1968). *A Writer Teaches Writing.* Boston: Houghton Mifflin.

Nagy, W. E. (1988). *Teaching Vocabulary to Improve Reading Comprehension.* Urbana, IL: National Council of Teachers of English.

Nagy, W. E., Herman, P. A., and Anderson, R. C. (1985). Learning Words from Context. *The Reading Research Quarterly* 20:233–253.

National Association for the Education of Young Children (1988). NAEYC Position Statement on Developmentally Appropriate Practice in the Primary Grades, Serving 5- Through 8-Year-Olds. *Young Children* 43:64–84.

Neill, D. M., and Medina, N. J. (1989). Standardized Testing: Harmful to Educational Health. *Phi Delta Kappan* 70:688–697.

Nelson, J. B., and Cleland, D. L. (1971). The Role of the Teacher of Gifted and Creative Children. In P. A. Witty (ed.), *Reading for the Gifted and the Creative Student.* Newark, DE: International Reading Association.

Newman, J., ed. (1985). *Whole Language: Theory in Use.* Portsmouth, NH: Heinemann.

Newman, J. M., and Church, S. M. (1990). Commentary: The Myths of Whole Language. *The Reading Teacher* 44:20–27.

Newport, J. F. (1990). What Is Wrong with Science Textbooks? *National Elementary Principal* 69:22–24.

Norton, D. E. (1990). Teaching Multicultural Literature in the Reading Curriculum. *The Reading Teacher* 44:28–40.

Noyce, R. M., and Christie, J. F. (1989). *Integrating Reading and Writing Instruction in Grades K–8.* Boston: Allyn and Bacon.

O'Sullivan, P. J., Ysseldyke, J. E., Christenson, S. L., and Thurlow, M. L. (1990). Mildly Handicapped Elementary Students' Opportunities to Learn During Reading Instruction in Mainstreamed and Special Education Settings. *Reading Research Quarterly* 25:131–146.

Ogle, D. (1986). K–W–L: A Teaching Model That Develops Active Reading of Expository Text. *The Reading Teacher* 39:564–570.

Otto, W., Wolf, A., and Eldridge, R. G. (1984). Managing Instruction. In P. D. Pearson et al. (eds.), *Handbook of Reading Research.* New York: Longmans.

Palinscar, A. S. (1984). The Quest for Meaning from Expository Text: A Teacher-Guided Journey. In G. G. Duffy, L. R. Roehler, and J. Mason (eds.), *Comprehension Instruction.* New York: Longman.

Paradis, E., Chatton, B., Boswell, A., Smith, M., and Yovich, S. (1991). Accountability: Assessing Comprehension during Literature Discussions. *The Reading Teacher* 45:8–17.

Paratore, J. R., Fountas, I. C., Jenkins, C. A., Mathers, M. E., Oulette, J. M., and Sheehan, N. M. (1991). *Grouping Students for Literacy Learning: What Works.* Boston: Massachusetts Reading Association.

Paratore, J. R., and Indrisano, R. (1987). Intervention Assessment of Reading Comprehension. *The Reading Teacher* 41:778–783.

Pearson, P. D. (1985). Changing the Face of Reading Comprehension Instruction. *The Reading Teacher* 38:724–728.

Pearson, P. D. (1985b). The Comprehension Revolution: A Twenty Year History of Process and Practice Related to Reading Comprehension. *Reading Education Report No. 57.* Urbana-Champaign: Center for the Study of Reading, University of Illinois.

Peters, C. W., and Wixson, K. K. (1989). Smart New Reading Tests Are Coming. *Learning 89* 17:43–44, 53.

Peterson, R., and Eeds, M. (1990). *Grand Conversations: Literature Groups in Action.* New York: Scholastic.

Petrosky, A. R. (1982). From Story to Essay: Reading and Writing. *College Composition and Communication* 33:19–36.

Phillips, L. M. (1989). *Using Children's Literature to Foster Written Language Development.* Technical Report No. 446. Champaign: University of Illinois at Urbana–Champaign, Center for the Study of Reading.

Pikulski, J. J. (1989). The Assessment of Reading: A Time for Change? *The Reading Teacher* 43:80–81.

Pinnell, G. S., DeFord, D. E., and Lyons, C. A. (1988). *Reading Recovery: Early Intervention for At-Risk First Graders.* Arlington, VA: Educational Research Service.

Pinnell, G. S., Fried, M. D., and Estice, R. M. (1990). Reading Recovery: Learning How to Make a Difference. *The Reading Teacher* 43:282–295.

Pogrow, S. (1990). The Effects of Intellectually Challenging At-Risk Elementary Students: Findings from the HOTS Program. *Phi Delta Kappan* 71:389–397.

Polya, G. (1945). *How to Solve It.* Princeton, NJ: Princeton University Press.

Prelutsky, J. (1983). *The Random House Book of Poetry for Children.* New York: Random House.

Putnam, C. (1991). Dramatizing Nonfiction with Emergent Readers. *Language Arts* 68:463–469.

Quintero, R., and Huerta-Macias, A. (1990). All in the Family: Bilingualism and Biliteracy. *The Reading Teacher* 44:306–312.

Raphael, T. E. (1982). Question-Answering Strategies for Children. *The Reading Teacher* 36:186–190.

Raphael, T. E., Englert, C. S., and Kirschner, B. W. (1989). Acquisition of Expository Writing Skills. In Jana M. Mason (ed.), *Reading and Writing Connections.* Boston: Allyn and Bacon.

Rasinski, T. V., and Fredericks, A. D. (1989). Dimensions of Parent Involvement. *The Reading Teacher* 43:180–182.

Rasinski, T. V., and Padak, N. D. (1990). Multicultural Learning through Children's Literature. *Language Arts* 67:576–580.

Readance, J. E., Bean, T. W., and Baldwin, R. S. (1989). *Content Area Reading: An Integrated Approach.* 3rd ed. Dubuque, IA: Kendall-Hunt.

Reinking, D. (1986). Integrating Graphic Aids into Content Area Instruction: The Graphic Information Lesson. *Journal of Reading* 30:146–151.

Reutzel, D. R., and Hollingsworth, D. M. (1988). Whole Language and the Practitioner. *Academic Therapy* 23:405–415.

Rhodes, L. K., and Dudley-Marling, C. (1988). *Readers and Writers with a Difference: A Holistic Approach to Teaching Learning Disabled and Remedial Students.* Portsmouth, NH: Heinemann.

Richek, M. A., and McTague, B. K. (1988). The "Curious George" Strategy for Students with Reading Problems. *The Reading Teacher* 42:220–226.

Rickelman, R. J., and Henk, W. A. (1990). Children's Literature and Audio/Visual Technologies. *The Reading Teacher* 43:182–184.

Robb, L. (1989). Books in the Classroom. *The Horn Book Magazine* 65:808–810.

Robertson, D. (1991). *Portraying the Disabled: A Guide to Juvenile Fiction.* New Providence, NJ: Bowker.

Robinson, F. P. (1946). *Effective Study.* New York: Harper.

Roblyer, M. D. (1988). The Effectiveness of Microcomputers in Education: A Review of Research from 1980–1987. *T.H.E. Journal,* 85–89.

Rosenblatt, L. M. (1982). The Literary Transaction: Evocation and Response. *Theory into Practice* 21:268–277.

Rosenshine, B., and Stevens, R. (1984). Classroom Instruction in Reading In P. D. Pearson et al. (eds.), *Handbook of Reading Research.* New York: Longmans.

Rosenshine, B. V. (1980). Skill Hierarchies in Reading Comprehension. R. J. Spiro, B. C. Bruce, and W. F. Brewer (eds.), *Theoretical Issues in Reading Comprehension.* Hillsdale, NJ: Lawrence Erlbaum Associates.

Roser, N. L., Hoffman, J. V., and Farest, C. (1990). Language, Literature, and At-Risk Children. *The Reading Teacher* 43:554–559.

Routman, R. (1988). *Transitions from Literature to Literacy.* Portsmouth, NH: Heinemann.

Row, B. D., Stoodt, B. D., and Burns, P. C. (1978). *Reading Instruction in the Secondary School.* Chicago: Rand McNally.

Rubin, A., and Hansen, J. (1984). *Reading and Writing: How Art the First Two 'R's' Related?* Reading Education Report No. 51. Champaign: University of Illinois at Urbana–Champaign, Center for the Study of Reading.

Samuels, S. J. (1979). The Method of Repeated Reading. *The Reading Teacher* 32:403–8.

Sanders, N. M. (1966). *Classroom Questions.* New York: Harper and Row.

Savage, J. F. (1978). What Do You Remember about Learning to Read? *New England Reading Association Journal* 13:6–10.

Savage, J. F. (1985). *Dyslexia: Understanding Reading Problems.* New York: Julian Messner.

Savage, J. F. (1992). Literature-Based Reading Instruction: It Works! *The New England Reading Association Journal* 28: 28–31.

Savage, J. F., and Mooney, J. F. (1979). *Teaching Reading to Children with Special Needs.* Boston: Allyn and Bacon.

Saxby, M. (1987). The Gift of Wings: The Value of Literature to Children. In M. Saxby and G. Winch, (eds.), *Give Them Wings: The Experience of Children's Literature.* Melbourne: Macmillan of Australia.

Schiro, M. (in press) *In Search of Excellence: Criteria for Evaluating Children's Mathematics Books.* Chestnut Hill, MA: Boston College.

Schmidtt, M. C. (1990). A Questionnaire to Measure Children's Awareness of Strategic Reading Processes. *The Reading Teacher* 43:454–461.

Schumaker, M. P., and Schumaker, R. C. (1988). 3, 000 Paper Cranes: Children's Literature for Remedial Readers. *The Reading Teacher* 46:544–548.

Schuman, D. R., and Fitzsimons, V. M. (1990). Reading As an Intervention for the Orthopedic Convalescent Child. *New England Reading Association Journal* 26:2–8.

Searfoss, L. W. (1975). Radio Reading. *The Reading Teacher* 29:295–96.

Sebesta, S. L., and Iverson, W. J. (1975). *Literature for Thursday's Child.* Chicago: Science Research Associates.

Sebesta, S. L. (1987). Enriching the Arts and Humanities through Children's Books. In B. E. Cullinan (ed.), *Children's Literature in the Reading Program.* Newark, DE: International Reading Association.

Shanahan, T. (1988). The Reading–Writing Relationship: Seven Instructional Principles. *The Reading Teacher* 41:636–647.

Shannon, P. (1983). The Use of Commercial Reading Materials in American Elementary Schools. *Reading Research Quarterly* 19:68–85.

Shannon, P. (1989). *Broken Promises: Reading Instruction in Twentieth Century America.* Granby, MA: Bergin and Garvey Publishers.

Shoop, M. (1986). InQuest: A Listening and Reading Comprehension Strategy. *The Reading Teacher* 39:670–674.

Simons, H. D. (1971). Reading Comprehension: The Need for a New Perspective. *Reading Research Quarterly* 7:340–361.

Sims, R. (1982). *Shadow and Substance: Afro-American Experiences in Contemporary Children's Fiction.* Urbana, IL: National Council of Teachers of English.

Sinatra, R. C., Stahl-Gemake, J., and Berg, D. N. (1984). Improving Reading Comprehension of Disabled Readers Through Semantic Mapping. *The Reading Teacher* 38:22–29.

Slavin, R. E. (1991). Synthesis of Research on Cooperative Learning. *Educational Leadership* 47:71–82.

Sloan, P., and Latham, R. (1981). *Teaching Reading Is . . .* Melbourne: Thomas Nelson.

Smith, D. D. (1979). The Improvement of Children's Oral Reading through the Use of Teacher Modeling. *Journal of Learning Disabilities* 12:39–42.

Smith, F. (1985). *Reading without Nonsense* (2nd ed.). New York: Teachers College Press.

Smith, F. (1988). *Understanding Reading* (4th ed). Hilsdale, NJ: Lawrence Erlbaum Assoc.

Smith, N. B. (1965). *American Reading Instruction.* Newark, DE: International Reading Association.

Smitherman, G., ed. (1981). *Black English and the Education of Black Children and Youth.* Detroit: Center for Black Studies, Wayne State University.

Snowball, D. (1989). Classroom Big Books: Links between Reading and Writing Nonfiction. *The Reading Teacher* 43:267.

Staab, C. (1991). Classroom Organization: Thematic Centers Revisited. *Language Arts* 68:108–114.

Stahl, S. A. (1992). Saying the ''p'' Word: Nine Guidelines for Exemplary Phonics Instruction. *The Reading Teacher* 45:618–625.

Stahl, S. A., Osborn, J., and Lehr, F. (1990). *Beginning to Read: Thinking and Learning about Print by Marilyn Jager Adams. A Summary Prepared by Steven A. Stahl, Jean Osborn, and Fran Lehr.* Urbana, IL: Center for the Study of Reading, University of Illinois at Urbana-Champaign.

Stauffer, R. (1969). *Teaching Reading As A Thinking Process.* New York: Harper and Row.

Stevens, R. J., Madden, N. A., Slavin, R. E., and Farnish, A. M. (1987). Cooperative Integrated Reading and Composition: Two Field Experiments. *Reading Research Quarterly* 22:433–445.

Strickland, D. S. (1989). Some Tips for Using Big Books. *The Reading Teacher* 41:966–968.

Strickland, D. S., and Morrow, L. M. (1990). Sharing Big Books. *The Reading Teacher* 43:342–3.

Strother, D. B. (1989). Developing Thinking Skills through Questioning. *Phi Delta Kappan* 71:324–327.

Sullivan, J. (1987). Read-Aloud Sessions: Tackling Sensitive Issues through Literature. *The Reading Teacher* 41:874–878.

Sumara, D., and Walker, L. (1991). The Teacher's Role in Whole Language. *Language Arts* 68:276–285.

Taylor, B. M., and Nosbush, L. (1983). Oral Reading for Meaning: A Technique for Improving Word Identification Skills. *The Reading Teacher* 37:234–237.

Taylor, W. (1953). Cloze Procedure: A New Tool for Measuring Readability. *Journalism Quarterly* 30:415–433.

Teale, W. (1990). Dear Readers. *Language Arts* 67:808–810.

Teale, W. H., and Sulzby, E. (1986). *Emergent Literacy: Writing and Reading.* Norwood, NJ: Ablex.

Thomas, K. F. (1985). Early Reading as a Social Interaction Process. *Language Arts* 62: 469–475.

Tierney, R. J., Carter, M. A., and Desai, L. E. (1991). *Portfolios in the Reading–Writing Classroom.* Norwood, MA: Christopher-Gordon Publishers.

Tierney, R. J., and Pearson, P. D. (1983). Toward a Composing Model of Reading. *Language Arts* 60:568–580.

Tierney, R. J., J. E. Readance, and Dishner, E. K. (1990). *Reading Strategies and Practices: A Compendium.* Boston: Allyn and Bacon.

Tierney, R. J., Soter, A., O'Flahoran, J. F., and McGinley, T. (1989). The Effects of Reading and Writing upon Thinking Critically. *Reading Research Quarterly* 24:134–173.

Tomkins, G. E. (1990). *Teaching Writing: Balancing Process and Product.* Columbus: Merrill Publishing.

Top, B. L., and Osguthorpe, R. T. (1987). Reverse Role Tutoring: The Effects of Handicapped Students Tutoring Regular Class Students. *The Elementary School Journal* 87:413–423.

Trachtenburg, P. (1990). Using Children's Literature to Enhance Phonics Instruction. *The Reading Teacher* 43:648–652.

Trelease, J. (1985). *The Read-Aloud Handbook.* New York: Penguin.

Trelease, J. (1989). *The New Read-Aloud Handbook* (2nd ed.). New York: Penguin.

Tunnell, M. O., and Jacobs, J. S. (1989) Using "Real" Books: Research Findings on Literature Based Reading Instruction. *The Reading Teacher* 42:470–477.

Tway, E. (1985). *Writing Is Reading: 26 Ways to Connect.* Urbana, IL: National Council for Teachers of English.

Tylor, E. B. (1992). *Primitive Cultures.* 5th ed. London: J. Murray Co.

U.S. Department of Education (1991). Report to the 13th Congress on the Implementation of the Education of the Handicapped Act. Washington, DC: U.S. Department of Education.

Unsworth, L. (1984). Meeting Individual Needs Through Flexible Whole-Class Grouping of Pupils. *The Reading Teacher* 38:298–304.

Uttero, D. A. (1988). Activating Comprehension through Cooperative Learning. *The Reading Teacher* 42:390–395.

Vacca, J. L., Vacca, R. T., and Gove, M. K. (1991). *Reading and Learning to Read* (2nd ed.). New York: Harper Collins.

Vacca, R. T., and Vacca, J. L. (1989). *Content Area Reading* (3rd ed.). Glenview, IL: Scott Foresman.

Valencia, S. (1990). A Portfolio Approach to Classroom Reading Assessment: The Whys, Whats, and Hows. *The Reading Teacher* 43:338–340.

Valencia, S., and Pearson, P. D. (1987). Reading Assessment: Time for a Change. *The Reading Teacher* 41:726–732.

Varnhagen, C. K., and Goldman, S. R. (1986). Improving Comprehension: Causal Relations Instruction for Learning Handicapped Learners. *The Reading Teacher* 39:896–904.

Walker-Dalhouse, D. (1992). Using African-American Literature to Increase Ethnic Understanding. *The Reading Teacher* 45:416–422.

Walshe, R. D. (1988). Questions Teachers Ask about Teaching Writing K–12. In R. D. Walshe and P. March (eds.), *Teaching Writing K–12*. Melbourne, Australia: Dellastar.

Watson, D., and Henson, J. (1991). Reading Evaluation—Miscue Analysis. In Bill Harp (ed.), *Assessment and Evaluation in Whole Language Programs*. Norwood, MA: Christopher-Gordon Publishers.

Watson, D. J. (1989). Defining and Describing Whole Language, *The Elementary School Journal* 90:129–141.

Weaver, C. (1988). *Reading: Process and Practice.* Portsmouth, NH: Heinemann.

Welsh, V. (1985). Why Change? A Teacher's Perspective. Paper presented at the 1985 Spring Conference of National Council of Teachers of English, Houston. ERIC Document ED 255 868.

Whisler, N. and Williams, J. (1990). *Literature and Cooperative Learning: Pathway to Literacy.* Sacramento, CA: Literature Co-op.

Whitin, D. J., Mills, H., and O'Keefe T. (1990). *Living and Learning Mathematics.* Portsmouth, NH: Heinemann.

Whole Language Council, Milwaukee Public Schools (1990). *Whole Language Assessment Guide.* Milwaukee: Milwaukee Public Schools.

Wiggins, G. (1989). A True Test: Toward More Authentic and Equitable Assessment. *Phi Delta Kappan* 70:703–713.

Wilson, P. T., Anderson, R. C., and Fielding, L. G. (1986). *Children's Book Reading Habits: A New Criterion for Literacy.* Champaign-Urbana: University of Illinois, Center for the Study of Reading, Reading Education Report No. 63.

Winch, G. (1982). The Use of Reading Schemes: A Comparative Study. In D. Burnes, A. Campbell, and R. Jones (eds.), *Reading, Writing, and Multiculturalism.* Sydney: Australian Reading Association.

Winch, G. (1987). The Supreme Fiction: On Poetry and Children. In M. Saxby and G. Winch, (eds.), *Give Them Wings: The Experience of Children's Literature.* Melbourne: Macmillan of Australia.

Wixon, K. K., Bosky, A. B., Yochum, M. N., and Alvermann, D. E. (1984). An Interview for Assessing Students' Perceptions of Classroom Reading Tasks. *The Reading Teacher* 37:354–359.

Wolf, A. (1977). Reading Instruction: Time Will Tell. *Learning* 5:76–81.

Wolf, D. P. (1989). Portfolio Assessment: Sampling Students' Work. *Educational Leadership* 36:35–40.

Wood, K. D. (1988). Techniques for Assessing Students' Potential for Learning. *The Reading Teacher* 41:440–447.

Wood, T. L., and Wood, W. (1988). Assessing Potential Difficulties in Comprehending Fourth Grade Science Textbooks. *Science Education* 72:561–574.

Woodcock, R. W., and Johnson, M. B. (1989). *Woodcock-Johnson Psycho-Educational Battery.* Rev. ed. Allen, TX: DLM/Teaching Resources.

Wuthrick, J. A. (1990). Blue Jays Win! Crows Go Down in Defeat! *Phi Delta Kappan* 71:553–556.

Yatvin, J. (1980). *Trade Books or Basals? Two Programs Measured against the Standard of What a Reading Program Should Be.* Urbana, IL: ERIC Clearinghouse on Reading and Communications Skills. ED 215 336.

Zarrillo, J. (1989). Teachers' Interpretations of Literature-Based Reading. *The Reading Teacher* 43:22–28.

Index

A

A, My Name Is Alice (Bayer), 107
Aardema, Verna, 86, 299, 360
ABC books, 125
Abe Lincoln Grows Up (Sandburg), 279
Abiyoyo (Seeger), 360
Abstract elements, assessment and, 385
Accepting pupils with physical
    handicaps, 343
Accountability, tests and, 414
Ace, the Very Important Pig (King-
    Smith), 279
Ackerman, Karen, 234, 346
Across Five Aprils (Hunt), 40, 217, 230
Activities
    centered on alphabet awareness, 119
    in questioning, 205
Adams, Marilyn Jager, 19, 26, 118,
    134, 158, 170, 183, 210, 322,
    335, 352
Adjustment(s)
    of instructional materials for slow
        learners, 333
    for learning disabled pupils, 339
Adler, David A., 191
Administrators, meetings with, 414
Advantageous seating for pupils with
    visual problems, 339
Adventures of Huckleberry Finn
    (Twain), 32, 367
Aekyung's Dream (Paek), 363
Aesop, 344
Aesthetic knowledge in reading-writing
    connection, 295
Aesthetic responses to literature,
    297–98

Affective response, impact of literature
    on, 12
Affixes, 164
Agard, John, 358
AHANA (African American, Hispanic,
    Asian and Native American)
    pupils, 356–58
    meeting needs of, 356
    multicultural literature for, 356
Ai-Ling, Louie, 361
Aiex, N. K., 403, 415, 416
Airport (Barton), 106
Alcott, Louisa May, 31–32
Aldo Applesauce (Hurwitz), 39
Alexander, Martha, 112, 113, 316
*Alexander, Who Used to Be Rich Last
    Sunday* (Viorst), 234
*Alexander and the Terrible, Horrible,
    No Good, Very Bad Day*
    (Viorst), 14, 144, 315
Alice's Adventures in Wonderland
    (Carroll), 32, 40
Aliki, 218, 230, 314, 318
Allard, Harry, 35, 179, 204
Allen, Pamela, 12, 148, 150
Allen, V. G., 372, 373, 380
Allington, R. L., 19, 26, 78, 91, 275,
    290
Allison's Zinnia (Lobel), 107
Almanacs, 259
Alphabet books, 119
    in nursery school programs, 106
    selected sample of, 107
Alphabet knowledge, 118–19
    in kindergarten, 118–19
    in reading readiness, 99
Alvermann, D., 395, 416

Amelia Bedelia books (Parish), 189,
    190, 374
American Association for the
    Advancement of Science, 215,
    253
American Guidance Council, 346
American history
    in children's fiction, 40
    trade books for, 230
American Library Association, 39, 44
American Newspaper Publishers
    Association Foundation, 264
American Tall Tales (Osborne), 36
American Tall Tales (Stoutenburg), 36
Amigo (Schweitzer), 204
Ammon, R. I., 253
Analogies
    in integration, 141–42
    teaching content words and, 241
Analytical Reading Inventory (Woods
    and Moe), 407
Anaphora, 183
Anaphoric relationships, 183
Anchondo, Mary, 374
And Now Miguel (Krumgold), 362
*And Then What Happened, Paul
    Revere?* (Fritz), 4, 40
*And to Think That I Saw It on Mulberry
    Street* (Seuss), 49
Andersen, Hans Christian, 31, 35, 37
Anderson, R. C., 12, 26, 60, 91, 123,
    134, 138, 147, 154, 155, 166,
    170, 171, 198, 200, 210, 211,
    349, 352
Anderson, T. H., 261, 268
Anecdotal records, 398
Angel Child, Dragon Child (Suart), 363

Page numbers in italics indicate figures; page numbers followed by t indicate tables.

Angel Island Prisoner 1922 (Cherin), 363

Angelucci, Enzo, 259

Anglund, Joan Walsh, 119

Animal, the Vegetable, and John D. Jones, The (Byars), 38, 197, 346

Animal Alphabet (Kitchen), 107

Animals, Animals (Whipple), 42

Animals Definitely Should Not Wear Clothes (Barrett), 34

Animals in children's fantasy, 37

Anna in Charge (Tsutsui), 363

Anne of the Green Gables (Montgomery), 32

Annie and the Old One (Miles), 142, 206, 363

Anno, Mitsumasa, 12, 107, 113, 234

Anno's Alphabet (Anno), 107

Anno's Counting Book (Anno), 234

Anno's Flea Market (Anno), 12

Anno's Journey (Anno), 12

Answer rating, in metacognition, 202

Anteater Named Arthur, An (Waber), 50

Anthropomorphization in children's fantasy, 37

Anticipation guides, 199

Antics! An Alphabet Anthology (Hepworth), 107

Antiphonal arrangements in choral reading, 285

Antonym searches, 144

Applebee, A. N., 178, 210, 389, 416

Appropriate instructional practice (NAEYC), 122

Arbuthnot, May Hill, 42

Arbuthnot Anthology of Children's Literature (de Regniers), 42

Archambault, John, 107, 285, 286, 316, 341, 363

Are You There God? It's Me, Margaret (Blume), 44, 79

Armbruster, B. B., 261, 268

Armstrong, William, 47, 369

Arnold, H., 16, 26, 287, 290, 411, 416

Arrow to the Sun (McDermott), 360, 374

Arroz con Leche: Popular Songs from Latin America (Delacre), 374

Art text, expository text in, 233

Articulation, reading aloud for, 272

Artist, An (Goffstein), 233

Artistic response to literature, 298

Artwork. *see* Visual media

Ashanti to Zulu: African Traditions (Musgrove), 107

Asher, Sandy, 318

Ashton-Warner, Sylvia, 151, 170

Assessing literacy development, 381–415

classroom-based assessment, 393–411

formal assessment, 387–93

general perspective on, 384–87

new views of reading and, 386

portfolio assessment, 411–14

reasons for, 383–84

Assessment, 383

changing nature of, 385, 387

difficulty with abstractions, 385

dimensions of, 384

of emergent literacy, 394

as part of learning, 384–85

process of, pupil voice in, 413

Atkinson, Mary, 373

Atlases, 259

Attention span, 96

Attitude and behavior problems

bibliotherapy for, 345

literature-based readings for pupils with, 344

pupils with, 343–45

teaching techniques for, 344

Atwater

Florence, 177

Richard, 177

Atwell, N., 306, 322

Atwood, Ann, 316

Atypical learners, 324–50

with attitude and behavior problems, 343–45

classroom teachers and, 348–49

gifted and talented, 345–48

with learning disabilities, 334–39

mainstreaming, 327–28

with sensory and physical problems, 339–43

slow learners, 328–33

support services for, 348

Au, K. H., 214, 253, 370, 380

Auckerman, R. C., 20, 22, 26, 335, 352

Audette, R., 350, 352

Audience identification in prewriting, 305

Audience reading, in teaching oral reading, 284–85

Audiovisual devices, 70–71

Auditory blending, 118

Auditory closure, 118

Auditory discrimination, 118

Auditory expressive function (speaking), 142

Auditory figure ground, 118

Auditory media, 70–71

Auditory memory, 118

Auditory perception, 118

Auditory problems, classroom accommodations for, 340–41

Auditory receptive function (listening), 142

Austin, M., 281, 290

Authentic situations, in whole language theory, 9

Author(s)

author/illustrator of the week/month, 50

learning about, 49–52, 303

sources of information about, 51, 52

study of, 6

writing letters to, 315–16

Author a Month, An (McElmeel), 51

Author groups, heterogeneous, 79

Author's Chair, 116–17, 312

B

Ba-Nam (Lee), 359

Babbitt, Natalie, 6

Babe Didrickson, Athlete of the Century (Knudson), 234, 299

Baboushka and the Three Kings (Robbins), 361

Baby Bears, The (Bullatz and Lomeo), 218

Baldwin, R. S., 211

Bancheck, Linda, 151

Bank Street Writer (word processing program), 308

Banks, J. A., 360, 380

Banks, Lynne Reid, 37, 188, 198

Bargain for Frances, A (Hoban), 196, 299

Barnitz, J. G., 368, 380

Barr, Linda, 346

Barrett, Judi, 34, 38

Barrett, T. T., 193, 210

Barton, Byron, 106

Basal readers, 16–19, 69

benefits of, 17–18

contemporary, 19

criticisms of, 18

Basal reading series

elements of, 17

supplementary material for parents, 130

versus trade books, 20–21

See also Conventional reading instruction

Basal reading tests, 390

Basic Reading Inventory (Johns), 407

Basketful of White Eggs, A (Swann), 42, 258
Bateman, B., 349, 352
Bayer, Jane, 107
Baylor, Beth, 360
Baylor, Byrd, 232, 298, 363
Be a Perfect Person in Just Three Days (Manes), 278
Beach, R., 298, 322
Beach, W., 182, 210
Bean, T. W., 211
Bear Called Paddington (Bond), 257
Bears (Rosenthal), 218
Bear's Toothache, The (McPhail), 304
Beast in Mrs. Rooney's Room, The (Giff), 305
Becoming a Nation of Readers (National Commission on Reading), 60, 123
Beginning of year assessment, of emergent literacy, 394
Behavior management strategies, 344
Behaviorism, 98
Behind the Blue and Gray: The Soldier's Life in the Civil War (Ray), 217
Bemelmans, Ludwig, 4, 12, 160
Ben and Me (Lawson), 230
Benjamin, Carol Lea, 318
Berg, D. N., 329, 353
Bergeron, B. S., 8, 26
Berghoff, B., 83, 83t–84t, 91
Bernard (Waber), 50
Bertrand, J. E., 416
Best Christmas Pageant Ever, The (Robinson), 39–40, 179
Bettelheim, B., 37, 56, 156, 170
BGF, The (Dahl), 282
Bible, the, 3
Bibliotherapy, 345
Bierhorst, John, 361
Big Bad Bruce (Peet), 196, 218
Big Books, 104, 109, 113–15
    shared reading lesson with, 115
    using as writing models, 314
Big Cats (Simon), 62
Big Red (Kjelgaard), 279
Big Wave, The (Buck), 230, 363
Biggest Pumpkin Ever (Kroll), 231
Bilingual texts, 374
Bill Peet: An Autobiography (Peet), 51
Biographies, multicultural, 262, 364
Birch, David, 234
Birdseye, Tom, 361
Bishop, R. S., 357, 380
Bissex, G. L., 123, 134

Blachowicz, C. L., 138, 170
Black and White (Macaulay), 33
Black English, 367–69
    black cultural experiences and, 368
    implications for teaching, 368
    phonological features of, 367
    respect for speakers of, 367
Black perspective, children's books with, 368, 369
Black Snowman, The (Mendez), 369
Blanchard, J. S., 72, 91
Blanco, Alberto, 374
Blanton, W. E., 204, 210
Bleich, D., 299, 322
Bloom, B. S., 193, 210
Blubber (Blume), 39, 48, 144
Blue, Rose, 39
Blueberries for Sal (McCloskey), 218
Blume, Judy, 38, 39, 44, 48, 79, 144, 165, 187, 344
Blyden, A. E., 342, 352
Bobo's Dream (Alexander), 112, 113, 316
Bond, G. L., 118, 134
Bond, Michael, 37, 257, 278
Bonsall, Crosby, 121, 178, 286
Book clusters, topic-related, 218–21
Book discussions, 395
Book reports
    kinds of, 317–18
    as written products, 316–19
Book review boards, 64
Bookfinder, the (American Guidance Council), 346
Books Are By People (Hopkins), 51
Books for the Gifted Child (Hauser and Nelson), 347
Books of Junior Authors and Illustrators, 51
Bored—Nothing to Do (Spier), 305
Bormuth, J. R., 224, 253
Borrowers, The (Norton), 38
Bosma, B., 34, 56
Bowman, B. T., 356, 376, 380
Boy (Dahl), 51
Boy of the Three Year Nap, The (Snyder), 361
''Boy Who Cried Wolf, The,'' 35
Boys' Life (magazine), 264
Bragomer, Reginald, Jr., 259
Branley, Franklyn M., 4, 218, 225, 232, 314
Brenner, Barbara, 369
Brian Wildsmith's ABC (Wildsmith), 107
Bridge, C. A., 151, 170

Bridge to Terabitha (Patterson), 39, 40, 297, 317, 346
Bridwell, Norman, 332
Brinckloe, Julie, 21, 232
Brittain, Bill, 279
Bromley, K. D., 300, 322
Brother Eagle, Sister Sky (Chief Seattle), 363
Brown, A., 201, 210
Brown, Marcia, 35, 196, 234
Brown, Margaret Wise, 104
Brown, Tricia, 373
Brown, V. L., 295, 322, 392, 416
Brown Bear, Brown Bear (Martin), 109, 114
Brown Bear, Brown Bear, What Do You See? (Martin), 314
Bruce, B., 14, 26
Bruchac, Joseph, 232, 253
Buck, Pearl S., 363
Buddy journals, 117
    in response to literature, 300
Bugs (Parker and Wright), 22
Bullatz, Sonja, 218
Bully for You, Teddy Roosevelt! (Fritz), 230
Bumps in the Night (Allard), 179
Bunnicula (Howe and Howe), 279
Bunting, Eve, 346, 364
Burger, Douglas, 146
Burke, C., 409, 417
Burling, R., 367, 380
Burnett, Frances Hodgson, 299
Burnford, Sheila, 188, 279
Burns, Paul C., 254, 407
Buros Mental Measurements Yearbook, 393
Burton, Virginia Lee, 37
Butterworth, Oliver, 279
Butzow, Carol M., 232, 253
Butzow, John W., 232, 253
Byars, Betsy, 38, 39, 146, 197, 279, 286, 341, 346

C

Caduto, Michael J., 232, 253
CAI. *see* Computer-aided instruction
Caines, Jeanette, 346
Caldecott, Randolph, 32
Caldecott Award, 39, 107, 113, 234, 361
Calhoun, Mary, 62
California State Department of Education, 4, 26
Calkins, L. M., 134, 208, 322
Call It Courage (Sperry), 79, 279

Calypso Alphabet, The (Agard), 358
Cam Jensen books (Adler), 191
Cambourne, B., 9, 26, 336, 352, 395, 403, 416
Cane in Her Hand, A (Litchfield), 341
Caps for Sale (Slobodkina), 12, 35, 103
Carbo, M., 157, 170, 202, 210
Caribbean Canvas (Lessac), 364
Carle, Eric, 42, 105–6, 231
Carl's Christmas (Day), 113
Carpenter, P. A., 137, 166, 171
Carroll, Lewis, 32
Cars and How They Go (Cole), 232
Carter, M. A., 385, 417
Cassedy, Sylvia, 318
Cassidy, J., 347, 352
Castillo, M., 398, 416
Cat in the Hat (Seuss), 121, 304
Categorizing, 241
Catling, Patrick Skene, 179
Cats and Kittens (Estep), 62
Cause-effect relationships
    comprehending expository text and, 226
    multiple, 192
    in reading comprehension, 191–92
    sample passage, 229
Cave Boy (Dubowski), 5
Caxton, William, 31
Cay, The (Taylor), 276, 367
Censorship, 44
Cesar Chavez (Faucher), 373
Chall, J. S., 156, 157, 170
Changes Changes (Hutchins), 113
Chapbooks, 31
Chapter books for oral reading, 278
Chapters, main idea of, 187
Characterization, 44–45
Charles, Oz, 243
Charlie and the Chocolate Factory (Dahl), 279, 368
Charlotte's Web (White), 33, 37, 45, 121, 279, 298, 344
Chatton, B., 217, 253
Checklists
    in classroom assessment, 398
    samples of, 399–402
Cheek, E. H. Jr., 19, 26
Cherin, Helen, 363
Chicka Chicka Boom Boom (Martin and Archambault), 107, 285
Chicken Little (Kellogg), 160
Chicken Soup with Rice (Sendak), 110, 119, 234
Chief Seattle, 363
Child behavior, in whole language theory, 11

Child of the Silent Night (Hunter), 341
Childhood development
    early experiences with print, 99
    early literacy and, 95–99
    language acquisition in, 98–99
    physical and mental, 95–96
    schemata in, 96–97
Children's Book Council, 130, 363
Children's Choice Award, 39
Children's Digest (magazine), 264
Children's literature, 28–52
    authors of, 49–52
    genres in, 33–43
    history of, 30–33
    literary elements in, 43–49
Children's Literature in the Elementary School (Huck), 279
Chilly Stomach (Caines), 346
Chinese Mother Goose Rhymes (Wyndham), 361
Chinese Word for Horse and Other Stories, The (Lewis), 363
Chocolate Moose for Dinner, A (Gwynne), 146
Choosing Books for Children: A Commonsense Guide (Hearne), 130
Choral reading(s)
    for ESL and bilingual pupils, 374
    refrain arrangements in, 285
    rehearsed, 285
    in teaching oral reading, 285–86
Choral speaking, 299
Christenson, S. L., 328, 352
Christie, J. F., 15, 26, 293, 319, 322
Church, J. C., 399–402
Church, S. M., 158, 171
Ciardi, John, 43, 316
Cinderella, 34, 37
CIRC. *see* Cooperative Integrated Reading and Composition
Cisneros, Sandra, 373
Civil Rights Movement, 357
Class books, for publishing pupils' writing, 310–11
Classics, 40
Classification, 247
Classroom
    environment of, 64–65
    parents in, 86–87
    space management in, 64–67
    vocabulary development in, 140–47
    in whole language theory, 10
Classroom-based assessment, 393–411
    informal reading inventories, 406–8
    miscue analysis, 408–11

pros and cons of, 403, 406
    teacher observation, 394–95, 398
Classroom floor plan, 66
Classroom library(ies), 6
    circulation of books in, 69
    of trade books, 68–69
Classroom mailbox, 315
Classroom management techniques, 328
Classroom newspaper, 310
Classroom Reading Inventory (Silvaroli), 407
Clay, M. M., 329, 352, 394, 416
Clay Flute, The (Rehnman), 361
Clear and Simple Thesaurus Dictionary, The (Wittels and Greisman), 144
Cleary, Beverly, 5, 38, 39, 50, 51, 63, 184, 196, 305, 316, 346
Cleland, D. L., 348, 352
Clemens, Samuel. *see* Twain, Mark
Clementina's Cactus (Keats), 113
Clifford (Bridwell), 332
Climo, Shirley, 361
Closed syllables, 159
Cloudy with a Chance of Meatballs (Barrett), 38
Cloze exercises, 154–55
    using, 155
Cloze test, 223–25
Clymer, T., 159, 170
CMI. *see* Computer-managed instruction
Co-teaching, 257
Coates, Laura Jane, 111
Cockrum, W. A., 398, 416
Coerr, Eleanor, 228, 332, 363
Cognitive activities, 294
Cognitive processing
    comprehending expository text and, 243–44
    integrating instruction, 192–93
    level of thinking in, 243–44
    levels of thinking in, 193–97
    in reading comprehension, 176, 185–97
    type of thinking, 243
    types of comprehension, 185–92
Cognitive psychology, 98
Cohen, Miriam, 120
Cole, Joanna, 225, 232
Coles, G., 334, 352
Collaborative word webbing, 81
Collier, Christopher, 40, 279, 360
Collier, James, 40, 279, 360
Colligan, Louise, 318
Color coded programs, 20
Colt, J., 69, 91

Combined reading program
 advantages of, 22–23
 designing, 21–22
Communities Large and Small, 225
Comparison—contrast
 comprehending expository text and,
  226
 as context clue, 153
Compartmentalization, 293
Competency testing, 391
Complete Nonsense Book, The (Lear),
 43
Compound words in structural analysis,
 164
Comprehension
 defined, 174
 of details, 187–89
 development of, in DRTA, 77
 link with vocabulary, 137
 of main ideas, 186–89
 of sequence, 189–90
 types of, 185–92
Comprehension matrix and profile,
 396–97
"Comprehension skills," 185
Compton's Encyclopedia, 259
Computer(s), 71–73
Computer-aided instruction (CAI), 72
Computer-managed instruction (CMI),
 72–73
Computer programs, for teaching
 reading, 20
Concept(s)
 of story in reading-writing
  relationship, 295
 work knowledge and, 138–40
Concept books
 for math, 234
 in nursery school programs, 105
 selected sample of, 106
Conferences, individual, in teaching
 oral reading, 283
Conferencing
 group thinking, 310
 importance in classroom assessment,
  395
 with peers, 308, 310
 with pupils
  in editing and revising, 307–8
  in writing, 306
Conoley, J. C., 393, 417
Conrad, S., 263, 269
Consensus model. *see* Combined
 reading program
Consonant phonemes, 159
Content, 206
 appeal of, to children, 14

censorship in, 44
 of curriculum, audience reading and,
  284–85
 of expository text, 228, 230–35
 in reading comprehension, 176
 of text in reading comprehension,
  179, 182
Content words, teaching, 241
Context clues, 114
 cloze exercises, 154–55
 exercise in, 153
 semantic, 152–54
 syntactic, 152–54
 in vocabulary development, 152–55
Context in reading comprehension, 203
Contractions, 164–65
Contributions approach, to multicultural
 literature, 360
Conventional programs
 basal readers in, 16–19
 literature-based programs and,
  15–19
 skill-development view, 15–16
 writing in, 293
Cooke, C. L., 199, 210
Cooney, Barbara, 81, 143, 190
Cooperative Integrated Reading and
 Composition (CIRC), 82
Cooperative learning, 78, 80–81
 paired practice and, 283
 using literature, 81
Cooter, Robert, Jr., 407
Cosby, W., 358, 380
Costello, Jacalyn R., 338
Council on Interracial Books for
 Children, 363, 369, 373
Count and See (Hoban), 106
Counting books
 for math, 234
 in nursery school programs, 106–7
Country Mouse—City Mouse (Aesop),
 344
Courage of Sarah Noble, The
 (Dalgliesh), 40, 243, 279
Cox, S., 358, 380
Creative dramatics, as oral response to
 literature, 299
Creative reading, 195
Crews, Donald, 106
Criscuolo, N. P., 319, 322
Criteria
 for group formation, 76, 78, 86
 in IRI, 407–8
Criterion-referenced tests (mastery
 tests), 390–91
 basal reading tests, 390
 pros and cons of, 390–91

Critical-creative comprehension,
 194–97
Critical-creative questioning, 204
Critical reading, 195–97
 of social studies text, 230
Critical thinking, 196
 in reading and writing, 294
Crook, P. R., 215, 219, *219, 220,* 253
Cross Country Cat (Calhoun), 62
Cross-grade library assignment, 111
Crow Boy (Yashima), 5, 230, 363
Culinan, B. E., 4, 26
Cultural dimensions of literacy, 356–64
 types of multicultural trade books,
  358–64
 value of multicultural literacy in
  classroom, 357–58
Culturally conscious literature, 368
Culture, learning to read and, 356
Cumulative arrangements in choral
 reading, 285
Cunningham, D., 267, 269
Curiosity, vocabulary development and,
 145
Curious George (Rey and Rey), 332
"Curious George Strategy for Students
 With Reading Problems," 332
Curriculum and instructional practices,
 NAEYC position paper on, 122
Curriculum area textbooks, readability
 of, 223

D

Daddy Is a Monster . . . Sometimes
 (Steptoe), 367
Dahl, K. C., 159, 170
Dahl, Roald, 6, 38, 51, 279, 282, 368,
 408
Dahos, Kalli, 42
Daily classroom schedule, 61, 63
Dale, E., 139, 170
Dales, B., 257, 269
Dalgliesh, Alice, 40, 243, 279
Dancing Teepees (Sneve), 364
Danny, Champion of the World (Dahl),
 6
Davey, B., 330, 352
Davidson, A., 223, 253
Davis, F. B., 138, 170
Davis, Z. T., 45, 56
Davison, A., 215, 219, *219, 220,* 253
Day, Alexandra, 113
Day In Space, A (Lord and Epstein),
 218

Day the Teacher Went Bananas, The (Howe), 35
Dayrell, Elphinstone, 111
de Angeli, Marguerite, 230, 279
De Groff, L., 73, 91
de Paola, Tomie, 42, 113, 230, 297, 316, 361, 363
de Poix, Carol, 373
de Regniers, Beatrice Schenk, 42
DEAR. *see* Drop Everything and Read
Dear Mili (Manheim), 6
Dear Mr. Henshaw (Cleary), 38, 305, 316, 346
DeClements, Barthe, 6, 39
Decoding
　comprehending expository text and, 239–40
　in reading maps, 238
Decoding ability, 183
　extra assistance for the learning disabled, 336
Decoding skills, reading-writing relationship and, 295
Deep reading, 347
Definitions as context clues, 153
DeFord, D. E., 329, 352
DeGroff, L-J., 311, 312, 322
Delacre, Lulu, 374
Demi, 363
Departmentalization, 87
Desai, L. E., 385, 417
Desert Mermaid, The/La Sirena del Desierto (Blanco), 374
Deserts (Seymour), 232
Design
　in expository text, 235–36
　in reading comprehension, 182
Details, comprehending, 187–89
Devine, T. G., 138, 170, 183, 210
Diaakiw, J. Y., 358, 380
Diagnosis, 383
Diagnostic—prescriptive approach, for learning disabled pupils, 335–36
Diagrams or maps, comprehending expository text and, 227
Dialect(s), 366
　in print, 367
Dialect speakers, 364–69
　Black English, 367–69
　regional dialect, 364
　social dialect, 365
　Standard English and, 366
Dialogue(s)
　as oral response to literature, 299
　as written products, 316
Diane Goode Book of American Folk Tales and Songs (Durell), 361–62

Dicey's Song (Voigt), 39, 190
"Dictionaries" of word knowledge, 138–39
Dictionary, use in vocabulary development, 165–66
Digraphs, 159
Dillard, J. L., 367, 380
Dinosaur Digs (Lasky), 314
Dinosaurs (Zallinger), 314
Diphthongs, 159
Direct experience, building schemata and, 245
Direct instruction
　on comprehension components, 328–29
　importance for slow learners, 328
　teaching content words and, 241
Direct questioning, in teaching story structure, 180
Directed Reading-Thinking Activity (DRTA), 77
Discussion, 299
Dishner, E. K., 281, 290
Displays, 6, 64–65, 68
Diverse learners
　bilingual and ESL pupils, 369–76
　dialect speakers, 364–69
　multicultural literature for, 354–76
Doctor DeSoto (Steig), 34, 231
Dr. Seuss. *see* Geisel, Theodore
Dolch, E., 170
Doll in the Garden, The (Downing), 146
Door in the Wall, The (de Angeli), 230, 279
Doorbell Rang, The (Hutchins), 234
Doubleday Children's Thesaurus, The (Steveson), 144
Doublet, Anne, 107
Dowhower, S. L., 275, 290
Downing, Mary, 146
Dragonwings (Yep), 363
Drama and dance, expository text in, 234
Drawing conclusions in reading comprehension, 190–91
Drop Everything and Read (DEAR), 61
DRTA. *see* Directed Reading-Thinking Activity
Drummer Hoff (Emberley), 114, 160, 178
du Boulay, G., 262, 269
Dubowski, Cathy, 5
Dubrovin, Vivian, 318
Ducks Don't Get Wet (Goldin), 231
Dudley-Marling, C., 64, 91, 336, 353
Duffy, G. G., 21, 22, 26

Dunn, K., 202, 210
Dunn, L. M., 392, 417
Dunn, R., 202, 210
Dupuis, M. M., 247, 253
Durell, Ann, 361–62
Durkin, D., 123, 134
Durr, W. R., 148, 170
Durrell, D. D., 118, 134
Dykstra, R., 118, 134
Dyslexia, 334

E

Early, M., 371, 380
Early American Christmas, An (de Paola), 230
Early childhood programs, 103–21
　beginning instruction in, 120–21
　kindergarten, 108–19
　nursery school, 104–8
Early Detection of Reading Difficulties (Clay), 329
Early literacy, 93–131
　childhood development and, 95–99
　early childhood programs, 103–21
　reading readiness/emergent literacy in, 99, 101–3
　role of parents in, 121, 123–31
Earp, N. W., 233, 253
Earrings (Viorst), 146
Ebert, M. J., 217, 253
Echo reading, 284
Eckert, Allan, 299
Edelsky, C., 21, 26
Editing and revising, 307–8, *309*, 310
　conferencing with pupils and, 307–8
　critical reading and, 307
　decisions in, 313
　proofreading in, 307
Educational television programs, 125
Eeds, Maryann, 61, 79, 91, 139, 148–50, 152, 170, 171, 272, 276, 290, 299, 306, 322
Efferent responses to literature, 297–98
Egawe, K., 83, 83t–84t, 91
Egyptian Cinderella (Climo), 361
Eight Hands Round: A Patchwork Alphabet (Paul), 107
Eissenberg, T. E., 391, 417
Eldridge, R. G., 84, 91
Elementary classroom
　grouping in, 83–84
　literature in, 1–24
Elementary Reading Attitude Survey, 392
Ellen Tebbits (Cleary), 196
Elley, W. R., 276, 290, 375, 380

Ellis, D. W., 112, 134
Ellis Island: New Hope in a New Land (Jacobs), 364
Emberley, Barbara, 114, 160, 178
Emberley, Rebecca, 374
Emergent literacy, 101–3
   assumptions about literacy, 103
   conventional programs and, 101–3
   reading readiness and, 99, 101–3, 102t
   reading-writing activities for, 117
Emma (Kesselman), 143, 233
Emotional factors in reading readiness, 99
Emotional response in creative reading, 195
Emperor and the Kite, The (Yolen), 37
Emperor's New Clothes, The (Andersen), 37
Empty Pot, The (Demi), 363
Encoding skills, reading-writing relationship and, 295
Encounter (Yolen), 48, 230
Encyclopedia, 259
Encyclopedia Brown mysteries (Sobol), 191
End of year assessment, of emergent literacy, 394
Englert, C. S., 254
English as a Second Language. *see* ESL (English as a Second Language) pupils
Enormous Egg, The (Butterworth), 279
Enumeration, 225
Environment, for reading aloud to pupils, 277
Epstein, Jolie, 218
Equal-ability pairs in paired learning, 81
ERIC Clearinghouse on Reading and Communications Skills, Indiana University, 130
ESL (English as a Second Language) pupils, 369–76
   language instruction for, 370–73
   reading instruction for, 373–75
   resource teachers for, 375–76
Estep, Don, 62
Estice, R. M., 329, 352
Ethnic additive approach, to multicultural literature, 360
Ets, Marie Hall, 218, 373
Etymology, 145
Evaluation, 383
Evaluative questioning, 204
Every Time I Climb a Tree (McCord), 41

Evslin, Bernard, 35
Evslin, Dorothy, 35
Examples as context clues, 153
Expectation of success, 9
Experience as context clue, 153
Expository text, 110–11
   comprehending, 212–49
   interactive model of comprehension and, 221
   narrative text and, 172–208
   reader-based features, 239–48
   text-based features, 222–39
   trade books and textbooks, 215–21
Expression
   meaning and, 273–74
   in oral reading, 273–74
   punctuation and, 274
   suprasegmental phoneme system and, 273–74
Eye dialect, 367
Eye Openers: Choosing Books for Kids (Korbin), 68
Eye-voice span in oral reading, 276

F

Fables, 35
Fairy tales, 35
   multicultural, 360–61
Familiarity with topic, reading comprehension and, 179, 182
Family, realistic fiction about, 38
Fantasy, 37–38
Farest, C., 375, 380
Farjeon, Eleanor, 41, 280
Farmer Boy (Wilder), 198
Farnan, N., 21, 26
Fast-Slow, High-Low: A Book of Opposites (Spier), 106
Fastest Friend in the West (Grove), 346
Father's Arcane Daughter (Konigsburg), 165
Faucher, Ruth, 373
Feedback in editing and revising, 310
Feelings, Muriel, 107, 358, 359
Felita (Mohr), 362, 373
Fielding, L. G., 147, 170, 198, 211
Figurative language, for ESL and bilingual pupils, 374
Filmstrips, for LEP pupils, 372
Find It! The Inside Story at Your Library (McInerney), 259
Finding Buck McHenry (Slote), 369
Fine, J., 263, 269
Fireflies (Brinckloe), 21, 232
First Book of Creative Writing (Mahon), 318

First Comes Spring (Rockwell), 106
First grade, 120–21
   first day in, 120
   literature in, 121
   skill-development exercises in, 120
Fisher, Aileen, 280
Fisher, B., 394, 417
Fisher, David, 259
Fitzgerald, J., 307, 310, 322
Fitzsimons, V. M., 342, 353
500 Hats of Bartholomew Cubbins, The (Seuss), 37
Flash cards, 150
Flashbacks, 190
Flecha al Sol [Arrow to the Sun] (McDermott), 374
Fleischman, Paul, 286
Fleischman, Sid, 279
Flesch, R., 156, 170
Flexibility in grouping, 85–86
Flood, J., 21, 26, 86, 91, 412, 417
Floor plan of classroom, 66
Florian, Douglas, 231
Flournoy, Valerie, 367
Flow charts, 180, *181*
Fluency
   marking phrases, 276
   modeling, 275
   in oral reading, 274–76
   repeated reading, 275–76
Fly Away Home (Bunting), 346
Fly with the Wind, Flow with the Water (Atwood), 316
Flynn, L. L., 81, 91
Flynt, E. Sutton, 407
Flynt-Cooter Reading Inventory for the Classroom (Flynt and Cooter), 407
Folk literature, multicultural, 361–62
Folktales, 34
   multicultural, 259–62
Follow-up
   in DRTA, 77
   by parents, 125
   in shared reading lesson, 115
For Reading Out Loud: A Guide to Sharing Books with Children (Kimmel and Segal), 68
Forbes, Esther, 40, 218, 230, 360
Forgan, H. W., 233, 253
Form selection, in prewriting, 305
Formal assessment, 387–93
   skill-development tests, 390–93
   standardized reading achievement tests, 387–90
Formal instruments for pupil assessment, 384

Fourth Floor Twins mysteries (Adler), 191
Fourth Grade Wizards (DeClements), 6
Fowler, G. L., 210
Fox, Paula, 196, 362
Francisco (Baylor), 360
Freckle Juice (Blume), 79, 165, 187
Fredericks, A. D., 128, 134
Free verse, 42
Freebody, P., 138, 170
Freedman, Russell, 216–17
Freeman, E. B., 102, 103, 134
Freeman, Ina, 228
Freeman, Y. S., 16, 26
Freight Train (Crews), 106
Freppon, P. A., 159, 170
Fried, M. D., 329, 352
Friedberg, Joan Brest, 341, 352
Fritz, Jean, 4, 40, 51, 230
Frog and Toad (Lobel), 121, 178
Frog and Toad Are Friends (Lobel), 316
Frog and Toad Together (Lobel), 408
Frog Prince Continued (Scieszka), 48
Frog Went a-Courtin' (Langstaff), 234, 258
From the Mixed-up Files of Mrs. Basil E. Frankweiler (Konigsburg), 165, 189, 196, 279
Frost, Robert, 43
Frustration reading level, in IRI, 406
Fuhler, C. J., 14, 15, 19, 26, 337, 352
Fujimoto, Patricia, 259
Fun with Words (Nuinberg), 146
''Function words,'' 148, 150, 151

G

Gag, Wanda, 5, 104
Galaxies (Simon), 232
Galda, L., 203, 210, 358, 380
Gale Publishing Company, 51
Garden of Abdul Gasazi, The (Van Allsburg), 338
Gardiner, John Reynolds, 196, 279, 299
Gates, A., 108, 134
Gates, Doris, 35
Geisel, Theodore S. (Dr. Seuss), 37, 49, 121, 178, 188, 303, 304
Generalizing
    in phonics, 159
    from specialized vocabulary, 251
Gennaro, Joseph, 225
Genre. *see* Literary genres
Gentile, L. M., 108, 134, 331, 332, 352
Geography, trade books for, 230

George, Jean Craighead, 79, 165, 230, 233, 314
Gera, Adele, 361
Gere, A. A., 253
Giff, Patricia Reilly, 305, 318
Gift of the Sacred Dog, The (Goble), 360
Gifted and talented pupils
    challenging reading for, 347–48
    defining, 346–47
    instruction for, 345–48
GIL. *see* Graphic Information Lesson
Gilberto and the Wind (Ets), 218, 373
Gilcrest, Cherry, 259
Gilfranconi, Ann, 359
Gingerbread Man, The, 19
Gipson, Fred, 232
Girl from Yamhill, A (Cleary), 51
Gladone, Paul, 218
Glossary, 235, 236
Goble, Paul, 359, 360
Goffstein, M. B., 233
Going Up (Sis), 234
Gold Cadillac, The (Taylor), 6
Goldin, Augusta, 231
Goldman, S. R., 328, 353
Good Dog, Carl (Day), 113
Good Hunting, Blue Sky (Parish), 359
Good Night, Owl (Hutchins), 5, 114, 115, 178, 314, 374
Goodall, John, 111, 113
Goodman, K. S., 8, 16, 26, 156, 170, 408, 417
Goodman, Y. M., 393, 409, 417
Goodnight, Moon (Brown), 104
Gove, M. K., 102t, 134
Government Printing Office, 130
Grade level of pupils, book selection and, 278–79
Gramatky, Hardie, 34, 37, 196
Grandfather Tan's Story (Tompert), 359
Grandma Didn't Wave Back (Blue), 39
Grandpa's Face (Greenfield), 369
Grannis, C. B., 33, 56
Graphemes, 159
Graphic Information Lesson (GIL), 239
Graphic materials in expository text, 237–39
Graphic organizers, *229,* 261
    for main idea, 188
    in paragraph comprehension, *242,* 242–43
    teaching content words and, 241
Graphophonic clues, 158
Graphophonic miscues, 409

Graphophonic patterns, 160
Graphs in expository text, 238–39
Graves, D. H., 116, 134, 312, 322
Graves, M. F., 199, 210
Greaney, V., 123, 134
Great Books Foundation, 196
Great Cat (McPhail), 62
Great Gilly Hopkins, The (Paterson), 279
Green, Carol, 259
Green Eggs and Ham (Seuss), 121, 178, 188, 303
Greene, Bette, 369
Greenfield, Eloise, 42, 369
Greisman, Jon, 144
Griff, Patricia Reilly, 39
Grillone, Lisa, 225
Grimm, Jacob, 31, 34, 37
Grimm, Wilhelm, 31, 34, 37
Group Assessment in Reading: Classroom Teacher's Handbook (Warncke and Shipman), 407
Group Comprehension Matrix, 396–97
Group oral reading, 282
Group prediction strategies, for cooperative learning, 81
Group thinking conferences, in editing and revising, 310
Grouping
    cooperative learning, 78, 80–81
    in elementary classroom, 83t–84t
    flexibility in, 85–86
    heterogeneous, 78, 79
    homogeneous, 76, 78
    paired learning, 81–82
    for small-group instruction, 75–82
    See also Pupil management
Grove, Vicki, 346
Guarin, Deborah, 160
Guided reading in DRTA, 77
Guilford, J. P., 193, 210
Gulliver's Travels (Swift), 30
Gurlnick, Elissa, 146
Gutenberg, Johannes, 3
Guy, Rosa, 316
Gwynne, Fred, 146

H

H. W. Wilson Company (publishers), 51
Hahn, A. L., 330, 352
Haiku, 42
Hailstones and Halibut Bones (O'Neill), 42
Hale, Janet, 363
Haley, D., 151, 170

Hall, David, 190
Hall, Donald, 230
Hamilton, Virginia, 279, 362, 369
Hammill, D. D., 295, 322, 334, 352, 392, 416, 417
Haney, W., 383, 417
Hans Christian Andersen Prize, 39
Hansen, J., 116, 134, 294, 296, 312, 322
Happy Prince, The (Wilde), 37
''Hare and the Tortoise, The,'' 35
Harris, A. J., 99, 134, 253
Harris, T. L., 388, 417
Harry (Zion), 332
Harry By the Sea (Zion), 192
Hatch, J. A., 102, 103, 134
Hauser, Paula, 347, 352
Have You Seen My Duckling (Tafuri), 151
Hawk, I'm Your Brother (Baylor), 363
Hawthorne, Nathaniel, 31
HBJ Health, 225
Heald-Taylor, G., 114, 134, 404–5, 417
Hearne, Betsy, 130
Hector Lives in the United States Now: The Story of a Mexican-American Child (Hewitt), 364
Helen Oxenbury's ABC of Things (Oxenbury), 107
Hello, Amigos! (Brown), 373
Henk, W. A., 70, 91
Henson, J., 409, 418
Hepler, S., 13, 26, 37, 56, 105, 134, 218, 253, 290, 417
Hepworth, Cathi, 107
Her Seven Brothers (Goble), 359
Herman, P. A., 154, 155, 166, 171
Heroes in traditional literature, 36–37
Heros and Monsters of Greek Myth (Evslin, Evslin and Hoopes), 35
Herringbone Technique, 244, 261
Hess, M. L., 253
Heterogeneous grouping, 78, 79
Hewitt, Joan, 364
Hickman, J., 37, 56, 105, 134, 218, 253, 290, 417
Hiebert, E. H., 69, 91
High fantasy, 38
Higher Order Thinking Skills (HOTS), 329–30
Highlights for Children (magazine), 264
Hill, Mary W., 130
Hippopotamus Ate the Teacher, The (Thaler), 35
Historical fiction, 40
Hittleman, D. R., 76, 91, 146, 170, 294, 322, 409, 417

Hoban, Russell, 196, 299
Hoban, Tana, 106, 234
Hobbit, The (Tolkien), 38, 279
Hobertman, Mary Ann, 333
Hodges, Margaret, 36
Hodges, R. E., 388, 417
Hoffman, J. V., 231, 253, 375, 380
Hogrogian, Nonnie, 299
Holdaway, D., 105, 134, 273, 290, 417
Holistic contexts, in whole language theory, 9
Holistic instruction for learning disabled pupils, 336–38
Hollingsworth, P. M., 10, 11, 26
Holman, Felice, 79
Holmes, B. C., 253
Holophrastic speech, 98
Holt Science, 225
Home: Where Reading and Writing Begin (Hill), 130
Homecoming, The (Viorst), 79
Homesick, My Own Story (Fritz), 51
Homogeneous grouping, 76, 78
Hoopes, Ned, 35
Hop on Pop (Seuss), 121
Hopeful Trout and Other Limericks, The (Ciardi), 43, 316
Hopkins, Lee Bennett, 51, 56
Horn Book, The (magazine), 51, 68, 130
Hoskisson, Kenneth, 180
HOTS. *see* Higher Order Thinking Skills
House is a House for Me, A (Hobertman), 333
House on Mango Street, The (Cisneros), 373
How a Book is Made (Aliki), 318
How Does Soda Get into the Bottle? (Charles), 243
How I Came to Be a Writer (Naylor), 51
How Many Days to America? A Thanksgiving Story (Bunting), 364
How Many Miles to Babylon (Fox), 362
How Much is a Million? (Schwartz), 234
How My Parents Learned to Eat (Freeman), 228–29
''How the Elephant Got His Trunk'' (Kipling), 35
How to Eat Fried Worms (Rockwell), 39, 279
How We Came to the Fifth World/Como Vinimos al Quinto Mundo (Rohmer and Anchondo), 374

Howe, Deborah, 279
Howe, James, 35, 279
Howell, Margaret, 345
Hoyt-Goldsmith, Diane, 361
Huck, Charlotte S., 30, 37, 56, 105, 134, 218, 253, 279, 290, 361, 417
Hudelson, S., 375, 380
Huerta-Macias, A., 376, 380
Hugh Pine (van de Wetering), 121
Hughes, Langston, 196
Humor, 191
Hundred Penny Box, The (Mathis), 369
Hungry, Hungry Sharkes (Cole), 225
Hunhardt, Dorothy, 106
Hunt, Irene, 40, 217, 230
Hunter, Edith Fisher, 341
Hurst, Carol Otis, 51, 56
Hurwitz, Johanna, 39
Hutchins, Pat, 5, 33, 109, 113, 114, 115, 151, 178, 234, 314, 374
Huynh, Queng Nhuong, 363
Hyman, Trina Schart, 44
Hynds, S., 182, 210, 298, 322

I

I Can Be A Librarian (Green), 259
I-Charts. *see* Inquiry Charts
I Know an Old Lady Who Swallowed a Fly (Rounds), 285
I Like the Library (Rockwell), 259
I Won't Let Them Hurt You (Barr), 346
Idalia, Rosario, 358
IDEA. *see* Individuals with Disabilities Education Act
IEP. *see* Individualized Education Plan
If the Dinosaurs Came Back (Most), 314
If You Are a Hunter of Fossils (Baylor and Parnall), 232, 298
If You Give a Mouse a Cookie (Numeroff), 192
If You Made a Million (Schwartz), 234
If You're Not Here, Please Raise Your Hand: Poems about School (Dahos), 42
Illustrations, in reading comprehension, 182
Immersion, in whole language theory, 9
In a Pumpkin Shell (Anglund), 119
In a Spring Garden (Keats), 43
In Other Words: A Beginning Thesaurus (Schiller and Jenkins), 144

In the Beginning: Creation Stories from Around the World (Hamilton), 279

In the Night Kitchen (Sendak), 44, 111

In the Year of the Boar and Jackie Robinson (Lord), 40, 363, 364

In Your Own Words: A Beginner's Guide to Writing (Cassedy), 318

Inappropriate instructional practice (NAEYC), 122

Incident at Hawk's Hill (Eckert), 299

Incredible Journey, The (Burnford), 188, 279

Incubation time, in prewriting, 305

Independent reading level, in IRI, 406

Index, 235, 236, 259

"Indian Father's Plea, An," 359

Indian in the Cupboard (Banks), 37, 188, 198

Individual Education Plan (IEP), 349

Individual reading—study carrels, 67

Individualized activities, 84, 85

Individualized Education Plan (IEP), 327

Individualized patterns, grouping and, 82, 84–85

Individuals with Disabilities Education Act (IDEA), 327

Indrisano, R., 395, 417

Inferential comprehension
  as level of thinking, 194
  schemata and, 198

Inferential questioning, 204

Inflexibility, avoiding, 67

Info (magazine), 264

Informal reading instruction, in home, 129

Informal Reading Inventory (IRI), 406–8
  reading levels determined by, 406

Informal Reading Inventory: Preprimer to Twelfth Grade (Burns and Roe), 407

Information knowledge, in reading-writing connection, 294

Informational books
  multicultural, 262, 364
  picture, 111
  for science, 232

InQuest (Investigative Questioning Procedures), 205, 385

Inquiry Charts (I-Charts), 231

Inquiry reading, for gifted and talented pupils, 347

Instructional connection, in reading-writing relationship, 296

Instructional questioning, 204

Instructional reading level, in IRI, 406

Instructional Story Plans, 333

Instructional tools, overreliance on, 18

Integrated activities, in combined reading program, 21

Integration
  analogies in, 141–42
  semantic mapping in, 141
  Venn diagrams in, 141
  in vocabulary development, 140–42

Interactive assessment, 395

Interactive model of reading comprehension, 175–77, 221

Interest centers, 65, 67

International Reading Association, 39, 130

Interpretative comprehension, 194, 198

Invented spelling, 116

Investigative Questioning Procedures (InQuest), 205, 385

Involvement in reading, impact of literature on, 12

Ira Sleeps Over (Waber), 50, 191, 194, 278

IRI. *see* Informal Reading Inventory

Irony, 47

Irving, Washington, 31

Is It Red? Is it Yellow? (Hoban), 106

Is Your Mama a Llama (Guarin), 160

Iverson, W. J., 47, 56

J

Jack and Jill (magazine), 264

Jacko (Goodall), 113

Jacob Have I Loved (Paterson), 38

Jacobs, Joseph S., 8, 15, 27, 34

Jacobs, William Jay, 364

Jambo Means Hello: A Swahili Alphabet Book (Feelings), 358

James and the Giant Peach (Dahl), 38, 368, 408

Japanese focus, trade books with, 363

Jeffers, Susan, 363

Jenkins, L. V., 389, 416, 417

Jenkins, William, 144

Jimmy Yellow Hawk (Sneve), 362

Jo, Flo, And Yolanda (de Poix), 373

John Midas in the Dreamtime (Catling), 179

Johnny Tremain (Forbes), 40, 218, 230, 360

Johns, J., 407

Johnson, Angela, 6, 286

Johnson, B. V., 194, 210

Johnson, D. D., 141, 170, 194, 210

Johnson, M. B., 392, 406, 417, 418

Johnson, N. M., 217, 253

Johnson, P., 388, 393, 415, 417

Johnson, T. D., 18, 26, 89, 91, 156, 158, 170

Joint Committee for Learning Disabilities, 334

Jones, Betty Millsaps, 234

Jones, M., 119, 134

Journals, in classroom assessment, 398

Journals as written products, 316

Journey (MacLachan), 346

Journey Home (Uchida), 360

Journey to Jo'burg (Naidoo), 368

Journey to Topaz (Uchida), 40, 360, 363

Joyful Noise, A: Poems for Two Voices (Fleischman), 286

Judge Rabbit and the Tree Spirit (Wall), 359

Julie of the Wolves (George), 79, 230, 233, 314

Jumanji (Van Allsburg), 304, 338

Junior Great Books program, 196
  for gifted and talented pupils, 347

Junior Scholastic (magazine), 264

Just, M. S., 137, 166, 171

Just So Stories (Kipling), 6, 35

Juster, Norton, 38, 278, 318

K

K-W-L (structured teaching technique), 246, 385

Kane, S., 263, 269

Kantor, Robert N., 223, 253

Kantrowitz, B., 19, 26

Kardaleff, P., 230, 253

Karolides, N. J., 298, 322

Katy and the Big Snow (Burton), 37

Kear, D. J., 385, 392, 417

Keats, Ezra Jack, 34, 43, 52, 113, 311–12, 368

Keegan, S., 79, 91

Keep the Lights Burning, Abbie (Roop and Roop), 225

Keepers of the Earth (Caduto and Bruchai), 232

Keifer, B., 196, 210

Keller, Ruth, 146

Kellogg, Steven, 36, 107

Kelly, P. R., 295, 298, 322

Kennedy, DayAnn M., 232, 253

Kesselman, Wendy, 143, 233

"Kid watching," 393

Kids Magazine, 264
Kiefer, B., 33, 56, 216, 253
Kimmel, E., 345, 352
Kimmel, Margaret Mary, 68, 91
Kindergarten, 103, 108–19
  alphabet awareness in, 118–19
  language development in, 109
  literature in, 109–15
  metalinguistic awareness in, 108–9
  perceptual training in, 117–18
  writing in, 115–17
King, Carole, 110
King-Smith, Dick, 279
King Who Rained, The (Gwynne), 146
King's Chessboard, The (Birch), 234
Kinney, M. A., 227, 253
Kinzer, C. K., 203, 211
Kipling, Rudyard, 6, 32, 35
Kirk, S. A., 339, 352
Kirschner, B. W., 254
Kitchen, Burt, 107
Kitchen Knight, The: A Tale of King Arthur (Hodges), 36
Kjelgaard, Jim, 279
Kleiman, G. W., 233, 253
Klein, M. L., 138, 139, 171, 177, 205, 211
Kliebhan, J. M., 339, 352
Kliman, M., 233, 253
Knots on a Counting Rope (Martin and Archambault), 286, 316, 341, 363
Knowledge background
  need for, 245
  in reading-writing connection, 294–95
Knowlton, Jack, 238
Knudson, R. R., 234, 299
Kolczynski, R. G., 296, 322
Konigsburg, E. L., 165, 189, 196, 279
Korbin, Beverly, 68, 91
Koshkin, Alexander, 361
Kossack, S., 263, 269
Krahn, Fernando, 113
Kramer, J. J., 393, 417
Kress, R., 406, 417
Krieger, E., 51, 56
Kroll, Steven, 231
Krumgold, Joseph, 362
Kurelek, William, 230
Kuskin, Karla, 190, 234

L

LaBarge, M. J., 199, 210
Label words, 109, 150
Lady with the Alligator Purse, The, 286

Lake, R., 359, 380
Lake at the End of the World, The (MacDonald), 279
Lamme, L. L., 253
Land I Lost, The: Adventures of a Boy in Vietnam (Huynh), 363
Langer, J. A., 199, 211, 389, 416
Langstaff, John, 234, 258
Language
  acquisition of, in childhood development, 98–99
  censorship in, 44
  impact of literature on, 14
  of poetry, 41
Language Arts (journal), 51, 68
Language background, 206
  comprehending expository text and, 239–43
  decoding ability, 183
  metalinguistic awareness, 182–83
  paragraphs, 184
  in reading comprehension, 176, 182–85
  selections, 184–85
  sentences, 183
  vocabulary, 183
Language connection, in reading-writing relationship, 295
Language development
  in kindergarten, 109
  in nursery school programs, 104–5
Language experience activities
  comprehending expository text and, 227
  for ESL and bilingual pupils, 374
Language experience approaches, to teaching, 20
Language factors, in reading readiness, 99
Language instruction for ESL pupils, 370–73
Lapp, D., 21, 26, 412, 417
Large-group instruction, 74–75
Larrick, Nancy, 130
Larsen, S. C., 392, 417
Lasky, Kathy, 314
Lass, B., 123, 134
Last Dinosaur, The (Murphy), 6
Latham, R., 278, 282, 290
Laubner, Patrice, 314
Laughlin, M., 230, 253
Laura Ingalls Wilder Award, 39
Lawson, Robert, 5, 37, 48, 84, 230
LEAP supplementary program (Sundance Publishers), 70
Lear, Edward, 32, 43, 279

Learner objectives, in holistic reading instruction, 336
Learning disabilities, 334–35
Learning disabled pupils, 334–39
  holistic reading and, 336–38
  reading programs for, 335–36
  writing for, 338–39
Learning Links, 70
Learning process in whole language theory, 10
Leaves in October, The (Ackerman), 346
Lee, Jeanne M., 359
Legend of Bluebonnet, The (de Paola), 363
Legend of Old Barara, The (de Paola), 361
Legends, 36
  multicultural, 360–61
Lehman, B. A., 215, 219, *219*, *220*, 253
Lehr, F., 158, 171
L'Engle, Madeleine, 38, 279
LEP. *see* Limited English Proficiency
Lerner, J. W., 339, 352
Lessac, Frane, 146, 364
Let the Balloon Go (Southall), 39, 341
Let the Circle Be Unbroken (Taylor), 368
Letters
  writing, 117
  as written products, 315–16
Leu, D. J., 203, 211
Level of text. *see* Readability
Levels of thinking
  in cognitive processing, 193–97
  critical-creative comprehension, 194–97
  inferential comprehension, 194
  literal comprehension, 193–94
  taxonomies for describing, 193
Levi, R., 413, 417
Levitt, Paul M., 146
Lewis, C. S., 38, 47, 279
Lewis, John, 363
Lewis, Richard, 42, 43
Lexical differences in social dialects, 365
Librarians
  classroom book collections and, 68
  teachers and, 257–58
Libraries (Fujimoto), 259
Library(ies)
  in literature-based programs, 255–68
  newspapers and magazines in, 262–65
  reading rate/reading efficiency and, 266–67

reference materials in, 258–62
teachers and librarians in, 257–58
Light in the Attic (Silverstein), 42, 338
Limericks, 42
Limited English Proficiency (LEP), 371
Lincoln: A Photobiography (Freedman), 217
Lindgren, Astrid, 38, 282
Linek, W. M., 403, 417
Linguistic labels, 198
Lion, the Witch, and the Wardrobe, The (Lewis), 38, 47, 279
Lion Dancer: Ernie Wan's Chinese New Year (Waters and Slovenz-Low), 364
Lipson, Eden Ross, 279, 290
Listen, Children (Strickland), 369
Litchfield, Ada B., 341
Literacy development
    assessing, 381–415
    parental reinforcement of, 127–28
    process of, 121
Literal comprehension, as level of thinking, 193–94
Literal questioning, 204
Literary elements, 43–49
    characterization, 44–45
    plot, 45
    setting, 43–44
    theme, 45, 47–49
Literary genres, 33–43
    fantasy, 37–38
    folktales and fairy tales, 34–37
    historical fiction, 40
    picture books, 33–34
    poetry, 41–43
    reading comprehension and, 178
    realistic fiction, 38–40
Literature
    advantage of using, 192–93
    in cultural life, 356–57
    discussing in teaching story structure, 180
    integrating with science, 233
    in kindergarten, 109–15
    language competency of LEP pupils and, 372
    multicultural. see Multicultural literature
    in nursery school programs, 104–5
    as part of language therapy, 338
    for slow learners, 331–33
    using to support process writing, 311–12
    using with the learning disabled, 337
    written products based on, 312–19

Literature-based program(s), 4–7
    book clusters in, 218–21
    changing view of assessment and, 387
    conventional instruction and, 15–19
    for emotionally handicapped pupils, 344
    expository text in, 215–16
    library in, 255–68
    organizing and managing, 57–89
    reading aloud in, 272
    reasons for using, 7–15
    research-based qualities of, 8
    skill-based programs and, 189
    synthesis with basal systems, 19–23
    textbooks, 216
    trade books, 216–18
Literature-Based Social Studies: Children's Books and Activities to Enrich the K-5 Curriculum (Laughlin and Kardaleff), 230
Literature-related materials in basal series, 17
Literature report cards, 81
Literature-rich classroom, writing in, 300–301, 303
Literature study groups
    heterogeneous, 79
    pupil-directed dialogue in, 207
Little House in the Big Woods (Wilder), 198
Little House on the Prairie (Wilder), 40, 198
Little Pigeon Toad, A (Gwynne), 146
Little Prince, The (Saint-Exupéry), 37
Little Red Riding Hood (Hyman), 44
Little Toot (Gramatky), 34, 37, 196
Little Women (Alcott), 31–32
Littles, The (Peterson), 38, 278
Lobel, Anita, 107
Lobel, Arnold, 107, 121, 178, 316, 408
Lomeo, Angelo, 218
Lon Po Po (Young), 338, 361
Lonely Dragon (Howell), 345
Lord, Beth Bao, 40, 363, 364
Lord, Suzanne, 218
Lord of the Dance: An African Retelling (Tadjo), 360
Losing Uncle Tim (Jordan), 346
Louis, D. R., 18, 26, 89, 91, 156, 158, 170
Love You Forever (Munsch), 297
Lowry, Lois, 38, 318
Lyle, Lyle, Crocodile (Waber), 50
Lyons, C. A., 329, 352
Lyric poems, 42

M

Macaulay, David, 33, 232
McCallum, R. D., 18, 26
McCauley, D. S., 374, 380
McCauley, J. K., 374, 380
McCloskey, Robert, 33, 52, 199, 218, 278
McCord, David, 41, 279
McCoy, K. M., 326, 328, 341, 352
McDermott, Gerald, 360, 374
MacDonald, Caroline, 279
McDonald, Betty, 278
McElmeel, Sharron, 51, 56
McGee, L. A., 227, 229, 253
McGee, L. M., 103, 134
McGuffey Eclectic Readers, 3
McInerney, Claire, 259
McKenna, M. C., 385, 392, 417
MacLachlan, Patricia, 40, 155, 196, 279, 341, 346, 408
McMillan, M. M., 331, 332, 352
McNeil, J., 211
McPhail, David, 62, 304
McPherson, M. D., 45, 56
McSwigan, Marie, 199
McTague, B. K., 332, 353
Madaus, G. F., 383, 417
Madden, L., 81, 91
Madeline (Bemelmans), 4, 12, 160
Magazines, 264–65
Maggie, Too (Nixon), 196
Magic Horse, The (Scott), 359
Magic Leaf, The (Morris), 363
Magic Window II (word processing program), 308
Mahon, Julia C., 318
Main idea
    comprehending, 186–89
    details and, 187–89
    graphic organizers for, 188
Main topic, 186
Mainstreaming of atypical learners, 327–28
Make Way for Ducklings (McCloskey), 199, 278
Manes, Stephen, 278
Mangrum, C. T., 233, 253
Mangubhai, F., 375, 380
Manheim, Ralph, 6
Maniac Magee (Spinelli), 279, 346
Mann, Horace, 20
Many Luscious Lollipops (Keller), 146
Manzo, A. V., 205, 211
Maps: Getting from Here to There (Weiss), 238
Maps and Globes (Knowlton), 238

Maps in expository text, 237–38
Marcella and the Moon (Coates), 111
Maria Teresa (Atkinson), 373
Marimoto, Jinko, 359
Martin, Bill, Jr., 107, 109, 114, 285,
    286, 314, 316, 341, 363
Marzano, R. J., 202, 211
Mason, J. M., 214, 253, 319, 322, 370,
    380
Massachusetts Department of
    Education, 197, 211
Mastery tests. *see* Criterion-referenced
    tests
Material management, 67–73
    audiovisual devices, 70–71
    basal readers, 69
    computers, 71–73
    patterns of selection and use, 69
    supplementary materials, 70
    trade books, 68–69
Mathematics, 63
    expository text in, 232–33
    trade books for, 234
Mathews, M. M., 19, 26, 171, 272, 290
Mathis, Sharon Bell, 369
Maurice's Room (Fox), 196
Mayer, Mercer, 113, 304, 338
Meaning, reading aloud for, 272
Meaning-building process for the
    learning disabled, 336–37
''Meaning connection,'' 294–95
Meaning orientation, 8
Meaningful use
    teacher involvement and, 146
    in vocabulary development, 146–47
    wide reading and, 146–47
Measurement, 383
    difficulties of dialect speakers with,
    366
Meddaugh, Susan, 144
Media center, 65
Media presentations in schema theory,
    198–99
Medieval Feast (Aliki), 230
Medina, N. J., 383, 417
Melting pot literature, 368
Mendez, Phil, 369
Mental development, 95–96
Merrill, Claire, 231
Metacognition, 206
    comprehending expository text and,
    246–47
    promoting, 246
    in reading comprehension, 176,
    200–202
    for slow learners, 329–30

Metacomprehension. *see* Metacognition
Metacomprehension Strategy Index
    (MSI), 201
Metalinguistic awareness, 182–83
    in kindergarten, 108–9
Mightiest of Mortals: Heracles (Gates),
    35
Miles, Miska, 142, 206, 363
Milliken Word Processor (word
    processing program), 308
Millions of Cats (Gag), 5, 104
Mills, H., 232, 254
Milne, A. A., 32, 37, 278
Mine's The Best (Bonsall), 121, 178,
    286
Minimal brain damage, 334
Mintoyne, Grace, 233
*Miracles: Poems by Children of the
    English-Speaking World*
    (Lewis), 42
Miscue analysis, 408–11
    categories of miscues in, 408–9
    conducting, 409
    as focus for listening to pupils read
    aloud, 410
    pros and cons of, 410–11
Miss Nelson Is Missing (Allard), 35,
    204
Miss Rumphius (Cooney), 81, 143
Mitchell is Moving (Sharmat), 143
Mitzi's Honeymoon with Nana Potts
    (Williams), 346
Mixed-ability pairs, in paired learning,
    82
Model(s)
    Big Books as, 314
    interactive, of reading
    comprehension, 175–77, 221
    of parent-teacher cooperation, 128
    parents as, 126
    in prewriting, 304
    teachers as, 8, 154
    for teaching multicultural literature,
    365
Modeling
    in instruction for the learning
    disabled, 337
    in whole language theory, 9
Modified cloze, 154
Moe, Alden J., 151, 171, 407
Mohr, Nicholasa, 362, 373
*Moja Means One: A Swahili Counting
    Book* (Feelings), 107, 359
Montgomery, L. M., 32
Mood, 47
Mooney, Jean F., 66
Moonlight (Omerod), 113

Moore, Clement Clarke, 42
Moorman, G. B., 204, 210
Morals, in children's literature, 47
More Books By More People (Hopkins),
    51
''Morning message,'' 117
Morphemes, 164
Morphemic analysis. *see* Structural
    analysis
Morphemic elements, 165
Morphett, M. V., 108, 134
Morris, Winifred, 363
Morrison, C., 281, 290
Morrow, L. M., 64, 91, 114, 134
Mortimer (Munsch), 190
Mosel, Arlene, 6, 363
Most, Bernard, 314
Mother Goose, 42
Motivation
    comprehending expository text and,
    247–48
    in reading comprehension, 202
    for writing, 304
Mouse On the Motorcycle, The
    (Cleary), 5, 184
Mouse's Marriage (Marimoto), 359
Mousetails (Lobel), 121
Movies about authors, 52
Mr. Popper's Penguins (Atwater and
    Atwater), 177
Mrs. Frisby and the Rats of NIMH
    (O'Brien), 45, 279
Mrs. Piggle Wiggle (McDonald), 278
MSI. *see* Metacomprehension Strategy
    Index
Mufaro's Beautiful Daughters
    (Steptoe), 230, 361
Muggie Maggie (Cleary), 316
Mullel, Tololwa M., 359
Mullis, I. V. A., 389, 416, 417
Multicultural literature, 358–64
    biographies and informational
    books, 362, 364
    cultural dimensions of literacy and,
    356–64
    diverse learners and, 354–76
    folktales and traditional literature,
    359–62
    integrating into curriculum, 360
    picture books, 358–59
    realistic fiction, 362
    teaching model for, 365
    value in classroom, 357–58
Mummies Made in Egypt (Aliki), 218
Munsch, Robert, 35, 190, 297
Murphy, Jim, 6
Murphy, S., 16, 26

Murray, D. M., 305, 322
Murray, Michele, 369
Musgrove, Margaret, 107
Music, expository text in, 234
My Brother Sam is Dead (Collier and Collier), 40, 279
My Grandmother's Story: A Collection of Jewish Folk Tales (Gera), 361
My Home/Mi Casa (Emberley), 374
My Kitchen (Rockwell), 106
My Little Island (Lessac), 146
My Nursery School (Rockwell), 105
My Side of the Mountain (George), 79, 165
My Visit to the Dinosaurs (Aliki), 314
Myths, 35

N

NAEP. *see* National Assessment of Educational Progress
NAEYC. *see* National Association for the Education of Young Children
Nagy, W. E., 138, 140, 147, 148, 154, 155, 166, 171
Naidoo, Beverly, 368
Narrative poems, 42
Narrative text, 110, 172–208
    expository text and, 172–208
Nate the Great series (Sharmat), 191
Nathaniel Talking (Greenfield), 42
National Assessment of Educational Progress (NAEP), 389
National Association for the Education of Young Children (NAEYC), 122, 130, 134
National Commission on Reading, 123
National Council of Teachers of English, 44, 130
National Geographic World, 264
Native American focus, trade books with, 363
Nativist theory of language acquisition, 98
Natural language-experience activity, 111
Natural reading, 8
Natural text, 8
Naylor, Phyllis Reynolds, 51, 278
Neill, D. M., 383, 417
Nellie Cameron (Murray), 369
Nelson, Gail A., 347, 352
Nelson, J. B., 348, 352
Ness, Evaline, 47, 188, 196
Neurological impairment, 334
Neurological impress, 8, 337

New Advocate, The (magazine), 51
New American Spelling Book, 3
New England Primer, 3, 67
New Kid on the Block (Prelutsky), 338
New Read-Aloud Handbook, The (Trelease), 130, 279
Newbery Medal, 31, 39, 190
Newman, J. M., 8, 26, 158, 171
Newport, J. F., 254
Newspapers, 262–64
    for reading and language instruction, 263
    ten ways to use, 264
Nixon, Joan Lowery, 196
Noisy Nora (Wells), 160
Norm-referenced measures, 387–88
Norton, D. E., 358, 365, 380
Norton, Mary, 38
Nosbush, L., 283, 290
Not-Just-Anybody Family, The (Byars), 146
Notetaking, 261
Nothing Ever Happens on My Block (Raskin), 47
Nothing's Fair in Fifth Grade (DeClements), 39
Novel-ties supplementary program, 70
Now One Foot, Now The Other (de Paola), 297
Noyce, R. M., 15, 26, 293, 319, 322
Nuinberg, Maxwell, 146
Numeroff, Laura Jaffe, 192

O

O'Brien, Edna, 359
O'Brien, Robert C., 37, 45, 279
October Child (Spense), 341
O'Dell, Scott, 40
Ogle, D., 246, 254
O'Keefe, T., 232, 254
Ol' Paul, The Mighty Logger (Round), 36
Old Yeller (Gipson), 232
Omerod, Jan, 12, 113
On Learning to Read (Bettelheim and Zelan), 156
On Market Street (Lobel and Lobel), 107
Once a Mouse (Brown), 35
Once Upon a Time: An Encyclopedia for Successfully Using Children's Literature with Young Children (Hurst), 51
One Fine Day (Hogrogian), 299
''One-liners,'' 282
One-to-many communication, 280

O'Neill, Mary, 42
Ongoing assessment
    in emergent literacy, 394
    in holistic reading instruction, 336
Open syllables, 159
Optical aids, 339
Oral language background of LEP pupils, 371
Oral reading, 270–88
    expression, 272–74
    fluency, 274–76
    by pupils, 280–87
    to pupils, 276–80
    silent reading and, 280–81
    as tool, 281
Oral response to literature, 298, 299
Oral tradition, 31
Organization and management, 57–89
    of materials, 67–73
    parents in classroom, 86–87
    of pupils, 73–86
    schoolwide patterns, 87–88
    of space, 64–67
    of time, 60–64
Organizing information, 261–62
    notetaking, 261
    into systematic format, 261–62
Orphan Boy, The (Mullel), 359
Orton-Gillingham method, 335
Osa's Pride (Gilfranconi), 359
Osborn, J., 158, 171
Osborne, Mary Pope, 36
Osguthorpe, R. T., 82, 92
O'Sullivan, P. J., 328, 352
Otto, W., 84, 91
Our Regions, 225
Out, Out, Out! (Alexander), 113
Outline format, 261
Owl Moon (Yolen), 111
Owl's Song (Hale), 363
Ox-Cart Man, The (Hall), 190, 230
Oxenbury, Helen, 107

P

Pace of reading, in reading aloud to pupils, 277
Padak, N. D., 358, 360, 380
Paddington Bear (Bond), 278
Paek, Min, 363
Paired learning, 81–82
    in oral reading, 283–84
    with parents, 126
Palinscar, A. S., 395, 417
Pancakes for Breakfast (de Paola), 113, 316
Paper Airplane Book, The (Simon), 231

Paradis, E., 395, 417
Paragraph(s)
    in expository text, 242–43
    main idea of, 187
    as part of language background, 184
    skills for developing, 295
Paratore, J. R., 78, 82, 91, 395, 417
Parent(s)
    attitudes toward, 122, 123
    changing roles of, 123
    as children's first teachers, 124
    in classroom, 86–87
    literacy workshops for, 129–30
    as models for reading, 126
    role in early literacy, 121, 123–31
    role in preschool years, 123–27
    role when children come to school,
        127–31
Parent conferences, use of portfolios in,
    414
Parent materials in basal series, 17
Parent-teacher cooperation, model of,
    128
Parent's Guide to Children's Reading
    (Larrick), 130
Parent's Guide to the Best Books for
    Children (Lipson), 279
Parish, Peggy, 189, 190, 359, 374
Parker, Nancy Winslow, 22
Parnall, Peter, 298
Participation, books involving, 105–6
Pat the Bunny (Hunhardt), 106
Patchwork Quilt, The (Flournoy), 367
Patent, Dorothy Hinshaw, 231
Paterson, Katherine, 38, 39, 279, 297,
    317, 346
Pattern(s), of expository text, 225–27
Pattern of organization
    reading comprehension and, 178
    schoolwide, 87–88
Patterned language, 114
Paul, Ann Whitford, 107
Paul Bunyan (Kellogg), 36
Peabody Picture Vocabulary Test, 392
Pearson, D., 198, 200, 210
Pearson, P. D., 138, 141, 170, 171, 174,
    200, 207, 211, 293, 294, 307,
    322, 323, 383, 386, 393, 417
Pearson, Susan, 316
Peck, Robert Newton, 257, 279
Pecos Bill, 71
Peer conferencing in editing and
    revising, 308, 310
Peer tutoring, 82
    in metacognition, 202
Peet, Bill, 196, 218

People Could Fly, The: American Black
    Folktales (Hamilton), 369
Perceptual factors in reading readiness,
    99
Perceptual training
    auditory, 118
    in kindergarten, 117–18
    visual, 117–18
Performance basis, of classroom
    assessment, 406
Personal responses (journals), 316
"Personal words," 151
Personalized activity, individual reading
    conferences as, 283
Peter Rabbit (Potter), 32, 40, 71, 315
Peters, C. W., 385, 417
Peter's Chair (Keats), 34, 368
Peterson, John, 38, 278
Peterson, R., 61, 79, 91, 139, 171, 272,
    276, 290, 299, 306, 322
Petrosky, A. R., 299, 322
PFS Write (word processing program),
    308
Phantom Tollbooth, The (Juster), 38,
    278
Philharmonic Gets Dressed, The
    (Kurstein), 190, 234
Philip Hall Likes Me, I Recon Maybe
    (Greene), 369
Phillips, L. M., 300, 304, 322
Phonemes, 159
Phonetic analysis
    debate on, 156–58
    in literature-based programs,
        158–60, 162
    phonics and writing, 162–63
    in vocabulary development, 155–63
Phonetic elements of English, and LEP
    pupils, 371–72
Phonics, 155, 158–63
    guidelines for instruction, 163
    in literature-based programs
        connected, meaningful discourse,
            159–60
        whole-to-part instruction, 160,
            162
    terminology of, 159
    writing and, 162–63
Phonological differences in social
    dialects, 365
Physical development in childhood,
    95–96
Physical education, expository text in,
    234
Physical factors in reading readiness, 99

Physical handicaps
    classroom accommodations for, 342
    instruction for pupils with, 341–43
Picture book(s), 33–34
    about teachers, 35
    multicultural, 358–59
    for oral reading, 278
Picture Book Studio, 71
Picture-writing aids, 20
Pictures/illustrations in expository text,
    237
Pikulski, J. J., 385, 406, 417
Pinballs, The (Byars), 279, 286, 346
Pinnell, G. S., 329, 352
Pippi Longstocking (Lindgren), 38, 282
Planning
    for audience reading, 284
    teacher/librarian collaboration and,
        258
Play week, oral reading and, 287
Plays and scripts, in teaching oral
    reading, 286–87
Plot, 45, 190
Plot diagrams, 180, 180
"Poet-tree," 64
Poetry, 41–43
    anthologies of, 42
    imagery in, 41–42
    main idea of, 187–88
    multicultural, 364
    for oral reading, 279–80
    as written products, 316
"Poetry" (Farjeon), 41
Pogrow, S., 329, 330, 353
Point of view, 48
Polar Express, The (Van Allsburg), 34,
    196
Portals to Reading program, 70
Portfolios
    assessment of, 411–14
        contents of portfolios, 412–13
        cornerstones of, 411–12
        how portfolios are used, 414
    summary sheet in, 412
    uses of, 414
Portraying the Disabled: A Guide to
    Juvenile Fiction (Robertson),
    341
Portraying the Disabled: A Guide to
    Juvenile Non-Fiction (Friedberg
    et al.), 341
Positive attitudes, wordless books and,
    112
Possum Come A-Knockin' (Van Laan),
    12
Postreading questions by teacher, 204
Potter, Beatrix, 32, 37, 65, 315

Prairie Boy's Winter (Kurelek), 230
''Predict-Test-Conclude'' strategy, 205, 206
Prehm, H. J., 326, 328, 341, 352
Prelutsky, John, 42, 56, 218, 338, 374
PReP (PreReading Plan), 199
Preparation for reading, in DRTA, 77
Preparation for reading aloud, 277
Preposterous characters in children's fantasy, 38
PreReading Plan (PReP), 199
Prereading questions, 204
Preston, F. W., 112, 134
Pretty Little Pocketbook, A (Newbery), 31
Prewriting
    decisions in, 313
    imagination in, 304
    for letters, 315
    in process writing, 304–5
Princess and the Pea, The (Andersen), 35, 37
Princess Furball (Huck), 361
''Print awareness,'' role of parents in developing, 124–25
Prior knowledge, importance of activating, 198
Problem—solution
    comprehending expository text and, 226
    sample passage, 229
Problem solving, for gifted and talented pupils, 347
''Process'' in reading comprehension, 175
Process knowledge, 295
Process writing, 303–12
    editing and revising in, 307–8, *309, 310*
    prewriting in, 304–5
    publishing in, 310–12
    using literature to support, 311–12
    writing in, 305–7
Product(s)
    in reading comprehension, 175
    of writing, 303
Project ABC (Idalia), 358
Pronunciation systems of LEP pupils, 371
Pseudographs (Graphic Information Lesson), 239
Psychological factors in reading readiness, 99
Public Law 94–142, 327, 349
Publishing
    decisions in, 313
    forms of, 310–11
    in process writing, 310–12

Pueblo Storyteller (Hoyt-Goldsmith), 361
Pupil(s)
    with attitude and behavior problems, 343–45
    attitudes of, 8
    competency of, testing, 280, 391
    familiarity with cloze tests, 224
    gifted and talented, 345–48
    interest of, reading aloud and, 277
    with learning disabilities, 334–39
    opportunity to select work for portfolios, 413
    records kept by, 398
    response to literature, 299–300, 300–302
    with sensory and physical problems, 339–43
    skills of, impact of literature on, 14–15
Pupil-directed dialogue, 207
Pupil-generated questioning, 202
Pupil management, 73–86
    flexibility in grouping, 85–86
    individualized patterns, 82, 84–85
    large-group instruction, 74–75
    small-group instruction, 75–82
Purpose in comprehending expository text, 247
Purposefulness in whole language theory, 9
Putnam, C., 134

Q

QAR (Question—Answer Relationships), 195
Quackenbush, Robert, 299
Quality of books, judging, 49
Question—Answer Relationships (QAR), 195
Questioning
    in metacognition, 201–2
    tips on, 203
Quintero, R., 376, 380

R

Rabbit Hill (Lawson), 5, 37, 48, 84
Radio reading in teaching oral reading, 285
Ragtime Trumpie (Schroeder), 364
Rainbow People, The (Yep), 361
Raintree Illustrated Science Encyclopedia, The, 259
Rainy Rainy Saturday (Prelutsky), 218
Rand, M. K., 64, 91

Random House Book of Poetry for Children (Prelutsky), 42
Ranger Rick (magazine), 264
Raphael, T. E., 195, 211, 254
Rasinski, T. V., 128, 134, 358, 360, 380
Raskin, Ellen, 47
Rawls, Wilson, 195, 279, 297
Ray, Delia, 217
Read-Aloud Handbook, The (Trelease), 68
''Read alouds,'' 6
    with LEP pupils, 372
Readability, 206
    in expository text, 222–23, 225
    in reading comprehension, 176–78
    using cloze for, 224
Readability checklist, 223
Readability formula, 222–23
Readability formulas, difficulties with, 223
Readance, J. E., 211, 281, 290
Reader(s)
    in basal series, 17
    response of, 5
Reader-based features, 206, 239–48
    cognitive processing, 185–97, 206, 243–44
    context, 203
    language background, 182–85, 206, 239–43
    metacognition, 200–202, 206, 246–47
    motivation, 202, 247–48
    in reading comprehension, 176, 182–203
    schemata, 197–200, 206, 244–45
    state of mind, 202
Readers (Webster), 3
Reader's theater, 286–87
Reading aloud
    to children, 125–26
    by pupils, 280–87
        alternatives to round-robin reading, 282–87
        oral versus silent reading, 280–81
        round-robin reading, 281–82
    to pupils, 276–80
        advantages of, 276–77
        books for, 279
        conditions and techniques for, 277
        goals of, 276
        selecting books for, 278–80
        suggestions for, 278
    in shared reading lesson, 115
    to younger pupils, 330
Reading behavior inventory, 404–5

Reading comprehension, 172–208
  cause-effect relationships in, 191–92
  expository text, 212–49
  interactive model of, 175–77, *176*,
    221
  product and process in, 175
  reader-based features in, 176,
    182–203
  role of teacher questioning in,
    203–5, 207
  sentence comprehension in, 184
  text-based features in, 176, 177–82
Reading corner, 65
Reading efficiency, reading rate and,
  266–67
Reading Miscue Inventory (Goodman
  and Burke), 409
Reading preparation, in shared reading
  lesson, 115
Reading programs
  effect of standardized tests on, 389
  for learning disabled pupils, 335–36
Reading rate
  comprehension and, 266
  flexibility and, 266–67
  reading efficiency and, 266–67
Reading readiness
  emergent literacy and, 99, 101–3,
    102t
  factors in, 99, 101
Reading Recovery (intervention
  program), 329, 394
Reading Report Card, The, 389
Reading Teacher, The (journal), 39, 68,
  201, 392
Reading—writing activities, for
  emergent literacy classroom, 117
Reading-writing connection, 291–320
  in each stage of writing process, 312
  process writing, 303–12
  relationship of, 293–96
  responding to literature, 297–303
  written products based on literature,
    312–19
Real-life experiences in schema theory,
  199
Realistic fiction, 38–40
  multicultural, 362
Really Rosie (musical play), 110
Rebecca of Sunnybrook Farm
  (Wiggins), 32
Reciprocal Questioning (ReQuest), 205,
  385
Reciprocal teaching, 395
Record keeping, computers and, 72–73
Record-keeping, tools in basal series,
  17

Red Pony, The (Steinbeck), 278
Reference materials
  dictionary as, 166
  learning to use, 260–61
  in library, 258–62
  organizing information, 261–62
  tools, 259–60
Reference sources
  alphabet books, 107
  for author information, 51
  books about children with
    handicaps, 341
  books about libraries, 259
  books about words, 146
  books about writing, 318
  books for mathematics, 234, 235
  books for reading aloud, 279
  books for science, 232
  books for social studies, 230
  books from Hispanic perspective,
    373
  books on ''tender topics,'' 346
  books with black perspective, 369
  concept books, 106
  multicultural trade books, 363
  for phonics elements in trade books,
    161–62
  poetry anthologies, 42
  for reading in the home, 130
Reformed alphabet approaches, 20
Regional dialect, 364
Rehnman, Mats, 361
Reinking, D., 239, 254
Reiss, John J., 106, 233
Repeated phonetic elements, 160
Repetition, 337
  in vocabulary development, 142–45
Repetition and patterns, for ESL and
  bilingual pupils, 374
Reports
  as oral response to literature, 299
  as written products, 314
ReQuest (Reciprocal Questioning), 205,
  385
Rereading in shared reading lesson, 115
Research
  children's literature and second
    language learning, 375
  related to cooperative learning, 81
  in whole language theory, 10
Resource teachers, for ESL and
  bilingual pupils, 375–76
Responding to literature, 297–303
  artistically, 298
  orally, 298
  in writing, 298–303

Response in comprehending expository
  text, 247
Reutzel, D. R., 10, 11, 26
Rey, H. A., 37, 332
Rey, Margaret, 37, 332
Rhodes, L. K., 64, 91, 336, 353
Rhyme, 41
Rhythm, 41
Richek, M. A., 332, 353
Richgels, D. J., 103, 134, *229*
Rickelman, R. J., 70, 91
Risk-taking in whole language theory, 9
Robb, L., 233, 254, 314, 322
Robbins, Ruth, 361
Robertson, Debra, 341, 353
Robinson, Barbara, 39–40, 179
Robinson, F. P., 254
Roblyer, M. D., 73, 91
Rockwell, Anne, 106, 259
Rockwell, Harlow, 105, 106
Rockwell, Thomas, 39, 279
Roe, Betty D., 407
Rogers, Jean, 230
Rohmer, Harriet, 374
Role playing in metacognition, 202
Roll of Thunder, Hear My Cry (Taylor),
  230, 299, 360, 369
Roop, Connie, 225
Roop, Peter, 225
Rootabaga Stories (Sandburg), 6
Roots in structural analysis, 164
Rosenblatt, L. M., 205, 211, 297, 322
Rosenshine, B. V., 76, 91, 185, 211
Rosenthal, Mark, 218
Roser, N. L., 375, 380
Rosie's Walk (Hutchins), 33, 109, 151
Rottenberg, C. J., 72, 91
Round-robin reading, deficiencies of,
  281–82
Rounds, Glen O., 36, 285
Routman, Regie, 68, 75, 91, 310, 322,
  333, 353
Row, B. D., 254
Royalty in children's fantasy, 37
Rubin, A., 294, 296, 322
Rudner, L. M., 391, 417
Runaway Mittens, The (Rogers), 230

S

Sadako and the Thousand Paper Cranes
  (Coerr), 228, 332, 363
Saint-Exupéry, Antoine de, 37
Sam, Bangs, and Moonshine (Ness), 47,
  188, 196
Samuels, S. J., 290
Sandburg, Carl, 6, 187, 279

Sanders, N. M., 193, 211
Sarah, Plain and Tall (MacLachlan), 40, 155, 196, 205, 279, 408
Savage, John F., 15, 26, 66, 272, 290, 335, 353
Saxby, M., 30, 45, 56
Saying Good-bye to Grandma (Thomas), 346
Scanning, 266
Schema, 197
Schema theory, 197, 244–45
    examples of, 96–97
Schemata, 206
    in childhood development, 96–97
    in reading comprehension, 176, 197–200
        expository text and, 244–45
Schiller, Andrew, 144
Schiro, M., 236, 254
Schmidtt, M. C., 201, 211
Scholastic Mazazines, 264
Scholastic's A+ Junior Guide to Good Writing (Colligan), 318
School, realistic fiction about, 39
Schoolwide organizational patterns, 87–88
Schroeder, Allan, 364
Schumaker, M. P., 76, 92, 332, 345, 353
Schumaker, R. C., 76, 92, 332, 345, 353
Schuman, D. R., 342, 353
Schwartz, David M., 234
Schweitzer, Byrd Baylor, 204
Science
    integrating with literature, 233
    trade books for, 231, 232
Science and Technology in Fact and Fiction: A Guide to Children's Books (Kennedy, Spangler, and Vanderwerf), 232
Science text
    expository text in, 230–32
    fictional trade books and, 231
    poetry and, 232
Science Through Children's Literature: An Integrated Approach (Butzow and Butzow), 232
Scieszka, John, 48, 299
Scott, Sally, 359
Scripts, as written products, 316
Searfoss, L. W., 285, 290
Sebesta, S. L., 47, 56, 234, 254
Second language learning principles, 371
Secret Garden, The (Burnett), 299, 301
Seed Is A Promise, A (Merrill), 231
Seeger, Pete, 360

Segal, Elizabeth, 68, 91
Seidman, James F., 233
Selections
    in expository text, 243
    as part of language background, 184–85
Self-selection of materials, 8
Semantic context clues, 152–54
Semantic mapping
    in integration, 141–43
    for slow learners, 329
Semantic miscues, 408–9
Semantic study, 144
Sendak, Maurice, 6, 33, 34, 44, 52, 110–11, 191, 234
Sensory and physical problems, 339–43
    auditory, 340–41
    physical handicaps, 341–43
    visual, 339–40
Sensory images in poetry, 110
Sentence(s)
    anaphoric relationships in, 183
    comprehension of, 184
    in expository text, 241–42
    length of, in readability formula, 222
    as part of language background, 183
    writing skills for, 295
Sequence, comprehending, 189–90
Setting, 43–44
Seuss, Dr. *see* Geisel, Theodore
Shablak, S. L., 267, 269
Shadow (Brown), 234
Shanahan, T., 296, 323
Shannon, P., 16, 18, 26, 67, 92
Shapes (Reiss), 106, 233
Shared reading lesson, with Big Book, 115
Shared stories
    for handicapped learners, 342
    with LEP pupils, 372–73
Sharmat, Marjorie Weinman, 143, 191, 318
Shiloh (Naylor), 278
Shipman, Dorothy A., 407
Shoop, M., 205, 211
Shopping Cart Art (Seidman and Mintoyne), 233
Shrake, K., 79, 91
Sight words
    deciding how to teach, 150–52
    ''personal words,'' 151
    selecting vocabulary, 148, 150
    teaching, 152
    in vocabulary development, 147–52
Sign of the Beaver, The (Speare), 279, 363

Signal words, 227
Silent reading, oral reading and, 280–81
Silvaroli, Nicholas J., 407
Silverstein, Shel, 42, 43, 187–88, 279, 305, 338, 374
Simon, Seymour, 62, 231, 232
Simons, H. D., 295, 323
Sinatra, R. C., 329, 353
Sing Down the Moon (O'Dell), 40
Sipay, E. R., 99, 134, 253
Sis, Peter, 234
Sister (Greenfield), 369
Skill development, CMI and, 73
Skill-development approach
    to reading comprehension, 185
    to reading instruction, 15–16
Skill-development tests
    criterion-referenced, 390–91
    in formal assessment, 390–93
    standardized skills tests, 392–93
Skimming, 266
Sky Is Full of Stars, The (Branley), 232
Slake's Limbo (Holman), 79
Slavin, R. E., 81, 92
Sloan, P., 278, 282, 290
Slobodkin, Louis, 218
Slobodkina, Esphyr, 12, 35, 103
Slote, Alfred, 369
Slovenz-Low, Madeline, 364
Slow learners, 328–33
    literature for, 331–33
    teaching strategies for, 328–31
Small-group instruction, 61, 75–82
    cooperative learning, 78, 80–81
    heterogeneous grouping, 78
    homogeneous grouping, 76, 78
    paired learning, 81–82
Small Worlds Close Up (Grillone and Gennaro), 225
Smith, D. D., 275, 290
Smith, Doris Buchanan, 279, 346
Smith, F., 8, 26, 171
Smith, N. B., 272, 290
Smitherman, G., 367, 380
Snake, The: A Very Long Story (Waber), 50
Snake In, Snake Out (Baucheck), 151
Sneve, Virginia Driving Hawk, 362, 364
Snow Treasure (McSwigan), 199
Snowball, D., 227, 254
Snowy Day, The (Keats), 34, 311–12
Snyder, Diane, 361
Sobol, Donald J., 191, 279
Social action approach, to multicultural literature, 360

Social context in comprehension, 203
Social dialect, 365
Social Education (journal), 230
Social factors in reading readiness, 99
Social studies text
     critical reading and, 230
     expository text in, 228, 230
Socially conscious literature, 368
Socks (Cleary), 63
Solution strategies for word problems in
     math text, 233
Song and Dance Man (Ackerman), 234
Song of the Stars, A (Birdseye), 361
Songs and chants for ESL and bilingual
     pupils, 373–74
Sound features in phonics, 160
Sounder (Armstrong), 47, 369
Soup (Peck), 257, 279
Soup and Me (Peck), 279
Soup for President (Peck), 279
Southall, Ivan, 39, 341
Space management, 64–67
Spangler, Stella S., 232, 253
Speare, Elizabeth George, 40, 43, 230,
     279, 363
Special Trade, A (Wittman), 34
Specialists, 63
Specialized words in expository text,
     240
Specific language disability, 334
Spense, Eleanor, 341
Sperry, Armstrong, 79, 279
Spier, Peter, 106, 113, 305
Spinelli, Jerry, 279, 346
Spirit Child, The (Bierhorst), 361
Spontaneous choral reading, 285–86
SSR. *see* Sustained silent reading
Staab, C., 63, 92
Stahl, S. A., 158, 163, 171
Stahl-Gemake, J., 329, 353
Standard English, dialects and, 366
Standardized testing, 383
     reading achievement tests, 387–90
          pros and cons of, 388–90
     of skills, 392–93
State of mind in reading
     comprehension, 202
Stauffer, R., 77, 92
Steig, William, 34, 139, 231
Steinbeck, John, 278
Steptoe, John, 230, 361, 367
Stevens, R. J., 76, 82, 91, 92
Stevenson, Pete, 144
Stevenson, Robert Louis, 42, 279, 280
Stimulus—response theory of language
     acquisition, 98
Stone Fox (Gardiner), 196, 279, 299

Stone Soup (Brown), 35, 196
Stoodt, B. D., 254
"Stopping By Woods on a Snowy
     Evening" (Frost), 43
Stories as written products, 313
Story boards for LEP pupils, 372
Story frames, story structure and, 180,
     180
Story maps, 46–47, 261
Story of an English Village (Goodall),
     111, 113
Story structure, teaching, *180*, 180–81,
     182
Story time, 61
Storybooks for math, 234
Storytelling
     activities in, 36
     folk literature and, 36
     as oral response to literature, 299
Stoutenburg, Adrien, 36
Stranger, The (Van Allsburg), 338
Strategies for questioning, 205
Strategy training for slow learners, 330
Streep, Meryl, 71
Strickland, Dorothy S., 114, 134, 369
Strother, D. B., 204, 211
Structural analysis, 155
     comprehending expository text and,
          239–40
     in vocabulary development, 163–65
Structural knowledge, in reading-
     writing connection, 294
Students. *see* Pupil(s)
Study guides, 245
Style, 48
Suart, Michele M., 363
Sullivan, J., 345, 353
Sulzby, E., 101, 134
Sumara, D., 9, 26
Summaries
     as context clues, 153
     in holistic reading instruction, 336
Summer of the Swans (Byars), 39, 341
Sunshine (Omerod), 12, 113
Sunshine Makes the Seasons (Branley),
     4, 218, 225, 232
Superfudge (Blume), 38
Supplementary literature-based
     materials, 70
Support services for atypical learners,
     348
Suprasegmental phoneme system, 273
Surfeit of Similes, A (Juster), 318
Sustained silent reading (SSR), 6, 8,
     61–62, 174, 248
Swann, Brian, 42, 258
Swift, Jonathan, 30

"Swing, The" (Stevenson), 42
Sword in the Stone, The (White), 36
Sylvester and the Magic Pebble (Steig),
     139
Symbolic thought, 96
Synonym(s)
     antonyms and, 241
     in cloze test, 224
Synonym searches, 143
Syntactic context clues, 152–54
Syntactic miscues, 409
Syntactical differences in social
     dialects, 365
Syntax, LEP pupils and, 372
Synthesized reading program, 23
Systematic format, for organizing
     information, 261–62

T

Table of contents, 235, 236
Tadjo, Veronique, 360
Tafuri, Nancy, 106, 151
Taking a Walk/Cammandro (Emberley),
     374
Tale of the Flopsy Bunnies, The
     (Potter), 65
Tales for the Telling (O'Brien), 359
Tales of a Fourth Grade Nothing
     (Blume), 38, 344
Tall tales, 36
Tape recorder
     in teaching oral reading, 283
     using in reading assessment, 411
Taped books
     for ESL and bilingual pupils, 374
     for slow learners, 330
Taped reading, 310, 337
Taste of Blackberries, A (Smith), 279,
     346
Tattercoats (Jacobs), 34
Taxonomies, for levels of thinking, 193
Taylor, B. M., 283, 290
Taylor, Mildred, 6, 230, 299, 360, 368,
     369
Taylor, Theodore, 276, 367
Taylor, W., 224, 254
Teacher(s)
     assessment of, use of portfolios in,
          414
     behavior of, in whole language
          theory, 11
     competency testing of, 391
     function in literature-based
          programs, 6
     importance for atypical learners,
          348–49

involvement of, meaningful use of
        words and, 146
    librarians and, 257–58
    observation by, in classroom-based
        assessment, 394–95, 398
    picture books about, 35
    role in classroom-based assessment,
        393–94
    sustained silent reading and, 6
Teacher from the Black Lagoon, The
        (Thaler), 35
Teacher modeling, 8
    in demonstrating context clues, 154
    in metacognition, 202
Teacher questioning
    comprehending expository text and,
        227
    critical/creative, 204
    evaluative, 204
    inferential, 204
    instructional, 204
    as key to reading comprehension,
        191
    literal, 204
    patterns of, 205
    postreading, 204
    prereading, 204
    in reading comprehension, 203–5,
        207
    during readings, 204
    techniques for, 205
Teachers editions in basal series, 17, 18
Teaching goals in holistic reading
        instruction, 336
Teaching strategies
    direct instruction on comprehension
        components, 328–29
    focus on metacognition, 329–30
    reading to younger pupils, 330
    semantic mapping, 329
    for slow learners, 328–31
    strategy training, 330
    taped books, 330–31
    think-alouds, 330
Teale, W. H., 3, 26, 101, 134
Team teaching, 87
Tebbits, Ellen, 50
Technical vocabulary in expository text,
        240
Telegraphic speech, 98
Tell Me a Story, Mama (Johnson), 6,
        286
Ten Little Rabbits (Grossman), 107
Tenth Good Thing about Barney, The
        (Viorst), 34, 346
Terminology, of phonics, 159

Test of Reading Comprehension, 392
Test of Written Language, 392
Testing, 383
    in basal series, 17
    See also Assessment; Standardized
        testing
Text-based features, 206
    content, 179, 182, 206, 228, 230–35
    design, 182, 235–36
    in expository text, 222–39
    graphic materials in, 182, 237–39
    level, 177–78
    readability, 206, 222–23, 225
    in reading comprehension, 176,
        177–82
    structure, 177–78, 206, 225–27
Text previews, 199
Text structure, 206, 225–27
    patterns of expository text and,
        225–27
    in reading comprehension, 176,
        178–79
    teaching, 228
Textbooks, 216
Thaler, Mike, 35
Thanksgiving Story, The (Dalgliesh), 40
Thematic units, 6
Theme(s), 45, 47–49
Theme groups, heterogeneous, 79
Theme projects, 62–63
Themes, in realistic fiction, 39–40
''They've Put a Brassiere on the
        Camel'' (Silverstein), 43
''Think alouds,'' 395
    steps in, 330
Thomas, Jane Rush, 346
Thomas, K. F., 104, 134
Thomas' Snowsuit (Munch), 35
Three Bears, The (Gladone), 218
Three Billygoats Gruff, The, 299
Three-Seated Space Ship, The
        (Slobodkin), 218
Through Grandpa's Eyes (MacLachan),
        341
Thurlow, M. L., 328, 352
Tierney, R. J., 281, 290, 294, 307, 323,
        385, 417
Tikki Tikki Tembo (Mosel), 6, 363
Time management, 60–64
    daily classroom schedule, 61
    math, 63
    small group activities, 61
    specialists, 63
    story time, 61
    sustained silent reading, 61–62
    theme projects, 62–63
    whole class work, 60

Time of Wonder (McCloskey), 34
Time-on-task, 328
Time order, expository text and, 226
Tiny Seed, The (Carle), 231
Tolkien, J. R. R., 38, 279
Tom Sawyer (Twain), 279
Tomkins, Gail E., 180, 299, 323
Tompert, Ann, 359
Tone, 48
Too Short Fred (Meddaugh), 144
Top, B. L., 82, 92
Topic selection in prewriting, 304–5
Trachtenburg, P., 161–62, 171
Trade book(s), 5
    adaptability of, 217
    advantages for slow learners, 332
    as benchmark measures in
        assessment, 408
    with Chinese focus, 363
    classroom library of, 68–69
    content areas in, 217
    defined, 4
    for ESL and bilingual pupils,
        373–74
    multicultural, 358–64
    purpose of, 4
    sharing with LEP pupils, 372–73
    as supplements to textbooks, 216–18
    topic selection in prewriting and,
        305
Traditional literature, multicultural,
        259–62
Transactional knowledge, in reading-
        writing connection, 294
Transformations approach, to
        multicultural literature, 360
Transitions from Literature to Literacy
        (Routman), 68
Treasure Island (Stevenson), 279
Trelease, Jim, 12, 27, 68, 92, 130, 279,
        290
True Story of the Three Little Pigs, The
        (Scieszka), 48, 299
Tsutsui, Yoiko, 363
Tuck Everlasting (Babbitt), 6
Tuesday (Weisner), 113
Tunnell, M. O., 8, 15, 27
Turbill, J., 395, 403, 416
Twain, Mark (Samuel Clemens), 32,
        279, 367
'''Twas the Night Before Christmas''
        (Moore), 42
Tway, E., 319, 323
26 Letters and 99 Cents (Hoban), 234
Tylor, E. B., 356, 380

U

Uchida, Yoshiko, 40, 360, 363
Under The Sea From A to Z (Doublet), 107
Unison arrangements in choral reading, 285
Unsworth, L., 86, 92
Ups and Downs of Carl Davis III, The (Guy), 316
U.S. Department of Education, 334, 353
Uttero, D. A., 81, 92

V

Vacca, J. L., 102t, 134, 223, 244, 254
Vacca, R. T., 102t, 134, 223, 244, 254
Valencia, S., 383, 386, 393, 411, 414, 417
Van Allsburg, Chris, 34, 196, 304, 338
van de Wetering, Janwillem, 121
Van Laan, Nancy, 12
Vanderwerf, Mary Ann, 232, 253
Varnhagen, C. K., 328, 353
Vasilissa the Beautiful (Winthrop), 361
VBE (Vernacular Black English). *see* Black English
Vegetable Garden (Florian), 231
Velveteen Rabbit, The (Williams), 143, 196
Venn diagrams
  for cooperative learning, 81
  in integration, 141
Vernacular Black English (VBE). *see* Black English
Verne, Jules, 32
Very Hungry Caterpillar, The (Carle), 105–6
Videos about authors, 52
Viorst, Judith, 14, 34, 144, 146, 234, 315, 346
Visit to the Library, A (Gilcrest), 259
Visual discrimination, 118
Visual expressive function (writing), 142
Visual figure ground, 117
Visual media, 71
  censorship in, 44
  in illustrating picture books, 33–34
Visual memory, 117
Visual-motor skills, 117
Visual perceptual development, 117–18
Visual problems
  classroom accommodations for, 339–40
  identifying undiagnosed problems, 340

instruction for pupils with, 339–40
Visual receptive function (reading), 142
Visual sequencing, 117
Vocabulary, 183
  selecting to teach, 148, 150
Vocabulary development, 135–68
  integration, 140–42
  meaningful use, 146–47
  repetition, 142–45
  word analysis, 155–66
  word-identification skills, 167
  word knowledge, 137–47
  word recognition, 147–55
Voigt, Cynthia, 39, 79, 190
Vowel phonemes, 159

W

Waber, Bernard, 50, 191, 194, 278
Wagon Wheels (Brenner), 369
Walker, L., 9, 26
Walker-Dalhouse, D., 369, 380
Wall, Lina Mao, 359
Walshe, R. D., 303, 310, 323
War Comes to Willy Freeman (Collier and Collier), 360
Warncke, Edna W., 407
Washburne, C., 108, 134
Waters, Kate, 364
Watson, D. J., 8, 27, 409, 417, 418
Way Things Work, The (Macaulay), 232
Weaver, C., 92, 409, 418
Webster, Noah, 3
Weighty Word Book, The (Levitt, Burger, and Gurlnick), 146
Weisner, David, 113
Weiss, Harvey, 238
Well, I Never! (Pearson), 316
Wells, Rosemary, 160
Welsh, V., 14, 27
Weston Woods Company (author information), 52, 71
What an Awful Mess! (Quackenbush), 299
What Do You Do with A Kangaroo? (Mayer), 304, 338
What Happened to the Dinosaur (Branley), 314
What's the Big Idea, Ben Franklin? (Fritz), 230
What's What: A Visual Glossary of the Physical World (Bragomer and Fisher), 259
When Will I Read (Cohen), 120
Where Do You Get Your Ideas? (Asher), 318

Where Do You Think You're Going, Christopher Columbus? (Fritz), 230
Where Food Comes From (Patent), 231
Where the Red Fern Grows (Rawls), 195, 279, 297
Where the Sidewalk Ends (Silverstein), 42, 338
Where the Wild Things Are (Sendak), 6, 33, 34, 191
Whipping Boy, The (Fleischman), 5, 279
Whipple, Laura, 42
Whisler, N., 81, 92
White, E. B., 33, 37, 45, 121, 279, 298, 344
White, T. H., 36
Whitin, D. J., 232, 254
Who Sank the Boat? (Allen), 12, 148, 150
Whole class work, 60
Whole Language Council, Milwaukee Public Schools, 408, 418
Whole language theory, 8–12
  advantages of literature in, 12, 14
  changes in assessment and, 385, 387
  conditions for learning, 9
  contrasted with conventional theory, 10–11
  philosophies of, 10
Whole-to-part instruction, 160, 162
Who's Counting (Tafuri), 106
Why Johnny Can't Read (Flesch), 156
Why Mosquitoes Buzz in People's Ears (Aardema), 86, 299, 360
Why the Sun and Moon Live in the Sky (Dayrell), 111
Wiederholt, J. L., 295, 322, 392, 416
Wiggins, G., 388, 418
Wiggins, Kate Douglas, 32
Wilde, Oscar, 37
Wilder, Laura Ingalls, 40, 198, 218
Wildsmith, Brian, 107
Williams, Barbara, 346
Williams, J., 81, 92
Williams, Margery, 143, 196
Williams, Robin, 71
Wilson, P. T., 147, 170, 198, 211
Wilsted, Joy, 124
Winch, G., 16, 27, 41, 56
"Wind, The" (Stevenson), 42
Winnie-the-Pooh (Milne), 32, 37, 278
Winograd, P. N., 151, 170
Winthrop, Elizabeth, 361
Wish Giver, The (Brittain), 279
Witch of Blackbird Pond, The (Speare), 40, 43, 230

Wittels, Harriet, 144
Wittman, Sally, 34
Wixson, K. K., 385, 417, 418
Wolf, A., 84, 91, 92
Wolf, D. P., 414, 418
Wonder Women of Sports (Jones), 234
Wood, K. D., 204, 210, 396–97, 418
Wood, T. L., 216, 254
Wood, W., 216, 254
Woodcock, R. W., 392, 418
Woodcock-Johnson Psycho-Educational Battery, 392
Woods, Mary Lynn, 407
"Word alerts," 144–45
Word analysis, 137, 138, 155–66
　phonetic, 155–63
　structural, 163–65
　using dictionary, 165–66
Word board, 65, 67
"Word for the Day," 144
Word frequency, 148, 149t–150t
Word games, vocabulary development and, 145
Word identification
　fluency and, 275
　skills for, 167
Word knowledge, 137–47
　comprehending expository text and, 240–41
　concepts, 138–40
　five stages of, 139
　for LEP pupils, 372
　vocabulary development in classroom, 140–47
Word length, readability and, 222
Word lists, in vocabulary development, 152
Word processing
　as aid to literacy development, 72
　in stages of writing process, 308
Word recognition, 137, 138, 147–55
　context clues, 152–55
　sight words, 147–52

Word sorts, content words and, 241
Wordless books, 111–13
　developing reading lesson with, 112
　in nursery school programs, 107
Workbooks in basal series, 17, 18
World Book Encyclopedia, 259
World culture, trade books for, 230
World Encyclopedia of Civil Aircraft (Angelucci), 259
World history, trade books for, 230
Wreck of the Zephyr, The (Van Allsburg), 338
Wright, Joan Richards, 22
Wright Brothers at Kitty Hawk, The (Sobol), 279
Wrinkle in Time, A (L'Engle), 38, 279
Write Your Own Story (Dubrovin), 318
Writing, 305–7
　about children's books, 303
　comprehending expository text and, 227
　conferencing with pupils and, 306
　decisions in, 313
　first-draft form, 306–7
　for gifted and talented pupils, 347
　in instruction for the learning disabled, 338–39
　in kindergarten, 115–17
　in nursery school programs, 107
　as "output activity," 8
　process of, decisions in, 313
　in response to literature, 298–303
　　basal and literature-based programs compared, 300–301
　　in buddy journals, 300
　　in the literature-rich classroom, 300–301, 303
　　personal perspectives and, 298–300
　teacher role in, 306

Writing center, 65, 116
Writing for Kids (Benjamin), 318
Writing instruction
　for ESL and bilingual pupils, 374–75
　in metacognition, 202
Writing web, 317
Written products
　based on literature, 312–19
　book reports, 316–19
　journals, 316
　letters, 315–16
　poems, 316
　reports, 314
　scripts and dialogues, 316
　stories, 313
Written records in classroom assessment, 398
Wuthrick, J. A., 92
Wyndham, Robert, 361

Y

Yashima, Taro, 230, 363
Yatvin, J., 18, 27
Yeh-Shen: A Cinderella Story from China (Ling), 361
Yep, Lawrence, 361, 363
Yolen, Jane, 37, 48, 111, 230
Young, Ed, 338, 361
Young World (magazine), 264
Ysseldyke, J. E., 328, 352

Z

Zallinger, Peter, 314
Zarrillo, J., 6, 27, 70, 92
Zeeley (Hamilton), 362, 369
Zelan, K., 156, 170
Zion, Gene, 192, 332